THE GREAT LANGUAGES

GENERAL EDITOR:

William J. Entwistle, M.A., Litt.D., Ll.D., D. em L.

King Alfonso XIII Professor of Spanish Studies in the University of Oxford

PUBLISHED

THE GREEK LANGUAGE (2ND ED.)
By B. F. C. Atkinson, M.A., Ph.D.

Under-Librarian of the University Library, Cambridge

THE FRENCH LANGUAGE (2ND ED.)
By A. Ewert, M.A.

Professor of the Romance Languages in the University of Oxford

THE GERMAN LANGUAGE (2ND ED.)
By R. Priebsch, Ph.D., and W. E. Collinson, M.A., Ph.D.

The former late Professor Emeritus of University College, London, and the latter, Professor of German and Honorary Lecturer in Comparative Philology in the University of Liverpool

THE SPANISH LANGUAGE, TOGETHER WITH PORTUGUESE, CATALAN, BASQUE
By William J. Entwistle, M.A.

RUSSIAN AND THE SLAVONIC LANGUAGES
By William J. Entwistle, M.A., and W. A. Morison, B.A., Ph.D.

The latter of the British Broadcasting Corporation, sometime Lecturer in the School of Slavonic and East European Studies, University of London.

THE CHINESE LANGUAGE
By R. A. D. Forrest, M.A.

Research Lecturer in Tibeto-Burman Linguistics at the School of Oriental Studies, University of London

IN PREPARATION

THE LATIN LANGUAGE
By R. L. Palmer

Professor of Latin, King's College, University of London

THE SEMITIC LANGUAGE
By W. J. Martin, M.A., B.D.

Lecturer in Semitics in the University of Liverpool

THE ENGLISH LANGUAGE
By Helge Kökeritz, Ph.D.

Professor of English in Yale University

THE CELTIC LANGUAGES
By Myles Dillion, Ph.D., and Sir Ifor Williams, M.A., D.Litt.

The former, Professor of Celtic in the University of Wisconsin, and the latter, Professor of Welsh at Bangor University College

SANSKRIT AND THE LANGUAGES OF INDIA
By Thomas Burrow, M.A., Ph.D.

Boden Professor of Sanskrit in the University of Oxford

RUSSIAN
AND THE SLAVONIC
LANGUAGES

RUSSIAN

AND THE SLAVONIC

LANGUAGES

by

W. J. ENTWISTLE, M.A.

*(Alphonso XIII Professor of Spanish Studies
in the University of Oxford)*

and

W. A. MORISON, B.A., Ph.D.

*(Sometime Lecturer in the School
of Slavonic and East European Studies)*

FABER AND FABER LIMITED

24 Russell Square

London

First published in mcmxlix
by Faber and Faber Limited
24 Russell Square, London WC1
Printed in Great Britain
by Percy Lund, Humphries and Co. Ltd. Bradford

CONTENTS

Old Russian (1100–1500)

PREFACE

Something like two hundred million souls use Russian as their maternal, their official, or their auxiliary tongue. The last group contains many of the fifty million speakers of the other Slavonic languages. The westward frontier of their influence stands, at the time this is written, where it did in the tenth century of our era, on a line descending from Mecklenburg to Trieste. Ten centuries ago the eastern limit scarcely advanced beyond the Dnieper; it now reaches to the frozen waters of the Sea of Okhotsk, so as to include within the Russian domain half of Asia, with immense resources as yet scarcely tapped. This is the centre of gravity of the land masses of the globe as much as London is the midpoint of the world's land and water connections. Few countries are so unlike in their situation and strength as Britain and Russia, but they are complementary and have much to do with each other.

To the demand for a knowledge of Russian Britain makes a gravely inadequate response, implying a misdirected language policy in education. From time to time there are large movements of students who wish to learn the language, but they retreat baffled by its remoteness and its difficulty. Those who pursue the study to the end are generally those who have had previous training in the rigours of language-work when acquiring French or German or the Classical tongues. These languages must often, in any case, be used by students in pursuit of data concerning the Slavonic peoples, so that there is a natural order of precedence for their acquirement. Russian is related to English, but at a distance due to four or more millennia of separation. Greek is relatively familiar to English scholars, and by the age of its documents and the archaic nature of the language it is fitted to lead up to the study of Russian, and to furnish the links needed to connect the oldest Russian words with our own. We have, for this reason, given Greek parallels as often as may be.

Our object is to offer a *rationale* of the Russian tongue. We do not simply describe it after the fashion of conversation-grammars, but we account for its present form by the process of development from what was the speech of our own remotest ancestors. The first chapter endeavours to assemble what may be known or conjectured concerning the speakers of the oldest Slavonic. They were not the only ancestors of modern Slavs, since their tongue has spread to many nations who, even within historic times, spoke other languages. We then endeavour to give a shadowy outline of the history of the un-recorded developments between about 2000 B.C. and A.D. 1000. All the ingredients were shaken together in that period, and the pattern of the language transformed. It is possible to offer a description of the common Slavonic tongue, from which Russian has arisen at the beginning of our millennium; a description the more certain since it is, in most particulars, the same as the description of extant literary documents written in Old Bulgarian. A form of this Old Bulgarian, with Russian modifications, served as the literary language of Russia until the middle of the eighteenth century, and it is still lodged in literary Russian as Latin is lodged in literary English. The chapter on Common Slavonic and Old Bulgarian is one of descriptive grammar. That which follows, on Russian, is designed chiefly to distinguish states of the language at different periods, and to trace the gradual evolution of literary Russian until, in the work of Puškin, it reached complete cultural maturity.

The chapters on West and South Slavonic languages are more briefly sketched. They are intended to show parallel and divergent develop-ments of the same Slavonic speech, and to serve to illustrate by likeness or contrast the development of Russian. But these languages have their own intrinsic interest, though no one of them has, like Russian, become international. They are vehicles of highly developed cultures. If Russia can boast in modern times three great novelists and one great poet, Poland and Bohemia have a longer history of achievement. Poland surpasses other Slavs in the amount and grandeur of its poetry; Czech thinkers have had profound influence on religion, education and poli-tics. The folk-poetry of the Serbs is consummately heroic and tender.

This book has been written under great stress, and cannot but show many faults. The war has absorbed the services of almost all the small band of competent students of Slavonic. One author has been wholly engulfed in public business, and the other partly, during the composi-tion of the work, which has been elaborated too often in hotel bed-rooms or railway carriages. Long neglect has left our libraries, despite the gallant efforts of their librarians, deficient in Slavonic works. Not infrequently we have been unable to consult essential works, and have had to rely on our own discretion. Apart from the excellent miniatures contributed by Sir Ellis Minns and Professor Jopson to the *Encyclo-pædia Britannica*, this is the first attempt to give in English an account of the Slavonic language-group. It is the first in any language to make the attempt along lines mainly historical and cultural rather than analytical. It will have the defects of first attempts; but, we hope, also some of the virtues.

We would close this preface by giving our sincere thanks to friends who have aided our task with counsel and help.

List of Abbreviations

A. acc. accusative.
abl. ablative.
act. active.
adj. adjective.
adv. adverb.
aor. aorist.
Arm. Armenian.
Av. Avestic (Zend).

B. Bulgarian.
Balt. Baltic.
BSl. Balto-Slavonic.

Ča. Ča-dialect of Serbocroat.
ChSl. Church Slavonic.
cond. conditional.
conj. conjunction.
CSl. Common Slavonic.
Cz. Czech.
CzSlk. Czechoslovak.

D. dat. dative.
D. dual.
dial. dialect.

E. East.
E. E-dialect of Serbocroat.
Eng. English.

F. fem. feminine.
fut. future.
F. French.

G. gen. genitive.
Germ. German, Germanic.
Gk. Greek.
Goth. Gothic.
Gt. Great.

I. instr. instrumental.
I. I-dialect of Serbocroat.
IE. Indo-European.
imper. imperative.
impf. imperfect.
indic. indicative.
It. Italian.

Je. Je-dialect of Serbocroat.

Kaj. Kaj-dialect of Serbocroat.

L. Lithuanian.
L. loc. locative.
Lat. Latin.
Latv. Latvian.
lit. literally.
LowWend. Lower Wendish.

M. modern.
M. masc. masculine.
Mid. middle.

N. North.
N. nom. nominative.
N. neut. neuter.

O. Old.
OB. Old Bulgarian.
OE. Old English.
OHG. Old High German.
OPr. Old Prussian.
opt. optative.

P. Polish.
P. pl. plural.
part. participle.
pass. passive.

Pers. Persian.
pf. perfect.
plpf. pluperfect.
prep. preposition.
pres. present.
pret. preterite.
pron. pronoun.

R. Russian.
Rum. Rumanian.
Ruth. Ruthenian (Ukrainian).

S. South.
S. Serbocroat.
S. sg. singular.
Skr. Sanskrit.
Sl. Slavonic.

Slk. Slovak.
Slov. Slovene.
Što. Što-dialect of Serbocroat.
subj. subjunctive.

T. (Osmanli) Turkish.
TT. Turko-Tatar.

UpWend. Upper Wendish.

V. voc. vocative.
vb. verb.

W. West.
Wend. Wendish.
WR. White Russian.

Phonetic transcriptions in square brackets. Sanskrit final -ḥ is, for convenience of comparison, represented by s. Cerebral or cacuminal ś.

   1 2 3. first, second, third person.

   = equals, equalling.

   / alternating with, constrasted with, or.

   * hypothetical form (asterisked).

   : : on the analogy of ($x :: y$ or $x : y :: a : b$, '*b* stands to *a* on the analogy of the relation between *y* and *x*').

   > derived from.

   < developing into.

When accents are written they do not always have the same meaning. In Lithuanian, Polish, Czechoslovak, Wendish, Slovene and Serbocroat, they are given in accordance with the principles of orthography in each language (save that the Serbocroat double grave accent is represented by the diaeresis), though it should be remembered that in Lithuanian, Slovene and Serbocroat the accents on vowels are omitted in ordinary print. For Russian and Bulgarian the acute accent (´) on a vowel denotes the stressed vowel, two accents on the same word meaning that both accentuations are found; for Common Slavonic the accents denote stress, and also rising (´) or falling (^) long intonation. Above a consonant or after it (´) is the sign of softening, and so it is before a vowel (e.g. *č š* are soft consonants, and *'a* is a softened vowel).

Chapter I

THE SLAVS

1. *The first Slavonic homeland.* To say where those who first spoke Slavonic were at home is beyond knowledge, but not beyond conjecture. A common element in several theories is that the original site must have been where yew and ivy were natives, since the names for these trees (R. *tis pljušč*) are native, and where the beech was a stranger, since its name is a Germanic loanword in all these languages (R. *buk*, cf. Germ. *Buche* ON. *bœkiskógr* 'beechwood'; and derivative R. *búkva* 'letter'). Now, the beech-tree does not flourish east of a line drawn through Königsberg*-Łomża-Siedlce-Lublin-Bukovina, and yew and ivy extend as far east as the line Ösel Island-Courland-Kaunas-Vilna-Kamenec Podolsk-Kišinev. Russia is entirely excluded from this reckoning, and so (though less decisively) is the valley of the Vistula. Within the two lines several emplacements are possible.

If we give weight to Ptolemy's statement that the Baltic was called the Slavonic Gulf because Slavs lay all along its shores (κατέχει δὲ τὴν Σαρματίαν ἔθνη μέγιστα οἵ τε Οὐενέδαι παρ' ὅλον τὸν Οὐενεδικὸν κόλπον), and add that the retention of the original name for 'sea' (R. *móre*) implies that the sea was never lost to sight, we may conclude that the first home was on the shores of the Baltic, between Königsberg and Riga. The Baltic peoples retain the word for 'sea' only in the Riga region, and it means rather 'lake'; the new name was L. *júres*. The Balts, however, cannot have suffered much displacement since the earliest times, and we must suppose that the Slavs extended no further than the middle course of the Niemen and Western Dvina, with the Lithuanians (*Lietuvà* 'Ripuarians', cf. Lat. *litus* 'shore' IE. **lei-* 'flow') on the upper courses. The special attraction of this theory is that it accounts satisfactorily for the long association which must have been experienced by the two language-groups, and for the fact that the Slavs were not drawn down the Dniester river-road to the Black Sea and Ægean at a much earlier date. Its disadvantage is that it has no vestige of support from archæology. River-names are often a criterion of ancient residence, and there are no Slavonic river-names in this region. On the other hand, there is none anywhere except the *Berezina* (R. *berëza* 'birch') and the *Desna* (OB. *dèsnŭ*='right'). The Oder, Bug, Vistula, Dnieper, etc., have names of non-Slavonic origin.

* Now Kaliningrad.

If the evidence of river-names were pressed too hard it would leave the Slavs no original foothold in the world!

Another emplacement satisfying the botanical conditions would be in Eastern Poland. Some, interpreting the conditions very strictly, place the primitive Slavs in Polesie, centring on the Pripet Marshes, a terrible region of frozen or soggy bogland where nothing but a primitive life of hunting and fishing would have been possible. Such a location would account for the long isolation of the Slavs, but not for their characteristic culture or even their physical increase. There would be strong temptation to descend the Dnieper water-road at all costs. Others extend the original home westward as far as the Vistula, and even with more hesitation as far as the Oder, so as to provide at least a foothold on solid ground. This corresponds, at least, to the first location recorded by a historian, namely Tacitus. It would be less easy to account for the silence of Greek writers, and, in fact, Niederle supposes that the Slavs were not wholly unknown. He identifies as Slavs the *Neuri* of Herodotus (whom Šachmatov identifies as Western Finns), and possibly also the *Budini* and *Ploughman-Scyths*. On·these points the evidence is far from clear. Herodotus mentions the *Neuri* as recent arrivals, who had driven the *Budini* eastward.·They act in concert with the *Anthropophagi* ('Cannibals', Mordvinians; Iranian *mard* 'man' *khvar* 'devour') and *Melanchlæni* (Čeremisses, who wear dark cloaks), who are certainly Eastern Finns. Hence the presumption that the *Neuri* were Western Finns. Herodotus notes that their language is unlike that of the Iranian Scyths, but he makes no note on the language of the *Neuri*, whom we are thus tempted to consider as linguistically akin to Indo-European, that is, as Slavs. We get no help from his description of their customs, of which the chief was shape-shifting, a form of wizardry as familiar to Finns and Lapps as to Slavs; nor can we identify the land plagued by serpents from which the *Neuri* descended one generation before Darius.*

The first Slavs practised a forest-agricultural culture in village-communities. Strictly archæological evidence is of a date much too late to throw much light on the conditions of 2000–1000 B.C., and the linguistic inferences are based on what has been preserved and what lost of the common Indo-European store. The Slavs were not sea-farers, though they may have had the sea in sight. They lost the original word for 'ship', and reduced their requirements to dug-out canoes (R. *odnoderёvka* Gk. μονόξυλον). At the opening of history the boats in use among the Slavs were called **oldija* OB. *aldiji ladiji* R. *lodjá*, **čĭlnŭ* (R. *čёln* 'canoe') and OB. *korablĭ* (a loanword,

---

* We have to thank Professor Drummond, University of Manchester, for verifying the botanical details.

Gk. καράβιον). There are no Slavonic words implying political, military or religious organizations more elaborate than the village unit. The words for 'prince', 'king', 'emperor' (R. *knjaž koról car*) are all loanwords of comparatively recent date, and only the South Slavs appear to have known a loose confederacy of village-communities (S. *žúpa* 'county, district, parish', *žùpân* 'lieutenant of the county', *župànija* 'district, county'). There was no word for 'priest', but a considerable number for 'wizard', including one of the terms for 'doctor' (R. *vrač*). Complex ritual begat high-sounding compounds in Sanskrit and Greek. Slavonic was almost devoid of such words, though they were readily remade when Christianity brought a lexicon of concepts expressed by Greek compounds (R. *Bogoródica* θεοτόκος, *licemér* 'hypocrite'). Personal names, however, were compounded (*Vladímir*, *Svjatopólk*, etc.), except in familiar forms.

On the other hand, the village-community was a rounded whole. It was a 'village' (P. *wieś* R. dial. *veś* OB. *vǐsǐ*, cf. Lat. *vicus* Gk. οἶκος) otherwise regarded it was a *mir*, i.e., 'village-community' 'world' 'peace', and it was a 'settlement' (R. *seló* P. *siedlisko*, cf. Lat. *sedere* 'sit'), since the shifting system of primitive agriculture required ever-renewed settlements. The earliest extant form, as still used in the Drawehn, by the lower Elbe, was that of a ring round a cleared space. It was only at a later date that communications developed, roads ran through the villages, and they began to take the form of a ribbon. The site was no doubt a clearing made in a forest, in which the oak was the principal object, and was revered as the seat of the god of thunder (R. *Perún*, L. *Perkúnas*, cf. Lat. *quercus*). Other trees were the birch, yew, ivy, lime, aspen, ash, etc. Among animals the bear was of special consequence. Its name was taboo, and it was alluded to as the 'honey-eater' (R. *medvéd*), partly through fear perhaps, and partly as a rival in the search for honey (R. *měd*) in the woods, from which was made hydromel or 'mead' (R. *měd* Gk. μέθυ). The wolf (R. *volk* Gk. λύκος) may have been a tribal-totem, since it appears as an element in names. The boar (R. *vepř*), stag (R. *olén*), beaver (R. *bobr*), mouse (R. *myš'*), duck (R. *útka*) and goose (R. *guś*) were familiar, though the last two may not have been domesticated. Among domestic animals were the sheep and the cow (R. *ovcá koróva* and *govjádina* 'beef' cf. Lat. *bos* Gk. βοῦς). The word *tur* (Lat. *taurus* 'bull') means 'aurochs', and has been displaced by *vol;* similarly *koń* 'horse' *kobýla* 'mare' and *sobáka* 'dog' have displaced older names doubtless known to the primitive Slavs (L. *ašvà* 'mare' Skr. *açva-* 'horse', L. *šuõ* 'dog' Gk. κύων). Terms for hunting and fishing are relatively late and few, and it seems that the villagers supported themselves principally by agriculture, like the modern Lithuanians. The name for 'grain' (R. *zernó* cf. Lat. *granum*

Eng. *corn*) is ancient. Though the specific names of cereals do not go back to the Indo-European period (R. *pšeníca* 'wheat' *rož* 'rye' *ovĕs* 'oats' *jačmén* 'barley' *próso* 'millet'), they are Panslavonic, and prove the intensity of the culture. The principal utensil was the hand-plough (OB. *ralo* 'plough' P. *radlica* 'ploughshare', cf. Gk. ἄροτρον Lat. *aratrum*), which the horse helped to pull (L. *arklỹs* 'horse' *árklas* 'wooden plough'); the plough with wheel and coulter (R. *plug* Germ. *Pflug*) came later from abroad. In addition to the word R. *mĕd* 'honey, mead' already quoted, the word for 'bee' (R. *pčelá* <OR. *bičela*, L. *bitìs bìtė*) proves that apiculture ascends with the Slavs to a primitive date.

Archæological data in the Slavonic field derive mostly from the first centuries of the Christian Era, and do not serve to confirm or refute inferences from language made concerning a much earlier time. They are worth mentioning because the first historical account gives a quite different picture. According to Tacitus the Slavs of the first century led a nomad life of rapine between the foothills of the Carpathian range and the confines of the Finns (*Venethi . . . quidquid inter Peucinos Fennosque silvarum ac montium erigitur latrociniis pererrant*). On the other hand, he describes the Lithuanians (*Aestii*), no longer in contact with the Slavs, as remarkable for their agricultural labours (*frumenta cæterosque fructus patientius quam pro solita Germanorum inertia laborant*). The vocabulary above cited is evidence that the Slavs were also ardent agriculturists, and their agitated condition in the first century A.D. must be put to the account of the Germanic invaders; the Goths had then recently arrived from Sweden and were pressing up the Vistula, and one or two centuries earlier the *Bastarnæ* must have thrust their way through Slavonic territory to reach the Carpathians and Black Sea. When the Slavs, and in particular the Russians, later appear as colonizers, it is by no means as hunters or nomads, but as land-hungry agriculturists following behind a line of foresters seeking for fur and honey. Their unit is the village-community, and the whole process corresponds to a way of life older than the German aggressions.

2. *Slavonic and Indo-European*. The science of language, like other sciences, is confined by its data. One may make inferences concerning geography, history, culture, etc.; but such inferences are not confirmed until supported by evidence proper to those studies, nor is it necessary for linguistic purposes that they should be confirmed. Archæology is silent concerning the primitive habitat of the Slavs, and has still less to say about the habitat of those who, possibly four thousand years ago, spoke a united Indo-European language. Arguments have been constructed in favour of places as diverse as the Baltic area, Central Europe, South Russia, and Central Asia. For our purposes, however,

a simple diagram giving relative positions will suffice (Tokharian being omitted as notably displaced):—

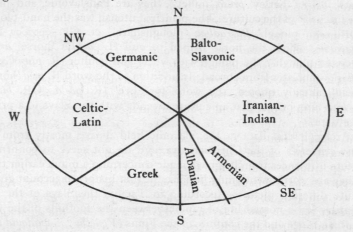

The diagram shows that Baltic and Slavonic languages form the north-western branch of the eastern (*satem*) branch of the Indo-European languages, in association with Indo-Iranian, Armenian and Albanian, but also in immediate contact with the most easterly of the western (*centum*) branch, viz. Germanic. With Greek, Latin and Celtic the relations are remote; but Greek, because of the great age of its literature and its marked conservatism in some respects, is particularly helpful in determining the historical meaning of certain Slavonic features. Omitting these remoter contacts and expressing immediate ones in more detail (though not necessarily in contemporary detail) we reach a distribution as follows:—

Germanic: Old Swedish	Baltic: Latvian
Gothic	Lithuanian
SLAVONIC	Old Prussian
	Iranian: Scythian (Ossetic)

Illyrian: Thracian?:   Sarmatian
Venetic?   Phrygian   Medic and Persian
(Albanian)   Armenian   Indian: Sanskrit*

* For the Indo-European family of languages see pp. 3–17 of R. Priebsch and W. Collinson, *The German Language* (London: Faber and Faber, 1934); A. Meillet, *Introduction à l'étude comparative des langues indo-européennes* (Paris, 1924); W. Schmidt, *Die Sprachfamilien und Sprachenkreise der Erden* (Heidelberg, 1926), pp. 42–43; A. Meillet and M. Cohen, *Les langues du monde* (Paris, 1924); K. Brugmann and B. Delbrück, *Abrégée de grammaire comparée des langues indo-européennes* (trsl. A. Meillet and R. Gauthiot, Paris, 1905). A. Carnoy, arguing on behalf of South Russia, gives the evidence in exceptionally agreeable form (*Les indo-européens: préhistoire des langues, des mœurs et des croyances de l'Europe*, Brussels-Paris, 1921).

It would seem that the terminations of the dative and instrumental plural and dual of nouns had not been precisely defined in the late Indo-European period. Apart from the interference of pronouns with the *o*- and *a*-declensions, the remaining evidence does not suffice to reconstitute the forms proper to these cases, and merely reveals elements more cumbrous and more independent than are used elsewhere in the paradigm. Two tendencies are perceived. There is a northern usage in -*m*- shared by the Germanic and Balto-Slavonic groups (OB. *vḷkomŭ* L. *viĺkams* Goth. *wulfam* OHG. *wolfum* <-*umiz*, -*amiz* 'to the wolves'), and a southern usage in -*bh*- (Skr. *açva-bhyam*, -*bhyas*, -*bhiṣ*, Arm. *gailov* 'to the wolves', Lat. *ovibus duābus*, Homeric Gk. ναῦφι, Gaulish *Namausikabo*, Irish *rigaib*=Lat. *regibus*). The element -*bh*- appears in OB. *tebĕ*=Lat. *tibi*, and the Gk. -φι is a postposition used in all numbers [cf. L. -*p(i)*: *dieviep* 'by God']; -*m*- occurs in the Lithuanian and Slavonic instr. sg. (L. *sūnumì* R. *sýnom*). Taken in sum, these vacillations are evidence of a certain degree of contact between Balto-Slavonic and Germanic before the separation of the Indo-European languages into the two main (*centum/satem*) groups. After this time there must have been a long separation of Germanic and Slavonic, since it is only with the beginning of our era, as the loanwords show, that German contacts again become important.

The *Veneti* were an Illyrian stock. The earliest recorded name of the Slavs is *Venethi* (Οὐενέδαι), and it is still applied by the Finns to Russians (*venäläinen*). It is not a self-adopted name, but clearly German (*Wenden*, *Windische Höhe* in Austria, ON. *Vindland*= 'Pomerania', etc.). One possibility is that the Slavs may have moved into an area formerly held by the Veneti, and so received their name. Another suggestion is that the word derives from Celt. **vindos* 'white'(?), which appears in place-names, and that the Germans borrowed it from the Celts. The fairness of the Slavs was noted by classical authors. The East Slavs first appear in history as a confederation of tribes under the name *Antes* (6th cent.). It has been explained as the plural of **As* or **Os* (cf. Ptolemy's "Οσιοι, 'Οσυλοί and the modern Ossetes of Caucasia); it may have been borrowed from Scythian neighbours.

The case for contact between the Slavs and the ancestors of the Armenians is perhaps stronger. F. C. Conybeare remarks (*Encyc. Brit.*, 11th ed., ii, p. 572): 'Armenian appears to be half-way dialect between the Aryan branch and Slavo-Lettic'. Comparison is made particularly difficult by the drastic changes that have affected Armenian sounds, forms and words, and by the refashioning of its vocabulary under Persian influence. Its history is not well known. There is nothing against the ancient account of this people as descended from the Phrygians who immigrated from Thrace.

The eastern Indo-European languages are united in a sound-shift which must have occurred towards the end of the period of common development.

IE. *k̯mtóm '100' OB. sŭto L. šĩtas Skr. çata Av. satəm/ Gk. ἑκατόν Lat. centum OIr. cet Germ. hund;

IE. *dek̯mt '10' CSl. desętĭ L. dešimtìs Skr. daça Arm. tasn/ Gk. δέκα Lat. decem OIr. deich Eng. ten.

In the first group of languages, known as the satem-group, the palatal gutturals of Indo-European have become sibilants, though they remain as gutturals in the second, or centum-, group. The effect of these changes is very marked, and was associated with other changes which tend to emphasize the mutual resemblance of the eastern languages. For instance the IE. *kʷ also palatalizes in the East but is otherwise developed in the West, in

IE. *kʷetwor- '4' OB. četyre Skr. catur Arm. č'ors/Gk. τέτταρες Lat. quattuor OIr. cethir OWelsh petguar.

Between Slavonic and the Indo-Iranian languages, within the eastern group, there is a special relation due to their sharing in the i u r k rule (sect. 31). The common method of representing languages by family-trees tends to give a wrong impression of their development. It shows them joined in some common origin, but otherwise quite isolated from each other. That is not how languages have developed in historic ages. The Romance languages remained liable to common movements long after they had begun to separate, and when they were fully developed they still shared some common trends and linked up through frontier dialects. In the remotest prehistory groups may have been smaller in relation to the vast earth, and so have tended to greater aloofness; but this tendency may have been balanced by the greater mobility of nomad hunters. The Turko-Tatar tribes of Central Asia cover great distances in their migrations. We should rather suppose the separation of the Indo-European peoples to be like the stretching of elastic. Their contact would be increasingly tenuous, but would hold until the break came, when they would fly apart with a great interval. So long as the contact was maintained, however thinly, an impulse to change felt in one centre might communicate itself to the others.

The case is that i u r k cause IE. s to become Skr. ṣ Iranian š Sl. ch[χ]/š. One account supposes that these sounds are not historically related, but arose separately in each language-area. If there was only one change involved, and it had a simple phonetic explanation, as in the change rs >rš in L. virsùs 'top' marsùs 'forgetful', one might suppose the resemblances to be fortuitous. But the sounds i u r k have almost no common features, and the i u r k rule must be the result of three or four different sound-shifts brought together in one grand result. Such coincidence over so wide an area must, we think, be due to contact. What is common is the development of *s* as far as the 'lingual' or 'cerebral' *ṣ* (the *s* of *horse* when the *r* is sounded) which survives in Sanskrit. Now the history of Spanish sounds shows that this *ṣ*, though it can be maintained for centuries, is nevertheless an unstable sound, with a tendency either to develop into the palatal sibilant *š* (the *s* of *sure*) or to relapse into the normal dorso-alveolar *s* (the *s* of *sore*); the same history shows that *š* may be pronounced further back in the mouth until it becomes the velar fricative [χ] Sp. *j* Sl. *ch*. These later developments belong to the separate histories of Iranian and Slavonic, but the movement as far as *ṣ* is common to Slavonic and Indo-Iranian.

This argument is not weakened by the fact that the Ashkun Kafirs, who lie between Iran and India, have in these cases *iš us rṣ kṣ*. Their language is little known and its history is not known at all. The group *us* may be due to a relapse, and *iš* shows, if anything, that the palatal *š* developed from *ṣ* first under the influence of the palatal vowel.

A common feature of syntax is the postposition of a weak demonstrative **jos/is* to serve almost as a definite article. CSl. **dobra-jego otĭca* L. *gēro-jo tĕ'vo* 'of the good father' resembles Avestic *stārǝm yǝm Tištrīm* 'the star Sirius'. The parallel, however, is not entirely convincing. In modern East Armenian the article is suffixed, and there is a considerable use of other pronominal suffixes, as in Common Slavonic (e.g. R. *dneś* 'today', with the demonstrative suffix *-sĭ* 'this').

There are also some remarkable coincidences of vocabulary between Iranians and Slavs. There is a group of words meaning 'corn' 'rich' 'distributor' which spring from the same root in Skr. *bhagas* 'distributor' *bhagavant* 'honourable' Phrygian *Zeus Bagaios* R. *bogátyj* 'rich' *ubógij* 'poor' P. *zboże* 'corn' Ruth. *zbíže* 'corn' WR. *zbóže* 'bread' Cz. *zboží* 'wares'. In Sanskrit and in Phrygian we see the natural use of these terms as applied to the deities who distribute well-being to their worshippers, but it is only in Iranian and Slavonic (OPers. *baga-* R. *bog* 'god') that the word has ousted the original term for the supreme deity (*Zeus*, L. *diẽvas*). Those who do not recognize in this semantic change any proof of interchange of ideas are none the less ready to admit as evidence of contact the following parallels:

R. *topór* 'axe' *sochá* 'plough' *sobáka* 'dog' *kur* 'cock' S. *vätra* 'fire'/Pers. *tabar*, Skr. *çākhā* Pers. *šakh* 'bough' (L. *šakà* 'bough' Goth. *hoha* 'plough'), Medic *spaka* (recorded by Herodotus), Pers. *khorūs*, Pers. *ātash* Skr. *atharī* Ossetic *art*.

These words seem to define the oldest stratum of culture borrowings in Slavonic.

That the East Iranians made a long halt in South Russia seems to be indicated by the presence of the word *dānu* 'water' in the names of the great rivers: *Danubius Danastris Danapris Tanais.* The Ossetic (Scythian) equivalent is *don*, which has prevailed in one instance. The Finnish languages show a number of examples of indebtedness to their southern neighbours in words which are not shared by the Slavs. One explanation of the movements reported by Herodotus as occurring in the hinterland of Scythia is that the Finnish peoples may have been pressing southward, and tending to cut the Dnieper line of communication between Slavs and Iranians. The loanwords mentioned are found in two series, according to Šachmatov. The older series is of such an archaic complexion as to be best explained by parallels from Sanskrit, before Iranian languages took their special complexion. Examples of this series are

Finnish *sisar* 'sister' Mordvinian *sazor*/Skr. *svasar* Pers. *khāhar*;

Mordvinian *azoro* 'lord' Zyrjenian *ozyr ozer* 'rich'/Skr. *asura* 'demon' Av. *ahura-*;

Mordvinian *veŕgas* 'wolf'/Skr. *vṛkas* Pers. *gurg*.

The other series is much later, and is definitely Scythian (Ossetic), as

Mordvinian *loman* 'man'/Ossetic *limän* 'friend';

Mordvinian *eŕdeks* 'oath' Permian *jord*/Ossetic *ard ärd*.

The evidence for the contact between Balts and Slavs must be given later. It is so intimate as to belong to the evolution of Slavonic proper. Some scholars have assumed the existence of a Balto-Slavonic language, but this theory has been strongly disputed by Meillet. However, in the same proportion as one admits the argument against their original identity of speech, one must admit that for a protracted symbiosis. The extraordinarily close parallelism of Baltic and Slavonic sounds, words and syntax, if not due to a common original tongue, implies long and intimate interchange and communication. When these languages differ it is usually because the Baltic group preserves the original Indo-European matter, while Slavonic innovates. Where and when this community of life took place, we cannot know for certain. If Herodotus be considered to have known nothing of the Slavs in the fifth century of our era, it may have been because they were then lying beside the Balts in the Baltic area. There may have been periods of contact followed by others of separation. These would allow for the separate development of Slavonic features, as well as the common development of the Balto-Slavonic characteristics. In the days of Tacitus Balts and Slavs were separated, and nothing seemed to have associated them in his mind. On the other hand, contact had been recovered before the first Russian chronicles were written.

3. *The Centre of Diffusion* (*1st–5th centuries* A.D.). Tacitus describes the Slavs as living by pillage in the region between the Germanic Peucini, on the Carpathian foothills, and the desolate territories of the

Finns. The Peucini were the rearguard of the Bastarnæ, who had thrust through Slavonic lands to reach the Black Sea. In the first century the Goths, immigrants from Sweden, were on the lower Vistula, and pressing hard on the Slavs. In the second century the Goths had occupied the upper Vistula valley, and were in touch with the Finns to the east of the Slavs. This location accounts for L. *gùdas* 'White Russian'. In the third century the Goths occupied South Russia with a strong kingdom which effectively barred the path of the Slavs to the south. A relic of their rule was the small body of Crimean Goths (R. *góty*) who continued to use that language until the sixteenth century. The Goths were overwhelmed by the Huns in 376, but were merged into the Hunnish kingdom, forming a still more potent bar to Slavonic migration. Consequently, no mass movements were possible until the Hunnish kingdom disintegrated on the death of Attila (453).

These five centuries were a period of agitation and compression. The Slavs were held within the quadrilateral of the Narew, Vistula, Carpathian foothills and middle Dnieper, subject to constant Germanic movements across the dry ground, and with the Pripet wastes for most of their patrimony. As they were populous (much more so than the Goths, for instance), it would seem that they were compressed like a spring, especially after they had lost the Vistula valley. Once the pressure was relaxed by the dissolution of the Hunnish empire, they expanded violently to the west, south and east, and they found in all directions chiefly empty land.

The superiority of the German tribes in war and some domestic arts led to a considerable number of loans to the Common Slavonic language. Military terms are R. *knjaż* 'prince' (Germ. *kuningaz* Finnish *kuningas* 'king'), *vítjaż* 'hero' (tribe of *Witings?*, ON. *Viking?*), *ljúdi* 'people' (cf. Germ. *Leute*), *Čud* 'Estonians' (Goth. *þjuda* 'people, heathen'), *meč* 'sword' (Goth. *mêki*), *šlem* 'helmet' (<*chelm-*), *polk* 'troop, regiment' (cf. Eng. *folk*). As to housing, the Slavonic house was a miserable half-buried hovel without heat. The Germans led them to add a room with stove (Frankish *stuba* OB. *istüba* R. *izbá* 'hut') in addition to the cold room (*séni* pl. 'vestibule', cf. *seń* 'shade, shelter'). The word might also be used for the room where steam baths were taken, though for this the Gk. Lat. *banea* R. *bánja* was more precisely apt. Other household words were R. *kúchnja* 'kitchen' (OHG. *kuchina* Lat. *coquina*), P. *komora* 'room, larder', Slov. *híša* 'house', P. *buda* 'booth'. To agriculture the Germans probably contributed the wheeled plough with coulter (R. *plug*), the words *vinó* 'wine' and *vinográd* 'vine', and *skot* 'cattle' (Germ. **skattaz*). They added to Slavonic some names for utensils (as R. *bljúdo* 'dish' Goth. *biups*, P. *misa* R. *míska* 'tureen' Goth. *mes* Lat. *mensa*), bread (*chleb*), the rudiments of exchange (OB. *cęta* 'coin' Goth **kinta*,

OB. *skŭle(d)zĭ sklęzĭ štĭlęgŭ* Goth. **skillings*, OB. *pĕnęgŭ pĕnędzĭ* Germ. *pfenning*) and the first Christian terms (R. *cérkoǔ* 'church'). The number '1000' (P. *tysiąc*) seems to have been borrowed at this time.

It will be noted that these words imply only a humble level of civilization, except when due to an ultimate Roman source, and that they suggest the Slavonic culture had suffered a decline. Tacitus describes the Balts (*Aestii;* the name was later borrowed by the Estonians for the name of their country *Eesti*) as enjoying a relatively flourishing agricultural civilization, raised above the German level. It is some confirmation of this difference of level that the Finns, borrowing at this time new words for their own rising standards, take them (when not from German) from Lithuanian, not from Slavonic. Examples are: Finn. *paimen* 'shepherd' *oinas* 'ram' *heinä* 'hay' *tarha* 'yard, fold' *seinä* 'wall' *silta* 'bridge' *ratas* 'wheel' *laiva* 'ship' *taivas* 'heaven, sky' *heimo* 'tribe' *perkele* 'devil', etc. The words are important because half a millennium older than the oldest Lithuanian records. *Taivas paimen* L. *diēvas* 'God' *piemuō* show an older stage of the vocalism (*ai > ie*); *heinä* L. *šiēnas* R. *séno* is proof of the former existence of a neuter in Lithuanian (since there is no final -*s* in this Finnish word, as in masc. *taivas*). The existence of a Baltic neuter is attested by Old Prussian. Slavonic loans to Finnish (*risti* 'cross' *pappi* 'priest' *pukana* 'pagan') were delayed until after the advent of Christianity.[*]

Towards the end of the period the Slavs emerge under their national names. The term *Wend* is not native, but is in universal use among the Germans, and was communicated by them to the Romans, and to the Finns (*venäläinen* 'Russian'). The most general word was *Slovĕne* (pl. of a sg. -*ĕn-inŭ*). Its etymology is doubtful: R. *slóvo* 'word' (**ǩleu-*, Gk. κλέος 'fame' Avestic *sravo* 'word' Skr. *çravas* 'glory') or R. *sláva* 'glory' are both possible. In the latter case the Slavs would be self-styled 'the glorious'. In the former case they would be 'those who speak', as against the 'dumb' R. *némcy* 'Germans' (*nemój* 'dumb'). A further consideration supporting this view is that the only discrimination known to the Slavs was R. *jazýk* 'tongue', the term used to denote the various tribes of Russian Slavs in the Kiev chronicle. The *Slovĕne*, who appear in Byzantine chronicles from the sixth century, are evidently Yugoslavs. They are allied with the *Antes* or *Antæ* who later retired to Russia, and were evidently East Slavs. Other forms of the word give the modern *Slovenes* of *Slovenia*, the *Slovaks*, and the *Slovinces* (*Wendish Slovenes*) of Lake Leba in Pomerania.

---

[*] See Meillet and Cohen, *Les langues du monde* (Paris, 1924, p. 177); A. Brückner, 'Slavisch-Litauisch', p. 86, *Die Erforschung der indogermanischen Sprachen*, ii, 3 (Strassburg, 1917).

The word *Serb* is also wide-spread, and has no certain explanation. There are the *Srbi* of the Balkans, and the Lusatian or Wendish Serbs or *Sorabs*. Mention of *Serb(l)ioi* in Russia in the tenth century may have been due to a mistake, and so also the *Sporoi* of Procopius in the sixth century (*Bosporoi?*). Niederle claimed as Slavonic the *Lugii* of eastern Germany, by virtue of R. *lug* 'meadow' (= P. *ług* 'lye' *ługowisko* 'marsh'/not P. *łąg* 'marsh, moor'), but this seems very questionable. The name of the Russians (*Ruś*) is most probably connected with Finn. *Ruotsi* 'Swede', and is an example of a name due to foreign political organization. So also is the name of the *Bulgars*. The Poles (P. *Polak*/R. *Ljach* L. *Leńkas* Magyar *Lengyel* OS. *Ledanin* T. *Lehistan* 'Poland') derive their name from (R.) *póle* 'field' or from some topographical word (cf. R. dial. *ljáda* 'fallow'). Most of the names of Russian tribes in the tenth century were of this nature: *Poljane* from *póle* 'field, plain', *Drevljane* from *dérevo* 'wood', *Sěverjane* from *séver* 'north'. The *Vjatiči* and *Radimiči* are explained as patronymics (*Vjatka Radim*). The Russian *Bužane* are evidently the dwellers on the Bug, as the *Havolane* are dwellers on the Hawel (cf. Germ. *Helvecones*). The Czechs (*Čechy*) have been connected with *četa* 'group'. The Croats (*Hrvati*) were found upon the Carpathians as well as in the Balkans in the tenth century. The name has been connected with a Germanic form of the name of that range.

What is characteristic of all these names is their lack of political and military implications. There are no truly national entities, no leagues, few patronymics. Under such conditions it is not at all improbable that the Slavs may have been partly implicated in the movements of other nations before their own mass movements of the sixth century. In Germany their tribes sometimes inherited German names, as *Slęzy Varnovi Havolane Rojane* (*Rugii*). The German *Silingi* left their name and land to the Slavonic *Silędzi* (whence P. *Ślązk*), from which comes MHG. *Schlesien* 'Silesia'. These mutual interchanges seem to indicate a period of joint tenancy between Germans and some groups of Slavs. The same seems indicated by the German-Slavonic parallelism of place- and river-names (e.g. *Elbe*/*Labe*). No doubt also Attila's empire included some Slav subjects, which may explain why the ambassador Priscus was offered a drink of μέδος (R. *mëd* 'mead') in Lower Hungary in 448. Inferences drawn from place-names in Hungary and the Balkans are open to objection, and are rejected by some authorities. Thus the old name of Lake Balaton was *Pelso* (Pliny and after), which might be due to Sl. *pleso* Cz. *pleso* 'mere, tarn' R. *plëso* 'river-reach'. The Tisza was also called *Potisus*, and Sl. *po-* is used of places adjoining rivers (cf. *Polabian* 'beside the Elbe'). The ancient *Dierna* or *Zerna* corresponds to the modern *Černa*, though folk-etymology may have been at work. There are also other apparently Slavonic place-names quoted before the fifth century. But all these may have had another explanation.

4. *The Slavonic Migrations (6th–10th centuries). Withdrawal in the West and South.* It was from Germany east of the Elbe that the principal German migrations set out. The Goths left for Russia in the third century. At the beginning of the fifth century the Vandals, Silingi, Alans and Suevi headed for Spain, and somewhat later the Burgundians moved across Germany to the Rhine and Rhône. The Lombards were also easterners. In consequence of these movements the whole region was depopulated. Little is known of the consequent Slavonic movement, save that it had reached the Elbe in the sixth century. Their *Serbian* name is preserved in that of *Zerbst*, south-east of Magdeburg. The method of advance may well have been infiltration, and the evidence already noted for the symbiosis of Slavs and Germans may have its explanation in the conditions of the immigration. In 805 Charlemagne attempted to stabilize the German-Slav frontier by his *limes sorabicus*, which was later continued to the Baltic at Kiel as the *limes Saxoniæ* (808). The frontier ran from Regensburg on the Danube to Bamberg on the Main, and thence through Erfurt to the Elbe near Magdeburg; keeping west of the Elbe to include the *Drawehn*, the line crossed the river not far from Hamburg and ended at Kiel. In front of the frontier were outlying Slavs at Fulda.

Behind the Elbe frontier, the Western Slavs seem to have been divided linguistically into two dialects by a line roughly from Frankfurt-on-Oder to Magdeburg. There were no great politically conscious masses, but only a number of tribes and clans. They are best represented by documents in the northern half. The principal bodies seem to have been the Dravanians beyond the Elbe. of which the last survivor reached the eighteenth century. His language was noted, and has importance in Slavonic philology as the matter of August Schleicher's study (*Grammatik der polabischen Sprache*, 1871), one of the basic texts of the discipline. The name *Polab* is something of a misnomer, since the historic site of that tribe was on the other side of the Elbe. The proper name should be *Dravanian* (P. *Drzewianie*). In this region, also known as *Wendland*, there are the townships of Lüchow and Wustrow (P. *Łuków Ostrów*). Between the Elbe and the Island of Rügen were a mass of tribes generically called Obodritic. The colonization of Rügen was especially thorough. The Slavs inherited the German name (*Rojane*) and maintained an important oracle at Arcona. The creation of this religious centre and of another at a place called Rethra was the utmost effort of centralization by the Western Slavs in the early Middle Ages. Between Rügen and Stettin were the tribes grouped as Veletians, and between Oder and Vistula were the Pomeranians (P. *pomorze* 'maritime country'). Of the Pomeranian

Slavs there have survived to our times two groups, the Wendish Slovenes of Lake Leba (about 200–250 souls) and the Cassubians (*Kaszuby*) on the west side of the Vistula estuary. The southern tribes have a large number of divisions, with names such as *Lužyčane, Serbište, Sorabes, Milčane, Slęzane*. In the region of Berlin were the Havolane, and near them the Sprevjane on the Spree.

These immigrants have had an important effect on German nomenclature in the district between Elbe and Oder. Names in *-itz, -za* and *-wind(en)* are reminders of former Slavonic inhabitants. Leipzig was once *Lipsk* (*lipa* 'lime-tree') and Dresden was **Dręždžane*, 'the people of the **dręzga*=marshy woods'. Such parallels as *Wrocław/Breslau Babimost/Bomst, Chojnice/Konitz* show how the Slavonic name has undergone purely German developments, and has not been borrowed and left invariable, like a wholly strange term.

The German reaction began in the ninth century, but was exceptionally strong between the twelfth and fifteenth centuries. It took the form of a war of extermination upon a religious pretext (*ut paganismus Sclavorum destrueretur*). The means of subjugation were fortress-cities, such as Hamburg, Dresden, Frankfurt and Königsberg. This last was in the territory of the Borussians (Old Prussians), since the German drive in Pomerania passed right through the Slavs to attack the Baltic peoples. King Bolesław the Brave (992–1025) began to constitute a state capable of resisting these aggressions in Poland, but the enemy was not decisively halted until the Teutonic Knights suffered a crushing defeat at Grünwald-Tannenberg in 1410.

In consequence of this Germanic reaction the Slavs found themselves back almost at their starting line in the Vistula valley, except for the outlying Lusatian Wends of Cottbus and Bautzen (*Khoćebuz Budyšin*) in the upper valley of the Spree, the Cassubians and Wendish Slovenes (P. *Słowińcy*) hard against the Polish border, and the so-called Polabs, who lost their language in the early eighteenth century.

Poland suffered a heavy defeat at Liegnitz by the Tatars, but they were able to recover sooner than the Muscovites and gradually gained a wide dominion in White Russia and the Ukraine. This, however, did not affect the language, since the Polish Government was polyglot. White Russian became a chancery language, not a literary tongue. Of more importance was the difference of cult. The Roman and Orthodox churches used Latin and Church Slavonic for their respective liturgies, and the latter was also the literary language of Russia. Orthodox subjects of the Polish kings were attracted towards the eastern power by the common language of their devotions. On this side the linguistic frontier seems to have been stable since the thirteenth century.

The Czechs and Slovaks penetrated into the valleys of northern tributaries of the Danube as a result of the dissolution of Attila's empire on his death (453). In Bohemia proper they found a natural geographic division, lying as it does in the quadrilateral of the Bohemian Forest, Erzgebirge, Sudetes, and Moravian highlands. The Moravians lie in three sides of a rhombus open to the Danube, but the Slovaks have no natural frontiers to the south. At first, however, the Slavs lay thinly over the whole space of 'Great Moravia', and connected through Slovaks south of the Danube with the Slovenes, while there were Slavs akin to the Bulgar Slavs in Hungary. These connections were snapped by the irruption of the Magyars into the plain of the Tisza under their leader Árpád (895–906), and the creation of Austria after Otto I's victory at Lechfeld (955). Vienna was reached by the German colonists about 1140, and after that a solid mass of Germans and Magyars cut off the Czechoslovaks from the South Slavs. Moreover they occupied the lowlands into which the Czechoslovak valleys led, and pressed upon their neighbours by the easiest way of entry. The Czechs and Moravians thus fell within the Austrian pressure-area, and the Slovaks within the Hungarian system. All regional differences were accentuated, and perhaps nowhere in the Slavonic world are there still so many tribal differences.

The Slavs were further constricted by the policy of their own kings. Some of the Premyslids, notably Ottakar II (1253–78), wishing to gain an urban and artisan population despite the reluctance of the Slavs to live in towns, introduced German colonies within the Czech quadrilateral. In this way Reichenberg (Liberec), Trautenau (Trutnov), Glatz (Kladsko), Teplitz (Teplice), Brüx (Most), Carlsbad (Karlovy Vary) and Eger (Cheb) became German. A reaction in favour of Czech language and nationality began in the fourteenth century and reached its height in the fifteenth. The language was then given official status beyond its narrower frontiers: Opava (1431), Těšín (1434), Moravia (·1480), Bohemia itself (1495). The Hussite reform and the ensuing religious wars gave a further outlet for national self-expression; but it was overwhelmed in 1620 by the defeat on the White Mountain. The victorious Austrians proceeded to stamp out not only the Protestant religion but also the Czech language, and in 1790 the patriotic Pelcl expected that one more century would see the extirpation of Czech identity. How that identity was re-established, largely through an athletic movement (the Sokols), which also stimulated art, music and the vernacular tongue, is a romance of our own time. The Slovaks, though linguistically close to the Czechs and Moravians, stood largely outside their political development.

5. The advance of the South Slavs took place along two lines: the ancestors of the modern Yugoslavs (Slovenes, Croats, Serbs) crossed the Danube plain and descended along the spine of Illyria; the ancestors of the modern Bulgars (Σκλαβηνοί Στλάβοι Σθλάβοι) came

across the Lower Danube in association with the Antes, who were East Slavs. According to Constantine Porphyrogenitus the Serbs came from White Serbia, north of the Carpathians, at an unidentifiable place called Boïκι. Similarly the Croats came from White Croatia, a region near the Vistula, called Διτзική, near the Βαγιβάρεια (for which *Babia góra* in the Beskides is a clever guess). Some suppose the first name might be derived from *Boiohæmum* 'Bohemia', and the third from *Bagoaria* 'Bavaria'. The Bulgarian Slavs presumably lay to the east of these groups, and in immediate contact with the East Slavs. The latter had advanced south-eastward in such numbers by the sixth century that Procopius speaks of the vast numbers of the Antes along the shores of the Black Sea and Sea of Azov.

The invasions from the north-east impinged on lands of vital importance for the Byzantine crown, and so were at once the cause for military and diplomatic action. They began in the early sixth century, chiefly by infiltration. The country districts had been depopulated by the internal decline of the Empire's manhood and by the Gothic seizure and evacuation of Mœsia. The chief method employed seems to have been infiltration, so that the military resistance offered by the Emperors proved incapable of stemming the immigration. The Antes retired to Russia, but the other Slavs filled Mœsia, the hinterland of Salonica, and Macedonia. Some elements descended into the Peloponnesus. In the middle of the sixth century these Slavs began to feel the weight of incursions by the Avars (R. *óbry*), operating from the middle Danube, and they welcomed the advent of the Bulgar tribesmen of Asparuch (670), who organized their unity, and strengthened their defences by redistributing population. Asparuch's horsemen were Turco-Tatars from the Great Bulgaria on the Volga, where a kingdom persisted as late as the thirteenth century. The name may be derived from *bulǧamak* 'mix, embroil', meaning either a 'mixed race' or 'the brawlers'. To their subjects they contributed a few personal names, as *Šišman Kardam Karan Asparuch*. But the modern Bulgarians, in race and language, are not Tatars but Slavs.

A Bulgarian empire was organized by Tsar Simeon (893–927), but brought to ruin at the end of the tenth century by the Emperor Basil II 'the Bulgar-slayer'. A second empire in the twelfth and thirteenth centuries was weakened by Serbian onslaughts from the west, and was finally obliterated by the Turkish conquest between 1340 and 1382 (capture of Sofia).

The Macedonian dialect of Thessalonica was used by the apostles Methodius and Cyril for their work in Great Moravia. Their disciples converted the Bulgars during the reign of Boris (852–84), and thereafter the language was a vehicle for a considerable literature of religious translations and homilies.

The date of the Serbian penetration is doubtful if we distrust the Byzantine assertion that they came at the 'invitation' of Heraclius (610–41). The Croats are stated to have come later still, in consequence of struggles with the Franks. In the tenth century their occupation of Dalmatia and Illyria led to a full, but sometimes enigmatic, description of their polity by Constantine Porphyrogenitus. The unit of occupation was the village-federation (*župànija*, now 'parish, district'), centred on one or more townships (κάστρον). The account Constantine gives of the hinterland is vague, but he is very detailed concerning the Dalmatian ports. The Croats extended from Zara (Zadar) to the Cetina river; from the Cetina to the Narenta (Neretva) were the Narentines, also known as Pagans; thence to the Pelješac (Sabbionetta) peninsula were the *Zachlumi* (S. *hûm* 'hill'); followed by the *Terbunians* between Dubrovnik (Ragusa, Epidaurum), fronted by the *Kanalitai* on the coast; and between Kotor and Bar were the *Diokletianoi* (*Dukljane*). Inland were the Bosnians on the *Bosóna* or *Bosthna*, and the Serbs of *Serblia* (Zeta, North Montenegro).

It was the development of a political instinct among the Serbs of Zeta which had the effect of unifying this region to some extent, despite the overwhelming natural obstacles. By the middle of the twelfth century the tribal centre had shifted from Zeta to the Raška, a tributary of the Ibar, which flows into the Western Morava. From the Raška Stevan Nemanja (1186–95) extended his rule as far as the Southern Morava (often called the Bulgarian Morava). With Stevan Dušan the Great (1333–55) Old Serbia in Northern Macedonia was firmly occupied, the Bulgarians were defeated, and a Serbian empire reached as far as the Ægean. Meanwhile the capital shifted under the influence of these victories: it was successively Novi Pazar (on the Raška), Priština, Prizren and Skoplje (on the Vardar, which leads to the Ægean).

Upon this period of expansion there followed an equally violent series of retreats. The Turks inflicted crushing defeats upon the Serbs on the Marica (1371) and at Kosovo (1389). The Serbocroat confederation was dissolved, and at first local princes continued the struggle. After the fifteenth century this was no longer feasible, and only partisans continued the struggle under the command of outlawed chiefs. But they never wholly subsided. Mass migrations gave some relief to the common folk. In the fifteenth century they crowded into Bosnia, Slovenia, Bačka and the Banat. In the sixteenth century they withdrew into Austrian lands (1520, '28, '47, '54, '62, '74, '82). The victories of Sobieski (1689) and Prince Eugen (1738) gave cover to two other big migrations. The War of Independence (1804–12) put an end to these movements into Austrian territory, but caused a general shift of population from Old Serbia into the new kingdom. The net result was greatly to reduce the Serbian element in the southern part of the old empire, with a consequent increase of the Bulgarian percentage. The rugged territory imposes differentiation, but the different dialect criteria have unrelated areas, due to their jostling together.

6. The East Slavs advanced from Polesie eastward, and in the tenth century lay in a vague territory which may be described as either an arc or a triangle based on the line Novgorod-Kiev. Their position was determined rather by natural than by human limits. They were agriculturists advancing behind fur-hunters, the latter being at this period much the more important. As such they found congenial conditions in the mixed forest region of central Russia which describes a triangle Leningrad-Kazań-Kiev. To the north lay the great conifer forests which could only be developed when the advance of the second type of Russian culture had provided a new base for the fur-hunters' advance. In neither capacity did the intruders much disturb the fishing and hunting economy of the Finnish tribes, which were reduced or assimilated without circumstances that have remained on historical record. Another diagonal (approximately from Kremenčug to Saratov), parallel to the southern limit of mixed forests, describes the limit of the wooded steppe. This was the debatable region of mediæval Russian history. Upon the open steppe, whether grassy or arid, the Slavs had no skill to live. They could not resist the raids of Turco-Tatar nomads who, with nothing to lose, were prompt to destroy the results of agricultural labour. Slavonic tribes were established on the western end of the wooded steppe, between Dniester and Dnieper, thanks to the Dnieper waterway, but even there were exposed to nomad raids, which ended in the destruction of Kiev itself by the Golden Horde in 1240. Russia had to be rebuilt from the mixed forest area, and the conquest of the open steppe did not occur until the settlers could be preceded by Slavonic semi-nomads, the Cossacks of the sixteenth century and after, who could meet the nomads on equal terms of livelihood and force. The analogy of American cowboys and Indians in the Prairie States will readily present itself.

The method of penetration in roadless country was by linking the waterways by portages (R. *vólok*). Two systems radiating from Novgorod were of special importance. The 'way from the Varangians to the Greeks' (*put iz Varjag v Greky*) started at the Gulf of Finland, ascended the Neva to Old Ladoga, thence by the Volchov to Novgorod; crossing Lake Ilmeń it ascended the Lovat and reached the upper Dnieper by a portage near Smolensk; thence it descended the Dnieper to Kiev, where fleets were gathered for the rest of the Dnieper navigation and the coastal sail to Constantinople. Subsidiary feeders to this 'way' were the Narva-Peipus-Velikaja route and portage, the Dvina, and the Pripet drainage-basin. From Novgorod there was access also to the Volga and so to the great markets of Kazań and Astrakhan (*puť v Bolgary i v Chvalisy*). Between Oka and Don there was also ready access for the dug-out canoes of the early Russians.

The *Antes* or *Antæ* were the first of the East Slavs to receive notice from history, since they were on the extreme right flank of the movement and came into conflict with the Goths and Byzantines. They are first mentioned as impinging on South Russia in the fourth century. In the sixth they lay along the Black and Azov coasts, divided into many tribes (ἔθνη τὰ 'Αντῶν ἄμετρα, according to Procopius); but their name disappeared after an expedition of extermination by the Avars in 602. It is possible that it may be the same as that of the later *Vjatiči*.

Discounting the Antes, our evidence is drawn from the tenth-century account of Constantine Porphyrogenitus and the tenth-century traditions recorded in the Kievite *Pověsť vremennych lět*. The Slavonic tribes lay thus: In the north were the *Slověne* or *Novgorodci* of the Ilmeń region, and between Novgorod and Smolensk were the *Kriviči* (Κριβιτζοί Κριβηταινοί; a patronymic? *krivój* 'crooked'; Latv. *Kreivija* 'Russia'). They held the portage region, at the headwaters of the Dvina, Dniester and Volga, and it is clear that they extended also to the headwaters of the Sož, Desna, Moskva, Kljaźma, and as far as Suzdaĺ and Vladimir. This is the North Great Russian dialect area, apart from the western part, which belongs to White Russia. In the latter a special branch of the Kriviči were the *Poločane* on the Polota, around Polock.

The Narva-Peipus route had an important centre at Pskov (OR. *Pĺskov* cf. Germ. *Pleskau*), with certain dialectal peculiarities in the mediæval and modern periods. Nearby was Izborsk, a fortress of the Kriviči.

Between the Dvina and the Pripet were the *Dregoviči* (Δρουγουβιτοί), called by a name of uncertain origin. They are the racial substratum of White Russian.

In the south the main tribes were the 'plainsmen', *Poljane*, who extended on the right bank of the Dnieper from the Teterev to Kiev, and the 'woodlanders', *Drevljane* (*dérevo* 'wood', Δρεβλενίνοι, Βερβιᾶνοι, with wrong initial) between the Teterev and the Pripet. On the eastern bank were the 'northerners', *Sěverjane* (Σερβίοι), of the Desna, around Černigov and Novgorod-Seversk. Minor tribes were found on the Southern Bug river, possibly because of the break-up of the Antes confederation. The names *Bužane*, *Dulěby*, *Velynjane* (in the province of Volhynia), and *Lučane* (*Ločane*, *Lutiči*, Λενζανῆνοι, cf. Luck) are grouped together between the headwaters of the Bug and of streams flowing into the Pripet. Lower down the Bug were the most exposed of the Russian tribes, the *Uliči* (Οὐλτίνοι) and *Tiverci*. These peoples formed the southern dialect region. The last two were probably disintegrated by the pressure of the nomads. After the destruction of Kiev, the principality of Galicia-Volhynia formed the basis for the modern Ruthenian speech.

In the east there were two tribal agglomerations, the *Radimiči* on the Sož and the *Vjatiči* on the Oka. The Kievite chronicle derives them both from Poland (*Radimiči že i Vjatiči ot Ljachov*) and explains their names as patronymics from Radim and Vjatko. There is nothing in their language to justify this derivation, but it may have been that they started later from Polesie, probably in the seventh century. The Vjatiči were the most populous of the Russian tribes, and they crossed from the Oka to the Don at an early date, descending that river and even founding Tmutorokań in the Kubań. They were so thickly established in the ninth century that they earned for the Don the name of the Slavonic River in Arabian writings. But they could not withstand the assaults of the Turco-Tatar nomads in the steppes, and gradually recoiled towards their tribal centre on the Oka. Moscow was within their limits, but bordered on those of the Kriviči, whence its central character. As the Kriviči extended eastward, the Vjatiči became rather southerners than easterners, and so form the racial substream of South Great Russian.

The Slavs proved unable to organize themselves for wholesale trade or for politics. This was done for them by the Swedes of the Rurikid dynasty, the original 'Russians' (*Ruś*, Gk. 'Ρῶς, cf. Finnish *Ruotsi* 'Swede'), the famous Varangians (R. *varjág*). Though they appeared in the Volga markets as dealers in slaves (mostly Vjatiči) in exchange for oriental wares, their organization was chiefly determined by the market of Constantinople. They controlled from north to south a movement of settlement from west to east. The Vjatiči lay outside the districts they pacified, and 'to go to the Vjatiči' (*v Vjatiči poiti*) meant, at Kiev, 'to be irrecoverably lost'. Furs were collected on the tributaries of the Dnieper and floated down to Kiev on canoes. At Kiev they were transhipped for the risky journey to Constantinople. The whole system was controlled by fortresses (R. *górod*, ON. *garðr*): Old Ladoga (*Aldegjuborg*—the lake was at first called *Nevo*), Novgorod (*Holmgarðr*), Pskov (*Pskov*), Polock (ON. *Palteskja*), Smolensk (Μιλινίσκα), Ljubeč ([Τε]λιούτζα), Černigov (Τзερνιγώγα), Vyšegorod (Βουσεγραδέ), Kiev (τὸ Κιοάβα, τὸν Κίαβον; ON. *Kœnugarðr* < *kœna*, a kind of boat; also Σαμβατάς < ON. *sandbakki-áss* 'sandbank ridge'), and the last friendly station on the river, Vitičev (Βιτετзέβη). Turko-Tatar origins have however also been proposed for the names of Kiev and other places (*Slavonic Review*, 1944).

The brilliant achievements of the Rurikids have tended to over-shadow their dependence on Slavonic initiative. They organized wholesale most of the resources gained by the latter, apart from those of the Vjatiči. They found a political framework in the ramifications of the Rurikid family, but they failed to centralize government under the Grand Prince at Kiev. Their assaults on Constantinople were more spectacular than happy, and they failed to devise a means of security upon the steppe. The Tatar invasion of the thirteenth century destroyed their essential assets which lay below the forest-line on the Dnieper, and the future Russia was reconstructed by Moscow, not by Kiev. It might even have been so in any case, since the north-south axis of the Varangian States was not so essential as the west-east trend of the Kriviči and Vjatiči. The Rurikids, however, performed one indispensable service. The conversion of Vladimir the Great (980–1015) and all his connections gave to Russia, in due course, unity of religion, of creed and of culture. It introduced the elements of Byzantine civilization along with the religion, and provided an order of men charged with its protection through the use of the Church Slavonic literary tongue. As opposed to the pagan Lithuanians in the west and Tatars in the east, the Russian felt himself essentially a Christian (R. *kresťjánin* 'peasant'); as against the Catholic Poles he asserted his Orthodoxy; and in both respects his country was 'Holy Russia'.*

7. *The Orient.* It will be seen that Russia lay almost entirely outside the range of the original Slavs. Herodotus (Book V) describes Russia from the Black Sea as far as the upper reaches of the Southern Bug, the Dnieper Falls, and the wooded steppe beyond the Don. At that time the Scyths were in possession of the lower courses of the Russian rivers, following a mixed economy of agriculture ('Ploughman'- and 'Farmer'-Scyths on the Bug and Dnieper) and nomadic pastoralism ('Royal' Scyths from the Crimea to the Don). Beyond them, between Don and Volga, lay the Sarmatians, and to the north were East Finnish tribes (Čeremisses and Mordvinians) and others of doubtful classification. At a later date the Sarmatians overwhelmed the Scyths, who are represented by the minute Ossetic group in the Caucasus today, and reduced all South Russia to nomadism. They were distributed into so many incoherent tribes that the word *Sarmatia* had, in the first and second centuries of our era, little more than a geographical sense. The Goths and Heruli dispossessed the Sarmatians in the third century after Christ, and were themselves submerged by

* See L. Niederle, *Manuel de l'antiquité slave* (Paris, 1923), i; A. Šachmatov, *Vvedenie v kurs istorii russkago jazyka* (Petrograd, 1916), i. Chronological appendix; Constantine Porphyrogenitus, Περὶ θεμάτων (c. 934), Περὶ ἐθνῶν (949); *Povésť vremennych lět*, ed. Šachmatov (Petrograd, 1916), i.

the Huns in 376. After Attila's death in 453 the Huns broke up into
two weak tribes, the *Utrigurians* and *Kutrigurians*, who occupied the
right bank of the Dniester.*

The succession of transient dominions recorded by ancient authors
is relevant to the history of Russian only as showing how the ground
was kept clear for the advance of the Antes in the sixth century. Our
principal source of pertinent information is, here also, the Kievite
chronicle, supplemented by the work of Constantine Porphyrogenitus.
Russia was occupied by two great groups of tribes: the Finnish (Finno-
Ugrian) tribes of the wooded country, who lived by fishing and hunting, frequently shifting their locations, and the Turco-Tatar tribes of
the steppes, nomad stock-breeders. They lay north-west and south-
east respectively, and it was the Finnish peoples who thus first felt the
Russian impact.

The Russian chronicler states:

> In Japhet's portion were settled the Ruś, Čjud and all tongues:
> Merja, Muroma, Veś, Mordva, Čjud beyond the portages, Perm,
> Pečera, Jam, Ugra, Litva, Zimĕgola, Korś, Lĕtgola, Lib. The
> Ljachove and Prusi and Čjud are established on the Varangian
> Sea (Baltic).

The list is repeated later as that of the tributaries of the Rurikids.
Apart from the Zimĕgola, Korś, Lĕtgola, Litva, Prusi and Ljachove
(*Zemgale*, *Kurzeme*, *Latgale*, *Lietuva* and Old Prussians, and the
Poles), these tribes are all Finno-Ugrians, and their numbers witness
to their extension in space and lack of coherence. Their racial centre
should probably be placed by the great bend of the Volga near
Kazań. The Čeremisses live north-west of the bend, and the Mord-
vinians to the south. The Ugrian group (Voguls and Ostjaks)
first migrated in order to live beside the Urals; thence the
Magyars detached themselves, first to the South Russian steppe
and then to conquer Hungary (895–906). The Permian group
(Votjaks and Zyrjenians) moved west, then north. The Finns and
Estonians went west. A last division occurred in the Ladoga region,
so that the Estonians (*Čud*) were separated from the Finns (*Sum*,
Finn. *Suomi* 'Finnish') and Karelians. In the middle space were
weak tribes: the Veś at the source of the Volga, the Merja near the
Oka and Volga confluence, and the Muroma near Murom on the
Oka. These were assimilated by the Kriviči and Vjatiči, so that in
time the West Finns lost all connection with the East Finns. About
18,000 Samoyedes, speaking a vast number of dialects distantly
related to Finnish, roam over the tundras between the Ob and the
Yenisei.

* H. Hübschmann, *Etymologie und Lautlehre der ossetischen Sprache*, Strassburg,
1887, with a comparative treatment of Ossetic and Iranian on pp. 115–117.

At the present day the Finno-Ugrian languages are spoken by about seven millions in Finland and the Soviet Union and ten millions in Hungary:

West:— Finns .. .. about 3,000,000
Karelians (Archangel, Olonec, Tveŕ,
Novgorod) 205,000
Ingrians (Leningrad area) 13,000
Vepsians (Olonec, Onega) 24,000
Vots 1,000
Estonians 1,450,000
Livs 2,000
East:— Voguls (Perḿ and Toboĺsk) ⎱ Ob-Ugrian 5,000
Ostjaks .. .. ⎰ group .. 19,000
Zyrjenians ⎱ 258,000
Votjaks ⎰ Permian group 450,000
Čeremisses (Vjatka, Kazań, Ufa) 375,000
Mordvinian (Mokša and Ersä) .. about 1,000,000

    6,802,000
Magyars 10,000,000

These languages are represented in Russian place- and river-names. Many of the latter end characteristically in *-ma*, *-da*, *-va*. Otherwise the Finns had little to offer to the Slavs, nor had the Slavs much to offer other than was represented by Lithuanian loanwords already borrowed to represent the simpler cultural concepts. The Russian words in Finnish show that Christianity became known first from Russia.

The Turco-Tatar group of languages extends from the Black Sea to the Sea of Okhotsk, linking up with Mongolian and Tungusic (Manchurian) to form the Ural-Altaic family of languages. There has been remarkably little differentiation among them in historical time, but one may distinguish between the North Turkish languages (TT) which have especially influenced Russian, and the Osmanli Turkish (T) which has operated upon Bulgarian and Serbocroat. The distribution of these peoples was in 1897 approximately as follows:—

Tunguses of Siberia.. 73,110
        Manchurians 1,500,000
                                ————— 1,573,110
Mongols of Siberia (Burjats) 332,554
        of the Volga (Kalmuks) 190,650
        Estimated total of all Mongolians 3,500,000
Turco-Tatars of Siberia: Yakuts 228,739
                Others 255,154

Turco-Tartars

of Central Asia:	Kazak-Kirghiz	..	4,026,066
	Kara-Kirghiz	..	215,682
	Turcomans	..	838,280
	Uzbegs ..	..	1,992,325
	Sarts	..	2,258,128
of Turkestan and	Kansu ..	..	1,604,311
	Others ..	..	500,127
Osmanli Turks in Turkey ..		..	10,000,000
in Russia	..	..	153,032
Azerbaijanis in Transcaucasia		..	1,475,553
in Persia ..		..	2,000,000
Others ..	..	..	29,902
Turco-Tatars in Russia: Kumiks, Nogais,			
		etc. ..	208,943
	Baškirs, Meščera,		
		etc. ..	1,492,944
Volga and Kama Tatars		..	1,693,925
Crimean and South Russian Tatars		..	220,237
Elsewhere in Russia	..	..	40,429
Čuvašes	..	..	843,755
Turko-Tatars in Rumania and Poland		..	97,276
			30,174,808

These figures show that the Turco-Tatar element is much more considerable than the Mongolian; Jenghiz Khan, on the other hand, was a Mongolian. Apart from Turkey, they are thickest in southern Central Asia, which came under Russian rule only in the last quarter of the nineteenth century. They are still relatively dense in the Volga-Kama region, around their old capital of Kazań, but there are few on the Irtysh and Tobol, the region comprised in the original Siberia (*Sibir̆*). In South Russia they are not numerous, but were able to control the open steppes for centuries thanks to their mobility. Their way of life was wholly unfamiliar to the early Russians and gave occasion for a large number of loanwords which will be examined in due course, but they touched Common Slavonic only in its latest epoch.

Between the fifth and eleventh centuries hordes of Turko-Tatars swept across the South Russian steppe to the mouth of the Danube: 376 Huns, about 482 Bulgars, 559 Avars (*Obri*), Magyars (left for Hungary in 895), mid seventh century Khazars across the Don (recorded as taking tribute from the *Poljane, Sĕverjane* and *Vjatiči* in 859; destroyed by Svjatoslav in 965), 968 Pečenegs (*Pečenĕzi,* Πατзινακῖται), 1061 Polovci, 1238 Golden Horde. Though the princes of Kiev were able to defeat several of these tribes they could not hold

the steppe, and new swarms poured into the waste places, defeating
the prime object of Kievite policy, which was to advance towards
Constantinople.*

8. *The Russian Expansion.* After the fall of Kiev the Tatar pressure
was exerted from the south-east and Russia was pressed back into the
central forests. She found compensation by opening up the great
conifer forests of the north-west, sending out fur-hunters from
Novgorod. Moscow, which had been a manor set among Finnish
tribes, was surrounded with wooden walls in 1156, and gradually drew
to itself the strength of the surrounding principalities of Vladimir,
Suzdaĺ, Rjazań, Rostov and Murom. Situated on the dividing line of
north and south Great Russian, where Kriviči and Vjatiči mingled,
Moscow had notable advantages as a capital of Russia, and the dynastic
policy of her rulers saved her from the disruption characteristic of the
other Rurikids. In 1478 Novgorod fell definitively to Moscow, and
with it the new North. The Tatar yoke was thrown off in 1480, and in
1552 Ivan the Terrible took the Tatar capital of Kazań, giving to
Russian expansion once more its eastern trend. He was able to seize
the whole Volga and Don basins. In 1581 Ermak began the conquest of
Siberia by seizing the Toboĺsk region, and in 1584 he was fighting on
the Irtysh. The seventeenth and eighteenth centuries witnessed the
assimilation of Siberia by fur-traders and miners as the advanced
guard of the Russian peasantry. They used river routes and portages,
and the explorers of North Russia were fully trained for the rigours of
Siberia: 1600 Mangazeja, 1607 Yenisei, 1632 Lena, 1640 Kamčatka,
1689 first treaty with China, Alaska, 1860 Amur river and Vladivostok.
The beginning of the trans-Siberian Railway in 1891 led to a rush for
Siberia, a land so empty that the Russian element constitutes over
80 per cent. of the whole population.

In Russia itself the frontier was gradually pressed out upon the
steppe by the half-nomad Cossacks, whose gains were consolidated by
long diagonal defensive works: 1571 Orel-Kulikovo, 1650 Belgorod-
Simbirsk, 1584 Penza-Samara, 1735 Dnieper-Donec. This brought
Russia to the limits of Kievite rule. 1774–91 recovery of the Black
Sea and Azov area. From this position expansion beyond Don
and Volga was made easy. In the early nineteenth century Russia

---

* See Meillet and Cohen, *Les langues du monde* (Paris, 1924): A. Sauvageot,
'Langues finno-ougriennes et langues samoyèdes' and J. Deny, 'Langues turques,
langues mongoles et langues tongouzes', with maps. The statistics are from the
census of 1897, which seems to be the last available with full linguistic classification. They require correction, but may be assumed proportionately instructive.
The two language-groups are often united as Ural-Altaic, and M. Pei, *Languages
for War and Peace* (New York, 1943) assigns to the Ural-Altaic languages
approximately 60,000,000: Magyars 9½ millions, Finns 4 millions, Estonians
1 million, Turks 18 million. J. Szinnyei, *Finnische Sprachwissenschaft* (Berlin-
Leipzig, 1922) gives the same figures as A. Sauvageot.

conquered the Caucasus area: 1653 Poti, 1803 Mingrelia and Georgia, 1805 Karabagh, 1813 Lenkoran, 1828 Erivan, 1859–64 Kuban and Terek and Daghestan, 1878 Kars. In the later nineteenth century Russia absorbed Central Asia: 1864 Taškent, 1868 Samarkand, 1873 Khiva, 1876 Kokand, 1881 Askhabad, 1884 Merv, 1885 River Murghab. The Central Asian Railway serves as the means for assimilating this area, but there is a much greater density of older inhabitants. The Russian percentage in Central Asia is only 9, as against 85 Turco-Tatars. In the Caucasus the Russians are the strongest group (34 per cent.), with 20 per cent. Turco-Tatars, 14 per cent. Kartvelians (Georgians proper) and 12 per cent. other Georgians.*

9. *Population and Frontiers.* It is particularly difficult at the time of writing to give anything like an exact estimate of the extent and density of the Slavonic-speaking peoples. Within one generation they have been the chosen victims of two German wars, the first of aggression, the second of extermination. Their political frontiers have violently fluctuated, and are at this time not definitely settled. It is true that the linguistic frontiers show a remarkable steadiness, when compared with the political; but in the period between the wars the tendency to identify nationality with language led to attempts to modify the linguistic pattern, and this process has been accelerated since the conclusion of hostilities.

(a) *Russian.* On January 17 1939 there were 109,278,000 souls in the Russian Republic (Great Russia and Siberia), 38,960,000 in the Ukraine, and 10,400,000 in White Russia, with a total of 158,638,000 Russians of all sorts. The figures for speakers of White Russian should be extended to include those of what was North-eastern Poland, and the Little Russian or Ruthenian of the Ukraine extended into Southern Poland and the eastern extremity of Czechoslovakia. Allowing for deductions of non-Russian elements on Russian soil, one may say that there are about 10 million who speak White Russian and about 40 million who speak Ruthenian. From the figures for Great Russia we have to deduct about 2,350,000 Finno-Ugrians and 5,733,000 Turco-Tatars, Mongols and Tunguses, and we must add a figure for the Russian-speakers of Caucasia (Azerbaijan, Georgian and Armenian Republics) and Central Asia (Turkmenian, Uzbeg, Tadjik, Kazak and Kirghiz Republics). Allowing, as in Niederle's calculation, 34 per cent. for the former and 9 per cent. for the latter, we reach the sum of

---

* L. Niederle, *Obozrěnie sovremennago Slavjanstva* (St. Petersburg, 1909), with map. This work is the source also of the ensuing paragraphs. Its data are those of 1897, but the totals are corrected for 1908. B. H. Sumner, *Survey of Russian History* (London, 1944), chap. i 'The Frontier'; B. Pares, *A History of Russia*, 3rd ed. (London, 1943, with map of the Muscovite expansions facing p. 100). Map of the Caucasus and Central Asia in C. Grant Robertson and J. G. Bartholomew, *Historical and Modern Atlas of the British Empire* (London, 1905).

4,227,000, and so calculate that the number of persons to whom Great Russian is a maternal tongue is about 105,500,000 souls. It is, however, a language of culture, administration and travel to all the citizens of the USSR, to whom must be added in this sense the Bulgarians and a large number of Yugoslavs, Czechs and even Poles. For the last three, however, the claims of German and French in the cultural field have generally seemed stronger.

Within the political frontiers of the USSR the Russian language has no definite boundary. It extends in a huge, irregular triangle to the basin of the Tobol in Siberia, and from thence along the trans-Siberian Railway to the Far East. It is, in the main, absent from the Tundras of the North and the dry steppes of the South and of Central Asia, where conditions do not favour the kind of life preferred by Russian settlers. The ground occupied is either wooded steppe or variegated forest, with penetration of the conifer forest and grassy steppe and long tentacles along all river-banks and the Central Asian Railway. The northern tribes are so sparsely distributed on the ground that a relatively small influx of Russians considerably alters the percentages. The Turco-Tatars are densely settled in the lands where abundant water is brought from the snows of the Pamir region, but a great waste thinly held separates them from the main body of Russians. Near the great bend of the Volga, however, in the region of Kazań, there is a great knot of both Tatar and Finnish peoples, representing the old Tatar hegemony, round which the tides of Russian migration have flowed. In the north-west there is a more definite frontier between Russian and Finnish. The Soloveckij (1439) and Belozero (1397) monasteries developed into semi-governmental centres of Russian industry and influence in the Middle Ages, and thanks to them the Russian language-frontier descends from the Kandalakša inlet of the White Sea to include Lake Onega; it crosses the Sviŕ and remains south of Lake Ladoga and the Neva, in such a way that Leningrad lies in a Finnish hinterland.

The western language-frontier has remained stable since the thirteenth century, and is described in much the same terms by both Russian and Polish investigators. The first section is Great Russian. It starts from Narva and follows the eastern side of Lake Peipus and all Lake Pskov; thence it runs west of the Velikaja River to a point between Ludza in Latvia and Opočka on the Velikaja. The political frontier followed the Velikaja, so that some Russians were included within Latvia. As the Slavs were intruders in all this region the frontier is a clear-cut line. Next comes the White Russian frontier from the headwaters of the Velikaja to the Narew. Here the historical conditions are different. The mediæval Polish-Lithuanian kingdom extended over White Russia, and White Russian was an official language of the Chancery. There has been considerable mingling of the three languages, and the frontier can be determined only by the preponderance of one over the others. The linguistic condition of certain cities is open to dispute, since in cities whatever is the national and official language is reinforced. A further complication is that many who signed census-forms felt more keenly their religious than their linguistic differences, and recorded not their language but their religion. The general trend of the frontier is to the south-west, with forward surges round Dvinsk (Daugavpils), Vilna (Wilno) and Grodno; from Grodno it drops south to Białystok and the Narew. It thus crosses a portion of Latvia (Latgale) and much ground claimed by Lithuania and recently held by Poland, and bisects the province of Białystok. In 1921, 56 per cent. of the inhabitants of Vilna registered as Poles, and in the whole province of Białystok the Polish proportion was 76.9 per cent.

The rest of the Russian frontier is described by Ruthenian (Little Russian). After the fall of Kiev (1240) the chief cultural and political centre was the principality of Galicia-Volhynia, and it is in documents emanating therefrom that we find the Ruthenian language taking its special character. When the power of the Tatars declined, the rulers of Poland were able to thrust far into the Russian Ukraine. In 1494 they held all the streams on both banks of the Dniester, and in 1657 they still held the river in all its course. At the time of the first partition, in 1772, the Polish frontier lay along the line of the river to approximately Kremenčug, and then cut back to the Dnieper near Kišinev. Here again conditions favoured the mingling of peoples, who were held apart chiefly by religious animosity. The present linguistic frontier runs by Bielsk, Biała and Chełm (Cholm), with Brest-Litovsk (Brześć-Litewski) on the Russian side. The precise allocation of Chełm is debatable. Thence the frontier curves south-west and south-west-by-west to include Tomaszów, Sanok and Przemyśl, and to touch the pre-war southern political frontier on the banks of the Poprad. In the three provinces to the east of this line there were 23.4, 16.8 and 22 per cent. of Poles in 1921; immediately to the west are some of the most densely Polish tracts (Kraków 93.1, Lublin 85.4 per cent.). Within the Poland of 1939 there were at least one million speakers of White Russian and four million Ruthenians.

From the Poprad valley and the Carpathians the Ruthenian frontier falls south-eastward across what was the tail of Czechoslovakia and the headwaters of the Tisza in Hungary to the sources of the Seret. It then swings east across Bukovina, including Czernowitz (Cernăuți), and touches the Dniester at Mogilev-Podolsk. The frontier follows the left bank of the stream continuously to the sea, apart from a wide bridge-head at Tiraspol. There is, however, a strong Russian minority between Dniester and Prut, and there are Bulgarian and Rumanian elements between Dniester and Bug. In the Crimea the majority was Tatar.

Ruthenian and White Russian are separated from each other by the Pripet and a line north of Černigov and Novgorod-Seversk, which both belong to Ruthenian. Independence has been claimed for both White Russian and Ruthenian. In the first case there seems little justification either in the structure of the dialect or in its cultural history. The special characteristics of Ruthenian are of comparatively recent growth also, since it began to take shape in the thirteenth century, but Galicia and Kiev have been notable centres for culture, and Ukrainian traditions and folk-songs have a marked individuality. Under the repressive measures taken by the last tsars to suppress the language, an isolationist movement was stimulated in the Ukraine. Regional autonomy has sufficed, in recent years, to quiet the modest desire for independence whetted by difference of dialect. On the side of Great Russian, White and Little Russian together mark out the Dniester as a unit of civilization. The White Russian border runs eastward from the sources of the Velikaja to those of the Dvina. It curves round the headwaters of the Dvina and Dnieper almost to Smolensk; thence south-south-east to the Desna near Novgorod-Seversk. The sources of the Desna and Oka fall within a transitional region between White and South Great Russian. The Ruthenian language-frontier takes up the line at Novgorod-Seversk, goes eastward to the Don, crosses at Pavlovsk, recrosses south of Bogučar, touches the Donec, and then travels south-south-east to about Stavropol. The southern frontier is marked by the Kuban river and delta. Much of this area represents the modern expansion of the dialect as a language of colonization in the steppe region.

Great Russian itself has dialects, though generally speaking for so wide-spread a language it is remarkably uniform. The most important division is that between the South and the North; that is, between the Vjatiči and Kriviči. The southern dialect is found in the upper basin of the Oka, buttressed on Gžatsk, Kaluga and Rjazań. It swings slowly southward to embrace the Don valley, and runs along the Volga from Kamyšin to Stalingrad (Caricyn). In the Caucasus it occupies the Terek valley. In the west it is supported against White and Little Russian by Kaluga, Orel, Karačev, Sevsk, Rylsk and Kursk. The rest belong to North Great Russian, but there is a band of transitional dialects between. The first of these is the north-western dialect of Pskov, through which North Great Russian shades into White Russian. Then follows the ancient dialect of Tveŕ (Kalinin) and Moscow, which reconciled historically the decidedly northern speech-habits of Novgorod and Vladimir with the decidedly southern Rjazań. This middle Russian is also found in the Sura valley, with Penza as its principal town, but with large non-Russian minorities. The literary language is that of Moscow, mainly North Great Russian, but with concessions to the South (*ákañe*).

(*b*) *Polish.* For about 25,000,000 people Polish is a mother-tongue. To these one may add some 4–5 millions in the United States and South America, and the associate languages of the Cassubians or Kaszuby (about 150,000) and the Wendish Slovenes of Lake Leba (200–250), the last relics of the old East Pomeranian speech. The eastern frontier has been described above. The northern ran through the southern third of East Prussia, including Goldap, Allenstein (Ołsztyn) and Graudenz (Grudziądz), whence it descended the Vistula to the sea. Between the sea and the Czech frontier the linguistic and political frontiers mainly agreed; since the war the political frontier has been moved considerably westwards to Stettin (Szczecin). Between Gdynia and Chojnice (Konitz) lie the Cassubians, with little enclaves into what was Germany at Bütow and Stüdnitz. Konitz was German-speaking, but Radnawitz, Flatau and Bomst (Babimost) were Polish enclaves in Germany. In Silesia the Polish language swung westward by Namslau, Oppeln and Neustadt, and at one time probably followed the Bober. Along all this border the linguistic percentages showed heavy infiltration of German elements. In Pomorze and Poznań there were about 18 per cent. of Germans in 1921, and in the city of Łódź the Polish majority was as low as 58.9 per cent. Polish extends into Czechslovakia in the Těšín (Cieszyn) and Poprád regions.

Apart from Cassubian, Polish has three main dialects: Great Polish of Poznania, Little Polish of Kraków, and Mazovian in the north-east. Warsaw lies on a belt of compromise between Mazovian and Little Polish. The Germans gave the name *Wasserpolaken* (*Wasserpolen*) to the speakers in Silesia of a highly Germanized form of Polish.

(*c*) *Wendish.* There were before the war about 115,000 speakers of the Wendish (or Sorabe or Sorb) dialect of Lusatia in the upper valley of the Spree. Their two principal towns are Cottbus (Khoćebuz) and Bautzen (Budyšin). On the east they hardly reach the Neisse, and on the west the line drops southward from Lubbenau (Lubnjow) on the Spree (Sprowja). They are all that remain of the tribes who spread Slavonic through Central and Southern Germany, and who were said to speak their own language in Leipzig as late as 1327. They are divided into two dialects (Upper and Lower).

(*d*) *Czechoslovak.* Czechs about 8,000,000; Slovaks about 3,000,000. Independence has been claimed for Slovak on the basis of certain formal differences, such as the first sing. pres. indic. in -*m*, but the argument is defective. Slovaks have only of late come to possess a cultural tradition capable of supporting a language, since they were long subject, politically and economically, to Hungary. Their language retains old stages through which Czech has passed, and it is the easternmost of a spectrum of Czechoslovak dialects. The official language (Czechoslovak) recognizes two forms, Czech and Slovak. Czech had official currency in the fifteenth century throughout much of the region. It may be divided into Czech proper and Moravian; and Moravian divides into a plethora of dialects, which shade into Polish along the common frontier. Czechoslovak Ruthenia belonged to the Russian-speaking area. There were in 1938 4–5 million non-Slavs in Czechoslovakia, including 3 million Germans. These occupied North-west and South-west Bohemia, inside the strategical bulwark of the Bohemian mountain border. There was thus a grave discrepancy between the defensible and the linguistic (and so, nationally self-conscious) frontiers.

In the north there was a deep German salient between Opava and Olomouc, corresponding to the Gesenke massif. Svitavy (Zwittau) and Landškroun (Landskron) formed a German-speaking island close to the passes that lead to Glatz. The frontier ran north-west from Olomouc to Vysoké, with many indentations. From Vysoké it ran west to the Elbe near Mělník. Thence via Třebenice and Louny south-westwards to Domažlice, with Pilsen (Plzeň) as the principal Czech bulwark. On the German side were the towns of Teplitz, Carlsbad and Eger (Teplice, Karlovy Vary, Cheb). From Domažlice the frontier ran south-east to Kaplice, with Budweis (Budějovice) as a German islet; north-east and south-east to Znojmo, with a German islet at Iglau (Jihlava), and along an arc to Břeclav and the Morava. Here it is continued by Slovak to the Danube at Bratislava (Press-burg), whence it continues in a very ragged line eastward by Nitra, Levice, Lučenec and Rožňava to Mihalovce, following the line of the hills, and clear to the north of the political frontier along the Danube and Ipoly.

(e) *Slovene.* The Slovenes number about 1,500,000 and have their cultural capital at Ljubljana. Their northern frontier is the northern frontier of the South Slavs and runs from Šmohor to St. Gothard through Beljak (Villach), Celovec (Klagenfurt) and Djekše. From either extreme it drops due south: from Šmohor through Resja (Resiutta) and Čedad (Cividale) to the Adriatic (Italian is buttressed here upon Udine, Gorizia and Trieste); from St. Gothard through Lendava to the Drava. The southern frontier is hard to define since it is made with the *kaj*-dialect of Serbocroat, which is transitional between Slovene and Serbocroat. It runs south-west towards Kočevje (Gottschee), which was a German islet, and then west to Podgrad and Buzet.

(f) *Serbocroat.* Speakers of Serb and Croat number approximately 12,000,000. There is a short western frontier from Buzet through Rovinj to Pulj (Pola). The Dalmatian coast and islands are Serbocroat as far as the Bojana river. The northern frontier descends the Drava to its confluence with the Danube. There are Serbocroat colonies along the Danube at Sombor and other points. Between Vukovar and the confluence with the Tisza the language-frontier lies evenly north of the river, and Serbian colonies extend north up the Tisza to Szegedin. Between Bečkerek and Bela Crkva the frontier runs south-east, with a salient to Modoš and outlying colonies in Hungary. It rejoins the Danube below Požarevac, but Rumanians occupy both sides of the Iron Gates. Finally the Serbocroat limit is reached at Zaječar on the Timok.

The eastern and southern frontiers cannot be drawn with consent, since Bulgars and Serbs both lay claim to the transition dialects in the band of country between the Timok and Prizren. They run southward from Zaječar to cover the Nišava valley and south-west to the head-waters of the Southern Morava near Vranje. From Vranje the fully Serbian districts lie north of Mitrovica, Novi-Pazar, Prijepolje, Podgorica and Skadar (Scutari), but there is a mixed region between this arc and the arc Kumanovo-Skoplje-Tetovo-Đakovica.

The dialectal variations of this area are important. Adjoining Slovenia is the region of the *kaj*-dialect, which is transitional between Slovene and Croat. (The literary language of this area and its capital, Zagreb, is a form of the *što*-dialect mentioned below.) Then comes the *ča*-dialect. Its frontier was formerly much more extended to the east. Now it leaves the Drava near Virovitica, ascends in an irregular line to Bjelovar and descends to the Sava at Sisak. Thence it follows the Kupa valley to Karlovac, where it bends southwards along the ridges to Zadar (Zara). After that, save for an enclave near Split, it is confined to the islands. Its southernmost limit is in the island of Lastovo (Lagosta) and the Pelješac (Sabbionetta) peninsula. The *ča*-dialect admits of further division into *i-* and *e*-dialects according to the treatment of CSl. *ě*. The rest of Yugoslavia belongs to the *što*-region, which is also divided into dialects (*je- i-* and *e-*) by the development given to CSl. *ě*. The *je*-dialect is westerly, and the dividing line is from Osijek on the Danube, through Lešnica and Kraljevo, to Mitrovica and Peć. West of a line joining the Bosna and Narenta *i-* and *je*-are found mixed. East of the *je*-dialect is the *e*-dialect of Belgrade and the Šumadija. The Šumadija is closed by a line from Smederevo to Kragujevac and Kraljevo. Next follow, eastward, the Kosovo-Resava dialects of Serbian, and the Serbo-Bulgar transition dialects which begin at Zaječar on the Timok and include the towns of the Southern (or Bulgar) Morava, notably Niš, Vranje, Skoplje and Prizren.

A Macedonian dialect is used in the new (federal) Yugoslavia as the literary and official language in Yugoslav Macedonia. It will be touched on in section 217.

(g) *Bulgarian.* Bulgarians number about 7,000,000. The northern frontier follows the Danube to its mouth. There is a Bulgar salient on the north bank of the Danube between Ismail and Taraklija, but on the southern bank there is an admixture of Rumanians in the Dobrudja and of Turks in the Deli Orman region. Bulgarians are numerous south of the political frontier, as far as the approaches to Constantinople and the River Marica. They also lie just inland from the Ægean all the way between the Marica and Salonica. From Salonica (Solun) the Macedonian dialects run through Ostrovo westwards to Chrupišta, whence north along the Albanian border through Ohrid to Prizren.

The principal division is into East and West Bulgarian by a line from Nikopol on the Danube to Salonica. The very archaic Rhodope dialects lie south of a line from Plovdiv to Burgas.*

* Apart from Slavonic sources, see Meillet and Cohen, *Les langues du monde* (Paris, 1924); Mario A. Pei, *Languages for War and Peace* (New York, 1944); A. Howard and E. Newman, *Pictorial History of Russia* (London, 1943), for population statistics.

Chapter II

BALTO-SLAVONIC AND
PROTO-SLAVONIC

10. *Definitions.* The unity of the Indo-European language ceased from a remote date, probably between 2500-1000 B.C. It is only from the end of the first millennium A.D. that we have any Slavonic records. There is thus a lapse of some 3000 years between a linguistic state which is known with tolerable accuracy by the comparison of a whole family of languages and our first dated information concerning this particular member of the group. Now Slavonic, despite its highly conservative appearance, was given to innovation. The Indo-European system of conjugation, for instance, has been discarded in Slavonic, and more than one system substituted in its place. Changes of this sort take place over long periods of time, and the trends are not constant, but operate variously each within its own bracket of time, after which they cease to have effect. To explain a given crux of late date we must not call to our aid a linguistic law which operated only at an early date; and so on. In fact we must keep to a chronology; and yet in this lapse of unrecorded time (3000 years) dates are too obviously lacking. A chronology, however, can and must be set up. It is partly relative: that is, it depends on propositions like 'the change x implies the previous change y, and that was due to z', which gives the relative chronology zyx; partly it is susceptible of approximate dating by comparison with neighbouring languages which have sure or approximate dates (see sections 2-5 of the last chapter). The two processes determine eras in the prehistory of the Slavonic languages for which we must now find suitable terms.

The earliest records are in Old Bulgarian. This was so like what must have been the common source of the existing Slavonic languages that Old Bulgarian forms are frequently quoted as the bases of each particular explanation. It is clearly an advantage to quote attested forms rather than ones due only to inference from the sum of the languages today; the attested forms are certain, the inferred ones can never be deemed certain until corroborated by actual examples. Still, it has to be remembered that not only was Old Bulgarian not the common parent, but even that it was a dialect with a very precise localization. We may define it by concentric arguments thus: (i) Old Bulgarian was a South Slavonic language, and opposed to East and West Slavonic, because the solution of CSl. *tort* was the characteristically SSl. *trat* (for the explanation of this convention see section 29 hereafter); elsewhere this solution is found only in Czechoslovak, which other criteria, e.g. the treatment of CSl. *t *d, assign to the WSlav group; (ii) within South Slavonic it was definitely Bulgarian because the result of CSl. *t *d was $št$ $žd$ (see section 40): OB. *nošti* 'night'/S. *nôć* Slov. *nôč* Cz. *noc* P. *noc* R. *noč'*; (iii) within Bulgarian it was a south-western dialect because CSl. OB. *ŭ* occasionally vocalized as OB. *o:* OB. *pĕsokŭ* 'sand' Macedonian dial. *pésok*/MB. *pjásăk;* (iv) but it was not one of those Macedonian dialects which represent CSl. *t *d by *k̂ ĝ*. In fact, Old Bulgarian was the dialect of the Slavs who lived near Salonica, the home of the apostles Methodius and Cyril, though it served for the evangelization of Greater Moravia. Middle Bulgarian continued this language in a stereotyped literary form, with some scribal peculiarities for each important scriptorium, and some conces-sions to the vernacular. It was not a stage in the evolution of Modern Bulgarian, which depends chiefly upon the eastern dialects, and which, as Rumanian loanwords show, had already assumed its characteristic forms while Middle Bulgarian was still perpetuating those of Old Bulgarian. The conventional style, however, persisted upon the pens of some writers well into the nineteenth century.

In countries which followed the Orthodox persuasion Old Bulgarian became the 'dead' language of the liturgy, and in this use it is properly called Church Slavonic. Church Slavonic was pronounced in Russia and Serbia in accordance with a tradition influenced by the verna-cular system of sounds, and with some other concessions to the vernacular: we may thus speak of Russian Church Slavonic and Serbian Church Slavonic. The vernacular concessions were more numerous in works for the instruction or entertainment of laymen, and this literary usage lasted in Russia until the middle, and in Serbia until the end, of the eighteenth century. This usage is of great impor-tance, since it was the channel through which Slavonic terms became embedded in the cultural vocabulary of vernacular Russian and Serbocroat. We thus speak of Russo-Slavonic and Serbo-Slavonic, and for a period there existed in Serbia a Serbo-Russo-Slavonic, arising from the substitution of Russo-Slavonic for Serbo-Slavonic as a literary language in the eighteenth century.

The languages of the Catholic persuasion do not pass through these stages, but the documents distinguish Old, Middle and Modern periods, as they do also for Russian and Serbocroat. The old period in these cases corresponds to the twelfth century or the second half of the eleventh, and so is younger than the oldest Old Bulgarian. Where the individual languages are not attested but can be reasonably assumed to exist in characteristic form, it is sometimes convenient to speak of Proto-Russian, Proto-Polish, etc.

When we compare the extant languages they first yield concor-dances in three groups: East (Russian, White Russian, Ruthenian),

West (Polish, Czechoslovak, Wendish), South (Slovene, Serbocroat, Bulgarian) Slavonic. These again show evidence of derivation from a single common original: Common Slavonic. Common Slavonic is thus the sum of all the inferences which can be drawn from the individual Slavonic languages. It is an abstract conception, though the inferences work out in fact to something very like the attested Old Bulgarian forms. Still, we sometimes have to keep in mind the circumstance that Common Slavonic is the result of abstract thinking, and is not a description of a language perfectly localized in time and place. If we consider the history of the nasal vowels, for instance, it is clear that CSL. ǫ ę persisted until the ninth century, but at that time the *tort*-formula had already divided into ESlav. *torot*/SSlav.Cz. *trat*/ P. *trot*. This is not to deny, however, that there was a language common to all Slavs when they lived between the Vistula and the Pripet in the sixth century of our era: that language can be properly called Common Slavonic, but it might not have been precisely such as is composed by the heads of the individual inferences from the modern tongues. OB.MB. *št* S. *ć* Slov. *č* P.Cz. *c* R. *č* imply CSl. *$t́$ (a *t* pronounced in the high palate), but the latter was probably no more than a transitional stage of the older *tj *$kt́$ *$gt́$, which can also be described as Common Slavonic.

Between the sixth century of our era and the Indo-European period, however, there extends a history which receives no light from the mere comparison of the modern speeches, but has to be described by comparison between Common Slavonic and common Indo-European. It is convenient to call this Proto-Slavonic, and to divide it into Primitive Proto-Slavonic (according to the first distinctively Slavonic features), Early, Middle and Late Proto-Slavonic, the last period opening with the Christian Era. The Early and Late Proto-Slavonic periods are those in which the first and second Slavonic palatalizations took effect, and the Middle is that in which a number of mutually linked vowel-shifts, anterior to the second palatalization, were worked out.

In addition to these terms, the term Balto-Slavonic is necessary to our studies to express the degree of agreement or parallelism between the Baltic and the Slavonic groups. It does not imply that there was one single undifferentiated language as the source of both groups, but that the two stood and stand so closely related in contents and development as to have a necessary bearing upon the explanation of each other's problems.

11. *Balto-Slavonic*. The Baltic languages (Lithuanian, Latvian and the now extinct Old Prussian, speakers of the first two numbering some two and a quarter and two millions respectively) agree with Slavonic in representing original palatal gutturals by sibilants like

other *satem*-languages, by reducing original aspirates to the corresponding unaspirated occlusives, and by declining certain cases in -*m*- as in Germanic, not in -*bh*- as in Indo-Iranian, Greek, Latin and Celtic. The declensional system of seven cases and three numbers is the same for each group. The genitive and ablative singular were originally distinct only for *o*-stems; for these stems they have been identified in Baltic and Slavonic on the basis of the ablative (in Sanskrit they are separate: *vṛksya vṛkāt*, as in Latin: *lupi lupo;* in Greek they are identified as genitives: λύκου/L. *vilko*). There was a neuter gender in Old Prussian, and though not present in any Lithuanian document it is found in Lithuanian loanwords in Finnish; in Slavonic there was also a strong tendency to identify the neuter with the masculine, which was averted by a reaction in favour of a formal distinction in adjectives and in nouns of the *o*-declension (NSM. -*ŭ*/ NSN. -*o*). The definite declension of adjectives by means of a postpositive demonstrative suffix is a notable common mark. In both Baltic and Slavonic the Indo-European middle and passive voices were rejected, and the effect secured analytically by associating the verb with the reflexive pronoun. Both formed the infinitive in *-tēi*, and both had a future in -*s*-, of which there remains barely a trace in the oldest Slavonic records. The participles are similarly declined. Otherwise, however, the two language-groups reconstituted the verbal paradigm in complete independence and upon quite different principles. A comparison between the accentual systems of Lithuanian and Serbocroat shows original identity as to place of stress and kinds of intonation (rising, falling), but also that the stress has shifted place in the *što*-dialect of Serbocroat, and that the intonation has changed in kind in Lithuanian (rising for original falling, falling for original rising tones).

These considerations show that Baltic and Slavonic are remarkably similar, but they do not prove identity. However, it is desirable to note that the likeness of words in the two groups is obvious whenever they are compared with words from other groups: R. *volk* 'wolf' L. *vilkas*/ Lat. *lupus* Goth. *wulfs*, R. *berëza* 'birch' L. *béržas*/OHG. *birihha* ON. *biork*, OB. *žeravi* 'crane' L. *gérvė*/Lat. *grus* Gk. γέρανος, R. *dérevo* 'tree' L. *dervà* 'resinous wood'/Gk. δρῦς, OB. *krŭvĭnŭ* 'bloody' L. *krùvinas*/Lat. *cruentus*, etc.

When the vocabulary of the two groups is examined it shows a wide area of coincidence, with certain irreducible differences. There are many words not paralleled elsewhere, as R. *lípa* L. *liepa* 'lime-tree', R. *begú* L. *bëgu* 'I run'. When words are examined by classes the agreement appears strongest in the basic vocabularies. Thus the names of trees are mostly held in common: birch, willow, lime, bird-cherry, fir (R. *el* OPr. *adle* L. *ēglė*), ash, apple (R. *jáblonja* OPr.

wobalne), nut, cane, mountain-ash, elm, and the names of grains: R. *zernó* 'grain, corn' L. *žìrnis* 'pea', R. (ChSl.) *zélie* 'weeds' L. *žolě*, R. *list* 'leaf' L. *laĩškas*, R. *pyréj* Cz. *pýr* 'couch-grass' L. (dial.) *pūraĩ* 'wheat', R. *rož'* 'rye' L. *rugiaĩ*. Passing over some discrepancies of formation and meaning, these coincidences are evidence that the speakers of both languages inhabited the same regions for a long time. They agree also in naming most parts of the body, and coincide in some notable innovations: hand (R. *ruká* L. *rankà*), finger, foot (R. *nogá* OPr. *nage* cf. Gk. ὄνυξ Lat. *ungula* Germ. *Nagel* 'nail'), head, mouth, throat, beard, shoulder, elbow, heart, entrails, tongue (R. *jazýk* CSl. *ęzy-kŭ* OPr. *insuwis*), body (R. *čérevo* 'body, belly' OPr. *kērmens*). For all these there must have been a certain community of thinking between the two groups. There is more discrepancy in the names of animals since these are subject to change through the preference of one breed over another. Held in common are the names for the bee (OB. *bičela* R. *pčelá* L. *bitìs*, and also R. *úlej* 'beehive' P. *ul* L. *aulỹs*, P. *skarzỹk* L. *korỹs* 'cell of a honeycomb'), wasp (R. *osá* L. *vapsà*), ox (OB. *govędŭ* R. *govjádina* 'beef' Latv. *govs*), sheep (R. *ovcá* L. *avìs*), domestic pig (OB. *prasę* L. *pař̃šas*), wolf, mouse, stag, eagle, thrush, (perhaps) goose, fly, etc. Other conspicuous coincidences are the words for stone (OB. *kamy* R. *kámeń* L. *akmuõ*), iron (R. *želézo* L. *gelẽžìs* OPr. *gelso*), gold (R. *zóloto* Latv. *zelts*), lake (R. *ózero* L. *ẽžeras*).

On the other hand a great number of common Slavonic words have no parallels in the Baltic tongues because they are due to Slavonic borrowing or innovation. They include the words for God, man, father, tooth, horse, mare, dog, bull, goat, bird, swan, liver, milk, friend, sun, moon, water, etc. Sometimes the older term survives in a restricted sense, as R. *dívo* 'wonder' cf. L. *Diẽvas* 'God', R. *tur* 'aurochs'/R. *Bog vol*. Very characteristic of the relations between the languages is the constant variation of detail in word-formation owing to the use of different forms of the root or different suffixes, as R. *son* L. *săpnas* 'dream, sleep', R. *ráno* 'early' L. *rýtas* 'morning', R. *jáseń* L. *úosis* 'ash-tree', or by different choice of related meanings. There are certain suffixes which regularly alternate, as Sl. *-dlo*/L. *-klas* (of tools: P. *radło* 'hoe' L. *árklas* 'wooden plough', both from *ar-*), Sl. *-ičĭ* (<*-iko*)/L. *-ikis*, Sl. *-itj-* (<*-eit-*)/L. *-aitis*. There are variations which elude explanation, as R. *guś* OB. *gǫsĭ*/L. *žąsìs* 'goose'.

The differences between Baltic and Slavonic are thus also important, and some of them ascend to a high antiquity. In Slavonic, but not fully in Baltic, IE. *s* was withdrawn into the palate by contact with *i u r k*, provided a vowel followed. This happened also in Sanskrit and most of the Iranian languages, and therefore is a feature of date before the final dispersion of the languages forming the Slavonic and Indo-Iranian groups; that is, considerably before 1000 B.C. At such a date, therefore, Baltic was already distinct from Slavonic: Balt. *s*/Sl. *ch* < *š* < *s* after *i u r k*. There was probably no complete Balto-Slavonic unity short of Indo-European date, but there was a symbiosis lasting over a vast period of time, and possibly still unbroken, or quite recently interrupted, when Herodotus described the Scythian (Iranian) culture of South Russia in the fifth century B.C. It overlapped some stages of Proto-Slavonic. The likeness induced in the two groups by this living together in prehistoric times (see Senn, in *Slavonic Yearbook* 1941, on possible historic influences) has several consequences for Slavonic studies: in all cases it is necessary to ascertain what is the Baltic evidence; where alternative explanations can be offered for Slavonic phenomenon, those are most probable which can also be offered for the Baltic parallel; no explanations contrary to Baltic can be offered for Slavonic facts until proof is given that the latter are entirely disconnected.

The reader may care to compare the following passage in Old Bulgarian (Matthew XIII, 24–26, transliterated from the Glagolitic of the Codex Marianus) with the corresponding text in Lithuanian:

inǫ pritŭčǫ prědloži imŭ glagolę: upodobi sę cěsarestvie nebeskoe člověku sěvŭšu dobro sěmę na selě svoemĭ. supęštemŭ že člověkomŭ pride vragŭ ego i vĭsě plěvelŭ po srědě pšenicę i otide. egda že prozębe trěva i plodŭ sŭtvori, tŭgda avi sę i plěvelŭ.	Kìtą prilýginimą sãkė jìs jíems tarýdams: Prilýgsta dangaũs karalýstė žmõgui sėjančiam gẽrą sėklą į sãvo diřvą. Bèt žmonėms bemiẽgant atėjo jõ príetelius ir užsėjo kukaliùs tarp kviečių ir atstójo. Ir kaĩp želmuõ paáugo ir vaĩsių nẽše, štaĩ, rãdos ir kukãliai.

In this (Modern) Lithuanian version the word *príetelius* (enemy) and the root of *karalýstė* (kingdom) represent borrowings from Slavonic.*

12. *Proto-Slavonic.* (*a*) *Primitive Slavonic.* The first distinctively Slavonic phenomenon to emerge was Sl. *ch*[χ] < IE. *s* after *i u r k* unless a consonant followed: R. *such* 'dry'/L. *saũsas*. This process

* See R. Trautmann, *Baltisch-Slavisches Wörterbuch* (Göttingen, 1923); A. Brückner, 'Das Litauische und seine Verwandten' in *Grundriss der indogermanischen Sprach- und Altertumskunde: ii, Die Erforschung der indogermanischen Sprachen; iii: Slavisch-Litauisch, Albanisch* (Strassburg, 1917). On Baltic generally see works by Berneker, Bezzenberger, Bielenstein, Brückner, Būga, Endzelin, Kurschat, Leskien, Lidén, Senn, Torbiörnsson. See also N. B. Jopson, 'The Syntax of Lithuanian compared with that of Latin and Greek', *Slavonic Review*, xxiv, No. 63. The case against 'Balto-Slavonic' is argued by A. Meillet, *Le slave commun* (Paris, 2nd ed. 1934), and the evidence is reviewed by A. Senn, 'On the Degree of Kinship between Slavic and Baltic', in *The Slavonic Yearbook* (xx, 1941).

does not normally affect Sl. *s* from IE. *k̂*. The beginnings of the change were set in times immediately post-Indo-European, since they affect also the Indo-Iranian group. After these sounds IE. *s* was pronounced higher in the mouth, becoming cacuminal (Skr. *ṣ*), then palatal (Avestic *š*), then velar (Sl. *ch*). Lat. *tonsorias* has passed through these stages in Spanish (*tiseras* is a common vulgarism, Med.Sp. *tixeras* [š], MSp. *tijeras* [χ] 'scissors'). The resulting *ch* was added to the group of velars before the first Slavonic palatalization.

13. (*b*) *Early Proto-Slavonic*. This period is characterized by the palatalization of IE. *k g* and Primitive Slavonic *ch* before *e/i* (*i̯*) to Sl. *č dž* (later *ž*) *š*: R. *volk* 'wolf'/OR. voc. *volče*, *Bog* 'God'/voc. *Bóže*, *duch* 'spirit'/*dušá* 'soul' <**duch-ja*. This is, of course, after the *satem*-palatalization of Indo-European date by which IE. *k̂ ĝ* >Sl. *s z*: R. *sto* 'hundred' Latv. *simts* L. *šìmtas* Skr. *çata* MPers. *sad*/Gk. ἑκατόν. The palatalization giving *č dž* is unknown to Lithuanian (R. *četýre* 'four'/L. *keturì*), but it arose separately in several languages of the *satem*-branch: Latv. *četri* Arm. *č'ors* MPers. *chehâr panj* 'five' (**penke*) Skr. *catur pañca*.

The original pronunciation of IE. *o e* seems to have been very open, at least in parts of the area, with a tendency towards *å ä* (Eng. *fall there*). It was so with Gk. ω η, represented in Doric often by α. In Balto-Slavonic *o a* fell together, but *e* remained; and later BSl. **å* was differently developed according to quantity, viz. BSl. short **å* >Balt. *a* Sl. *o*, BSl. long **å* >Balt. *o* Sl. *a*. OB. *ě* was so open that no sign was used in the Glagolitic alphabet to distinguish it from *ja*. In Sanskrit the three vowels became one *a* (thus BSl. *o* >*å*=*å* <*a*, *e*/Skr. *o* >*å* >*a*=*a*=*a* <*ä* <*e*), *e* remaining long enough to cause the palatalization of IE. *k g* before it; the vowels had been identified by the Vedic period (c. 1000 B.C.) By analogy, we may infer as probable that the Early Proto-Slavonic period should be dated before 1000 B.C.

One consequence of the palatalization was that a following *ě* became *a*: R. *slýšať* 'hear' (for *-ěti*). There is no way of dating this change, though it may quite well have followed shortly after the first palatalization.

14. (*c*) *Middle Proto-Slavonic*. By reason of a number of related changes in the Middle Proto-Slavonic period (1000–1 B.C.?) the Slavonic languages gained their special vowel-complexion. The order of these changes may be debatable in some cases, but that they occurred in series is clear enough. If we compare OB. *kamy* 'stone' with L. *akmuõ* Gk. ἄκμων 'anvil', it is evident that we must proceed from **-on* to *-y*, and this implies the stages **-ōn* >**-ūn* (vowel closed by the nasal in final syllable) >**-ū* (nasal vowel) >**-ų* (denasalized vowel) >*-y* (mixed vowel for back vowel). In final syllables vowels were closed one degree before *n* or *s*; all syllables closed by a nasal gave

nasal vowels (possibly first in final syllables, as in Lithuanian), and the nasal element disappeared from the narrower vowels; the soft vowels were distinguished from the hard or normal vowels, and hard vowels after a palatal element became soft; *ū* and *u* were pronounced more centrally, so as to become 'mixed' instead of 'back' vowels; diphthongs became monophthongs, and the CSl. *ě* came into being as a common result of *ē* and *ai, oi*. The most probable order of changes seems to have been: (i) *on os ons* final >*un us uns*, (ii) rise of nasal vowels in closed syllables: *į ų ǫ = ą̇ ę*, (iii) loss of -*n* -*s*, (iv) shift of back vowels (*u o* but not *ǫ* <-*ont*) to front vowels (*i e*) after a palatal element (*j*): *ju jo >ji je*, (v) denasalization of the narrow vowels (*ų į*), (vi) development of Sl. *y ŭ ĭ*, (vii) reduction of diphthongs to monophthongs: *ou eu oi ai ei >u ju œ i*, (viii) final *œ̂ >ě/œ́ >i*, otherwise *ě* only, e.g. OR. loc. sing. *volcě* cf. Gk. οἴκοι 'at home', (ix) identification of *ē̦ >ě = ě <oi ai*.

With regard to denasalization, it should be noted that there are several categories of nasal vowels. The escape of air through the nose results from the lowering of the uvula, and this may be varied according to three grades, numbered 1 2 3 by Jespersen. Grade 1 is a slight lowering of the uvula throughout the whole discourse, and gives what is called a 'nasal accent'; 2 is the normal lowering as for nasal consonants and Portuguese nasal vowels; 3 is a deep lowering which touches the tongue when raised and prevents the formation of narrow nasalized vowels, as in French and Polish. It follows that in Middle Proto-Slavonic the grade of lowering was increased, with the result that the narrow vowels were eliminated. (In Fr. *fin*, to preserve tne nasalization the vowel has been opened to [ɛ̃].) There were no narrow nasals in Slavonic when Germanic words in -*ing* and -*ung* were borrowed in the first years of the Christian era.

It is possible also to give a relative order for some changes in conjugation. The perfect must have been lost at a very early date, since only faint traces of it survive (R. *ved* 'after all' cf. Gk. οἶδα < **woid-* pf. 'I know'). Indo-European distinguished durative from perfective aspects by means of stems (*e*-grade/zero-grade: Gk. λείπω/ ἔλιπον). Slavonic used zero-grade stems to make present tenses, and so broke down the original method of distinguishing aspect; by way of compensation it extended the use of the *s*-aorist, and gave it new forms. The aorist acquired the sense of a past definite, and led to the creation of a new imperfect (Sl. *běachŭ* 'I was' corresponds partially to Lat. *fueram* 'I had been': ? **bhē-ēsom/*bhu-esam*). A new distinction of aspect (imperfective/perfective) was built up by associating simple verbs and verbs compounded with prefixes, and a new durative or iterative was made by using the suffixes -*va*- -*yva*- -*ja*-. This procedure was completed in the latest Common Slavonic period, and was beginning to undermine the imperfect and aorist tenses at the opening of the historic period in Russian and Polish.

15. (d) *Late Proto-Slavonic.* This period covers the entry of the Germanic loanwords into Common Slavonic vocabulary (1st–6th cent. A.D.) They were affected by a process similar to the second Slavonic palatalization, by which in original Slavonic words the velars *k g ch* >*c dz* (later *z* in some languages) *š/š*, under two sets of circumstances: these are (i) after *i ĭ ę*, provided no *o* *oi ǫ *ū >*y* followed, and (ii) before *ai *oi >*ě/i*. The first is exemplified by R. *ovcá* OB. *ovica* <*ovĭka 'sheep', R. *otéc* OB. *otĭcĭ* <*otĭkŭ 'father'. It would seem to be older than the other group (represented by OB. *vlkŭ* 'wolf' loc. sing. *vlcě* nom. pl. *vlci*), which has not been carried out in West Slavonic when a *v* intervenes: R. *cvet* 'flower'/Cz. *květ*, R. *zvezdá* 'star'/P. *gwiazda*. R. *knjaž* 'prince' OB. *kŭnędzĭ* <Germ. *kuningaz* (Finn. *kuningas*) would appear to be due to antecedent *ę*, and R. *cérkov* 'church' OB. *crky* < Germ. *kirihha (Kirche)* to the following *i;* the first is one of the oldest Germanic loanwords (about 1st cent. A.D.), and the latter one of the latest (about 6th cent.), since the former was due to military prowess of the Migration Age, and the latter to the Christianization of some German tribes, leading to their adoption of Gk. κυριακή.

16. *Slavonic divisions.* It is customary to divide Slavonic into East, West and South. Of the unity of East Slavonic there is no doubt; White Russian and Ruthenian are essentially forms of Russian which have developed within the historical era in almost all particulars. South Slavonic is also closely-knit, though there is evidence of cleavage between Slovene with Serbocroat, on the one hand, and Bulgarian on the other. The unity of West Slavonic is most doubtful, since there are fundamental divergencies between Polish and Czech, while Czech sometimes continues trends of South Russian (CSl. *g* >Cz.Ruth. *h*) and sometimes of South Slavonic (e.g. treatment of *tort*, denasalization of *ǫ ę*), and Slovak has some close contacts with Slovene dialects of the north-east and with Russian. The conception 'West Slavonic' thus describes a sum of coincidences, without excluding important differences. Polish, Polabian and perhaps Wendish are sometimes classified as Lechitic.

The main criterion applied is the development of CSl. *ť *ď (*tj, *kt *gt+front vowel, *dj) giving ESl. *č ž* WSl. *c dz z* SSl. Slov. *č j*, S. *ć đ*, Macedonian dial. *k ǵ*, B. *št žd:* R. *noč* 'night' *mežá* 'boundary' /Cz. *noc mez* P. *miedza*/S. *nôć mèđa* B. *nošt meždá*. With regard to *y*, it remains in E and WSl. (but in CzSlk. and Ruth. has changed value in later times), and disappears in SSl.: R. *syn* 'son'/S. *sîn*. The *jers* (*ŭ ĭ*) when in strong position give ESl. *o e*/WSl. *e*/SSl. *a* or *ă:* R. *son* 'dream' *deń* 'day'/P. *sen* Cz. *den* P. *dzień*/S. *sän dân*. SSl. *e i* have been hardened, but remain soft in ESl. (save in Ruthenian) and WSl. (save in Czech, where *e* has hardened); in ESl. *t d ŕ* remain before them, but in WSl. (Polish and Wendish) they palatalize (e.g. P. *ć dż rz: ciało* 'body' *dzień* 'day' *rzecz* 'thing'/R. *télo deń reč'* 'speech'). The nasal vowels *ǫ ę* persist only in P. *ą ę*, after notable vicissitudes; otherwise they give ESl.Cz.S. *u e*, Slov. *o e*, MB. *ă e*. Other distinctions arise from the *tort* formula, i.e. when *o/e* precedes *r/l* between consonants. In such cases ESl. *torot*, etc., shows characteristic 'full vocalism'/P.Wend. *trot* shows metathesis/CzSlk.SSl. *trat* shows metathesis and change of vowel. Sonant *r l* existed in Old Bulgarian (spelt *rŭ rĭ lŭ lĭ*), and exist in Czechoslovak; Serbocroat and Slovene have sonant *ŗ*; in Serbocroat sonant *ļ* has been vocalized as *u:* R. *pólnyj* 'full' P. *pełny* Cz. *plný* S. *pün* B. *păln-*. In ESl. initial (*j*)*e-* under certain conditions >*o:* R. *oléń* 'stag'/S. *jèlen*. In the field of syntax SSl. *da*+finite verb largely replaces E. and WSl. use of the infinitive. The accent is free in E. and SSl. (but has been shifted in *što-* and *kaj*-Serbocroat and in Slovene); it is generally bound in WSl. (CzSlk. initial, Wend. initial with tendency to secondary accent on the penultimate, P. penultimate, free in Cassubian and Polabe.) CSl. *g* >voiced *h* in CzSlk. Upper Wend., WR., Ruth., and >[γ] in Southern Great Russian. Quantity is retained only by CzSlk., Slov.S., though much altered; tone by Slov.S.

Chapter III

THE ALPHABET

17. *The problem.* Writing in or about the year A.D. 914, the Bulgarian monk Chrabrŭ defined the problem of spelling Slavonic in these terms:

> Hitherto the Slavs had no books. While yet pagans they read and wrote cryptically by means of marks and cuts. When converted to Christianity, they expressed the Slavonic speech unsystematically in Roman and Greek writing. But how could they accurately write in Greek letters *bogŭ, životŭ, dzělo, crkŭvĭ, čajanije, širota, jadŭ, ǫdŭ, junostĭ* or *językŭ*, and others like them? So, after many years, God sent them a saintly philosopher, Constantine, also called Cyril, a just and true man, and he made for them 38 letters, some according to the value of the Greek letters, others according to the Slavonic tongue.

An excellent example of the 'unsystematic' use of the Roman alphabet is the papal bull of 1136 in Polish, which is distinguished for the large number of equivalent renderings for single Slavonic sounds. In Greek, the Emperor Constantine Porphyrogenitus's transcriptions of Slavonic names and words show the highest degree of accuracy that could be obtained along such lines.

The Slavonic palatalizations had produced a number of sounds for which there were no Greek or Latin equivalents: *č* (roughly Eng. *ch* in *church*), *dž* (Eng. *g* in *George*) which had become an affricate *ž* (Eng. *z* in *azure*), *š* (Eng. *sh* in *shin*), *c* (Eng. *ts* in *bets*), *dz* (Eng. *ds* in *beds*). The Greek alphabet had a sign χ for the Slavonic voiceless velar fricative, to which the Roman responded by *ch*, which had been adopted by German and is treated as a single letter when it occurs in Slavonic. Gk. β had become fricative *v*, and so raised a problem about representing *b* in Cyrillic, which was not felt by those who used Roman as their basis: they opposed to occlusive *b* fricative *v* or *w* (*uu* used in mediæval Latin to represent a Germanic sound). Similarly, Roman *u* represented Sl. *u*, but Greek required the two letters ου, sometimes written as a ligature ȣ, since Gk. υ was a 'mixed' vowel of the nature of French *u*, German *ü*.

Under Mediæval Latin conditions the letters *i j* were frequently used to denote palatal glides, and they offered a chance of specialization: vocalic *i*/semivocalic *j*. Gk. η ι were both vocalic *i* in the ninth century, and so the Greek alphabet offered one resource less than the Roman. Neither, however, was quite adequate to express the subtle

nuances of Slavonic pronunciation, according to which the whole
series of consonants was divided into 'hard' (i.e. normal) and 'soft'
(i.e. accompanied by a palatal off-glide). The velars were hard, and
their palatalizations (*č dž ž š c dz* etc.) were all soft. Hardening of
these palatals is a feature of the independent histories of the Slavonic
tongues. The labials (*p b m*) did not change timbre when softened, but
under some conditions developed a palatal consonant (*l*) between
themselves and the following vowel. The sounds produced upon the
teeth or gums (dentals or alveolars: *t d l r n s z*) were liable to more
serious modification, since they could be 'hard', or 'soft' (before
front vowels), or converted into palatals (before the semivowel or
glide *j*), without quite losing unity of timbre. This happens sporadically in some pronunciations of English, as the *t* in *note* (hard) *nature*
(soft) *try* (palatal) or the first *n* in *unite* (hard) *union* (soft) *onion*
(palatal). To cope with this situation neither model alphabet offered
adequate resources. Roman *i j* were made to serve more or less
adequately. In Old Bulgarian a circumflex to the right of a letter
indicated softening or palatalization, as *zeml^o izměn^enümŭ;* but the
usage was not entirely consistent nor did it descend to later Cyrillic
alphabets.

The Slavonic vowels were no less troublesome. There was nothing
in Greek or Latin answering to Sl. *ě*, the two *jers* (*ŭ ĭ*) or the two
nasals (*ǫ ę*). Moreover, the Slavonic vowels were often preceded by a
palatal on-glide resembling the semivowel [j] when initial or after
another vowel; this involved making signs for *ja ju je jǫ ję*. After a soft
consonant, which had an off-glide [j], the vowel inevitably began with
a palatal on-glide, and this raised the question whether this feature
should be marked in the consonant or in the vowel. Complete
consistency in this respect eluded even John Hus, the founder of the
modern Czech alphabet.

Latin supplied no signs for stress, tone or quantity. The Greek
signs were originally tonal, but in the ninth century represented stress.
Old Bulgarian spelling does not record these distinctions systemati-
cally, though Russo-Slavonic documents make frequent use of the
acute accent to mark stress. It is possible that Old Bulgarian,
like Modern Bulgarian, lacked precise distinctions of tone and
quantity, and the fall of the stress-accent was taken for granted in
an alphabet for the use of natives who knew perfectly well where the
stress fell. To distinguish quantity, Hus was able to use the acute
in the sense given to it by Old English and Old Norse usage.
The tonal diacritics used for Serbocroat and Slovene are entirely
modern.

Finally, as the Old Bulgarian alphabet was designed to serve for
translations from Greek religious works, signs had to be included for

purely Greek sounds: φ (which only developed later in Slavonic from final $v >f$, $chv >f$ or $p\ddot{u}v >f$) ψ ξ θ υ γ (in its mediæval Greek value before front vowels) ω.

18. *Comparative table of Slavonic alphabets.*

Glago-litic	Old Cyril-lic	Num-erical Value of OC	New Cyril-lic	Trans-litera-tion	Latin	Notes
✦	ⰀА	1	а	a	a	Long vowels (Cz. á, etc.) are not separately noted in this table.
					ä	Slovak [æ] after labials.
Ⰱ	в		б	b	b	
ⰂѴ	к	2	в	v	v w	CzSlk.S.Slov.v/P.Wend.w.
Ⰳ	г	3	г	g h	g h	CzSlk.UpWend.Ruth.h.
			ґ	g		Ruth.g.
Ⰴ	д	4	д	d	d	
					ď	CzSlk.ď (palatalized).
			ђ		dj ď	S. (palatalized).
Ⰵ	є	5	е	e	e	
					ě	Cz.[jɛ],Wend.[iə].
			ё	ë	R.[jɔ]. The diacritic is not as a rule used.
			е	je		Ruth.
			э	ê	R.WR., without palatal on-glide.
					é	UpWend. closed [e]
ⰆЖ	ж		ж	ž	ž ż	P.ż. Hus used dot. Arm. Av.
Ⰴ	ѕ	6		dz	dz	Arm.Ѕ =t.
					dź	P. (palatalized), Wend.
Ⰸ	з	7	з	z	z	Gk.minuscule ʒ=ζ.
					ź	P. (palatalized), Wend.
Ⱄ	и	8	и	i y	i	Ruth. transliteration y=[e]. O B. also stands for ji jï.
	і	10	і	i	i	WR. i used instead of и. P.i is often a sign of the palatalization of the previous consonant. O B. also stands for ji jï.
			ï	ï		Ruth. [ji].
			й j	j	j	S. Cyrillic j from Latin. Sign of palatalization in S. dj lj nj.
	ћ			ǵ		Gk. γ (palatalized).
Ⰹ	к	20	к	k	k	Gk. minuscule ϰ, Arm.
Ⰾ	л	30	л	l	l	P. l is palatal.
					ł	P. 'hollow' or 'dark' ł.
					ĺ	Slovak long sonant.
			љ		lj	S. palatal; sometimes written ļ.
Ⰿ	м	40	м	m	m	

Glago-litic	Old Cyril-lic	Num-erical Value of OC	New Cyril-lic	Trans-litera-tion	Latin	Notes
Ⱏ	И	50	Н	n	n	Gk. cursive ν
					ń ň	P.Wend.ń,Cz.ň (palatalized).
			Њ		nj	S. palatal; sometimes written ŋ.
Ⰹ	o	70	o	o	o	
					ó	P. [u], UpWend [uɔ]; CzSlk. long [o:].
					ô	Slovak ô=uo.
Ⱂ	п	80	П	p	p	
Ь	ρ	100	р		r	
					ř rz	Cz.ř is palatal [ř], Wend.ř [š], P.rz [ž/š].
					ŕ	Slovak long sonant.
Ⱄ	с	200	с	s	s	
					ś	P.Wend. palatalized sibilant.
ⱳ	тⰲ	300	Т	t	t	Arm. ա and Sl. ш due to Gk. minuscule ∝.
					ť	CzSlk. ť (palatalized).
			ħ		ć	S. palatalized affricate ťś.
Ⱘ	оу	400	у	u	u	Gk. ου=OB. оу, ligature ȣ = Cyrillic у.
			ў	ŭ		WR. semivowel.
					ů	Cz. [u:], formerly uo.
Ⱇ	Ф	500	ф	f	f	Originally only in Gk. words.
Ⱈ	х	600	x	ch	ch h	S.Slov. h.
					kh	UpWend. init. aspirated k.
Ⱁ	ѡ	800	o		o	Gk. ω in Gk. words.
Ⱌ	ц	900	ц	c	c	Hebrew צ, ץ; Arm. ց.
Ⱍ	ч	90	ч	č	č cz	P.cz. Arm. ċ ; Av. Ⲩ (written right to left).
			џ	dž	dž dž	P.dž. Only Serb uses џ; other languages дж.
Ⱎ	ш		ш	š	š sz	P.sz. Hebrew שׁ Arabic ش Av. ⲏⲟ.
Ⱋ	щ		щ	št šč	št šč	OB.MB.št; S.št is not a ligature.
					szcz	(ШТ); R.OCz. šč (R. often [š':]); P.szcz. Always a ligature in Av.ⲱⲟ(št),ⲭⲟ (šč).
Ⱏ	ъ		ъ	ŭ ǎ ' -		OB.ŭ; MB.ǎ (with the sound of Rumanian ǎ); R. generally not transcribed as it only indicated the normal (hard) pronunciation of a previous consonant, but represented by ' when indicating hardness of a consonant before a soft vowel; limited to this use in the modern orthography, which uses ъ or the apostrophe.

Glagolitic	Old Cyrillic	Numerical Value of OC	New Cyrillic	Transliteration	Latin	Notes
ⰟⰉⰟⰊ	ЪІ ЪИ		Ы	y	y	Mixed [ɨ], pronounced with tongue retracted but lips unrounded.
Ⱐ	ь		ь	ĭ ' -		OB.ĭ; R. ' above or after consonant; MB. transliterated ' where occurring (e.g. *Bot'ov*). (The acute accent represents length in CzSlk. vowels and sonants, and OP. vowels; but represents only softening of consonants and stress or rising tone of vowels in transliterations.)
Ⱑ	ѣ		ѣ	ě		In Glagolitic also ja; Arm. ƚ=(j)e.
Ⱓ	ю		ю	ju 'u		The Cyrillic sign results from contraction of Gk. ιου. The transliteration 'u is here used for OB. after consonants.
	ꙗ		я	ja 'a		For Glagolitic see above. Sometimes 'a.
	ѥ			je		Sometimes 'e.
Ⱔ	ѧꙗꙗ	900		ę	ę	P.ę [ɛ̃] is a later development.
Ⱘ	ѫ		ж	ǫ ǎ	ǫ	P.ą [ɔ̃]; OB.ǫ; MB.ǎ; Av.ą (nasal) was written Ⱇ.
Ⱗ	ѩ			ję		
Ⱙ	ѭ		ѭ	ją ja		OB.jǫ; MB.ja (ѭ replaced by я in 1923).
	ѯ	60		ks	x	Gk. minuscule ꙃ=ξ, in Gk. words; Cz. x occasionally in foreign words and names; P.x occasionally found.
	ѱ	700		ps		Gk. words only.
Ⱚ	ѳ	9	ѳ	f		Gk. words only; now disused in R.
Ⴟ	ѵ	400	v	ü		In Gk. words only.

In rendering Old Bulgarian words (except when quoting texts) the present writers have adopted Leskien's method of attempting a phonetic version rather than a letter-for-letter transliteration. Thus, *l'ubŭ* for *ljubŭ*, *prvŭ* (with sonant *r*) for *prŭvŭ*, and so on. On the other hand the softness of such OB. consonants as *č*, *š* and the rest has not normally been indicated by a tick, since (as explained later) these consonants were always (at any rate originally) soft. *L' ń ŕ* followed by front vowels (e.g. *koń*) indicate an original *lj nj rj* and (as certain evidence would suggest) a pronunciation differing somewhat from *l n r* followed by front vowels.

Other languages (e.g. Russian) are transliterated letter for letter, so far as the system of transliteration permits. Except in

Chapter V, Russian has been transliterated to facilitate comparison.

In some works OB. ϱ is represented by the sign q, and the Russian hard and soft signs (ъ ь) are used (e.g. by Leskien) for OB. $\breve{u}$ $\breve{\imath}$.

19. *Glagolitic* (OB. *glagolŭ* 'word') *and Cyrillic.* Chrabrŭ's account prepares us to expect an alphabet of personal and scholarly character, but not two alphabets mutually related and with marked idiosyncrasies. The older was possibly the Glagolitic, in which the most ancient texts are redacted. It has continued in liturgical use in some parts of Yugoslavia. It may have been the alphabet of the Moravian mission of Methodius and Cyril (863 ff.), the fruits of which were gathered by the Latin Church. Yet, about 914, it was possible for a Bulgarian monk to suppose there had only been one alphabet, the Cyrillic, and to attribute it to Methodius's brother Constantine (or Cyril). Its identification with Orthodox Christianity causes it to be the only alphabet in use among the Russians or Serbs. A difference of dialect reveals itself: Glagolitic agrees with East Bulgarian in considering *ja* to be a function of *ě* (which corresponds to *ea* in Rumanian loanwords from Slavonic), with only one sign for both, but Cyrillic and West Bulgarian distinguish two vowels. Glagolitic is based on Greek minuscule writing of the ninth century, as may be seen in the equivalents of *g d k n t;* but it is also characterized by arbitrariness, which leads to the creation of new letters where there is no need (*v m s f*) and a riot of fancy expressed in small circles. Cyrillic is just as obviously marked by prudence and boldness in its use of the Greek uncial. The style, indeed, shows rather too much firmness in its heavy downstroke and serifs, with scarcely visible connecting hairlines. The letters *b v k, a l*, and *n i* are not easily distinguishable at times.

Provision was made in Glagolitic for the transcription of purely Greek sounds in Greek words (γ θ υ φ ω). Other letters were added for this purpose in Cyrillic (ξ ψ).

To solve the special problems offered by Slavonic the authors of these alphabets, and especially of Glagolitic, seem to have relied heavily on their inventive genius. The opening of the upper loop to give an occlusive *b* in Cyrillic and the use of the element ь in the consecutive letters *ŭ y ĭ ě* seem to be examples of such a procedure. It is noteworthy that the Cyrillic inventor should have accepted the Glagolitic resolution of Sl. *y* into *ŭ+i*. He concurred in the need to distinguish certain vowels which begin with a palatal on-glide or semivowel, and increased the series from *ju jọ ję* by adding *ja je*. The series was left incomplete, however, in respect of *ji jĭ*, which are represented by a simple vowel sign (*i*) in Old Bulgarian texts. The author of Glagolitic obviously recognized an *a*-quality in the vowel *ě*, a quality which may be found in modern East Bulgarian, and is recorded in Rumanian loanwords as *ea*. In Cyrillic the sound of *ě* was represented by a new letter and distinguished from *ja*, but the Glagolitic sign was adapted to represent *ę*, which presumably had for the Cyrillic author a very open quality (such as nasal [ã]). Both transcriptions seem to find an *o*-quality in the hard nasal (*ǫ*).

Were hints taken from other alphabets than Greek? The alphabet-makers were Biblical scholars and so were likely to know something of the Hebrew alphabet. Constantinople was a cosmopolitan capital, where there had reigned an Armenian dynasty, and Syrians and perhaps some Parthians might be 'met in the streets. An Armenian alphabet had been formed to preserve the Christian scriptures. It was indebted to the Greek uncial and also to the script used by the Sassanian monarchs to preserve the Zoroastrian Avesta. The letter *š* is probably due to Hebrew, though the same sign is found in other Semitic alphabets (Arabic and Ethiopian), and also in Avestic. In Avestic *št* and *šč* are always ligatures. It is odd that this combination of two sounds should have been placed in the Slavonic alphabets, though the simple elements were clearly understood. Signs for *ž* were formed for Armenian and Avestic, not wholly unlike the Slavonic ones. The dental affricate *c* was to be found in Hebrew in a shape not too unlike that used in the Cyrillic and Glagolitic scripts. The sign used in Cyrillic for *dz* has a dental quality (*t*) in Armenian. The sign for palatal affricate *č* resembles Cyrillic, but not Glagolitic, in the Armenian and Avestic alphabets. Armenian scribes found a sign for *je/e*, and in the Avestas there is a nasal vowel sign for *ǫ*. Whether the Slavonic alphabet-makers incurred such debts or no, they certainly impressed on their letters two distinct and colourful personalities, and removed their work from obvious comparison with any other alphabet than the Greek.

20. *Later Cyrillic.* A new epoch was opened in the early eighteenth century by the use of Peter the Great's Russian 'civil alphabet' (*graždánskaja ázbuka/pečát*). It was extraordinarily conservative: it recognized, as Russo-Slavonic had already done, that there were only two Russian sounds corresponding to the four Slavonic characters for *ǫ/u ę/ja*, but it left two characters for *f*, two for *e* and *i*, and retained the two *jers* which had no longer an· alphabetical value; it failed to provide a sign for *jo*, continued the Russo-Slavonic tradition of representing a central dialect under northern conditions (so that *g* has three values: *g v h*, and there is no proper representation of the variations of *a o e* under and away from stress), and was even retrograde in abandoning the use of the stress accent, found sporadically in older Russo-Slavonic texts. The whole phonetic complexion of a Russian word depends on the fall of the stress. It was an advantage to distinguish the letter *i* from the second half of a diphthong (й), and,

as *e* always had a palatal on-glide, to provide a reversed *e* to express the predominantly foreign sound without this glide. The system was simplified by the provisional Government in 1917, when ѣ ѳ і were discarded together with otiose ъ.

What was chiefly gained from the 'civil alphabet', apart from legibility and a certain degree of approximation to the West, was a final cleavage between the liturgical and lay use of cultured speech. Modifications were introduced for Ruthenian (*g/h je/e ji/i*) and White Russian (*ŭ*, i for *и*), and the Russian alphabet has been applied to a wide range of non-Slavonic languages within the Soviet Union. In Bulgaria the Old Cyrillic naturally lasted long. After attempts at simplification, a system was established in 1923 in which there were two signs (ъ and ѫ, not always used etymologically) for *ă* ([ɐ] as in Eng. *above*), *ě* had two sounds, and the *jers* were often otiose. On February 15 1945 the orthography was reformed as follows: ѫ and ѣ are abolished, being replaced by ъ, е and я (except in сѫ 'are', which is now written са); ъ is dropped at the end of words; and ь is only used to indicate softness before an o. A very important modification of the 'civil alphabet' was effected by Vuk Stefanović Karadžić for the transcription of Serbian at the beginning of the nineteenth century. There being no distinction of 'hard' and 'soft' vowels and consonants in Serbian, he was able to isolate the semivowel *j* and use for it a letter borrowed from Roman type. He also added signs for *ć đ lj nj dž*. Croat provides Roman equivalents for all the Serbian signs, and so is normally used in comparative grammars.

Rumanian was officially written in Cyrillic until about 1860. It conformed to Bulgarian idiosyncrasies (e.g., the alternation of *ea/e*, *f* for final *ch*, etc.), and provides Latin equivalents for Slavonic sounds (*â î*, *ă* as in Bulgarian, final unstressed *i* non-syllabic, *c*+front vowel=Sl. *č*, *ţ*=Sl. *c*, *g*+front vowel=Sl. *dž*, *j*=Sl. *ž*, *ş*=Sl. *š*). This alphabet has, in its turn, influenced the new Turkish alphabet.

21. *Germano-Latin alphabets* (*Czech, Polish, Wendish*). Glagolitic extended as far as Bohemia in occasional use; notable examples are a Passionale (14th cent.) and a Bible (1416). Generally speaking, however, the model to be followed in Central Europe was the Roman alphabet, as it was understood in the Middle Ages and as it had been adapted to represent German sounds. The form taken by letters until the end of the eighteenth century was Gothic (known to the Slavs as 'Swabian'). The Roman letters had variable values (e.g. *c g*) and entered into numerous combinations to express Romance sounds; further combinations gave sounds peculiarly Germanic; and between Latin, Romance and Germanic there were resources for expressing most Czech and Polish sounds. The history of these alphabets differs from those of the Balkans and Russia chiefly because they were not

rationalized by any single mind until the Czech Hus (c. 1374–1415) issued his alphabet for Czech. There has been no commensurate reform of Polish, which largely continues the mediæval tradition of double letters for single sounds, together with some elements of Hus's diacritical system. Before Hus, Czech and Polish development was essentially on the same lines: (i) to single Latin letters were assigned more than one sound, so that the 25 letters could express almost double their number of sounds: OCz. *cas=čas*, OCz. *zen=žeň*, OCz. *kazy=káží*, etc. As the equivalences were only approximate a considerable number of Latin approximations were possible for any one Slavonic sound, as P. *c ch che z zi* (1136) for *c;* while one Latin letter might have to express many sounds, as P. *z* (1136) for *z s ž š dz dž c č*. Each approximation throws some light on the nature of the Slavonic sound, and sometimes on its historical transformations. (ii) The attempt was made to standardize the expression of Czech and Polish sounds (in Bohemia from the 14th–16th centuries) by assigning to each Roman letter its own Latin sound, and using combinations to express the remaining Slavonic sounds. These combinations were very numerous, as they were in the earliest Romance spellings, but there was a tendency to eliminate most of them in favour of a single convention in each case. For instance *č* could be expressed by OCz. *c cc s cs sc zs sz ch chz chs sch cz czz tcs czi* and (after Hus had introduced his *č*) by *ċ č cž cž tc*, and *ž* by OCz. *z s ss zz ż ž ž zi*. Polish and Hungarian orthography of today arises from selection from these possibilities: *č*=P. *cz* Hungarian *cs*. Hus assigned Latin senses to Latin letters, taking *ch* to be a ligature expressing a single sound; he distinguished between *c* and *k*, but allowed to *g* its two mediæval values; and he added diacritics to modify the primitive sounds. He showed palatalization by a point in *ṅ ḋ ṫ ċ ż ṡ ṙ* and velarization in *l̇*, while length was marked by a comma above the vowel. P. *ż* retains the point. The Moravian Brethren adopted Hus's system in the main and so secured its acceptance more generally, but they introduced modifications in their Bible of Kralice (1579–83). They preferred a looped *l* to a dotted one, and this has given P. *ł*. The remaining points signified palatalization; the Brethren preferred chevrons (ˇ) to dots in some cases, and in others added commas ('): Cz. *č ň ž ř š/ť ď*. They allowed some double letters sporadically and used *v y* somewhat irregularly. All in all, however, they gave a powerful impetus to the use of the reformed spelling, and there radiated from it an influence over Poland into Lithuania and Latvia, as well as southward into Slovenia and Croatia. Consistency and analogy operated some improvements in Czech spelling in the nineteenth century. For example, *g* was reduced to a single value, and *galilegský gegj* have become *galilejský její*, while *y au w* were replaced by *j ou v: dey obauwati*/MCz. *dej obouvati*. The resulting phonetic accuracy is so great that it is convenient to use the Czech alphabet for most purposes of comparison between Slavonic languages, with only occasional recourse to a phonetic alphabet.

Upon these principles Czechoslovak and Polish have reached the following solutions of the cruces of Slavonic spelling:—The palatals are Cz. *č* P. *cz*, Cz. *ž* P. *ż*, Cz. *š* P. *sz*, Cz.P. *c*, P. *dz dż*,(OCz. *šč*) P. *szcz* (cf. Magyar *cs=č zs=ž s=š sz=s c <cz=c*). West Slavonic palatalization of dento-alveolars gives Cz. *ŕ* P. *rz*, Cz. *ň* P. *ń*, Cz. *t ď* P. *ć dź*, OCz. *l/ł* MP. *l/ł*. Followed by a vowel these palatals are written *ni* etc. in Polish, e.g. *koń* 'horse' G*S. konia*. In addition to these letters there are P. *ś ź* to indicate softenings of *s z*. Both use *ch* [χ] in the German sense, and Cz. *h* is a voiced fricative (<Sl. *g*), whereas P. *h* is voiceless and frequently pronounced [χ].

The development of vowel signs is rather more complex, since it covers developments within the historical record of the separate languages. In Mediæval Polish and in Czech new quantities developed and sometimes led to closing of long vowels by way of diphthongs; quantity has wholly disappeared from Polish, and it is only the change of quality that is denoted. Hence P. *ó* is [u], but was originally a lengthened *o;* Cz. *ů* is [uː] through OCz. *uo*, and is still long. An acute accent on a Czechoslovak vowel is a sign of its length: *á é í ó ú ý;* Cz. *ě* represents [jɛ] or ['ɛ]. The Slavonic 'mixed' narrow vowel *y* is represented by P. *y*, and was so represented by Hus, though Cz. *y* has since become simply [i]. This is an example of specialization between two alternative symbols of the Roman alphabet. For most of the Middle Ages, however, *i/j/y* were interchangeable, and *y* was sometimes dotted in the attempt to make a distinction. It was Hus who established the distinction of *i* and *y* for Czech in 1406; before that the sound *y* had been represented by *ui* (OCz. *Buitsow Buistrice* for *Bydžov Bystřice*), as in the Old Slovene of the Freising manuscripts, in accordance with OHG. *ui=* MHG. *ü*. The two weak *jers* had ceased to be vocalic before Czech or Polish documents arose, and so presented no alphabetic problem.

The two nasal vowels had been replaced by simple vowels before the first Czechoslovak documentation, but nasalization has persisted in Polish. In the twelfth century they still preserved the Common Slavonic differences, though with a strong tendency to come together. In the Bull of 1136 Sl. *ǫ ę* are represented by loosely approximate Roman spellings: *an am en em un um o u e: Balowanz Dambnizia Deuentliz Lunciz Sodouo Chomesa Chrustov= Białowąs Dąbnica Dziewiętlic Łęczyca Żądowo Chomięża Chrząstow*. From approximately the values of nasal [å] and [ä], the two nasals coalesced in a single sound which began to be written with strokes on either side or a through-stroke in the thirteenth century: *Gøbin* (1253)= *Gąbin, Køblou*

(1285) = *Kębłow*. This letter took other forms, such as φ, and in the sixteenth century was α, as well as *av aú ú*. By this time a distinction of length had developed, and the short nasal vowel was denoted by ę borrowed from the Mediæval Latin alphabet, in which ę = æ. This led to placing a subscript *iota* beneath the apparently Greek long nasal (ą), which was latinized as ą. To the distinction of length connoted by ą/ę was added a distinction of quality: front/back, and at last the quantitative difference disappeared in the eighteenth century, leaving MP. ą [ɔ̃]/ę [ɛ̃]. Thanks to the Polish practice a cedilla is used in Slavonic grammars as a sign of nasalization, and in Lithuanian as a sign of former nasalization.

The Lithuanian and Latvian languages were spelt under the influence first of Polish and German, then of Czech. The Lithuanian palatals are *č š ž dž* (formerly *cz sz ż dż*) and dental *c dz*. The former nasal vowels ą ę į ų are now long simple vowels. L. *i u* are short vowels and *e o ū y* [iː] are long; *a* and *e* may be long or short. The diphthongs *ie uo* are written *ė ů* in older works, in which a hard l (ł) may also be discerned. On the Lithuanian accents see section 22. In Latvian soft *k g n l* are distinguished by an apostrophe placed above or below; long vowels are indicated by a bar (ā), and *o* stands for the diphthong *uo*.*

Note.—The Slovak authorities now propose to introduce a reform of the spelling that will make it more phonetic and, incidentally, increase the difference to the eye between Slovak and Czech. According to the new system, softness before *i* will in all cases be indicated, so that the present *ti di*, for instance, will be written *t'i d'i*. This will permit the abolition of the letter *y*, the present *ty*, for instance, being written *ti*. Other points are the replacement of *ô* by *uo*, and *s* by *z* when so pronounced.

---

* See *Encyclopædia Britannica*, s.v. 'Alphabet'; A. Leskien, *Grammatik der altbulgarischen (altkirchenslavichen) Sprache* (Heidelberg, 1909) and *Litauisches Lesebuch* (Heidelberg, 1919); I. Taylor in *Archiv für slavische Philologie*, v. pp. 191 ff.; J. Łoś, 'Stosunek pisma do mowy' in *Krótka Gramatyka historyczna Języka Polskiego* (Lwów, 1927); J. Gebauer, *Historická Mluvnice Jazyka Českého* (Prague, 1894), i *passim*. On the transliteration of Russian see articles by W. A. Morison, N. B. Jopson and C. B. in *The Slavonic Review*, Vols. xii and xiii.

Chapter IV

COMMON SLAVONIC AND OLD BULGARIAN

A. SOUNDS

22. *Stress, Tone, Length.* Old Bulgarian orthography does not suffice to show how the stress fell, or whether there were changes of musical pitch, or whether syllables varied in length. It is known that OB. *o e ŭ ĭ* represent originally short vowels, and that all others represent original long vowels or diphthongs; but it is not certain that in the ninth to eleventh centuries OB. *o e* were shorter than OB. *a ě*. There is no distinction of quantity in Modern Bulgarian. The Greek tonic accents had become marks of stress; the circumflex was used in Old Bulgarian to denote palatalization of consonants, and the acute as a mark of stress was chiefly in use in Russia. In Modern Bulgarian the stress is free, and the same was probably true of Old Bulgarian. On the other hand, by comparing certain features of Russian, Modern Bulgarian, Czechoslovak, Slovene and Serbocroat, it becomes clear that Common Slavonic possessed free stress, musical tones (including a distinction between rising and falling long tones), and long and short quantities.

Words are organized by varying the stream of outgoing breath either in energy of utterance (stress) or in musical pitch (tone) or in the length of particular syllables (quantity). Though in theory these are three different accidents of words, they are in practice mutually related. A stressed syllable has a higher tone and is absolutely longer than an unstressed syllable. Cz. *starý* 'old' (stressed short/unstressed long) has absolute proportions of about 5 : 4; so that the quantity ascribed to syllables is strictly relative. If the energy of stress is increased above a certain unit there is increasing difference in tone and quantity between the stressed syllable and the others; but everything then comes to depend on the stress, and tone and length cease to be formal elements of word-formation. This has happened in Russian and Modern Bulgarian. Under such circumstances tone and length are more readily available for other uses throughout the sentence, such as expressing emotion. When the stress is relatively weak, as in Indo-European or Lithuanian or Common Slavonic, or when it is fixed, as in Czechoslovak upon the first syllable, conditions favour the retention of length and tone as evidently constituent parts of each word. But even so there must be stress. Unstressed tones are indifferent, and it is only under stress that distinctions appear. These distinctions are latent in unstressed syllables, as may be seen when stress is, for any reason, attracted upon them. We know, for instance, that the infinitive ending -*ti* was intrinsically unstressed in Common Slavonic, but had a latent rising tone, since it had power to attract the stress from a previous falling tone. We can also discover latent stress by comparing one form with another; e.g., for the nom. sing. fem. Gk. -η we can compare Gk. λίμνη κορυφή so as to conclude that the latent tone of the η in the first word was acute or rising.

Because of their interrelations both stress and tone are included under the one concept of accent. The word is sometimes used ambiguously or indifferently, and sometimes defined as 'stress accent' or 'musical accent'; it hardly serves an independent purpose, but it does recognize the connection inevitably existing between stress and tone.

Tone is also affected by quantity. A short quantity is assumed to be a unit of length, and therefore a short stressed element has a high tone, but no differentiation within it. A long syllable or vowel is assumed to have two units of length, and the tone may rise or fall from the first unit to the second (*oó/óo*). The interval may cover about five semitones. In Greek script the rise under stress of the short is equated to the rise within the vowel of a stressed long, and both receive an acute accent ('); the falling long is analysed as due to an initial rise and later fall (*óò*) which gives for result the circumflex accent (^). In contracted words this is a matter of historical record: Homeric ὀράω/ὀρόω becomes Attic Gk. ὀρῶ. In transcribing Lithuanian, unfortunately, the Greek accents were applied to corresponding grammatical forms, so that Gk. ἑκυρά-ᾱς 'stepmother' provided a visible parallel to L. *mergà mergõs* 'maid' (the acute accent being reserved for stressed longs). But *mergõs* is pronounced with a rising tone, and L. *nósis* 'nose' has a falling tone, which is quite contrary to the facts of Greek, Slavonic and Indo-European.

The free Slavonic accent is best exemplified in Russian, though it also occurs in Bulgarian, *ča*-Serbocroat and Cassubian. It may fall on any syllable; numbering from the end we have : R. 1 *nogá* 'foot', 2 *térem* 'attic', 3 *stískivať* 'compress', 4 *ukládyvajut* 'they pack up', 5 *zadërgivajutsja* '(curtains) are drawn', 6 *výdvinuvšiesja* 'drawn out', 7 *vospítyvajuščiesja* 'being educated'. The accent is not constant as between related words (R. *stekló* 'glass', *stekólnyj* 'of glass', *stëklyško* 'little glass') or within the declension of a single word (R.N.S. *sestrá* 'sister' NP. *sëstry* GP. *sestër*). In Russian the phenomenon known as *ákañe*, that is the reduction of *a o e* in unstressed syllables, shows two grades of reduction. The syllables immediately before and after the stressed syllable (especially the pretonic) are middling in clearness and tone, and those further away are more relaxed. Thus R. *doróga* 'road'/*dorogá* 'dear' are distinguished as [darógə]/[deragá], the pretonic being more tense than the posttonic. When we allow for rising and falling tone in long stressed syllables, we find that the Common Slavonic word must have been organized thus:

(a) With rising tone   (b) With falling tone

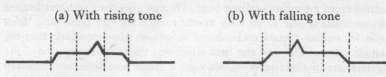

It is because of this relative prominence of the pretonic and post-tonic syllables that the Slavonic accent-shifts have occurred. Syllables of middle stress and tone are not so unlike the lower portions of rising and falling tones as to preclude confusion due to a slight anticipation or retraction of the peak of intonation. Hence R. *volk* 'wolf' *vólki*/*volkám* shows the stress attracted to a following unstressed syllable with latent rising tone, while in *što-* and *kaj-* Serbocroat the stress is attracted away from the last syllable of all words: R. *zimá* 'winter' *ča-*S. *zīmä*/*što-*S. *zima*. There is free accent in Sanskrit also, and, by a curious device, the Vedic texts are accented not by showing the stressed syllable but by marking the lower tone of the syllable immediately preceding (*anudâtta*) and the falling tone of the syllable following (*svarita*): Skr. *ag-ni-nà* (stress on *ni*) 'by fire'. It seems probable, therefore, that the Russian system represents not only Common Slavonic but also Indo-European practice.

Greek submitted to a trisyllabic rule whereby the accent could fall only on one of the last three syllables, and then only according to quantity. Thus Greek evidence for Indo-European stress and intonation, invaluable for the final syllable, is untrustworthy elsewhere, as one may see on comparing Skr. *bháramanas*/Gk. φερόμενος 'borne'. Classical Latin also depends on quantity. In pre-classical Latin, Irish, the Germanic languages, Magyar, etc., there is another type of accentuation which depends on a physiological consideration. During the utterance of a word there is a diminishing flow of breath from the lungs, so that end syllables are lower and more relaxed than any others. This is noted for long syllables in Vuk Karadžić's accentuation of Serbocroat: in S. *jèlênâ* (*GP.*) 'of the deer' there is only one high tone and stress accent, the first; the other two syllables are of indefinite tone and no stress, but are marked with falling intonation because of the lowering due to diminishing breath. Conversely, the same considerations make the first syllable of the word relatively clear and emphatic. If the stress elsewhere be weak, or in emphatic utterance, the first syllable is thus fitted to attract stress to itself. This has happened to West Slavonic, in Czechoslovak and Wendish, in historic times (cf. Latvian); but the development is clearly later than the Common Slavonic period, because the law of strong and weak position of *ŭ ĭ* applies to these languages as much as to any other (see section 27). The initial stress has been attributed by some scholars to imitation of near-by German; but as it conforms to a general law of breath there seems no binding need to admit foreign influence. With primary initial stress Czechoslovak develops also secondary stresses, which often fall on the penultimate: Cz. *nepovezu neobyčejný pronásledováte*. In the Wendish region these penultimate secondary accents increase in energy, and in Polish they become primary. In this way, Polish penultimate accentuation (cf. Welsh) is to be derived from an earlier West Slavonic initial stress still operative in Czechoslovak (cf. Irish), but neither principle is Common Slavonic.

With regard to the Baltic languages there are scholars who have heard two peaks in certain tones. While Leskien heard the first vowel of L. *bŭdas* 'manner' as steadily rising, Sievers (*Grundzüge der Phonetik*, 5th ed., para. 607) explained it as rising slightly, falling, and finally rising to a peak ($\wedge\!\!\vee$). L. *árti* 'to plough' (long falling tone) corresponds to Latv. *aȓt*, which Endzelin described as beginning clear and loud, then interrupted by a glottal stop or relaxing of breath, then ending abruptly ($\searrow . \wedge$ or $\vee\!\!\wedge$). The facts are uncertain, but if true they offer a hope of accounting for the peculiar intonation-shift of Lithuanian. It is not from a high-toned syllable to a middle-toned one as in Slavonic, but within the syllable itself, in such a way that the rising stress has become falling and the falling rising; that is, *oó* has become *óo*, and *óo* has become *oó*. This would be more easily understood if the lower element had its own peak.

The evidence concerning accent is evidently defective, and it is not feasible to do more than indicate the origins of intonation in general terms together with some historical principles of wide application. One may learn the original stress from Sanskrit, but nothing about tone; from Greek one may learn much about stress and tone, but only on the last syllable; from Lithuanian one may learn about stress, but only the converse of the original tone; from Russian and Bulgarian about stress, but not tone; from Serbocroat and Slovene about stress and tone, but only after discounting their characteristic accent-shifts. The process by which acutes change to circumflexes and *vice versa* is known as metatony.

Original long vowels have a rising intonation in Slavonic: S. *brät -a* R. *brát -a* 'brother' cf. Skr. *bhrātṛ*. Final -*a* of the feminine *ā*-stems stands for an original long vowel, and so has a rising intonation which attracts the stress under certain conditions. The rising stress also occurs in Slavonic with short vowels functionally lengthened, and with original long diphthongs (as *-*ēi* in infinitives in -*ti* and in loc.

sing. OB. *nošti*, *ča*-S. *noči* R. *noči* 'night'). The falling tone appears in original short diphthongs, as S. *cvijet* OB. *cvětŭ* 'flower', S. *zúba* 'tooth' (G*S*.) (diphthong **om*, Gk. γόμφος 'nail' Skr. *jámbha-*), and as a result of contraction, as G*S*. *-a* L. *-o* $<$IE. **ōd* $<$**-o-ed*, L*S*. *-ě* $<$IE. **-o-i* (OB. *městě* 'in a place', cf. Gk. 'Ισθμοῖ οἶκοι 'at home' οἶκοι 'houses'). This agrees with the Greek account of the circumflex as being due to a combination of rising-falling tones.

One principle of Slavonic accent-shift is connected with the names of Fortunatov and de Saussure. It is: An original falling tone or a tone that became (by metatony) falling in early Slavonic times yields its stress to a following syllable if this be of a rising tone. An original short syllable behaves in this respect like a falling syllable. The law affects Lithuanian also, as L. *bařzdą* (A*S*.) 'beard' (with falling tone on the root syllable) /*barzdà* (with stress attracted to the rising tone; the *-à* represents an original *-*ó*), R. *bórodu* (A*S*.)/*borodá*, CSl. **bŏrdǫ*/ **bôrdǎ*. This was due to a shift from one peak to another. In the acc. sing. the falling stress was followed by a (latently) falling unstressed syllable ($\wedge$: —), so that there was no second peak; but in the nominative ($\wedge$: $\diagup$) became (— : $\diagup$). The loc. sing. **-ŏi* and nom. pl. **-oí* differed in accentuation; this gave different results when the diphthong became a monophthong in the Middle Proto-Slavonic period: the rising accent gave *-i*, the falling gave *-ě*.

In words falling within the *tort*-formula there were two possible accentuations which have left different results in Russian, Czechoslovak and Serbocroat. In Common Slavonic these words had *o*/*e*+ *r*/*l* between consonants: as CSl. **vórna* 'crow' **bérza* 'birch' **vôrnŭ* 'raven' **dêrvo* 'tree' [cf. L. *várna béržas* /*vařnas deřvą* (A*S*.)—always remembering that the Lithuanian accent means the exact opposite of the Slavonic as to tone]. Analysing the long Slavonic vowels as double units we find here opposed *oó*/*óo*. In Russian two syllables arise in these cases (*tort* $>$*torot*), and the syllables receive stress accents corresponding to the units of the original long: R. *voróna berëza*/*vóron dérevo*. In Czechoslovak the difference is expressed in length: *oó* $>$**ó* *óo* $>$**o*, Cz. *vrána břiza*/*vran* dřevo*. In Serbocroat the rising tone has become a short falling tone, and the falling tone remains a long falling tone, in conformity with the law eliminating all original rising tones from the language: (*ekavski*) S. *vräna brëza*/*vrân drêvo*. Thus the results in Czechoslovak and in Serbocroat are opposed as to length, since the original rising tone gives Cz. long/S. short, and the original falling tone gives Cz. short/S. long; but the fact is that Czechoslovak records an effect of quantity only, and Serbocroat primarily one of intonation. The principle of course worked outside the *tort*-formula

* This word is only found in literature. The ordinary form is *havran*, with a prefix found elsewhere in Slavonic.

(CSl *býti/dûchŭ cf. L. búti/daũsos fem. pl., Cz. býti/duch S. bïti/dûh 'to be'/'spirit'). In this case, however, there is no appeal to Russian for controlling evidence.

23. *Vowel system.* The Slavonic vowels were distinguished in quantity (long/short) and in quality (hard/soft):

Long:	a ě yu i ǫ ę	hard: a o yu ŭ ǫ
short:	o e ŭ ĭ	soft: ě e i ĭ ę

The vowels *ŭ ĭ* were extra-short or 'fugitive'. Counting from the end, each odd one in consecutive syllables was in weak position and did little more than help to express the hard or soft quality of the previous consonant; each even one was in stronger position, and tended to develop into a full vowel. Weak or strong, they served, along with the other vowels, to separate consonants in such a way that Common Slavonic and Old Bulgarian were characterized by a regular alternation of consonants and vowels. Since they were frequently found at the end of words, all Old Bulgarian words ended in a vowel. Their disappearance in some circumstances in the course of the history of the separate languages has led to new consonant-groups, which have usually suffered assimilative changes or fresh reduction to single consonants, and their loss has led to the numerous final consonants of the modern languages. Their action is so distinctive that it is convenient to treat them always together, and to adopt the term *jers* (from R. *er/eŕ*) to cover them both.

Length is deemed to have been a feature of Common Slavonic because it is a sum of inferences from the history of the modern languages. Proto-Slavonic diphthongs were eliminated in the Middle Proto-Slavonic period (see sect. 14). The two nasal vowels result from diphthongs in which the second element was a nasal sonant (*n/m*).

The distinction between 'hard' and 'soft' is purely Slavonic, but most important for linguistic history and for the structure of the present-day languages. It is almost only in South Slavonic that it has to a large extent been lost. The 'hard' consonant is the velar, dental or labial in its normal enunciation; the 'soft' consonant is the velar, dental or labial followed by a palatal off-glide, and implying a following vowel of the 'soft' series, with a palatal on-glide. Palatal consonants were originally 'softened' forms of velars, and so classed as 'soft' and requiring soft vowels to follow. But at various stages in Slavonic history the palatal consonant has absorbed the whole of the glide, with the result that a hard vowel follows, and the palatal is, in this sense, 'hardened'. In Russian, for instance, *č š ž c* were all originally soft, but now only *č* remains soft.

From the standpoint of their formation in the mouth soft vowels are front (or palatal), and hard vowels are back (or velar). Sl. *y* is a 'mixed' vowel [ɨ], since it is formed partly like *u* and partly like *i*; but it behaves like a hard vowel.

The antithesis 'front/back' played a great part in the organization of Indo-European. It takes the fundamental form of three alternative vocalizations of any given root: *e/o/*O (*zero*). This is well exemplified in Greek: ἔχω 'have, hold'/ὄχος 'container, chariot'/ἔσχον 'held', representing IE. *seĝh-/*soĝh-/*-sĝh-. The *e*-grade generally marked imperfect tenses, the zero-grade denoted the aorist, and the *o*-grade served to make perfect tenses, deverbal nouns and, after them, denominative verbs. The vocalizations take various forms in consequence of lengthening or the adding of semivowels or sonants to make diphthongs. In the case of diphthongs the zero-grade appears as vocalic, since the second element persists when there is no *e/o* present: Gk. λείπω/λέλοιπα/ἔλιπον 'leave' includes the semivowel *i̯* and represents an alternation *ei/oi/i*. The vowel *a* does not enter into these morphological alternations, which include the series: *e/o/*O, *ē/ō/ə, ei/oi/i, eu/ou/u, er/or/r̥, el/ol/l̥, en/on/n̥, em/om/m̥, we/wo/u, re/ro/r̥*.

It is characteristic of Slavonic to have retained the ancient principle of vowel-alternation and to have made a totally different application of it. The historical development of Slavonic vowels ruined the symmetry of the Indo-European system. Those listed became *e/o/*O, *ě/a/o* or -, *i/ě* or *i/ĭ, u* or *ov/u* or *ov/ŭ*, etc. The loss of the perfect and the application of present meanings to aorist stems damaged the system on the side of semantics. The consequences of vowel alternation, however, remain embedded in Slavonic vocabulary, particularly as affecting verbs and verbal nouns: R. *berú/bratĭ* 'take'/ -*bor* 'taking', *nestí* 'bear'/*nóska* 'bearing', *nosít* 'bear' (iterative), *slóvo* 'word' <*k̂leu-/sláva* 'glory' <*k̂lōw-, statĭ 'become, begin' <*sthā-/stojáĭ* 'stand' <*sthə-*, etc. To these have to be added purely Slavonic correspondences, such as the lengthening of vowels in the stem of iterative verbs: R. *vynosítĭ* 'endure, carry out'/*vynášivatĭ* 'wear out (clothes)', *uchodítĭ* 'go away'/*ucháživatĭ* 'flirt with' (*a* <*ō*). Such words form related groups in all Slavonic languages without conforming to the old strict formula.

24. *Oral Vowels and Diphthongs. A* O. IE. *a o* > BSl. *å; BSl. *ā* > L. *o uo* Latv. OPr. *a* Sl. *a*, BSl. *ā* > L. Latv. OPr. *a* Sl. *o;* IE. *ə* > L. *a*/- Sl. *o*/-.

IE. *māt̄ē(r)* L. *mótė* 'wife' Latv. *māte* CSl.OB. *mati* R. *matĭ* 'mother' (Gk. μήτηρ Lat. *māter*);

IE. *dō-* L. *dúoti* 'give' OPr. *dāt* CSl.OB. *dati* R. *datĭ* 'give' (Gk. δίδωμι Lat. *dō*);

IE. *ak̂-* L. *ašìs* 'axle' CSl.OB. *osĭ* R. *osĭ* 'axle' (Gk. ἄξων Lat. *axis*);

IE. *to(d) L. tàs (masc.) 'that' OPr. s-ta (neut,) CSl.OB.R. to (Gk. τό);

IE. *sthətós L. statýti 'place' CSl.OB. stojati R. stojáṫ 'stand' (Gk. στατός);

IE. *dhughətḗr L. duktḕ 'daughter' CSl. *dŭkti̧ >*dŭ̧li OB. dŭšti MB. dăšterjá R. doč' 'daughter' P. córka Cz. dcera S. kćî <*dći (Gk. θυγάτηρ).

The pronunciation of Sl. o is usually very open [ɔ]. In Polabe and the Pomeranian dialects it is still further opened to å (cf. Eng. follow/fall): Slovak plietol/Polabe plitål 'plaited'. Though this å is of secondary origin, the sound å is the mid-point phonetically between a and o[ɔ], and must be passed when either sound passes into the other under the full tension of a stressed syllable. So we must take it into account in the series R. górod 'city' P. gród/Cz. hrad and in the development of Pomeranian (Staro)gard to Polabe gord. An unstressed relaxed a coincides with a relaxed o in the Russian ákańe. The distinction between a/o is, in Slavonic, purely due to original quantity, whereas the Baltic languages are somewhat discrepant in their evolution, having admitted also the qualitative criterion. IE. ə is treated like IE. ă in the few cases in which it survives. When lost, its disappearance may cause a circumflex tone to become acute: IE. *-anɔ- >CSl. -ǫ̑-.

OB. rǫka 'hand' (nom.) rǫko (voc.) reflects the distinction between IE. -ā/-ă. L. nom. rankà (instead of *rankó) is due to the shortening of final vowels which have a rising tone. VS. raṅka.

IE. ai oi >L. ai ie Proto-Sl. *oi >*œ >CSl. ě, final ě or i, IE. āi > CSl. ě; IE. au ou >L. au Proto-Sl. *ou >CSl. u, IE. ōu >CSl. u.

L. ai was formerly in more extensive use, as may be seen from Finnish loanwords like paimen/L. piemuō 'shepherd'. There may have been Slavonic influence in the development ai >ie (see Senn, Slavonic Yearbook, xx, 1941). The older position with regard to IE. ai oi was L. ai/Sl. *oi. Examples are L. snaigalà 'snowflake' sniẽgas 'snow'/ CSl.OB. sněgŭ, L. tiẽ (NAFD) 'those'/CSl.OB. tě. For the Slavonic development see section 14. It depends to a certain extent on intonation: at the end of the word the falling tone is represented by ě and the rising tone by i: OB. ti vl̦ci 'those wolves', cf. Homeric τοί λύκοι (NPM), Gk. οῖκοι/οῖκοι 'at home' (LSM) OB. vl̦cě; OB. beri berěte 'take' (imperatives) Gk. φέροις φέροιτε. IE. āi occurs in *gʷenāi (DLSF of *gʷenā 'woman') OB. ženě. The reduction of these diphthongs to monophthongs of the palatal type gave rise to the second Slavonic palatalization (section 38). Examples of the diphthongs in u: L. raũdas 'red' raudà 'redness'/CSl.OB. ruda R. rudá 'ore', L. ausìs 'ear'/R. úcho (cf. Lat. ruber rufus, auris), OB. synu (LSM) <ōu (Skr. sūnāu) 'son'.

The back vowel *o* changes to the corresponding front vowel (*e*) when preceded by a palatal glide: thus V*SF. duše* 'soul' corresponds to *ženo* 'woman' <*-ǎ*, and *je* takes the place of older **jo(d)* Skr. *yad*. The diphthongs in *i* develop as **joi* > **jei* > CSl.OB. *ji* (N*PM*) and **jai* > **joi* > CSl.OB. *ji*.

When *o* is lengthened it becomes *a* and when weakened it may apparently become *ŭ:* OB. *tvoriti* 'create'/*tvarĭ* 'creation, creature' *tvańati* 'form'; OB. *togda/tŭgda*, 'then'.

25. *E*. IE. *ē* > L. *ė* [e:] CSl.OB. *ě*, R. *e*, Ruth. *i ï*, P. *e 'a* (Polabe *e a o*), Cz. *ě e i*, Slov. *e*, usually [e], S. (*i*)*je i e*, MB. *ě* (WB. *e* EB. *e/ja*); IE. *e* > L. *e* [æ] CSl.OB. *e*, R. *e ë* [jɔ] *o-* init. in some cases, P. *e 'o*, Cz.S.MB. *e*.

> IE. **dhē-* L. *dě́ti* 'put, lay' CSl.OB. *děti* R. *det́* (formerly spelt *dět́*);

> IE. **wēra* R. *véra* 'faith' Ruth. *víra* P. *wiara* Cz. *víra* S. *vjëra vïra vëra;*

> IE. **weĝhō* L. *vežù* 'convey' CSl.OB. *vezǫ* R. *vezú vëz,* P. *wiozę wieziesz*; R. *odín* 'one' *ózero* 'lake' Cz. *jeden jezero*.

Since 1917 R. *ě/e* have been written with the one letter *e*. When stressed it represents a relatively short *e* preceded by a palatal glide: open [ɛ] when followed by a hard consonant, close [e] when followed by a soft consonant. Another letter is required to denote *e* without palatal on-glide, viz. ə. The two vowels (*ě e*) have been pronounced identically for many centuries, but evidence of their original difference is seen in the fact that only *e* can give *ë* before a hard consonant (apart from examples due to analogy) or *o* initially. In Polish *ě* may appear as *ia* and *e* as *io*. Cz. *ě/e* differ as [jɛ]/[ɛ], and the former when long has given a diphthong *ie* which has ended in *í*, cf. Ruth. *í* S. *ije i*. CSl. *e* was certainly soft, and had a palatal on-glide; its quality was probably short and open [ɛ]. The fact that in Glagolitic script no distinction was made between *ě* and *ja* suggests either that *ě* had a more open pronunciation than *e*, viz. *ä*, preceded by a glide, or that *ě* had a double value as in Modern East Bulgarian. Whether *ě* was longer than *e* in Old Bulgarian is not certain, but it must have been so in Common Slavonic. Its value would thus seem to have been *jä*, with a tendency to become *ja*, and *a* after a palatal consonant. On the other hand, Šachmatov argued that CSl. *ě* was long and closed like Lithuanian *ė*, though his conclusions are not widely accepted. In Proto-Slavonic, *ě* < *ē* differed from *ě* < **œ* < **oi ai*, since it had a different effect upon velar consonants in contact. The identification of the two *ě*'s must have been one of the last developments of the Middle Proto-Slavonic period. The later development of *ě* is most plausibly based on a diphthongal pronunciation *ie* deriving from the CSl. monophthong *ě*: from *ié* come the pronunciations in *je*, while *ie* develop S. *ije i* Cz.Ruth. *i*.

IE. *ej* >L. *ej* CSl.OB. *ĭj;* IE. *ew* >*ow* >L. *av* CSl.OB. *ov.*

IE. **trejes* CSl.OB. *trĭje* 'three' (Gk. τρεῖς);

IE. **wejō* L. *vejù* 'drive, twist' CSl.OB. *vĭjǫ* R. *v́ju* 'twist';

IE. **newos* CSl.OB. *novŭ* 'new' (Gk. νέος/Lat. *novus*). L. *naũjas* <**neujos*/OPr. *nava-* <**newo-*.

These are not diphthongs, since the *j w* belong to the following syllable, but the effect is similar to that in the diphthongs *ei ou*. In the first case *j/i* serve to close *e* to *ĭ*, and in the second *w/u*, being back sounds, attract the front vowel *e* into the corresponding place among back vowels.

IE. *ei* >L. *ei* *ie* CSl.OB. *i;* IE. *ou eu* >L. *au* CSl.OB. *u/ju.* Sl. *u* may take the place of an expected *ju* (**plewō* >*plovǫ* : : **pleutēi* > *pluti*, not **pluti*) because of analogy. Goth. *iu* L. *au* Sl. *ju.*

IE **ĝheima* L. *žiemà* CSl.OB. *zima* R. *zimá* 'winter' (Gk. χεῖμα Lat. *hiems,* cf. *Hima-laya*);

IE. **ei-* L. *eīti* CSl.OB. *iti* 'go' (Gk. εῖμι Lat. *ire*);

IE. **bheudhō* Goth. *biuda* L. *baudžiù* 'punish' CSl.OB. *bl̃udǫ* R. *bljudú* 'observe' (Gk. πεύθομαι);

Goth. *þiuda* L. *tautà* 'folk' OR. *Čuď* 'Estonians'.

After a palatal, *ě* became *a:* R. *stoját* 'stand' *slýšať* 'hear' (<-*ěti*). At the beginning of words the palatal on-glide became virtually a consonant, so that initial *ě* >*ja:* OB. *jadŭ* 'ate' <**ēd-* (pf. stem, cf. Lat. *ēdi*). Sl. *e* weakens to *ĭ:* OB. *mĭněti* 'think'/Gk. μένος Lat. *mens.* Final -*ē* >CSl.OB. -*i* in IE. **mātē(r)* CSl.OB. *mati* R. *mať* 'mother'; cf. IE. **dhughǝtēr* 'daughter' OB. *dŭšti.*

26. *Ū Ī.* IE. *ū* >L. *ū* CSl.OB. *y;* IE. *ī*> L. *y* CSl.OB. *i.*

IE. **sūnus* L. *sūnùs* CSl.OB. *synŭ* R. *syn* 'son';

IÉ. **dhūmos* L. *dúmai* (pl.) CSl.OB. *dymŭ* R. *dym* 'smoke' (Gk. θυμός Lat. *fūmus*);

IE. **gʷīwos* L. *gývas* CSl.OB. *živŭ* R. *živ* 'alive'.

L. *y* is long *i* [i:]. Sl. *y* [ɨ] is defined by John Hus (1406): 'ponendo principium linguæ sub inferioribus dentibus et in medio elevando linguam per modum circuli'. The lips are unrounded and form a fissure opening as if for *i,* but the back of the tongue shapes the mouth cavity as if for *u;* the vowel is thus one of the 'mixed' (back-front) order. The early approximate spellings recognized these two elements. The Latin rendering was by *ui* (*Buistrice*), adopted from the Old High German *ui*=*ü.* After a labial consonant the vowel sounds almost as a diphthong, since the *u*-element is reinforced by the labial. The Glagolitic and Cyrillic spellings recognized one element as *i,* but did not identify the other with *u;* in them it was represented by the hard *jer* (*ŭ*), which may have resembled the [ʌ] in Eng. *but,* an obscure relaxed short vowel pronounced a little behind the middle of the mouth cavity. This Slavonic vowel developed during the Middle

Proto-Slavonic period (section 14) and has remained in Russian and Polish. It was alive in the Czech of Hus, and so has a place in his spelling; later it became equivalent to *i*, as it is in Slovene, Serbocroat and Modern Bulgarian. In Ruthenian the vowel и (transliterated *y*) is described as a closed *e* [e] as in Germ. *geht* Fr. *été*, and so differs from *i* and *ï* [ji]. To English ears it sounds like the [ɪ] of *milk*.

OB. *krai* 'district' corresponds to CSl. **krajĭ* (*-jĭ* < *-*jŭ* < *-*jos*), and OB. *i*(*že*) to CSl. **jĭ-*. As, after another vowel, there must have been a palatal on-glide in the Old Bulgarian *i*, and its pronunciation may have been *jĭ ji*, it is generally convenient so to transcribe it.

CSl.OB. *y* also arises from the denasalization of certain flexions (**ont *unt *ōn *ūn*); CSl.OB. *i* derives from diphthongs in **ei *oi *ai* and from palatalized forms of them, as well as being the soft alternative for hard *y;* CSl.OB. *u* derives wholly from diphthongs (**au *ou *eu*).

27. *Ŭ Ĭ* (*the Jers*). IE. *ŭ*, L. *u*, CSl. *ŭ*, OB. *ŭ o -*, R. *o -*, P.Cz. *e -*, Slov. *a/e -*, S. *a -*, MB. *ă -;* IE. *ĭ*, L. *i*, CSl. *ĭ*, OB. *ĭ e*, R. *e ' -*, P. *e ' -*, Cz. *e -*, Slov. *a/e -*, S. *a -*, MB. *ă/e/-*.

IE. **swepnos/supnos* L. *sāpnas sāpnis* CSl.OB. *sŭnŭ* 'sleep, dream' R. *son* (pl. *sny*) P.Cz. *sen* Slov. *sèn* [sʌn] S. *sän* MB. *săn* (Gk. ὕπνος Lat. *somnus*);

IE. **muskos* L. *mùsos* (FP) 'mould' CSl.OB. *mŭchŭ* 'moss' R. *moch* P. *mech* Cz. *mech* Slov. *mâh* S. *mähovina* MB. *măch* (Lat. *muscus*);

IE. **dejen- *dein- *din-* L. *dienà* CSl.OB. *dĭnĭ* 'day' R. *deń* (pl. *dni*) P. *dzień* Slov.S. *dân* MB. *den;*

IE. **liptos* L. *lĭpti* 'stick, adhere' CSl.OB. *lĭpnǫti* (Gk. λίπος); CSl.OB. *lĭvŭ* 'lion' R. *lev* P. *lew* Cz. *lev* Slov. *lèv* S. *läv* MB. *lev* (Gk. λέων Lat. *leo*);

CSl.OB. *ĺubŭvĭ* (acc.) 'love' R. *ljubóv* S. *ljûbav* MB. *ljubóv.*

It is difficult to fix the values of these sounds in Old Bulgarian, since usage was fluctuating. The only certainty is that the inventors of both alphabets thought these sounds unlike any Greek *u* or *i*, and so requiring a new pair of signs (Cyrillic ъ ь). For Common Slavonic it is fairly certain that their value, as descendants of IE. *ŭ ĭ*, must have been of the nature of extra-short *ŭ ĭ*. When *jers* result from the shorten- ing of *o e* (see above), they may not have had the same timbre as original *ŭ ĭ*. Furthermore, the *jers* had strong and weak variants. They were weak in final position, in initial syllables followed by syllables with full vowels, and at each second *jer* from the last in consecutive syllables; in other positions the *jers* were strong (though still extra- short, dull vowels). A *jer* was strong also when its disappearance would leave a difficult group of consonants. When strong a *jer* becomes a vowel in the modern languages; when weak it disappeared. The *jers* in roman letters are strong in the following list: *sŭnŭ dĭnĭ dĭnĭsĭ šĭvĭcĭ šĭvĭcĭmĭ sŭ-šĭvĭcĭmĭ* Cz. *sen* 'sleep' *den* 'day' *dnes* 'today' *švec* 'cobbler' *ševcem* OCz. *s-ševcem*. When a weak *ĭ* disappeared the preceding consonant was palatalized in Russian and Polish (OB. *kostĭ* 'bone' R. *kosť* P. *kość*), but it is hard in Czech (*kost*) and South Slavonic (Slov.S. *kôst* MB. *kost*). Before *ŭ* the consonant was normal, so that the loss of the *jer* left it unmodified. The 'hardening' of *ĭ* was complete when Serbian documentation began in the twelfth century, so that Serbian scribes used only one sign (ь) for both *jers*, and sometimes doubled it to represent strong position.

The values which would satisfy the modern developments are [ʌ] and ['ə] or [ə], as in Eng. *but the* [bʌðə]. These are obscure relaxed vowels pronounced in the middle of the mouth, the one slightly more to the back than the other; in a 'broad' phonetic transcription they may both be represented by [ə]. (The English front dull vowel lacks the palatal on-glide which was certainly present in Common Slavonic, though lost in the southern languages.) Another dull vowel is [ɐ] as in Eng. *about*, to pronounce which the jaw is slightly lowered and the arch of the tongue is precisely central. In Modern Bulgarian *ŭ ĭ* came together in the middle position as *ă*, which is occasionally opened as *a*, and is so always in Serbocroat. In Slovene *a* is a normal development, but also *e* [ʌ]. In West Slavonic [ʌ] and [ə] came together in the forward position [ə], and developed from there to the forward vowel *e*, with palatal on-glide in Polish and Slovak, but not in Czech. In Russian the *jers* continued to be distinguished as back/front vowels, and so developed into the open vowels *o/e* respectively; when they disappeared they became - '-, that is, *ŭ* disappeared entirely and *ĭ* remained as a palatal quality in the preceding consonant. It is clear from the transliterations by Constantine Porphyrogenitus (see section 82) that the Russians had reached this solution by the middle of the tenth century. In reading Church Slavonic, Russians gave the values *o/e* to the *jers* as written except when final, and so many words can be recognized as of clerical origin by *o/e* where the Russian colloquial would have no vowel.

In Old Bulgarian the *jers* are found in a transitional stage. (i) After the sibilants *š ž št žd č c dz=z* and after *ř* the soft *ĭ* is often replaced by the hard *ŭ*: *šĭdŭ/šŭdŭ* 'having gone' *prišĭlŭ/prišŭla* 'having come'. (ii) In strong position *ŭ/ĭ* sometimes became *o/e* as in modern dialects of south-west Bulgaria: *sĭ/se* 'this' *rabo-tŭ* 'this slave'/*rabŭ rodo-sĭ* 'this race'/*rodŭ dĭnesĭ* 'today'/*dĭnĭ crkovĭ/crkŭvĭ* 'church' *ko mně* 'to me'/*kŭ doždŭ/dŭždĭ* 'rain' *plotĭ/plŭtĭ* 'flesh'. In the declension of the *i*- and *u*-stems *e/o* appear frequently instead of the expected *ĭ/ŭ* in the endings *-emĭ -emŭ -echŭ/-omĭ -omŭ -ochŭ*, but this is due to substitution of forms from the *jo/o*-stems (*-emĭ -emŭ/-omĭ -omŭ*) and analogical extension to *-echŭ/-ochŭ*, rather than to a development of *ĭ/ŭ*. It takes place sometimes in weak position. (iii) The *jers* are frequently lost. This occurred in Common Slavonic in the combinations *s-n z-n*, as OB. *desnŭ* 'right'/L. *dešině*. So also *p(ĭ)sana* 'written' *k(ŭ)to* 'who' *m(ŭ)nogo* 'much' *t(ĭ)ma* 'darkness' *v(ĭ)si* 'all' (pl.). In Russian the loss of soft *jer* was much later than in Old Bulgarian. (iv) Interchange of the *jers*. The hardening of the sibilants and *ŕ* during the Old Bulgarian period was a contributory cause to this interchange, but it could be effected by the influence of a labial consonant, a preceding or following vowel, and not only in weak position but also in strong position. Examples are *tĭmě/tŭma* 'darkness' *vŭ nasŭ* 'in us'/*vĭ tebě* 'in thee' *bĭrati/bŭrati* 'take' *vĭzĭ-/vĭzŭ-/vŭzŭ-/vŭzĭ-* 'up' *dĭbrĭ/debrĭ/dŭbrĭ* 'glen' *sǫdĭba/sǫdŭba* 'judgment' *jesmĭ/jesmŭ* 'am'. The practice of each principal codex differs upon these points.

CSl. *ŭ* derives also from Proto-Sl. final *-*un*, and from *-*on* > *-*un:* IE. *sūnum > *sūnun > **sūnu̯* > CSl.OB. *synŭ* (acc.) 'son', IE. *tokom > *tokon > *tokun > **toku̯* > CSl.OB. *tokŭ* R. *tok* 'flow'. It is also found alternating with *o:* OB. *togda/tŭgda* 'then', and in some cases represents, or may represent, IE. **m̥*.

CSl. *ĭ* derives also from Proto-Sl. final *in:* IE. *noktin CSl. *noktĭ **noži̯* OB. *noštĭ* (acc. sg.) R. *noč′* 'night' L. *năktĭ*). It serves for weak forms of roots in *e:* O.B. *mĭněti* 'think'/Lat. *mens;* and before *j* beginning the next syllable IE. *e* > CSl. *ĭ:* IE. *trejes CSl.OB. *trĭje* 'three'. It is also the palatal that arises from *ŭ* after *j* or palatal on-glide: Proto-Sl. *otĭko *otĭkŭ CSl.OB. *otĭcĭ* R. *otéc* 'father' (Gk. ἄττα), ASM. of *jo*-stems **-jom* **-jon* **-jŭ* **-jĭ* OB. *mečĭ* 'sword' *krai* (= *kraji̯*) 'country'. Initially or after a vowel the palatal glide becomes a full consonant *j*, which combines with *ĭ* to give OB. *i* (*kraji̯* > OB. *krai,* **nmen(t)* > **ĭnmen(t)* > *jĭmę > OB. *imę* 'name'); another treatment is shown by Cz. *jméno*, where the *ĭ* is treated as a normal weak semi-vowel.

28. *Nasal Diphthongs and Nasal Sonants.* IE. *am an anə om on,* CSl.OB. *ǫ.* R. *u,* P. *ǫ ę,* Cz. *u ou,* Slov. *o,* S. *u* MB. *ă;* IE. *em en,* CSl.OB. *ę,* R. *ja,* P. *ǫ ę,* Cz. *ě e í á a ja,* Slov. *e,* S. *e,* MB. *e;* IE. *m̥ n̥* CSl. *ę* (but in some cases *ŭ*).

IE. *anətis L. *ántis* 'duck' CSl.OB. *ǫty* OR. *utovĭ* MR. *útka;*

IE. **ang-* L. *angà* 'aperture' CSl.OB. *ǫglŭ* 'corner R. *úgol* Cz. *úhel* Slov. *ôgel* S. *ügao* MB. *ăgăl* (Lat. *angulus*);

IE. **angust-* L. *añkštas* 'narrow' CSl.OB. *ǫzŭkŭ* R. *úzkij* P. *wąski* Cz. *úzký* Slov. *ózek* S. *üzak* (Lat. *angustus*);

IE. *ĝombhos L. *žaṁbas* 'edge' CSl.OB. *zǫbŭ* 'tooth' R. *zub* P. *ząb* Cz. *zùb* Slov. *zôb* S. *zûb* MB. *zăb* (Gk. γόμφος 'nail' Skr. *jámbhas* 'tooth' Albanian *dhëmp* 'tooth');

IE. *penkʷe *pente L. *penkì* 'five' CSl.OB. *pętĭ* R. *pjat́* P. *pięć* Cz. *pět* Slov. S. *pêt* MB. *pet* (Gk. πέντε Skr. *pañca*);

IE. *dek̑mt L. děšimt 'ten' CSl.OB. desęti R. désjat́ P. dziesięć
Cz. deset Slov. desêt S. dësêt MB. déset (Gk. δέκα Lat. decem
Arm. tasn Skr. dáça);

IE. *k̑mtóm L. šimtas CSl.OB. sŭto 'hundred' R. sto.

In pronouncing m n there is a stoppage of the air-passage through
the mouth, either by closing the lips or by raising the tongue to the
teeth, but the breath passes freely through the nose because the
uvula has been lowered. These sounds are therefore uninterrupted,
and can stand by themselves as vowels do. In this usage they
are sonants (m n̩) and make syllables, as in Eng. London seven
atom solemn (rapidly pronounced). The mouth-stoppage makes
them narrower than the oral vowels, and so they combine with a
preceding vowel to make a diphthong when a consonant follows.
M n have also a purely consonantal value when initial of a word or
syllable.

The uvula may be little depressed or much depressed (see section
14). When little or normally depressed all sorts of nasal diphthongs
and vowels are possible, but when much depressed the uvula makes a
stop at the back of the mouth for all but the most open nasal vowels.
That is the case with Slavonic. Though all nasals must have been
possible at an early period in Proto-Slavonic, there came to be
increasing depression of the uvula so that in Common Slavonic only
two vowels remained in this category (ǫ ę, with soft forms jǫ ję).
Narrower vowels had to be widened to the measure of these nasals if
they were to survive as nasals; in final positions (see section 31) this
did not occur, and the vowels were denasalized. Germanic ung/ing
gave CSl. ǫ/ę under this compulsion. In some Old Bulgarian manuscripts ě is found in place of ę, which may be evidence (along with
R. ja) that the pronunciation of the front nasal was very open, approximately nasal ä. It must have been the same with the back nasal
(approximately nasal å). The ǫ for u in certain Old Bulgarian forms
(nǫditi/nuditi 'constrain' gnǫšati/gnušati 'abominate') is supposed to
be due to the preceding nasal. O is found for ǫ in the work of a scribe
who pronounced nasals lightly. In Russian the nasal vowels were
alive in the ninth century when Scandinavian loanwords were
adopted (varingr R. varjág 'Varangian', sund OR. Sud, R. pud cf. Eng.
'pound'), since the vowels in these words developed like the Slavonic
nasals in Russian. In Polish of the twelfth century there were two
nasal vowels of very open timbre, which came together as one in the
thirteenth century, and thereafter developed differences of quantity
which led at last to differences of quality (P. ą ę—see section 142).
After the Polish nasal vowel a nasal consonant intrudes itself before
some following consonants: P. ręka 'hand' is pronounced [rénka] and
dąb 'oak' [dɔmp]; but wąski 'narrow' [vŏski].

In the modern Slavonic languages other than Polish the nasal resonance has disappeared from these vowels, and *ǫ* has suffered closure to Slov. *o* R.Cz.S. *u* MB. *ă*. A nasal consonant or resonance tends to narrow the timbre of a vowel, and so, when the uvula is much depressed, to eliminate the nasality, unless a phonetic reaction occurs. Final nasals are discussed later (see section 31).

29. *Liquid Diphthongs and Sonants*. (*a*) Tort. CSl. **tort* R. *torot* P.Wend. *trot* Polabe *tort* Cz.Slov.S.OB.MB. *trat;* CSl. **tolt* R. *tolot* P.Wend. *tlot* Polabe *tlåt* Cz.Slk.Slov.S.OB.MB. *tlat;* CSl. **tert* R. *teret* P.Wend. **tŕet* Polabe *trit* Cz.Slov.S.OB.MB. forms based on *trĕt;* CSl. **telt* R. *telet* or, more often, *tolot* P.Wend. *tlet* CzSlk.Slov. S.OB.MB. forms based on *tlĕt.*

CSl. **gôrdŭ* R. *górod* 'town' P. *gród* Pomeranian (*Staro*)*gard* Polabe *gord* Cz. *hrad* Slov.S.OB.MB. *grad* (S. *grâd*) OB. *gradŭ;*

CSl. **górchŭ* R. *goróch* 'peas' P. *groch* Cz. *hrách* Slov. *gràh* *ča*-S. *gràh što*-S. *gräh* OB. *grachŭ* MB. *grach;*

CSl. **kórva* R. *koróva* 'cow' P. *krowa* (dial.)*karw* 'old ox' *Karwin* Cz. *kráva* S. *kräva;*

CSl. **sôldŭ* R. *sólod* 'malt' P. *słód* Cz. *slad* S. *slâd;*

CSl. **gôldŭ* R. *gólod* 'hunger' P. *głód* Polabe *glåd* Cz. *hlad* S. *glâd;*

CSl. **sólma* R. *solóma* 'straw' P. *słoma* Polabe *slåma* Cz. *sláma* S. *släma;*

R. *koróĺ* 'king' P. *król* Cz. *král* S. *krâlj* OB. *kraĺ;*

CSl. **bêrgŭ* R. *béreg* 'bank' P. *brzeg* Polabe *brig* Cz. *bŕeh* S. *brijeg;*

CSl. **bérza* R. *berëza* 'birch' P. *brzoza* Polabe *bréza* Cz. *bŕíza* S. *brëza* (*e* for *je* after *r*);

CSl. **melkó* R. *molokó* 'milk' P. *mleko* Polabe *mlåka* (gen.) Cz. *mléko* S. *mlijèko;*

CSl. **želza* 'gland' R. *železá* Cz. *žleza* OB. *žlĕza.*

On the effect of intonation see section 22. When the tone fell from a peak at the beginning of the syllable it gave rise to stress on the first of the two Russian syllables and falling tone in Serbocroat; shortening occurred in Czechoslovak. When the tone rose to a peak at the end of the syllable it gave rise to stress on the second of the two syllables in Russian, was converted into a short falling tone in Serbocroat, and caused a long vowel in Czechoslovak.

R. *koróĺ* 'king' develops as if it were a Common Slavonic word, but it is the name of *Karl* (*Charlemagne*) used as a common noun, and so only came into circulation when the Common Slavonic unity had been broken. The processes which gave the different consequences of CSl. *tort* were, however, still operative, and were carried through for this word also. The lateness of the whole development accounts for the lack of Slavonic unity in this respect. The long vowel in S. *králj* is due to metatony.

It is customary to speak of the *tort*-formula to allude to the whole group of these changes. By '*tort*-formula' is understood all cases in which *o/e* before *r/l* stood between consonants (*t* is any consonant) in Common Slavonic. The effect of *r/l* was greatly to open the preceding vowel *o* to CSl. **tårt*, though this may not have been the case in the East Slavonic area. P. *karw* 'old ox' *Karwin ch(r)abry/chrobry* 'brave' are evidence that this *å* was current in Proto-Polish. OP. *ze błota* 'from the marsh' *ode młodosći* 'from youth'/*w święto* 'on the festival' prove that the initial consonant-groups involved were different, since those of the *tort*-formula required a vowel of support for the consonant of the preposition. Rozwadowski has explained that the metathesis was still incomplete, so that *błoto* 'marsh' was approximately *bəloto*, and the disappearance of the fugitive vowel strengthens the preceding semi-vowel, e.g. *ze błota* 'from the marsh'. In Russian this condition has persisted, and *r/l* have vowels on either side. In Czechoslovak and South Slavonic **år* >**rå* >*ra;* the metathesis has been completed for all the *tort*-series. In Polabe and Cassubian CSl. **år* has often remained or, more probably, reverted to *or;* the change **år* >*ar* is also current.

There are discrepancies of development due to special circumstances within each language. R. *molokó* 'milk' must be due to the influence of the hollow *ł;* similarly R. *polón* 'booty'/OB. *plěnŭ*, etc. *Telot* is also found: Goth. *hilms* R. *šelóm* 'helmet, rooftree'/OB. *šlěmŭ*, R. *železá/ żelozá* 'gland'. There are similar alternatives in Czech: Cz. *žleb/žlab* 'trough' *člen/článek* 'limb, member'.

(*b*) *Initial Ort-*. CSl. **ort-* >*rat- rot-;* CSl. **olt-* >*lat- lot-* (OB. also *alt-*); CSl. **ert- elt-* >*rět- lět-*.

IE. **ar-* L. *árklas* 'plough' CSl. **ordlo* R. *rálo* P. *radło* Cz. *radlo* Polabe *rådlö* Slov. *rálo* S. *rälo* B. *rálo* (Gk. ἄροτρον Lat. *aratrum*);

IE. **arəm-* 'shoulder' CSl. **ormę* R. *rámo* Cz. *rámě* Slov. *ráme ráma* S. *räme* (Lat. *armus* Goth. *arms*);

CSl. **orvĭnŭ* OB. *ravĭnŭ* 'even' R. *róvnyj ravnína rovésnik* P. *równy* Cz. *rovný rovina* Slov. *ráven* S. *rávan rȃvnî* MB. *ráven* (OPr. *arwis* 'true');

CSl. **orbŭ* OB. *rabŭ* R. *rab* 'slave' *rabóta* 'work', Cz. *rob* 'slave';

CSl. **orz-* R. *roz- raz-* P. *roz-* Polabe *rüz-* Cz. *roz-* Slovak *roz- raz-* Slov.S.B. *raz-;*

CSl. **oldĭja* R. *loďjá ladjá* 'large boat' Polabe *lüda* Cz. *lodí loď* Slovak *loď* Slov. *ládja ča-*S. *làja što-*S. *lȃdja* OB. *al(ŭ)diji ladiji* (L. *aldĭjà*);

CSl. *olni R. loní 'last year' P. łoni Cz. loni Slov. láni S. lâni láni (Lat. olli <*olnei);

CSl. *elbędĭ/olbodĭ R. lébed 'swan' (with e for ja in the unstressed syllable) Slov. lebéd OB. lebędĭ MB. lébed/P. łabędź OCz. labuď MCz. labuť Slov. labód S. läbûd (OHG. elbiz 'swan' Lat. albus).

Examples of these initial groups are fewer and more difficult to determine than those of tort. Metathesis takes place, and CSl. *o became *ă. In many cases the initial tones are not known, but they seem, when we can recognize them, to have affected the choice of o/a. An original rising tone seems to have given rat- lat- in all languages but a falling tone gave rot- lot- in East and West Slavonic: CSl. *ólkomŭ (cf. L. álkti) R. lákom 'dainty' P. łakomy Cz. lakomý S. läkom/CSl. *órstŭ R. rost 'stature' P. rość Cz. rùst S. râst OB. rastŭ.

(c) R L. IE. ŗ L. ir ur CSl. *ĭr *ŭr OB. rĭ rŭ = ŗ; IE. ļ L. il ul CSl. *ĭl *ŭl OB. lĭ lŭ = ļ.

IE. *wrb(h)es- L. viřbas 'stalk' CSl. *vĭrba 'willow' OB. vrba R. vérbá P. wierzba Cz.Slov.S. vrba MB. vărbá (Lat. verbena);

IE. *wrs- L. viršùs 'top' CSl. *vĭrchŭ OB. vrchŭ R. verch P. wierzch Cz. vrch Slov. vřh S. vřh MB. vărch;

CSl. *gŭrstĭ OB. grstĭ 'handful' R. gorsí P. garść Cz. hrst S. gřst MB. grăst;

IE. *wļkʷos L. vilkas 'wolf' CSl. *vĭlkŭ OB. vļkŭ R. volk P. wilk Cz. vlk Slov. vôlk S. vûk MB. vălk (Gk. λύκος Lat. lupus);

CSl. *dĭlgo OB. dlgo 'long' R. dólgo P. długo Cz. dlouho Slov. dólgo S. dügo MB. dălgo (Gk. δολιχόν);

CSl. *dŭlgŭ OB. dlgŭ 'debt' R. dolg P. dług Cz. dluh Slov. dôlg S. dúg MB. dlăg.

In pronouncing r the tongue-point makes one or several stoppages of the breath-stream at the teeth or gums (there is also a uvular r which has no place here) resulting in continuous vibrations which characterize the sound; for l the front of the tongue blocks the air at the teeth or gums (or the back of the tongue may do so in the hard palate or velar region), and air escapes continuously along one or both sides. Thus r and l are continuous sounds, like vowels, and are capable of forming vowels or diphthongs. They actually did so in Indo-European, as we may infer from the regular correspondences between languages. Original *ŗ *ļ came to be pronounced with the help of short vowels, and these are different in the different groups, but consistent within each. The existence of IE. *ķŗd- *wļkʷ- is inferred from the correspondences: Gk. καρδία 'heart' Lat. cordis (gen.) OIr. cride OB. sŗdice, Skr. vŕkas 'wolf' Germ. Wulf L. vilkas OB. vļkŭ, and others of the kind. They existed also as weak alternatives in the permutations er/or/ŗ, el/ol/ļ, and so had an important share in Indo-European word-building and conjugation.

In Balto-Slavonic they were vocalized by means of short *u i*. What were the conditions governing the choice between these vowels is not sufficiently known; the fact is that CSl. **ŭr/*ĭr* and **ŭl/*ĭl* form pairs of the hard/soft variety. In Russia, Poland and Pomerania these diphthongs persisted. Old Russian orthography keeps the short vowel before the consonant when Old Bulgarian spelling places it after: OR. *vŭlkŭ chŭlmŭ pĭrstŭ* 'wolf, hill, finger'/OB. *vlĭkŭ chlŭmŭ prĭstŭ*. In part of the Slavonic area, however, from Bohemia to Bulgaria, the vowel again disappeared, leaving a new *r̥ r̥/l̥ l̥*, which was spelt with a following *jer* in Old Bulgarian. In rare cases the *jer* was omitted: OB. *vrchu* 'above'. In unstressed syllables OB. *rŭ* stood also for Gk. αρ ερ ιρ ορ υρ: OB. *trŭtorŭ* (Gk. τάρταρος). It is also found separating letters that form a group in Greek: OB. *nar(ŭ)da* (Gk. νάρδου) *orŭganŭ* (Gk. ὄργανον) *sŭrĭtĭ* (Gk. σύρτις). There may have been some slight dialectal difference in pronunciation, but in general the sonant pronunciation of OB. *rŭ/rĭ lŭ/lĭ* is established. Using the device of the *tort*-formula, we may say that these are instances of CSl. *tŭrt*.

CSl. *trŭt*, OB. *trŭt* OR. *trŭt*. In these cases the liquid *r/l* was followed by a short vowel *ŭ/ĭ* derived from an original IE. *u/i*. In strong positions these vowels tended to become full vowels (OB. *o/e* R. *o/e*); in weak positions they tended to disappear and leave sonant *r̥/l̥*. Thus in Old Bulgarian the *tŭrt* and *trŭt* series tended to fall together, wherever the vowel of the latter was in weak position; but in other languages (Russian, for instance) they were held apart. Examples are: OB. *krŭvĭ* 'blood' *krŭvenŭ* (Lat. *cruentus*) S. *kȓv* R. *krovǐ* P. *krew* OB. *krĭstiti* 'baptize' *plĭtĭ plŭtĭ* 'flesh'.

30. *Initial Vowels*. At the beginning of a word, especially after a pause, the stream of breath is fuller than later on, and as the mouth gets ready to form an initial vowel the escape of some air may produce an anticipatory sound. In Greek this is recognized as of two kinds, distinguished as the hard and soft breathing. In English, and still more in German, the breath is obstructed and comes with an explosion; the obstruction is liable to be heard as a glottal stop (the glottal stop is heard in the Glaswegian's *wa'er* for *water*), or as an aspiration. In Slavonic the 'attack' is gentle, and should result in a semivowel appearing fugitively before a vowel of the same order. This is largely what occurs, save that the front semivowel *j* is liable to appear also before back vowels, and the back semivowel **w >v* is not much in evidence.

Initial *ĭ* can be detected in the compounds *iz-ĭmǫ ot-ĭmǫ/*ĭmǫ >*jĭmǫ >*OB. *imǫ* 'I shall take'. Similarly, L. *ĭs* 'out' shows that the corresponding Slavonic preposition has developed **ĭz >*jĭz >*OB. *iz;* **ņment >*ĭnmę >*jĭmę >*OB. *imę* 'name'. Cz. *jmouti jméno* result from treating these initial vowels as syntactical medials, that is, as occurring within phrases pronounced with a single breath. Initial *e ę:* OB. *jestŭ* 'is' *jezero* 'lake' *językŭ* 'tongue'. In Russian *e* almost always has palatal on-glide. Initial *ě* >*je/ja:* IE. *ēd-* OB. *jasti* 'eat' R. *jesí* Ruth. *ísty* P. *jeść* Cz. *jisti* S. *jěsti;* in these cases *je* is explained by analogy.

Before the back vowels *ŭ y ǫ* it would be natural to expect **w* >*v*, as in CSl. *vy-* <**ūt*, OB. *vŭ(n)* <**ŭn*, *vǫza/ǫza* 'bond', P. *wąż*/R. *už* 'adder', P. *wąski*/R. *úzkij* 'narrow', (Cz. *pavouk*/R. *paúk* 'spider'). But the examples are not numerous, and in their stead we have *j-* prefixed: OB. *jǫ-/ǫtrĭnĭ* 'inner' *jutro/utro* 'morning'.

As the vowel *a* occupies a middle position in the mouth, it can combine with either semivowel or neither. OB. *ja-/a-* are frequently found alternating: OB. *ja-/aviti* 'reveal', *ja-/agnĭci* 'lamb'; OB. *ajĭce jajĭce jaje* 'egg' R. *jajcó* P. *jaje* Slov. *jájce* S. *jáje* MB. *jajcé/OCz. vajce* MCz. *vejce* (Lat. *ovum*).

31. *Final Vowels.* In principle all Common Slavonic words end in vowels. A few prepositions, having no independent life of their own, end in consonants, as *iz-* 'out', and others recover a final consonant in syntactical combinations, as *sŭ* 'with' (**sŭn*) in OB. *sŭ-ńimĭ* 'with him' (**sŭn·jimĭ*); modern final consonants are due to the loss of the *jers.* Differences of timbre in Old Bulgarian stood in some cases for older distinctions of tone in the final vowels. The *jers* were liable to confusion, and in the 3*SP.* pres. indic. (IE. **-ti *-nti*) only Old Russian preserved the *ĭ;* in Modern Russian it has been hardened, as in OB. *nesetŭ nesǫtŭ* 'bring'; and elsewhere the hard *-t* has been eliminated, as in P. *pisze piszą* 'write'. With the relaxed tension natural in the final position vowels tended to close: so *-ē(r)* >*-i* in OB. *mati* 'mother' *dŭšti* 'daughter'; they tended also to be shortened, as R. *mat doč'* and infin. *-t́*/OB. *-ti.* (On final **oi *ai* see section 24). On the other hand, final *-o* was retained in order to distinguish between the masculine and neuter *o*-stems, and this reaction has been a principal cause of the preservation of three genders in Slavonic. There was nothing in the *o*'s of IE. **wlkʷom* (ASM.)/**jŭgom* (ASN.) to cause the Slavonic divergence between OB. *vlkŭ/igo.* Original final long diphthongs were **āi *ōi* >L. *-ai -ui* CSl. *-ě -u* (DSFM.): L. *stírnai* 'doe' *výrui* 'man' OB. *ženě* 'woman' *vlku* 'wolf'; final **-ōis* >**ū* >CSl. *-y* (IPM.): L. *výrais* OB. *vlky.*

Within the word a consonant following a nasal diphthong normally belongs to the next syllable, but in final position a *t* or *s* may close the syllable in which the nasal stands. Final *-t* disappeared without trace, but final *-s* tended to narrow the previous vowel, with compensatory lengthening, so that IE. **-āns *-ōns* >CSl. *-y*, and **-ons *-uns* >**-ū* > CSl. *-y*, **-ins* >*-ī* >CSl. *-i:* OB. *rǫky* (APF.) 'hands' *toky* (APM.) 'streams' *nošti* (APF.) 'nights' from **ronkāns *tokons *noktins.* OB. *rǫky* (GSF.)/L. *rankōs* <**ronkās* appears to derive from a form

containing an *n* (**-āns?*), perhaps borrowed from the *n*-stems. In the
jo- and *ja*-stems there is a discrepancy between the Slavonic language-
groups, since *GSF.APM.NAPF.* -*ę* is found only in South Slavonic;
West and East Slavonic have -*ě: OB. konę* (**konjons*)/P. *węže* 'snakes'.

When the nasal closed the syllable it ceased to be a consonant, and
survived only as a nasalization of the vowel; the vowel was narrowed
one grade, that is, *a* becomes *o*, *o* becomes *u*. This involved the
denasalization of all but the most open vowels. Hence: OB. *synŭ tokŭ
kamy* (**sūnun *tokon *kamōn*)/*ženǫ berǫ* (**ženām ?*berām*)*; front
vowels: OB. *noštĭ* (ASF.) (**noktin*)/*imę* (**nmen*).

32. *Semiconsonants or semivowels. W J.* IE. *w* (*u̯*), L. *v* Sl. *v;* IE.
i (*i̯*) L. *j* Sl. *j*.

> IE. **newos*/**neujos* L. *naũjas* CSl.OB. *novŭ* R. *nov* 'new'
> (Gk. νέος Lat. *novus*);
>
> IE. **jōunos* L. *jáunas* CSl.OB. *junŭ* R. *júnyj* (OR. also *un*)
> 'youthful' (Lat. *juvenis*);
>
> IE. **jugom*/**jung-* L. *jùngas* CSl. **jĭgo* OB.R.Slov. *igo* Cz. *jho*
> 'yoke' (Gk. ʒυγόν Lat. *jugum*);
>
> IE. **trejes* CSl. *trĭje* OB. *trĭje trije* 'three'.

Initially or between vowels these were fully consonantal, though
apparently not pronounced with tension, and so often denoted *u̯ i̯;*
(Eng. *w y* are relatively tense). Between a consonant opening a syllable
and a vowel they were semi-consonantal, beginning in the close
position of the consonant and opening up to the vowel. After a vowel
in the same syllable they were semi-vocalic, beginning in the open
position of the vowel and closing towards the close position of the
consonant. Though semivowel and semiconsonant are mid-points
in the same distance between consonant and vowel, it is the direction
of the movement which has proved important in the history of most
languages; the semivowel forms diphthongs with the preceding
vowel, which it modifies in time, but the effect of the semiconsonant
is usually (though not always) upon the previous consonant. The
sound represented by *j* is one of the most potent in Slavonic linguistic
history, and it was a weakness of the Old Bulgarian alphabets that they
gave no adequate equivalent.

As observed in the last section, *w j* develop initially before original
simple vowels.

The pronunciation of *w* was bilabio-velar (i.e. with lips rounded and
tongue raised towards the velum). It was in this position that *ŭ- ū-*
initially gave *wŭ- wū-* >CSl. *vŭ- vy-*, and it was in this position that
IE. *e+w* (opening the next syllable) became *ow* >CSl. *ov:* IE. **newos*
CSl.OB. *novŭ* 'new', IE. **k̂lew-os*/*-es-* CSl.OB. *slov-o*/*-es-* 'word' (Gk.
κλέος). The bilabio-velar pronunciation is reflected in Ptolemy's
Οὐενέδαι Οὐιστούλα (Wends, Vistula), but in the sixth century it had

become labiodental *v* (pronounced between the upper teeth and lower lip) and was represented by the Byzantine value of β: Σκλαβηνοί (*Slověne*). In certain positions *v* is pronounced *w* (*u*) in Slovak, Slovene, Serbocroat, Ruthenian and White Russian.

Consonantal *j* also affected the development of vowels before it, so that *ej* > *ij* (**trejes* > *trĭje*) > *i*(*j*) [OB. *tri*(*j*)*e*], *ŭj* > *yj* (*dobrŭ-jĭ* > OB. *dobryi* R. *dóbryj* 'good'). It combined with a following *ĭ* to make *i*, and converted a following *ŭ* to *ĭ* before giving *i* (**jugom* > **jŭgo* > **jĭgo* > *igo* 'yoke'/Cz. *jho*); a following *o* became *e* and *joi* > (*j*)*i* (OB. *znajite* 'know ye' < **znajoite*).

33. *Sibilant. S.* IE. *s* L. *s* (*š* after *r*) CSl.OB. *s š ch;*

IE. **Sēd-* L. *sĕdĕti* CSl.OB. *sĕdĕti* 'sit' (Gk. ἕζομαι Lat. *sedēre*);

IE. **esti* L. *ēsti* CSl.OB. *jestĭ* 'is' (Gk. ἐστί Lat. *est*)

IE. **nebhes-* CSl.OB. *nebese* (*GSN.*) 'sky' (Gk. νέφεος);

IE. **jōunos* L. *jáunas* CSl.OB. *junŭ* R. *júnyj* 'youthful' (Lat. *juvenis*);

IE. **wr̥sus* L. *viršùs* CSl. **vĭrchŭ* OB. *vr̥chŭ* R. *verch* 'top' (Lat. *verruca* < **versuca*);

IE. **-isu* L. *akmenysè* CSl.OB. *kamenĭchŭ* 'stones' (*LP.*) (Skr. *-iṣu : matiṣu*);

IE. **snusus* CSl.OB. *snŭcha* R. *snochá* 'daughter-in-law' (Skr. *snuṣā* Lat. *nurus* Gk. νυός);

IE. **rēksom *rēksn̥t* CSl.OB. *rĕchŭ rĕšę* (1*S*.3*P*. aorist)/*rĕste* (2*P*. aorist) 'said';

Proto-Sl. **duchja* CSl.OB.R. *dušá* 'soul';

IE. **sodos* CSl.OB. *chodŭ* 'way' R. *chod;*

IE. **misdh- *mizdh-* CSl. *mĭzda* 'wage' (Gk. μισθός Goth. *mizdō*).

The Indo-European language was poor in fricatives, and only the one, sibilant *s*, is certainly demonstrated. Before voiced consonants it became voiced (*z*), but the voiced sibilant had no separate existence in the sound-system.

The development of Sl. *s* < IE. *s* is quite distinct from that of Sl. *s* < IE. *k̑;* they must have been different sounds at the moment when their lines of change crossed. After *i u r k,* even at a distance, IE. *s* > Skr. *ṣ* (*matiṣu snuṣā r̥ṣi-* 'seer', *r̥kṣas* 'bear'), called 'lingual *s*'. Other terms are 'cacuminal' and 'cerebral'; they imply that in these instances the tip of the tongue was raised from the lower teeth towards a point in the high palate, as in Castilian *s*. Such an *ṣ* readily becomes *š* and is generally heard as *š* by foreigners unacquainted with it; the sibilant is then pronounced in the high palate, but with the back of the tongue. This is the development in Avestic: Av. *dašina-* Skr. *dákṣinas* OB. *desnŭ* 'right (hand)' (Lat. *dexter* Gk. δεξιός). If the friction with the back of the tongue slips further back in the mouth, as far as the soft palate or velum, then the sound produced is the velar sibilant *ch*, which is the Slavonic conclusion unless a consonant follows. (See sections 2 and 12).

From the hard Proto-Sl. *ch* there developed a soft *š* before front vowels by the first Slavonic palatalization (*vide supra*). The conditions under which *ch* occurred involved certain case- and personal-endings, and so allowed for the working of analogy. The velar sibilant occurs normally in the locative plural, without restriction to the combinations involving *i u r k*. Similarly it seems that initial *s* might become *ch* (*chod*), and thus give rise by palatalization to *š* (OB. *šĭdŭ* 'having gone'), though these developments may have been due to the analogy of compounds (e.g. R. *prichód* 'arrival' *uchodít* 'depart') in which original *s* was preceded by *i* or *u*. Original *ks-* may have given rise to some instances of initial *ch-/š-:* IE. **(k)s(w)eks* Skr. *ṣaṣ* Avestic *khšvaš* L. *šešĭ* CSl.OB. *šestĭ* R. *šesť* 'six'.

34. *Aspirate Occlusives.* In Indo-European the simple occlusives *k g k̂ ĝ t d p̂ b* were accompanied by aspirates of the same formation, viz. *kh gh k̂h ĝh th dh ph bh.* They were most fully conserved in Sanskrit, where the system was applied to the new order of palatal consonants, so that beside Skr. *c j* there were also Skr. *ch jh.* In Greek the voiced aspirates became unvoiced, and only χ θ φ remained. In Balto-Slavonic the aspirates were identified with the corresponding simple consonants in all cases. A doubt has been raised in favour of the survival of *kh* by A. Meillet (*Introd. à l'étude comparative des langues indo-européennes*, Paris, 1924, p. 64), as a result of comparing R. *chóchot* 'laughter' *chochotát* 'laugh' with Skr. *kakhati* 'he laughs' Gk. καχάζω<*χαχάζω Lat. *cachinnus* OHG. *huoh* Arm. *khakhankʿ*. The word is inconclusive, however, as it may represent in each case imitation of the sound of laughter. In what follows, the aspirates will not be separately discussed.

35. *Velars and Postpalatals. K G.* These sounds are caused by raising the back of the tongue, a relatively sluggish muscular mass, to contact with the velum or soft palate, which gives a duller resonance than the hard palate or hard teeth in the front part of the mouth. There is, in consequence, a considerable area in which contact may be made at different points without changing the essential timbre of the consonants. As between the *k*'s (*c*'s) in Eng. *keen ken/con* there is the difference that the first sound is pronounced well forward in the velum (prevelar) or immediately behind the hard palate (postpalatal), while the second is pronounced towards the middle of the velum (medio-velar). The effect of a *w* upon *k* (Eng. *quad*) is to shift the point of contact lower down the throat (postvelar).

In many languages the distinction between postpalatal and medio-velar *k g* occurs as an accident of pronunciation, and has no effect upon linguistic structure. In others, such as the Romance group, the postpalatal pronunciation of *k* *g* (before front vowels *e* *i*) was accentuated and tended to come as far forward as the high palate (mediopalatal). But in the high palate it is not possible to retain the occlusive pronunciation intact, and a change is made to another order of sounds. In raising the back of the tongue to the velum and lowering it again, a relatively short distance is traversed, without influencing the total sound, which is essentially defined by the contact of tongue and velum. But in the high palate the tongue has to rise and fall an appreciable distance, and the contact is at the extreme of possible movement; the contact becomes momentary, and the total sound includes a long sibilant off-glide. Instead of occlusion there is affrication or semi-occlusion. Such sounds are sometimes described by phoneticians as composed of two others, an occlusive and a fricative; but they are not of double length, and they are formed with on-glide, tension, and off-glide like any other consonants. The explanation also falls foul of the fact that the existence of complete occlusives in the high palate is rather a matter of theoretical symmetry than of actual experience of languages. In such a region occlusives immediately become unstable, and are transformed to sounds of other orders.

The cause of this development is that *e* *i* are vowels formed by raising the tongue forward towards the hard palate and gums. Energy is saved by lifting the tongue for *k* *g* not against the middle velum, but more forward in the palate. But, having begun such movements, the tongue may continue to develop its forward utterance even beyond the place where *e* *i* are formed, and so give rise to dental affricates. Moreover, in any affricate the moment of contact is brief in comparison with the off-glide, and it may be eclipsed altogether, so that the affricate becomes a fricative. Few languages have gone so far as Castilian, which has given to the fricative an interdental value. To sum up these possible developments (using *ḱ ǵ ch́* for *k g ch* modified in a forward direction), we have

	Velar	Postpalatal	Mediopalatal	Dento-alveolar	Interdental
Occlusive	*k g* →	*ḱ ǵ* →	(*k̂*) (*ĝ*)		
Affricate			↓*č dž* →	*c dz*	
Fricative	*ch*	*ch́* →	↓*š ž*	↓*s z* →	θ ð

All but the last occur in Slavonic. The *satem*-palatalization gives *s z*, the first Slavonic palatalization gives *č* (*d*)*ž* (and *š* from *ch*), and the second gives *c* (*d*)*z* (and *ś/š* from *ch*).

The Semitic languages distinguish between velar and postvelar pronunciations: Arabic *k/q*, Arabic *j* <*g* (Hebrew *g*)/*ġ*. In Indo-European languages the postvelar pronunciation is an accident due to a following *w* (Eng. *quad quantity*). But *w*, while resembling the velars in the position of the tongue, resembles the labials in being pronounced by both lips, and so it is capable of transforming *kw gw* into *p b*. The western languages of the Indo-European family reveal no trace of a distinction between velar and postpalatal *k g*, but they do show the postvelar either as such or as a labial. The eastern languages distinguish between the two orders of *k g*, and treat as an accident the presence of *w* after either order. Exactly how the distinction between the two kinds of *k g* arose is not known, since we lack all evidence of states previous to the point of divergent development. In order not to beg any questions the forward variety is denoted IE. *k̂ ĝ* and the backward IE. *k g*.

36. (*a*) *The satem-palatalization.* IE. *k̂ ĝ*, L. *š ž*, Latv.OPr. *s z*, CSl.OB. *s z*, Iranian *s z*, Arm. *s c'*, Skr. *ç j*/Gk. κ (but *k̂w* >Gk. ππ) Lat. *c* = *k g* Ir. *c g* Germ. *h k;* IE. *k g* BSl. *k g*.

IE. **k̂mtóm* L. *šimtas* 'hundred' Latv. *simts* CSl.OB. *sŭto* R.P.Cz.S.MB. *sto* (Skr. *çatam* Avestic *satəm*/Gk. ἑκατόν Lat. *centum* Ir. *cet* Goth. *hund*);

IE. **dek̂mt* L. *dēšimt* 'ten' Latv. *desmit* CSl.OB. *desętĭ* R. *désjať* (Skr. *daça* Arm. *tasn*/Gk. δέκα Lat. *decem* Ir. *de(i)ch n-* Goth *taihun*);

IE. **ek̂wos *ek̂wa* L. *ašvà* 'mare' (Skr. *açvas*/Gk. ἵππος Lat. *equus* Ir. *ech* Goth. *aihw-*);

IE. **ĝn-*ĝnō-* L. *žinóti* 'know' Latv. *zināt* CSl.OB. *znati* R. *znať* (Skr. *jñā-* Arm. *c'anot'* 'acquaintance'/Gk. γιγνώσκω Lat. (*g*)*nosco*);

IE. **ĝheim-* L. *žiemà* 'winter' Latv. *ziema* CSl.OB.R.etc. *zima* (Skr. *hima-* Gk. χεῖμα χειμών Lat. *hiems*);

IE. **kru- *kreu-* L. *kraũjas* 'blood' CSl.OB. *krŭvĭ* (acc.) R. *krov* (Skr. *kravíş-* Gk. κρέας Lat. *cruor* Ir. *crū*);

IE. **jugom* L. *jùngas* (with infixed *n*) 'yoke' CSl.OB. *igo* (Eng. *yoke*);

IE. **ghordhos* L. *gardas* 'enclosure' CSl. **gordŭ* OB. *gradŭ* R. *górod* Ruth. *hórod* P. *gród* Cz. *hrad* Slov.S.MB. *grad* (ON. *garðr* 'garth' Eng. *yard*);

IE. **snoigh^wos* L. *sniẽgas* 'snow' CSl.OB. *snĕgŭ* R. *sneg* P. *śnieg* Cz. *sníh* Slov. *snêg* S. *snijeg* (Gk. νίφα (acc.) Lat. *nix nivis*).

The distinction between the velars and postpalatals is clear from the above examples. Slavonic *s z* represent phonetically the extreme of change, and intermediate stages may have been like those stabilized in Lithuanian (*š ž*) and Sanskrit (*ç j*), while yet others are possible. Hence IE. *s* (>Sl. *s š ch*) never coincided with *s* <*k̂* during the formative period of either sound.

There are some words which retain the velar pronunciation of *k̂ ĝ* for reasons hard to discover: CSl.OB. *svekry* 'mother-in-law' R. *svekróv*/Skr. *çvaçrūs* Lat. *socrus*, CSl.OB. *gǫsĭ* 'goose' R. *guś*/L.

žąsìs Latv. *zuoss* OPr. *sansy* G. χήν Lat. (*h*)*anser* Germ. *Gans*. The explanation that CSl. *gǫsǐ* was borrowed, in respect of the initial, from the German seems improbable, and it is best to admit that a phonetic law may not be carried through in all its instances through some resistance, which may not itself be known.

37. (*b*) *First Slavonic palatalization*. IE. *k g* (before *e i*) L.OPr. *k g* Latv. *c dz* CSl.OB. *č* *dž* >*ž* (and Proto-Sl. *ch+e i* >CSl. *š*).

IE. *ketwores* L. *keturì* 'four' CSl.OB. *četyre* R. *četýre* (Skr. *catur* Arm. *č'ors*); L. *ketviȓtas* 'fourth' OPr. *kettwirts* Latv. *ceturtais* CSl. *četvȋrtŭ*;

IE. *gʷenā* OPr. *genno* (voc.) CSl.OB.R. *žena* 'woman';

IE. *gʷīwos* L. *gývas* OP. *gijwans* (AP) Latv. *dzivs* CSl.OB. *živŭ* 'alive' R. *živ* (Skr. *jīvati* 'lives');

Vulgar Lat. *ceresia* (*č*) R. *čeréšnja* 'cherry'.

Sounds resulting from palatalization were 'soft' in Common Slavonic and originally in Old Bulgarian. It is not necessary to indicate this 'softness'. CSl. *č* must be understood as *č'*, CSl. *ž* as *ž'*, etc. Only *s z* may have been originally hard or soft.

The development of a postpalatal occlusive into a mediopalatal affricate is very natural. The presence of the same developments in Sanskrit and Armenian, together with the fact that they are anterior in Slavonic to the Middle Proto-Slavonic period (see section 13), is evidence of high antiquity.

38. (*c*) *Second Slavonic Palatalization*. Proto-Sl. *k g ch* (i : after *i ĭ ę* ‹*in* and before *ǐr*; ii : before *ě i* ‹*ai oi*); CSl.OB. *c dz z s* (WSl. *š*).

i: Proto-Sl. *ovĭka* CSl.OB. *ovĭca* 'sheep' R. *ovcá*;
Proto-Sl. *otĭkŭ* CSl.OB. *otĭcĭ* 'father' R. *otéc*.

Goth. *kirihha* (OHG. *chirihha*) OB. *crky* 'church' R. *cérkoǔ*;
Germ. *kuningaz peningaz* CSl.OB. *kŭnę(d)zǐ pěnę(d)zǐ* 'prince, coin' R. *knjaž* OR. *pěnjaž*;

ii: L. *káina* Proto-Sl. *koina* CSl.OB. *cěna* 'price' R. *cená* (Gk. ποινή);

Germ. *Kaisar* CSl.OB. *cěsaȓi* 'king' R. *caȓ*;
L. *gailùs* 'sharp' OB. (*d*)*zělo* 'vehemently';
OB. *rokŭ* 'destiny' *bogŭ* 'god' *duchŭ* 'breath'/LS. *rocě bo(d)zě dusě*/NP. *roci bo(d)zi dusi* (*mucha* 'fly'/DLS. Slovak dial. *musě muse*/Cz. *mouše* P. *musze*);
OB. *cvětŭ* 'flower' (*d*)*zvězda* 'star' R. *cvet zvezdá*/P. *kwiat gwiazda* Cz. *květ hvězda*.

These sounds also were soft in Common Slavonic and originally in Old Bulgarian.

The second palatalization does not take place after *e ě* (R. *čelovék* 'man'), and it seems to have been impeded when after the velar came *y o ǫ* (OB. *kŭnęgyńi* R. *knjaginja/knjaź*). Both forms operated upon Germanic loanwords, but they do not seem to have been entirely contemporaneous. It is disputed which was earlier, but it is to be noted that, while the first type was completely carried through, the second shows an incomplete process in e.g. P. *kwiat gwiazda*. P.Cz. *š* from *ch* may be due to the analogy of the first palatalization, since *s* is found in Slovak dialects.

In Russian *ky gy chy* have become *ki gi chi* (OR. *Kyev* MR. *Kiev*) and thus given rise to new examples of *k ǵ ch* before a front vowel. The consonants have been softened, though not changed in timbre, but the development has permitted the restoration of *k g ch* in declension before case-endings *ě i* (that is, L*SMN* DL*SF* NA*PM*).

39. *Dentals and Alveolars.* The tongue-tip is a lively organ which forms clear sounds against the teeth, gums (alveoli) and front palate. It also reaches to the high palate, but in that region the mid-back of the tongue functions more readily, and dentals which develop so far back are liable to conversion into palatals such as develop from the velars. In contact with the teeth and gums the tongue is more protruded than for the articulation of the front vowels. Their effect is thus to withdraw the tongue-tip to the front of the hard palate immediately behind the gums (which is the effect of *e i ę* on a preceding dental), or into the high palate (which is the effect of *j*). Owing to the resonance, however, it is possible to maintain these distinctions without complete separation of timbre. In Common Slavonic this is what occurs; the dentals and alveolars have three shades: hard or normal before back vowels, soft or palatalized before front vowels, and palatal before *j*. [We may compare, for illustration, Eng. *t* in *tone* (*t*), *tune* (*t́*), and *try* (*t̬*)]. In the individual languages, including Old Bulgarian, the palatals *t́ d́* appear as back-tongue palatals, but of different kinds in each region. They have no common source as such palatals, and one must suppose that in Common Slavonic they were tongue-tip palatals of dental timbre. Hence Common Slavonic must be credited with a triple series of these sounds; *t t́ t̬, d d́ d̬, l ĺ l̬, n ń ň, r ŕ ř*, etc.

In Old Bulgarian manuscripts a semi-circle placed to the right of a letter is a sign both of soft and of palatal utterance. The South Slavonic languages have eliminated softness, so that there remain of these Common Slavonic sounds only the normal varieties, save for certain back-tongue palatals. In Russian, apart from these back-tongue palatals, the tendency has been to reduce the three orders to two: hard/soft. In Polish and Czech there has also been reduction to two: hard/palatal.

40. *T D*. IE. *t* BSl. *t;* IE. *d dh* BSl. *d;* CSl. **t́* (before *e i*) P. Up Wend. *ć* LowWend. *ś;* CSl. **d́* (before *e i*) P. UpWend. *dź* LowWend.

ź; CSl. *ť (before j; also from *kí *gí) R. č P.Wend.Cz. c Slov. č S. ć
OB. šť(<*š'ť'š/<*íš') MB. št; CSl. *ď (before j) R. ž (<*dž) P. dz
Cz. z (<dz) Slovak dz Slov. j S. đ OB. žď MB. žd.

    IE. *trejes CSl. trǐje 'three';

    IE. *dō- L. dúoti CSl.OB. dati 'give' R. dať;

    IE. *mātē(r) L. móté 'wife' CSl.OB. mati 'mother' R. mať/
P.UpWend. mać LowWend. maś;

    CSl.OB. dědŭ 'grandfather' R. ded/WR. dźed P. dziad Up
Wend. dźed LowWend. źed;

    CSl. *svěťa 'candle' R. svečá/P. świeca Cz. svíce/Slov. svéča
S. svijèća OB. světša MB. svešt;

    IE. *noktis L. naktìs CSl. *noťĭ 'night' R. noč'/P.Wend.Cz.
noc/Slov. nôč S. nóć OB. noštĭ MB. nošt;

    IE. *magtis CSl. *moťĭ 'might' R. moč' etc.;

    IE. *medhja CSl. *meďa 'boundary' R. mežá/P. miedza
Slovak medza Cz. mez/Slov. méja S. mèđa OB. mežda MB. meždá.

The different results from CSl. *ť *ď serve to mark off Russian
from West Slavonic and West Slavonic from South Slavonic, and so
are used as the main criterion for classifying the Slavonic languages.
They do not indicate the unity of the South Slavonic block. In Istria
the pronunciation is still largely dental and occlusive, but in Serbia it
is more affricate. A palatal sibilant off-glide in Slovene resulted in a
palatal consonant (č) for the voiceless sound, while the voiced dj
ceased to be affricate, resulting in j, which extends into ča-dialects.
In Bulgarian the sibilant palatal off-glides were both voiceless and
voiced, so that *ť >*íš' >*š'íš' >ší, and *ď became žď by parallel
stages. On the other hand the treatment of soft ť ď divides the main
Slavonic groups by associating White Russian with Polish and
Wendish.

    41. L R N. IE. l r n CSl.OB. l r n; CSl. *ŕ *ŕ R. ŕ P. rz=ž Wend.
š ś r Cz. ř.

    CSl. *elbędĭ/*olboďĭ OB. lebędĭ R. lébeď 'swan' P. łabędź Cz.
labuť S. läbùd;

    IE. *leiĝh- L. liežiù 'lick' OB. ḷizati ližǫ R. lizáť P. lizać (Gk.
λείχω Lat. lingo);

    Germ. Karl R. koról 'king' P. król S. krâlj;

    L. rankà 'hand' CSl.OB. rǫka R. ruká P. ręka Cz. ruka;

    R. reč' 'discourse' P. rzecz 'thing' Cz. řeč 'speech';

    IE. *newos CSl.OB. novŭ 'new' R. nov P. nów Cz.S.MB. nov;

    R. koń 'horse' P. koń Cz. kůň S. kònj.

It is normal in speech for these sounds to approximate to the
articulation of the following sound. The liquid l moves from the gums
to the high palate, where it becomes [λ]. Hus described the 'hollow'
or 'dark' ḷ/l as it existed in Czech: 'unde sciendum, quod l generatur

apponendo linguam ad superius palatum sive dentes æqualiter tenendo, seu inferiores extra protendendo, vel e contra; sed *l* generatur linguam in fine sub dentibus ponendo et superiores dentes ultra inferiores protendendo'. Thus *l* was pronounced by the tongue-tip, and *l̦* by the arched back of the tongue. The sound has died out in Czech, but it is the normal or 'hard' Russian *l* (*l̦* being represented by a following soft *jer* or soft vowel); in Polish hard *ł* is distinguished alphabetically from soft *l*. Where [λ] has developed in Serbocroat it is represented by *lj*.

The development of CSl. *ŕ *r̄ into a vibrant followed by a sibilant off-glide is highly characteristic of West Slavonic. In Czech this vibrant remains, the off-glide having the nature of *ž/š* according to circumstances. Elsewhere the glide has eliminated the vibration (P. *rz = ž/š* Wend. *š š*), though there are some instances in Wendish in which the vibrant persists without the glide. The result in Slovak is a hard *r*.

As for *n* there are three distinct sounds commonly represented by one letter, viz., the alveolar *n*, the palatal *ň*, and the velar *ṅ*. The latter commonly arise before palatals or velars, and as there is only a mechanical adaptation it is not often denoted alphabetically (but cf. Skr. *pañca* 'five' Gk. ἄγγελος= Lat. *angelus* 'messenger'). In Indo-European they had no existence independently of alveolar *n*. As they were due to the nature of the following consonant they fell out of Slavonic, because they formed diphthongs with the preceding vowel, and were reduced to nasal vowels. (R. *bank ángel* and similar words retain alveolar *n* even before velars, though the more difficult group in *punkt* probably has velar *n*.) New varieties of *n* arose, however, by softening alveolar *n*, and they developed a palatal articulation (Cz. *ň* P. *ń* S. *nj*) which restored the palatal nasal to the alphabet. The distinction between palatal *ň* and soft *ń* is subtle (cf. Eng. *onion/ union*). Russian *ń* is the soft variety, i.e., it is pronounced by the tongue-tip, not the arched back.

Sl. *s*, however it originated, is liable to these nuances: OB. *nosŭ* 'nose' *nositi* (*š*) 'carry' *nošǫ* <*nosjǫ* 'I carry'.

42. *Labials. P B V M.* IE. *p b m* L. *p b m* CSl.OB. *p b m;* Proto-Sl. *w* L. *v* CSl.OB. *v;* CSl. *pj *bj *vj *mj* R.Slov.S. *pl* etc./P.Wend.Cz.MB. *p'(p)* etc./OB. *pl p.*

IE. *penkʷe* L. *penkì* 'five' CSl.OB. *pęti* R. *pjaṫ* P. *pięć* Cz. *pět* S. *pêt* MB. *pet* (Gk. πέντε);

IE. *nebhos* L. *debesìs* 'cloud' (*d* by substitution) CSl.OB.R. Slov.S.MB. *nebo* 'sky' P. *niebo* (Gk. νέφος), MGk. καράβι R. *korábl* 'skiff'/P. *korab* Cz. *koráb;*

CSl. *zemja zeḿa* OB. *zem(l)'a/*R. *zemljá* S. *zèmlja* 'land'/P. *ziemia* Wend. *zemja* Cz. *země* MB. *zemjá;*

IE. *bheudhō* CSl. *bjudǫ* OB. *bludǫ* 'guard' R. *bljudú.*

F was not a Common-Slavonic sound. It derived later from unvoicing of final *v* after the loss of the *jers*, from the Slavonic combinations -*pŭv*- and *chv*, from Gk. φ θ and Germanic and Romance *f*. The remaining labials we must suppose to have come down to Common Slavonic unaltered as to timbre, but with three nuances, like the dentals, which may be denoted *p* (before back vowels), *ṗ* (before front vowels), and *p̃* (before *j*) etc. It is, of course, impossible for a labial to become a palatal proper; but by *ṗ* we understand a labial followed by a palatal off-glide due to the prepalatal position taken by the tongue, and by *p̃* a labial with the tongue in so tense a position that when its articulation could be heard it was a palatal consonant, *j* in the more relaxed utterance, but *l̆* in the more tense. The palatal consonant made itself heard when the closure of the lips ceased a fraction of time before the tongue proceeded from its position of expectancy to form the front vowel itself. The two varieties of palatalized articulation were marked in Old Bulgarian by semi-circles to the right of the letter. In Russian they are unmarked, since here again, after the rise of the specifically palatal groups *pl̆ bl̆ vl̆ ml̆*, the labials were reduced from three orders to two: hard/soft. The quality is known from the following vowel.

43. *Final Consonants. S N T D.* All Indo-European final consonants were lost in Common Slavonic, with the result that, in principle, all Common Slavonic and Old Bulgarian words ended in a vowel. By the twelfth century the most common of these vowels, the two *jers*, had disappeared, leaving new final consonants in all the modern languages. These have been reduced from the two series of voiceless and voiced consonants to the single series of voiceless consonants everywhere but in Serbocroat and, to some extent, in Slovene and Ruthenian. Thus, for instance, MR. *chod* 'way' is pronounced [χɔt], Cz. *zub* 'tooth' [zup].

The most interesting final consonants are those used in flexions: -*d* of the ablative, -*s* of the nominative and plural, -*n* of the *n*-stems, -*t* 3 pers.sg.pl. of verbs, -*nt* of the *nt*-stems. Though all have gone, there is reason to believe that they did not disappear at the same time. Thus final -*n* closes the vowel one grade (see section 31). Therefore, since 3 pl. *-ont* > CSl. -*ǫ*, it is evident that *n* cannot have been final at the relevant period: the development must have been *-ont* > *-ǫt* > -*ǫ*, because otherwise it would have given *-y*. On the other hand, *-ons* > CSl. *-y*. The effect of *s* is to lengthen a previous vowel before disappearing, and the effect of *n* is to close it. The order of development can only have been *-ons* > *-ūn* > *-y*.

Prepositions and some other proclitics had no independent life in the sentence, but formed part of the same breath-group as the word following. Therefore their consonants were not really final, and might stand, either in all cases or in some. Thus OB. *iz/is* L. *ìš* 'out' (cf.

Lat. *ex* Gk. ἐξ) persists, but there are also forms in *ŭ* due to the general analogy of vocalic endings (whence R. *izo-* in compounds). IE. **op *ob* L. *ap ab* CSl.OB. *o ob* 'concerning, against' had other forms in *obŭ obĭ* due to IE. **abhi*. Final *-t* has dropped in IE. **ūt* CSl. *vy-* 'out'. OB. *vŭ* 'in' *kŭ* 'to' *sŭ* 'with' recover their original *-n* before pronouns beginning with a vowel and in compounds, and an analogical *n* is found after other prefixes in certain compounds, e.g., R. *raznuzdát* 'unbridle'/*uzdá* 'bridle'.

44. *Influence of Consonants on Vowels.* A major feature of Slavonic linguistic history has been the creation of palatal consonants from normal velars or dentals. At first these function as hard/soft pairs, but as the palatal consonant attains independence it tends to become its own norm, giving rise to new hard consonants. Old Bulgarian was in process of hardening a considerable number of its palatals (*š ž št žd c z* etc.), and the hardening (or normalizing) process has become general in South Slavonic, and quite advanced in Czech. Even in languages which, like Russian and Polish, maintain the alternation hard/soft with scruple, there are cases of hardening, such as P. *rz*. Now a soft consonant requires a soft vowel and a hard consonant a hard vowel. The appearance of hard vowels after palatals is a sign of the hardening process. It probably went back in part to a very ancient date when **slyšěti* became *slyšati* (see section 13). Examples from the Old Bulgarian period are: CSl. **stojěti*/OB. *stojati* 'stand', CSl. ?**čěsŭ*/OB. *časŭ* 'hour'. A foreign *e* in hiatus was liable to pass into *o:* OB. *Vitĭleomŭ*/Gk. Βηθλεέμ 'Bethlehem'. A difficult case is OB. *Rimŭ* R. *Rim* P. *Rzym* for 'Rome'. It is explained as **Rūm-* >N.S. **Rymŭ*, but L.S. **Rymě* >*Rimě* (by influence of the front vowel *-ě* upon the preceding back vowel), and so N.S. *Rimŭ*. The *y* in P. *Rzym* is due to a later Polish process of hardening.

45. *Consonant Groups.* Consonant groups are simplified thus: (i) double consonants become single, (ii) of two occlusives, only the second survives, (iii) occlusive+sibilant assimilates to the sibilant. These changes leave as groups only sibilant+occlusive, and those involving *l r* as the second element. The loss of the *jers* in historic times led to the formation of new groups in the individual languages. In Polish they attain notable complexity (e.g. P. *państw sprzymierzonych* 'of the Allied States', with seven successive consonants). But in Polish, as in all the Slavonic languages, the instinct to simplify or eliminate groups has been at work. Adjacent voiced and voiceless consonants are subject to assimilation, which is usually regressive (e.g. *pd* > *bd*), and this assimilation is indicated in Serbocroat spelling. The voicing of consonants before sonants—common in the Romance languages—is rare in Slavonic, though, for instance, Slovak *my sme* 'we are' is pronounced [mi zmɛ].

(i) Double consonants were found in some nursery words like *atta Gk. ἄττα 'daddy' OB. otĭcĭ, and in forms like *essi 'thou art' OB. jesi. Those arising in compound words have not as a rule been reduced, though there is e.g. OB. bezakonije 'lawlessness' (<bez zakon-). It has been interestingly suggested that the word besěda 'speech, conversation' represents bez sěd- with the sense of 'sitting without', i.e., 'outside'; cf. R. besédka 'arbour'.

(ii) Occlusive+occlusive: *pt *bt *tk >OB. t k, as OB. netĭjĭ 'nephew'/Lat. neptis, dlato 'chisel' <*dolto <*dolbto, OB. okryti 'uncover'/ot(ŭ)kryti. OB. potŭ 'sweat' may be from *poktŭ (pek- 'bake'), and if so it shows t <*kt. CSl. *kĭ *gĭ (see section 40). OB. gd in kŭgda kogda 'when' is a recent group, if the latter element stands for goda, as has been suggested.

(iii) Occlusive+sibilant: *kch *tch >OB. ch, *ps *ts >OB. s, as in OB. rěchŭ 'I said'/rekǫ, ochoditi 'depart'/ot(ŭ)choditi, osa 'wasp'/ Lat. vespa OE. wǽsp wǽps, věsŭ 'I led'/vedǫ.

Sibilant+occlusive: sp st sk, zb zd zg remain. By the two palatalizations *sk *zg gave (i) *sč >šč and *zdž >ždž (OB. št žd) and (ii) sc zdz (OB. st zd): OB. iskati 'seek' gives (i) ištǫ P. iszczę (by the first palatalization), and dŭska 'board' gives (ii) LS. dŭstě P. desce (by the second palatalization).

Consonant+nasal: *tn *dn *pn *bn >OB. n, *dm >OB. m, *bdm > OB. dm: OB. sŭnŭ 'sleep'/IE. *supnos, damĭ 'I shall give' <*dadmĭ/ Gk. δίδωμι, sedmŭ 'seventh'/Gk. ἕβδομος.

Consonant+l/r: tl dl >WSl. tl dl/SSl.ESl. l, as in vedla 'led' (fem. past part. of vedǫ) Cz. vedla P. wiodła/SSl.ESl. vela; Cz. křidlo OP. krzydło MP. skrzydło LowWend. kšidło/OB.S. krilo R. kryló (with hardening of the vibrant in Russian). Original *sr *zr >CSl. str zdr: OB. sestra 'sister'/L. sěserį (acc.) Lat. soror (*sesor), OB. Izdrailĭ 'Israel'.

46. Dissimilation. Original *-tti/dti (infinitives) >OB. etc. -sti: OB. mesti 'throw'/metǫ, pasti 'fall'/padǫ.

B. FORMS AND THEIR USES

(i) VERBS

47. Simplifying the Paradigm. A verb is that part of a sentence which is grammatically equipped to express phenomena. The sentence itself expresses phenomena, i.e., the changes and states of experience as our minds rest upon them, but it does so with full circumstantiality in each case. From the sentence it is possible to abstract concepts which can serve to denote circumstances of other phenomena: the names of parties to the events (nouns) or substitutes for those names (pronouns), terms denoting their qualities (adjectives) or qualities of the

activity or state (adverbs). There remains, however, the essentially phenomenal element, which is the verb. The verb must be equipped grammatically for the purpose, and it is from the ancient Greek (preferably Homeric) conjugation that we get the best idea of how the Indo-European language equipped its verbs. In Greek the vowels *o/e* are preserved, and with them one of the principal artifices of the parent tongue, viz., vowel-alternation. They fall together with *a* in Sanskrit, but otherwise the Sanskrit conjugation helps to complete the evidence of the Greek. From certain discrepancies between them it would seem that the Indo-European system was looser in structure, less precisely ordered in a paradigm, and possessed of alternative possibilities of growth.

The Indo-European verb provided means of relating the phenomenon in several ways. The act or state described might be represented as proceeding simply from the subject as source or agent (active voice), or as affecting and, so to say, returning to, the subject (middle voice). The middle voice was based on the active, generally by means of additions to the flexion (e.g. Gk. active δείκνυμι/middle δείκνυμαι 'show'). There was also a grammatical device (passive voice) to enable the logical object to be expressed as subject. The passive voice employed chiefly forms from the middle, with a few specially its own, and so must be regarded as incompletely stabilized in the Indo-European period. In Balto-Slavonic these secondary voices were eliminated. The return to the subject was more simply expressed by the reflexive pronoun: L. *si* (dat.) CSl.OB. *sę* (acc.). It satisfied the requirements of the middle voice to associate the active with the reflexive pronoun, and it was used also for the passive which depended formally on the middle. It had the great advantage of applying one single form for the new conceptual element, in place of the very mixed and various collection of forms used in Indo-European. As an enclitic the reflexive would stand after the first substantial word of the sentence, but its association in thought with the verb has led to its taking in Russian an invariable place behind the verb. In Old Bulgarian it might still be separated by a particle, and in other Slavonic languages it is still relatively free.

The speaker regarded his expression in various ways (moods), whether as a statement or enquiry about facts (indicative), as an energetic utterance to be obeyed (imperative), as a nearer or remoter notion (subjunctive/optative), the actuality of which was not asserted. Expressions of the verbal idea in nouns and adjectives constituted the infinitive mood, so called, but are developments on another line of distinction. The infinitive itself appears to have been very loosely constituted, since its forms are independent in each group of languages. They have in common only a general tendency to be formed by endings analogous to case-endings. In Balto-Slavonic the infinitive was given definite form as *-tēi, supine *-tum. The system of participles (verbal-adjectives) is very complete, though largely reduced to invariable gerunds in the modern languages by loss of flexion. Of the four finite moods only the indicative survived fully articulate in Slavonic, and forms of the optative were used instead of the imperative. The imperative and subjunctive completely vanished.

It was also possible to distinguish between certain types of activity (aspects) and between times (tenses). As to aspect, the phenomenon might be one precisely delimited (perfective) or not delimited (imperfective). The former usage also covered absolute and abstract assertions, as in proverbs, and is called aorist in Greek (ἀόριστος 'indeterminate'), a word which is inconvenient in view of the use of the aorist for actions or states defined as to time and space. Such definition is more common in past time than in the present, so that the notion of aspect tended to become one of tense, especially when the suffix -s- (sigmatic aorist) opposed the aorist formally to the present. Most languages show increasing clearness in distinctions of time, while those of aspect become too complex for grammatical flexion. In addition to the perfective/imperfective criterion, phenomena may be repetitive (iterative aspect in Slavonic), or defined as to their beginning (Latin inceptives), or as to their ending only (Fr. *il vient d'arriver* 'he has just arrived'), or as something towards which the subject is in motion, or that is due to will or obligation, etc. In past tenses there is more room for definition of aspect than in present or future time: the past is known, and therefore we can profitably use forms which describe a past activity or state as indefinite (imperfect) or definite (past definite, past, or aorist) or continuing in effect into present time (past indefinite or perfect). If a present event has to be defined as beginning to be and ending later (perfective) that can only be in future time. Hence in Slavonic the present perfective performs the duties of an English future; cf. such Greek futures as βαλῶ, λαβῶ.

The Indo-European parent tongue made use of the alternation o/e/O to denote noun/imperfective verb/perfective (aorist) verb: Gk. λοιπός 'remaining'/λείπω 'I remain'/Homeric λίπον 'remained'. An adverbial prefix IE. *e- served to mark past time, and was added to the imperfective as well as to the perfective forms: Gk. ἔλειπον (impf.)/ἔλιπον (aor.). To express the perfect the o-grade of stem was used, with reduplication of the initial (vowel of support e): λέλοιπα. In a very primitive verb, the verb 'to be', distinctions of this sort were made by quite different words (e.g. Lat. sum/fui); but even when the root was the same the vowel-gradation made the aorist as independent of the present as the noun was of the verb. In process of time the aorist and present were associated, along with the perfect, in a paradigm felt to be the conjugation of one and the same word; and this association was strengthened with the rise of the s-aorist: late Gk. ἔλειψα. But originally they were independent, and the distinction imperfective/perfective -e/O was valid also in present time. In Slavonic this is so; root-thematic verbs may be of either vowel-grade in the present tense: R. berú 'I take'/žgú 'I burn'; or they may use the vowel grades to express the distinction between the present and aorist: R. berú/bral 'took'. The s-aorist imposed itself in new forms in Slavonic, and upon it was formed a new imperfect tense. The augment, if it ever affected the tribes who later formed the Baltic and Slavonic branches, has left no trace, save perhaps in the form discussed in section 51. The perfect has disappeared save for OB. vědě 'I know' (IE. *woidai cf. Gk. οἶδα), which remains in the Russian vedí 'after all'.

One further distinction effected by the verbal paradigm was that of nearness to the speaker and his hearer; this was the distinction of person, complicated by number: three persons and three numbers. It was effected by personal endings. The most primitive series was that of the athematic verbs, in which the three persons seem to be represented by possessive or possessive-demonstrative pronouns. Thus Sl. dami (*dad-mĭ) would have been originally 'my giving'. The personal endings expressed also tense, with a primary series for the present and future, secondary series for the aorist and imperfect, and another series for the perfect. The last drops out of Balto-Slavonic with the loss of the perfect, but the others remain.

48. *Classes of Conjugations, Verbal Suffixes*. It is from these elements that the Slavonic conjugations have been built. The infinitive-aorist stem is in each case independent of the present stem, but customary associations have hardened into definite paradigms. The principal types of conjugation are:

A. *Athematic*. A number of very simple verbs retain in the present tense the use of a primitive series of personal endings, which are attached without intervening vowel to the bare stem. They have all felt a strong attraction to the thematic conjugations, and only *es- 'to be' persists in being athematic in the modern tongues. This verb is notable also as using other roots (*bhū- *bhē- *bhondh- etc.) to complete the paradigm, and by playing a most important part in the conjugation of other verbs.

B. *Thematic*. With thematic verbs the basic principle is that the alternating vowels o/e are added to the root, to make a stem or base (theme) for the attachment of the personal endings in the present tense. The thematic vowels are also found outside the present, though absent from the sigmatic aorist in Greek.

Classification of thematic verbs is best done on the basis of the infinitive, distinct treatments of the present tense generally supplying sub-classes. The infinitive ends CSl.OB. in -*ti* preceded either by no suffix (*zero*-grade of suffix) or by one of five. So we may classify thematic verbs by the infinitive suffix, viz., (i) *zero* (ii) *n* (iii) *ě* (iv) *i* (v) *a* (vi) *ova*.

(i) *Zero-suffix:* infin. -*ti*. The present varies according to the nature of the last vowel or consonant of the root. The thematic *o* is found in 1*SPD* 3*P*, otherwise *e*. This leads to the modifications required by Slavonic principles of hardness and softness. There are seven sub-classes, defined by the last sound of the root:

1. *k g ch*. Infin. *-*kti* *-*gti* > *-*ti* (R. *č'*/WSl. *c(i)* Slov. *či* S. *ći* OB. *šti;* see section 40); present, first palatalization (*č ž š*) before thematic *e:* OB. *pešti* 'cook' *mošti* 'be able', S1. *pekǫ mogǫ* 2. *pečeši možeši*, R. *peč' moč'*, *pekú mogú, pečéš' móžeš'*. OB. *vrěšti* 'thresh' < **verch-*, S1. *vrchǫ*, S. *vŕći*, S1. *vŕšěm*.

2. *t d*. Infin. *-*tti* *-*dti* > -*sti* (section 46); present, palatalization in Polish. OB. *vesti* 'lead' *vedǫ*, R. *vestí vedú*, P. *wieść wiodę wiedziesz*.

3. *p b v*. Infin. *-*vti* > -*ti:* OB. *žiti* 'live' *živǫ*, R. *žíť živú;* *-*pti* *-*bti* > -*ti*, or with intrusive *s* -(*p*)*sti:* OB. *greti* 'scratch' *grebǫ*, R. *gresti* 'row' *grebú*, S. *grèpsti*.

4. *s z*. OB. *nesti* 'carry' *nesǫ*, R. *nesti nesú;* OB. *vesti*, 'convey' *vezǫ*, R. *vezti vezú*.

5. *m n*. Infin. nasal vowel (section 28): OB. *pęti* 'stretch' *dǫti* 'blow' < *penti *domti, *pinǫ dŭmǫ*, R. *vzjať* 'take' *vožmŭ*, P. *dąć dmę*.

6. *l r*. Infin. *tort*-formula (section 29): present, palatalization in Polish and Czech (section 41): OB. *klati* 'split' *mrěti* 'die', *kolǫ mirǫ*, R. *kolóť meréť koljú mrú*, P. *mleć* 'grind' *mrzeć, mrę mrzesz, mielę mielesz*, Cz. *mřiti mru mřeš*.

7. *vowel*. Present, suffix -*j*- or -*v*- (after *o*): OB. *biti* 'strike' *pěti* 'sing' *pluti* 'swim' *kryti* 'hide', *bijǫ pojǫ plovǫ kryjǫ*, R. *bju pojú króju, duť* 'blow' *dúju*.

(ii) *n*. Infin. -*noti*, present -*nǫ*. There are two sub-classes, due to the presence of a vowel or consonant before the nasal:

1. *vowel:* OB. *minǫti* 'pass' *minǫ*, R. *minúť*.

2. *consonant:* OB. *dvignǫti* 'move' *dvignǫ*, R. *dvinúť* (cf. *dvígať*), P. *ginąć* 'perish' *ciągnąć* 'pull'. In this sub-class the *n* is not found in the asigmatic aorist (OB. *dvigŭ*), but it appears in the sigmatic form (OB. *dvignǫchŭ*).

The nasal suffix has a perfective value. It resembles the nasal infix of Greek and Latin (Lat. *jungo* 'join'/*jugum* 'yoke'), but the nasal infix is not common in Slavonic: OB. *bǫdǫ* 'shall be', *sędǫ* 'shall sit', *lęgǫ* 'shall lie down', *grędǫ* 'come'/*sěsti lešti*, R. *búdu sjádu ljágu sesí leč'*.

(iii) *ě*. Infin. -*ěti*/after palatal -*ati* (section 25); present, suffix -*ěj*- or -*i*-:

1. *ěj:* OB. *uměti* 'know how to' *umějǫ*, R. *umét uméju*. Compare Lat. *manēre, maneo*.

2. *i:* OB. *trpěti* 'suffer' *trpl'ǫ trpiši*, R. *terpét terpljú térpiš'*; OB. *mŭčati* <**mŭčěti* 'throw'. The suffix is usually durative, and denotes a state.

(iv) *i* <**-ej-*. Infin. -*iti:* OB. *nositi* 'carry' *nošo* (section 41 *ad finem*) *nosiši*, R. *nosít nošú nósiš'*, *vozít* 'convey' *vožú, govorít* 'speak' (*góvor* 'talk, rumour, patois'). Often denominative, the suffix is iterative and causative. It commonly follows a root in the *o*-grade. (cf. Gk. ποτεῖται 'flutters'/πέτεται 'flies', Skr. *patáyati/pátati*).

(v) *a*. Infin. -*ati*; present, -*aj*-/-*j*-/root; also -*j*- in both stems.

1. -*aj*-: OB. *dělati* 'do' *dělajǫ*, R. *délat délaju*, Cz. -*eti* <-*ati* after palatal (*sázeti* 'plant'). These are denominatives, and mean to perform the action of the noun: R. *igrá* 'game' *igrát* 'play' (cf. Gk. τιμή τιμῶ τιμάω 'honour', Lat. *honos honorare*).

2. -*j*-: OB. *pisati/pĭsati* 'write' *pišǫ* <**pisjǫ* (sect. 41) *pišeši*, R. *pisát pišú*, Cz. *psáti piši*, P. *orać* 'plough' *orzę orzesz*.

3. *zero:* OB. *birati* 'take' *zŭvati* 'call' *kovati* 'forge', *berǫ zovǫ kovǫ*, R. *brat zvat lgač* 'tell a lie', *berú zovú lgu*, P. *brać biorę bierzesz*.

4. -*j*- in both stems: OB. *lajati lajǫ* 'bark, scold', R. *lájat láju*.

(vi) *ova*. Infin. -*ovati;* present, -*uj*- <**-ou-j*- (cf. Gk. δουλεύω 'serve'/δοῦλος 'slave'). These words are often denominatives: *obědovati* 'eat a meal'/*obědŭ* 'meal'. OB. *kupovati* 'purchase' *kupujǫ*, R. *torgovát* 'traffic' *torgúju*. After a palatal: OB. *kralevati* 'reign', R. *nočevát* 'pass the night'.

49. *Slavonic Aspects*. In addition to the principal distinction between perfective/imperfective, Slavonic offers two varieties of the latter, viz., durative/iterative; within the perfective series it is also possible to distinguish between momentary/terminative types, and within the terminative between ingressive/finitive according as definition is given to the beginning of the action or to its conclusion. The simple verbs of the first thematic class are for the most part imperfective in the sense of durative; they denote an act or state without limiting its continuance: R. *nestí* 'be carrying' *ittí* 'be going'. There are, however, some of them which are proper to momentary, and so perfective, action: R. *past* 'fall' *dat* 'give' *leč* 'lie down' *det* 'put' *sest* 'take one's seat' *stat* 'take one's stand' (pres. *stánu*, class ii). The nasal suffix (*n*, class ii) is generally perfective, and is used on a considerable scale to supply perfectives for the durative imperfectives of

the *ě*- and *a*- classes (iii, v) R. *gljadét* 'look'/*gljánut*, *dvígat* 'move'/ *dvínut*, *kidát* 'fling'/*kínut*, *trógat* 'touch'/*trónut*. There were, however, a certain number of imperfectives in the *n*-class: R. *gíbnut* 'perish' *mérknut* 'grow dark, fade' *tonút* 'sink'. In the *i*-class (iv) the denominatives are generally durative imperfectives (*chvalít* 'extol'/*chvalá* 'praise'); but the deverbatives, when based on a simple durative verb, are iteratives: *vodít* 'lead'/*vestí*, *nosít* 'carry'/*nestí*, *chodít* 'go, walk'/*šid-* 'be going'. The same discrimination is applied to the *a* (-*aj*-) class: they are durative when derived from nouns, but iterative when derived from verbs. This is, indeed, the principal source of iterative imperfective verbs: R. *byvát* 'be'/*byt letát* 'fly, fly around'/ *letét* 'be flying'. Otherwise the *a*- class is composed of durative imperfectives (iii 2–4), and they serve in pairs with perfectives in -*it*, of which there are a considerable number: *rešát* 'decide'/*rešít*, etc. Similarly, in the *ova*-class, the denominatives are durative, the deverbatives are iterative. The general effect of these suffixes, however, with the exception of *n*- and sometimes *i* < **ej*, was to supply additional imperfective verbs; for additional perfectives recourse was had to prefixes.

The effect of a prefix was to define the simple verb, and so to make it perfective: *nesti* 'carry'/*donestí* 'carry to a destination', *bit* 'strike'/ *izbít* 'beat to pieces, smash'. The prefix might define the action either by its end (*do- pri-*), or by its beginning (*vy- iz-*), giving either ingressive or finitive perfectives. An unexpected reversal of procedure occurs with *kupít* 'make a purchase' (perfective)/*pokupát* 'buy'. The prepositional prefix usually has, in addition, its own proper value, which it will be convenient to discuss later (section 74); but even so it normally makes the verb perfective. The ingressive sub-class is important because it is the ground upon which the perfective verbs have given equivalents for the future tense of other languages; the finitives serve to give definition in past time, in contrast to the unfinished duration of the imperfectives. In this way the tense-scheme of a Russian verb is obtained from the perfective/imperfective pair: perfective past definite, imperfective imperfect, imperfective present, perfective future (present tense in form), the imperfective future being expressed periphrastically. The grouping is mostly effected by denuding of individual meaning one of the prepositional prefixes, most frequently *po-*. It then does no more than define the verb. Examples are: R. *napisát* 'write down' *sdélat* 'do' *pročitát* 'read' *poiskát* 'make a search' *zarabótat* 'earn' *ukrást* 'steal' *výpit* 'drink up' *raskrýt* 'uncover'.

From these perfectives it is possible to obtain new iterative imperfects, thanks to the extensive use of the Slavonic suffixes *va yva ja*, as also from simple perfectives: *dat* 'give'/*davát*, *podát* 'serve'/ *podavát*, *nadét* 'put on'/*nadevát*, *výbrosit* 'throw out'/*vybrásyvat*, *ostanovítsja* 'stop'/*ostanávlivatsja*, etc. (It should be noted that *-ivati* acts like *-jivati* upon preceding consonants.) While it is always necessary to unite the imperfective and perfective forms of the verb in order to complete its full paradigm, it is sometimes necessary to add the iterative form as a third member of the group.

Some pairs are wholly unrelated: R. *brat/vzjat* 'take', *bit/udárit* 'hit', *klast/položít* 'put', *lovít/pojmát* 'catch', *govorít/skazát* 'say'.

The Slavonic imperfective aspect normally covers both the habitual and the durative present senses (e.g. Eng. 'I go'/'I am going'), but for a few simple words special forms are employed to distinguish these senses (e.g. R. *chožú* 'I go'/*idú* 'I am going'; cf. *letát letét* above). The words specialized to the habitual sense have disappeared from some languages, but in Czech, Polish and colloquial Russian they have had a considerable vogue, and led to a wide development of iteratives. A striking example is Cz. *on chodívává*, meaning 'he keeps going at irregular intervals'. The frequentatives of colloquial Russian (as distinct from those also admitted by the literary language) are only used in the past tense; e.g. *on govárival* 'he used to say'. In Russian only the imperfective (and, if there is one in the literary language, the iterative imperfective) can be used to form the compound future or in conjunction with such verbs as *to begin*.

A small number of verbs embrace both aspects in one form and may therefore be described as perfective-imperfective. Such is R. *ženítsja* 'to get married' (of a man).

Anything approaching a complete exposition of Slavonic aspects and their use e.g. in Russian would, even if within the capacity of the present writers, take up far more space than could be afforded in this book. Students of Greek will notice similarities between the use of the Slavonic perfective infinitive, imperative and participles and the forms of the Greek aorist, and distinctions of 'aspect' are plentiful in West European languages, including English (e.g. *I have come/I came/I was coming/I used to come*). Those who can read Russian should not fail to consult V. V. Vinogradov's Русский Язык (Moscow-Leningrad 1947) for a detailed examination of this complicated question, which, as Vinogradov says (*op. cit.* p. 477), is 'one of the most difficult and debatable and one of the least investigated departments of Russian grammar'. Here however is some indication of the position: The Russian *on chodíl* may be iterative, meaning 'he used to go', but may also mean 'he was (on a definite occasion) walking up and down'; the form of this verb with e.g. the prefix *s-* (*schodít*) may be the imperfective corresponding to the perfective *sojtí* 'to go down' but is also used as a perfective verb meaning 'to pop down'; in metaphorical expressions the non-iterative imperfect is used instead of the iterative, e.g. *nerédko nës* (instead of the frequentative *nosíl*) *vsju otvétstvennost'* 'he frequently bore the whole responsibility'; in certain negative constructions the imperfective is preferred to the perfective, and e.g. the negative imperative of a perfective verb may convey a warning: *ne poskol' zniś* '(take care you) don't slip'; the imperfective is frequently encountered when the foreign student would expect a perfective. Some of the at first sight anomalous uses of the imperfective for the perfective may perhaps be compared with the 'vivid' use of the French imperfect for the past definite.

50. *Personal Endings.* The chief formal distinction between nouns and verbs is due to the opposition of nominal case-endings and verbal personal endings. These serve to distinguish not only person, but also number and voice, and they belong to two series: primary/secondary. They were:

IE.	S1.	2.	3.	P1.	2.	3.	D1. 2 3.
Primary: athematic	-*mi*	-*si*	-*ti*	-*mos*/*mes* -*men*	-*te*	-(*o*/*e*)*nti*	-*w*- -*t*-
thematic	-*ō*						
Secondary:	-*m*	-*s*	-*t*	-*mo*/*me*	-*te*	-(*o*/*e*)*nt*	
OB. primary thematic	-*ǫ*	-*ši*	-*tŭ*	-*mŭ*	-*te*	-(*o*/*e*)*tŭ*	
secondary	-*ŭ*	-	-	-*mŭ*	-*te*	-*ǫ*/*e*	-*vě* -*ta* -*te*
OR. primary thematic	-*u*	-*š'*	-*t́*	-*me*/*mo*/*my*/*mịa*/*m* -*te*		-(*u*/*ja*)*t́*	-*vě* -*ta* -*ta*
MR.	-*u*	-*š'*	-*t*	-*m*	-*te*	-(*u*/*ja*)*t*	

The original force of the endings may have been possessive. IE. **es-mi* was probably 'my being' = 'I am', and **ei-mi* 'my going' = 'I go'. It is easy to recognize the first personal possessive in the termination, not the nominative **eĝo(m)*. The second and third singular would then also be possessives, but their form recalls the demonstratives in *s* and *t* which indicate nearer and remoter distance. The first person of the plural is a modification of the singular, and the first person of the dual is also recognizably the dual pronoun; but the other persons are more enigmatic.

S1. The ending -*mi* serves to give a name to the whole class of athematic verbs as 'verbs in -*mi*'. Thematic verbs end in -*ō* (Gk. φέρω), to which -*mi* was later added in Sanskrit (Skr. *bhárāmi* = Lat. *fero*, cf. Arm. *berem*). The Slavonic -*ǫ* may represent a subjunctive **-ām*, or an **-ō* to which **m* has been added: hence CSl.OB. *berǫ* 'I take', R. *berú*/L. *dìrbu* 'work' ⟨*uo* ⟨-*ō*⟩. In the secondary series -*om* > Sl. -*ŭ*. In the modern Slavonic languages, and especially in Czech, Slovak, Slovene and Serbocroat, there has been a notable extension of -*m* to certain classes or to all verbs. This originates in the -*aj*- class (v 1) which contracted -*aje*- to -*a*- (OB. *dělajetŭ*/Cz. *dělá* 'does'). Except for *S1.* (OB. *dělajǫ* OCz. *dělaju*) the tense showed endings like those of Cz. *dám*, which had been assimilated to the thematic class: hence Cz. *dělám* : : *dám*.

P1. OB. *nesemŭ* 'carry' R. *ljúbim* 'love' Ruth. *pytájemo* 'ask' P. *piszemy* 'write' Cz. *nesem(e)* Slov. *govorímo* 'say' S. *gòvorîmo* MB.

nósim 'bear' *bắrzame* 'hurry'. The source of most of these variations must have been an alternation of *-*mos*/*mes*, so that *-*mos* >-*mŭ* -*m* *-*mes* >*me*. Ruth. -*mo* may be compared with Skr. -*ma* <*-*mo*. In a strong position, such as might occur syntactically, *ŭ*+*j*- (initial of the next word) would become *y*, whence OB. -*my*. The pronoun *my* 'we' would also influence this ending as in Polish. MB. -*me* starts with the athematic verbs. L. *dìrbame* has no final *s*.

*D*1. L. -*va* Sl. -*vě* [Skr. -*vas* (prim.)/*va* (sec.), Avestic -*vahi*/*va*, Goth. *habōs* 'we two have'/*habaiwa* (subj.)]. With this conflict of testimony one cannot go beyond the assertion that the first person dual was something involving *w*. The corresponding pronoun was CSl.OB. *vě* (*va* 'ye two'); other parallel formations were *dŭva* 'two' *oba* 'both' and the NA*D*. *M*. -*a*/FN. -*ě* of *o*- and *a*-stems. Hence the change of vowel in Slov. *mìdva govoríva* 'we two say'.

*S*2. OB. *jesi* 'thou art' Ruth. *jesý* P. *jesteś* Cz. *jsi* S. (*jè*)*si* is difficult to explain. IE. *es-si >Homeric ἐσσί Skr. *assi* have the same short vowel as in the thematic -*si*, but the Old Bulgarian form implies *-*sī*, which might derive from *-*sai* (*S*2. middle, Skr. *bhárase* Gk. φέρεαι Goth. *bairaza*). L. *esì* is short, but appears to have been shortened from *esíe <*essai. (Cf. Gk. future: ἔσομαι ἔσει or ἔση). The disappearance of the middle voice from both Baltic and Slavonic makes some scholars reluctant to accept an explanation based upon a middle-voice survival. They prefer to consider that a short vowel has been lengthened. Slavonic languages other than Old Bulgarian show a short vowel in the thematic conjugation, which would naturally depend upon -*sĭ*, but might be due to shortening of -*sī* in final position. However the long vowel originated in the athematic conjugation, it was doubtless from thence that it spread to the thematic. Some thematic verbs offered the case of *s* following *i* (e.g. *chvališi* 'thou praisest'), and this was generalized to all thematic conjugations as OB. -*ši* (R. -*š'* P. -*sz* Cz.Slov.S.MB. -*š*). The secondary ending -*s* disappeared.

*P*2. L.CSl.OB. -*te* P. -*cie*. Skr. -*tha* (prim.)/-*ta* (second.) makes a distinction not observed in Gk. φέρετε/ἐφέρετε. Both *th* and *t* would give BSl. *t*.

*S*3. OB. *nositŭ* 'bears' R. *nósit*/P. *czyta* 'reads' Cz. *nese* Slov. *govorí* 'says' S. *gòvorî* MB. *nósi* Ruth. *pytáje* 'asks'/*chvalýt* 'praises' OR. *nosit́*. MR. *jest́* 'is' and OP. *jeść* (1350) retain the soft ending which has gone out of Russian in historical times. The soft form is sometimes found in Old Bulgarian (-*tĭ* for -*tŭ*), but the instances may be due to scribal error. A hard -*tŭ* is implied by those languages which have no personal ending, and it must therefore be supposed to ascend to Common Slavonic date. Thus CSl. *-*tĭ*/*tŭ* for IE. *-*ti*. It is difficult to explain -*tŭ* otherwise than as an example of the liability to confuse *jers* in final position. It has been suggested that it represents the secondary middle -*to*, but there is little plausibility about such a survival; or it may be a demonstrative *tŭ* 'that one'. Even so the loss of personal ending would only be explained by the hardening of the *jer*. The secondary ending -*t* is lost, so that secondary $S2 = S3$. The *ŭ* in strong position may become *o*, and before *j*- may become *y* (OB. *možeto sĭ* 'this one can', *proslavity jĭ* 'he will glorify him').

$P3$. IE. *-*nti*. There has been the same treatment of final *jer* as in the singular. This person has been lost in Lithuanian; the $S3$ is used instead. The thematic vowel and nasal coalesced in a nasal vowel (OB. *nesǫtŭ* 'they carry'), which was not palatalized after a suffixed *-*j*- as in class v (*znajǫtu*). OB. *naricajǫ* (Codex Suprasliensis) is an early form without final -*t*, which has disappeared from Polish, Czechoslovak, Slovene and Serbocroat, with compensatory lengthening of the vowel. R. *suť* 'are' contains the only survivor in the plural of the Old Russian soft final *t*.

$D23$. It is difficult to be certain what were the terminations of these persons. Skr. (prim.) 2. -*thas* 3. -*tas*/(second.) 2. -*tam* 3. -*tām* correspond only imperfectly with Gk. $D23$. φέρετον/2. ἐφέρετον 3. ἐφερέτην. There is no third person in Gothic or Lithuanian: the second person is represented by L. -*ta* Goth. -*ts*. OB. $D2$.-*ta*/3.-*te* differs from OR.$D23$.-*ta*; there is a tendency in Old Bulgarian to associate these endings with the dual of the demonstrative *tŭ* (*M. ta FN. tě*), and to import into the conjugation a distinction of gender: $D23.M.$ -*ta* *FN*. -*tě*. It is so in Slovene for all three persons.

The dual survives only in Slovene and Wendish (Wend.$D1$. -*mej* cf. *mej* 'we two').

51. *Athematic Verbs.* **Es/s/ēs*- 'be'. The present tense runs:

	$S1$.	2.	3.	$P1$.	2.	3.	$D1$.	2.	3.
IE. **es-*	-*mi*	-*si*	-*ti*						
**s-*				-*mos*	-*te*	-*onti*	-*w-*	-*t-*	-*t-*
OL. *es-*	-*mi*	-*i*	~-*ti*	-*me*	-*te*		-*va*	-*ta*	
OB. *jes-*	-*mĭ*	-*i*	-*tŭ*	-*mŭ*	-*te*		-*vě*	-*ta*	-*te*
s-						-*ǫtŭ*			
MR.			*esť*			(*suť*)			

OB. *jesmŭ* is found alongside *jesmĭ*, but rarely. OPr.$S1$. *asmai* 2. *assai/essei* make it probable that L. *esmì* stands for *esmie, a middle form (Gk. ἔσομαι); but OB. *jesmĭ* must be the active (Gk. εἰμί), while *jesi* may represent a middle ending (see section 50, $S2$). The accent originally fell on the stem in the singular and on the ending in the plural and dual, but the vocalized form of the stem was restored by analogy to all persons but the $P3$. *sǫtŭ*. Macedo-Bulgarian *set* Slovak dial. *sa* may represent an alternative CSl. *sęt- (Skr. *santi* Dorian Gk. ἐντί). A reduced form of the $S3$. *jestŭ* appears in the negative form *ně* 'is not'/*něstŭ* (*němĭ něsi* etc.). In the modern languages the stem is variously treated. In Polish the tense is rebuilt on $S3$. *jest* (*jestem* etc./

są); in Wendish the first syllable is lost (som); in Czech it is reduced (jsem etc.); and Serbocroat shows a double conjugation (jèsam/sam and even su/jèsu). From the same stem is formed the present participle: OB. M. sy F. sǫšti (<*sonts *sontjā), L. ēsąs (GS. sañčio F. santì).

The formation of the Slavonic imperfect makes it probable that there was a past tense in *ēs- akin to Homeric Gk. ἦα(<*ēsm̥)'was', Skr. āsam, and used as an auxiliary like Lat. -eram in fueram 'had been'. In Common Slavonic and Old Bulgarian it had no existence apart from the imperfect tense. It may have run (with secondary thematic endings)

IE.?	*ēs-	-om	-es	-et	-mos	-te	-ont	-w-	-t-	-t-
ProtoSl. (j)a-ch-	ŭ				-omŭ		-ǫ	-ově		
š-		-e	-e		-ete				-eta	-ete

The long vowel in Sanskrit is due to the augment, but of this there is no other trace in Balto-Slavonic. In Greek perfect-endings are used, so that the stem may be a lengthened perfect (cf. *ed/ēd- Lat. ēdi 'ate' OB. jadętŭ 'they eat'). Initial *ē- >ja- (section 25) because of the palatal on-glide, and this glide must have dropped between vowels, perhaps starting with forms like děla(j)achŭ 'did'.

*Bhū-/bheu-/bhewā- etc. The past tenses of 'to be' are formed from variants of one root, and are thematic throughout. IE. *bhū- gives Gk. φύω 'grow' (poetically πέφυκα ἔφυν 'am') Lat. fu-i 'was' L. buvaũ infin. búti, and OB. aor. bychŭ infin. byti past partic. act. byvŭ bylŭ. The imperfect is from *bhē- Eng. be, OB. běachŭ (?*bhē-ēsom)/ běchŭ. The conditional OB. bimĭ (bi bi bimŭ biste bǫ) is not easy to account for, and was replaced in the Old Bulgarian era by bychŭ, which has been reduced to an invariable by in Russian. These are mostly perfective-imperfective verbs; the perfective OB. bǫdǫ (*bheu-n-d/dh-, with suffixed -d- or -dh- and infixed -n-) R. búdu was specialized to express the future. The imperative was CSl.OB. bǫdi.

This verb acquired extraordinary importance in Slavonic from its use as an almost universal auxiliary. The present tense with the participle in -lŭ of a principal verb formed the perfect tense of that verb; it has generally ousted the aorist in East and West Slavonic; běachŭ/běchŭ+-lŭ made the pluperfect, later analysed into the perfect of byti+-lŭ; imperfective verbs formed their future (at first future perfect) by bǫdǫ+-lŭ or infin. -ti, but chŭtěti 'wish' iměti 'have' were also used as auxiliaries of the future (S. -ću); bimĭ+-lŭ expressed the conditional, later giving place to the aorist bychŭ and thence to the invariable by (originally aor. S23.).

One other feature of this verb is the unique survival in it of a former future formed by means of the suffix -sj-, which was desiderative in effect as in Lat. esurio (*-sjō) 'desire to eat, be hungry'. To L. búsiu would correspond CSl. *byšǫ, and to the future participle L. búsęs corresponds OB. (*M. byšę*) N. *byšǫšteje/byšęšteje*, which was used to render Gk. τὸ μέλλον 'what will be, the future'. OCz. *probyšúcný* 'useful' is derived from this future participle by adding a prefix and an adjectival suffix.

52. **Ei/i-* 'go'. Gk. εἶμι OL. *eimi* are athematic, but OB. *idǫ* (<*jĭdǫ* <*ĭdǫ*) has passed over to the thematic class, thanks to a formative suffix *-d-* <*-d-* or *-dh-*. OB. infin. *iti* corresponds to L. *eīti*, but the *-d-* was inserted in Russian, giving *idtí ittí*. P. *iść, idę, idziesz*, with analogical infinitive.

*Sthā- 'stand' **dhē-* 'put'. Gk. ἵστημι τίθημι. The first has become thematic by the addition of the suffix *-j-* followed by the thematic vowels: L. *stóti*/R. *stojat* (<*stə-jěti*). The second had a present athematic in OL. *demi*, etc., but thematic in Slavonic, with the aid of the perfective present suffix *-n-*, R. *dénu (deĭ)*.

*Dōd- 'give' **ed/ēd-* 'eat' **woid-* 'know' Sl. *iměti* 'have'. These run:

			S1.	2.	3.	P1.	2.	3.	D1.	2.	3.
OB.	da-	ja-	vě-	-mĭ	-si	-stŭ	-mŭ	-ste		-vě	-sta	-ste
	dad-	jad-	věd-						-ětŭ			
	im-a-			-mĭ	-ši	-tŭ	-mŭ	-te		-vě	-ta	-te
	im-								-ǫtŭ			

IE. **dedōmi* >Skr. *dádāmi* (with a different vowel of reduplication from Gk. δίδωμι) suffered an unusual metathesis to **dōd-* in Balto-Slavonic: OL. *duomi* ML. *dúodu* CSl.OB. *damĭ* <**dad-mĭ*. The second *d* was assimilated before *m* and *v* (section 45), dissimilated to *s* before *t* (section 46), and so remained only in the third person plural. Before *t* this gave endings unlike those of the thematic verbs, and in all languages (except R. *dast*) the *s* has fallen away by analogy. That has left athematic only *damĭ* and its descendants. *Damĭ* has, however, exerted a powerful influence on the thematic conjugations in some languages, wherever *a* appears in the final syllable, especially in contracted verbs and those of the *va*-class (VI). From these it has even passed to the whole set of paradigms in Slovene and Serbocroat. *P3. dadętŭ* is from **-ṇti*. Alongside *damĭ* there appeared the thematic *dajǫ*. OB. *jamĭ* and *věmĭ* have the same characteristics as *damĭ*. The perfective OB.*S2.* *izě* 'ate' has *ě* (not *ja*) since the vowel is not then initial. *Imamĭ/imějǫ* is a thematic verb partially attracted into the athematic verb. Present participles: OB. *jady* (G*S.* *jadǫšta*) Cz. *jeda;* imperative OB. *daždĭ* < **dadjĭ jaždĭ* R. *eš'* Ruth. *ĭdž;* aor. *dachŭ* (*S2.* *dastŭ* from the present) *jasŭ/jachŭ;* impf. *daděachŭ jaděachŭ*. The aorist and imperfect correspond to no ancient formula.

*Woid- Gk. οἶδα 'know' was an unreduplicated perfect, with perfect personal endings. It has generally been assimilated to *damĭ* in Old Bulgarian, but there survived a middle **woidai* (Skr. *vede*) in CSl.OB. *vědě* (R. *ved*).

An isolated athematic form is OB. *sętŭ* 'says he' $<$ **kens-ti* Lat. *censet*, and a sporadic imperative OB. *viždĭ* 'lo' (R. *viš'* $<$ *viž'*).

53. *Thematic Present Indicative.* The paradigm may be summarized thus:

		S1.	2.	3.	P1.	2.	3.	D1.	2.	3.
IE.	*bher-	-ō	-esi	-eti	-omos(i)/omes	-ete	-onti	-owes	-et(h)es	-etes
Skr.	bhar-	-āmi	-asi	-ati	-āmas(i)	-atha	-anti	-āvas	-athas	-atas
Gk.	φερ-	-ω	-ειϛ	-ει	-ομεν/ομεϛ	-ετε	-ουτι		-ετον	-ετον
OB.	ber-	-ǫ	-eši	-etŭ	-emŭ	-ete	-ǫtŭ	-evě	-eta	-ete/eta
	zna-	-jǫ	-ješi	-jetŭ	-jemŭ	-jete	-jǫtŭ	-jevě	-jeta	-jete/jeta
(iv)	chval-	-jǫ	-iši	-itŭ	-imŭ	-ite	-ętŭ	-ivě	-ita	-ite/ita
(iii 2)	slyš-	-ǫ	-iši							
OR.	ber-	-u	-eš'	-et'/e	-em/emy/emo/eme	-ete	-ut́/u	-evě/eva	-eta	-eta
Arm.		berem			beremk'		beren			
L.	dìrb-	-u	-i	-a	-ame	-ate		-ava	-ata	

Concerning classes of verbs and stems see section 48. The two classes with suffix *-i-* (iii 2, iv: from **ī* and **ej*) have in the *P*3. -*ętŭ*, which seems to have been borrowed from the athematic verbs, since **-int-* would have given **-it-*. The thematic vowel *o* originally applied to *SPD*1.*P*3., but in Slavonic *PD*1. have gone over to thematic *e* (as in Armenian); *P*3. retains thematic *o*. Final consonants of root verbs (class i) which are liable to hard/soft alternation formally oppose *S*1.*P*3. to other persons, and as the present participle has the hard vowel it is commonly said to be 'formed from the stem of the third person plural'. That is not scientifically stated; it is formed from the hard or normal stem.

*S*1. The occurrence of the nasal element has not been satisfactorily explained. If not due to the subjunctive *S*1. **-ām*, it was not, as in Sanskrit, an extension of athematic *-mi*, though probably connected, albeit remotely, with the first personal pronoun. The Lithuanian *-u* represents IE. **-ō*. *S*2. -*ši* represents the normal Slavonic evolution of *s* after *i* and before a front vowel in *chvališi* 'praisest', and from such words spread to others like *bereši*, where it was not due to sound-laws. R. -*š'* shows the short final vowel to be expected from IE. **-si*, but, in view of Old Bulgarian, it is generally considered a shortening of -*ši*, though this is not a necessary conclusion. OB. -*ši* is then accounted for by the influence of *jesi* 'art', if this represents a middle **essai/essei* (section 51). In consequence of these developments there is an opposition in OB. -*ši/si* (athematic) which the modern languages have largely eliminated by extending *š* to the athematic verbs. So Cz. *dám dáš dá* is thematic except in *S*1., and this in its turn has enabled *dám* to extend the suffix -*m* to the thematic conjugations in Czechoslovak and Serbocroat. *SP*3. -*t* $<$ IE. **-ti* occurs in Old Russian and was the development to be expected, but Old Russian also has forms without *t*, partly due perhaps to the aorist (in which final **-t* drops). *P*1. has a range of alternate forms in Old Russian (cf. section

50), to which Middle Russian added -*mja*. D1. -*vě* is found with -*va*, on the analogy of *dŭva* 'two' and other duals in *a*. The confusion of D23. -*ta*/*te* is found in Old Bulgarian, and is normal in Old Russian. Because of the conflict of evidence between Greek and Sanskrit it is not possible to determine exactly the Indo-European form for these two persons.

54. *Imperative* (*Optative*). In the imperative proper the idea of an action is announced in an emphatic tone; the tone implies expectation that the action will be carried out by the person who hears it. There is thus no need to specify the person by using a personal ending, or employ any sign of mood. As with the vocative for names of things, the bare stem suffices. At most, it is convenient to distinguish between singular and plural: Gk. φέρε φέρετε. Other persons are not properly addressed in this fashion, but rather become objects of an expression of nearer or remoter contingency (subjunctive or optative). The remoter contingency is of the nature of a wish that the action announced may take place. Hence, in some languages, the use of the imperative *SP*.2 goes with that of the subjunctive or imperative in other persons. The expression of a wish is, however, also appropriate to second persons, and is less brusque than a command. In Slavonic the optative has wholly ousted the imperative. In Lithuanian, subjunctive [*dìrbčiau dìrbtum*(*ei*)etc.] and imperative (*dìrbk*) remain distinct, but have been refashioned from other materials than in Slavonic.

The optative was formed with an element -*i*-:

thematic:	S1.	2.	3.	P1.	2.	3.	D1.	2.	3.
OLat. s-iē-	-m	-s	-t						
s-ī-				-mus	-tis	-ent			
Skr. s-yā-	-m	-s	-t	-ma	-ta	(syus)	-va	-tam	-tām
OB.		daždĭ			dadimŭ etc.				
hematic:	*-m	*-s	*-t	*-mo/me *-te		*-nt	*-w-	*-tom	*-tām
Gk. φερ-ο-ι-	-μι	-ς	-	-μεν	-τε	-εν		-τον	-την
OB. ber-i-	-	-							
-ě-				-mŭ	-te		-vě	-ta	-te/ta
slyš-i-	-	-		-mŭ etc.					

From the Old Latin paradigm it would appear that the athematic suffix was *-*jē*- in the singular and *-*ī*- in the plural, with the weak form of the stem. This seems to have resulted in Sl. *-*jĭ*-/-*i*-, so that *S*23. *dad-jĭ* 'give' became OB. *daždĭ* (*jaždĭ věždĭ viždĭ*), with P2. *dadite*. In the thematic paradigms the optative suffix -*i*- was preceded by the *o*-grade thematic vowel, forming a diphthong. This diphthong was differently treated according to its position, since final *-*oi* >CSl. -*i*/medial *-*oi*- >CSl. -*ě*-. Preceded by a palatal element, however, the group *-*joi* >CSl. *i* : *slyšite* 'hear ye', *znajite* 'know ye'. Partly perhaps on the analogy of the athematic imperatives with short final vowel, the *S*2. -*i* has been shortened in modern Slavonic languages, and has usually disappeared save as a softening of the stem-consonant

(R. *buď* 'be'/OB. *boḍi*), and the plural has been reformed upon this singular (R. *budte* 'be ye', Cz. *piš pište* 'write').

55. *Present Participles and Gerunds.* (*a*) *Active.* The formative element is *-nt-*. Before this suffix came a vowel: Gk.Skr.BSl. *o*/Lat. *e:* Gk. ὤν 'being' <*sonts*, OB. *sy*/Lat. *-sens* (*praesenš*) <*sents*. In the feminine there was used an additional suffix *-jā:* Gk. οὖσα<ὄντια< *sontja*. In Lithuanian and Slavonic the oblique cases of the masculine and neuter have received the additional suffix *-jo-:* OB. *idy* 'going' GSMN. *idošta*, and those of the feminine continue the use of *-jā-:* L.GSF. *sùkančios* OB. *idoštę.* OB.NSF. *idošti* (with *i* from the reduced form of the suffix *-iə*) is due to the analogy of the other cases. A preceding palatal transformed *o* (from *-ons* *-onts*) into *ę:* OB. *znaję* 'knowing'/fem. *znajošti* GSMN. *znajošta.* Verbs with present in *-i-* have *-ę-* like the 3 pl.pres.: *sědę fem. sědęšti.*

Being adjectives, all participles have definite and indefinite declensions in Old Bulgarian (section 70), and the pres.part. *-y-jĭ* tended to be confused with the past part. *-ŭ-jĭ*, which also gave *-y-jĭ* by the lengthening of *ŭ* before *j*. To remove this difficulty there was a tendency to replace *y* by *ę*, especially in the Codex Zographensis (*gręḍęi* 'coming=*gręḍę-jĭ*/*gręḍy-jĭ*, which also represented *gręḍŭ-jĭ*). In the modern languages the indefinite present participle has become a gerund through the disuse of its cases: R. *nesjá* 'bearing' (*-ę*), *búdučí* 'being' (OB. *-ošti*). In Modern Bulgarian the gerund is *-ajki/ejki* (dial. *k* <*tĭ* OB. Standard B. *št*).

The participial declension was important in Old Bulgarian for certain syntactical reasons which have ceased to be influential. There was little subordination of clauses. Each clause tended to have equal value, as in Homer's Greek. Each finite verb was a principal verb. But by way of compensation we find nouns associated with participles, which were not finite parts of the verb and so did not constitute main clauses. In this way there arose equivalents for indirect discourse, the absolute construction, and other subordinate clauses; e.g.:

OB.: *egda že synŭ tvoi* izědy *tvoe iměnĭe sŭ ljubodĕicami pride.*	When thy son, having devoured thy goods with harlots, came.
vĕdĕachǫ gospodja samogo sǫšta.	They knew He was the Lord (indirect discourse, cf. Gk. μέμνημαι ἐλθών 'I remember I went').
sĕjǫštjumu ova padǫ pri pǫti i *pridǫ pŭticę nebesĭskyjǫ i pozo-bašę ja.*	As he sowed, these fell by the wayside and the birds of heaven came and ate them (dative absolute, Gk. αὐτοῦ σπείροντος).

[L.: *sākè tavè šìrgēli* pragĕrusį. They said you had watered the
horse.

mán važiúojant *snìgo*. As I drove (to me driving) it was
snowing.]

The choice of case for the absolute construction has been varied in
the various Indo-European languages. In English it is now the
nominative; in Latin it was the ablative, in Greek the genitive, and in
Balto-Slavonic the dative. The construction comes fully into existence
when one case is fully specialized.

When conjunctions became more varied and more frequently used
the need for participial subclauses, and so for participial declension,
was much diminished.

(*b*) *Passive*. Formed from the present stem with the suffix -*m*-:
L. *nēsamas* 'borne' OB. *beromŭ* 'taken' *znajemŭ* 'known' *chvalimŭ*
'praised'. It is possible that the suffix may have been originally *-*mn*-,
the *zero*-grade of *-*men*-. OPr. *poklausimanas* 'being asked' is an
isolated example of the fully vocalic suffix, which provides middle
participles in Sanskrit and Greek: Skr. *bháramanas* Gk. φερόμενος.
The *zero*-grade is found in Lat. *alumnus* 'nurseling' (*alo* 'nourish').

56. *Infinitive and Supine*. Infin. probably *-*tēi* L. -*ti* (dial. -*tie*, -*t*)
CSl.OB.Cz.Slov.S. -*ti* R. -*t* -*ti* P. -*ć* [*-*kti* *-*gti* >OB. -*šti* R. -*č'*
P.Cz. -*c*(*i*) Slov. -*či* S. -*ći*]; supine *-*tum* L. -*tŭ* CSl.OB. -*tŭ* Cz. Slov. -*t*.

L. *búti* 'be' OB. *byti* R. *byt* P. *być* Cz. *býti* Slov.S. *biti*

L. *nèšti* 'carry' OB.Cz.Slov. *nesti* R. *nestí* P.*nieść*

OB. *mošti* 'be able' R. *moč'* P. *móc* S. *mòći*

L. *dúotų* 'give' (Lat. *datum*); OB. *sŭpatŭ* 'sleep' Cz.Slov. *spat*.

The tenses hitherto discussed belong to the present system; those
that follow are based on the aorist stem. With the loss of the aorist in
many Slavonic languages the aorist stem is to be found in the infinitive,
and consequently it is from the infinitive stem that the other parts of
the conjugation seem to derive. Yet the infinitive does not seem to have
been a settled part of the paradigm in Indo-European. The situation
then must have been like that of present-day Finnish, in which the
verbal root is modified by several suffixes to make nouns from which
the infinitive is derived by means of several different case-endings. The
verb Finn. *saa*- 'get, receive' admits the four suffixes -*da* -*de* -*ma* -*min*,
to which may be added the case-endings of the nominative, inessive,
instrumental, elative, adessive, abessive, instrumental or translative,
making in all ten infinitive forms. In Vedic about a dozen infinitives
can be distinguished. The accusative and dative cases are predominant,
and among other forms are encountered Skr. *dātum* (Lat. *dātum*) *dāváne*
(Gk. δοῦναι <δοϜέναι) *dātáve* (with -*tu*-+*ai*) 'give'. Homeric Greek has
a similar variety of infinitives used interchangeably, and Classical

Greek, though restricting each form to a particular use, still offered four infinitives in each voice: present, future, aorist (λῦσαι 'loose') and perfect. The Slavonic infinitive corresponds to the aorist only.

The supine was the accusative of direction of motion from a *u*-stem noun, and was suitable for use after verbs of motion: Slov. *óče grê spàt* 'father goes to bed' (literally 'to sleep'), cf. Lat. *spectatum ire* 'to go to see'. There is nothing to correspond to Lat. *mirabile dictu* (loc.) 'wonderful to say' (literally 'in the telling').

The infinitive was also a nominal case, but it is more difficult to determine the declension, though the case is clearly locative. An original *-tēi* would satisfy the Lithuanian and Slavonic forms, since Lithuanian would allow shortening of the final vowel resulting from this diphthong. In Russian *-ti* remains when the suffix was accented under the de Saussure-Fortunatov rule. The ending was originally unaccented, but has a rising tone which attracted to itself a previous falling stress; this occurred when the penultimate syllable had a short vowel or a long falling vowel. Thus *nêsti* became *nêsti* (Roman type indicating the stressed syllable). The final vowel, if unstressed, is always shortened in Russian (*brat* 'take'), and there are a number of doublets resulting from analogy (R. *vesti/vesí* 'lead'). The special development of **kt *gt* (verbs of class i 1) leads in Polish to a distinction between infin. *-c/ć*. In Modern Bulgarian the infinitive has been lost, save for a few traces. As in Modern Greek and other neighbouring tongues, a finite construction is preferred: MB. *toj možá da spi* 'he was able to sleep' (cf. MGk. φοβοῦμαι νὰ τὸ πῶ 'I am afraid to say so', Rum. *doresc să lucrez* 'I want to work').

For the types of infinitive see section 48. In verbs of class ii, formed with the perfective present suffix *-n-*, the infinitive keeps the suffix, which is not found in the participles or the older forms of the aorist tense.

57. *Past Participles.* (*a*) *Active I.* IE. **-wos/wes/us-* and **-wot/wet-* (fem. with additional suffix **-jā;* masc. with additional **-jo-* in oblique cases); L.*M.* *-ęs* N. *-ę* F. *-usi*, CSl. OB.*M.* *-(v)ŭ* F. *-ŭši* (with *-i-* from **-iə-* as in the pres. part.).

L.*M.* *sùkęs* N. *sùkę* F. *sùkusi* 'having turned' (*GSM. sùkusio*) (cf. Gk. εἰδώς εἰδότος, Homeric F. ἰδυῖα 'knowing' <**weidwos *weidwotos *widusjā*); CSl.OB. *davŭ* F. *davŭši* 'having given' (*GSM. davŭša*); *nesŭ* 'having borne', *dvigŭ* 'having moved' (class ii), *bivŭ* 'having struck' (i 7), *chvali/chvalivŭ* 'having praised' (iv).

The Lithuanian past participle has been influenced by the present participle active in the nominative singular of the masculine and neuter, so as to end in **-ents*. In Slavonic **-wos* >-*vŭ* and **-us* >-*ŭ* give the two suffixes in use, but after *j* the *ŭ* palatalizes and the suffix is -'ĭ (*chvalĭ*), and at a later date an analogical form was recreated for this verbal class (*chvalivŭ*). In the feminine the *zero*-grade suffix *-us- was followed by an additional *-jā/iə (*nesŭši*), as in the Homeric-Greek form cited. The masculine oblique cases are in *-us-jo-, doubtless as the result of remodelling the declension, since the Greek parallels show a change of suffix in that gender from *-wos to *-wot.

(b) *Active II*. IE. *-lo/lā, CSl.OB. M. -lŭ N. -lo F. -la.

CSl.OB. *neslŭ* 'having borne' *dviglŭ* 'having moved' *minǫlŭ* 'having passed' *šĭdlŭ* OB. *šĭlŭ* 'having gone'.

The proper function of this suffix seems to have been to derive adjectives from verbs, as Lat. *credulus* (*credo*) 'believing', cf. R. *gnilój* (*gniĭ*) 'putrid'. Apart from Slavonic it enters the verbal paradigm only in Armenian, where it serves to form the infinitive: Arm. *el* 'to be'. It has become specialized in Slavonic to form periphrastic tenses, viz., the perfect, pluperfect, future perfect and conditional. In some languages it helps to form the future, for which other languages prefer to use the infinitive. The auxiliary is omitted in the Modern Russian perfect tense; in Serbocroat and in direct speech in Bulgarian it is retained for all persons, and in Polish and Czech normally for the first and second person. The *l* when final gives WR. -ŭ Ruth -v S. -o (Ruth. *pytáv pytála* 'asked' S. *pitao pitala*).

(c) *Passive in -tŭ*. The suffix *-to/tā served to form verbal adjectives from nouns or verbs, as in Lat. *barbatus* (*barba*) 'bearded' *sceleratus* (*scelus*) 'criminal' *genitus* (*gen-*) 'begotten'. In Slavonic it was attached to root verbs ending in *i ě rě* (CSl. *er) ę, which also take -tŭ in 23.S. aorist: OB. *jętŭ* 'taken' *klętŭ* 'accursed' *načętŭ* 'begun' *pětŭ* 'sung' *rasprostrtŭ* 'spread'. These verbs show the *e*-grade of the nasal and vibrant diphthongs (*em *en *er), and o/e-grades of the diphthong in *i* (*oi *ei). OB. *otvrstŭ* 'open' *uvęstŭ* 'crowned with a wreath' *izvěstŭ* 'known, sure' show this suffix in purely adjectival forms.

(d) *Passive in -enŭ*. It is applied to root-verbs (i) not included above, notably to the *o*-grade nasal diphthong (*om): OB. *nesenŭ* 'borne' *pečenŭ* 'cooked' *nadŭmenŭ* 'swollen' (-dŭm-, *dǫti* <*domti*). In the other verbal classes those with infinitive stems in *a ě* elide the vowel of the suffix: OB. *danŭ* 'given' *dělanŭ* 'done' *povelěnŭ* 'ordered'. Those ending in *i/y* transform these to *ĭj/ŭv* in hiatus before the suffix: OB. *bijenŭ/bĭjenŭ* 'beaten' *obŭvenŭ* 'shod'. The proper function of this suffix also was to make adjectives from verbs: OB. *plnŭ* 'full' Lat. *plenus*.

Possibility was implied by the suffix -*ĭnŭ*, but most often impossibility with a negative prefix: OB. *neizdrečenĭnŭ* (*ne-iz-reč-*) 'unspeakable'. In OB. *izvěstĭnŭ* 'known' the suffix does not seem to add to the participial meaning.

58. *Verbal Noun in -ĭje-*. This suffix was added to participial stems in -t/n-: OB. *dělanije* 'deed' *raspętĭje* 'crucifixion' R. *délańe*

raspjátie (the latter a form from Russian Church Slavonic). (Gk.-ιον, Lat.-*ium*).

59. *Aorist.* (*a*) *Asigmatic.* This aorist is found only with verbs of classes i and ii. Verbs of class ii (-*n*- in present and infinitive) have no nasal in the aorist stem:

		S1.	2.	3.	P1.	2.	3.	D1.	2.	3.
IE.		*-om	*-es	*-et	*-omo/me	*-ete	*-ont	*-ow	*-etom	*-etām
Gk. Homeric	λαβ-	-ον	-ες	-ε	-ομεν	-ετε	-ον		-ετον	-ετην
OB.	*nes*- 'bear'	-ŭ	-e	-e	-omŭ	-ete	-ǫ	-ově	-eta	-ete
	dvig- 'move'	-ŭ			-omŭ		-ǫ	-ově		
	dviž-		-e	-e		-ete			-eta	ete

The personal endings are of the secondary series, and the tense is thematic. The *o/e* alternation affects the final consonant under the conditions of the first Slavonic palatalization: OB. *tekŭ/teče* 'flow', *dvigŭ/dviže*. It is an old type of aorist, depending upon Indo-European vowel-mutation for a stem characteristic of the tense, and it has not survived in the modern languages. Even in Old Bulgarian the tendency was to use for it one of the two variants of the sigmatic aorist, i.e. the aorist formed by means of a tense-suffix *-s-.

Since Slavonic did not maintain the Indo-European vowel mutation *o*/O unimpaired, it was not in a position to discriminate precisely between the imperfect and aorist of the original tradition. In Greek the second aorist (so called, but really the first in order of time) is found with only a comparatively narrow range of verbs which clearly distinguish between the vocalism of the present and aorist stems: Gk. λείπω 'leave', impf. ἔλειπον/aor. ἔλιπον, λαμβάνω 'take', ἐλάμβανον/ ἔλαβον, but λύω 'loose', ἔλυον/ἔλυσα (sigmatic aorist, since the asigmatic would evidently coincide with the imperfect). It is a nice point in dealing with each separate Slavonic verb to decide whether the form surviving as an asigmatic aorist was originally aorist or imperfect. Imperfects are OB. *padŭ* 'fell' *běgŭ* 'ran' *idŭ* 'went'.

Verbs of the first class ending in a vowel (i 5–7, see section 48) have no asigmatic aorist.

(*b*) *Sigmatic, without vowel of support.*

		S1.	2.	3.	P1.	2.	3.	D.1	2.	3.
IE.	*-s-	-m̥/om	-s/es	-t/et	-mo/omo	-te/ete	-nt/ont			
Gk.	ἔδειξ-	ἔλυσ-	-ᾰ	(ᾰς)	-ε	(-ᾰμεν)	-(ᾰτε)	-ᾰν		-ᾰτον	-ᾰτην
Skr.	*ádik-ṣ-*	-am	-as	-at	-āma	-ata	-an	-āva	-atam	-atām
OB.	*ně-s*- 'bear'	-ŭ			-omŭ	-ete	-ę	-ově	-eta	-ete
	zna-ch- 'know'	-ŭ	-	-	-omŭ			-ově		
	zna-									
	zna-s-					-te			-ta	-te
	zna-š-						-ę			
	ję-s- 'take'	-ŭ			-omŭ	-te	-ę	-ově	-ta	-te
	je-		-tŭ	-tŭ						
	da-ch- 'give'	-ŭ			-omŭ			-ově		
	da-s-		-tŭ	-tŭ		-te			-ta	-te
	da-š-						-ę			

The personal endings were secondary in Indo-European, but it is not quite certain whether they were attached to the suffix -s- directly or by means of the thematic vowels o/e. Gk. ἔλυσα implies IE. *-s-m̥, and ἔλυσαν implies IE. *-s-n̥t/nnt; but $S2.$, $P12.$, $D23.$ have been provided with the vowel -a- by analogy, and $S3.$ ἔλυσε implies IE. *-s-et, and was doubtless influenced by the forms of the asigmatic aorist (ἔλιπε). In Sanskrit the vowel -a- is found in all persons representing *o/e. In Old Bulgarian the personal endings vary. $P3.$ represents *-s-nt for all verbs; $P2.$ -te $D2.$ -ta $3.$ -te are attached directly to the suffix in verbs ending in a vowel (classes i 7, iii–vi) and in the athematic conjugation. $SPD1.$ have the thematic vowel o in all instances.

The treatment of the second and third persons singular is especially complex. In root-verbs ending in a consonant (i 1–4), which have an asigmatic aorist, there is no sigmatic $S23.$ The vowel of the root may be lengthened by compensation for loss of a final consonant. Thus $S1.$ *nek̑-s-om >*nes-som >OB. ně-sŭ 2. *nek̑-es >nes-e 3. *nek̑-et > nes-e. Verbs ending in an original diphthong (*em *en *er *el *ei *oi) may borrow from the present $S3.$ -t, and extend its use to $S2$: OB. $S23.$ jętŭ pitŭ (i 5–6, cf. section 57, past part. -tŭ). Similarly $S3.$ *dōd-s-t >OB. dastŭ (jastŭ bystŭ), which takes the place of $S2.$ *dōd-s-s; but a compound of jasti has aor. $S23.$ iz-ě.

Verbs whose infinitive -ti is preceded by a vowel (i 7, iii–vi) conjugate like znachŭ: $S1.$ *ĝnō-s-om >OB. zna-ch-ŭ 2. *ĝnō-s-s >zna 3. *ĝnō-s-t >zna, since both final consonants fall. So also OB. brachŭ bra 'took', glagolachŭ glagola 'said', velěchŭ velě 'commanded', chvalichŭ chvali 'praised'.

The remaining complications are due to the varying treatment of IE. s in Slavonic. The s remains when not preceded by i u r k and when not affected by analogy: *nek̑-s-om >OB. ně-s-ŭ but *ēd-s-om/ OB. ja-ch-ŭ : : by-ch-ŭ <*bhū-s-om. When preceded by i u r k original s becomes ch before a back vowel and š before a front vowel, but remains s before a consonant: *tek-s-om >OB. tě-ch-ŭ, *tek-s-nt >OB. tě-š-ę, *tek-s-te >OB. tě-s-te. Analogy is at work in *ĝnō-s-om/OB. zna-ch-ŭ and other verbal stems ending in a vowel other than u/i. (See section 33.)

(c) Sigmatic, with vowel of support -o-.

OB. id-o-ch- $S1.$ -ŭ 2. 3. $P1.$ -omŭ 2. 3. $D1.$ -ově 2. 3.
  -s-   -te   -ta -te
  -š-   -ę

It will have been noted that most verbs had a vowel before the personal endings of the aorist, either because of a suffix (classes iii–vi), or because the root ended in a vowel (i 7) or a diphthong which had become a vowel (i 5–6). On that analogy a vowel was added to consonant-stems also (i 1–4, ii), viz. -o-. In class ii it was attached to the aorist-stem, if consonantal: *dvig-o-chŭ*, but to the infinitive stem when the aorist was vocalic: *mi-no-chŭ*, with elision of *o* after *o*. On this analogy, the infinitive-stem of consonantal roots in this class was employed: *dvig-no-chŭ*. As there were no sigmatic forms of *S*23. in these classes of verbs, there were none either in the secondary aorists.

60. *Imperfect*. (See section 51). A tense of purely Slavonic formation, it runs:

zna- sě- děla- chvala- + *-ach-*⎫ S1. *-ŭ* 2.   3.   P1. *-omŭ* 2.   3. *-o* D1. *-ově* 2.   3.
                    -aš-⎬   *-e* *-e*   *-ete*   *-eta* *-ete*
chotě- + *-ch/š-*⎭

The formation of this tense is a debated problem in Slavonic. The theory here followed is that the ending represents **jachŭ* ⟨**ēsom* attached to an aorist-stem, and it has the important support of Lat. *ju-eram* ⟨**esam*, while the lengthened root **ēs-* is attested by Gk. Homeric ἦα Skr. *āsa* ⟨**ēsm̥* (perf.). The use of *o/e* between the root and the personal endings is then according to the practice of asigmatic aorists, as also the ending **-nt*, and the fact that there are only the two derivatives of IE. *s*, viz. *ch* before *o* and *š* before *e*. The difference from the sigmatic aorist is steadily maintained, though it became difficult to retain, and in the early history of the extant languages the confusion of imperfect and sigmatic aorist is a common feature.

This explanation is, however, not without serious difficulties. If *s* is to give *ch/š* it must be preceded by *i* (according to the rule concerning *i u r k*, section 33). But there is no *i* in **ēs-*. In the initial syllable of an independent word *ě* ⟩*ja-*, but we do not know at what period this occurred, and whether this **j-* would suffice for the purposes of the rule. Besides, **jachŭ* does not survive anywhere as an independent word, and in the termination *-achŭ* there is nothing to represent the supposed **j-*. Some scholars, in consequence, have turned to a theory that the imperfect is a late, and somewhat arbitrary, set of variations upon the sigmatic aorist. That theory, in its turn, gives no help in explaining the differences between the imperfect and aorist endings, though these differences are at once intelligible from the postulated **ēsom*.

A point of initial divergence for the various theories is found in the doublets of Old Bulgarian: *děl-achŭ/aachŭ chot-ěchŭ/ěachŭ b-ěchŭ/ěachŭ*. As to the last pair, *běchŭ* 'was' is an aorist (*S*23. *bě* P2. *běste* 3. *běšę*, etc.) used as an imperfect, and *běachŭ* is evidently a new formation on the analogy of thematic verbs. In Old Bulgarian forms these verbs appear to demonstrate the derivation of the contracted forms from the longer uncontracted ones. But great uncertainty prevails, with intermediate states like *slověaše* 'said' *idaaše* 'went', etc.

The vowel of support in the imperfect is *a/ě*. That is readily understood of verbs which have these vowels in the infinitive-stem (iii 1, v vi). When the vowel of the infinitive is *i*, the imperfect is perhaps in *ě: *chvaléachǔ*; which leads to *chvalaachǔ*. In other cases the use of *ě* as a new formative element is evident: *nes-ě-achǔ* (after a palatal, *a: teč-a-achǔ*), *mǐr-ě-achǔ*, *bor-ě-achǔ*, etc. Where *ě* is a formative element only, it is attached to the present-stem, not to the aorist: *dvign-ě-achǔ*.

The sigmatic aorist introduced a formal distinction between the aorist and the present tense which was not expressed by the Indo-European *o*/O-grades of the same root. The aorist thus became identified with perfective past time, and required some correlative form for imperfective past time. The notion of time thus came to be more prominent than aspect when comparing aorist and imperfective with the present. But the forms of the imperfect were fluctuating, and were easily confused with those of the aorist. Interchanges of form once being admitted, the distinction of aspect in past time could not be consistently maintained, and a welcome awaited any other method of attaining this end. This was given by the new Slavonic distinction between imperfective and perfective verbs through prefixes (perfectivating imperfective verbs) and the suffixes -*va/yva/ja*- (imperfectivating perfective verbs). These pairs allowed both time and aspect to be adequately represented, since the functions of the aorist were fulfilled by the past of a perfective verb, and those of the imperfect by the past of an imperfective verb. Tenses with their functions adequately performed by other means were menaced with dissolution, the more so as their personal endings were otherwise unsupported, and were ambiguous (*S*2. and 3.). Their *raison d'être* had been lost, and there existed a simple analytical way of expressing past time through the auxiliary and the participle in -*lǔ*. At length both tenses disappeared from East and West Slavonic, apart from Wendish, and from Slovene among the South Slavonic languages.

(ii) NOUNS, ADJECTIVES, PRONOUNS

61. *Declension.* By means of declension nouns are equipped to play their parts in the sentence. It is necessary to define the relation of the named parties to the main phenomenon, i.e. to show how the nouns are related (or 'fall', Gk. πτῶσις Lat. *casus*) to the verb, whether as source of the phenomenon (subject), or wholly determined by it (object), or affected in some way, as by receiving (recipient). These relations may be expressed, as in English and Chinese, by position and by the use of 'empty' words; but in Indo-European they were indicated by elements suffixed to the stem. In addition to these main relations there are others of secondary importance which Indo-European and such other languages as Finnish and Basque represent

by case-suffixes. To define the relation of noun to noun within the sentence the adjectival genitive case was employed, signifying either possession or an attribute. Relations of place (*in*, *from*, *to*) seemed easy to define, and also the concept of agency or instrument; from these come the adverbial cases: locative, ablative, accusative of motion, instrumental. In Finnish or Basque this kind of adverbial definition can be carried to great length. There is no limit to the number of modifications possible in a Basque noun, but Finnish and Esthonian declensions are considered complete with fifteen or sixteen cases, including the inessive, adessive, abessive, illative, lative, elative, translative, caritative, etc. Such refinements show dissatisfaction with the cruder definition possible through the Indo-European case system. The Indo-European cases confuse different relations under the same symbol, so that, for instance, the same sign serves for both the possessive and the partitive genitives. The symbols themselves were not so firm as to resist decay, and all languages show some reduction in the number of cases originally available. Balto-Slavonic identified the genitive and ablative cases, which were only differentiated in the *o*-stems. The use of prepositions to supplement the defective information provided by case-endings has led in many languages to reliance upon the preposition for this purpose, and the consequent disuse of case-endings.

In the agglutinative languages number appears as a symbol which is lacking in the singular and present in the plural, but is additional to the case-suffixes. In Indo-European, however, the ending expresses both number and case, and there are very few symbols which, like the Gk. —δε and —φι, can be used in any number. The fusion of case and number, and the modifications often needed in the stem, close the declensional system. The various declensions then run parallel to each other, number to number and case to case, and invite comparison. While the Slavonic conjugations tend to isolate the tenses and moods, giving a separate history to each, there is a continual going to and fro between the declensions.

The first cause of declension in pronouns was possibly different. As different words are used for 'I' the actor and 'me' the sufferer, it is possible that, to a primitive mind, these two situations seemed essentially different. 'Thou' and 'thee' are also distinct words, but they observe a relationship. 'My' the possessor and 'to me' the recipient are in that sort of relationship to 'me' the sufferer; and so a declension is formed; but it is one very different from that of the nouns.

Adjectives are declined by apposition to their nouns. In Balto-Slavonic they were made definite by means of a suffixed demonstrative article, so that they have two declensions, an indefinite noun-type declension, and a definite compound noun-pronoun type, in which the nominal cases tend to disappear. The adjective reproduces various different noun-declensions, and the rules of concordance between adjective and noun give rise to the category of gender in grammar. In consequence of this fact, declension is said to reveal gender as well as number and case.

Apart from these three declined categories there are numerous indeclinable words in a sentence (adverbs, prepositions, conjunctions, interjections) which often have the form of nominal cases.

62. *Noun-declensions.* (a) *Suffix-less, athematic consonant-stems.* IE. **ĝhan-s* AS. *ĝhan-m̥* 'goose' **ĝhwēr-s -m̥* 'animal', Gk. χήν–ά θήρ–ά μῦς 'mouse' χθῶν 'earth', Lat. *rex* <**rēg-s* DS. *-i* 'king' *cor(d) -i* 'heart'. In this type of declension the root ends in a consonant to which the case-endings are directly added. It must have been widely developed in the original tongue, but has almost disappeared in Slavonic. CSl. **kry* <**kruw-s* 'blood' gave way to its own accusative *krŭvĭ*, and so is classed among the *i*-stems in Old Bulgarian; so also OB. *gǫsĭ* 'goose' *zvěrĭ* 'animal' *myšĭ* 'mouse'. In this way the *i*-stems (suffixless, athematic vowel-stems) remained as the oldest surviving type of Slavonic declension. Its subsequent diminution to the advantage of the *jo*-stems (thematic) belongs mainly to the history of the separate languages. The consonant-stems tended to be lost in all languages by the effect of suffixes which transferred words to other declensions: OB. *sr̥dĭce* 'heart' (suffix **-iko*) *zem(l)'a* 'earth' (suffix **-jā*) Gk. καρδία 'heart' (suffix **-jā*) Lat. *cruor* 'blood' (suffix *-or*).

(b) *Suffixless, athematic vowel-stems. I-Stems.* There were roots ending in *u* and *i*, taking the case-endings without intervening vowel. Those in *-u* [see (e) below] have been fused with thematic *o*-stems, no longer constituting a separate declension in the modern tongues. The identity of the *i*-stems remains, but they have been much diminished by transfers to the *jo-/jā*-stems which have the advantage of better defined case-endings. In historic times there has been a tendency to identify this declension with the feminine gender, and indeed each declension with a definite gender. That tendency was in play before the historical record opens, since the neuters of this class (Gk. μέλι Lat. *mel* 'honey'), together with the *u*-neuters (Gk. μέθυ 'mead' Lat. *cornu* 'horn'), did not survive as such into Old Bulgarian. There remained a few masculines: OB. *gospodĭ* 'lord' *pǫtĭ* 'road' *gostĭ* 'guest' *ogńĭ* 'fire' *ludije/ludĭje* (pl.) 'folk', etc. They have since passed mostly into the *jo*-declension. Feminine words were liable to transfer by means of suffixes: OB. *ovĭca* (suffix **-ika*)/Lat. *ovi-s -m* 'sheep'. On the other hand the class has been augmented by means of the numerous *i*-suffixes listed in section 78. The suffixed vowel seems to have been liable to alternation, giving the variants *i/ei/oi* and *u/eu/ou*, as NS. **ponti-s* GS. **pontei-s* LS. **pontēi*, and **sunu-s *sunou-s* *sunēu*. The *i*-stems have greatly influenced the declension of consonant-suffix words.

(c) *Consonant-suffix, athematic words.* -R- -N- -NT- -S- -Ū. R: IE.
mātē(r) 'mother' *dhughǝtē(r)* 'daughter' L. *móte* 'wife' *duktě* OB.
mati dŭšti (CSl. *dŭťi*) R. *mať doč'*. Only these two words, both feminines, survive in Old Bulgarian. Cz. *net'* 'niece' is an *i*-stem (Lat.
neptis) assimilated to the two *r*-stems. Even the two *r*-stems tend to
give way, as in S. *mâjka* P. *matka* 'mother', and most of the words
originally belonging to the group have joined other declensions: OB.
otĭcĭ 'father' R. *otéc*/Lat. *pater* is due to a baby-word (Albanian *at*
'father' Gk. ἄττα 'daddy') plus thematic suffix *-iko*, OB. *bratrŭ bratŭ*
'brother'/Lat. *frater, sestra* 'sister'/L. *seser-*, R. *svëkor* 'father-in-law'
(declined as an *o*-stem)/Lat. *socer*, OB. *zętĭ* 'son-in-law' R. *zjať* L.
žéntas/Lat. *gener* Albanian *dhëndër* 'bridegroom'.

N: masc. Gk. ἄκμ-ων A*S.* -ονα 'anvil' Lat. *hom-o -inem* 'man' L.
akm-uō ~-eni 'stone' OB. *kam-y -enĭ -plamy* 'flame'. The accusative
singular imposed itself on the nominative even in Old Bulgarian:
N*S.* *kamenĭ plamenĭ korenĭ* 'root' *jelenĭ* 'hart', etc., so that the original
-y ⟨*-ōn* is imperfectly represented in the texts. The transference of
all masculine *n*-stems to the *jo*-declension became easy thereby:
kamenĭ : : koňĭ 'horse'. A N*S.* *di* 'day' may be preserved in P. *dziś*
'today' (?*di sĭ* 'this day'), and would answer to Lat. *di-es*. OB. *dĭnĭ* is
thus seen to be a masculine *n*-stem, R. *deń* P. *dzień* etc.

N: neut. Lat. *nomen* 'name' OB. *imę* 'name' G*S.* *imene vrěmę* 'time'
brěmę 'burden' *plemę* 'tribe' *sěmę* 'seed', etc., R. *ímja* etc. With the
withdrawal of the masculine words, the *n*-neuters form a clearly
defined class in all Slavonic languages.

NT: neuters of exclusively Slavonic formation, with a precisely
defined sphere of meaning, viz., the young of humans and animals:
OB. *otroçę* 'child' G*S.* *otroçęte telę* 'calf', etc., R. *ditjá* 'child' G*S.*
ditjáti.

S: neuters with suffix *-os/es-:* IE. *nebh-os* G*S.* *-es-os* NAP. *-es-a*,
Gk. νεφ-ος *-εος* (ους) *-εα* (η) OB. *neb-o -ese -esa* 'sky, heaven' *slovo*
'word' *tělo* 'body' *drěvo* (CSl. *dêrvo*) 'wood' *liko* ⟩*lice/ličes-* 'face'
kolo 'wheel' *divo* 'wonder' *luto* 'trouble' *čudo* 'miracle' *istesa* (pl.)
'kidneys'. This class of words is masculine in Lithuanian (*měn-uo*
-esis 'month'), but the Slavonic masculines have passed to other
declensions (OB. *měsęcĭ* with suffix *-iko* R. *mésjac*). The ending
NA*S.* *-o* resembles that of *o*-stem neuters in *-o*, and all these words
tend to pass into the *o*- declension; but they figure in it with double
stems *neb-/nebes-* in several languages, occasionally carrying one stem
through the singular and another through the plural. OB. *neb-u -omĭ*
occur, and, on the other hand, *těles- drěves- ličes-* are found only in the
oldest stratum of documents. The words *oko* 'eye' and *ucho* 'ear' also

belong to this class (*oces- uses-*). Alongside the stem with suffix they also have the bare stem in the plural: OB. *oka ucha;* but in the dual have been assimilated to *i*-stems: *oči uši*. They are very important physical doublets, and have been the cause of most other dual survivals in the modern tongues: R. *óči úši pléči* 'shoulders' *koléni* 'knees'.

Ū : Sl. *y/ŭv-*. IE. **swekrū-s* 'mother-in-law' **snusū-s* 'daughter-in-law' Skr. *çvaçr-ūs* GS. *çvaçr-vās* Gk. νυός Lat. *socrus nurus* OB. *svekr-y* AS. *-ŭvi, neplody* 'barren woman' *luby* 'love' *cěly* 'healing' *žrny* 'corn-mill' *loky* 'puddle' *crky* 'church'. The words either refer to females or are abstracts (with few exceptions) and so feminine. As with the *-y* resulting from **-ōn*, this NS. *-y* < **-ūs* yielded to the AS. *-ŭvi*, so that even in Old Bulgarian it maintained itself with difficulty. By way of *-ŭvi* these words were transferred to the *i*-stems: R. *svekróv ljubóv cérkov*. A further shift was to the feminine *a*-declension: R. *snochá* 'daughter-in-law' P. *snecha* S. *snàha svěkrva crkva*.

(*d*) *Suffix -ā/jā-, athematic.* Formerly abstract or collective suffixes, and so giving rise to neut. pl. *-a*, they apparently became feminine through the inclusion of **gʷenā* 'woman' Sl. *žena*. Names of offices are abstracts and belong to this class, but those which are normally held by men give rise to an *a*-class of 'natural' masculines, which is well-represented in Slavonic: OB. *sluga* 'servant' *vladyka* 'ruler' cf. Gk. κρίτης 'judge' Lat. *agricola* 'farmer'. A feminine *ī*-declension is exemplified by Skr. *patn-ī* 'wife' AS. *-īm* GS. *-yās/sen-ā -ām -āyās*. From the genitive onwards cases are those of *ja*-stems. In Old Bulgarian and elsewhere there are noms. in *-i* < **-iə/ĭji:* OB. *bogyńi* 'goddess', *sǫdĭji* (masc.) 'judge', whence by assimilation to the *ja*-stems: R. *sudjá* P. *sędzia*, etc.

(*e*) *Thematic o/jo-stems and athematic u-stems.* In Slavonic the *u*-stems are masculine only; the thematic declension is masculine and neuter but not feminine. Owing to the contamination of the two declensions it is hard to be certain which Slavonic words belong by origin to the *u*-declension. The best criterion is the genitive singular which opposes Sl. *u/a*. By this criterion can be identified OB. *synŭ* 'son' *volŭ* 'ox' *vrchŭ* 'top' *domŭ* 'house' *medŭ* 'honey' *polŭ* 'half' and some others (cf. L. *sūnùs* Gk. μέθυ Lat. *domus* L. *viršùs*). In cases formed by a vowel, a diphthong developed: NP. **sūnewes* OB. *synove*. These longer endings proved attractive because they were distinctive, and tended to extend over the thematic declension, as much as other cases tended to be sacrificed to that declension. Their use is sometimes also associated with the masculine gender in the modern languages, since the *u*-stems included no neuters. Soft forms were in *-eve:* OB. *vrači* 'wizard' NP. *vračeve, zmĭji* 'snake' NP. *zmĭjeve*.

The thematic *o/jo*-stems are masculine and neuter: masc. **-os* > L. *-as* CSl. *-ŭ*, soft **-jos* > **-jŭ* > **-jĭ* > *-'ĭ*/neut. **-om/jom* > *-o/e*: IE.

*wl̥kʷos 'wolf' L. vil̃kas OB. vl̥kŭ R. volk, OB. koňĭ R. koň 'horse', OB. krajĭ 'country'/*sed- OB. selo 'field, farm' R. seló 'village' lice 'face' znamenije 'sign'. To the root were added the thematic vowels o/e before the case-ending, and when this is vocalic there have resulted diphthongs which give Slavonic monophthongs. The e-grade occurred originally in the vocative singular only, and involved the first Slavonic palatalization of velars (k g ch >č (d)ž š: OB. Bože 'O God'); the o-grade formed a diphthong which gave ě/i and the second palatalization in the locative singular and nominative and locative plural (k g ch >c (d)z s/š: LS. Bo(d)zě LP. Bo(d)zěchŭ NVP. Bo(d)zi).

NAVSN. -o/e was due to a reaction against the sound-law which caused ASM. *-om to become -ŭ. Without this reaction masculines and neuters would have become identical; but that, in a language trusting to flexion to elucidate its meaning, was inconvenient. Masculine gender pertained not so much to males as to things conceived as self-moving, and so capable naturally of being the subject of a verb, since they could cause its phenomenon. There were other things naturally inert, and so provided only with the accusative sign *-om. If by convention they became the subject of a sentence they still did not take the sign of the agent -s, like the masculines. But if *-om >-ŭ in all cases this distinction between the self-moving and the inert, so important for primitive thinkers that they deified the one and ignored the other, would disappear. That it did not disappear was due to the reaction towards neut. -o/e. This affected also the adjectives, and therefore also the concord of noun and adjective, and so preserved the notion of three genders in Slavonic, against the general tendency to reduce to two: masculine/feminine as in Lithuanian or French, epicene/neuter as in Dano-Norwegian and some Greek adjectives.

A circumstance favouring the retention of o in the neuter was that the neuter of the demonstrative *tod >Sl. to retained the vowel, which was only closed to ŭ by a final *m n or s (see section 31).

63. Gender. The first important distinction between nouns seems to have been made between animates and inanimates. It is all that appears in Hittite, a very early form of Indo-European. As animates the barbarian mind regards all things apparently self-moving, i.e. not only men and animals, but water, fire, the sky, etc., as inanimates, all that are inert or receptive. But concerning the same thing there exist different points of view. Children and the young of animals are often deemed inert, but so too are women (Germ. Weib neut.), while the sky is both self-moving (L. diēvas 'God' Gk. Zεῦς Lat. dies) and inert (R. nébo), according to the standpoint of the speaker. The inert class (neuters), as we have seen, would not naturally be subjects of verbs, and so differed from the other (masculines) by not taking the *-s of the nominative. In all this sex is not a consideration. The distribution of

Slavonic words between the masculine and neuter still follows, in the main, the animistic criterion. The feminine gender was added by reason of a suffix specialized to abstract and collective terms, which happened to contain the key-word of female sex (*$g^w en\bar{a}$ 'woman'). In the collective sense it was suited to express the plural of inert things (neuters), at first, as Greek syntax shows, in the singular. Because of this category of feminine words the animate declension became more distinctively male. Even the introduction of the sexual criterion, however, does not suffice to give grammatical gender. It creates more categories of nouns, but has no syntactical importance until adjectives are differentiated to correspond to the nouns. In Slavonic the adjectival declensions were much simplified, so that the opposition of genders was according to an obvious pattern: OB. nov-ŭ/o/a 'new' or t-ŭ/o/a 'that'. This pattern clearly distinguished the nominative neuter from the masculine, and so maintained both these genders, despite the identity of their oblique cases.

In Slavonic there has been a continuous process of adaptation of declension to gender.

64. *Number*. Indo-European had three numbers: singular/plural/dual distinguished by the conceptions unit/many/pair. All three remained in Old Bulgarian, but the dual as such is used only in Slovene and Wendish among the modern languages. Its meaning was compromised very early by a shift from the notion of 'pair' to that of 'two things', not necessarily paired, and consequent normal association with OB. dŭva 'two' oba 'both' (cf. L. mù-du 'we two'). But with 'two' signified by the numeral, there was evidently little need of repeating the numerical idea in the noun, the more so since the nominative dual endings were such as could readily be confused with other cases. In the modern languages the dual remains concealed in plurals of exceptional formation or as the apparent genitive singular after certain numbers (2–4, and similarly 22 23 24 etc.).

On the other hand the opposition unit/many is open to cavilling, since there are objects which, when unit is added to unit, still retain the notion of unity, e.g. sand and its grains, peas in a basket, heads in a crowd, etc. In such cases the antithesis is not so much 'unit/many' as 'singulative/collective'. This criterion has had free play in the Slavonic languages. The collectives are either plural or singular in form, and in some instances original singular collectives have later come to be construed as plurals, thus adding to the number of plural suffixes recognized by the modern languages. From such a collective if an individual was to be signalized, it had to be picked out by a kind of isolating process, either by using a word with no collective value (OB. človĕkŭ 'man'/ludije 'people', dĕtištĭ 'child'/dĕti 'children'), or by a singulative suffix (as OB. graždane 'citizens'/graždaninŭ 'citizen').

65. *Paradigms of Nouns.* The following paradigms from Slavonic and other languages are given for comparison, and as a basis for subsequent notes on cases:

I-stem

	SN	A	G	Ab	D	L	I	V
IE. *ow-i-	s	m	es	d	ei	e/i	ē?	-
		n	os		ai		m-?	
-ei-		*N*.i	s					
Gk. πολ	ıς	ıν	εως		ει			ı
Lat. ov-	is	im	is	ī(d)	(e)i	i		
L. nakt-	is	į	ies			yje	imi	ie
nakč-					iai			
CSl.OB. *M. pǫt-*	ĭ		i		i		ĭmĭ	i
F. kost-							ijǫ	
OR. *put-*	´				i		´m̆	i
kost-							´ju	
							iju	

Consonant-stem

	SN	A	G	Ab	D	L	I	V
IE. *māte(r)	-	m̥				i		-
*mātr-			es		ei	i	ı	
			os					
			s					
Gk. μητηρ/ποιμην	-							
μητερ/ποιμεν-		α	ος		ı			
μητρ-			ος		ı			
ὀνομα/νεφος	-	-						
ὀνοματ/νεφε-			ος		ı			
Lat. *homo*	-							-
homin-		em	is		i	e		
L. *mótè*	-							
moter-		i	s		iai	yje	ia	ie
L. *akmuõ/mènuo*	-							
akmen-		i	s		iui	yje	iu	ie
mènes-			io					i
CSl. *mati*	-						-	
mater-		ĭ	e		i	i/*e	ijǫ	
OB. also								
OR. *mati*	-						-	
mater-		´/e	e		i	i	´ju/iju	
CSl.*kamy/korę/dinĭ*								
kamen/din-		ĭ	e		i	e	ĭmĭ	
imę/telę/slovo	-							
imen/telęt sloves-			e		i	e	ĭmĭ	
OB. also							emĭ	
OR. *vremja*	-	-						-
vremen-			e/i		i/e?		´m̆	

PNV	A	G	Ab D	I	L	DNAV	GL	DI
s / s / s	ns	om/ōm on/ōn	-bh/m-		su	e/ē? ī ī	os	-bh/m-
ες ις / s / vs	εις īs is	εων ium ių	ibus ims	imis	εσι yse	εε ει i	εοιν im	εοιν
je	i	ιjï	īmŭ	īmï	īchŭ	i	ïju	īma
je je	i	´i ij	´m	´mi	´ch	i	´ju iju	´ma
es	ns ns	ōm	-bh/m-		su	i?	jos?	-bh/m-
ες	ας	ων			(ποιμεσι) ασι	ε		οιν
α	α	ων			σι	ε		οιν
es	es	um	ibus					
s	is	ų	ims	imis	yse	i		im
s ai	is ius	ų ių	ims iams	imis iais	yse	iu		im iam
*e	i	ŭ	īmŭ emŭ	īmi	īchŭ echŭ	*i	*u	*īma
e/i	i	-/´i/ii	´m	´mi	´ch	i?	´ju/iju	´ma
e	i	ŭ	īmŭ	īmi	īchŭ	i	u	īma
a	a	ŭ	īmŭ emu	y	īchŭ echu	ě	u	īma
a	a	-	´m	y ´mi?	´ch? och ech	i?	u?	´ma

U-stem

	SN	A	G	Ab	D	L	I	V
Skr. çvaçrū-	s	m						
çvaçrv-			ās		āi	ām	ā	
çvaçr-								u
OB. svekry	-							-
svekrŭv-		ĭ	e		i	e	ĭjǫ	

A-stems

IE. *ekw-	ā	ām/ān	ās		āi	āi	ā(m)	a
Gk. χωρ-	α	αν	ας		ᾳ			
Lat. mens-	a	am	ae	ā(d)		ae		a
L. rank-	a	ą	os		ai	oje	a	a
žem-	ė	ę	és		ei	ėje	e	e
CSl. rǫk-	a	ǫ	y				ojǫ	o
rǫc-					ě	ě		
struj-	a	ǫ	ę/ě		i	i	ejǫ	e
sodij-	i							
OR. žen-	a	u	y		ě	ě	oju	o
duš-	ja	ju	ě		i	i	eju	e

U- and O-stems

IE. *sūnu-	s	m	s					-
*sūnew/u-					ei	-/i		-
*sūnow/u-								-
*sūnv-			es/os		ei			
*medh-	u	u						
*wl̥kw-o-	s	m/n	sjo/so			i	-bh/m-	-
-e-						i		-
-ō-				d	i		(m)	
Gk. πηχ-	υς	υν	εως		ει			
ἀστ-	υ	υ						
λυκ-ο-	ς	ν	ιο/υ					
λυκ-ε-								-
λυκ-					ῳ			
Lat. mang-	us	um	ūs	ū(d)	ŭi	ū		
gen-	u	u						
lup	us	um	ī	ō(d)	ō			
jug-	um	um						
L. sūn-	us	ų	aus		ui	uje	umi	au
vyr-	as	ą	o		ui	e	u	e
eln-	is	į	io		iui	yje	iu	i
CSl.OB. syn-	ŭ	ŭ	u			u	*ŭmĭ	u
							omĭ	
synov-					i			
OB. grad-	ŭ	ŭ	a		u	ě	omĭ	e
sel-	o	o						
CSl. kraj-	ĭ	ĭ	a		u	i	emĭ	u
lic-	e	e						
OR. volk-	-	-	a		u/ovi		oḿ	
volč-								e
volc-						ě		
kon-	'	'	ja		ju	i	eḿ	ju
					jevi			

PNV	A	G	Ab D	I	L	DNAV	GL	DI
s / as	nãm		bhyas	bhis	su	āu	os	bhyām
i	i	ŭ	amŭ	ami	achŭ	i	u	ama
ās	ās	?	-bh/m-		āsu	ai		-bh/m
αι / ae	α(ν)ς / ās	ῶν / ārum	is/(ābus)		αις(ασι)	α		αιν
os / es	as / es	u̯ / iu̯	oms / ėms	omis / ėmis	ose / ėse	i / i		om / ėm
y	y	ŭ	amŭ	ami	achŭ	ě	u	ama
ę/ě / ę	ę/ě / ę	ĭ	amŭ	ami	achŭ	i / i	u	ama
y / e	y / e	- / -	am / jam	ami / jami	ach / jach	ě / i	u / ju	ama / jama
es		ns	-bh/m-		su/si?			
ū	ū	ōm / ns	-bh/m-		isu			
s		m		is		(u)	u(m)	
εες/εις / εα/η	εις / εα/η / νς/υς	εων			εσι	ει		εοιν
		ων		οις	οισι	ω		οιν
ūs / us / i / a	ūs / ua / ōs / a	uum / ōrum		ubus/ibus	īs			
ūs / ai / iai	us / us / ius	u̯ / u̯ / iu̯	ums / ams / iams	umis / ais / iais	uose / uose / iuose	u / u / iu		um / am / iam
	y		*ŭmŭ / omŭ	ūmi	*ŭchŭ / ochŭ	y		ŭma
e / i	y / a	ŭ	omŭ	y	ěchŭ	a / ě	u	oma
a / š	ę/ě / č	ĭ	emŭ	i	ĭchŭ	a / i	u	ema
ove	y	ov/-	om	y	och	a	u	oma
i	ě	'/ev?	em	i	ěch / ich	ja	ju	ema

66. *Singular cases.* (*a*) *Accusative.* (i) Bare stem, neuters: **nmen* >
OB. *imę* 'name' (cf. Gk. ὄνομᾰτ- < **(o)nomnt-*) R. *ímja*, **telent* >OB.
telę 'calf', IE. **klewos* >OB.R. *slovo* 'word'. The same principle
applied to neuters of the *u/i*-stems (Gk. μέθυ μέλι, Lat. *cornu animal(i)*),
but these were lost in Slavonic, changing their gender or their
declension. The suffix -*os/es*- shows *o/e*-gradation, and it was only by
popular analogy that the -*o* of *slovo* came to be understood as a case
ending, like the -*o* of *igo* 'yoke'. That the accusative case is, in a way,
basic in the declension appears from this use of the stem without
modification, and from the fact that the accusative form runs through
all genders, whereas the nominative form is restricted to animates
(masculine and feminine).

(ii) IE. **-m/n* (consonant after a vowel, sonant after a consonant):
IE. **pontim* >OB. *potĭ* 'road' R. *puí*, OB. *svekrŭvĭ* (<**-uwm*) 'mother-
in law', **ronkām* >OB. *rǫkǫ* 'hand' R. *rúku*, **sūnum* >OB. *synŭ* 'son'
R. *syn*, **ghordhom* >OB. *gradŭ* 'city' R. *górod*, **jugom* >OB.R. *igo*
'yoke'; **māterm* >**māterim* OB. *materĭ* 'mother', **akmenm* >OB.
kamenĭ 'stone'. The Indo-European languages are divided in their
testimony concerning the quality of the Indo-European final nasal.
Balto-Slavonic, like Greek seems to suggest a dental nasal (**n*), but
Latin and Sanskrit suggest a labial (**m*). In the same way, Hebrew
and Portuguese favour final *m*, but Arabic and Spanish favour final
n; it is an idiosyncrasy of each individual language to prefer one or the
other nuance of a relaxed final nasal consonant.

Concerning neuter **-om* >Sl. -*o* and **-os* >-*o* see section 62 *ad fin.*

(iii) *Genitive-accusative.* In the singular of the *o*-stems the accusative and nominative both resulted in -*ŭ*. Things cannot properly
be agents, and where an inanimate thing is concerned there is no
ambiguity likely to arise from this identity of forms. The notion
'inanimate' is here taken in the current sense, and not in the primitive
sense of objects apparently self-moving, like fire, water, hand or
foot. But with animates, especially with persons, it is necessary to
have distinct flexions in languages where position is not decisive. It
is necessary to know whether 'Peter robs Paul' or 'Paul robs Peter'.
To get over the difficulty the distinctive G*S.* -*a* was used for the
accusative of persons, and sometimes of animals, in the singular of
the *o*-stems. The usage then spread to other stems: N*S.* *synŭ* G-A*S.*
syna. Finally, during the development of the modern languages, it
spread to the plural, where there was no confusion of forms. The
inclusion of trees among animates is not unnatural (Ruth. *dub* 'oak'
G-A*S.* *dúba*), but the extension to games is odd: P. *grać w bridża*
'play bridge'. Another unexpected extension is to coins. In Old
Bulgarian the usage was still fluctuating, and both forms were found
in the *o*-stems.

The accusative completes the action of the verb, and when that is a verb of motion the accusative gives the direction of the motion. In this way the accusative alternates with other spatial cases (locative and ablative) to answer the questions *quo? ubi? unde?* When a preposition is used, the original construction was to regard the case as completing the verbal action in a general sense, while the preposition was adverbial, and gave a finer definition to the verbal idea. The preposition, thus used, did not 'govern' the case. When the preposition later came to be associated with the noun it took over the cases as they had syntactically developed.

(b) *Nominative*. (i) The accusative form served for the nominative of neuters.

(ii) Stem, with lengthened final vowel (*M.F.*): IE. **mātē(r)* > OB. *mati* 'mother' R. *mat́*, **akmōn* > OB. *kamy* 'stone', **korēn?* > OB. *korę* 'root', **gʷenā* > OB. *žena* R. *žená* 'woman'. The agreement of Sanskrit with Balto-Slavonic shows that the loss of -*r* after a lengthened vowel goes back to Indo-European times: Skr. *mātā* L. *mótė* OB. *mati;* final -*ē* was here further narrowed to Sl. -*i*. The opposition OB.N*S. mati*/A*S. materi* tends to be eliminated in the modern language by the use either of the nominative for both cases (R. *mat́*), or the accusative (Cz. *máteř* = *máti*). L. *akmuō* 'stone' *piemuō* 'shepherd' may show that the long final vowel generated a diphthong, which became a monophthong later in Slavonic: **-ōn* > L. -*uō* > **-ū* > CSl. -*y* (cf. the development of P. *ó* Cz. *ů*). Even in Old Bulgarian the acc. sg. was substituted for the nom. -*y* -*ę: kameni koreni*. This practice has become general in the modern languages.

(iii) **-s:* lost in Slavonic, sometimes with closure of the preceding vowel: IE. **pontis* > OB. *pǫti* 'way' R. *put́* [cf. Gk. πόντος 'sea' Lat. *pon(t)s* 'bridge'], IE.**swekrūs* > OB. *svekry* 'mother-in-law', IE. *sūnus* > OB. *synŭ* 'son', R. *syn*, IE. **wl̥kʷos* > OB. *vl̥kŭ* 'wolf' R. *volk*, **konjos* > **konjŭ* > **koń-i* > OB. *koni* 'horse' R. *koń*.

The nominative is strongly indicated in a sentence as the source of all that follows. In Old Bulgarian, in consequence, it was often accompanied by a suffixed demonstrative *si* 'this'/*tŭ* 'that' : OB. *dinisi* 'this day, today', *rabŭtŭ* 'this slave' (with *ŭ* opened in strong position to *o : rabotŭ*). Hence the suffixed article in North Great Russian and perhaps in Modern Bulgarian. The nominative is rarely used with prepositions; but there exists the idiom in Russian and Polish (but not Czechoslovak): R. *čto éto za kníga?* (nom.) 'what sort of book is this?' (cf. Germ. *was ist das für ein Mann?*)

(c) *Vocative*. The vocative hardly merits the name of flexion. It does not enter into the sentence, but stands to it in apposition, urgently calling to it the attention of someone. The expression of urgency was the heightened tone; there being no syntactical relations to define, no flexion was required. Most vocatives are of the same form as the nominative, but sometimes without the lengthened vowel or with a shortened vowel: VS. *g^wenā/NS. *g^wenā OB. ženo/žena. Personal names are often in the vocative in place of the nominative, especially children's names. Hence comes the order of personal nominatives in -o: *Marko Danilo* etc. The thematic stems express the vocative by the e-grade of stem, without case-ending: OB. *vlče* 'O wolf!' Neuters have no vocative case-ending, but use the nom.-acc. In the plural and dual the nominative is used for the vocative. The special value of the case is inferred from the high tone.

(d) *Genitive.* (i) IE. *os/es/s; Gk. prefers *-os, Balto-Slavonic, like Latin, prefers *-es, the sibilant being lost in Slavonic (section 43): OB. *matere kamene imene slovese telęte svekrŭve* all from *-es; *pǫti* from ?*-eis [see section 62(b)], L. -iēs (GS. *akiēs* 'eye'/NS. *akìs*); *synu* from *-ous, L. -aūs. The flexion -i (*pǫti*) has prevailed over -e in R. *máteri imeni ditjáti*, helped by the analogy of the dative in -i, whereas P. *imienia* Slov. *iména* R. *néba* have come to be inflected like o-stems. The feminine ā/jā-stems offer considerable difficulty. The suffix had a rising tone (á/já), which would combine with the falling tone of the genitive ending (*-ès) to give a circumflex (*-âs), which is represented by the circumflex in Greek (τιμῆς) and by rising tone in Lithuanian (*dainōs*). But this would give Sl. *-a. The closing of the vowel to -y (OB. *rǫky*) is hard to explain, but seems to indicate the presence of a nasal, as also the flexion -ę in South Slavonic ja-stems/ EWSl. -ě: -y <*-ōns ę <*-jōns. The source of this nasal termination may have been the declension in -ōn (cf. L. *akmeñs*/*-ons), and the reason for substitution the circumstance that the gen. sg. would be otherwise indistinguishable from the nom. sg. (-a). The discrepancy in the soft stems (SSl. -ę/EWSl. -ě: gen. sg. OB. *dušę*/OR.WSl. *dušě*) has been explained as due to the occurrence of a special quality of nasal ě not encountered elsewhere in Slavonic, save in the acc.pl. of ja/jo-stems and the nom.pl. of ja-stems. In the acc.pl. the nasal is in place, and denasalization in East and West Slavonic must be due to the dialectal timbre of the vowel. In final position, where these sounds occur, the enunciation is relaxed, and this relaxation might combine with the effects of analogy to give a timbre otherwise unparalleled.

(ii) Ablative of the thematic declension IE. *-ōd (masc.neut): OB. *grada sela kraja.* It was only in this declension that the genitive and ablative were distinct: Skr. GS. *kāntasya*/AbS. *kāntāt* from *kāntas* 'beloved', Lat. *lupī*/*lupō(d).* In Balto-Slavonic the genitive and ablative have been identified in all conjugations, but in the o-stems the identification has been upon the basis of the original ablative in *-ōd. This contained a final postposition akin to Lat. *de* 'away from', and possibly in the form of *-ed, giving with the thematic vowel

-o-ed *-ōd* >L. -o CSl.O.B. -a/soft -ja. The postposition resembles Gk. -θε<*-dhe (ἐξ ἁλόθεν 'from the sea'), but is opposed in meaning to Gk. -δε('Αθήναζε='Αθήνας-δε 'to Athens').

The uses of the genitive in Slavonic correspond to both original cases. The proper sense of the genitive seems to have been to name the whole thing of which something is a part (partitive genitive): R. *ja choču vodý* 'I want (some out of all) water', *vagón pólon ljudéj* 'a carriage full of people'. What one negates is usually something partial; hence the Slavonic genitive after negatives: R. *net déneg* 'there is no money'. The genitive of point of time corresponds to the Latin ablative: R. *pérvogo márta* 'on the first of March'. Another use of the genitive is the adnominal or adjectival: R. *dom otcá* 'father's house' (possessive), *pjať rubléj* 'five (a five-group of) roubles', *stakán čáju* 'a cup(-ful) of tea'. Hence the use of the genitive with secondary prepositions like R. *bliz* 'near' *ókolo* 'round', etc., which are frequently nouns made invariable in some case and used as adverbs, whence also as prepositions. The proper sense of the ablative is removal from a thing or situation. It is thus used with verbs of deprivation, avoidance, fear, etc.; of the point from which measurements are made; and so of the point of reference from which a comparison is made: R. *on slabée menjá* 'he is weaker than I (measured from me he is the weak one)'. So the genitive occurs with the prepositions R. *bez* 'without' *ot* 'away from', *s* 'down from', *u* 'by'.

The adjectival use of the genitive was overshadowed in Common Slavonic by the facility with which adjectives were made from nouns. The possessive 'God's' was not as a rule *Boga* 'of God' but *Božiji* (R. *Bóžij*).

(*e*) *Dative.* IE. *-ei/ai* CSl.OB. *-i:* OB. *materi kameni imeni telęti slovesi svekrŭvi; ročě* (?*-âi* ⟨*-āi* ⟨*-ā-ei*) *duši; synovi* (?*-ew-ei*); *pǫti kosti* (=*i*+?) OB. *vḷku* may derive from *wḷk^w ōi* (?*-o-ei*), in which the long vowel has developed at the expense of the short semivowel (as in Gk. λύκῳ Lat. *lupō*), being closed by it in Slavonic to *-ū* >*-u.* In Polish and Czechoslovak *-ovi* has been construed as all case-ending, and so as an alternative for *-u:* P. *dębowi*/OP. *synu* (MP. *synowi*) (*dąb* 'oak' is an *o*-stem, *syn* 'son' is a *u*-stem), Cz. *Janovi bratrovi* 'brother' (of persons), *hadovi* or *hadu* 'snake' (of animals)/ *hradu* 'city' (of things).

The dative is the case of the recipient, whether actually the receiver of the verbal activity or affected by and interested in it (ethic dative).

(*f*) *Instrumental.* IE. *-bh/m-:* OB. *pǫtīmi kamenīmi imenīmi* (*synŭmi* is not attested) *rabomi krajemi* (cf. Anglo-Saxon *cwic* 'alive' D*SMN. cwicum*). This element *-m-* was probably an agglutinated suffix, and is found also in the dual and plural (dat.instr.). Its use was parallel to that of *-bh-* in Sanskrit, Greek, Latin, Celtic and other languages. The latter appears in Homeric Greek in a rudimentary form (-φι) which can be added to singular or plural cases: βίηφι 'by force' κλισίηφι 'in the huts'. In Latin it is restricted to the plural (*deabus regibus manibus diebus*), where it gives both dative and ablative by means of the same vocalism. In Sanskrit it is plural and dual only, and shows differences of vocalism: I*P*. *-bhis* DAb*P*. *-bhyas* IDAb*D*. *-bhyām*. In Slavonic the vowels vary: I*S*. *-mǐ* I*P*. *mi* D*P*. *-mǔ* DI*D*. *-ma*. The Lithuanian series (I*S*. *-mi* I*P*. *-mis* D*P*. *-ms* DI*D*. *-m*, the latter with changes of tone) do not sufficiently elucidate the problem of the original forms in Balto-Slavonic or Indo-European.

(ii) IE. *-m/jam:* OB. *rǫkǫ/rǫkojǫ* <*ronkā-m/jam* (L. *rankà* denasalized), *strujejǫ*. Cf. Skr. *dhis* 'thought' I*S*. *dhiy-ā*, whence *kāntā* I*S*. *kānt-ay-ā*, which gives an alternation *-ā/ayā* in the instrumental, as in Slavonic). Both types of suffix are found in Old Bulgarian, but the shorter are absent from some documents and may be due to dissimilation. Once established, this instrumental of the *a*-stems sets a pattern for other feminines: *kost-ǐjǫ/ijǫ mater-ǐjǫ/ijǫ svekrǔv-ǐjǫ/ijǫ*, which have no shortened forms.

The instrumental has the meanings 'by means of' (instrumental proper) and 'accompanied by'. Both senses are united in the English preposition *with*, in the Greek dative and the Latin ablative. As denoting time within which something occurs the instrumental is doubtless sociative: R. *vesnój* 'in the spring' *útrom* 'in the morning'. It is used for the standard of measurement: R. *ja gódom stárše egó* 'I am a year older than he', and in the locution *čem . . . tem* 'by how much . . . by so much; the more . . . the . . .' Similarly sociative is the instrumental of place where (*ubi?*), and with the prepositions R. *za* 'after' *méždu* 'among' *pod* 'under' *s* 'with'. An extension of the same usage causes the instrumental to follow the verb 'be', when not expressing identity but only a relation between subject and predicate: R. *kogdá ja byl málčikom* 'when I was a boy' (cf. L. *tù búsi vilkù* 'you'll become a wolf'). True instrumentals are found in phrases like R. *menjá zovút Ivánom* 'they call me John', *êto služílo mne predlógom* 'this served me as a pretext'.

(*g*) *Locative*. (i) IE. *zero*-ending: OB. *kosti* (*-ēi*) *synu* (*-ēu*). The consonant-stems should end in their consonants according to this principle of formation, but *materi* has the *-i* of the *i*-stems, and *svekrǔve kamene imene telęte slovese* have a suffixed *-e* of uncertain origin. It might be connected with the suffixed *-e* in Lithuanian, which gives an appearance of uniformity to Lithuanian locatives: *-yje/oje/ėje/uje*.

(ii) IE. *-i:* OB. *rǫcě* (*-ā-i;* cf. L. *rankoj-ė*, where *-oj-* <*āi*) *struji gradě* (*-o-i*) *kraji*. Gk. loc. οἴκοι 'at home'/N*P*. οἶκοι 'houses' shows by the accentuation of the stressed syllable that there was a difference of intonation between these two diphthongs, viz. loc. *-ói*/nom. pl. *-oi*.

The locative is a spatial case, defining place where (*ubi?*), and is a source of adverbs as an extension of this usage. It now occurs only with prepositions, and is often called the 'prepositional case', but the term suggests an exclusiveness which does not in fact exist. The chief prepositions associated with the locative are R. *v* 'in' *na* 'on' *o*/*ob*/*obo* 'concerning' *po* 'after' *pri* 'in the presence of, in the time of, near'. It is opposed to the accusative of motion, as indicating place of rest.

67. *Plural Cases.* The plural differs markedly from the singular in the ease with which its flexions fuse together. The nominative and accusative cases remain distinct, but the genitive presented a termination which ran through all declensions, and the dative, instrumental and locative show substitution of one declensional vowel for another even in Old Bulgarian. In Russian this has been carried to a logical conclusion by which the endings of the *a*-stems have been adopted by most words in other declensions, the instrumental showing more resistance than the dative and locative. In the declension of the definite adjective there was already identity of flexion for all three genders in Old Bulgarian. A psychological support for this usage is the circumstance that sex is important in individuals, not in masses.

(*a*) *Nominative.* (i) IE. **-es:* OB. *pọtĭje* (**-ejes*), *kamene synove* (**-ewes*) (masculines). OB. *materi* is modelled on feminine *i*-stems, but OR. *matere* Cz. *mateře* implies CSl. *matere*. The *i*-stems, when feminine, use the acc.pl. for the nominative: OB. *kosti* (<**-ins*), and this is the explanation also of *svekrŭvi* and *dušę*. It might apply also to OB. *rọky*, nom. and acc.pl., but CSl. *-y* could perhaps derive from **-ās *-ā-es*), as L. *rañkos* certainly does.

(ii) IE. **-oi* (with rising tone), masc. *o*-stems: OB. *gradi krai* (=*kraji*). This is due, as in Latin and Greek, to the analogy of the demonstrative NPM. **toi* 'those'/Skr. *devās* 'gods'. The modern languages, especially Polish, show much interchange between *-i*/*ove*. Some *o*-stems are found with the termination *-ove* even in Old Bulgarian: *duchove* 'spirits'.

(iii) IE. **-ā* CSl.OB. *-a*/*ja:* neuters: OB. *imena telęta slovesa iga*/ *pola lica*. This flexion was that of a nom.fem.sg. of a collective noun, and as such still took a singular verb in Gk. ἀδυνατόν/ἀδυνατά ἐστι 'it is impossible'. As in the singular, the same flexion is used for the nom. voc.acc. of neuters. The distinctively plural endings of other cases have been attached by analogy of the masculines to the neuter paradigm.

As a collective feminine noun, the plural of a neuter was originally a different word from the singular, and so might have a different accentuation. Gk. φῦλον/φυλή 'race, clan, tribe' are different words formed from the same root in the relationship **-om/ā* and differently accented. Hence perhaps some of the accent-shifts encountered in

Slavonic neuters (apart from those due to the workings of de Saussure's law), such as R. *ózero/ozёra* 'lake' *nébo/nebesá* 'sky'. In S. *sèlo/sёla* the difference reveals itself as one of tone-quality.

Such independent words could also be formed alongside masculines, giving mixed paradigms: R. *rog/rogá* 'horn' *véčer/večerá* 'evening' (cf. Lat. *locus/loca*).

In the plural the vocative is identical with the nominative.

(*b*) *Accusative*. (i) IE. **-ns*, consonant after vowels, sonant after consonants: IE. **pontins* OB. *pǫti kosti;* IE. **māterns* OB. *materi kameni svekrŭvi;* IE. **sūnuns *ghordhons* (cf. Cretan λύκονς) OB. *syny grady; *krajons >*krajens* OB. *kraję/*OR.WSl. *krajě.* On the alternatives *ę/ě* see section 66 (*d*). The vowel of the ending was lengthened by final *s* before this disappeared (see section 31), and the nasal timbre remained only with the most open vowel.

(ii) **-s/ns:* *a/ja*-stems. L.NPF. *stírn-os* A. *-as* implies N. **-ās* A. *-as,* the latter without nasalization. Without nasal are also Goth. *gibōs* 'gifts' Skr. *senās* 'armies', though both accusatives have the long vowel of the nominative. In Old Prussian (*-ans*), Greek (*-ᾱς* Cretan τίμανς), Italic and Slavonic the termination has been assimilated to accusatives in **-ns,* with lengthening and closure one grade of the vowel and its consequent denasalization in Common Slavonic: **ronkans >*ronkons >*-ū >*OB. *rǫky, dušę/*EWSl. *dušě.* APF. *rǫky=* NPF. *rǫky* (? *<*-ās*), and on this analogy *dušę* was extended to the nominative, and then all feminines (*kosti materi svekrŭvi*) used the accusative instead of the original nominative.

(*c*) *Genitive.* IE. **-ŏm/ŏn:* CSl.OB. *-ŭ/*soft-(*j*)*ĭ:* OB. *materŭ kamenŭ imenŭ telętŭ slovesŭ svekrŭvŭ rǫkŭ synovŭ gradŭ; pǫtĭjĭ; strujĭ dušĭ; koňĭ.* The vowel of this flexion was short in Slavonic, and also in Latin (*oviŭm*), though the latter is said to have resulted from a shortening of **-ōm.* Whether that be true of Latin, there is no ground for believing that the Slavonic termination has been shortened, since long nasal finals are carefully preserved. On the other hand Gk. -ων L. -*ŭ* quite as definitely indicate an original long vowel. It is necessary to suppose that both existed in Indo-European.

Final -*ŭ/ĭ* dropped in the later languages, and the case was left without characteristic flexion. Reaction set in against this state of affairs. As in the dat.sg. and nom.pl., the ending of the *u*-stems was treated as a flexion (*-ov/ev*) and extended over the *o*-stems: R. *stolóv* 'chairs' *saráev* 'sheds', P. *wujów* 'uncles' *cieniów* 'shades', Cz. *mužů* (formerly *mužŭv*) 'men', Slov. *učiteljev* 'teachers'. The *i*-stems naturally added the case-ending to the -*ĭ* of the stem, giving -*ĭjĭ,* which also was treated as wholly flexion. The first semivowel was in strong position, and so led to a suffix *-ej,* which spread to other declensions: R. *lošadéj* 'horses', whence *caréj* 'tsars' *moréj* 'seas' (both *jo*-stems), *sudéj* (from *sudjá* 'judge'). In Serbocroat the *i*-declension has GP. *-î* (*stvárî* 'things'), but for all other declensions the language has developed, in a way not satisfactorily explained, a suffix *-â* for the gen. pl.: S. *jèlênâ* 'stags' *žénâ* 'women' *pleménâ* 'tribes', etc.

Owing to the lightness of final *-ŭ* there appear certain accent-shifts in some genitives: R. *vrémja* 'time' NP. *vremená* GP. *vremën*, *sestrá* 'sister' NP. *sëstry* GP. *sestër*, S. *žèna* 'woman' NP. *žëne* GP. *žénâ*. In West Slavonic the final syllable of the gen. pl. is affected by the law of lengthening (and later closing of vowel) in compensation for the loss of final *jer*, e.g. P. *pora* 'season' GP. *pór;* and in some words this form has analogically affected the other cases: P.GP. *gór* 'of the mountains' : : NS. *góra*.

In the plural the ablative has been confounded, as to usage, with the genitive; as to form, with the dative.

(*d*) *Dative and Instrumental.* IE. **-bh/m-:* OB. *-mŭ -mi: pǫtĭ-mŭ -mi*, *mater-ĭmŭ -ĭmi* and *materemŭ, svekrŭv-amŭ -ami, rǫka-mŭ -mi, struja-mŭ -mi, synŭ-*mŭ -mi* and *synomŭ, grado-mŭ, kraje-mŭ.* The corresponding forms in other languages are: L.DP. *-ms* IP. *-mis* Goth.DP. *-m* Lat.DAbP. *-bus* <**-bhŏs*, OIr.DP. *-ib* <**-bhis*, Homeric -φι <**-bhi*, Arm.IP. *-vk͑ -mbk͑*, Skr.DP.*-bhyas* <**-bhjŏs* IP.*-bhis.* The parallelism of the two series is obvious, but so also are the discrepancies of detail. The Slavonic dative depends on **-mŏs*, parallel to Lat. **-bhŏs*, and independent of the Lithuanian flexion. The long final vowel of the instrumental in Slavonic has no parallel in noun declensions, but corresponds to the **-bhei*-suffix in Lat. *tibi.*

A *jer* before the flexion was in strong position in the dative, but weak in the instrumental. In the dative, therefore, there was a tendency to replace it by a full vowel (*materemŭ imenemŭ synomŭ*), as also in the locative plural. The *a- o-* stems have a full vowel in such a position. In Russian the vowel *a* has spread over all declensions in the dative and locative. In the instrumental it is also general, and has met with resistance only from the *i*-stems: R. *lošadmí* (cf. P. *kośćmi* Cz.Slov. *kostmi*).

The dat. instr. loc. of *ū*-stems in Old Bulgarian were remodelled on *a*-stems.

(*ii*) IE.IP. **-ō-is:* *o*-stems: OB.IP. *grady sely/kraji.* The vowel of the diphthong is closed by the final **-s.* Gk. λύκοις results from both instrumental and locative (Homeric -οισι) and has a short thematic vowel as in the locative. There is a short vowel in L. *výrais;* long in Skr. *devāis.* In Latin the ending was used also of the dative and ablative, and was extended to the *a*-stems also.

(*e*) *Locative.* IE. **-su/si?:* OL. *-su* ML. *-se* CSl.OB. *-chŭ*, OB. *pǫtĭchŭ, svekrŭvachŭ* (with *a* from *a*-stems), *ženachŭ/strujachŭ, syn-*ŭchŭ/ochŭ, graděchŭ/krajichŭ.* The consonant **s* followed an *i* in the

i-stems and the *o*-stems (*-*oisu*) and so gave Sl. *ch*, which was generalized to all stems (as with *ženachŭ*/*g^{w}enāsu:* Skr. L*P*. *senāṣu*); in
the *u*-stems it followed *u*, with the same consequences (Skr. *bhānuṣu*).
Vocalization of *jer:* OB. *materechŭ synochŭ domochŭ*.

68. *Dual Cases*. The dual has the appearance of being incomplete in
Indo-European. Only three case-flexions had been developed (NVA,
GL, DI), and they were transmitted imperfectly. The genitive was the
first to be lost, since it is almost unrecorded in Greek and has been lost
in Lithuanian; its form, on the other hand, is less doubtful than that of
the other two.

(*a*) *Nominative-accusative-vocative*. The vowels *e i* occur, and
probably also the semivowels *i u* forming a diphthong with final stem
vowels. OB. *poti* may represent original *-ī*, L. *naktì* having been
shortened. OB. *kameni* is attested, but not *materi*. The *o*-stems had,
in the masculine, *-ō:* CSl. -*a*/soft *ja:* OB. *grada kraja*. The feminine
a-stems have *-a-i* (Skr. -*e: sene*), giving CSl. -*ě*/soft -*i:* OB. *rǫcě
struji*. The neuters seem to have been formed with the element *-i*,
which was lost to the *i*-stems by the loss of neuters in that declension.
In the *o*-stems, neuter *-o-i* >CSl. -*ě*/soft -*i*, and so coincide formally
with the feminine: OB. *selě*/*lici*. The consonant-stems would naturally
have shown -*i* in this place (OB. *tělesi* 'two bodies'), but the historically
justified ending is rare. They generally show -*ě* (OB. *imeně* 'two
names') borrowed from the neuter *o*-declension.

(*b*) *Genitive-Locative*. IE. *-ou-:* OB. *potiju/potiju*, etc. Arcadian
μέσουν 'in the midst' preserves this ending (cf. OB. *meždu* GLD. with
the same meaning). Skr. -(*y*)*os: devayos* 'gods' *senayos* 'armies'
bhānvos 'suns'. In Lithuanian the gen. pl. is used instead of the gen.
dual. The adverb L. *pusiaŭ* 'in two halves' is an old locative dual, and
trace of a distinction between G*D*. *dviejaus* L*D*. *dviejau* 'two' have
been noted. OIr. G*D*. *fer scél* rest upon *-ou*.

(*c*) *Dative-Instrumental*. IE. *-bh/m-*, L. *-m*, CSl. *-ma:* OB. *potǐma
ženama gradoma* etc. Skr. -*bhyām* (*senābhyam bhānubhyām*) is closer
akin than Celtic -*bhim*, but there was no palatal glide or final nasal in
Slavonic. Nor did it show differences of tone as in Lithuanian (L.D*D*.
sūnùm I*D*. *sūnum̃*), which may not have been primitive. Gk. -ιν (λύκοιν)
is on a different line of development. Gothic dat. *twáim* 'two'.

In Serbocroat the flexion -*ma* has come to be used for the DIL*P*. of
all declensions. The same type of extension occurs also dialectically in
Czech and Slovak, but in most modern languages this flexion is
restricted to the case of the numerals, taking its rise in the dual
declension of CSl.OB. *dŭva* 'two'.

69. *Numerals*. There are no characteristics of the numeral declensions not found elsewhere, but they are drawn from several different
parts of speech, and in their use they form a closely associated group.

They also conserve some of the oldest features of the language to which they belong. These are reasons for treating them as a group.

1: *oĭ-nos 'sole'? Lat. ūnus Gk. οἴνη 'ace', *oi-wos Gk. οῖος 'sole', *oi-kos Skr. ekas 'one'. From *oinos come L. vienas CSl.OB. inŭ (which is rarely used) and the prefix ino- 'one, other'; with *ed- (neut. sg. of a pronominal root *e-) the latter gives OB. jedinŭ/jedĭnŭ R. odín (neut. odnó) 'one'. OB. jedĭnŭ, with the short vowel in the second syllable, is definitely later than jedinŭ, though it is as hard to account for long as for short quantity in this place. 1st: L. pìrmas (pirm 'before') OB. prvŭ, with difference of suffix; cf. Eng. first Goth. fruma frumista Lat. pri(s)mus prius Gk. πράμος πρόμος. The root is *pr̥-, with suffix -m/v-.

2–4: (2 is a pronominal o-stem, 3 an adjectival i-stem, and 4 an adjectival consonant-stem):

E. *duō   L.NAMD. dù/F.dvì   GD. dviėjŭ   DD. dviem   ID. dviĕm
   OB. M.dŭv-a FN.-ĕ   -oju   -ĕma   (so also oba 'both').
E. *trejes L.NP. trȳs   A. trìs G. trijŭ   D. trìms I. trimìs LM. trijuosè/F. -josè
   OB.M. tr-ĭje/FN.-i -i   -iji/iji   -ĭmŭ   -ĭmi   -ichŭ
E.*kwetwores. OB.M. četyr-e/FN. -i -i   -u

OB. dŭva follows the pronominal declension. The following noun was in the dual, but the dual endings of nom. acc. were later confused with plurals in -i (oči 'eyes') or with gen. sg. -a/ja. When so understood these forms began to appear after 3 and 4 also. 2nd: L. añtras, cf. Goth. anþar/OB. vŭtorŭ (? <*n̥-tor-). 3rd: tretĭjĭ. 4th: četvr̥tŭ. The suffix -tŭ is used to make the remaining ordinals.

5–9: are collective nouns in *-is in Slavonic, but L. keturì etc. are adjectives. 5: *penktis >OB. pętĭ. 6: *ks(w)ekstis OB. šestĭ. 7: *sebdmis (Gk. ἕβδομος) OB. sedmĭ. 8: *oktmis OB. osmĭ (Gk. ὀκτώ Lat. octō have the form of duals, meaning possibly 'both sets of fingers'). 9: *newn̥- OPr. newīnts L. devynì OB. devętĭ (with the initial of 10).

10–19: *dekm̥t(i)- OPr. dessimpts L. děšimt OB. desętĭ. This is a consonant-stem as appears from loc. sg. desęte 'in the teens'. 11: jedinŭ na desęte, 12: dŭva na desęte, etc. When standing alone it is assimilated to the i-stems and to the numerals 5–9: gen. loc. sg. desęti. Other cases are: GP. desętŭ/desętii (occasionally found), IP. desęty (on the analogy of the o-stems), NP. desęte/desęti, NAD. desęti/desętĕ, GD. desętu.

20–90: are composed of 2 with nom. du. desęti (dŭva desęti), 3–4 with nom. pl. (tri desęte/desęti), 5–9 with gen. pl. (pętĭ desętŭ). MR. pjatdesját shows both parts declined as i-stem nouns (gen. pjatidesjati, etc.). 40: MR. sórok (see section 117).

100: *km̥tóm L. šim̃tas CSl.OB. sŭto. This is a neuter o-stem, giving 200: dŭvĕ sŭtĕ (dual), 300: tri sŭta (plural), etc. The difficulty here is to account for the ŭ. It seems better to accept it as Slavonic rather than to have recourse to borrowing from Avestic sata or

Scythian (Ossetic) *sädä*, which leave the difficulty unresolved. The expected development is found in L. *šĩmtas*.

1000: L. *tūkstantis* OB. *tysǫšta/tysęšta* R. *týsjača* P. *tysiąc* S. *tïsûća* < Goth. *pūsundi*. It is a feminine noun. Also S. *hîljada* MB. *chiljáda* < MGk. χιλιάδα.

10,000: OB. *tĩma*, cf. Tokharian *tumane tmām̥* and TT. *tumaṅ* 'cloud, mist, ten thousand warriors'.

The collective (distributive) numerals have in the masc. sg. the forms 2: OB. *dŭvojĭ*, 3: *trojĭ*, 4: *četverŭ*. In the last instance the *r* is part of the root (*četyre*), but it has led to -*rŭ* being generalized as a suffix for distributives: 5: *pętorŭ*, 6: *šestorŭ*, 7: *sedmorŭ*, 8: *osmorŭ*, 9: *devętorŭ*, 10: *desętorŭ*. Numerals of this type are used in both Old Bulgarian and the modern languages, for instance, with *pluralia tantum:* S. *dvŏja kŏla* 'two carriages' (formally neut. p. from sg. *kŏlo* 'wheel'). A derived form in -*ica* is found in the instr. sg. OB. *četvoricejǫ* 'fourfold' *sŭtoricejǫ* 'a hundredfold'.

70. *Adjectives and Participles.* (a) *Indefinite.* Adjectives and participles are either definite or indefinite, i.e. are either accompanied by a postpositive article (-*jĭ* <*-jos* *-i-*) or not. In Slovene, Serbocroat and Bulgarian the distinction is still so maintained: as in Slov. *nòv klobúk* 'a new hat'/*nôvi klobúk* 'the new hat'. This does not hold in Slovene apart from the nom. acc. sg. masc., owing to the confusion in other case-forms of the two declensions. Elsewhere the definite adjective has become attributive, accompanying the noun whether defined or not; the indefinite is simply predicative. In the predicate the nominative case is much the most common, and the others are rarely used. Thus, though a full declension survives in theory in Russian, for example, scarcely any case but the nominative is found in practical use. There are traces of a Russian predicative dative (see section 106); an accusative is found in appositional predicates of the type Cz. *našel jsem potok rozvodněn* 'I found the brook swollen'. In adverbs there are traces of yet more cases: R.*GSN. snóva* 'anew', P.*DSN. po francusku* 'in French'.

Indefinite participles gradually shed their cases with the exception of a few fixed forms, and so became gerunds, without declension.

There is only one declension of indefinite adjectives, composed of the *o*- and *a*-noun declensions: OB. *nov-ŭ -o -a*, soft. *pěš-ĭ -e -a*. Only *trije* remains as an *i*-stem adjective, and *četyre* as a consonant-stem adjective. The vocative in -*e* occurs only when the adjective is used as a substantive, as OB. *bezumĭne* 'O fool!'/*o rode nevěrĭnŭ* 'O faithless generation!' In the same way are declined the participles in -*lŭ -tŭ -nŭ -mŭ*. The other participles follow the soft declension in almost all cases, but they, and the comparative form of adjectives, show variations of suffix which may be represented thus:

	NSM.	NSN.	ASM.	GSMN.	NSF.	ASF.	GSF.	
E. *sent/sont-	s	-	-m̨		-jā	-jām	-jās	(i)
*snt̥-				-os/es				
*weid-	-wōs	-wos						(ii)
			-wotm̨	-wot-es/es				
*wid-					-us-jā	-us-jām	-s-jās	
*magh-	-jōs	-jos	-josm̨	-jos-os/es	-is-jā			(iii)
*mag-		-is						
Gk.	ὤν	ὄν	ὄντα	ὄντος	οὖσα < *ὄντια			(i)
ειδ-	-ώς	-ός	-ότα	-ότος				(ii)
Homeric ιδ-					υἶα < *-υσια			
ηδ-				ίω < *-ιοσα				(iii)
Lat. suav-	-ior < -iōs	-ius < *-ios	-iorem	-ioris				(iii)
.. suk-	-ąs	-ą	/ -antι	-ančio	-anti	-ančią	-ančios	(i)
suk-	-ęs	-ę	/ -usι	-usio	-usi	-usią	-usios	(ii)
ger-	-es-nis							(iii)
OB. id-	-y	-y	/ -ǫšt-	ǐ ja	-i	-jǫ	-ję/WSl.-jě	(i)
daj/sěd-	-ę	-ę	/ -ǫ/ę-št-					
ved-	-ŭ	-ŭ	/ -ŭš-					
da-	-vŭ	-vŭ	/ -vŭš-	-ǐ -ja	-i	-jǫ	-ję/WSl.-jě	(ii)
javl-	-ǐ	-ǐ	/ -ǐš-					
miñ-	-ǐjǐ	-e	/ -ǐš-	-ǐ ja	-i	-jǫ	-ję/WSl.-jě	(iii)
nově-	-jǐ	-e	/ -ǐš-					

(i) The present participle active [section 55 (a)] took a weak form of the root in the oblique cases of the masc. neut., but in Slavonic these cases have been remodelled and that form of the root no longer appears. Verbs of classes iii b and iv have the extended suffix -ęšt-. Russian gerunds derive from the nominatives (masc. sg. -ę >-ja, fem. sg. *-łi >-či).

(ii) The past participle active is derived from *-wos/us-. There was a long vowel in nom. sg. masc./short in nom. sg. neut., both of the o-grade of the suffix, as may be seen from Greek. The fem. showed the zero-grade of suffix with an additional suffix -jā (nom. -i <*-iə). The fem. *-ŭs- caused the suffix of the masculine and neuter to become *-(w)ŭs- > CSl. -ŭ after consonants/ -vŭ after vowels. In the oblique cases of these genders the additional suffix -jo- was employed. In the oblique cases of all genders and the nom. sg. fem. the influence of i/j palatalized Sl. *ch to Sl. š : davŭši etc.

(iii) The comparative was formed by *-jos/is-. By palatalization of the vowel *-jos became *-jes, whence, for instance, neut. OB. miñe 'less' (-'e <*-jes). On the analogy of the zero-grade, *-is, the masculine came to be formed in *-jis-. In the oblique cases this suffix received further suffixes (*-jo/ja-), like the participles, and the nom. sg. fem. is in -i <*-iə.

The comparative suffix is either added immediately to the stem (CSl. *chudī 'worse' <*chud-jis, cf. OB. chudŭ 'bad', definite comparative chuždīji), and in such an event any other adjectival suffix is usually dropped before the comparative is formed (OB. *vysokŭ* 'high' comp. *vyšji̇̆*, *krĕpŭkŭ* 'strong' comp. *krepli̇̆ji̇̆*); or else the stem takes the ending *-ĕ-* before **-ji̇̆s* (*novŭ* 'new' comp. *novĕji̇̆*). The feminine forms are nom. sg. *chuždĭši vyšiši novĕji̇̆ši*, etc., and the masc. neuter. oblique cases are gen. sg. *chuždĭša vyšiša novĕji̇̆ša*, etc.

The superlative is expressed in Old Bulgarian by *nai-*+the comparative, or, in a less purely superlative sense, by *prĕ-*+positive: OB. *naivyšji̇̆* 'highest' *prĕvelikŭ* 'very great'.

(*b*) *Possessives and adjectives of origin.* These are formed from masculine names or titles by means of the suffix *-ov/ev-* and from feminines by *-in-*: R. *Ivánov* 'John's' S. *òčev* 'father's' *bratòvljev* 'brother's R. *séstrin* 'sister's'. To some extent these duplicate the uses of the genitive case: S. *òčev könj=könj òca* (rare) 'father's horse', and there are ambiguities (R. *Ivánov* 'John's' or 'Johnson'). A number of masculines also employ *-in-* (R. *Fomin* 'Tom's' *brátnin* 'brother's'), and this is usual with diminutives. These words are self-defined though the following noun may be definite or indefinite. They are consequently declined partly according to the indefinite paradigm, partly according to the definite (I*SM.*, and oblique cases of the plural).

(*c*) *Definite adjectives.* Formed by suffixed article **-i- *jos* >*-ji̇̆*:

		SNV	A	G	D	L	I
L.*M. ger-*	{	-as-	-ą-	-o-	-a-	-a-	-uo
		-is	-ji	-jo	-jam	-jame	-ju
F.	{	-o-	-ą-	-os-	-a-	-o-	-ą
		-ji	-ją	-ios	-jai	-joje	-ja
CSl.*M.dobr-*	{	-ŭ-	-ŭ-	-a-	-u-	-ě-	-y-
		-ji	-ji	-jego	-jemu	-jemĭ	-jimĭ
N.		-o-je	-o-je				
F.	{	-a-	-ǫ-	-y-	-ě-		-ǫ/o-
		-ja	-jǫ	-ję	-ji		-jǫ

WSl.G*SF.*NA*PF.*APM. -jĕ
Soft: S*M. pĕš-ĭ-ji̇̆* N. -e-je F. -a-ja; P*M.* -i-ji N. -a-ja F. -ę-ję; D*M.* -a-ja NF. -i-ji

As the demonstrative element comes last the declension depends mainly upon it, and the detailed commentary on cases may be left to the next section. The adjective proper has a nominal declension: OB. *novŭ -o -a* 'new' (like *gradŭ selo žena*) *tŭštī tŭšte tŭšta* 'empty' (like *koni̇̆ lice struja*).

The subsequent development of this paradigm in the modern languages was due largely to the fusion of the two endings of each case into a single compound form. In Old Bulgarian they appeared still sufficiently distinct, but there were certain effects of assimilation and interplay between vowels. Apart from merely scribal differences from the above paradigm, such as the use of *i e* with the values *ji̇̆ je*, Old

Bulgarian shows the following developments: N*SM.* *-yi* (*-yĭ*)/*-ii* by lengthening of the vowel before *j:* G*SMN.* *-aago -ago -ajego*, D*SMN.* *-uumu -umu*/*-ujemu*, L*SMN.* *-ěěmĭ -ě*(*j*)*amĭ -ěmĭ*/*-ějemĭ*, by assimilation. In later manuscripts are found also G*SMN.* *-ogo* : : *togo kogo* (hard demonstrative declension for the soft *jego*), D*SMN.* *-omu -emu*: OB. *živogo* 'living' *drugomu* 'another' *slěpomu* 'blind'. The ending I*SF.* *ǫjǫ* is comparatively rare: OB. *čistojǫ* 'pure'; in most cases there has been dissimilation to *-ojǫ*/*ejǫ* (*věčinojǫ* 'eternal'), and even *-ujǫ:nebesĭskujǫ* 'heavenly'.

In the comparative the NA*SM.* was not distinguished from the indefinite form; thus, *novějĭ* 'newer' fem. *novějĭši*, def. masc. *novějĭ* fem. *novějĭšija*.

PNV	A	G	L	D	I	DNA	GL	DI
ie-	-uos-	-ų-	-uos-	-ies-	-ais-	-uo-		-ie-
-ji	-ius	-jų	-iuose	-iems	-iais	-ju		-jiem
os-	-ąs-	-ų-	-os-	-os-	-os-	-ie-		-o-jom
-ios	-ias	-jų	-iose	-ioms	-iomis	-ji		
i-	-y-	-y-	-jichŭ	-y-	-y-	-a-	-u-	-y-
-ji	-ję			-jimŭ	-jimi	-ja	-ju	-jima
a-ja	-a-ja					-ě-ji		
y-	-y-					-ě-		
-ję	-ję					-ji		

71. *Paradigms of the Demonstrative Declension.* These run:

	SNV	A	G	Ab	D	L	I
IE. *s- M/F.*	-os/ā						
t- M.		-om		-ōd		-oi/ei	-ōm
toi-							-mi
tos/tes-			-(j)o	-mōd	-mōi	-mi	
t- N.	-od	-od					
t- F.		-am					-ajā(m)
tos/tes-			-(j)ās		-(j)aj		
L.*t- M.*	-às	-ą̃		-õ	-ám	-amè	-úo(mì)
F.	-à	-ą̃	-ōs		-aī	-ojè	-ą́
j- M.	-ìs	-į̃		-õ .	-ám	-amè	-úo(mì)
F.	-ì	-ą̃	-ōs		-aī	-ojè	-ą́
OB. *t- M/N.*	-ŭ/o	-ŭ/o	-ogo		-omu	-omĭ	-ěmĭ
F.	-a	-o	-oję		-oji	-	-ojǫ
k-	-ŭ(to)		-ogo		-omu	-omĭ	
c-							-ěmĭ
onŭ/jedinŭ/inŭ							
M/N.	i(že)/je(že)		jego		jemu	jemĭ	jimĭ
F.	ja(že)	jo	eję		jei		jejǫ
s- M/N.	-ĭ/e		-ego		-emu	-emĭ	-imĭ
F.	-i	-ijo	-eję		-e(j)i		-ejǫ
č-	-ĭ(to)		-ĭso		-ĭsomu	-emĭ	-imĭ
			-eso		-esomu	-esomĭ	

kyjĭ N. koje F. kaja P.M. cii N. kaja F. kyję; D.M.? F. cěji; mojĭ; tvojĭ; svojĭ, našĭ, vašĭ; čijdŭvojĭ, trojĭ, obojĭ.

	SN	A	G	D	L
	MN.				
OB. *vis-*	-ĭ/e	-ĭ/e	-ego	-emu	-em
F.	-a/ja	-ǫ	-eję		-eji

PNV	A	G	L	AbD	I	DNVA	GL	DI
oi	-ons			-bh/m	-ōis	-ō(u)		-bh/m-
		-sōm	-su					
ā	-ā					-oi		
ās	-ās	-āsōm	-āsu		-bh/m-	-ai		
iē	-úos	-ų̆	-uosè	-fems	-aĩs	-uŏ(du)		-fem-
	-ùs							-iēm-
ōs	-às	-ų̆	-osè	-óms	-omìs	-iē(dvi)		-óm-
								-ŏm-
iē	-uŏs	-ų̆	-uosè	-fems	-aĩs	-uŏ(du)		-fem-
ōs	-às	-ų̆	-osè	-óms	-omìs	-iē(dvi)		-ŏm-
i/a	-y/a		-ĕchu	-ĕmŭ	-ĕmi	-a/ĕ	-oju	-ĕma
y	-y					-ĕ		
/ja(že)	ję/ia		ichŭ	jimŭ	jimi	ja/i(že)	jeju	jima
ę(že)	ję					i(že)		
/i	-ĭję/i		ichŭ	jimŭ	jimi	ĭja/iji	jeju	jima
ĭę/iję	-iję					-i(j)i		

	I	PNV	A	G	L	AbD	I
	-ĕmi	-i/ja	-ję ja			-ĕchŭ	-ĕmŭ	-ĕmi
	-ejǫ	-ję	-ję					

N*S*.: Balto-Slavonic has made uniform the stem of the demonstrative: OB. *tŭ to ta*/Gk. ὁ(ς) ἡ το Skr. *sas sā tad*. Final -*d* has dropped without affecting the quality of the vowel, and upon Sl. *to* has been stayed the whole neuter gender (see section 63). OB. *tŭ* is also used freely with nouns as a suffix, and can be doubled with itself (*tŭtŭ*), thus giving R. *tot*. OB. *i*- (the so-called anaphoric pronoun) 'he' appears in the nom. only with the enclitic -*že* and in the relative sense 'who, which'. The interrogatives *kŭ*- 'who?' *čĭ*- 'what?' take the enclitic -*to* in the nominative.

G*S*.: Skr.*MN*. *tá-sya* (Homeric τοῖο ⟨**to-sjo*) F. *tá-syai*. It is unlikely that this genitive should have survived, developing through *tojo > *toho > to *togo* (pronounced [tavó] in Russian), though the theory has been propounded. L.*M*. *tõ* indicates IE.Ab. *tõd, Sl. *ta; the vowel would have been reformed on the basis of D*S*. *tomu* L*S*. *tomĭ*, after the addition of a particle -*go* = Skr. *gha*. Under the influence of the *o*-stems, this case occasionally appears ending in -*a* (OB. *sega jega toga*), which has been normal in Serbocroat and Slovene since the fifteenth century. Polish and Wendish show the soft form influencing the hard: P.LowWend. *tego*. GFS.L. *tõs* ⟨**tās*/OB. *toję* ⟨**tojā*-; this stem serves for all the oblique cases of the feminine singular in Slavonic. WSl. -*ě*. OB. *čĭso* ⟨**ki-s(j)o*, with vowel also opened to *česo*. This has given a new stem *čĭs/čes*- to the dat. loc. It remained so anomalous that the declension of *čĭto* 'what?' has been remodelled on *kŭto*: G*S*. *čego* etc.

DL*S*.: Skr. *MD*. *tá-smai* L. -*smin* FD. -*syai* L. -*syām*, OPr. *stes-se* -*mu -sias -siei*. The *s* has been dropped in Lithuanian and Slavonic on the analogy of the other cases. In the dat. masc. -*u* has been imported from *o*-stems; L*SM*. *tomĭ* ⟨**to(s)mi*. DL*SF*. *toi* (*toji*) is refashioned upon the stem of the genitive: *toj-. The stem *toi- was original in I*SM*. *těmĭ* ⟨**toi-mi*.

The conspicuous features of the plural are the identity of all genders in the oblique cases, and the fusion of the genitive with the locative. In these cases the demonstrative stem was *toi- > Sl. *tě*- and *jĭ > OB. *i*-. The use of the latter to make the definite declension of the adjective spread this fusion of genders into the adjectival declension, the more so since the indefinite cases were less and less seen. It was an encouragement to the tendency to unify the oblique cases of the noun-declensions also.

Like *tŭ* 'that' are declined *ovŭ* 'this', *onŭ* 'that, yon, he', etc., *takŭ* 'such', *kakŭ* 'what like?' *kŭto* 'who' *někŭto* 'someone' *nikŭto* 'no one' *kŭžĭdo* (gen. *kogožĭdo*) 'each' *jedĭnŭ/inŭ* 'one' *samŭ* 'self'. The correlatives (*kolikŭ* 'how great?' *tolikŭ* 'so great' *jelikŭ* 'as great' *mŭnogŭ* 'much' *drugŭ* 'other') show vacillations between nominal and pronominal forms. OB. *jeterŭ* 'a certain one' is declined as a noun. The soft declension has *sĭ* 'this' (which was originally an *i*-stem, cf. L. *sĭs* <*kis*), *čĭ(to)* 'what?' (Lat. *quid*), the possessives (OB. *mojĭ tvojĭ svojĭ našĭ vašĭ*), the collective numerals *dŭvojĭ trojĭ*, *sicĭ* 'such', *kyjĭ* 'which', *čĭjĭ* 'whose'. OB. (*š*)*tuždĭ* 'strange' also received a pronominal declension. Traces of the demonstrative *sĭ* are found in R. *dneś* 'today', *segódnja* 'today', *do sich por* 'hitherto', *sijú minútu* 'this minute', P. *dziś* 'today' *latoś* 'this year', etc.

In OB. *vĭsĭ* 'all' R. *veś* (Skr. *viçva-* 'all-' IE. *wis-*) the *s* should have passed into Sl. *ch* (its position after *i* is evident in L. *vìsas*, OPr.NSF. *wissa*), and the pronoun should have followed the hard paradigm of *tŭ*. Of *vĭchŭ*, the ISMN. NAPM. GP. would be (by the second palatalization) *vĭs-ěmĭ -i -ěchŭ*, with soft *ś*, which has spread to the other cases and involved change of the final hard vowels to soft: NSM. *vĭsĭ* GSMN. *vĭsego*. In West Slavonic the second palatalization of *ch* is *š*: P. *wszech* Cz. *všech*, and so P. *wszego* Cz. *všeho*. An acc. sg. fem. *vchu* is found in Old Russian.

72. *Personal Pronouns.*

	N	A	G	D	L	I	PN	A	G	L	D	I	DN	A	GL	DI
às																
		mán-è ⎱	-ę̃s	-	-yjè	-imì		mēs								
									mù-s	mú-sų	-mysè	-ms	-mìs	mù(du)		mù-
		táv-è						jũs	jù-s	jú-sų				jù(du)		jù-
		sáv-è ⎰														
B.																
azŭ	mę/mene	men-e					my									
			mĭn-ě	mŭn												
				-ojǫ			n-y		-asŭ	-amŭ	-ami			-a	-aju	-ama
													vě			
	tę/sę															
	teb/seb-e teb/			-ě												
		seb-e														
			tob/													
			sob	v-y	-y				-asŭ	-amŭ	-ami	-a		-a	-aju	-ama
			-ojǫ													

clitics: D*S*. mi/ti/si DI*D*. na/va

	N	A	G	D	L	I	PN	A	G	L	D	I	DN	A	GL	DI
R.																
z)	m-ja			-i			-y									
	men-e	-e														
		-ě		mŭn-ě		-oju										
								n-y/as	-as		-am	-ami	-ě ⎱		-aju	-ama
y	-ja		-i													
	teb/	-e		-ě/e												
	seb-e	-ě		tob/	-oju											
				sob-ě/e	v-y	-y/as							-a? ⎰			

OB. *jazŭ/azŭ* OR. *ja(z)* L. *àš* Skr. *aham* Avestic *azem* Ossetic *äz* Arm. *jes*/Gk. ἐγώ(ν) Lat. *ego* (OIr. *me-* Welsh *mi*). The Old

Bulgarian texts show almost exclusively *azŭ*; Old Lithuanian and Old Prussian have OL. *eš* OPr. *es*. The final nasal is attested in other *satem*-languages, and the original form of the Slavonic word may have been *ēĝom*: *ēzŭ* >*jazŭ* >*azŭ*, the *j*- being lost because of its position at the beginning of a word never compounded. There is, however, no other ground for admitting the existence of the long *ē* in this word, and as *azŭ* is the older in attested examples, one may think of a simple change (*azŭ* from *ezŭ* <*ēĝom*) to a more open vowel, as in L. *àš*. Another suggestion is that the change may have been the work of a prefix *ā*- (as in Skr. *ā-çis* 'blessing'), or of the conjunction *a*. IE. *tū* L. *tù* CSl.OB. *ty* 'thou'.

The oblique cases in the singular are formed from the roots *m*-, *tew/tw/t*-, *sew/sw/s*-, of which the latter groups are entirely parallel. The accusative has a suffixed *-m* (*mę/tę/sę*), which is not the usual accusative flexion, but akin to the *-m* suffixed to the nominative. GS.: *me-ne*, with suffixed *-ne*, cf. Skr. *máma* (*mána*). The corresponding forms should have been *teve/seve* (cf. Skr. *táva/sáva*), but the *b* of the dative has been substituted. R. *menjá* is probably due to AS. *mja* <*mę* and GS. *-ja* of the *jo*-nouns. DS.:Skr. *máhyam* Lat. *mihi* indicate an original form of the nature of *meghi*; OB. *mĭně*/ OR. *mŭně* L. dial. *mùni* probably owes its *ĭ* to the following *ě*. OB. *tebě/sebě* OPr. *tebbei/sebbei* Lat. *tibi/sibi* show a *bh*- phoneme (*bhei*) akin to that in Skr. *túbhyam*. In Polish and Czech there has been an exchange of cases: the original datives serve as genitive-accusatives: P. *ciebie/siebie* Cz. *tebe/sebe*, and the instrumental stem is applied to the dative: P. *tobie/sobie* Cz. *tobě/sobě*. The enclitic forms of the dative were IE. *moi/toi/soi* >CSl.OB. *mi/ti/si*. The locative has been identified with the dative in Slavonic/Skr. *máyi* etc. L. *manyjè*. IS: OB. *mŭn/tob/sob-ojǫ*, Skr. *má-y-ā*, etc. The termination is that of the instr. sg. of *a*-stems (*-ā-jam* >CSl.OB. *-ojǫ*: OB. *rǫkojǫ* Skr. *kāntayā*, see section 66 *f* ii), and the vowel of the stem is assimilated to the *o* of the flexion: OB. *mŭn*- for *mĭn*-, whence *mŭn/mĭn*- are found as alternative stems for the dative and locative also; *tob/sob*-. Conversely, the final consonants of these stems show influence of the dative on the instrumental. Cz. *teb/seb-ou* show a later assimilation to the genitive stem.

NPD.: IE.P. *mes* *wei/*wōs* *jūs*, D. *wē* *wō/*woi* (cf. OEng. P. *wē* D. *wit/P. ĝē* D. *ĝit*). OB. *my* has the vowel of the second person *vy* <*wōs;* L. *mēs* continues an original form. OB. *va* <*wō* and *vě* < *woi*. In the acc. and oblique cases there has been change of stem: *nō(s)* *n(s)/*wō(s)* *u(s)*. L. *mùs* has been influenced by *jùs* as to its vowel. ȮB.AP. *ny vy* later give way to the gen.-acc. *nasŭ vasŭ* (<*nōs-sŭ* *vōs-sŭ*). AD. OB. *na* (cf. Gk. νώ) is the only instance in Slavonic of an acc. dual differing from the nominative.

(iii) INDECLINABLES

73. *Adverbs.* (*a*) *Manner.* No use is made in Slavonic of tne method of forming adverbs from adjectives by means of suffixes, such as Eng. *-ly* Fr. *-ment.* The two principal sources of adverbs (and 'improper' prepositions) are the accusative and locative cases used invariably. There are more of the latter in West Slavonic than in Russian, which is evidence of regional preferences. The accusative adverb arises simply enough out of the 'interior' accusative, i.e. that idiom by which the noun of the action expressed by the verb is given as accusative of that verb (e.g. Gk. ἁμάρτημα ἁμαρτάνειν 'to sin a sin, commit an error'). To the noun an adjective might be attached, and the noun then omitted (Gk. μεγάλα [ἁμαρτήματα] ἁμαρτάνειν 'to commit great faults, sin grievously'). The noun need not have the same root as the verb, but only be cognate in meaning (Gk. νίκην/μάχην νικᾶν 'to win a victory/battle'); and in the ensuing uncertainty when the noun was omitted only the neuter was appropriate, sg. pl. in Greek, sg. only in Slavonic: *-o/e.* This is the normal adverb in Russian: *choroší* 'well' *ráno* 'early' *mílo* 'nicely' *dúrno* 'badly' *krájne* 'extremely', etc. The comparative is also a neuter: *bólee* 'more' *ménee* 'less'. This type of adverb was also normal in Old Bulgarian, and among words specialized for use as adverbs were OB. *tako* and *sice* 'so' *kako* 'how' *jako* 'as' *inako* 'otherwise' *pače* 'rather'. From *i-* and *u*-stems come accusatives like OB. *blizĭ* 'near' *nizŭ* 'down' *ašutĭ* 'in vain' *soprotivĭ* 'against' *ǫtrĭ* 'within' *vasnĭ* 'perchance' *iskrĭ* 'near' *pravĭ* 'truly' *strmĭ* 'rightly'. The correlatives *lubo . . . lubo* 'whether . . . or' are accusatives, and *protivǫ* 'against' is an accusative of the feminine *a*-stems. OB. *čĭto* 'why' (cf. Lat. *quid*) must also be reckoned an accusative.

The locative case has the metaphorical extension of 'in a certain way', and so is suitable for adverbial formations. Compare *-wise* in Eng. *otherwise.* The *o/a*-stems have *LSN. -ě:* OB. *godě* 'suitably' *dobrě* 'well' *zŭlě* 'ill' *dolě* 'under' *gorě* 'above' *kromě* 'outside, besides' *pozdě* 'late' *vŭně* 'outside', together with the prepositions *skvozě* 'through' *razvě* 'besides' (which govern the A and G). Locatives of *u*-stems have the suffix *-u:* OB. *vrchu* 'above' *dolu* 'down' *vŭnu* 'out'. As the genitive has the same flexion, these might be classified as genitive-locatives. OB. *meždu* 'between' is gen.-loc. dual of *mežda* 'boundary'; *vičera* 'yesterday' is a form of the genitive of *večerŭ* 'evening'. Other adverbs in *-a* are OB. *nyńa/nyně* 'now' *jedva* 'hardly'. OB. *doma* 'at home' (Gk. οἴκοι Lat. *domi*) corresponds to Lat. *domō* in form.

Various uses of the instrumental fit that case to be a source of adverbs. IP. of *o*-stems: OB. *maly* 'little' *latinĭsky* 'in Latin' *pravy* 'rightly'. The case was specially employed to designate language, as

OB. *gričĭsky* 'in Greek' R. *po-gréčeski*. The instrumental suffixes in -*m*- are used in both plural and dual forms, and sometimes alternate with datives: *vĭsĭma* 'quite', *tolĭmi/tolĭma* 'so greatly', *jelĭmi/jelĭma* 'as greatly' [see (*d*) below], *radĭma* 'on account of', *bŭchŭmŭ/bŭchŭmĭ/ bŭchŭma/bŭšĭjǫ* (ISF.) 'quite'. In the singular the instrumental is found in *jedĭnojǫ* 'once' *vŭtoricejǫ* 'for the second time', etc.

(*b*) *Time*. Adverbs of time perhaps take the form of Lat. *id temporis*, that is to say an interrogative, relative or demonstrative neuter followed by the genitive of the matter measured: -*gda* possibly from *goda*, gen. sg. of *godŭ* 'time'. They may be followed by the enclitic *že*: OB. *tŭgda/togda* 'then' *kŭgda/kogda* 'when' (Lat. *quum temporis*) *inŭgda/inogda* 'at some time' *jegdaže* 'when' (relative). The suffix -*da* appears in OS. *kada* 'when' Slov. *kdáj kàdar* (cf. L. *kadà* Skr. *kadā*). OB. *nikŭda* 'never' seems a cross between *kŭgda* and *kada*. Most modern Slavonic languages preserve traces of CSl. *kŭdy. From the locative come OB. *lani* 'last year' *utrě* 'in the morning' *lětě* 'in summer'.

(*c*) *Place*. A suffixed -*de* (< *-*dhe*, cf. Skr. *kúha* 'where') appears in *kŭde* 'where' *sĭde* 'here' *onŭde* 'yonder' *ide*(*že*) 'where' (relative) *vĭsĭde* 'everywhere'. With suffixed -*že*: *do-ideže* (*do-ńĭde-že/do-ńĭžde*) 'till, up to'. This -*de* appears as -*dě* in R. *gde* (formerly spelt *gdě*) S. *gdjě* 'where', perhaps on the analogy of the locatives in *ě*.

Place whence (*unde?*) is represented by means of -*ǫdu/ǫdě* < IE. *-*n-dhe*, which occur in the reverse order in Gk. -θεν < *-*dhe-n* (οἴκοθεν 'from home'): OB. *tǫdu* 'thence' *kǫdu/kǫdě* 'whence' *jǫdu*(*že*) 'whence' (relative) *sǫdu/ovǫdu* 'hence' *vĭsǫdu* 'from all sides' *iz vŭnǫdu* 'from without' *ǫtrĭjǫdu* 'from within'. (There is no suffix corresponding to Gk. -θι in οἴκοθι 'at home' or -δε in οἴκαδε 'homewards').

Place whither (*quo?*) is represented by means of -*amo*, which is purely Slavonic: *tamo* 'thither' *kamo* 'whither' *jamo* 'whither' (relative) *inamo* 'to some other place' *vĭsěmo* 'to all places'; cf. Gk. τῆμος 'then'.

An isolated form is *tu* 'there', cf. the demonstrative *tŭ* 'that'.

(*d*) *Degree*. Suffixes -*lĭ/li/lě/lĭma*: OB. *tolĭ* 'so far, so much' *do kolě* 'how long?' *seli* 'to this extent' *otŭ seli* 'from now on', etc. This is the source of the adjectival pronouns *kolikŭ* 'how great?', etc. (see section 71).

(*e*) *Miscellaneous*. Other common adverbs are OB. *tače* 'then' *pače* 'rather' *obače* 'however' *ješte* 'still, yet' [< **e/ot-s-kᵘe* > **je/o-sče*, whence P. *jeszcze* MB. *ošte*, S. *jöš*(*te*) by confusion of forms], *paky* 'again', etc.

74. *Prepositions*. The parent language can hardly be said to have possessed prepositions. These serve in modern languages to define precisely the relations between various parties and the activity expressed by the verb, but under primitive conditions that definition

was given, with all the clarity then desired, by the cases. To the sentence thus formed, however, it was possible to add certain small adverbs which were felt to be attached chiefly to the verb, and to define its meaning more closely, but sometimes might be considered specially to affect a noun. In the former case the particle was generally found at some distance from the verb (tmesis); in the latter it commonly followed the noun (postposition). Two forms sometimes used as postpositions in Slavonic languages are *radi* 'on account of' and *děla/*dila* 'for', both governing the genitive (cf. Lat. *gratia* and *causa*). In Homer's line

ἀμφὶ δέ οἱ κυνέην κεφαλῆφιν ἔθηκεν

'he placed a helmet on his head'

the adverb-preposition ἀμφὶ refers as much to the noun as to the verb, though separated from both, and the general relations of the two nouns to the verb are defined by their cases (acc. loc.). In all languages a more precise union has been sought, either by associating the preposition with the verb as a prefix (Gk. ἀμφέθηκεν) or with the noun as a preposition (Gk. ἀμφὶ τὴν κεφαλήν). The number of possible verbal prefixes has remained static since early times, and they have taken forms which occasionally differ from those in use as prepositions. At an early date it was also possible to attach prepositions to nouns, chiefly deverbals, as OB. *pamętĭ* 'memory' *pradědŭ* 'great-grandfather' *sǫsědŭ* 'neighbour' *sǫlogŭ* 'consort' *prorokŭ* 'prophet'. The power to make these compounds was soon lost. The vowel of the nominal prefix is usually long, but is short in the corresponding verb, as *pamętĭ/pomĭněti* (*ō/o).

It was possible to double a preposition (MB. *v*, pr. *văf*; *s*, pr. *săs*) and to use them in combination (R. *iz-pod* 'from under'). Further, since the union between the preposition and its noun is very close, and sometimes even marked by the transfer of the stress to the preposition, the consonant of the preposition was not really final, and hence survives (OB. *iz vŭz bez*). The prepositions *sŭ*, *kŭ* and *vŭ* originally ended in *n*, which appears in Slavonic as the initial of a pronoun beginning with a vowel (OB. *vŭ ńemĭ*).

In addition to these simple forms, which are almost unanalysable, there are others derived from adverbs, which are themselves evidently cases of neuter adjectives, either simply so, or compounded with a preposition. Such formations differ from language to language, according as they go out of use or additions are made. Their syntax is uniform, since they obviously must be followed by the case which expresses the dependence of nominalia upon other nominalia (nouns, adjectives, pronouns), i.e. the genitive. Some adverbial prepositions of this secondary type have gained such currency as to be classed among those in most frequent use.

Here is a list of the most usual prepositions and prefixes of Old Bulgarian. The so-called 'improper' prepositions (adverbial, based or apparently based on noun-cases, etc.) are indicated by an asterisk. Those occurring in OB. as prefixes only are indicated in the list by hyphens. The translation is rough and ready, particularly in the case of the prefixes. The prefix *vy-*, though not found in OB., has been included because of its importance in other languages.

bez bezŭ (G) 'without' [L. *bè*, Skr. *bahíš* 'outside'; ? $<$*IE. *blizŭ blizĭ* (G) 'near' [cf. Lat. *fligere* 'strike'].   (*bheĝh-s*].

črěsŭ (A) 'through, over, beyond' ($<$*čersŭ*), RChSl. also *črězŭ* by assimilation [L. *skeřsas* Gk. ἐγκάρσιος 'oblique'].

děla (G) 'because of, for' (postposition) [connected with *dělo* 'matter, affair'].

do (G) 'up to, as far as, till' [Eng. *to*, Gk. -δε, OLat. -*do*]. Prefix *do-*.

iskrĭ (G) 'near' [? from *ĭz*+a form of *kraji* 'edge, end'].

iz izŭ (G) 'out of, from' [CSl. *(j)ĭz*, L. *ĭš;* corresponds in usage rather than form to Lat. *ex*, Gk. ἐξ]. Prefix *iz-* 'out'.

kromě (G) 'besides, except' [LS. of *kroma* 'edge'].

kŭ(n) (D) 'to, towards' [$<$*kom*= Skr. *kam*].

meždu (I) 'between, among' [LD. of *mežda* 'border'].

na (L) 'on' (A) 'on to' [cf. Gk. ἄνω, ἄνα, Lat. *an-*, Goth. *ana;* ? Sl. form $<$*nō* $<$*ono* $<$*ana* (cf. L. *nuō*, which however means 'from')]. Prefix *na-*.

nadŭ (L) 'above' (A) 'down on to' [*na*+suffix *dŭ*].

o ob obŭ (L) 'around, about' (A) 'against' [L. *abi-;* cf. Skr. *abhí*, Goth. *bi*, Lat. *ob;* or Gk. ἀμφί Lat. *amb-*]. All forms found as prefixes; also *obi- obi-*.

ǫ- 'into', e.g. *ǫtoku* 'woof' [see *vŭ(n)*].

ot otŭ (G) 'away from' [L. *ati-;* Lat. *et* Gk. ἔτι in ablaut]. Prefix *otŭ- ot- o-* 'away'.

pa- 'after, then, secondly', etc.; e.g. *pamętĭ* 'memory' [see *po*].

po (D and A) 'across, over' and distributive functions [L. *pa-*, while preposition *pō* corresponds formally to *pa-;* Lat. *po-*, Gk. ἀπό]. Prefix *po-* with various meanings; frequently used to form perfectives.

podlgŭ (A) 'along' [*dlgŭ* 'long'].

podŭ (L and A) 'under, beneath' [*po*+*dŭ;* cf. *nadŭ*]. Prefix *podŭ-*.

pra- 'before', etc.; e.g. *praotĭcĭ* 'forefather' [see *pro*].

prě- 'through, across, above' [L. *peř* 'through', Lat. *per* Gk. περί].

prědŭ (L and A) 'before, in front of' [*per*+*dŭ;* cf. *nadŭ podŭ*] Prefix *prědŭ-*.

prěmo (D) 'against, opposite' [? Gk. πρόμος 'in front', Goth. *fram* 'forward'].

prězde (G) 'before' (time) [<*perd-je*, comparative form].

pri (L) 'by, at' [L. *priĕ, pri-;* cf. Lat. *prae*]. Prefix *pri-*.

pro (A) 'for' [L. *pra-*, while preposition *prō* corresponds formally to *pra-;* Skr. *pra-,* Lat. *pro,* Eng. *for*]. Prefix *pro-* 'through'.

protivǫ (D) 'against, opposite' [Latv. *pret,* Skr. *práti,* Gk. προτί πρός, Lat. *pretium*].

radi (G) 'for the sake of' (postposition) [cf. OPers. *rādiy*].

raz- razŭ- 'apart' [cf. Skr. *árdhas* 'part, side, half', L. *ardýti* 'divide, dissolve'; ? <*orz* <*ordh-z*].

razvě (G) 'apart from' [L. of *razvŭ;* cf. *raz-*].

skvozě (A) 'through' [?].

sǫ- 'with'; e.g. *sǫlogŭ* 'consort' [see *sŭ(n)*].

sŭ(n) (I) 'with' (G) 'down from' (A) 'to the extent of' [OPr. *san-* L. *san- sǫ-* Skr. *sam* Gk. ἅμα ἀ- ὁ-; IE. *som/sm*]. Prefix *sŭ(n)-* 'together, down'.

u (G) 'by, at' [despite difference of meaning, apparently the same as the following]:

u- 'away, down' [L. *au-* Skr. *áva* Gk. αὐ Lat. *au-*].

vŭ(n) (L) 'in' (A) 'into' [? <*n̥-;* cf. L. *i̯,* Gk. ἐν, Lat. *in,* Eng. *in*. The form *ǫ- (jǫ-)* from *on-* corresponds to Gk. ἀνα, Goth. *ana,* Eng. *on*].

vŭně (G) 'outside' [Loc.; cf. adv. *vŭnŭ* 'outside'. Cf. Gk. ἄνευ; or from *ud-no,* cf. *vy-*].

vŭz vŭzŭ (A) 'up, along, against' [L. *ùž* 'behind, for'; IE. *ubs/ups,* Eng. *up*]. Prefix *vŭz-* 'up'. This appears as *vŭ-* in *vŭstati* 'rise'.

(*vy-* 'out', found in ChSl. and other Sl. languages but not in OB. proper [Goth. *ūt,* IE. *ūd/ūt*]).

za (L and A) 'behind' (G) 'because of' [?]. Prefix *za-* 'behind', etc.

75. Conjunctions and Particles. The construction of Old Bulgarian sentences was of the type called paratactic, which is well represented in the Homeric poems. Sentences were normally given equal values in the discourse. There was little subordination, and almost nothing in the way of parenthesis. The large body of fully declined participles did offer a method of subordination, notably in the case of the dative absolute, but as the indefinite participles gradually developed into gerunds this resource was diminished in the modern languages. There was more than compensation, however, in the more precise conjunctival value assigned to the conjunctions, which co-ordinate or subordinate in Russian, for example, much as they do in French or English. In Old Bulgarian most of these conjunctions were present,

but their use is more akin to that of Homer. Subordinating conjunctions and relative pronouns were still clearly of demonstrative or
interrogative origin, and were employed in clauses so simply arranged
that they might be deemed coordinate. In Homer, for instance, the
Myrmidons are compared to wolves thus: οἱ δὲ λύκοι ὥς ὠμοφάγοι,
τοῖσίν τε περὶ φρεσὶν ἄσπετος ἄλκη ('like ravening wolves in whose hearts
there is unspeakable daring'), where τοῖσιν might easily be a demonstrative, and the sentence run: 'like ravening wolves—for them there
is unspeakable daring in their hearts'. So it is with the OB. *iže* 'who',
which may often be rendered 'and he', introducing a co-ordinated
statement. This is not to say, of course, that the relative is not of
Indo-European origin. OB. *i(že)* answers to Gk. ὅς Avestic *yō* Skr.
yas, and other Slavonic particles are of similar antiquity.

In South Slavonic and Russian the verb was normally initial in a
principal clause, which is the best position for narrative, since it gives
prominence to the succession of events. The final position seems to
have been more common in West Slavonic. There was thus a measure
of regional preference within the general order of the Indo-European
phrase (as exemplified by Homer), according to which the first place
was given to the most significant element of a clause. In subordinate
and especially in relative clauses the first place was taken by the
particle, and the verb was frequently delayed to the end. The position
of the subject with reference to the verb was free; a dative generally
preceded an accusative, an attributive or possessive genitive preceded
its noun, but a partitive genitive followed, and adjectives preceded
their nouns when attributive, but stood alone and later when predicative.

The principal particles and conjunctions in Old Bulgarian were
those listed below. Particles never found in isolation are indicated by
a hyphen:

    a 'but';+conditional 'if'. *a-bychŭ* etc. 'so that'. *a-cě* 'although':
a-li 'but'. [Skr. *át* 'then, and', L. *ō* 'and, but'; IE. *ōd/ōt* from
the pronoun stem *e-/o-*].

    ako (aky) 'as, when, that' [? from pronoun-stem *e-/o-;* cf.
Lat. *e-quidem*].

    ašte 'if, whether'. *ašte i* 'even if'. *ašte li* 'or else, otherwise'.
ašte da ne 'if not'. *ašte li da* 'if however'. *iže ašte* 'whoever'.
[? *ōt* (see *a*)+*jed* ⟨*jo-* ⟩*aĭed*].

    bo 'for'. *i-bo* 'and indeed'. *u-bo* 'therefore'. *ne-bo-nŭ* 'and
indeed'. [In ablaut to the *ba* found in other languages; cf. L. *bà*
'yes, good', Gk. φή].

    cě (in *a cě, cě i* 'and indeed, although' [cf. Gk. καί Skr. *ca*).
    da 'that, so, and, but'. *da-že ne* 'before'. *jako da* 'so, in order
that'. *da ako (da jako)* 'but when' [cf. Gk. δή].

i 'and, also'. *i*— *i*— 'both—and—'. *daže i do* 'till' [IE. **ei*, loc. of **e-/o-;* cf. Gk. εἰ 'so, if'].

jako 'as, that'. *jako že* 'as' [neuter of *jakŭ* (see section 73)].

jeda 'lest, that not'; used like Latin *num.* [?].

li 'whether'. *li—li—* 'whether—or' [? <**ŭloi;* Latv. *lai* 'let'; cf. Lat. *vel*].

ne 'not'. *ne-že* 'than' [IE. **ne*, Skr. *na*, Lat. *ne-*, L. *nè*].

ni 'not indeed'. *ni—ni—* 'neither—nor' [IE. **nei*, Lat. *ni*, Goth. *nei*, L. *neï*].

nŭ 'but' [L. *nù* 'now', Eng. *now;* connected with *nyně* 'now' *novŭ* 'new'].

ta (ta-že) 'and then' [from the pronoun *tŭ;* cf. Skr. *tād* 'as a consequence'].

ti 'and' [cf. Goth. *þei* 'that, so that'].

-žde (found e.g. in *tŭ-žde* 'the same') [<**dje* <IE. **djod* from pronoun-stem **djo*].

že 'and' [cf. Gk. γε, L. *-gi, -gu*].

-žĭdo (found in *kŭ-žĭdo* 'each' *iže koli-žĭdo* 'whoever', etc.) [?]. The pronouns are also used as conjunctions; e.g. *to* (neut. of *tŭ*) 'so', *jimĭže* (INS of *iže*) 'because', *po ńeže* (ANS of same) 'because', *za ńe* 'for', *se* (neut. of pronoun *sĭ*) 'behold'.

C. WORDS

76. *Preferences.* The inner circle of human relationships does not alter, and is represented in Slavonic by words drawn from the primitive stock: OB. *mati* 'mother' *dŭšti* 'daughter' *synŭ* 'son' *brat(r)ŭ* 'brother' *svekry* 'mother-in-law' *zęti* 'son-in-law' (Lat. *gener* Albanian *dhëndër* 'bridegroom') R. *mat́ doč́ syn brat svekróv zjat́.* Some of them are assimilated to more common declensions: OB. *snŭcha* 'daughter-in-law' *sestra* 'sister'/Lat. *nurus soror*, S. *svëkrva* 'mother-in-law'. In a rudimentary society relationships are traced through the mother; later, relationship to the father as head of the house is of more consequence. Traces of these two states of society are found in Slavonic: OB. *ujĭ* P. *wuj* 'uncle' was properly 'mother's brother', cf. Lat. *avunculus/patruus* and *avus* 'grandfather'; R. *zolóvka* (dim. of dial. *zólva*) S. *zäova* 'sister-in-law' is linked with Gk. γάλως Lat. *glos* 'husband's sister'; S. *jêtrva* 'husband's brother's wife' corresponds to OL. *jentė* Lat. pl. *janitrices* Homeric εἰνατέρες. Another tendency very strongly represented in Slavonic is to let nursery names persist: OB. *otĭcĭ* 'father' is a diminutive of a baby-word (Gk. ἄτ.α), as it were 'daddikins', and similarly throughout the inner circle of relatives: R. *djádja* 'uncle' *tëtka* 'aunt' *déduška* 'grandpa' *bábuška* 'granny'. In several languages *mati* and **dŭti* give place to diminutives like S. *mâjka máma* P. *córka.*

The large family was the village-community (see section 1). This
has left certain important terms: OB. *vĭsĭ* 'village', cf. Gk. οἶκος Lat.
vicus, originally the community's 'long house', whence came OPr.
waispattin 'wife' L. *viēšpats* 'master of the house' (Skr. *viçpatis*).
CSl.OB. *gospodĭ* 'master' is not quite clear in its etymology, but
may be compared with Lat. *hospes* <*hosti-potis*, so that, as it were,
'guest-master' was substituted for 'house-master'. OB. *domŭ* 'house'
(Lat. *dŏmus* Gk. δόμος δέμω 'build') refers primarily to the edifice;
it is absent from the Baltic languages in the simple form. The
more elaborate groups had names in Indo-European which died out
in Balto-Slavonic through disuse, and though the power of making
compound epithets was retained actual compounds were few, a fact
which denotes an absence of religious organization. Only names were
given the solemn and sacerdotal value associated with such compounds.

Though the parts of the body are permanent their names are liable
to certain changes, on account of modesty, humorous depreciation of
one's own, the use of slang equivalents. Other parts, however, by
exciting no such reactions, retain very old names. So OB. *językŭ*
'tongue' L. *liežùvis* Lat. *lingua* Goth. *tuggo* Eng. *tongue*, all apparently
representing modifications of a single root; OB. *sŭdĭce* 'heart' L.
širdìs Lat. *cor(d)* Gk. καρδία Eng. *heart*, OB. *brvĭ* R. *brov́* 'eye-brow'
Gk. ὀφρύς Eng. *brow*, OB. *nosŭ* 'nose' L. *nósis* Lat. *nasus* Eng. *nose*, are
all primitive names for these things. Unlike these, the word for 'hand'
varies from language to language, apparently for the sake of greater
vividness: OB. *rǫka* R. *ruká* L. *rankà* seems to mean 'the gatherer'
(L. *renkù* 'I gather'). OB. *usta* (pl.) 'mouth' was originally' lips' (Skr.
osṭhas). OB. *noga* 'foot'/L. *nagà* means 'hoof' (Gk. ὄνυξ L. *nãgas*
'nail') and OB. *zǫbŭ* 'tooth' R. *zub*/L. *dantìs* meant 'peg' (Albanian
dhëmb 'tooth' Gk. γόμφος 'nail', L. *žãmbas* 'edge', Ossetic *zämbin*
'yawn'). These two substitutions are the result of ancient slang. The
fact that Lithuanian participates in the one case but not in the other
exemplifies two characteristics of the Balto-Slavonic group: their
agreement in one set of highly characteristic innovations, and the
equally large number of innovations which are peculiarly Slavonic.
It has led to the suggestion that their unity was interrupted for a
while and then resumed; a suggestion which attempts to bring under
one formula their striking likenesses and differences.

The originality of Slavonic is well brought out by a long series of
names for animals which must have been quite familiar in the ancient
communities: OB. *koňĭ* 'horse' *kobyla* 'mare' *volŭ* 'ox' (Ossetic *gal*)
baranŭ 'ram' (? Ossetic *wärig* 'lamb' Arm. *garn* Pers. *barra* Skr. *urana-*
Gk. ἀρήν) *koza kozĭlŭ* 'goat', R. *sobáka* 'dog' (Medic σπάκα), OB.
ptica 'bird' *ryba* 'fish', *zmĭjĭ* 'snake' (? 'the earthy'). In the case of OB.
medvědĭ 'bear', literally 'honey-eater', a taboo has prevented the use of

the normal name for this dangerous animal. On the other hand, old survivals include: OB. *turŭ* 'aurochs' (OPr. *tauris* Lat. *taurus* Gk. ταῦρος) and *govędŭ* 'ox' R. *govjádina* 'beef' (Lat. *bos* Ir. *bo* Eng. *cow* ⟨*$g^{w}ou$-⟩, *ovĭnŭ ovĭca* 'sheep' (L. *avìs* Gk. οἴς Lat. *ovis*), *agnĭcĭ* 'lamb' R. *jagnënok* Lat. *agnus, vlna* 'wool' R. *vólna, svinĭja* 'sow', *vlkŭ* 'wolf' R. *volk, myšĭ* 'mouse', *orĭlŭ* 'eagle' R. *orël*, R. *drozd* 'thrush', OB. *žeravĭ* 'crane' L. *gérvė* (Gk. γέρανος Lat. *grus*), *gǫsĭ* 'goose' R. *guś, ǫty* 'duck' R. *útka* L. *ántis* (Lat. *anas* Gk. νῆσσα), *mucha* 'fly' L. *musẽ* (Gk. μυῖα), *osa* 'wasp' (Lat. *vespa*), *bĭčela* R. *pčelá* 'bee' L. *bitìs* (Germ. *Biene* OEng. *beo*), and the bee's product OB. *medŭ* R. *mëd* L. *medùs* 'honey, hydromel'.

Names of trees are generally stable, unless the name is transferred to another species as a result of travel. One notes, for instance: OB. *brĕza* 'beech' R. *berëza* L. *béržas* (Ossetic *bärz*), *želǫdĭ* R. *žëlud* 'acorn' L. *gìlė* (Lat. *glans*), *ablŭko* 'apple' L. *óbuolas* (Abella was a place-name in Campania). The oak is exceptionally variable, either because of difference of species or because of the religious awe which it often inspired. OB. *drĕvo* 'tree'/L. *dervà* 'pine-wood' corresponds to Gk. δρῦς 'oak' δόρυ 'cut trunk, spear-shaft', but the Slavonic term was *dǫbŭ* R. *dub*/L. *ážuolas*. Minerals include: OB. *solĭ* 'salt', *zlato* 'gold' R. *zóloto* Latv. *zelts*/L. *áuksas* (Lat. *aurum* ⟨*$ausum$), **$sĭrebro$* 'silver' R. *serebró* L. *sidâbras*/Lat. *argentum* Gk. ἄργυρος), *želĕzo* 'iron' L. *geležìs* (Gk. χαλκός 'copper'), *ruda* 'metal, ore' (ON. *rauði* Finnish *rauta* 'iron', ON. *rauðr* 'red').

A number of other words, when compared with Lithuanian equivalents, help to define the originality involved in the creation of Slavonic: R. *vysókij* 'high'/L. *áukštas* OB. *umŭ* 'intelligence'/L. *prōtas*, OB. *bolĭjĭ* 'greater' R. *bólše* 'more' [Gk. βέλτερος Lat. (*de*)*bilis* 'weak', with negative prefix *de*-]/L. *didèsnis, dobrŭ* 'good' (Lat. *faber* **$dhāb(e)r$-*)/L. *gēras*, R. *pesń* 'song'/L. *dainà*, OB. *lŭžĭ* 'lie'/L. *mēlas*, OB. *črnŭ* 'black'/L. *júodas, godŭ* 'year'/L. *mētas, pastuchŭ* 'shepherd'/ L. *piemuō, prijatelĭ* 'friend'/L. *draũgas, slnĭce* 'sun'/L. *sáulė, človĕkŭ* 'man'/OL. *žmuo*. The list would be much lengthened by adding those words in which Slavonic differs from the Baltic languages in some detail, as OB. *novŭ* 'new'/L. *naũjas* (**$newos$/*neujos*) or OB. *sŭmrtĭ* 'death' R. *smerí*/L. *mirtìs*. The correspondences, however, are not less striking: OB. *mirŭ* 'peace' L. *mieras* (obsolete), *mĭgla* 'mist' L. *miglà* (Ossetic *mĭy* Zend. *maeya* Gk. ὀμίχλη), *devętĭ* 'nine' L. *devynì, slava* 'glory' L. *šlovẽ/garbẽ*, R. *koróva* 'cow' L. *kárvė, nesti* 'bear' L. *nèšti, sladŭ-kŭ* 'sweet' L. *saldùs*, etc.

77. *Borrowings.* (*a*) *Iranian.* For these see section 2. The name of 'God' OB. *Bogŭ* might be purely Slavonic, and some of its derivatives are used in historic Slavonic senses. But the transfer of meaning involved between material notions like 'bread', 'distributor', 'rich', to

the spiritual concept 'God' is something which unites Iranians and Slavs. The word for 'dog' R. *sobáka* Medic *spaka* contrasts with L. *šuõ* Skr. *çvan* (Lat. *canis* Gk. κύων English *hound*), and shows that in such transactions the whole of the respective groups were not necessarily involved. Other probable Iranianisms were R. *sekíra* 'axe', *topór* 'axe' *sochá* 'plough' *kur* 'cock' S. *vätra* 'fire'. L. *šveñtas* OB. *svętŭ* 'holy' R. *svjatój* corresponds to Avestic *spəntō*, and OB.R. *slovo* 'word' to Avestic *sravo;* these may be coincidences. There may be other instances of borrowing which cannot now be demonstrated, but remain as curious coincidences. Thus OB. *zobŭ* 'tooth' R. *zub* coincides in every way with Skr. *jambhas* 'tooth', and there is a connecting link in Ossetic (Scythian) *zämbin* 'yawn, gape'/Gk. γόμφος 'peg', and OB. *volŭ* 'ox' with Ossetic *gal* (*g* < **w*, *a* < **o*). The former coincidence is particularly striking. The latter offers evidence of contact with East Finns: Čeremiss. *volek*, Vogul *volov vulu*. It may have had a centre of diffusion in Scythian territory.

(*b*) *Germanic and Occidental.* From their German neighbours the Slavs obtained words that expressed the superiority of German military organization, together with others, both of German and Romance origin, which expressed the greater domestic comfort of the west. Among Germanic military words were R. *vítjaž* < **witeng-*'heto' (possibly the *Witings*); OB. *mečĭ* 'sword' R. *meč* Finnish *miekka* OL. *mečius* < Goth. *mēki*, *brady* '(hal)berd' < Germ. *barta*, *šlěmŭ* 'helm(et)' < Goth. *hilms*, *plkŭ* 'troop' R. *polk* cf. Eng. *folk*, *kŭnę(d)zĭ* 'prince' R. *knjaž* < Germ. **kuningaz*, OB. *kralĭ* R. *korólĭ* < *Karl*. OB. *kopĭje* 'spear' probably came through the Germans from Gk. κωπίον 'haft'. The precise military terms *sŭtĭnikŭ* 'centurion', *desętĭnikŭ* 'decurion' and *leǵeonŭ* 'legion' may be of later literary importation.

The Slavonic hut had only one poorly-heated room (OB. *sěnĭ* 'cold room, vestibule'). A warm room was added by imitation of the Germans (OB. *istŭba* R. *izbá* 'room with stove', Frankish *stuba*, now 'hut'), and other terms were OB. *chyzŭ* 'house' *chlěvŭ* 'store-room' (Goth. *hláiw*), P. *buda* 'bothy', and from Romance through German: P. *komora* R. *kómnata* 'room'(< *caminata*), Cъ. *kuchyně* 'kitchen'. So also OB. *koliba* 'hut' (Gk. κάλυβη) S. *cigla* 'brick' (Lat. *tegula*) OB. *baňa* 'bath' (Lat. *banea*, *balneum*, Gk. βαλανεῖον βάνεια). The loanwords also indicate an improved standard of living in respect of food: OB. *olŭ* *olovina* 'ale' (which may not be a loanword) *chlěbŭ* 'bread' (Goth. *hláifs*); and utensils (notably *bludo* 'dish' Goth. *biups*), *kadĭ* 'vat' R. *kádka* (Gk. κάδος), R. *bóčka bočënok* 'barrel' (? < Gk. βουττίς < Lat. *būtis*), R. *miska* 'tureen' dim. of *misa* (Goth. *mes* Lat. *mensa*). Lat. *cucullus* 'cowl' gave various derivatives, including R. *kúkla* 'doll'; another sign of improved clothing was the word B. *gúnja* 'cloak' (< Lat. *gunna* < Celtic). A considerable number of loanwords attest the advance in agriculture and commerce: R. *plug* 'plough with coulter'/*sochá* 'wooden plough' and *ra(d)lo* 'hand-plough, hoe' (Germ. *pl(u)og Pflug*), *vinó* 'wine' and *vinográd* 'vine' originally 'vineyard', OB. *vrtogradŭ* 'orchard', R. *skot* 'cattle', OB. *osĭlŭ* 'donkey' R. *osël* (Lat. *asellus*, dim. of *asinus*), *pastyrĭ/pastuchŭ* 'shepherd', *kupiti* 'buy' (Goth. *káupōn*), and also the fruits R. *čeréšnja* 'cherry' (*ceresia*), *pérsik* 'peach' (*persicum*), with the vegetable Cz. *locika* 'lettuce' (Lat. *lactūca*) and OB. *jelejĭ* 'oil' (Gk. ἔλαιον). Communications and money were improved to support trade: R. *korábĺ* 'ship' [Gk. καράβι(ον); a further borrowing seems to have given the ON. *karfi* 'galley'], a word taken over when Gk. β was still occlusive *b;* but ON. *elliði* 'ship' seems to come from the native Slavonic **oldĭja*. R. *týsjača* 'thousand' (Goth. *pūsundi*) shows an intellectual advance in counting; OB. *pěnędzĭ* 'penny' *skŭlędzĭ* 'shilling' *dinarŭ* 'denarion' *kodrantŭ* 'quadrans' show how money superseded barter.

Not many words are free from the material bias of the above list, but there are a few which imply new distinctions of thought: OB. *chǫdogŭ* 'skilled' (Goth. *handugs*), *listĭ* 'guile', *čuždĭ* 'strange' (Goth. *piuda* 'people'), *ludĭje* 'people' (Germ. *Leute*). A special interest attaches to OB. *crky* 'church' R. *cérkoú* (Germ. *kirihha* <Gk. κυριακή) because it comes late in this series; it must have been borrowed after the conversion of the Goths, but before the break-up of the Slavonic community. *Cæsar* (Goth. *Kaisar*) was borrowed as OB. *cěsarĭ* and later again as *kesarĭ*, the latter connoting the Roman Emperor. R. *buk* 'beech-tree' may have been an ancient Germanic loanword, but *búkva* 'letter' evidently connoted a rune scratched on beech-bark; it must, therefore, have been borrowed later than the introduction of runes into Germany in the first centuries of our era, as a distant imitation of Roman writing. OB. *kŭńiga* S. *knjĭga* R. *kniga* 'book' has been connected with Arm. *knikʿ* 'seal', Assyrian *kunukku* 'seal' and *kanīku* 'something sealed', though not without difficulty, for want of intermediary forms in Syrian. The Slavonic word may belong to the same series ('sealed tablets or pages'). Owing to the geographical difficulties involved by this explanation, and to certain doubts concerning the link between Armenian and Assyrian, another source has been suggested, viz. Goth. *kannjan* 'make known', whence **kannjainga* MidLowGerm. *kenninge* ON. *kenning* (*F.*) 'doctrine, proclamation'.

Germanic *k g* are affected by the second Slavonic palatalization (section 38), and *-ing* gives CSl. *-ędzĭ*. Latin words commonly show Romance articulation: R. *čeréšnja* has *c = č;* OB. *kaležĭ* 'cup' shows a voiced and palatalized internal *c* in Lat. *calicem;* Cz. *locika* and its congeners develop Lat. *-ct-* as CSl. **-kt-* before a front vowel, so that the *ū* of Lat. *lactūca* may have been borrowed with its Gallo-Roman value *ü;* OB. *židovinŭ* 'Jew' shows the Romance pronunciation of *j* in *judæus*. In some cases these loanwords bear traces also of their passage through Germanic: OB. *pastyřĭ* with *y* $<$ *u* possibly due to Germanic/ Lat. *pastorem*, P. *mnich* 'monk' (cf. *Munich München*/Lat. *monachus*) *klasztor* 'cloister' (Germ. *Kloster*). West Slavonic takes its terms for religious organization from Latin, though they also penetrate into other parts: OB. *olŭtařĭ* 'altar' OR. *pogan* 'pagan'. Greek words show the iotacism of the Byzantine language, and fricative β $>$ Sl. *v*, a fact which makes the *b* in *korábl* so outstanding.

(c) *Byzantine.* (i) *Loanwords.* As a result of the missions of St. Methodius and St. Cyril the stream of external influence was diverted from Germany to Byzantium. It entered primarily the South Slavonic region, moulding the whole cultural vocabulary of Old Bulgarian, but it also reached northwards through Slovenia towards Poland. Hence it is that even the Latin Christianity of the Western Slavs has certain basic words from Church Slavonic, though the vocabulary of organization is essentially Latin. Russian Christianity, of course, is directly dependent on Old Bulgarian models.

Just as the Germanic loanwords in Slavonic include some which are of Roman origin, and among these are some Greek words adopted into Latin usage, so the Byzantine Greek element includes some words which are Latin by origin. Some have been mentioned above: *leǵeonŭ* 'legion', *sŭtĭnikŭ* translated from 'centurion'. A precise date of borrowing cannot usually be given. R. *ídol* 'idol' is Gk. εἴδωλον, but there is nothing to show whether this term, undoubtedly Christian in the meaning adopted, came as a result of the evangelization of the Goths in the fourth century or of the Slavs in the ninth. Concerning the majority, on the other hand, there is not much doubt. They belong to the lexicon of technical terms which refer to features of biblical society, the organization of the Orthodox Church, or theological ideas. There was probably another vocabulary, of which little trace remains, viz. that of diplomacy. The treaties placed under the name of Oleg by Russian chroniclers show a strong preponderance of Byzantine technical terms. Men of affairs were perhaps less inhibited than clerics, and may have been more prone to borrow such words as suited their needs. The most remarkable feature of the Byzantine loans to Slavonic is, indeed, not their number but the scruples of the learned borrowers in preserving as much as possible the Slavonic flavour of their language. It was for this reason, probably, that Russian and the other Slavonic languages have not developed, like English, into mixed speeches, as a synthesis between Slavonic essentials and Greek superstructure. The Slavonic missionaries preferred translation to direct transfer, and sought to increase the mental content of their tongue as much as possible by deploying its native resources.

The direct loans are, however, quite numerous. They include words in *archi-* (*archijereji* 'archpriest' *architᵛiklinŭ* 'chief of the feast'), *jevangelije, litürgija, aromatŭ, angelŭ, üpokritŭ, vlasfimisati* 'to blaspheme', etc. With these are included some Jewish terms like *sǫbota, pascha, fariseji,* and the system of dating was Latin: *inŭdiktŭ, aprili, dekębři,* etc. There was also a Slavonic series of names for months contrived to fit the Latin calendar, so that, for instance, Cz. *listopad* 'leaf-fall' corresponds to November/OB. *nojębři.* A large body of personal names are also Byzantine and Christian. Other borrowed words are: OB. *litra* 'pound' *drachma apostolŭ dijavolŭ*/Sl. *běsŭ zilotŭ* 'zealot' *psalmŭ kedrŭ* 'cedar' *onagrŭ* 'wild ass' *alavastrŭ aerŭ igemonŭ* 'leader' *igumenija* 'abbess'.

These words observe the rules of Byzantine pronunciation. The Gk. β is fricative (*vlasfimija* Gk. βλασφημία). Byzantine iotacism had caused Gk. η ι υ ει οι υι to coincide in the pronunciation *i;* hence OB. *ikonomŭ* (οἰκονόμος) *igumenija* (εἰγουμένη) *klirosŭ* (κλῆρος) *idolŭ* (εἴδωλον) *stichija/stüchija* (στοιχεῖα). The alphabet included special signs used to transcribe Gk. υ γ (when palatal) φ θ. The latter pair were pronounced as *f*. Their more popular equivalents would have been *p t*, hence OB. *fropitŭ* (προφήτης), and sometimes colloquial usage imposed itself, as OB. *Fezda* Gk. Βηθεσδά.

(ii) *Imitations.* R. *medvéd* 'bear' and *chlebosólstvo* 'hospitality' ('bread-saltness') are among words which give witness of powers of composition undiminished since the Indo-European period, but not generally in use. They were summoned to aid the clerics who had to make intelligible to Slavonic converts the leading ideas of Greek theology. They include many striking examples: OB. *licemě́rŭ* 'hypocrite' (Gk. προσωπολήπτης) *pakybytije* 'second birth' (Gk. παλιγγενεσία) *jedinočędŭ* 'only begotten' *žestosr̥dije* 'hardness of heart' *chranilište* 'phylactery' *ližesŭvědětelĭstvovati* 'bear false witness' *kuroglašenije* 'cock-crow' *bezočĭstvo* 'shamelessness', together with *prorokŭ* 'prophet' and a considerable number of words in *blago-* (Gk. εὐ- ἀγαθο-), *bez-* [Gk. ἀ(ν)-] and *bogo-* (Gk. θεο-): *blagoobrazinŭ* 'fair' (Gk. εὐσχήμων) *bezakonije* (*bez*+*zakon-*) 'lawlessness' (Gk. ἀνομία) *Bogorodica* 'Mother of God' (Gk. ἡ Θεοτόκος) *bogočitĭcĭ* 'godfearing' (Gk. θεοσέβης).

(*d*) *Turko-Tatar.* While Turko-Tatar contacts are not to be supposed effective in Common Slavonic times, some tribes were in contact with those peoples during the period of migrations, and some loanwords were adopted at an early date and have a wide extension. One such is OB. *sanŭ* R. *san* 'honour' (T. *san* 'appearance, dignity'). This was so far acclimatized as to give derivatives as if it were a Slavonic root: OB. *sanovitŭ sanoviniku* R. *priosánitsja* 'to assume a dignified air'. Until Russian colonists spread into the great forests, the ancient fur-trade passed through Tatar hands, and so T. *samur* 'sable' appears in OB. *samurinŭ* S. *sàmur*/R. *sóbol* P. *soból*, etc. A loanword generally accepted by the Slavonic tongues is OB. *bisĭrŭ* 'pearl, bead' R. *biser* S. *bìser*, etc. The source seems to be Arabic *buṣra* 'imitation pearl' (found in Ibn Foslan). At so early a date it would probably have entered Slavonic across Persia and the Tatar steppe, and so be a Turko-Tatar loan to Slavonic, though it does not form part of Osmanli Turkish. (The intermediate form may have been TT. **büsre*).

78. *Word-formation.* The oldest method of forming new words from old seems to have been by way of vowel mutations according to the grades *o/e/zero* (section 23). When certain primitive adverbs had come to be attached to their verbs in the form of prefixes they gave new derived verbs, perfective in value, and also the nouns of agent or action akin to those verbs (section 74). The power to compose new verbs on this model persists, but nouns of the type OB. *sǫlogŭ* 'consort' *sŭborŭ* 'assembly' have become petrified because of the loss of the verbal sense of the original verbal noun. Verbs are also formed by means of suffixes. The most important are those used to form the conjugations (section 48), and they sometimes differ in the two stems involved in each conjugation. There remain to be considered those suffixes which form, or once formed, derived nouns and adjectives. When derived from verbs by means of suffixes they are sometimes called deverbatives; when from nouns, denominatives. Most of them are thematic, i.e. involving the vowels *o/e*, but some give *i*-stems, and the feminine suffix *-ā/jā* was of the greatest importance. Suffixes which form nouns are distinct from those which form adjectives. Among the latter the participles form a clearly defined group, and another is composed of the diminutive and augmentative suffixes, which also express affection or contempt.

The following paragraphs give the principal noun and adjective suffixes (many of them compound) of Old Bulgarian, together with examples of their use. Not all of them are simple suffixes, e.g. *-inikŭ* < *-ĭn-ik-*, *-ĭstvo*, *-ĭstvĭje*, etc.; nor were all of them 'active' in Old Bulgarian.

-*a*: *rabŭ* 'slave'—*raba* 'female slave'
    gybnǫti 'perish'—*paguba* 'destruction'
-*ařĭ* (from Latin through Germanic): *ryba* 'fish'—*rybařĭ* 'fisherman'
-*atŭ*: *krilo* 'wing'—*krilatŭ* 'winged'
-*čĭji*: *šarŭ* 'colour'—*šarŭčĭji* 'painter'
-*elŭ*: *kysnǫti* 'grow sour'—*kyselŭ* 'sour'
-*ělĭ*: *kǫpati* 'bathe'—*kǫpělĭ* 'bath'
    pekǫ sę 'I worry' (lit. 'bake myself')—*pečalĭ* 'worry'
-*enŭ*: *zelĭje* 'herb'—*zelenŭ* 'green'

-ĕne: slovĕne 'Slavs'
    zemĺa 'land'—zemĺane 'countryfolk' (<*-ĺĕ-)
-ĕnŭ: drĕvo 'wood'—drĕvĕnŭ 'wooden'
    koža 'leather'—kožanŭ
-eži: grabiti 'rob'—grabeži 'robbery'
 -ę: osĭlŭ 'ass'—osĭlę 'young ass'
-ica: bogorodica 'Mother of God' (roditi 'bear')
    vrataři 'doorkeeper'—vratarica 'female doorkeeper'
    čr̥nŭ 'black'—čr̥nica 'nun'
-ikŭ: učenŭ 'learned'—učenikŭ 'pupil, disciple'
-ina: globokŭ 'deep'—globina 'depths'
    maslo 'oil'—maslina 'olive-tree'
-inŭ: graždaninŭ 'citizen' (from graždane; see -jane)
    vojevoda 'duke'—vojevodinŭ 'pertaining to the duke'
    golobĭ 'dove'—golobinŭ 'pertaining to a dove'
 -ište (<*-isče/-isko found in other languages):
    pozorŭ 'show'—pozorište 'theatre'
    žiti 'live'—žilište 'dwelling-place' (based on l-participle)
 -ištĭ (<*-ītjo-): robŭ 'slave'—robištĭ 'young slave'
-itŭ: mastĭ 'fat'—mastitŭ 'fatty'
    plodŭ 'fruit' (u-stem)—plodovitŭ 'fruitful'
-ivŭ: strachŭ 'fear'—strašivŭ 'timid'
-izna: glava 'head'—glavizna 'chapter'
  -ĭ: medŭ 'honey' (u-stem) *ĕd- 'eat'—medvĕdĭ 'bear'
    tvoriti 'create'—tvarĭ 'creation, creature' (a <*ō)
    studenŭ 'cold'—studenĭ 'coldness'
-ĭba: služiti 'serve' (sluga 'servant')—služĭba 'service'
    alkati 'hunger'—alčĭba
    drugŭ 'friend'—družĭba 'friendship'
 -ĭčĭ: tvoriti 'create'—tvorĭčĭ 'creator'
    slĕpŭ 'blind'—slĕpĭčĭ 'blind man'
    gradŭ 'city'—gradĭčĭ 'small town'
    *otŭ 'father'—otĭčĭ 'father' (originally a diminutive)
    (L. avìs 'sheep')—ovĭca 'sheep'
    jaje 'egg'—jajĭce 'egg'
-ĭda: pravŭ 'right—pravĭda 'righteousness'.
-ĭja: bratrŭ 'brother'—bratrĭja 'brothers, fraternity'
-ĭje: prositi 'beg', p.p.p. prošenŭ—prošenĭje 'request'
    žiti 'live'—žitĭje 'life'
    sŭdravŭ 'healthy'—sŭdravĭje 'health'
    bezŭ zakona 'without law'—bezakonĭje 'lawlessness'
 -ĭji: sodŭ 'court'—sodĭji 'judge'; see section 62(d)
 -ĭjĭ: bogŭ 'God'—božĭjĭ 'God's'
 -ĭkŭ: tęgostĭ 'heaviness'—tęžĭkŭ 'heavy'

-ĭlivŭ: *obida* 'offense'—*obidĭlivŭ* 'offensive' (Serbocroat *-ljiv* would indicate that the form was—*ĭl'ivŭ*)

-ĭlŭ: *svĕtŭ* 'light'—*svĕtĭlŭ* 'bright'

-ĭnica: *grĕchŭ* 'sin' *grĕšĭnŭ* 'sinful' (see -ĭnŭ)—*grĕšĭnica* 'female sinner'

tĭma 'darkness'—*tĭmĭnica* 'prison'

-ĭniku: *vrata* 'door'—*vratĭnikŭ* 'doorkeeper'

-ĭń̆ĭ: *bratrŭ* 'brother'—*bratrĭń̆ĭ* 'brother's'

doma 'at home'—*domašĭń̆ĭ* 'domestic'

nynĕ 'now'—*nynĕšĭń̆ĭ* 'present'

-ĭnŭ: *vĕra* 'faith'—*vĕrĭnŭ* 'faithful'

nedǫgŭ 'illness'—*nedǫžĭnŭ* 'ill'

prijęti 'accept', p.p.p. *prijętŭ*—*prijętĭnŭ* 'acceptable, agreeable'

-ĭskŭ: *žena* 'woman'—*ženĭskŭ* 'womanly'

slovĕne 'Slavs'—*slovĕnĭskŭ* 'Slavonic'

-ĭstvĭje: *cĕsarĭ* 'emperor'—*cĕsarĭstvĭje* 'empire'

-ĭstvo: *cĕsarĭstvo* 'empire'

bogŭ 'God'—*božĭstvo* 'divinity'

bogatŭ 'rich'—*bogatĭstvo* 'wealth'

-ja: *gospodĭ* 'master'—*gospožda* (<*-dja) 'mistress'

suchŭ 'dry'—*suša* (<*-chja) 'drought'

-jane (probably analogical from forms like *zemĺane;* see -ĕne):

graždane 'citizens' (<*gordjane)

Rimŭ 'Rome'—*Rimlane* 'Romans'

-jĭ: *voditi* 'lead'—*voždĭ* 'leader' (<*vodjĭ)

strĕgǫ 'I guard' (<*stergǫ)—*straži* 'guard' (<*storgjĭ)

prorokŭ 'prophet'—*proročĭ* 'prophet's'

-k-: *kamykŭ* 'stone' (cf. *kamy*)

językŭ 'tongue' (cf. OPr. *insuwis*)

biti 'beat'—*bičĭ* 'whip'

klĕtĭ 'larder', dim. *klĕtĭka*

-lo (<*-dlo): *orati* 'plough'—*ralo* 'plough' (<*ordlo)

-lo: *grebǫ* 'I row'—*greblo* 'oar'

-lŭ: *krǫgŭ* 'circle'—*krǫglŭ* 'round'

(cf. *dalŭ*, p.p.a., 'having given')

-nĭ: *dati* 'to give'—*danĭ* 'tribute'

-nŭ: *solĭ* 'salt'—*slanŭ* 'salty' (<*solnŭ)

(cf. p.p.p. *danŭ* 'given')

-oba: *zŭlŭ* 'evil'—*zŭloba*

-okŭ: *vysokŭ* 'high', cf. *vyše* 'higher' from *vys-je*

-ostĭ: *nagŭ* 'naked'—*nagostĭ* 'nakedness'

bujĭ 'crazy'—*bujestĭ* 'craziness'

-*ota*: *toplŭ* 'warm' (from *top-lŭ*, cf. *topiti* 'to heat')—*toplota* 'warmth'

    sujĭ 'vain'—*sujeta* 'vanity'

-*ovŭ*: *Avraamŭ* 'Abraham'—*Avraamovŭ* 'Abraham's'

    spasitelĭ 'saviour'—*spasitelevŭ* 'saviour's'

    lĭvŭ 'lion'—*lĭvovŭ* 'of a lion' (cf. *Lvov*)

 -*rŭ*: *moknǫti* 'get wet'—*mokrŭ* 'wet'

-*sli*: *jamĭ* 'I eat' (<*jad-mĭ*)—*jasli* (pl.) 'manger' (<*jad-sli*)

-*slo*: *čisti* 'count' (<*čit-ti*)—*čislo* 'number' (<*čit-slo*)

    mazati 'smear'—*maslo* 'oil' (<*maz-slo*)

-*snĭ*: *pěti* 'sing'—*pěsnĭ* 'song'

-*šĭnĭ*: see -*ĭnĭ*

-*tajĭ*: *orati* 'plough'—*ratajĭ* 'ploughman' (<*ortajĭ*)

-*telĭ*: *pisati* 'write'—*pisatelĭ* 'writer'

    prijati 'favour'—*prijatelĭ* 'friend'

 -*tĭ*: *mrěti* 'die' (* <*mer-*)—*sŭmrtĭ* 'death'

    mazati 'smear'—*mastĭ* 'salve' (<*maz-tĭ*)

    stradati 'suffer'—*strastĭ* 'passion' (<*strad-tĭ*)

-*to*: *pęti* 'stretch' (from *pen-*)—*pǫto* 'fetter' (from *pon-*) (cf. p.p.p. in -*tŭ*)

 -*ŭ*: *grměti* 'to thunder'—*gromŭ* 'thunder'

-*ŭkŭ*: *slaždĭ* 'sweetness' (<*slad-jĭ*)—*sladŭkŭ* 'sweet'; strictly speaking this is an old *u*-stem, cf. L. *saldùs*, with suffix -*k*-: *sladŭ-kŭ*)

    načęti 'begin', p.p.p. *načętŭ*—*načętŭkŭ* 'beginning'

    pętŭ 'fifth'—*pętŭkŭ* 'Friday'

 -*y*: *plodŭ* 'fruit'—*neplody* 'barren woman'

    lubŭ 'dear'—*luby* 'love'

-*yńi*: *rabŭ* 'slave'—*rabyńi* 'female slave'. [Soft *ń* on analogy of oblique cases based on -*yn-ja;* see section 62(*d*)].

-*znĭ*: *žiti* 'live'—*žiznĭ* 'life'

    bolěti 'be ill'—*bolěznĭ* 'illness'

    bojati sę 'fear'—*bojaznĭ* 'fear'

A few foreign suffixes have been borrowed embedded in the words they formed in the original tongue, such as Germ. -*ung*, T.- *luk*. Only one has come into general use, viz. Lat. -*arius* (via Germanic), which had definite cultural connotations, and referred to arts more highly developed in the west. The common adjectival suffix -*isko* is found in the same uses as Germ. -*isch* Eng. -*ish*, and may represent—though not certainly—a Slavonic debt to Germanic. It provided a ready means for transferring Greek words in -ισκος.

Some of the suffixes listed above were, as we have said, not active, i.e. they were no longer used freely to form new words. In all the existing languages the principal weight is laid on suffixes formed from a primary suffix augmented by a thematic vowel, and still more upon compounds of primary suffixes: R. *-skij* of adjectives, *-stvo* of abstracts, *-ushka* of affectionate words, etc. The use of suffixes in Slavonic, therefore, is seen to involve a transformation of the primitive system which is just as radical as any of the other transformations making up Slavonic historical grammar.

79. *Changes of meaning.* Vocabulary is augmented also by giving new senses to old words. In this process certain habits of our minds are involved, and they are generally independent of the evolutionary development of sounds and forms. It will suffice to give a few examples, which may be multiplied at the reader's leisure. The meaning may suffer a slight shift: R. *vinográd* 'vine' /not 'vineyard', *rot* 'mouth'/ Cz. *ret* 'lip'. Often a particular term is generalized or a general term particularized: R. *dérevo* 'wood, tree' is generalized from the meaning 'oak' or 'pine', *pišú* 'I write' means a particular way of making scratches, OB. *dǫbǔ* 'tree' is generalized from the Slavonic term for 'oak', R. *orël* 'eagle' is particularized from the concept 'bird' (Gk. ὄρνις), as being *the* bird *par excellence*. Such developments gain in interest when they can be associated with some change in social outlook: OB. *balǐjǐ* 'doctor' originally meant 'sorcerer' (*bajati* 'utter spells'), cf. R. *vrač* 'doctor' in association with *vráka* 'twaddle'; but R. *lékař* (Goth. *lekeis*) implies a definite advance in medical science, and *dóktor* implies status in an organized profession (not necessarily medical). Because of a taboo the Slavs called the bear 'honey-eater' (R. *medvéd* / Ossetic *ars* Av. *areša* Skr. *ŗksis* Gk. ἄρκτος Lat. *ursus* <*urcsos*). Petrified descriptions occur in R. *ótrok* 'lad, infant' ('not speaking'; cf. Lat. *infans* and MGk. ἄλογος 'horse') and *némec* 'German' originally 'foreigner' ('the dumb person'). The use of abstract for concrete and concrete for abstract is another resource of the vocabulary-maker, and interesting new words arise also from petrified metaphors, as R. *liceprijátie* 'partiality' ('face-acceptance').

Chapter V.

RUSSIAN

PROTO-RUSSIAN (TO ABOUT 1100)

80. *Russian characteristics*. (See also section 16.) Russian may be recognized by the occurrence together of the following eight characteristics: (1) the accent is free and there are no fixed distinctions of quantity or tone, (2) initial CSl. *e*- gives R. *o*- in some cases, (3) *y* is preserved with something like its primitive value, except in Ruthenian, (4) the *jers* cease to be vocalic in weak position and in strong position give *o/e*, (5) the nasal vowels are denasalized (R. *u/'a*), (6) full-vocalism: *polnoglásie* (CSl. **tort* >R. *torot*, etc.), (7) solution of the palatal dentals (CSl. **t̃ *d̃* <**tj *dj* give R. *č ž*, (8) occlusive *g* in North and Standard Great Russian/fricative in South Great Russian, Ruthenian and White Russian (as also in Czechoslovak and Upper Wendish).

These features will be illustrated as they arise in the following paragraphs. For the present it is to be noted that they existed in Russian before records began to be made, though they reveal themselves somewhat tardily in written sources. The Slavonic community began to disintegrate in the sixth century, and lost its identity of speech by the ninth. Between the ninth and the opening of the twelfth century Russian completed its formation as regards all its leading characteristics; but it was not noted down until the first chancery document appears, about 1130. The language of the chanceries was removed from colloquial Russian of the time by certain conventions proper to official Russo-Slavonic, but it was none the less a living language of business, and not deliberately foreign in the manner of Church Slavonic proper. Documents in Russian Church Slavonic open with the Ostromir Codex of the Gospels (1056–57). It is only by faults reflecting the local speech-habits that these works give evidence of the Russian tongue of their writers, but such signs grow more numerous as the centuries pass and Church Slavonic is more Russianized. However, neither the religious nor the official speech was meant to reflect accurately the characteristics of the colloquial, and it is only by degrees that the eight criteria above given are revealed in dated writings, though there can be no doubt that they existed before records began.

This unrecorded era is Proto-Russian. We can know something of it in the ninth century by reason of Scandinavian contacts, in the tenth from the pages of Constantine Porphyrogenitus, who ruled from 912 to 959, and in the eleventh by inferences made from the earliest liturgical works executed on Russian soil.

81. *The Varangians.* According to the *Povĕsť vremennych lĕt* the Varangians first established themselves in Russia in the year 6370 = A.D. 862. The name is that of the *Waring* tribe (ON. *Væringjar* Gk. βάραγγοι, possibly from ON. fem. pl. *várar* 'pledge, troth'). The Russian term is варяг (*ja* < *ę* < Germ. *in(g)*). Similarly OR. Судъ 'Bosporus' from ON. Swed. *sund* 'sound, strait' (*u* < *ǫ* < Germ. *un*) shows that nasal vowels were still alive in ninth-century Russian. Had they not then existed Germ. *in/un* would not have been represented as single vocalic sounds but as combinations of vowels and nasals, as happens when they are borrowed in loanwords of Modern Russian. By the middle of the tenth century (see section 82) the nasal vowels had been denasalized in Russian. The invaders were also known as Русь (Gk. 'Ρῶς 'Ρούσιοι Arab. *Rûs*/Finnish *Ruotsi* Estonian *Rootsi* 'Sweden'). The word is of disputed origin. In Constantine Porphyrogenitus' account 'Ρωσιστί undoubtedly means 'Swedish', as do the corresponding terms in Finnish. It may mean 'ruddy' or 'rowers' or possibly be a place-name (*Roper/Ropin* in Upland). More adventurous etymologies have been proposed from Iranian. As the Volga was called the 'Ρῶς and there are river-names like *Orša* and as there were ancient tribes of *Roxolani* and *Aorsi* in South Russian, an attempt has been made to derive the word from Iranian *ors/uors* 'white' and *rukhs* 'light'. The first settlement of the invaders was at *Aldegjuborg* (Old Ladoga), a name which seems to show that the metathesis of Sl. *al-/ol-* at the beginning of words was not complete in the ninth century. Cf. ON. *ellidi*/R. ладьй 'boat'.

The fullest account of the Varangian influence on Russian is in V. Thomsen's *The Relations between ancient Russia and Scandinavia* (Oxford, 1891). Over ninety personal names of Scandinavian origin are listed by the Russian chroniclers: *Rurik Oskold/Askold Dir Oleg Olga Igoŕ* (ON. *Ingvarr* Gk. "Ιγγωρ) *Rogvolod* (ON. *Ragnvaldr*) etc. They form a third part of Russian names, standing alongside the old Slavonic compound names and others of Byzantine Christian origin, whether Greek or Hebrew. Common nouns are fewer and refer to specifically Viking objects which have mostly gone out of use:

OR. аскъ/яскъ 'box' MR. ящик, гридь 'personal attendant', кнутъ 'whip', ларь 'chest', луда 'cloak' стягъ 'banner', шнека 'longship', тиунъ/тивунъ 'steward, manager', йбедникъ 'officer', йкорь 'anchor', dial. кербь 'flaxbundle', рюжа 'bow-knot', скива 'slice of bread'.

ON. *askr* OSwed. *asker* MSwed. *ask*, ON. *grið(maðr)*, ON. *knútr* OSwed. *knuter*, OSwed. *lar* MSwed. *lår*, ON. *lodi*, ON. *stöng* OSwed. *stang*, ON. *snekkja*, ON. *þjónn* OSwed. *þiun*, ON. *embætti* OSwed. *æmbiti*, Swed. *ankari*, ON. *kerf* Swed. *kärfve*, Swed. *rysja* (Finnish *rysä*), Swed. *skifva*.

It will be noted that the Russian forms stand closer to Swedish than to Old Norse. R. стул 'chair' has an initial *s* better explained by ON. *stóll* Swed. *stol* than by Germ. *Stuhl*, though the vowel is more German than Nordic. In Modern Russian ящик кнут стул ларь якорь are current, along with ябедник in the sense of 'slanderer'.

OR. Угры *Ǫgry = Hungari* is additional evidence of the nasal vowel in ninth-century Russian, at the time when the Magyars swept across South Russia. (MR. венгры is from P. *Węgry*.) It was also the time of Magyar borrowing from Slavonic. They seem to have used the Slavonic princely title of *vojevoda*, and the name *Lebedias* may derive from лебедь 'swan'. Other words are Hungarian *rab* 'slave' *járom* 'yoke' *borona* 'harrow'. From the Ossetic come various Magyar terms for commerce, communications and war.

82. *Constantine VII's description of Russia.* This description was executed in the middle of the tenth century, and it gives Greek equivalents of place-names, with some personal names. The latter are the less reliable, since they would be replaced by Old Bulgarian equivalents. Thus Constantine's Σφενδοσθλάβος = Святославъ is not evidence for the existence of a nasal diphthong in the Russia of his day; it is contradicted by the more veritable transcriptions of the place-names. These include Νεμογαρδά = Новъгородъ (ON. *Hólmgarðr*) (Σ)μιλινίσκα = Смольньскъ, Τελιούτζα = τὰ Λιούβτζα? = Любечь, Τζερνιγώγα = Чьрниговъ, Βουσεγραδέ = Вышегородъ, Κιά(ο)βα = Кыевъ = Σαμβατάς = ON. *Sandbakki-áss* 'sandbank-ridge'? ON. *Kœnugarðr* (ON. *kœna* 'boat'), Βιτετζέβη = Витечевъ, cf. ON. *Palteskja* = Полоцкъ. The Emperor also recorded Russian tribal names, which sometimes reveal features of interest in the common nouns on which they are based: Κριβηταινοί/Κριβιτζοί, Λενζανῆνοι/Λενζενίνοι, Οὐλτίνοι, Δερβλενίνοι = Βερβιᾶνοι (R. дерево 'wood'), Σερβίοι (an error, for Сѣверяне), Δρουγουβιτοί (Ruth. дряговина = 'marsh', cf. *Dresden* <*dreždžane* < ?*dręzg-jane* 'people of the marshy woods').

More valuable still is the list of falls of the Dnieper, which is at the same time our first list of common nouns in an authentically Russian form. The Emperor distinguished between their Russian names (Σκλαβινιστί) and the Scandinavian equivalents ('Ρωσιστί). According to Russian traditions represented in the *Povésť vremennych lět*, the subjects of the principality of Kiev recognized themselves as Russians in the eleventh century, so that the Emperor's evidence is interesting as coming before the fusion of the peoples. He sometimes confuses the two languages, and his lists are not quite complete. Rearranged, they give the following:

Rapids Modern Names	Constantine's Names		Old Swedish	Russo-Slavonic
1.	(N)'Εσσουπῆ		(Sof eigi)	не съпи
2. Surskij, Lochanskij	Οὐλβορσί	'Οστροβουνίπραχ	Holmfors	островьный прагъ
3. Zvonec(kij)	Γελανδρί		Gellandi	(звонéц)
4. Nenasytec(kij)	'Αειφόρ	Νεασήτ	Aiforr	неясыть
5. Volnyj, Volninskij	Βαρουφόρος	Βουλνήπραχ	Bárufors	влъньный прагъ
6. Tavolžanskij	Λεάντι	Βερούτζη	Leande	вьручи
7. Lišnij	Στρούκουν	Ναπρεζή	Strukum	напрязи?

The Scandinavian name for the first fall is not given, but *sof eigi* would serve to translate the Russian 'sleep not'. Then follow 'island fall', 'yelling, roaring', 'ever violent' (ON. *eyforr*), 'wave fall', 'laughing' (ON. *hlæjandi;* probably because of its stony bottom), 'small rapid' (Swed. *strukk* 'a small rapid which may be ascended with oars', *strâk, struk* ON. *strok stryk* 'a rapid current in a river, especially where it is narrow'). The Slavonic name of the fourth fall is explained as 'pelicans' fall' (OR. неясыть 'pelican'), but it may be an error for R. ненасы́тный 'insatiable'. The last name is not readily explained. Sobolevskij gives R. напрязи OB. *napręzi*, without interpretation (*napręzi* is found in the Ostromir Codex as 2*S.* imper. of OB. *napręšti* 'bend, strain'). Thomsen suggested Sl. **bŭrzŭ* 'quick', with *na* 'at, on'.

When we consider the whole group of words preserved by Constantine Porphyrogenitus, we are able to establish several features of the Russian of about 949. The nasal vowels had been denasalized (Νεασήτ/OB. *nejęsytĭ*, Βερούτζη/OB. *vĭrǫšti*). At the end of words the *jers* had ceased to be vocalic (Νεασήτ, πραχ) and also in the weakest medial positions (Βουλνη- OR. вълньный). In other positions they are represented by *e/u* (Βερούτζη = *vĭruči*, Βουλνη- σουπη ⟨*vŭln- sŭpi*, Τζερνηγώγα = *Čĭrnigov*). CSl. **ĭ* >R. *č* appears in Βερούτζη = вьручи/ OB. *vĭrǫšti*, and the pronunciation of fricative *g* (*h*) appears in πραχ/ R. порóг 'rapid, fall'. The use of Old Bulgarian forms of words in cultured conversation appears from γραδ (R. гóрод) and πραχ (R. порóг). R. ы is heard as a mixed (front-back) vowel; generally with the frontal element dominant (ι η), but with the back element developed after a labial (ου : Βουσεγραδέ). There is evidence also of full vocalism in Δερβλενινοί R. деревляне/OB. *drěvo*.

83. *Russian Sources. Ostromir's Codex.* The Greek treaties of Oleg and Igoŕ, recorded in the *Povĕsŕ vremennych lĕt* under the dates 911 and 945, would be of the highest importance for the history of the

language were they not preserved in a manuscript no older than the fourteenth century. It is not safe to make more than a limited use of them. The vocabulary, at all events, may be noted. Both dates are before the Christianizing of the Russians (988 ff.), so that the Greek words in them are not due to the intervention of Church Slavonic; they are, moreover, specimens of the language of diplomacy and affairs. The princes still bore Scandinavian names, though they were to give a Slavonic name (*Svjatoslav*) to the next ruler. They were in process of adopting the Russian language for their state business, but must have had an open mind in the matter of borrowing necessary terms from without. The borrowing, had contact remained on this level of business, might have been unlimited; it was probably due to scholarship that so much of the Russian vocabulary remained Slavonic, though often not Russian.

The Greek loans to these documents include untranslated words: грамота 'document' = γράμματα, епитимія 'penalty, penance' = ἐπιτιμία, коубара 'skein' = κουβάρα, литра 'litre' = λίτρα, харътия 'documents' = χαρτία, хламида 'cloak' = χλαμύς, полаты (fem.pl.) 'palace' = παλάτι(ον). The method of translation is also employed: глава in the sense of 'chapter, article' (κεφάλαιον), златьникъ to denote the Byzantine *solidus* (χρύσινος), ровьно in the sense of 'a copy' (τὸ ἴσον).

In the last quarter of the eleventh century a number of large works were executed in Kiev and Novgorod, all religious in character and Church Slavonic in language. Among them were the famous *Gospels* written by the priest Grigorij for Ostromir in 1056–57, the two collections (*Shorniki*) associated with the name of Svjatoslav (1073, 1076) and the Menologies (*Minei*) of 1096 and 1097. The evidence of these works must be taken later in discussing the separate histories of Russian sounds, but something may be said of them jointly here. It is not in the text but in the colophon that the scribe freed himself to some extent from his inhibitions against the use of the vernacular, and hence it is in the colophon to the Ostromir Codex that we find in the words Володимира Новѣгородѣ proof that the first full vocalism (*tort >*torot*) had already taken place. In the text, however, there is abundant evidence of the second full vocalism [*tŭrt >*tŭrŭt;* see section 88 (*a*)]: вълъкъ = волк 'wolf', зырьно = зернó 'grain', вьрътоградъ = вертогрáд 'garden', мълъва = молвá 'rumour'. The confusion of the two *jers* appears in дьнь = дьнь 'day' and шъдъ/шьдъ 'having gone'.

The scribe uses for *u* and *ja* of whatever origin the Slavonic signs for ǫ and *u*, ę and *ja*, and employs genitive forms like земля [= OB. *zem(l)ʹę*]. The vocabulary of the Codex is highly Græcized, but that feature belongs rather to developments in Old Bulgarian. The other documents show slightly different scribal traditions.

176 RUSSIAN

84. *Early Dialects*. There is not much evidence for early dialect differences in Russian. These could be expected to follow tribal lines, and the most important tribes must have been the *Kriviči* of the Novgorod region, the *Dregoviči* in White Russia, the *Poljane* at Kiev, and the *Vjatiči* on the Oka, who correspond respectively to the modern North Great Russians, White Russians, Ukrainians, and Muscovites. The fricative *g* (*h*) of the Ukraine was attested by Constantine Porphyrogenitus in 949 (see section 82), but the phenomena called *ákańe* (weakening of atonic *a o*) *jákańe íkańe* (alteration of atonic *e*) continued to pass unrecorded until Muscovite documents opened in the fourteenth century. R. лóшадь 'horse' (TT. *alaṣa*) may have been a term from the language of the Vjatiči, since it was brought from them by Vladimir Monomach to Kiev in 1103. To standard R. *žd* corresponds Kievite *žč* MRuth. *šč* in дъжчь MRuth. дощ 'rain', WR. *žč* (which appears as *ždč* in 1588): дъжчѐвнымъ (1296), and *žg* in Novgorod and Pskov, and probably also in Polock and Smolensk: дъжгъ (1095). The dialect of Novgorod was remarkable for its *čákańe* (*č* for *c*) and *cókańe* (*c* for *č*): црево 'belly' чвѣтъ 'flower' коньчь 'end' (1095), and in Pskov there was a further confusion of *ž/z š/s*, which may be attested from the fourteenth century. In Novgorod and Pskov *l* took the place of -*vl*-: присталивати 'appoint' (1270), Ярослали), and *i* took the place of *ě* occasionally as in Modern North Great Russian (человикомъ 'to the men', 1355). To sum up, in the earliest period the language was almost undifferentiated, but measured by the standard of Kiev, Novgorod and the North-west showed some divergent tendencies.

The language of the *Dregoviči* is not to be considered in the formation of the Russian dialects. Though they occupied the White Russian area, there is no sufficient evidence that their speech-habits directly moulded the White Russian language. This arose during the Middle Ages, partly through divergent tendencies within Russian itself, but more particularly because of the close association between White Russia and Poland, and the use of White Russian as a Polish chancery idiom.

To a less extent the language of the *Poljane* of Kiev has similarly to be discounted. The city was utterly destroyed in 1240, and the Ruthenian or Little Russian language was built up in the places to which the relics of this people retired, namely, in the principality of Galicia and in the district of Volhynia. Here, in the gospels and liturgical works of the fourteenth century, we see emerging slowly the characteristic features of the Ruthenian dialect or language, such as the reduction to *i* of *ě*, *e* and *o* in certain cases. The Kievite books show chiefly Church Slavonic. Apart from that they are but slightly differentiated from Common Russian. We have to attribute to Kiev, however, one feature of Modern Great Russian, i.e. the pronunciation of *g* in some cases as a voiced *h*. In Old Bulgarian *g* was an occlusive, but it was fricative in Kiev as early as the tenth century. From this fact there arose a clerical habit of reading Church Slavonic with a weak fricative *g* (a voiced *h*). This pronunciation became appropriate for one or two religious words: бог-а [bɔχ gen. bɔ́ha] 'God', господь 'Lord', and sometimes богатый 'rich' господин 'Mr.' благо- 'eu-'. In Old Russian there occurred spellings without *g*, as осподь осударь/государь 'ruler'. Except for very recent instances, where x appears, г is found for *h* in foreign words and place-names: герой Гекла Гуль Гималайские горы (hero, Hekla, Hull, Himalayas). In this use it is pronounced as an occlusive. Neville Forbes had occasion to point out that Гуль represents *Hull* and not the neighbouring *Goole*.

There remain the North and East Russians, the *Kriviči* and *Vjatiči*. With the extension of Novgorod's trading interests the *Kriviči* spread eastwards to the north of the *Vjatiči*, thus converting the distinction into one of North and South. There was sufficient intercommunion to keep these two branches together as Great Russian, with only sporadic divergencies in the North-West dialects. Where they joined along the Moskva and Kljaźma, a mixed North-South dialect arose; and at the point of convergence of all influences, though with a preponderance of the North in the literary tradition, lay Moscow. Moscow gave to Great Russian the rule of the greatest common agreement.

OLD RUSSIAN (1100–1500)

A. Sounds

85. *Stress.* Russian stresses are free to fall on any syllable of the word, and can be shown to fall on any of the last seven (section 22), though there are not many withdrawn past the fourth last place. They vary within a declension or a paradigm. This mobility was also found in the parent Indo-European language, and where comparison is possible it appears that (apart from instances noted below and largely due to de Saussure's law) the Russian stress falls on the same place as in the original tongue. Thus we may compare R. жена Gk. γυνή 'woman, wife', R. сноха Gk. νυός 'daughter-in-law', since the accent on a final syllable in Greek is trustworthy, and has not been altered for reasons of quantity. Other sources of confirmation are Bulgarian and the *ča*-dialect of Serbocroat, in which the accent-shifts of Slovene and *što*- and *kaj*-Serbocroat have not taken place. One general cause of accent-shift belongs to the Common Slavonic tradition, i.e. that illustrated in part by Fortunatov or de Saussure's 'law' that a final unaccented syllable with rising tone draws to itself the stress from a previous accented syllable with a falling long vowel or short vowel (see section 22). This principle is exemplified by the infinitive ending *-ti*,

the feminine suffix *-*ā* (which is also that of neuter plurals), some case-endings and the 1 sg. pres. indic. of verbs: R. нести 'bear' вода 'water' церева 'trees' пишу 'I write'. Hence certain accent-shifts in declension and conjugation, some of them analogical: вода/*AS*. воду дерево < *dêrvo/церева сад 'garden', *GS*. сада/*LS*. саду пишу/ пишешь, etc.

Some other general causes helped to modify the original accentuation in Russian. It is probable that when final *ŭ ĭ* became still shorter in the Middle Proto-Slavonic period they ceased to be substantial enough to bear an accent: R. ход 'motion' < *chódŭ*/Gk. ὁδός. As this occurs in the genitive plural of nouns it sometimes leads to a third accentuation within the declension: сестра 'sister'/*NP*. сёстры *GP*. сестёр (*ё* always bears the stress in Russian). Analogy interferes on a considerable scale, so that, for instance, both сестрами and сёстрами occur, and there was formerly a *NP*. сестры. (Cf. L. *sesuō sēsers seserŭ seserimĭs*). So also we have, by de Saussure's law, *NS*. земля/*AS*. землю/*NP*. земли/*GP*. земель. Prepositions and the negative не sometimes take the stress from a following word and sometimes shift it. In colloquial Russian there is some fluctuation in this matter: не брал/ не брал 'did not take', к зиме/к зимѣ 'towards winter' (the latter current in the eighteenth and early nineteenth centuries). There are a considerable number of words and expressions for which two different accents are current: высоко 'high' глубоко 'deep' далёко 'distant' нужды *GS*. of нужда 'need' из лесу 'out of the wood'. In неровён час (idiomatically equivalent to 'I shouldn't be surprised if something unpleasant happened') we have preserved in a fixed phrase an accentuation which is both popular and archaic; in other parallel cases the opposition is between literary and colloquial only: силён 'strong' короток 'short' (the forms with initial stress being literary). The accent frequently shifts from numerals: на три 'into three', etc.

In these fluctuations there is sometimes seen a difference in usage between North and South Great Russian, and the latter does not, for the most part, transfer the accent to a preposition. In a few cases difference of accentuation is used to express difference of meaning: большой 'great'/больший 'greater', чудный 'wonderful'/чудной 'strange', еще 'yet'/ещё 'still, moreover', честный 'honest'/честной 'noble'. Not all of these refinements are admitted in the literary tongue. It may be added, as an encouragement to students, that Russians themselves frequently appear uncertain as to the correct accentuation of the less common words and forms; and one may regret that ordinary print does not employ some simple system (such as that of Spanish) to indicate the fall of stress. Accents are used in print to avoid ambiguity; e.g. дорога 'road'/дорога 'dear', стоит 'costs'/стоит 'stands', потом 'with sweat'/потом 'then'.

The principal historic feature of Russian stress has been its increase in intensity, especially in the original East Russian area of the *Vjatiči*. This is not revealed in the spelling, which fails to mark stress, but it can be seen in its consequences. The increase of the importance of the stressed syllable diminished the distinctions existing in other syllables, both as to length and to tone. No Russian developments are due to the original length of unstressed syllables, nor, apart from the *tort*-formula and one dialect feature (a new acute *o* resulting from metatony giving *uo:* e.g. dial. *mʊo'žyš*) is there any trace of tone. Great and White Russian, unlike Ruthenian, did not even share the West Slavonic tendency to lengthen the vowel of a syllable that had become final through loss of a *jer* (lengthening by compensation).

It is not that quantity and intonation have ceased to be important for Russian. On the contrary the increase of stress has increased distinctions of pitch and length in stressed syllables, and the fact that these elements are not constituents of single words leaves them free for use throughout the sentence. Russian sentences are distributed among four types according to their tonal patterns, corresponding to assertions, questions, questions and statements with some implication (including commands), and requests. Apart from these formalized patterns there are also the variations of tone and length which express emotion of any kind. In short, the loss of tone and length as structural elements in each word has proved to be an economy of resources in the language, so that they can be applied to other purposes elsewhere.[*]

The Russian word is organized by its principal stress, thus: In the first syllable there is a copious use of the breath stream, so that, whether accented or unaccented, it is relatively clear and tense. Relaxed syllables follow, but the pretonic (immediately before the main stress) shows a distinct rise in tone and increase of clarity. The tonic syllable is the longest, clearest and highest in pitch; as a rule, that is, and when not pronounced with any special intention which may cause the pitch to drop. From the stressed syllable there is a continual drop. The posttonic stands relatively high in the scale, but is much lower than the pretonic in Russian, and can be treated as low, not medium. If the descent continues through two or more syllables followed by a final syllable, that final may show a slight secondary accent, with increase of clarity: человѣческѡго 'human' (G*SM.*) всемйлостивейшемý 'all-merciful' D*SM.*). The distinction between low, medium and high tone and stress may be brought out by numbers denoting increase of intensity: голо́вушка 'little head' (2311), го́лову 'head' (A*SF.*) (311), нá сторону 'to the side' (3111), сторонá 'side'

---

[*]On types of Russian intonation see S. C. Boyanus, *A Manual of Russian Pronunciation* (London, 1935), pp. 49–80, and for examples consult S. C. Boyanus and N. B. Jopson, *Spoken Russian* (London, 1939).

(123), where 1 represents the lowest tone and stress, and 3 the highest. The relative unimportance of the posttonic is well exemplified by these figures.

These distinctions are influential in the phenomena known as *ákańe jákańe íkańe*, which are characteristic of original East Russian, now South Great Russian, and of the Moscow dialect, as opposed to the *ókańe* of North Great Russian. As the Northern dialects prevailed among educated circles, even in Moscow, during the Middle Ages and the early part of the modern period, Russian spelling is marked by *ókańe*, and is discrepant from the standard pronunciation. In unaccented syllables the vowels are somewhat relaxed. In the North, however, the relaxation is not such as to affect their timbre, so that *o* unstressed is still recognizably *o*; the more intense stress of the dialect of the *Vjatiči* attacked the timbre of unaccented vowels, and in particular caused *o* to be pronounced like *a* under certain conditions. The vowels affected are *o a e* along with their soft forms (*jo*) *ja je*. In the stressed syllable in standard Russian *o a e* are pronounced [ɔ] [a] [ɛ before hard consonants/e before soft consonants]. In the pretonic, *o a* fall together in a sound like *a*, though it is somewhat relaxed. All other syllables are low in stress and tone, and the relaxation is such that both vowels become [ə]. Unstressed *e* and pretonic *ja* are pronounced [ji]; posttonic *ja* is [jə]. Between soft consonants *'o 'a* are pronounced [ö æ] under the stress, [ö] representing something like the sound sometimes heard in Fr. *note bonne*, and not unlike that in Eng. *nut bun*, [æ] more or less like the vowel in Eng. *sat*. Though this pronunciation is recommended by S. C. Boyanus (*op. cit.*), not all speakers narrow *e* before soft consonants, and unstressed *e* is frequently pronounced [ɛ], especially when final.

The evidence for the early existence of *ákańe* will be given later (section 86). The examples are late in making their appearance simply because Moscow documents open late. There is nothing to forbid the idea that *ákańe* was one of the primitive features of Russian dialects. In the same way, the occurrence of *ákańe* in White Russian does not lend itself to early documentation, though it may have been old. The original foci of Russian civilization both belonged to *ókańe* regions, namely Great Novgorod in the land of the *Kriviči*, and Kiev in that of the *Poljane*.

One other feature of Russian accentuation is the varied treatment of the *tort*-groups [see section 29 (*a*) and section 88 (*a*)]. The diphthong **or* was long, and was resolved in Russian into two short syllables *oro*. The result was to divide the accentuation \ : — for a falling tone, and —: / for a rising tone. As tones are converted into stresses in Russian it follows that the original falling long diphthong gives a stress on the first syllable in Russian, and the original rising long diphthong gives a stress on the second syllable in Russian: *tórt >tórot, *tórt >torót. Examples have been give in section 29 (a and b).

86. *Oral Vowels. A.* R. hard a/soft я. Between palatals the soft stressed vowel has the value *ä* [æ], as in дядя 'uncle' пять 'five'. Otherwise, when stressed, the sound is that of a relatively open *a* with a palatal on-glide. The survival of this pronunciation requires a comment. The Slavonic languages distribute all sounds between two orders, back and front. In this instance there should be a regular opposition of *a/ä*. It appears sporadically in Old Russian manuscripts and in certain modern dialects, and the natural trend would be from *ä* to *ě*, as in Czech. In Glagolitic documents OB. *ja/ě* were not distinguished, and were represented by one sign, of which the Cyrillic transcription is *ě*. It is not easy to interpret this feature. The use of a special sign for *ja* in pure Cyrillic documents may be due to a dialectal divergence, or it may be due to a reaction towards a sound recognizably associated (e.g. in the declensions) with hard *a*. The Ostromir codex, which is in Cyrillic, uses *ja* not *ě* as a feminine and neuter ending. This illustrates the Russian conservation of the *a*-timbre, which is shared with Polish and South Slavonic (apart perhaps from some Old Bulgarian), as opposed to Czech and Glagolitic: R. душа 'soul' воля 'will' (so in Ostromir's codex) P. *dusza wola*/Cz. *duše zeměa* 'land' Glagolitic OB. *dušě zem(l)ě*. It should be mentioned here that the *a* resulting from *ě* after palatals is by some believed originally to have resulted phonetically only before hard consonants (e.g. **kēs-* > nom. *časŭ* 'time'/loc. **čěsě*), the generalization of *a* being the result of analogy. This would explain the survival of *e* in certain Polish words.

Old Russian manuscripts show that usage was still fluctuating, since *e ě ja* (or *a* after certain palatal consonants) are seen to exchange: кнезя/князя (gen.) 'prince' 1478, чесехъ/часѣхъ (loc.) 'times' 1478, нечистия/нечистие 'uncleanness' c. 1310, Костромя/Костромѣ (loc.), сердца ваше/сердце 'heart', имя моя/мое 'my name'. The substitution of *ja* for *e/ě* is particularly common in documents from Galicia-Volhynia. In respect of neut. -*ńje* (куроглашенья 'cock-crow' 1266) this has led to MRuth. -*nnja* -*llja*: каміння 'stone-heap' весілля/весілé 'marriage'. Those north-western dialects which confuse *č/c* make *ja* into *e* between palatals (NWR. *ṕeṫ*/standard R. [ṕæṫ] пять 'five), and the same is true of the western dialects of Ruthenian, in Galicia. In these dialects e is found for я between palatals. In others there has been a further closing of the vowel to Ruth. i. Examples have been noted in Dobrilo's Gospels (1164), but are not so clear of doubt as to be fully probatory.

Племянник 'nephew'/племенной 'tribal' shows the influence of плéмя 'tribe'. For крóме 'except' пóсле 'after' there are the equivalents окромя́ опосля́, cf. OP. *kromia* Ruth. пíсля. OR. нельзѣ/MR. нельзя́ 'it is impossible' shows the correct dative construction in Old Russian, and in Modern Russian -я from a formerly unstressed ending.

In a few cases я is pronounced like ё : ея́ 'of her' (now spelt её) and certain verbs such as masc. тря́с/fem. трясла́ 'shook' : : нёс/несла́ 'bore'.

O. R. o, Ruth. o i. Russian *o* is found in both accented and un-accented syllables in North Great Russian. This kind of pronunciation is called *ókańe*. Among the *ókańe* centres are found the very important cities of Great Novgorod, Jaroslavĺ, Vladimir, Suzdaĺ, Nižnij Novgorod (Gorkij), and also the capitals of the South, notably Kiev. It follows that this dialect had an immense cultural preponderance in the mediæval period, and imposed its orthography upon all others. But in the original East Russian of the *Vjatiči*, now South Great Russian, *o* is reduced in unaccented syllables to [a] and [ə], as shown in section 85, and this is associated with modifications of *ja* and *e* (e.g. *e >ja*). The whole process, but particularly the pronunciation of unstressed *o* as *a*, is here referred to as *ákańe*. Now, *ákańe* may be combined with other South Great Russian characteristics or with North Great Russian elements. In the first case it serves to define the South Great Russian dialects, whose northern frontier is a vast arc from Gžatsk to Rjazań, and thence via Atkarsk to the line of the Volga between Kamyšin and Stalingrad (Caricyn). The central dialects are those which combine *ákańe* with northern peculiarities, and they include the cities of Kalinin (Tveŕ) and Moscow. It is in comparatively recent times that the *ákańe* of Moscow has imposed itself as the cultured usage in despite of the *ókańe* of official classes in that city. This pronunciation is reflected in the English *Muscovy/ Moscow*. It should be noted that in a few foreign words unstressed *o* is pronounced [ə], e.g. in поэ́т 'poet' [pɔɛ́t]. Many people pronounce ра́дио 'radio' [rádɪɔ].

Documentary evidence for *ákańe* is late, but begins with the first records from the Moscow chancery in the fourteenth century. In view of the official *ókańe* even there, these examples must be considered evidence of a firmly-established colloquial usage, which may have been of quite ancient date. Examples are: апустѣвшии/опустѣвшии 'depopulated' 1339, and the ultracorrections (*o* for *a*) толáнтъ 'talent', предлогаютъ/предлагаютъ 'offer' 1393. In the fifteenth century these confusions are quite common: па/по, пасле/после 'after' (unstressed prepositions) пага́ный/пога́ный 'pagan' (Lat. *paganus*). Hence, in Modern Russian, ла́сков 'amiable'/ChSl.OB. *laskavŭ* Ruth. ла́скав, о́вод 'gadfly'/P. *owad*. The CSl. prefix **orz-* should give OB. *raz-* R. *roz-*. Many examples of *raz-* in Russian are undoubtedly due to Church Slavonic influence, but it is hard so to account for the almost complete absence of *roz-*, which is of the rarest occurrence: рóздых 'rest' рóзыск 'inquest' рóспись 'list', all with *o* under stress. It is difficult to see in рабóта 'work' заря́ 'dawn' words of literary origin (ChSl. *zarja/zorja* P. *zorza* Cz. *zoře* S. *zòra* Ruth. зоря́, which is also found in North Great Russian dialects). There are other cases of the alternation *a/o:* ýтро 'morning' OR. зáутрок 'breakfast'/MR. зáвтрак, плáтит 'he buys' (frequently pronounced плóтит), пальтó 'overcoat' (Fr. *paletot*)/colloquial pl. *pólty*. These are examples showing the working of *ákańe* as much in ancient as in modern times.

After the fall of Kiev in 1240 the principal literary centre of South Russian was Galicia with Volhynia, in contact with Polish and Slovak areas. It was here that some of the leading peculiarities of Ruthenian began to appear in thirteenth-century documents, and among them the modification of *o e* to *i* in certain cases and of *ě* to *i* universally. In Ruthenian, as in Polish and Czechoslovak, *o e* were lengthened by way of compensation for the loss of a final *jer*, giving new long vowels *ō ē*. These vowels developed into diphthongs (*uo/ie*), which, becoming single vowels again, naturally resulted in narrower vowels than their originals (*u/i*). So Cz. *kůň* 'horse'/OB. *koňĭ* P. *mój* 'my' (with *ó*= [u])/OB. *mojĭ*. The development *ō* >*u* is found in юдѣюмъ/dat. pl. *-otŭ* 'to the Jews' 1266, унукумъ 'to the grandchildren' друздъ/R. дрозд 'thrush'. It is a feature of northern Ruthenian dialects and of the neighbouring South White Russian. The general line of development in Ruthenian, however, was apparently:

ō >*uo* >*uö* >*ue* >*ui* >*ü* >*i* Ruth. i : ніс 'nose' ⟨*nosŭ*/gen. нóса.
ē >*ie* >   *'i* Ruth. ï : сїм 'seven'/сéмий 'seventh'.
     or *i* Ruth. i : гребінь 'comb'/gen. грéбеня.

The spelling with *ї* is used, for instance, in Smal-Stockyj's *Ruthenische Grammatik* after consonants capable of softening (*n l t d s z c*): сїм/гребінь. The official Soviet orthography for the Ukraine, however, uses ï only for [ji] at the beginning of the word or after a vowel. So it does not distinguish between ніс 'nose' ⟨*nosŭ* and ніс 'bore' ⟨ *nes(l)ŭ*.

The development occurred also where a *jer* was lost within the word: Ruth. ліжко 'bed'/R. лóже. In the initial syllable *uo >**vuo-* > Ruth. *vi-*: Ruth. він 'he' вівця 'sheep'/R. он овцá. Ruth. воná 'she' is due to analogy.

Substitution of *u* for *o* occurs in R. муравéй 'ant'/OB. *mravĭjĭ* P. *mrówka*, журáвль 'crane'/P.*żóraw* and a handful of other words.

In a few cases initial *o-* prefixes a *v:* R. вóсемь 'eight'/OB. *osmĭ*, óстрый/вóстрый 'sharp', вот 'behold'/P. *oto*. The same thing occurs universally in the Czech of Prague: *vokno* 'window'/literary *okno*, *von/on* 'he', etc.

A characteristic of many Russian speakers is their labialization of *o* (and also of ə). Before they pronounce the vowel their lips rapidly pass through the position for *u;* the result is a sort of *w* between the consonant and vowel which is particularly noticeable after labials, though not restricted to them. Thus R. мóжет 'can' [m^{w}óžət], дом 'house' [d^{w}ɔm], бэ пэ (names of letters) [b^{w}ε p^{w}ε], об э́том 'about this' [ab^{w}étəm].

E. R. ѣ (disused since 1917), е ё э о, Ruth. e e i ï. R. э was introduced in the seventeenth century to denote *e* without palatal on-glide. It has been in general use only since the nineteenth century, when its function was to represent foreign *e* in French, German and other western loanwords: э́хо 'echo' поэ́т 'poet' эги́да 'ægis' экра́н 'fire-screen' эшафóт 'scaffold' эрцге́рцог 'archduke'. As a genuine Slavonic survival this sound is restricted to an epideictic *e*-(cf. Gk. ἐκεῖ 'there'. Lat. *equidem*): э́тот 'this' э́кой 'such' э́так 'thus', and the exclamations: эй, эх. Ruth. e also lacks palatal on-glide, but this is due to the hardening of previous consonants (л н р ц) and in the older state of the language the *e* was as in Great Russian. In standard Russian unstressed *e* is pronounced like unstressed и, i.e. [ɪ], and if preceded by a 'hardened' consonant undergoes the same change as и to ы; e.g. страни́це ('page', locative), pronounced [. . . tsɨ]. When stressed it is pronounced after 'hardened' consonants like ə: центр 'centre' [tséntr]. *E* is also pronounced ə in a great many modern borrowings; e.g. оте́ль 'hotel'.

OB. ѣ/e were probably distinguished as [æ]/[ε], since the former could pass into *ja*, but the latter could not. In Modern Bulgarian the (pre-1945) ѣ is *e* or *ea* (*ja*) in the eastern dialects according to circumstances, but e remains steadily *e*. Now, it seems doubtful whether these distinctions of quality held good even for the oldest Russian, since confusion of the two letters occurs both in the North and in the South from the twelfth century. It was especially true of the Novgorod region that these sounds tended to be indistinguishable: семене/сѣмене 'seed' тесный/тѣсный 'narrow' 1157, корѣне/корене 'root' ижѣ/иже 'who' 1157, all from Novgorod. In 1073 there occur ведение/вѣдѣние 'knowledge', домѣ/доме (V*S*.) 'O house'. In documents from Galicia-Volhynia the confusion is also found, though rarely as ѣ for e, since there was a secondary difference of quantity involved: на местѣ and на мѣсте/на мѣстѣ are found in 1164. From this it is clear that the quality of the two vowels must have been almost indistinguishable, though there was a difference which appears in their mutations. R. e may become ё, but R. ѣ cannot, except for a few analogical cases: сѣдлó 'saddle' pl. сѣдла. Before a single letter e came to be used for them both, the lexicon had consecrated a number of etymologically wrong spellings; сѣкира/OR. секира 'axe' (cf. Lat. *securis*), as if from сѣчь 'hack', змѣй/OR. змья змея 'snake', врéмя/OR. *vrĕmę* 'time', etc. In a few instances R. *ja* answers to OB. *ĕ*: R. прямо 'straight'/OB. *prĕmo* 'against', adj. suffix R. -янный/OB. -*ĕnŭ*. The first divergence may be due to alternating forms *prĕ-/prę-mo-*, the second to the analogy of similar adjectives in -*an*-, as кóжаный 'leather'.

The Russian discrimination between the two sounds, valid in full only for the Proto-Russian period, was probably between a diphthong [iɛ] and a palatalized monophthong ['ɛ].

Initially CSl. **e* > R. o: одúн 'one' óзеро 'lake' олéнь 'stag'/S. *jèdan jězero jèlen*. This may have occurred at first only when initial *e* was followed by a non-palatal consonant. The development is not without parallels in other Slavonic languages, but its general validity is a leading characteristic of Russian, and when it fails to appear the cause may lie in some analogy. ON. *Helgi Helga* became R. Олéг Óльга, which shows that this mutation was still active in the ninth century. Similarly Gk. Ἑλένη >Олéна. It may be that there were doublets *o/e*- as far back as the Common Slavonic period, and that Russian generalized *o* where other languages generalized *je*-. In Modern Bulgarian there are found the doublets *óšte/éšte* 'still' and *edvá*/dial. *ódvaj* 'scarcely'.

While there was still a distinction of some sort between ѣ and е, but the latter, whatever its origin (OB. *e* or *ĭ*), had come to represent one sound (that is, certainly in the twelfth century, and possibly in the eleventh), stressed *e* began to be dispalatalized before a hard consonant and to take a sound like *o*: блажонъ/блаженъ 'blessed' жонъ (GP.) 'of women'. The instance чоловѣка/человéка (GS.) 'man's', recorded in 1073, may be due to other causes; but it is clear that the modern requirement that the *e* should be stressed did not apply in the beginnings of the movement; съкáжомъ 'we shall say' стойщомъ (DP.) 'standing' are also twelfth-century examples. Instances of this trend are quoted from Polikarp's Gospels (1307), which come from the South-West; but it is possible they should be discounted as due to White Russian influence: чóрный 'black' ничóго (GS.) 'of nothing'. The change was operative also in White Russian. In Polish there is a similar development from *e* to *o*, but under different conditions. It is there effected by certain following hard consonants, and does not depend on stress.

To account for the modern standard usage which restricts this change to stressed syllables is not easy. A plausible explanation is that which takes account of *ákaňe*. In the Moscow dialect, as we have seen (section 85), *o* and *e* are quite distinct in stressed syllables, but in unstressed syllables both are modified. There are instances in which the change occurs before soft consonants, but these are to be explained by analogy: несёте : : несёт 'you bear/he bears', тётя : : тётка 'aunt', etc.

On the other hand there are many instances of the permanence of *é*. The most substantial class is that of Church Slavonic words: нéбо 'sky' лев 'lion'/Лёв or Лев 'Leo'. Personal names vary: Пётр Олёна/ Олёна Орéст. The negative prefix не- remains constant. The consonant before *e* was originally soft; the hard consonant following might be the originally soft ж ш, but not щ ц ч, of which only the last is now deemed soft (see section 95). Hence: отéц 'father' печь 'cook' лещ 'bream'/идёшь 'goest' падёж 'murrain'. Before й the change is probably due to analogy: бо́льшо́й 'pig'/сам-третéй 'self and two others' (both from -*ĭjĭ*). There are sporadic instances to the contrary: мятéж 'revolt'/тёща 'mother-in-law' (the former probably under the influence of Church Slavonic, the latter possibly on the analogy of тётка 'aunt'). Further, loss of *ĭ* led to consonant-groups in which the first consonant remained soft long enough to prevent this modification of *e*: верх/OR. вьрьхъ (by second full-vocalism) вéрьхъ 'top'. Where the orthography used before 1917 showed e in place of the etymological ѣ, there was no change: трескъ 'crack' блескъ 'gleam' нéкогда 'there is no time'. No cause can be assigned for the preservation of *e* in шест 'pole' вéтошь 'rags'/P. *wiotki* 'frail'.

The dialects of North Russia are, of course, liable to be influenced by the standard usage, but they belong to the region of *ókańe*, so that the above account does not apply to their own historical conditions. They show some peculiarities. The *o*-sound appears in unaccented syllables, and in final syllables. At Olonec one hears *žoná* 'woman' *plemjánniček* 'nephew' *čolovék* 'man' *ĕgó* 'his' *sĕstrá* 'sister' *pólĕ* 'field'. An accent-shift in the second person plural of verbs has led to doublets: *esté* 'are' *spité* 'sleep' *chotité* 'wish'/*estë spitë chotitë*. There is a similar shift in White Russian: *stoičĕ*/стóйте 'stand'. Here also *ákańe* rules. In addition to *o*, thirteenth-century documents from the South-West show a further development *ju* (жю/же 1266 ядущю 'eating'). In Ruthenian *o* occurs chiefly after palatals: чоловíк 'man' чогó 'of what' чотúри 'four' жóвтий 'yellow'/ньóго 'him', without restriction to the stressed syllable. The cases are too sporadic to constitute a rule.

There remains the development of *ĕ* > *ī* (*i*) in Ruthenian, which begins to appear in documents from Galicia-Volhynia in the twelfth century. It is paralleled by Cz.S. *i* in Cz. *vίra* S. *vīra* < *vĕra*: Ruth. вίра 'faith'. CSl. *ĕ* was a long vowel. CSl. *e* was lengthened in this dialect when a syllable became closed by a consonant owing to the loss of *jer*. We have seen that the same applied to *o*, and the principle of compensatory lengthening is held in common with West Slavonic. This mediæval *ē* tended to become a diphthong *ie* and then to close to *i*, but with an on-glide which is preserved initially, after vowels, and after consonants capable of softening. Fourteenth-century examples are: видинья/вѣдѣние 'knowing' свидѣнье/свѣдѣние 'testimony' 1307, with и for MRuth. i.

Soviet orthography, as already explained, only uses the sign ï initially and after vowels: Ruth. ï'хати 'travel', доброï (gen.sg.fem.) 'good' <EWSl. *dobrojě*/OB. *dobroję*, тїло (Smal-Stockyj's тїло) 'body' <*tělo*.

U. R. y. The Russian sound also arises from CSl. *ǫ* (section 87). When stressed between soft consonants it represents a sound between *u* and closed *o* for which the phonetic symbol is [ü]: люди [lü'dɪ], etc. (This is not the German *ü*.) In similar circumstances я ё also suffer modification [jæ jö], as already explained.

Y I. R. ы и *WR.* ы i *Ruth.* и. The retention of the mixed front-back vowel [ɨ] is characteristic of Great Russian, White Russian and Polish. Its soft companion was [i]. The distance between [i] and [ɨ] was not so great as to prohibit all confusion: непостыжна 1097/непостижимый 'incomprehensible', тисяча 1266/тысяча, нинѣ/ныне 'now'. The vibrant *r* has had a tendency to harden itself and the following vowel: рикати/рыкáть 'bellow', ригати/рыгáть 'belch', користь/корысть 'profit'. Russian has created a new group of postpalatals (*k ǵ ch́*), with consequent change from *y* to *i:* Кыевъ/Кíев, кыкати 'screech' (13th cent.)/кíкать.

In the Galicia-Volhynia dialect the letters ы/и ceased to represent distinct sounds, and their confusion began as early as the twelfth century: погыбый/погибий 'ruined' просыти/просити 'beg' 1164; синъ/сынъ 'son' occurs somewhat later. The two sounds approximated on a middle value which is described by some authors as a very close [e], but is quite like the [ɪ] of Eng. *milk*. Only the one letter is required in Modern Ruthenian. To mark the difference of this sound from [i] the letter *y* is used in transcriptions of Ruthenian.

In standard Russian и is also pronounced [ɪ] when unstressed. When preceded by the prepositions or prefixes в and с the resultant pronunciation (noted in the spelling in the case of compounds) is ы: сызнова 'anew' < с(ъ)+из—, в Итáлии 'in Italy' [vɨtá . . .]. After 'hardened' consonants the pronunciation of both stressed and unstressed и is ы : цинк 'zinc' [tsɨnk].

Jers. As explained in section 27, CSl. *ŭ/ĭ* occurred in strong and weak positions. In the latter case they ceased to be vowels in Russian at a very early epoch. The hard *jer* (ъ) served to show that the preceding consonant had its normal value. As in this function it was otiose, it was discarded in the 1917 spelling-reform. It remained, however, in words where a hard consonant occurs before a soft vowel, so that there is a sort of glottal stop between them; in this case an apostrophe may be used instead of ъ: с'едáть 'eat up'. The soft *jer* (ь) is still used to denote soft quality in the previous consonant. In the 2nd personal ending -шь the *jer* is merely traditional, and does not soften *š*, which has hardened during the development of Modern Russian; so also the *jer* in рожь 'rye' and some other words. In words like бьёт 'he strikes' the *jer* serves to show an intrinsic softness of the *b* apart from the softness of the vowel following; to some observers it seems to be pronounced like a very brief *ĭ:* [b′ĭjót].

In strong position the *jers* became *o/e* respectively, and follow all subsequent developments of these vowels in Russian. Ruth. *o e* $\langle$ *ŭ ĭ* are not liable to compensatory lengthening; hence instr. sg. *-om* $\langle$ *-ŭmĭ*.

In the middle of the tenth century the *jers* in final position had weakened so much as to be unperceived by the informants of Constantine Porphyrogenitus; in some medial positions, as we have seen, they seem still to have been sounded. From Russian sources it is possible to attest full vowels for semivowels in the first half of the twelfth century: врѣменемъ 'with time' на небесехъ 'in the heavens' кровоточивая 'sanguifluous'. The examples drawn from the second half of the twelfth century are too numerous to admit of mistake or analogy: цьрковь/цьркъвь 'church' сладокъ/сладъкъ 'sweet' 1157, исперва/испьрва 'from the first' съмерть/съмьрть 'death' весь/вьсь 'all' плоть/плъть flesh' 1164. These examples are drawn from North and South Russia. After *r*, and more rarely *l*, the vowel obtained may be ы in West and South Russia, but not in the North or East: крывавъ 'bloody' 1588/кровавый.

It was the practice to read the internal *jers* of Church Slavonic liturgical books as *o/e* respectively, and this has led to the retention of these vowels in many words where the *jer* occurred in weak position. Loss of the *jer* in the combination *jĭ* has led to the creation of descending diphthongs in Russian where there were two syllables in Common Slavonic: CSl.OB. *mojĭ*/R. мой. In White Russian and Ruthenian descending diphthongs of the other order have resulted from the vocalization of *l* and *v* as *ŭ* (WR. ў). Thus the Russian dialects are distinguished from Common Slavonic and Old Bulgarian by the possession of new diphthongs, which are, in Great Russian, in practically every case, due to the loss of the *jers*. Moreover, loss of *jers* within words upset the balance of Common Slavonic, which had established an almost exact alternation of vowels and consonants. New consonant-groups arose, and required a considerable effort of adjustment which will be studied later (see section 97). At the end of words the loss of *jer* left consonants final. That was never the case in Common Slavonic or Old Bulgarian, save for some proclitic prepositions, and it brought into play a new principle of unvoicing all final voiced consonants (see section 96). It follows that the *jers*, though their own history is brief in Russian, have proved to be a leading cause of readjustment over the whole language.

Secondary *jers* arose in Russian when the loss of final *jers* would have resulted in final consonant-groups which the spirit of the language did not then permit. The resultant (so-called) fill-vowel in Modern Russian is an *o* or an *e* which appears and vanishes like the vowels resulting from original *jers*. In such cases an *o* is inserted (i) between a guttural and *l n r*, (ii) between *s z* and *k g;* elsewhere the fill-vowel is *e*. Thus: огóнь 'fire' G*S.* огня́ (OB. *ogńĭ*); досóк, G*P.* of доскá 'board' (OB. G*P. dŭskŭ*); сестёр, G*P.* of сестрá 'sister' (OB. G*P. sestrŭ*). There is of course much scope here for analogy.

In one case an original *e* has been treated analogically as a *jer;* this is the word лёд 'ice', G. льда/OB. *leda.*

87. *Denasalization.* CSl. ǫ/ę R. у/я. This process was carried through in the first half of the tenth century, as already noted (sections 81, 82). In the ninth century OSwed. *ankari* 'anchor' *sund* 'haven' gave R. **ękoŕ *sǫd* (with nasal vowels), which have evolved to я́корь Судъ, and similarly Lat. (*H*)*ungari* Gk. Οὔγγαροι corresponded to ninth century. **Ǫgry* > Угры. But Constantine represented by Νεασήτ Βερούτζη OR. неясыть вьручи/OB. *nejęsytĭ vĭroŝti.* His use of nasals in certain proper names was due to identification with the same names in the Balkans, where the nasal vowels lingered on. The Ostromir Gospels (1056-57), though ostensibly copying Old Bulgarian, constantly confuse ǫ/u ę/ja. Four signs existed to express two sounds. Gradually two of the signs were eliminated, leaving у and я. The sounds *u ja* thus derived have the same history as the oral vowels *u ja.*

88. (*a*) *Tort. Full-vocalism (Polnoglásie).* When *r/l* followed *o/e* between consonants in Common Slavonic they are found with these vowels on either side in Russian. The result is conventionally designated *torot*, and the accent falls on the first or second of these syllables according to its original intonation (see section 85). This is called primary full-vocalism, and is as old as our documentation. It is attested by the colophon of the Ostromir Codex (Володимира Новѣгородѣ) in 1057, and in Svjatoslav's miscellanies of 1073 and 1076: полоньникъ 'prisoner' вереди 'sores' беремя 'burden'. The fact that Constantine records γραδ πραχ/гóрод 'city' порóг 'rapid' must be discounted as due to the Slavicized vocabulary of the upper classes in Kiev, and the same is true of врéмя 'time' and the many other examples in Modern Russian of words which do not conform to this rule of full-vocalism. Examples of the rule are: гóрод 'town' горóх 'pea' гóлос 'voice' головá 'head' солóма 'straw' терéть 'rub' железá 'gland'. Russian loanwords to Finnish do not show full-vocalism, but forms corresponding to **tort:* Finnish *palttina* 'linen' *talkkuna* 'flour prepared with hot water' *värttinä* 'distaff'/R. полотнó толокнó веретенó. These contacts date from the sixth century; they seem to imply that the *r/l* was more than normally resonant since it leads to

doubling the following consonant, so that the pronunciation may have been approximately *torṛt *telḷt, from which sonants the later vowels may have developed.

R. молокó 'milk' ⟨*melko/Cz. mléko and other instances show that *telt ⟩tolot must be regarded as the normal Russian development, due to the depalatalizing effect of velar l (*telt ⟩*tolt ⟩tolot). Instead of -ele/olo- there sometimes appears -elo-: шелóм 'ridge-piece, helmet'/ шлем 'helmet' (from OB.).

(b) *Ort*. Words in this series are divided according to their vowel (o/a), but in either case they suffer metathesis of the liquid r/l. To account for the different treatment of vowel is difficult. It seems to depend on intonation, but as tone becomes evident only under stress, the proof depends on amassing enough examples of stressed initial syllables of this type, and to do so is possible only for *ort- and *olt-; even so it involves some conjectures and some discrepancies. The most probable account is that a rising tone on this syllable gave R. la- ra-, and a falling tone ro- lo-, while re- le- result from *ert-/elt-. Examples of rising tones are: рáло 'hoe' L. árklas 'plough', рáтай 'farmer' L. ariù 'plough', лань 'deer' L. álnė, лáкомый 'dainty' L. álksti 'to hunger'/алкáть, рáка 'shrine' Lat. arca. Falling tones: лодья ладья 'boat' S. lâdja лóкоть 'elbow' L. alkúnė S. lâkat, лони 'last year' cf. Lat. olli ⟨*olnei, рóвный 'level' OPr. arwis 'true', рост 'growth' рости/ расти 'grow', роз/раз- ⟨*órz-. Some variations in the last series may be due to Church Slavonic influence, but not all. An example of *elt- (with e in the second syllable replacing unstressed я) is лéбедь 'swan' ⟨*elbendi/olbondi- ⟩S. läbûd.

Apart from some unaccountable instances we thus find that CSl. *órt/órt- appears in Russian as rot-/rat-. To explain the vowel, Vondrák assumes a difference of time; namely, he supposes that before the emergence of Sl. o there was a BSl. a which gave *árt- ⟩ rat-; when Sl. o had developed, then CSl. *órt- ⟩ R. rot-. This metathesis was still under way up to the ninth century, as is witnessed by the alternations OB. aldĭji 'boat' ON. ellidi (probably borrowed in Russia)/R. лодья, ON. Aldegja/Ladoga, Lat. arca/R. рáка 'shrine', R. алкáть/лáкомый 'dainty'. It is a very bold step to remove the rat-metathesis 1500 or 2000 years, into a Balto-Slavonic period. The explanation assumes we know the value of the common Balto-Slavonic vowel; but we cannot. The hypothesis advanced in section 24 is that IE. *a *o gave BSl. *ā̆, from which all divergent developments are readily understood (Baltic o = Sl. a, Baltic a = Sl. o). Further, the explanation is independent of tone, which is the only certainty we are within measure of possessing about this matter. We may suggest alternatively the following: *órt- and *órt- are necessarily long syllables because of the liquid diphthong; but after metathesis the syllable would only be long if the vowel itself were long. Now in Common Slavonic *a* : *o* : : long : short. After metathesis, the rising tone may have preserved the length of the vowel for a while (as it does in the Czech *trát* ⟨*tórt*) thus giving *rat-*; the falling tone allowed the vowel to be shortened (as Cz. *trat* ⟨*tŏrt*). In due course distinctions of quantity disappeared from Russian, and so here remained only a distinction in the quality of the vowel.

(c) *Türt. Secondary full-vocalism.* The same vocalic resonance after *r/l* is found in manuscripts from the eleventh to the fourteenth centuries when preceded by ъ/ь. These spellings correspond to sonant *r̥/l̥* between consonants in Old Bulgarian, there represented in writing by *rŭ lŭ rĭ lĭ*. In Russian, as in Common Slavonic, there was no sonant, but only an extra-short vowel before the liquid, making with it a diphthong before a following consonant. With the generation of a fugitive vowel after the liquid there arose in Russian the forms *tŭrŭt tĭrĭt tŭlŭt tĭlĭt*. These are very frequently recorded in the text of the Ostromir Codex (1056–57): мълъва 'rumour' мьрькнѫти 'grow dark' вълъкъ 'wolf' зьрьно̂ 'grain'. Sometimes the second vowel is represented by an apostrophe (вьр'ху 'on top'); sometimes the liquid is not flanked on both sides by the same vowel (вьрътоградъ 'garden'). Often there are vacillations: мрътвъ/мрьтвъ/мьрьтвъ 'dead'. In this way a fugitive vowel was reintroduced into Russian at the same time as the Common Slavonic *jers* were either being vocalized as *o/e* or eliminated. These secondary full-vocalisms were also resolved. A tendency to treat them like *torot* was manifest in the fourteenth century: молонья 'lightning' 1344, доложьнующе 'indebted' 1370. This result is found in a few instances in Modern Russian: столо́б/ столб 'pillar' беревно́/бревно́ 'beam, balk' по́солонь 'following the sun'/со́лнце 'sun' верёвка 'cord'/OB. *vr̥vĭ* су́меречный 'crepuscular'/ су́мерки 'dusk'. That, however, is the exceptional solution. The normal development is that the first vowel becomes *o/e* and the second may affect the quality of the consonant. The hard *jer* is no more than the sign of a normal consonant, and so disappears without trace. The soft *jer* palatalized the consonant for a while, and so impeded the passage of *e* to *ě* before it; finally the consonant assimilated to the next following. So OR. пьрьвый 'first' became *pér̦vyj*, where soft *r̦* impeded the development of *ě* under the accent, and then *pér̦vyj* пе́рвый (pronounced [p̦erv-] by some). An exception is found in чёрный 'black' ⟨чьрьнъ.

Outside Russian territory this tendency had some success in Poland and Upper Lusatia. P. *wierzch* 'top' has a soft *r̦* due to an intrusive soft *jer;* cf. also OP. *cerekew/cirekew* 'church'.

WR. маланнй 'lightning' shows *ákańe* (-ala- for -olo-) and WR. смяро́тны 'fatal' shows *ja* for *e* (*jákańe*) and hardening of *r* (*ro* for *rě*.)

89. *Initial Vowels*. There are a few cases of loss of vowels in initial position: Ruth. мáти 'have' грáти 'play'/R. имѣ́ть игрáть, Ruth. ще 'yet'/R. ещё. The prefix *iz*- was liable to be confused with *z*-, and hence also with *s*-. In Modern Ruthenian з із зі зо are interchangeable. For initial *o-/je-* see section 86 E.

90. *Final Vowels*. Loss of final vowels is more frequent, especially in connection with *j*. Thus in the adjectival and demonstrative declension *-ji* becomes *-j*, *-jĕ* becomes *-j*, *-ju* becomes *-j*, after the vowels of the adjectival or pronominal stem: G*SF*. дóброй (<*-ojĕ*) DL*SF*. дóброй (<*-oji*), I*SF*. дóброй (<*-oju*). The process of change cannot be traced, but was probably complete in the fourteenth century. Mediæval manuscripts have no й, and their и represents both *i* and *j*. Reduction of *-ĕje* is found in яснéй 'brighter' and other comparatives. The reflexive *-ся* is reduced to *-сь* after a vowel, except in certain participial and imperative forms, чтóбы to чтоб 'in order that', *vĕdĕ* to ведь 'but, why, after all', and final *-o* is lost in тут 'where' вот вон 'lo'. Нáдо 'necessary' represents an older на добѣ.

91. *Contraction and Assimilation of Vowels*. The Russian language on the whole resists contraction of dissimilar vowels in hiatus, but there are instances of such in the *ókańe* region of the North, where *igrát* 'he plays' *momú* (D*SM*.) *movó* (AG*SM*.) 'to my, of my' correspond to игрáет моемý моегó.

There appears to be assimilation in the word сидѣ́ть 'sit'/OB. *sĕdĕti*. The *i* in the Russian root is probably due to the *i* in the present tense endings (OB. *sĕdiši sĕditŭ*). Ruthenian presents the same phenomenon (сидíти), so that the *i* is not to be explained as due to the phonetic representation of the reduced vowel. Another instance perhaps due to a following stressed *i* is дитя́ 'child'/pl. дéти (OB. *dĕtę* pl. *dĕti*). Šachmatov accounted for дитя́ as due to the influence of дитúна 'lad' (now spelt детúна), cf. Ruth. дитúна дитя́. Other examples of this sort of assimilation are мизúнец 'little finger' (CSl. **mĕziničĭ*), снигúрь/снегúрь 'bullfinch' (Ruth. снíгур Cz. *snĕhýř*), витúя 'orator' (OB. *vĕtĭjĭ*).

In Владúмир (-мíръ 'world')/OR. Володимер (with *e* for *ĕ*), *e* has been replaced by *i* by popular etymology. *-mĕrŭ* (cf. Gk. -μωρος) meant 'glorious in the possession of' (e.g. 'power', *vlad*-). Cf. the place-name Житóмир (жúто 'corn').

92. *Velars and Postpalatals*. (*a*) *Palatalization of* к г х. In sections 36–38 we saw that successive palatalizations of *k g ch* into palatal affricates and dental fricatives and affricates left them only in contact with hard vowels in Common Slavonic. The hard vowels are normally back vowels, but Sl. *y* is a mixed (back-front) vowel [ɨ], akin both to *u* and to *i*, and represented by all early scripts as a combination of the two (*ui*, *ŭi*, etc.). It is somewhat variable. The *u*- element comes out

strongly after a labial consonant in Russian, giving rise to an almost perceptible diphthong. After a velar consonant (*k g ch*) the *i*-element must have become more and more evident in Old Russian, at least from the beginning of the twelfth century. No new letters were involved. The combinations *ky gy chy* gave way to *ḱi ǵi chi* (ки ги хи).

The earliest examples of this change are фуники/*funiky* (APM.) 'palms' сикими/*sikymi* (IP.) 'such', both of 1073. These examples are somewhat isolated. In the first half of the twelfth century the postpalatals *ḱ ǵ ch* were established in South Russia; небесьскімъ 'heavenly' 1144, секира 'axe 1164, великии 'great' 1220. In the Novgorod region the date of their establishment was somewhat later, at the end of the twelfth century, and the West Russian evidence (from Smolensk) is also somewhat later than that of the South. Ризкии 'of Riga' латинескимъ (DP.) 'Latin' княгини 'princesses' (Smolensk 1229), праздьники 'festivals' Римьскимь (IS.) 'Roman' (Novgorod 1282). For a period the two pronunciations *ky gy chy*/*ḱi ǵi chi* were concurrent: въ Кыевѣ 'in Kiev' кычеть 'cries like a cuckoo'. In the Moscow region посельскымъ (DP.) 'of messengers' Симановьскыи 'Simanov's' are examples found in documents of 1447–53. There are some relics of the old velar pronunciation in dialects of today. The softened pronunciation showed some tendency to spread to other combinations, as to *ḱu* in кюръ/кур 'cock' 1357 and to *ḱa* in всякяя/всякая (NFS.) 'every' 1405; and there are similar substitutions of soft for hard velars in modern dialects. Phonetic changes tend to develop beyond their original causes. The postpalatals *ḱ ǵ* approach the middle palate where the most backward varieties of *t d* (*ť ď*) are pronounced, and so lead to interchange (as in the Macedo-Bulgarian dialects): Овдотья for *Ovdókja* Eudocia', OR. Дюргии/Геóргий dial. *ándel* cf. Cz. *anděl*/áнгел 'angel'.

The emergence of soft *ḱ ǵ ch* has had an important effect upon the Russian declension. There remained in Russian from Common Slavonic the difference between the two orders of vowels: hard/soft. The soft vowels demanded soft consonants before them, and the soft consonants corresponding to hard *k g ch* had been determined by the Slavonic palatalizations. But it is characteristic of linguistic changes that their first motives are in time forgotten, and they remain as anomalies. English and French 'irregular' verbs, for instance, are for the most part verbs conjugated according to older, forgotten principles, which now seem merely anomalous. Old Russian stems ending in a velar presented the anomaly, as it then seemed, of an unstable final consonant, no longer understood as a necessary form taken by the velar in certain cases. The softening process gave a new and more intelligible alternation: hard/soft : : *k g ch*/*ḱ ǵ ch*. These new consonants therefore replaced the older palatals: OR. токъ 'flow'

L*S*. тоцѣ N*P*. тоци/MR. тóк-е -и, OR. бóгъ 'God' бозѣ бози/MR. бóг-е -и OR. духъ 'spirit' дусѣ дуси/MR. дýх-е -и, OR. рукá 'hand' DL*S*. руцѣ G*S*.NA*P*. рукы/MR. рýк-á -é -и. The vocative singular, however, in so far as it survives, is a form used outside the sentence, and so independent of declension. It suffered the first Slavonic palatalization, which remains in Бóже 'O God' Óтче 'O Father', and was more widespread in Old Russian: OR. точе. The usage is now archaic, save for the emotional use of бóже, and restricted to religious expressions.

(*b*) *Velar Fricatives.* CSl. *g* has acquired a fricative pronunciation (voiced [h] or [γ]) in South Russia, White Russia, Upper Lusatia, Slovakia and Bohemia. It is a characteristic which marks off an important area among the Slavonic tongues and cuts across their triple division, though it must be observed that the link between these languages is purely formal; the development may have been independent in the various languages, and occurred e.g. in Czech after the first written records. As remarked in section 84, a fricative pronunciation of *g* (voiced [h]) is found also in Great Russian in a few words which are of a religious cast and have been affected by the Kievite style of elocution. It has also, as there remarked, caused г to be used for foreign *h*. Though influenced by literary preferences, this substitution has not failed to produce really popular effects. Thus государь 'ruler' loses its initial by weakening of fricative [h], and then contracts as an enclitic to сýдарь >су/съ: какъ-су мнѣ царя не жалѣть? 'How am I not to pity the Tsar?' (Avakkum, 17th cent.). Cf. óлух 'dolt' for óглух (the form of this word in Ruthenian) from глухóй 'deaf'. In the official documents of the Polish-Lithuanian court г was *h*, and to reproduce occlusive *g* it was necessary to write кг : кгды 'when'. In those which use Latin script *h* is normal though *g* is also found: *Hodovica* 1371 *Haliciensis* 1375/*mogilla* 'grave-mound' 1378 *Jurgi* 1451. In Modern Rutherian a special letter has been invented to denote the rarely occurring occlusive.

In the declension of pronouns and adjectives G*SMN*. -*go* appears in conformity with Old Bulgarian orthography, and until 1917 the spelling -*ago* was used if the ending was unstressed. But the normal pronunciation is -*vo*. In some old forms of the language the pronunciation may have been -*ho*, as it is still in Olonec dialects in the North. The fricative is as characteristic of the North as of the South in this instance. Šachmatov's explanation starts from the pronominal G*S*. -*so* (cf. *-sjo* in Gk. τοῖο <*tosjo*) found in OB. *čiso česo.* Parallel with this would be G*S*. **koso* D*S*. **kosmu* L*S*. **kosmĭ*, of which the latter developed into *komu komĭ*, leading to an analogical loss of *s* in **koo*, whence by intrusion of *h* to separate the syllables: *koho.* The substitution of *v* for fricative *g* is found in North Russian dialects in other instances also: *kovdá tovdá*/когда тогда 'when, then', *vospodín* (Perḿ) 'sir'/господи́н. The pronunciation *-vo* has been established in the Moscow region since the fifteenth century: великово (*GSM.*) 'great' 1432. A form in *v* is also found, outside the Russian area, in Cassubian. Some who do not care to begin with **-so*, but prefer to explain *-go* as a particle, offer the sequence: *-ogo >-oho >-oo >-ouo >* *-ovo*. A third theory connects the *v* with the suffix of possessive adjectives: *-ov;* a fourth explains it by assimilation and dissimilation: *nóvogo >nóvovo* (assimilation), *dorogógo >dorogóvo* (dissimilation). The matter remains obscure.

The fricative values [χ γ] are liable to occur when the velar occlusive, after loss of *jer*, stands before another occlusive. The first occlusive is relaxed into a fricative, voiced before a voiced consonant, voiceless before a voiceless one. So it may be with кто 'who' где 'where' тогда 'there', and normally is in лёгкий 'light'. In the declension of the latter the [γ] is carried through by some speakers: indefinite лёгок [lóγək] comp. лéгче [léχči]. OB. *mękŭkyjĭ*/R. мя́гкий 'soft' is explained as *kk >χk >γ-k* (by analogy) in the indefinite form мя́гок. So too ко́готь 'claw' дёготь 'pitch-tar' may have fricative *g* from the gen.sing. *-gt-*. The fricative pronunciation is attested from the fourteenth century: хто мя́хки 1307, мягки/мя́хкы 1354.

The sound [γ] also occurs in standard Russian when x is followed by a voiced consonant (not a sonant), e.g. до́брых друзе́й 'of good friends' [dóbrɨγ druźéj], and in the word бухга́лтер 'bookkeeper' borrowed from the German [buγáltɪr].

93. *Dentals and Alveolars. T D, L R N.* In section 39 it was shown that these sounds probably existed in three varieties in Common Slavonic, viz. hard or normal, soft before front vowels, and palatalized by the semi-vowel *j.** In Russian ч ж took the place of **t̂ *d̂* before our records open. Thus Constantine VII's Βερούτзη 949 corresponds to OR. вьручи/OB. *vĭrǫšti.* Their history in Russian is among the sibilants. CSl. soft **t̂ *d̂ *r̂* persist in Great Russian, harden in Ruthenian, and have usually become *ć dź r* (hard) in White Russian: *dźe* 'where' *dźéŭka* 'maiden' *ćipér* 'now'/R. где де́вка тепе́рь P. *gdzie*

---

*The terms 'palatalized' and 'palatal' are used in discussions of Slavonic phonetics in a slightly different sense which should perhaps be pointed out. There Russian 'soft' consonants are described as resulting from palatalization in the sense of a certain tongue-position (described *e.g.* by Boyanus *op. cit.*). The soft ('palatal') consonants of Polish are formed with a slightly different tongue-position, Polish soft *s* for instance sounding very like German *ch* in *ich* [ç]. Broch (*Slavische Phonetik*) describes the soft consonants of Czech as *rand-palatal;* in forming them the tongue assumes a position midway between that of Russian and Polish. Thus Russian не, Polish *nie* and Czech *ně* do not represent identical sound-groups even if we assume the vowels to be identical; and the difference, though not easily perceptible by foreign ears, is immediately apparent to native speakers.

dziewka. The development is modern. It is not found in the Lithuanian Statute (1588) nor in any sixteenth-century documents that are free from Polish influence.

· The soft and palatalized varieties of *l r n* constitute the soft forms in Russian. In the case of *l*, the hard form is not the normal alveolar of Western Europe, but the hollow or 'dark' *l* something like that heard in Eng. *milk*. This *l* tends to become a semivowel when it closes a syllable, either at the end of the word or before another consonant; and the semivocalic *u* tends to develop further into the consonant *v*, and *vice versa*. The result is an oscillation *l/u/v* which is widespread in North, West, and South-West Russia, from the fourteenth century at least. So in WR. *byŭ* 'was' *dźeŭčýna* 'girl' *ŭlećéła* 'flew away' the letter *ŭ* (ў) is a semivowel, standing for older *l/v/u*. Ruth. вовк 'wolf' вовна 'wool' дав 'gave' show *l* > *ŭ* > *v* (pronounced *ŭ*). The reverse development *v* > *ŭ* > *u* is attested in mediæval manuscripts: уторникъ/ вторник 'Tuesday' ноугородского 1282, у праздьникъ 'on the festival' 1355 (Novgorod), укусивъшю 'having tasted'/вкус 1386 (Pskov), узяти/взять 'take' у корабль 'into the boat' 1164 (Galicia-Volhynia). Apart from Novgorod this phenomenon is rare in Great Russian dialects, and it is only found in the North in those dialects which confuse *č/c*, and in the South in the case of initial *v-*: удовá 'widow' унýк 'grandson' усё 'all'. R. зáвтра 'tomorrow' зáвтрак 'breakfast'/ ýтро 'morning' show *v* for *u*. The interchange *u/v* is especially frequent in Ržev, with examples continuous from the thirteenth century, and very rare in Moscow.

One property of the Russian *r* is to withdraw a following *i* from the front [i] to the mixed [ɨ] position; in other words, to harden *ŕi* to *ry*: крылы (I*PN*.) 'with wings' 1219/OB. *krily*. This leads to vacillations: грыб/гриб 'mushroom', крынка/кринка 'pot' (OB. *krinica*). There are also corresponding vacillations between *ŕa/ra*, *ŕu/ru* and *ŕë/ro*: красть/крясть (Novgorod) 'steal', трость/NGtR. трёсточка 'walking-stick', OR. рушити/рюшити 'collapse'. The hardening of *ŕ* is normal in White Russian.

94. *Labials*: *P B V F M*. The labials also formed a triple series in Common Slavonic, which has been resolved in Russian as *p ṕ pĺ*, *b b bĺ*, *v v́ vĺ*, *m ṁ mĺ*: под 'under' купить/куплю 'buy' дóбрый 'good' дóблесть 'valour', земля́ 'land', ловить/ловлю 'catch'. As *f* was not a Common Slavonic sound it has not developed beyond a distinction between hard and soft: *f/f*, though there is an analogical development of the verb потрáфить 'please'/потрáфлю (I*S*. pres.).

A Russian (and Modern Slavonic) *f* results from the unvoicing of *v* which has become final by loss of final *jer* (see section 86). It is also used to represent Gk. φ θ as ф ѳ, of which pair the latter has not been used since 1917, and also Germ.Fr.Eng. *f*. It is unlikely that the

Russians ever made the attempt to pronounce Gk. θ as an interdental fricative, so that the retention of this letter in such words as Θομά 'Thomas' Θεοφίλъ 'Theophilus' θεοκράτія 'theocracy' (until 1917) was merely due to orthographical conservatism. Examples of φ are: филосо́фия = Gk. φιλοσοφία флиѓгель Germ. *Flügel* 'wing' (of a building) фунт = Germ. *Pfund* 'pound' фло́ра = Lat. *flora* фура́ж = Fr. *fourrage* 'forage'. The sound [f] also arises through contact between *v* and a voiceless consonant: второ́й 'second' [ftaró j] всё 'all' [fśə].

In South-West Russia there was a general tendency to represent Gk. φ θ by the genuine Slavonic sound *ch* [χ]: Нехталимля 'of Naphtali' c. 1226, Хома/Фома́ Ходоръ/Фёдор Хролъ/Флор (14th cent.). This is still a feature of Modern Ruthenian. In North Russia there was a tendency to reproduce *chv* as *f* (as in Modern Serbocroat and Bulgarian), and to extend this process to *ch:* малафия 'Malachias' (14th cent.) фристофоръ 'Christopher' (c.1428). уѳачена/ухва́чена 'grasped' 1588. In dialectalisms like *dóbryf mojéf*/до́брых мойх we see this confusion of *ch/f* affecting even indigenous words.

On the pronunciation of *GSMN.-go* as -*vo* see section 92 (*b*).

95. *Sibilants.* R. с/з ш/ж ц/(*dz*) ч/(*dž*) щ/(*ždž*), the forms in brackets occurring for the most part as the result of assimilation to voiced consonants. All the sibilants, apart from those representing IE. *s/z*, have resulted from the softening of other consonants. Hard consonants are normal consonants, and soft consonants are essentially modifications of hard consonants. In process of time, therefore, the sibilants came to be accepted not as modifications but as normal consonants of their own kind, and so 'hardened', The process was already at work in Old Bulgarian, and perhaps in Common Slavonic. In Old Bulgarian there was the alternation hard *s z/* soft *ś ź*, but all other sibilants were soft: OB. *š' ž' ć dž č' š't ž'd* . It is not usual to mark this softening in transcription since it is implied in the consonant itself. Some of these have hardened in Russian: *š ž c* are hard, but *č* remains soft; щ is a compound of *šč* and so soft (many pronounce it as a double soft *š'š'*); soft *ž'* may still occur when the spelling has зж or жж or when ж is followed by a soft consonant: дро́жжи [dróž':ı] 'yeast', жди́те [ž'd'ıt'ı] 'wait'.

The surest evidence for the hardening of these consonants is the appearance of *y* after them in place of the older *i*. This occurs from the beginning of the fourteenth century: слышышь 'thou hearest' 1300, жывота (gen.) 'life' 1389, языцы 'tongues' 1397. The letter *č* is also hardened in some Modern Russian dialects and even in old documents: рѣчы 'speeches' 1588. In standard Russian it is regarded as soft. The use of и or ь after sibilants and of hard vowels after ч is not a guide to their actual quality in present-day Russian, but is due to conservative spelling and to the analogy of other declensional or conjugational forms. Thus слы́шишь [slɨ́šɨš] 'thou hearest' is pronounced with hard consonants and vowels, and the first syllable of ча́до [č'ádə] 'child' with soft ones. When *s*+*č* come into contact in the sentence or appear in compounds they develop to *šč*, and do not take the pronunciation [š':] which many speakers give to щ : с че́стью 'with honour' (*šč*-). Брошю́ра 'brochure' is spelt thus because ю is the traditional way of transliterating French *u* (and German *ü*); the pronunciation is -шу-. Compared with Russian *š ž*, English *sh zh* (e.g. in *leisure*) are relatively soft.

The pronunciation *ždž* occurs for зж with some speakers in words like выезжа́ть 'ride out' (P. *wyježdżać;* ⟨*-zdj-*); and in the case of those who pronounce щ as *šč* it may come by assimilation to a following voiced consonant: вещь была́ [v́ež'dž' biłá] 'the thing was'.

It is in its wealth of sibilants that Common Slavonic differs most markedly from Indo-European. By successive palatalizations consonants of other orders, velars and dentals, have continued to pass into the sibilants. As the modern sibilants have many origins, it may be helpful if we list the Russian sibilants in relation to their sources:

ч (*č*): IE. **k* (*kʷ*) by first palatalization; CSl. **č:* теку́/течёт 'flow', **otĭko(s)*/о́тче 'O father'.

CSl. **tj *kt *gt*, OB. *št:* свеча́ ⟨**světja* 'candle', ночь (⟨ **noktis*) 'night', течь 'flow' ⟨**tekti*, мочь 'power' ⟨**magtis.*

(*dž*): This voiced partner of *č* has become *ž* in Russian; for *ždž* see above.

щ (*šč*): (pronounced by many as a long soft *š*): IE. **sk*, by first palatalization, CSl. **sč'* OB. *št:* ищу́ ⟨**isčǫ*/иска́ть 'seek' P. *iszczę* OB. *ištǫ.*

CSl. **stj *skt* ⟩**št*, OB. *št:* ращу́ ⟨**orstjǫ*/расти́ть 'grow' OB. *raštǫ.*

R. сч : счёт 'bill, account' ⟨*sŭčĭtŭ.*

OB. щ/R. ч in loanwords: мо́щи 'relics' мо́щный 'mighty'/ мочь 'power', по́мощь 'help'/по́мочи (pl.) 'braces'; the strictly literary participles in -щий : несу́щий 'bearing' /могу́чий 'mighty'; посещу́/посети́ть 'visit'.

ц (*c*): IE. Proto-Sl. **k* by second palatalization, CSl. *ć:* (a) оте́ц (⟨**otĭko(s)* ⟩*otĭcĭ*) 'father' овца́ ⟨**ovĭka ovĭca* 'sheep', (b) цена́ ⟨**koina* 'price' рука́ OR.DLS. руцѣ NAP. руци 'hand' (MR. руке́ ру́ки); цвет 'flower'/Cz. *kvĕt.*

CSl. **ť* WR. *ć:* WR. *nalehać*/R. налега́ть 'press', cf. P. infin. -*ć.*

(*dz*): This voiced partner of *c* has become *z* in Russian. CSl. **ď* WR. *dž : dźe* 'where'.

ш (*š*): Proto-Sl. *ch* by first palatalization: душá 'soul'/дух 'spirit'.
CSl. **sj* >*š:* ношéние 'carrying'/носи́ть 'carry'.

ж (*ž*): IE. **g* (**gᵂ*) **gh* by first palatalization, CSl. **dž* >*ž*: бог 'god'/
бóже могу́ 'can'/мóжешь.

CSl. **zj* >*ž:* вожу́/вози́ть 'convey' (**vozjǫ*).

CSl. **d* OB. *žd:* межá 'boundary' (**medja*). OB. *žd* is borrowed
in мéжду 'among' надéжда/надёжа 'hope' and many other
words. In the Church Slavonic word иждивéние 'expense'
the *žd* represents *ždž* <**zdž*, being formed from the prefix
iz-+root **dživ-* (<**giv-*) >*živ-* 'live'.

с (*s*): IE. **s:* семь 'seven' IE. **k̂* by *satem*-palatalization: сто
'hundred'.

Proto-Sl. *ch* by second palatalization: дух 'spirit' OR.L*S*.
дусѣ N*P*. дуси.

з (*z*): IE. **s* before voiced consonants: гнездó 'nest' <**nizdo* <**ni-
sd-* (form affected by analogy).

IE. **ĝ* **ĝh* by *satem*-palatalization: везти́ 'convey' (**weĝh-*).

IE.Proto-Sl. *g*, by second palatalization, CSl. *dz:* бог 'god'/
OR.L*S*. бозѣ N*P*. бози.

CSl. **gẃ:* звездá 'star'/*P. gwiazda:*

It is by means of the sibilants that the oldest Russian dialect-
divisions are established. They are named by using the suffix -*kańe* in
association with the characteristic mark. Thus White Russia is the
region of *cékańe* and *dzékańe*, that is, where CSl. **t́* **d́* give *ć dź:* WR.
dźeń 'day' *byváć* 'be'. North Russian was distinct from South Russian
because of *čákańe* and *cókańe* (see section 84), that is, the use of *č* for
c and of *c* for *č:* цоловекъ/человéк 'man' чарь/царь 'tsar'. This
was a characteristic of the old Novgorod dialect, and there went
with it a tendency to substitute *i* for *ě* in stressed syllables. In the
districts of Bielsk and Brześć the confusion of sibilants goes further.
It affects *z/ž c/č sc/šč:* слузбу/слу́жбу 'service' 1530. In modern
dialects *zelézo* and *zémcug* are heard for желéзо 'iron' жéмчуг 'pearl'.
A similar feature appears in Polish (Mazovian) dialects.

96. *Final Consonants*. In principle there were no final consonants in
Common Slavonic or Old Bulgarian; every word ended in a vowel,
even though that vowel might be extra-short (*jer*). When the *jers* fell
away in Russian, consonants very frequently became final, and they
suffered one general law: final consonants, other than *m n l r*, are
unvoiced. *M n l r* are unvoiced in certain cases also, e.g. final after
a voiceless consonant: теáтр 'theatre'. By the unvoicing of *v* a Slavonic
f was acquired.

The *jers* were weakest in final position, and therefore most readily
confused. The hard *jer* was, however, a mark of normality in the
previous consonant; the tendency to be observed is that of the

hardening of final consonants which were originally followed by *ĭ*. The soft quality of such consonants could be maintained best when there were examples of it in more sheltered positions in a declension or conjugation, as, for instance, кость 'bone' by analogy with GDL*S*. кости, etc. Lacking such support *m̆ t̆ n̆* may change to *m t n* in final position. The hardening of final *m* occurs in the instr.sg. -*mĭ*/R. -мъ : богом 'by God', and the loc.instr.sg. of pronouns and adjectives: I*S*. том L*S*. тем of *M*. тот *N*. то 'that'. The athematic 1 sg. -*mĭ* was also affected: дам 'shall give' ем 'eat'. Similarly 3 sg. pl. -*tĭ* hardened in Russian as in Old Bulgarian, but only fully after 1350: несёт 'he bears'. Early instances are: стоить 'costs' уморять 'they will kill' 1354. This development is considerably younger than the hardening of final -*m*, which is amply exemplified in the Ostromir Codex (1056–57). There are exceptions: OR. есмь 'am' MR. есть 'is', суть (obsolescent) 'are', семь 'seven' восемь 'eight' (which were originally *i*-stems, and so analogous to кость). They are found hardened in Ruthenian and some White Russian dialects: семъ осмъ (Skorpina's Bible), Ruth. сім; вісім [*vi*- for *(*v*)*o*- < *o-] must be analogical, though the oblique forms have anomalously осьм-.

Final -*n̆* is hardened in gen.pl.fem. of some *ja*-stems: вечéрня 'vespers' G*P*. вечéрен. Final *b̆ v̆* also tended to harden: кровъ 'blood' (15th cent.), любовъ 'love' церковъ 'church' 1562. Ruth. любóв цéрков гóлуб 'pigeon'.

Final -*l* following another consonant drops in the -*l* participle: умер 'died' нёс 'bore'/умерлá неслá P. *umarł niósł;* the same thing occurs in colloquial Czech.

In several modern Great and White Russian dialects final -*st*/*śt* have been reduced to -*s*/*ś*: *mos póes šeś straś*/мост 'bridge' пóезд 'train' шесть 'six' страсть 'passion'; the same feature is found in Modern Bulgarian.

97. *Simplification of Groups and Assimilation.* Within the word the loss of the *jers* had the effect of creating a great number of new groups of consonants in Old Russian, which have largely been simplified.

(i) Three-consonant groups are simplified by loss of the middle term, and longer groups are similarly reduced; assimilation may supervene. Examples are: *lvt* полторá 'one and a half' (14th cent.), *rv́n* бéрно 1317 берно (14th cent.)/бревнó 'beam', *zdn* горáзно 'cleverly' 1356, *stb* избá 'hut' (14th cent.), *st́g* зга 'path' (cf. *st́zja* стезя́), *sístv* ество 'being' 1282 (*jestĭstvo*), *plsk* Псков. Бéрце 'shin' derives from *berdĭce < **bedrĭce;* cf. бедрó 'hip'. Перчáтка 'glove' derives from пёрст 'finger' by a similar reduction: *ršč* > *rč*. Under this heading may also be listed the frequent pronunciation of ч + consonant as ш : что [štə], конéчно 'of course' [kańéšnə], etc. When the group occurred at the beginning of the word, it might be the first consonant which was lost: чан 'vat' (*ščan* at Olonec) for *dŭščanŭ*, стакáн 'drinking-glass' for *dŭstŭkanŭ*, хорь 'pole-cat' P. *tchórz* Cz. *tchoř* for *dŭchoři*, пéрѧц 'pepper' for *pĭpĭr-*.

(ii) Double consonants were made single: Руской 'Russian' for *Rusĭskŭjĭ*. In mediæval manuscripts when the same consonant ends one word and begins the next, sometimes only one consonant is written. The doublet -*nn*- is, however, favoured: отмéнный 'superior'. In Ruthenian -*nn*- -*ll*- -*tt*- arise in part of the area as a result of palatalization: життя́/житѭ 'life' бажáння/бáжанє 'wish'. It should be noted that in Modern Russian double consonants are usually pronounced double, i.e. lengthened as in Italian: оттýда [at:údə] 'thence', etc. There are a few exceptions, such as рýсский [rúskəj] and some foreign words like комиссáр [kəmɪsár]. In the words гостúная 'drawing-room' гостúница 'hotel', on the other hand, a double *n* is heard.

(iii) The quality of the first consonant may become that of the second: *ún* нивѣныхъ (*GP*. adj.) 'of the fields', *vź* вьзя вьзяти 'take' 1164, *rb* прискърьбьнъ/прискóрбие 'affliction' 1215, *bú* любьве 'love' *ŕstv* царъство 'kingdom' 1307. In Modern Russian the distinction between hard/soft is most thoroughly maintained by *l*: сúльный 'strong' больнóй 'sick' большóй 'great'/NGtR. *bolšój*. With *t d ŕ* the results are various: чéстный 'honourable' G*S*. дня 'of day' сéрдце 'heart'/судьбá 'judgment' свáдьба 'wedding' тьма 'darkness' гóрький 'bitter' I*P*. людьмú 'by people' (свадбѣ 1354). *Ŝ* remains in письмó 'letter'/OB. *pismo* 'writing' восьмóй 'eighth', but *ś ź* are generally hardened before hard consonants: G*S*. ослá 'of a donkey' здáние 'building'. *M n p b v* are commonly hardened. It is very rare for this kind of assimilation to be due to a previous consonant; instances are: *jsk* галелѣиськую *ńsk* Сидоньськая (14th cent.), MRuth. -ський. There are numerous cases where the modern spelling fails to indicate softness, e.g. in the с of лесть, or indicates a non-existent softness, e.g. in the ending -нький and the reflexive -ся; cf. Ruth. пíсля [píśla] 'after', etc. Many speakers pronounce сюдá 'hither' [sudá].

(iv) Assimilation by voicing or unvoicing: *sd* здѣ MR. здесь 'here' (and so also *šb šg*, though it may not so appear in the spelling), *kd* гдѣ 'where' нѣгдѣ 'somewhere, *tb* свадбѣ D*S*./MR. nom. свáдьба 'wedding' 1354, *bč* пьчела, MR. пчелá 'bee' 1334, *dk* рѣтка 'rare' 1406 MR. рéдка, *dch* зáтхлый 'stuffy' (cf. дух 'breath'), *zk* ускими (I*P*.) 'narrow' 1307/ýзкий.

(v) Assimilation of point of articulation. The sibilants are either alveolar or palatal, and they readily exchange to suit following consonants: *žsk* Ризкии 'of Riga' 1229, *čs* нѣмецкыи (MR. немéцкий) 'German' 1284, *sl* шлити 'pour off, decant' 1284/MR. слить. The reflexive -*sja* assimilates to a preceding *t* in Ruth. dial. женýтца 'they hurry' póблятца 'they become' etc. ветчина́ 'ham' is supposed to be from *ветшина from vetŭch- 'old'.

(vi) Prefixes set up the most noticeable opposition to assimilation, though the tendency at first was for them to follow the general rule. In od- for ot- the d was supported by the analogy of prefixes ending in d (над под перед), and it has sometimes been acknowledged by the orthography: одъ вѣка 'from eternity (cf. P.Cz.S. od). With regard to bez- iz- ob- raz- vz- the reaction against losing their identity by assimilation appears in the thirteenth century. The Ostromir Codex (1056–57) has such forms as везаконие 'unrighteousness' (bez-z-). In the thirteenth century the double consonants reappear: рассудити 'arbitrate' иссыпати 'strew out' 1354. When a conventional sign is inserted between the prefix and the verb (расъсядуться 'they will take their seats') the effect is more marked, and still more when the original consonant is restored (разсказъ 'story'); but the latest orthography has gone back to thirteenth century principles (рассказ). Some examples of simplification remain, e.g. of zz in развева́ть 'gape'/ зев 'jaws'. In vulgar speech there is a false simple verb zorít 'ruin' resulting from the spelling раззорить for разори́ть.

98. *Epenthesis and Dissimilation*. In Russian, as in the other Slavonic languages, the groups sr/zr are expanded to str/zdr: струя́ 'stream'/ Gk. ῥέω(<*sr-.) Встре́тить 'meet' derives from (v(ŭ)z- >vs-+rĕt-).

The groups kt gd kk dissimilate in those words in which the first occlusive becomes a fricative before the second occlusive: хто 'who' мяхкы 'soft' 1305)/MR. кто где (sometimes pronounced [χtɔ] [ɣdɛ]). Similarly affricates lose either the occlusive or the fricative element to dissimilate from what follows: čt >št што (MR. что, sometimes pronounced [štɔ]) 'what' 1164, čš >tš лутьшии 'better' (13th cent.)/ лу́чший.

Dissimilation at a distance occurs with l---l r---r: уларь 'surplice' 1282/Gk. ὡράριον, gen. февларя (14th cent.) MR. февра́ль/Lat. *Februarius*, верблюд 'camel'/Cz. *velbloud* (ultimately the same word as *elephant*), пе́репел 'quail'/Perḿ dial. *pelepel*.

Two sibilants in contact may be dissimilated by making the first j: OR. бѣиство 'flight'/*běžĭstvo, WR. gen. малайца́ 'youth's'/*maładźcá R. молодца́; cf. P.gen. ojca <oćca 'father's', whence nom. ojciec by analogy.

Here may perhaps be mentioned the word близору́кий 'short-sighted', from a form близо-зоркий influenced by рука́ through popular etymology.

B. FORMS

(i) VERBS

99. *Simplifying the Paradigm.* What had been achieved in this way by Common Slavonic has been described in section 47. Russian is the Slavonic language which has carried the process of simplification forward to its extreme limit. The dual number disappeared from verbs, and subsequently from nouns. By relying on the perfective/ imperfective mechanism and by use of the compound past tense for the simple, Russian eliminated the imperfect and aorist tenses. The system of auxiliaries was simplified; some were eliminated and another reduced to a fixed form. The reflexive particle lost its freedom of place. The indefinite participles were confined to one or two forms, which became gerundial, and with that change Russian did away with the syntactical use of the participles where subordinate sentences are now found. The West Slavonic languages have retained more of the old auxiliaries, and the South Slavonic (apart from Slovene) have, like the WSl. Wendish, kept the old imperfect and aorist.

(a) *Loss of the Dual.* In the twelfth century the dual verb regularly went with a dual subject or two subjects: Никонъ и другыи чрньць отъидоста 'Nikon and the other monk departed'. The only difference from Old Bulgarian was the failure to distinguish between 2D. -ta/ 3D. -te. In documents of the thirteenth century plural verbs began to make their appearance in such circumstances: та два была іехали 'they two had travelled'. From the middle of the fourteenth century the use of the plural is so frequent as to assure us of the breakdown of the verbal dual: аще будемъ грубо написали 'if we (two authors) have written crudely' 1355, двѣ птицѣ продаються 'two birds are sold', та готоваша 'they two made ready' 1358. The dual has entirely disappeared from the modern verb, save for a particle -sta (<jesta 'ye two are') in пожа́луйста [pažálstə] 'please, be so kind as to', which is now classed among the adverbs.

(b) *Loss of the imperfect and aorist.* The imperfect was not colloquial Russian at any time within the embrace of our documents. It is absent from the *Russkaja Pravda*, a work which makes much use of the vernacular. In modern dialects there is no trace of the tense.

In Old Russian manuscripts the forms of the imperfect and aorist are confused, and the aorist is used in imperfect contexts in such a way as to show that it was losing its special virtue. It occurs, but comparatively rarely, in treaties and letters of the thirteenth and fourteenth centuries; an example is грамота псана бысть 'the document was written' 1284. In the *Russkaja Pravda* the perfect appears where the aorist is to be expected, and in Mstislav's deed (1130) there are four perfects but not one aorist. Soon after the fourteenth century this tense passed into disuse, and is now found only in fragmentary relics. In the north-western dialect of the heroic ballads it is found: бысть князь весел и радостен 'the prince was joyous and glad'. The 3 sg. ended in a vowel, and this is sometimes found with an added -*j* by confusion with the imperative: он не знай/*zna* 'he knew not'. The exclamatory particle чу 'hist!' has been explained as 2*S*. aor. of *čuti* 'perceive'. The aorist is also no doubt reflected in the use of such monosyllabic, undeclined forms as хлоп 'banged' прыг 'jumped' (e.g. я в негó трах бекассúнником 'I blazed away at it with small shot') and possibly in the use of the imperative as a past tense (see section 104).

Apart from the vernacular disuse, Russo-Slavonic works bear witness to the decay of the tense by the confusion of forms. Aor. 3*P*. -*ša*/Impf. 3*S*. -*še* 3*P*. -*chu* are used interchangeably. To the aor. 3*S*. - (without personal ending) there is frequently added the -*t* of 3*S*. present. These vacillations are common in the fourteenth century, especially in North Russia. In the sixteenth and seventeenth centuries the tense had fallen into complete confusion, both as to number and to person: жена же молишася (3*P*.) 'the woman prayed', мы обрѣтохъ (1*S*.) 'we discovered'. Even educated folk using Russo-Slavonic were unable to maintain control over a tense for which they had lost all instinctive capacity.

(c) *Loss of auxiliaries*. (i) *Perfect Tense*. The first and second persons are determined by the conditions of the discourse, but the third person embraces the universe. It is generally defined by means of a noun or a demonstrative pronoun; and, that being so, there is the less need for definition by flexion. The function of the auxiliary in the compound perfect tense (participle -*lŭ*+present tense of 'to be') was to bear this otiose personal ending. Even in the oldest Old Bulgarian manuscripts the loss of the auxiliary with the third person is noted.

For the first or second person there was need of definition so long as the genius of the language did not demand the use of the personal pronoun: далъ есмь 'I gave', судилъ есмь 'I judged' 1284. (It will be remembered that only the first and second persons have personal pronouns of their own; the third person is a demonstrative.) In the twelfth century personal pronouns rarely appear, and the personal endings of the auxiliary contribute to the meaning. The pronouns, when they are inserted, are emphatic or distinctive: азъ грѣшьныи Ѳеодоръ написалъ 'I, the sinner Theodore, have written'. Increasing use of the pronouns before the verb went with decreasing use of the auxiliary: язъ далъ рукою своею 'I have given with my own hand' 1130, мы вашее братие (gen.) не обидѣли ни грабили 'we have not injured or despoiled your brethren', ты его товаръ узялъ 'thou hast taken his goods' c. 1300. On the other hand, full forms of the tense are found as late as the seventeenth century: дали есми 'we have given' 1567, ночевала есмь 'I (fem.) spent the night'.

(ii) *Pluperfect*. This was originally past of the perfect, and its auxiliary was naturally the imperfect 'was' (бяхъ). With the disappearance of this tense the pluperfect could not be expressed thus. First, the past of the auxiliary was expressed by the compound perfect (былъ есмь), and then the auxiliary of the auxiliary decayed, leaving only был to mark pluperfect time. From the end of the fifteenth century this evolution is found complete, and it is the norm in the sixteenth: насадилъ былъ Богъ рай = *Deus plantaverat paradisum* 'God had planted a garden'. In folk-tales and ballads жыл-был ('there lived once upon a time') is originally a pluperfect of remote time maintained in popular use by the effective jingle. In colloquial Russian there occurs a sort of pluperfect formed with the past tense of 'to be' and the past gerund, e.g. выпивши было '(I) had had a drink or two'. See also the special use of было (section 107).

(iii) *Conditional*. The auxiliary *bimĭ* was quite unknown in Old Russian. It was giving ground in Old Bulgarian to *bychĭ* (3 sg. *by*). In Russian this auxiliary continued to be regularly inflected as late as the fifteenth century, but the 3 sg. бы came to be used as an invariable conditional particle (sometimes abbreviated to б) for all persons and numbers. This idiom first makes its appearance in the thirteenth century: аще бы въ Турѣ быша силы былы 'if there had been strength in Tyre' 1215, аще Богъ отець вашь бы былъ, любили бы мя ксте 'if God were your father, ye would have loved Me' 1354. In Skorpina's Bible the usage is still unfixed, and full forms are found in some Modern Ruthenian dialects. Бы has become an enclitic in Modern Russian. It is attached to conjunctions, and suffers abbreviation: чтóбы/чтоб 'in order that'.

The little word бы plays a very important part in the structure of Modern Russian. Its principal use being to form conditional clauses, it should be noted that in Russian, as almost universally in Slavonic, the conditional is used in the protasis as well as the apodosis: А что бы вы сдѣлали, ѐсли *бы* выиграли? 'And what would you do if you *won*?' [On the other hand, the use of the 'conditional' in reported speech does not occur; in Russian, as in all the Slavonic languages except Bulgarian, the tense of the reported statement is that of the statement as made, so that 'He said: "I am ill"' (English: 'He said he *was* ill') becomes 'He said he *is* ill', and 'He said: "I shall come" ' (English: 'He said he *would* come') appears as "He said he *will* come'].

Ѐсли бы may be followed by the infinitive instead of the *l*-participle: Ѐсли бы закрыть окнó, бы́ло бы ду́шно 'if one were to shut the window it would be stuffy', ѐсли бы знать! 'If only we knew!' In ѐсли бы не солдáты 'if it hadn't been for the soldiers' even the infinitive is omitted, and бы appears to perform the function of a finite verb (cf. 'but for the soldiers'); so to in лишь бы порядочный человек 'provided only he were a decent fellow', только бы скорее! 'if only we could do it without delay!', надо бы дать '(we) ought to give', ему бы жениться на ней 'he ought to marry the girl', можно бы устроить, если захотеть 'it could be arranged if one wished' and so on. (For this use of the infinitive with если see also section 106). In добро бы охотились, а то ведь ... 'it wouldn't be so bad if you really hunted, but as it is ...' бы seems to stand not only for the conditional verb but also for the conditional conjunction (было бы ... если бы).

The construction with the *l*-participle often expresses 'ought': шёл бы домой 'you ought to go home'. With pronouns and adverbs, together with the particle ни 'nor', it expresses 'who*ever*', '*no matter when*' and so on: что бы там ни говорили 'whatever they may say' (там 'there' apparently reinforcing the meaning), во что бы то ни стало 'cost what it may'. Finally, it often occurs where other languages (e.g. French) would use the subjunctive: не было ни одного, который находился бы под судом 'there wasn't a single one on trial', я хочу, чтобы ты пришёл 'I want you to come'. Чтобы with the *l*-participle often corresponds to the French *pour que* with the subjunctive (and чтобы with the infinitive to *pour* with the infinitive); it also expresses the optative: чтоб ей пусто было! 'damn her eyes!' (lit. 'may it be empty to her!')

(iv) *Future Simple.* The present tense of a perfective verb is a future, since no event can be actually occurring and completed; the completion, its perfective aspect, lies in the future. With imperfective verbs Common Slavonic allowed a considerable range of auxiliaries, expressing *willing, necessity, motion, beginning*, etc. In Modern Standard Russian all these have been reduced to буду (perfective of 'to be', and, more colloquially, стану)+the imperfective or, if there is one, the frequentative infinitive. In the dialects of Vologda, Kostroma and and Jaroslavĺ one finds иму, as in иму делать 'I shall do (have to do)', which becomes a flexion in Ruthenian: питатиму 'I shall ask'. *Hòću* 'I will' has given the future flexion in Serbocroat; this auxiliary is not represented in Russian vernacular, documents or dialects, but is attested in Nestor's Chronicle. Начьну 'I shall begin' is attested as an auxiliary in the thirteenth century.

The perfective future sometimes expressed possibly: тебя не поймёшь 'one cannot understand thee' ('you're not to be understood'). It may also express a frequentative present: уж как разбежится, так никак её не остановишь 'once (the horse) starts galloping there's no way of stopping it'.

(v) *Future Perfect.* The tense denotes a future condition anterior to a future consequence. It is expressed in Old Russian by буду + part. -*lŭ*:

аще кде буду изгрубилъ 'if anywhere I shall have offended' 1307, кто будетъ началъ тому платити = *qui cœperit is pendet* 'he that begins must pay'. In Modern Russian there only remains the obsolescent бу́де 'if, provided that'.

(*d*) *Reflexive-Passive.* R. -ся/-сь (enclitic). The particle is now attached to the verb in all cases. Its older freedom is attested as late as the sixteenth century: все то ся пригожаетъ 'all of that is fitting'. The so-called reflexive verbs occur in Russian with all the meanings (many of them not truly reflexive) found in other languages: reciprocal, passive and so on. A curious Russian usage occurs e.g. in ему́ не чита́ется 'he doesn't feel like reading'. In some cases the true reflexive uses, or may use, the full form of the pronoun ((себя́)); e.g. он застрели́лся / застрели́л себя́ 'he shot himself'. On the other hand there is a difference of meaning between он лиши́лся жи́зни 'he lost his life' and он лиши́л себя́ жи́зни 'he took his life'; and 'to feel (ill, etc.)' is only чу́вствовать себя́ (больны́м, etc.) The reflexive suffix -ся is normally pronounced -ca, even when stressed.

(*e*) *Gerund.* The loss of the cases of the indefinite participles is associated with the elimination of all but nominative forms of the indefinite declension of adjectives. The definite declension of participles suffered the same change of sense as the definite adjectives, namely, the suffixes ceased to mark the definite article, but only the attributive function. By this process the definite participles have come to be mere adjectives and are virtually unrelated to the verbal conjugation. The indefinite participles, reduced to single surviving forms, have no longer the adjectival value they possessed in Common Slavonic, but are gerunds. Their loss of case-endings has also unfitted them to give the dative absolute construction or to form clauses subordinate to a principal verb.

100. *Classes of Verbs.* The distinction between perfective, imperfective and iterative verbs has been discussed on the basis of Russian examples in section 49 and need not be repeated here. The classes of conjugations are detailed in section 48 on the basis of Old Bulgarian. The infinitive is the determining criterion of class, and the present indicative of sub-class. In the present section the verbs are given their modern forms, which represent the end of the evolutionary process. The mediæval forms will be discussed in following paragraphs.

A. Athematic. See section 101. This class, which has been very greatly reduced in Russian, is represented by есть 'is' суть 'are' дам 'shall give' ем 'eat' весть 'knows' ведь 'for'.

B. Thematic. (i) *Root-infinitives.* (1) *k g:* The infinitive endings **-kti *-gti* give R. -*č'* (sections 93 and 39). In the present indicative 23*S.* 12*P.* show the first palatalization (*k/č g/ž*). In the past tense (participle in -*l*), the -*l* is dropped in the masculine after *k g*. Hence мочь 'be able' 1*S.* могу́ 2*S.* мо́жешь past мог/могла́, течь 'flow' 1*S.* теку́ 2*S.* течёшь [despite the soft *jer*, *š* is hard and so changed *e* to *ë* whenever the final syllable is accented; see section 86(*E*)] past. тёк/текла́. Verbs of this class in *g* are: бере́чь 'take care of' стере́чь 'guard' жечь 'burn' стричь 'shear' лечь 'lie down', and in *k*: влечь 'draw' печь 'bake' толо́чь 'pound' воло́чь 'drag' сечь 'cut, flog'. Толо́чь (<**tolkti*) shows reduced vocalism in 1*S.* толку́ (<**tŭlko̜*); воло́чь here has first full-vocalism: 1*S.* волоку́, together with a remodelled present (iv) волочу́. Жечь has 1*S.* жгу 2*S.* жжёшь, passive participle жжённый, past жёг жегла́, past part. жёгший. Лечь has 1*S.* ля́гу (from *leg-*, with infixed *n*), past лёг.

(2) *t d:* Infin. **-tti* **-dti* become *-sti/sť*. In the present tense the vowel alternation affects the quality of the dental *t d/ť d́*, but does not change its timbre as in Polish (*ć dź*). In the past in *-l* the combinations **tl* **dl* simplify to *l*. Hence: мести́/месть 'sweep' 1*S.* мету́, past, мёл мела́; вести́/вѣсть 'lead' 1*S.* веду́ past вёл. In *t* are: плести́ 'plait' гнести́ 'press' (про)че́сть 'read through' 1*S.* -чту́ цвести́ 'blossom' (приоб)рести́ 'acquire', and in *d:* класть 'put' красть 'steal' пасть 'fall' брести́ 'wander' блюсти́ 'guard' прясть 'spin' сесть 'sit down'. (perfective, 1 p.sg. ся́ду from *sed-* with infixed *n*). Расти́ 'grow' has *st* in the stem and so represents **-stti*, 1*S.* расту́. Иду́ 'go, walk' has a suffixed *d*, since the original root was the athematic **ei/i-*. Its infinitive идти́/итти́ is an orthographic device for apparently forming the infinitive on the present; it represents the athematic **eiti* >OB. *iti*. The past шёл, part. ше́дший, is from *šĭd-/chod-*. Е́ду 'ride, drive' has an infinitive from another root: е́хать. Бу́ду 'shall be' is a defective verb; its infinitive быть belongs to class B(i) 7.

(3) *p b v: bt* (and also *pt*) took an intrusive *s* in Russian from the last group, giving **bst*, which simplified to *st:* грести́/гресть 'row' 1*S.* гребу́ past грёб гребла́, скрести́ 'scrape'; *vt* simplified to *t:* жить 'live' (unless the infinitive comes from another form of the root, viz. **gʷī-*) 1*S.* живу́ past жил part. жи́вший. Forms involving -шиб- (e.g. ошибся 'was mistaken') have infinitive in -ить (ошиби́ться).

(4) *s z:* нести́/несть 'bear' 1*S.* несу́ past. нёс, везти́/везть 'convey' 1*S.* везу́ past. вёз. So also in *s:* пасти́/пасть 'feed, pasture' трясти́ 'shake', and in *z:* ползти́ 'crawl' грызть 'gnaw' лезть 'clamber'.

(5) *m n:* The nasal consonants were preserved before vowels, but became nasal vowels (later denasalized) before the consonants of the aorist-infinitive system. Hence: мять 'crush' 1*S.* мну, жать 'squeeze' 1*S.* жму. In *m* are: (при-н)я́ть 'receive' 1*S.* приму́, снять 'take off, photograph', обня́ть 'embrace', and in *n:* жать 'reap', (рас)пя́ть 'crucify', (на)ча́ть 'begin'. клясть 'curse' has 1*S.* кляну́.

(6) *l r:* The infinitive shows full-vocalism, and the present may have a suffix *-j-:* мере́ть 'die' 1*S.* мру past. мёр, and also пере́ть 'push'

тере́ть· 'rub' (про)стере́ть 'extend'/поро́ть 'rip, whip' 1S. порю́, боро́ться 'struggle' поло́ть 'rake' коло́ть 'split' моло́ть (<*melti) 'grind' 1S. мелю́.

(7) *Vowel-stems:* These have been all more or less altered in Russian, as OB. *ŕuti* 'roar' *revǫ* R. реву́/реве́ть. In the present tense a semivowel is developed, which is normally -*j*- but occasionally -*v*-. Examples are: знать 'know' 1S. зна́ю, пить 'drink' 1S. пью (and so бить 'hit' вить 'wind' лить 'pour' шить 'sew'), гнить 'rot' 1S. гнию́, выть 'howl' 1S. во́ю (*ŭj*- >R. *oj*); so too мыть 'wash' ныть 'ache', рыть 'dig', крыть 'cover' and also петь (<*poiti) 'sing' 1S. пою́). OB. *pluti* 'swim' 1S. *plovǫ, sluti* 'be called' 1S. *slovǫ*, have elsewhere infinitives *plyti slyti;* from these forms Russian has refashioned its presents; плыть плыву́, слыть слыву́. The thematic derivatives of the athematics **sthā*- 'stand' **dō*- 'give' **dhē*- 'put' are not easy to classify. Стать 'stand still' has 1S. ста́ну with the *n*-suffix (ii), and деть 'put' has 1S. де́ну; the infinitives might be regarded as belonging to the present group. Даю́ 'give' might be at home here or in (v 4); it has an imperfective infin. дава́ть. Быть 'be', past. был, is a defective verb of this class.

The above list of verbs includes all the principal 'irregular' verbs in Russian. The term 'irregular' is a misnomer, since these verbs obey linguistic laws as strictly as any others. But they are short and they are in frequent use. The latter condition helps to maintain dissimilar forms, which have been learned separately in childhood and have not been questioned; less frequent words are liable to normalization. In these words old phonetic laws have operated without reaction.

(ii) *n*. (1) Roots ending in a vowel before the suffixed -*n*-: мину́ть 'pass'. (2) Roots ending, or originally ending, in a consonant before suffixed -*n*-: ки́нуть (<*kyd-) 'throw' дви́нуть 'move' (OB. *dvignǫti*) ти́хнуть 'grow quiet' шепну́ть 'whisper', etc. With the loss of the aorist the suffix was carried through the conjugation. For ста́ну де́ну cf. (i 1). R. осле́пнуть/OB. *oslipnǫti* 'become blind' is due to the analogy of слеп 'blind'. These verbs denote the end of a process or momentary acts, and so are perfectives. They frequently form pairs with those of other classes, especially in -*at*: perf. ки́нуть/imperf. кида́ть 'throw'. A secondary suffix -ану́ть is very active in the modern colloquial language.

(iii) *ě*. (1) Infin. -*et*/*jat*, pres. -*ej*-: уме́ть 'know how to' 1S. уме́ю 2S. уме́ешь, име́ть 'have' сме́ть 'dare' спеть 'ripen' греть 'warm' зре́ть 'ripen'/ве́ять 'waft' 1S. ве́ю 2S. ве́ешь, се́ять 'sow'. (2) Infin. -*et*/*at*, pres. -*i*-: ви́деть 'see' 1S. ви́жу (**dj* >**dž* >R. *ž*, see section 93) 2S. ви́дишь, сиде́ть (CSl.OB. *sěděti*) 'sit' гляде́ть 'look'/лежа́ть 'lie' 1S. лежу́ 2S. лежи́шь, бежа́ть 'run' 2S. бежи́шь (1S. бегу́ 3P. бегу́т are forms of root *běg*- without suffix), держа́ть 'hold'. Хоте́ть 'wish' has 1*S*. хочý (**tj* > R. *č*), which is continued by analogy in 2*S*. хóчешь; 3*S*. хóчет; but the plural shows *t* and suffix *i*: хот- и́м -и́те (-я́т).

(iv) *i*. Люби́ть 'love' 1*S*. люблю́ (**bj* > *bl*, see section 94) 2*S*. лю́бишь, вопи́ть 'wail' 1*S*. воплю́ (**pj* > *pl*) 2*S*. вопи́шь (also вопия́ть 1*S*. вопию́ 2*S*. вопие́шь), лови́ть 'catch' 1*S*. ловлю́ 2*S*. лóвишь, ходи́ть 'go, walk' 1*S*. хожý (**dj*) 2*S*. хóдишь (so also ла́дить 'fit' гла́дить 'stroke' води́ть 'lead' годи́ться 'be of use' горди́ться 'be proud'), вози́ть 'convey' 1*S*. вожý (**zj*, see section 95; so also ла́зить 'clamber.'), плати́ть 'pay' 1*S*. плачý (**tj*) 2*S*. пла́тишь, носи́ть 'carry' 1*S*. ношý (**sj*) 2*S*. нóсишь, пусти́ть 'allow' 1*S*. пущý (**stj*) 2*S*. пу́стишь. The present tense of гнать 'to drive' (OB. *ženo̧*) is гоню́, гóнишь . . .

(v) *a*. (1) Infin. -*at́*, pres. -*aj*-: де́лать 'do' 1*S*. де́лаю 2*S*. де́лаешь. This is an active class of verb formations, embracing a large number of words. There has been no contraction of these verbs in standard Russian. The verb мýчить 'to torture' has an alternative present tense мýчаю etc. (2) Infin. -*at́*, pres. -*j*-: писа́ть 'write' 1*S*. пишý (**sj*) 2*S*. пи́шешь. This also is a very large class. The consonant is softened by the suffix -*j*-, resulting in the alternations: *s/š ch/š sk/šč t/č l/l̓*. A few verbs in -*evat́* belong to this group: блева́ть 'vomit' 1*S*. блюю́ 2*S*. блюёшь (OB. *blujo̧* < **bhlēw-j-/blǐvati* < **bhluw-* with analogical softening of *l*. (3) Infin. -*at́* (generally with *zero*-grade of root), pres. *e*- *o*- or *zero*-root: брать 'take' 1*S*. берý, звать 'call' 1*S*. зовý, жрать 'devour' 1*S*. жру, лгать 'tell lies' 1*S*. лгу 2*S*. лжёшь. (4) Infin. -*j-at́*, pres. -*j*-: ла́ять 'bark' 1*S*. ла́ю.

(vi) *va*. Infin. -*ovat́*, pres. -*uj*-: торгова́ть 'trade' 1*S*. торгýю 2*S*. торгýешь. A very active verbal suffix, with an analogical soft variant in -*evat́*: ночева́ть 'pass the night'.

101. *Athematic Verbs*. **Es-/s-*. The present tense is as follows:

		*S*1	2	3	*P*1	2	3	*D*1	23
OR.	1ес-	-мь/ми	-и	-ть	-м-ъ/ы/о/е	-те	су(ть)	-вѣ/ва	-та
				1е					
MR.				есть			(суть)		
Ruth.			еси́	есть					
		е	е	е	є		є	є	

MR. суть is obsolescent, and есть is found only under special conditions (sometimes for all persons). *S*2. еси́ *P*2. есте́ are found in the North Great Russian dialect of the folk-ballads (*byliny*). Normally the verb is omitted, though the speaker may make a pause: это — мой сын 'this is my son'. There is a growing tendency to express the copula by means of the present tense of the verb явля́ться 'to appear' followed by the instrumental. The principal use of есть is to express 'to have': у меня́ (есть), 'there is beside me' = 'I have', есть ли у вас 'have you?' Negative: нет/нету. The shortened form of the third person singular may be used in Ruthenian with any personal pronoun. Participial adjective: су́щий 'extant, real'.

The rest of the paradigm is from other roots, which were thematic. Infin. быть,/Ruth. бу́ти (the y is due to analogy), past. был Ruth. був (*v* < *l*) бу́ла; past part. бы́вший/Ruth. бу́вший; future R. Ruth. бу́ду, imper. будь бу́дьте (Ruth. also *P*1. бу́дьмо), gerund. бу́дучи. It will be noted that the two stems have been assimilated in Ruthenian. The aorist (быхъ) existed in Old Russian, and has been specialized as a conditional particle in the form of the third person singular (бы/б). The imperfect form was бяхъ (*S*3. бяше/бяшеть).

The 3 p.sg. of the future tense is used idiomatically in the sense of 'that is enough': будет вам вздор моло́ть (lit. 'it will be to you to grind nonsense') 'that's enough nonsense out of you'. For a special use of the neuter singular of the past tense of this verb and its iterative быва́ть see section 107. For the part this verb plays in the formation of the imperative see section 104.

102. *Ēd-, *dōd-, *woid-. The Russian present tenses corresponding are:

Indicative

		*S*1	2	3	*P*1	2	3	*D*1	23
OR.	да-/дад-	-мь	-си	-стъ	-м-ъ/ы/о/е	-сте	-я(ть)/-у(ть)	-вѣ/ва	-ста
MR.	е-/да-/ед/дад-	м	-шь	-ст	-йм	-йте	едя́т/дадут		
				весть					
Ruth.	ї-/да-	-м	-ш/сй	-сть	-мо́	-сьте́	їдя́ть/дадуть		
	оповї-	-м	-ш	-сть	мо́	сьте́	-дя́ть		

Imperative

		*S*1	2	3	*P*1	2	3	*D*1	23
OR.	да-/дад-		-жь	-жь	-имъ, etc.	-ите		-ивѣ/ива	-ита
MR.	да-		ешь/й			ешьте/-йте			
Ruth.	їд-/оповїд-/да-		-ж/-й		-жмо/-ймо	-жте/-йте			

From the stem *woid- there remains in Russian only the fixed phrase Бог весть 'God knows' and the particle ведь 'for', but there is a full conjugation of a derivative verb оповісти 'tell' (perfective) in Ruthenian. S2. -š is from the thematic conjugation in Modern Russian and Ruthenian, and the plurals of the present indicative are thematic in Russian, while the imperative дай corresponds to the present даю (infin. давáть, imperative давáй). Dissimilation of dt >st gives the st of the third person singular and second person plural; similarly WR. S3. есць дасць (ć <ť). In the imperative *ědĭ according to Russian principles *ď becomes ž, which is unvoiced to š in final position: S2. ешь, similarly P2. éшьте. In Ruthenian the d of the stem had been restored by analogy of the third person plural of the present indicative, and this has preserved the ž. Ruth. S2. їдж. The plural forms are fashioned upon the singular.

The expression (в)ишь 'look' is now an exclamation. It may represent an original imperative of the otherwise thematic verb вúдеть 'see': OB. viděti imper. viždĭ (<*vid-jĭ) OR. viži.

For the use of дать and its imperfective давáть in the formation of the imperative see section 104.

103. *Thematic Present Indicative.* This tense runs:

			S_1	2	3	P_1	2	3	D_1	23
OR.	вед-	'lead'	-у	-ешь	е(ть)	-ем-ъ/ы/о/е	-ете	-у(ть)	-ев-ѣ/а	-ета
MR.	тян-	'pull'	-ý	-ешь	-ет	-ем	-ете	-ут		
	дѣла-	'do'	-ю					-ют		
(iv)	говор-	'say'	-ю	-йшь	-йт	-йм	йте	-ят		
(iii 2)	слыш-	'hear'	-у					-ат		
Ruth.	пас-	'pasture'	-ý	-ёш	-ё	-ёмо	-ётé	-ýть		
	дарý-	'present'	-ю	-еш	-е	-емо	-ете	-ють		
(iv)	хвал-	'praise'	-ю	-йш	-йть	-имó	-итé	-йть		
(iii 2)	бол-	'feel sore'								

The second series of endings is found in verbs of classes (iv) -iť, pres. -i-, and (iii 2) -eť Ruth. -iti, pres. -i-. All other verbs follow the first pattern. When the stress falls on the ending, R. -e- becomes -ё-: берý 'take' S2. берёшь. Conjugations are sometimes confused in ákańe dialects, since the relaxation of unstressed vowels tends to make them neutral: ljúbjut 'they love' smótrjut 'they look'/любят смотрят. The pronunciation ю is now recommended for the standard language. The change of conjugation (from v 2 to iv) in S2. хóч-ешь 'wishes' 3. -ет/ P1. хот-úм 2. -úте 3. -ят is of long standing in Slavonic. Between S1. бег-ý P3. -ут and the other persons (S2. бежúшь etc., infin. бежáть iii 2) there is a difference of stem: *běg-/běgj-. Орý/орю 'plough' are doublets (cf. Lat. aro/Lith. ariù).

The number of conjugations admitted for Russian may be extended considerably if we take into account the modification of stems. The principal changes have been noted in section 100, and need here only be summarized. The vowels of the personal endings were of *o*-grade in *S1.P3.*, but of *e*-grade elsewhere. When the stem ends in *k/g* this causes the first Slavonic palatalization to take effect. In other than velar root-verbs there is often an element *j* in the suffix which affects the preceding consonant: **sj *zj *tj *dj *bj *pj *stj *skj* then become *š ž č ž bl᾽ pl᾽ šč šč* in *S1*. ношу́/но́сишь 'carry', плачу́ 'pay'/пла́тишь, пущу́ 'allow'//пу́стишь, хожу́ 'go, walk'/хо́дишь, etc. 3*P*. -ят, which results from a specifically Russian development of *-ętŭ*, does not have this effect: но́сят. In some verbs *t* and *d* present their Old Bulgarian mutations: обрати́ть 'turn'/1*S*. обращу́, etc. *S1.-ǫ* had a rising intonation which attracted a preceding stress when the penultimate syllable was falling or short. Thanks to this rule (Fortunatov-de Saussure) the stress shifts in the present tense of many Russian verbs. (See section 103A.)

S1. -u/-ju and *P3. -ut/jut -at/jat* have been denasalized. *S2. -š'* probably continues a Common Slavonic form of this person (**-sĭ* Gk. -σι Skr. -*si*) as distinct from OB. -*ši*. The sibilant has hardened in Russian, and did so early enough to allow the passage of *é >ë:* идёшь 'goest', unless this is to be explained on the analogy of the other persons. In the more phonetic Ruthenian spelling the soft *jer* is omitted. *SP3. -t* has hardened in Russian and White Russian, but remains soft in Ruthenian. The hardening process comes after the year 1350 (see section 96). An alternative form of *-et* was *-e* in Old Russian, which is now the norm in Ruthenian and White Russian; but Ruth. *-it* persists. The only trace of this in Great Russian is in the survival of OR. *je* 'is' in не́ту 'there is not' не́когда 'there is no time' (**ne je tu*, **ne je kogda*) and similar words, and бу́де 'if, provided that' (obsolescent), де (enclitic expressing reported speech ⟨**děje* 'says'). In Old Russian manuscripts these forms are frequently encountered in Galicia-Volhynia, though probably not then dialectal marks: су 'are' иму 'have' 1164, купи 'will buy' (13th–14th cent.). By way of compensation the present *-t* is found intrusively in Old Russian aorists: бя́шеть 'was'. *P1.MR. -m/*WR.Ruth. *-mo* shows divergent preferences from among the alternatives current in Old Russian texts. *P2. -te* attracts the accent in White and North Russian dialects, and is then liable to change timbre: WR. дасце́ 'ye give' есце́ 'ye are'/дасцо́ есцо́.

There is an obsequious use of the *P3.* with a singular subject: господи́н мирово́й судья́, е́жели пожела́ют, мо́гут . . . 'the justice of the peace, if he chooses, may . . .'

The tendency to keep a stem stable leads in dialects to *mogú mógeš'*, *možú móžeš'*/могу́ мо́жешь, and other deformations of a like character; cf. colloquial Cz. *můžu můžeš*.

Imperfective presents are presents; perfective presents are futures. In Old Russian, however, there were a few ambiguous words: бегу 'am running/shall run', рожу 'bear (a child)', молвлю 'speak', крещу 'christen'; cf. MR. жёнится 'he is getting/will get married' (perfective-imperfective verb) and a few others.

Concerning the decline of the dual number see section 99 (*a*). *D*1. *-va* : : два 'two' is used interchangeably with the original *-vě*. Russian has not gone so far as Slovene, which has imported a distinction of gender into this person on the analogy of *M. dva NF. dvě*. *D*23. *-ta;* Russian did not distinguish 2. *-ta*/3. *-te* within historic times.

The 2 p.sg. is used in Russian where English has *you* or *one*, French *on*, German *man*.

103A. *Accent.* The present tense of all Russian thematic verbs is stressed uniformly on the same syllable throughout save in the case of those verbs which move the stress to the ending of the 1 p.sg. as a result of the Fortunatov-de Saussure law or the workings of analogy. Accepting for practical purposes the stress of the infinitive as a standard, what happens is that in *some* verbs stressed on the ending the stress moves back one syllable in all persons save for the first person singular, thus: (вести́ 'lead' веду́ ведёшь . . ./) тяну́ть 'draw' тяну́/ тя́нешь . . . ; писа́ть 'write' пишу́/пи́шешь . . . ; (говори́ть 'speak' говорю́ говори́шь . . . /) кури́ть 'smoke' курю́/ку́ришь . . . There is no shift in the present tense of verbs not stressed on the last syllable of the infinitive: осве́домить 'to inform' осве́домлю etc.

It should be noted that in some cases difference of accent is the sole indication of difference of aspect: узнаю́ 'I recognize' (inf. узнава́ть)/ узна́ю 'I shall recognize' (inf. узна́ть); cf. среза́ть 'to cut off' (imp.)/ сре́зать (perf.)

Perfective verbs with the prefix вы- stress this prefix in all forms; the cause lies no doubt in the original long vowel.

104. *Imperative.* The thematic imperative runs:

			*S*2	3	*P*1			2	*D*1	2
OR.	вед-	'lead'	и	и	$\left\{\begin{array}{l}\text{ѣ-}\\\text{и-}\end{array}\right\}$	мъ/мы/мо/ме		те	вѣ/ва	та
	хвал-	'praise'								
MR.	вед-	'lead'	й					йте		
	крикн-	'shout'	и					ите		
	бу́д-	'be'	ь					ьте		
	де́ла-	'do'	й					йте		
	ляг-	'lie down'	–					те		
Ruth.	пита́-	'ask'	й		ймо			йте		
	пас-	'pasture'	й		і́м			і́ть		
	уч-	'teach'	й		і́м			і́ть		
	гля́д-	'smooth'	ь		ьмо			ьте		
	мов-	'speak'	–		мо			те		

The formation of the Slavonic imperative from the Indo-European optative has been discussed in section 54, and the athematic imperative (MR. ешь ёшьте) in section 102. OR. дажь 'give' survives in North Russia in *daž' Bog* 'God grant', but it was misunderstood as early as the fourteenth century, when it was analysed as *daj+že*: хлѣбъ нашь даи же намъ днесь 'give us this day our daily bread'. The athematic endings combined with the tendency to shorten final vowels in such a way as to spread the endings -ь -ьте (after cons.)/-й -йте (after vowels) to all verbs in which the accent falls on the stem, save when the consonant-group would be too difficult (as in крикни). Вы́веди 'lead out' is due to the analogy of веди́ and other forms.) Examples go back to the thirteenth century: бу́дте 'be ye' наполньте/MR. напо́лните 'fill'. Ляг 'lie down' is exceptional in Russian in the hardness of the consonant, but this type is frequent in Ruthenian: вір 'believe' мов 'speak'.

The imperative is regularly stressed like the infinitive; i.e. писа́ть ∴ пиши́, кри́кнуть ∴ кри́кни.

The imperatives were originally of two types: CSl. *-i-ěte/-i-ite*. The tendency to reduce these to the single type *-i-ite* was strong in the oldest documents, such as Ostromir's Codex (1056–57) and the Menologies of 1095 and 1097. This type alone has survived in Modern Russian, and that only when stressed or after difficult consonant-groups. In Ruthenian only the type *-i-ěte* has survived under stress (in the form -и -іть), with an arbitrary reduction of final *e* to *jer*. This *e* remains in the type пита́-й -йте.

The introduction of palatal *k' ǵ ch'* in Russian has permitted the restoration of a stop in the imperative: OR. помози 'help' пьци 'bake' /MR. помоги́ пеки́. The older forms persisted into the fourteenth century. WR. поможи́ Ruth. печи́ are also analogical forms; instead of the second palatalization proper to the imperative they show the first palatalization proper to the present indicative (2*S.*).

There are various ways of expressing 1*P.* and 3*SP:* пусть (and colloquially пуска́й) войдёт/войду́т 'let him/them come in', да здра́вствует 'long live' (lit. 'that it be healthy', ChSl.), войдём 'let us go in' (indic.), or with -те borrowed from 2*P.* войдёмте, дава́й(те) + indic. 'let us' (lit. 'give'). The negative 1 *P.* uses бу́дем: не бу́дем(те) есть друг дру́га 'don't let's devour one another'.

The particles *-ko -ka* are used to strengthen imperatives of the second person in colloquial usage: по(й)ди́-ка 'come on.'

The imperative of пожа́ловать 'to grant' (пожа́луй) is used for 'I dare say, I don't mind'. The past tense of the verb пойти́ 'to go' is used as a peremptory imperative: пошёл прочь! 'clear off!'

Unique in Slavonic is the Russian use of the imperative in the sense of the conditional: не будь я так осторо́жен, я бы . . . 'had I not been so

careful I should have . . .', выиграй я сто тысяч 'if I were to win
100,000', and with the sense of a perfective past: он пойди и скажи
'he went and said'. It has been suggested that the latter use is a
reflexion of the vanished aorist. As is clear from these examples, the
2 p.sg. of the imperative is not restricted in use to this person; it may
in fact be used with all persons, even the 2 p.pl. with a plural reference:
вставай, ребята! 'get up, lads!' This is another example of the way
in which a diminution of forms has in Russian been compensated by a
growth in function. The Russian imperative, which, as we have seen,
derives from the optative, has inherited, or developed, the functions of
this mood; examples are: провались я сквозь землю 'may I sink
through the earth', будь я подлец, если я . . . 'may I be a scoundrel
if I . . .', дай бог память! 'may God give me memory!' The imperative
may express 'let': дай я попробую 'let me have a go', но скажи я хоть
одно слово 'let me say so much as one word' ('if I so much as say . . .').
With как ни it expresses 'however (much, etc.)': как ни храбрись
'however much you may steel yourself', как там ни философствуй
'however much one may philosophize . . .'

The imperative давай ('give')+the imperfective infinitive is used in
a way corresponding to the English 'start to': сели вместе за стол и
давай пить 'they sat down together at the table and started drinking'.

105. *Present Participles and Gerunds*. In section 55 it has been shown
that the pres. part. IE. *-onts* >*-ons* and the past participle IE. *-wōs*
both gave CSl. *-y*, but the soft pres. part. *-jonts* >*-jons* >-(*j*)ę was
free from this confusion (type: *znaję* R. зная 'knowing'). This led to
the extension of the soft form at the expense of the hard by means of
the alternation -*ja/a*: OR.NMN. веда *F.* ведучи/OB. *vedy vedǫšti*
'leading'. This participle continued to be declined in Old Russian
(GMN. ведуч-а *F.* -ѣ). As the definite declension became attributive,
i.e. the form normally associated with a noun, the oblique cases of the
indefinite declension lost their usefulness, and the participle was
reduced to two fixed forms based on the masc.-neut. and fem.
respectively: неся 'carrying' (forms in -*a* have died out) стоя 'standing'
плача (-*a* for -*ja* after a palatal) 'weeping'/будучи 'being' знаючи
'knowing'. The form in -чи is found in colloquial speech [e.g.
припеваючи '(live) in clover'] and in folk-poetry; it is also the only
form in the case of будучи 'being'. A second distinguishing feature of
the gerund is its timelessness, and that is recorded in Russian from
the thirteenth century: иде князь поимя съ собою мужи новгородьскы
'the prince went, taking (having taken) with him men of Novgorod'.
So in Kotošichin (17th cent.): поидучи въ городъ 'having gone into
the city'. In Modern Russian the gerund of a perfective verb expresses
the perfect: войдя 'having entered'. Some gerunds are used adverbially,
e.g. молча 'silently'. The Ruthenian gerund is in -чи.

The definite participle has a uniform stem, and has become entirely adjectival in function. The same is largely true of the present passive participle in *-m-:* любимый 'favourite' ведомый 'known'. In Standard Russian the form of the active participle is in -ущий -ящий/ащий, of which the consonants represent OB. *št* <*tj*, except for a few words which have become pure adjectives and retain the Russian -ч: висячий 'hanging, pendant' горячий 'hot'.

Хотя 'although' is a gerund (from хотеть 'wish') which has become a conjunction; ведомо 'indeed, notoriously' is the neuter of an indefinite pres. part. passive, now classified as an adverb. Its genitive survives in без моего ведома 'without my knowledge'.

106. *Infinitive and Supine.* OR. infin. вести весть, sup. весть. The supine in *-tŭ* persisted in Russian manuscripts down to the fourteenth century: идеть искатъ кунъ (*GPF.*) 'he goes a-hunting martens' 1282, поидеть торговатъ 'he'll go a-trading'. The supine governs the genitive. The infinitive is found instead of the supine as early as the Ostromir Codex (1056–57): идж положити место 'I go to prepare a place'. In some North Great Russian dialects there are infinitives in *-t* which are more likely due to hardening of *-t́* than to survival of the supine.

As regards the infinitive, *-ti* is found in Great Russian folk-songs, White Russian and Ruthenian. It was predominant in all Old Russian documents, but *-t́* is found more frequently as the centuries advance. In Modern Russian *-ti* is only preserved under stress, and is then usually accompanied by an alternative form in *-t́*. Root-infinitives in **-kti *-gti* end in *-č'* (class B i 1): печь 'bake'.

Though the infinitive is a younger form than the aorist, the loss of that tense has caused the basic secondary stem of Russian verbs to be considered that of the infinitive, so that it is upon the infinitive that past participles and verbal nouns are built.

The infinitive may be used as a peremptory imperative: молчать! 'shut up!' It appears to replace a finite verb in such a sentence as не выписывать же сюда для твоей подагры целый медицинский факультет 'we can't go and send for the whole faculty of medicine to deal with your gout'; understood is, no doubt, the copula and a dative pronoun ('it is not for us to . . .'). The latter (Dative and Infinitive) construction, with attraction of case, led to the now obsolescent Predicative Dative, of which the following is an example from the былины:

По правой ехать—богатому быть,
По левой ехать—женатому быть,
А прямо-то ехать—убитому быть.

('Take the road to the right and be rich; take the road to the left and be wed; take the road straight ahead and you're dead.') These lines also exemplify, with omission of 'if', the use of the infinitive in place of a conditional clause: (если) éхать 'if you travel, if one were to travel'. For the use of the infinitive with бы see section 99 c iii. Cf. не зайти ли? 'what about dropping in?'

107. *The Past Tense.* By the elimination of the imperfect and aorist and the loss of the auxiliary the original past part. active in -*lŭ* has become a veritable past tense, which shows not the person but the gender of the subject: *SM. -l N. -lo F. -la PMNF. -li.* Root-verbs in *d t* lose these before *l;* those in *k g b s z r* eliminate the -*l* of the masculine: *M.* мог 'could' *F.* могла. In White Russian *l* closing a syllable vocalized to -*ŭ*, and this vowel is written -*v* in Ruthenian (section 93). With бы this tense expresses a condition. The particle may follow the verb or a pronoun or a conjunction: хотéл бы/я бы хотéл 'I should like', чтóб(ы) 'in order that', хотя бы 'even if', хоть бы 'not even'. The pluperfect was represented by past part. -*l+bylŭ*, but is so no longer. It is now rendered by the simple past, if necessary with the help of adverbs like ужé 'already'.

The paucity of formal past tenses is compensated for not only by means of the aspects but also by a number of interesting developments. One of these is the use of the perfective present (=future) following a (usually drawled) как ('how'), which provides the equivalent of a vivid past tense eminently suitable for dramatic narrative: да ка-ак выскочит опять . . . 'and jumped out again'. The same effect is produced with the imperative, with or without как: да вдруг нелёгкая её дёрни сходить в баню 'and suddenly the Devil induced her to go to the bath-house', вдруг она как наклонись 'suddenly she bent down'. Another is the use of бывáло (from the iterative бывáть 'to be') with the present, past or future to express a frequentative action in the remote past: читáю, бывáло 'I used to read', он говорил, бывáло 'he would say', так, бывáло, и закричý 'and so I would start yelling', бывáло, когдá он начнёт говорить 'when he used to start talking'. The past tense with было expresses, to quote Vinogradov, 'an interruption in the accomplishment of an action'; e.g. я хотéл было остáться дóма, но не вытерпел 'I intended to stay at home, but couldn't stick it', послы было уéхали из Москвы; их воротили 'the ambassadors had started to drive out of Moscow; they were turned back'. As may be seen, this construction may approximate to a pluperfect.

107A. *Accent.* There is shift of stress in the past tense of a great many verbs with monosyllabic infinitives (and infinitives in -ти and -чь) and their compounds; all other verbs stress past tense and infinitive uniformly, with the exception of родилá 'she gave birth'/родить. In the case of simple verbs the shift is of two types; either to the ending, e.g. везти 'convey' вёз/везлá везлó везли, or to the feminine ending only, e.g. дать 'give' дал дáло дáли/далá. In compounds the stress may move to the prefix in the masculine, neuter and plural, e.g. продáть 'sell'/прóдал прóдало прóдали/продалá. In some of the verbs discussed here the stress may shift to the reflexive suffix -ся, e.g. поднять 'raise'/пóднял/поднялся, and the reflexive -сь may cause a shift as compared with the unreflexive form, e.g. звáло 'called' (neut.) /звалóсь 'was called'.

108. *The Past Participle and Gerund.* The past part. active in Old Russian was *SMN.* ведъ *F.* ведъши, *MN.* бывъ *F.* бывъши, and was declined. The indefinite declension has gone out of use, and only -в, -ши, -вши have survived as past gerunds: быв/бы́вши 'having been' читáв/читáвши 'having read' нёсши 'having carried' шéдши 'having gone'.

In the older stage of the language a stem ending in a nasal vowel transformed this into a consonant before the masculine suffix: OR. начьнъ 'having begun' възьмъ 'having taken'. In some Great Russian dialects the nasal is interpolated before -*ši: vzěmši/vzjamši.* Normally however the analogy of the gerunds in -*v/vši* has eliminated these nasals: начáв взяв. In like manner dentals have been replaced by *v:* OR. ѣдъ ѣдъши 'having eaten'/MR. ев éвши. For the colloquial use of this gerund in a sort of pluperfect see section 99 *c* ii. Another colloquial use occurs e.g. in у моегó Васю́тки всегдá у́хо вспу́хши от э́того 'my Vasjutka's ear is always swollen as a result' (вспу́хнуть 'to swell up').

The definite declension of the active past participle has become definitely adjectival: умéрший 'having died, dead'. Усóпший 'deceased', lit. 'having fallen asleep', presents the *p* of the root which has disappeared from this verb in Russian: усну́ть 'fall asleep'/OB. *usŭpe* 'he fell asleep'. With imperfective verbs this form is commonly used in narration where other languages prefer present participles: кни́га, лежáвшая на столé 'a book (that was) lying on the table'.

109. *Past Passive Participle.* R. -т/(е)н: мыт 'washed' сдéлан 'done' рáнен 'wounded' [cf. section 57 (*c*) (*d*)]. The definite forms are мы́тый сдéланный, i.e. the *n*-participle adds to itself the suffix -*ĭn-*. In a few words a single *n* is encountered; their use is purely adjectival: учёный 'learned, a savant', пи́саная красáвица 'a dazzling beauty'. From the forms in -*nn*- are formed predicates in -*nen:* откровéнен 'frank'. By means of this participle the passive may be expressed: кем э́та пье́са напи́сана? 'by whom was this play written?' In the case of verbs in -*iť* (class iv) the suffix -*en* is added to the -*i*-, producing -*jen* which causes palatalization: заплати́ь 'pay' заплáчен, etc. For *t* and *d* the OB. *št žd* frequently appear: победи́ть 'conquer' побеждён.

109A. *Accent.* The stress of participles in -áнный regularly moves back one (and occasionally more than one) syllable as compared with the corresponding infinitive, if the latter is stressed on the final syllable; e.g. продáть 'sell'/прóданный, передáть 'hand over'/

переданный. The short (predicative) forms of these participles frequently stress the ending of the feminine; e.g. проданá переданá/ прóдан пéредан -о -ы. The participle of verbs in -ить may be accented -ённый (победи́ть побеждённый) or may move the stress back one syllable (потопи́ть 'sink' потóпленный), and there are cases where the stress is moved *forward* in the participle; e.g. освéдомить 'inform' осведомлённый (cf. imperfective осведомля́ть). The short form of participles in (unstressed) -енный are stressed on the same syllable as the long form; the short form of those in (stressed) -ённый moves the stress to the ending of the feminine, neuter and plural: осведомлён/ осведомлен-á -ó -ы́.

110. *Verbal Nouns.* The verbal noun is formed from the passive past participle by means of the suffix *-ije*. Frequently *-ije* is found, through the influence of Church Slavonic, which transmits the Old Bulgarian principle of lengthening *ĭ* before *j:* битьё 'whipping' делéние 'division, sharing', etc.

111. *Imperfect and Aorist.* These are found only in Old and Middle Russian:

		S_1	2	3	P_1	2	3	D_1	23
OR. вел-	impf.	-яхъ	яше	-яше	-яхом-ъ/ы/о/е	-ясте	-яху	-яхов-ѣ/а	-яста
				-яшеть		-яшете	-яхуть		-яшетъ
						-яшьте?			-яшьтъ
	aor.	-охъ	-е	-е	-охомъ, etc.	-осте	-оша	-оховѣ, etc.	-оста

The loss of the imperfect and aorist is discussed in section 99(*b*). The third person plural of the imperfect tended to take the place of the corresponding form of the aorist, since it suggested the usual correspondence of $S_1.P_3$. in the present tense, but in the dual and plural the second person endings of the aorist intruded into the imperfect. In the third person singular the final *-t* of the present was added by analogy to the imperfect ending at random, and without limitation to the circumstances in which *-tŭ* appears in this tense in Old Bulgarian. The longer forms of the imperfect (OB. *-ĕachŭ* etc.) and the older forms of the aorist (asigmatic *-ŭ* and sigmatic *-sŭ/chŭ*, without *o*) were probably unknown in colloquial use. In secular documents the aorist disappears from South and West Russia from the twelfth century, but persists in North Russia until the fifteenth century, and is still occasionally encountered in North Great Russian folk-songs.

(ii) NOUNS, ADJECTIVES, PRONOUNS.

112. *Gender and Declension.* (See section 61–63). In the Old Russian period the declensions remained as they were in Common Slavonic, but there was at work a tendency, which completed itself in Middle

Russian, to remodel the declensional system in such a way as to correspond with gender. Gender, as we have seen, originated in primitive classifications of words to which particular marks were attached. There was the distinction between what seemed to move itself and what was moved by others. The former class offered conceivable subjects for sentences, and the latter could hardly be other than objects. Hence the difference between masculine (common gender) and neuter was marked by the presence or absence of a particular sign for the nominative case. Later the notion of sex became a classifier, along with collectivity and abstraction. Sex was not merely female, but anything that seemed animate and receptive. Hence the feminine gender, and by contrast the association of male sex with the masculine gender. As a consequence of this process, gender in Common Slavonic was confusing in its logic, since it resulted from the application of different criteria at different epochs. It did express itself in the concord of nouns and adjectives, that is, in the likeness of flexional terminations. The tendency then declared itself to make these concords more regular. Words began to be redistributed among the declensions by their genders; that is to say, a given declension would have a given gender in its accompanying adjectives and demonstratives. This process has been continued in Russian with a gathering momentum, which virtually reached its goal at the close of the Middle Russian period.

In this process the plural and the singular fared somewhat differently. First in the demonstrative and adjective, and then in the noun, the oblique cases of the plural tended to flow together and to adopt the best characterized pattern: that of the *a*-stems. With few exceptions, the dat. instr. loc. pl. of all Russian nouns is the same: *-am -ami -ach*. They were still distinct in the Middle Russian period, but with a strong tendency to unite. In Old Russian each declension had its proper endings for these cases, but also had alternative endings which suggest the final solution. In the plural, therefore, the distinction of gender and declension is confined in Modern Russian to the nom. acc. gen. The distinction of the genitive has been preserved chiefly by a reaction which assigned to masculines the *-ov-* termination of *u*-stems.

Distinctions akin to gender were also set up by the division between animate and inanimate entities. In the masc. *o*-declension the nominative and accusative both resulted in OB. *-ŭ*. The primitive animistic conception which classed such things as fire, wind and water among living bodies had died out. Their inanimate nature was evident, and when they stood as subjects to verbs there was no inconvenience in using the same flexion for the nominative as for the accusative, in the same way as with neuters. But with persons it was often important to distinguish between an agent and a patient. For this purpose the genitive in -*a* was used for the patient, first of a person, and then, by extension, of an animal. The confusion due to flexion did not, however, occur in the feminine *a*-declension or in the masculine plural, and it was only by analogy that the genitive-accusative was applied to masculine plurals, and then to some feminines. It is now used in the singular and plural of masculine nouns and the plural of feminine nouns denoting things that are or were animate: я вижу солдáта 'I see a soldier', я люблю собáк 'I am fond of dogs'. The extension was sooner made for persons than for animals. In Ruthenian an older stage of the process survives for animals (and trees, games and coins); they use the genitive-accusative in the singular and the nominative-accusative in the plural.

(i) The old *i*-declension has become wholly feminine, apart from the one word путь 'way'. In Old Bulgarian, masculines and feminines of this declension differed in the instr. sg. and nom. pl. In the plural the distinction existed in Old Russian but was eliminated in Middle Russian; so that there is but one formal difference: I.S. путём/лóшадью 'by the horse'. All other masculine *i*-stems have been transferred to the *jo*-declension: гость 'guest' зять 'son-in-law' гóлубь 'pigeon' червь 'worm'. In the sixteenth century тетеревь 'grouse' was still associated with the *i*-stems in some of its forms, but it has passed to the *o*-declension as MR. тéтерев. In dialects путь has either passed into the *jo*-class or has changed its gender in order to remain within the feminine *i*-class (cf. Cz. *pouť* fem. 'pilgrimage').

The feminine *uv*-stems have been added to the *i*-declension. When the A.S. любóвь 'love' кровь 'blood' цéрковь 'church' came to be used for the nominative, a process already active in Old Bulgarian, the transfer was easy. They differ from *i*-stems in the instr. pl., where they have -*jami*/-*ami*/-'*mi*. Бýква 'letter' has passed to the *a*-declension, and жёрнов 'mill-stone' to the *o*-declension possibly under the influence of кáмень 'stone'.

Feminine *r*-stems have also been assimilated to the *i*-declension. There are only two words involved: мать 'mother' and дочь 'daughter'. The point of contact was A.S. мáтерь дóчерь. In the instr. pl., as a result of the invasion of the *i*-declension by *a*-flexions, two forms are concurrent: матер-ьми́/я́ми. Only the nom. sg. remained distinctive as OR. мáти/MR. мать (by reduction of final vowel). In the sixteenth century the acc. sg. was мáтерь, but it has been assimilated to the non. sg.: MR.A.S. мать Ruth. мать/мáтір [*i* < *ē* < *e* with compensatory lengthening, see section 86(*E*)]. Examples of this identification come from the early sixteenth century: язъ Отаоья Семенова дочь 'I O., S.'s daughter' 1525/отпустилъ Емгурееву дочь (A.S.) 'he sent away E.'s daughter' 1503. In Ruthenian there are alternative *i*-declensional

forms based on the nom. sg.: NA*S*. мать GDV. мáти. The use of
мáтка дóчка, without a specially diminutive intention, was well-
established in the sixteenth century, and tends to transfer these words
to the *a*-declension.

The great bulk of feminine words belongs to the *a*-declension.
Russian has resisted the tendency to convert the alternatives -*a*/*ja*
into -*a*/*ě* (as in Czech), but has, on the contrary, reassimilated words
in *-*ija* to -*ja* (CSl.OB. -*ǐji* -'*i*) : ладья́ 'boat' богѝня 'goddess'/OB.
aldǐji bogyńi. No difficulty has been found, however, in treating as
masculine male names in -*a*. These are either (i) names of offices, etc.,
held by males only which have become the titles, etc., of the males
holding the offices (abstract to concrete): судья́ 'judge' воевóда 'general'
слугá 'man-servant' ю́ноша 'youth' убѝйца 'murderer' пья́ница
'drunkard', and (ii) the diminutives of personal names: Сáша 'Sandy'
Алёша 'Alick' Вáня 'Jack'. The latter might have the form of the
vocative: Данѝло 'Danny'. These masculines are said to have a
'natural' gender.

(ii) Neuter forms are also readily distinguishable. The main bulk
are in *o*/*e*. To them were added original consonantal neuters in -*s*-:
нéбо 'sky' тéло 'body' слóво 'word' дéрево 'tree' дѝво 'marvel' чýдо
'miracle' лицó 'face' óко 'eye' ýхо 'ear'. For the most part the transfer
has been complete, but the -*s*- is found in the pl. небесá чудесá, and it
occurs in derivatives: чудéсный 'wonderful' небéсный 'heavenly'
телéсный 'bodily' словéсность 'literature'. The word колесó 'wheel'
has generalized the oblique suffix (*koles*-). Assimilations are found in
Old Russian as early as the Ostromir Codex (1056–57), but the oblique
stem in -*s*- is still noted in fourteenth-century documents: словесьмъ
небесѣхъ/словомъ лицахъ 1377. Neuter *n*- and *nt*-stems assimilated
their flexions to the *i*-declension, but remained distinct by reason of
their stems. All *nt*-stems were neuter. Masculine *n*-stems were
attracted into the *jo*-declension by the coincidence of the accusative
case: кáмень (A*S*. for N*S*.) 'stone' was already common in Old
Bulgarian and is the only form known to the Ostromir Codex (1056–
57)/OB. *kamy*. The course of assimilation was (i) to masculine *i*-stems
and then (ii) to *jo*-stems. In the sixteenth century день 'day' кáмень
ячмéнь 'barley' кóрень 'root' пень 'stump' (an original *jo*-stem)
мишéнь 'target' (Pers. *nišān*) were still declined as *i*-stems, and rarely
confused with *jo*-stems. The *i*-declension nom. pl. -*ǐje* was confusable
with the collective -*ǐja*: камéнья. Novgorod seems to have led the
way towards assimilation with *jo*-stems: отъ сѝнего кáменя 'from the
blue stone' отъ берéзового пня 'from the birch stump' 1532. The
process was only completed in the eighteenth and nineteenth centuries.
Стéпень 'grade' became feminine, and *plamy* 'flame' became neuter:
плáмя. Кáмень gen. кáмня 'stone' loses its *e* by analogy.

Ancient usage put the young in the neuter (Gk. παιδίον 'child' Germ. *Mädchen* 'girl'), and so diminutives in *-ko* are 'natural' masculines: Федо́рко 'Teddy' дя́дько 'nunks'. They tend to pass into the *a*-declension (ба́тюшка 'daddy'/NGtR. *bátjuško*), but *-ko* is a very frequent termination in Ruthenian names. 'Natural' masculine diminutives in *-ja* have sometimes been confused with *nt*-stems (NAS. *-ja*) and declined like дитя́ 'child': Ван-я G. -я́те D. -а́ти.

(iii) By reason of these changes the Russian masculine gender, apart from 'natural' masculines, was confined to one single type: *o/jo*-stems, represented by the endings NS. -ъ -ь/й. The one other contributory cause was the fusion of the *u*- and *o*-declensions. That was a process carried through case by case, and so falls for discussion later. It has the effect, however, of establishing a number of contrasts between the declension of the masculines and the neuters, since only among masculines are *u*-stem case-endings current. The masculine declension admits or has admitted of the genitive-accusative in the singular, of gen. loc. voc. sg. in *-u* for some words (loc. *u* being always stressed), of dat. sg. in *-ovi*, nom. pl. in *-ove* >*-ovja* and gen. pl. in *-ov*.

The fusion of *u*- and *o*-stems had begun in Proto-Russian and Old Bulgarian, and, even earlier, in Common Slavonic. The adjectives in *u* had been wholly assimilated to *o* in Common Slavonic: OR. бъдръ MR. бодр 'alert' остръ 'sharp'/L. *budrùs aštrùs*. In Old Russian there are many instances of *u*-flexions for *o*-stems: GS. отъ льну 'from flax' 1073, GS. воску 'of wax' 1331, DS. Данилови 'to Daniel' 1270, мастерови 'to the artisan' 1230, Полоцку 'at Polock' 1407, NP. посоловѣ 'envoys', Татарове 'Tatars', GP. бѣсовъ 'of devils', манастыревъ 'of monasteries' (12th cent.). On the other hand, the distinction concerning declension was still alive in the sixteenth century. The most serviceable criterion is GS. *-u*. In the sixteenth century there are about forty words found with this genitive only: боръ 'fir-forest' берегъ 'bank' бродъ 'ford' верхъ 'top' годъ 'year' домъ 'house' дѣлъ 'share' зубъ 'tooth' ледъ 'ice' ленъ 'flax' лѣсъ 'forest' медъ 'honey' миръ 'peace' мостъ 'bridge' пиръ 'feast' полкъ 'troop' полонъ 'captivity' полъ 'half' рогъ 'horn' родъ 'family' рядъ 'rank' станъ 'station' торгъ 'market' часъ 'hour' and other less familiar words. Some of these words had, doubtless, been attracted into the *u*-class; зубъ/Gk. γόμφος is an example. Primitive *u*-stems were верх (L. *viršùs*) дом (Lat. *domus*) мёд (Gk. μέθυ) пол and possibly бор пир стан торг. In Modern Literary Russian the *o*-flexions have triumphed generally, apart from GP. *-ov/ev*, some locatives and certain adverbial phrases. There is an analogical soft locative in -ю : на корню́ 'unreaped, unfelled'.

113. *Number.* (a) *Loss of the dual.* When the notion of the dual as referring to pairs weakened, the principal support of this number was the characteristic words два 'two' о́ба 'both'. Their dual terminations

formed a jingle with those of the following nouns: Ламехъ оуби
два брата Енохова . . . рече Ламехъ своима женома (sic) 'L. slew
E.'s two brothers . . . L. said to his (two) wives' 1377. Their dual
declension still survives in part. Instead of N*M.* два *NF.* двѣ the
modern forms are *MN.* два *F.* две (but the old neuter survives in
двѣсти '200'). Plural forms are used for the gen. dat.: GL. двухъ/ОВ.
dŭvu D. двум. The instrumental form is двумя, formed from GL.
dvu+(DI. *-ma*+IP. *-'mi* >)*-mja*. This ending has spread to тремя
четырьмя; Ruth. двома has provided an instrumental flexion for 3–9.
(Cf. Ruth. всіма/всіми instr. pl. of весь 'all'.)

The instability of the dual appeared evident in the thirteenth
century. Dual and plural forms were mixed: з обема береги (I*P.*)
'with both banks', помози рабомъ своимъ (D*P.*) Ивану и Олексию
написавшема (D*D.*) книги сия 'help thy servants I. and A. who have
written these documents'. Occasionally a dual termination is attached
to one of the nouns forming a habitual pair: святого апостола (G*S.*)
Петру (G*D.*) и Павла (G*S.*) 'of the holy apostles Peter and Paul'.

In the North Great Russian dialect of Archangel the ending *-ma*
serves for the instrumental plural: с девкима 'with the girls'. Elsewhere the oblique cases have wholly disappeared, and only the
nominative-accusative remains. It is freely used in the feminine
a-declension in Ruthenian: Ruth. (дві) годині 'two hours' (дві) мусі
'two flies'. For the *o*- and *a*-stems the forms had been: *M.* -*a NF.* -*ĕ*
(which latter also served for *n*- *nt*- *s*-stems); -*i* served for *i*- *uv*- *r*- *ja*-
jo-(*N*) *n*-(*M*) stems, and -*y* for *u*-stems. Of all these only -*a* -*i* survive,
but they are felt to be plurals or, after 2–4, genitive singulars. The use
of this construction with 3 and 4 began to be general in the sixteenth
century. Два брата 'two brothers' began to be construed as G*S.* -*a*,
and on that analogy was formed две сестры (G*SF.*) 'two sisters'/
sestrĕ NA*P.* сёстры. Through loss of the sense of duality this led to
три стола 'three tables' четыре села 'four villages'/N*P.* сёла. As for
оба 'both', it has the same construction, but *F.* обе is also found with
the plural: обе сестры/сёстры 'both sisters'.

The other principal support of the dual was the existence of certain
obvious bodily pairs: очи 'eyes' уши 'ears' колени 'knees' плечи
'shoulders'. This -*i* was taken to be the nom. pl. of an *i*-stem in the
genitive (очей) but of an *o*-stem in other cases. In the singular око ухо
have passed from the *s*-declension (*očes*- *ušes*-) to that of neuters in *o*.
Confusion of declension is as early as the Ostromir Codex (1056–57):
G*S.* очесе L*S.* оцѣ/очесе L*D.* очию (preserved in MR. воочию 'before
one's eyes, obviously')/очесоу.

There were other obvious pairs in M*D.* -*a:* бока 'sides' глаза 'eyes'
берега 'banks'. The -*a* resembled the neuter plural, and so gave rise to
a heteroclite declension of things which do not form pairs: since глаз :

глазá : : лес : лесá 'woods' : : гóрод : городá 'cities' : : пи́сарь : писаря́ 'writers'. This pattern has been applied even to recent loanwords: инспекторá 'inspectors'. It has lead to double plurals: учи́тел-и/-я́ 'teachers', and to differentiation: óбразы 'forms'/образá 'ikons', хлéбы 'loaves'/хлебá 'corn', цветы́ 'blossoms'/цветá 'colours'. The final accentuation of these plurals is one of their characteristics.

(b) *Collectives and singulatives.* Collective suffixes were *FS.* -a -*ĭja NS.* -*ĭje*, declined originally as singulars. So OR. господа 'gentry, gentlemen' was a feminine singular (G*S.* отъ госпо́ды 'from the lords'), and so also сторожа 'watchmen, guard' хозяева 'hosts' (apparently based on the genitive хозя́ев; the singular is хозя́ин), and national names like Татарва 'Tatars'; in -*ĭja:* братья 'brothers' княжья 'princes' (вся княжья Руськая 'all the Russian princes' 14th cent.) зятья 'sons-in-law' дядья 'uncles'; and in -*ĭje:* деревье 'trees' каменье 'stones' (which coincides with the nom. pl. of masc. *i*-stems) столпье 'pillars'. It was seldom that these were taken to be plurals in Old Russian: каменьихъ 1144, быша камения 'there were stones'. In Modern Russian they have become a form of the plural, and extended to сыновья́ 'sons'/*synove*. There still remain as collective singulars трапьё 'rags' дубьё 'cudgels'.

The notion of plurality entered by way of syntax, since the accompanying verb was often put in the plural in Old Russian: гдѣ суть (pl.) дружина (coll. sg.) наша 'where are our bodyguard'. Hence it became natural to oppose брат дéрево кáмень кол 'stake'/брáтья дерéвья камéнья кóлья as singular/plural. They helped also to reinforce the influence of the dual -a upon the o-stems: домá/дóмы 'houses' годá 'years' рогá 'horns', and with -*ov-:* сыновья́ 'sons' сватовья́ 'matchmakers' кумовья́ 'god-parents'.

A singulative is the result of a grammatical device for picking out one from a collectivity or a plurality. The suffix employed was -*inĭ:* господá 'gentry'/господи́н 'gentleman', дворя́не (and also дворяня on the analogy of the collectives)/дворяни́н 'nobleman', горожáне 'townsfolk'/горожáнин 'townsman'. National names form pairs of this sort: англичáне/англичáнин. There existed OR.*MP.* госпóдие/*FS.* coll. господа. The latter drove out the old nom. pl. of a masc. *i*-stem, and caused its remaining cases to be declined according to the feminine *a*-stems.

These plurals are a feature of Great Russian dialects, and begin to appear in the fourteenth century: отъ братии моихъ 'from my brothers' 1362. They are foreign to White Russian and Ruthenian.

See overleaf for Section 114
Paradigms of Nouns

114. *Paradigms of Nouns.*

I-stems

		SNA	GDL(V)	I	PNV
OR. *F.*	кост-	ь	и	ью/ию	и
M.	пут-			ьмь	ые/ше
MidR. *F.*	рѣч-	ь	и	ью	и
MR. *F.*	лóшад-	ь	и	ью	и
M.	пут-		й	ём	й
Ruth. F.	чáст-	ь	и	ию	и
	рíч-	—			

Consonant-stem

		SNV	A	GL	D	I	PNV
OR. *F.*	мат-	и					
	матер-		ь	е/и	и	ью/ию	е/и
N.	имя	—	—				
	имен-			е/и	и	ьмь	а
M.	горожан-						е
MidR. *N.*	имя	—	—				
	имен-			и	и	емъ	а
MR. *F.*	мат-	ь	ь				
	мáтер-			и	и	ью	и
N.	врéмя дитя́	—	—				(дéт-и
	врéмен- дитя́т-			и	и	ем	á
Ruth. F.	мáт-	и/ь	ь	и	и		
	мáтер-			и	і	ю	і
			мáтір				
N.	ягня́	—	—		(DL)	м	
	ягня́т-			и	и/і		а

A	G	D	I	L	*D*NAV	GL	DI
и	ьи/и	ьмъ	ьми	ьхъ	и	ью/ию	ьма
и	ей	емъ	ьми	ехъ	(очи		очима)
и.	éй	я́м	ьми́	я́х	(óчи)		
й			я́ми				
и	ий	ям	ями	ях			
	ам	ами	ах				

A	G	D	I	L	*D*NAV	GL	DI
и	ъ/ьи/ии	ьмъ	ьми	ьхъ	и	ью/ию	ьма
а	ъ	ьмъ	ьми	ьхъ	и	у	ьма
			ы	ѣхъ/охъ			
е/ы	ъ	ьмъ/омъ	ьми/ы	ьхъ/охъ			
а	ъ	емъ	ы	ѣхъ			
G	éй	я́м	ьми́/ями́	я́х			
G	éй	ям	ьми́	ях)			
á	(ён)	ам	áми	áх			
i	ий	ям	ями	ях			
а	—	ам	ами	ах			

A-stems

		SN	A	G	DL	I	V
OR.	жен-	а	у	ы	ѣ	ою	о
	душ-	я	ю	ѣ	и	ею	е
MidR.	вод-	а	у	ы	ѣ	ою	о
MR.	жёнщин-	а	у	ы	е	ой/ою	
	а́рми-	я	ю	и	и	ей/ею	
	зе́мл-	я́		й	é	ёй/ёю	
Ruth.	годи́н-	а	у	и	i	ою	о
	бу́р-	я	ю	i	i	ею	е

O/U-stems

		SN	A	G	D	L	I	V
OR. *M.*	вълк-	ъ	G	а	у/ови		ьмь	
	вълц-					ѣ		
	вълч-							е
	кон-	ь	G	я	ю/еви	и	ьмь	ю
MidR. *M.*	город-	ъ	N	а	у	ѣ	омъ	
N.	сел-	о	о					
MR. *M.*	наро́д-	—	N	а	у	е	ом	
N.	сел-	о́	о́					
M.	оле́н-	ь	G	я	ю	е	ем	
	сара́-	й	N					
N.	мо́р-	е	е					
								о́тче
Ruth. *M.*	ли́с-	—	G	а	ови	i	ом	е
	ду́х					ду́сі		ду́ше
N.	о́зер-	о	о	а	у	i	ом	
M.	учи́тел-	ь	G	я	еви	i/ю	ем	ю
N.	со́нц-	е	е	я	ю	i/ю	ем	

PNAV	G	D	I	L	DNAV	GL	DI
ы	ъ	амъ	ами	ахъ	ѣ	у	ама
ѣ	ь	ямъ	ями	яхъ	и	ю	яма
ы	ъ	амъ	ами	ахъ			
ы	—	ам	ами	ах			
и	й	ям	ями	ях			
	земель						
и	—	ам	ами	ах			
і	—	ям	ями	ях			

PNV	A	G	D	I	L	DNAV	GL	DI
ове	ы	ъ/овъ	омъ	ы	охъ	а	у	ома
и					ѣхъ			
и	ѣ	ь/евъ	емъ	и	ихъ	я	ю	ема
ы	ы	овъ	омъ	ы	ѣхъ			
а	а							
ы	N	ов	ам	ами	ах			
сёл-а	а	—						
и	G	ей	ям	ями	ях			
и	и	ев						
я́	я́	ей	я́м	я́ми	я́х			
сыновья́		сыновей		сыновья́м				
и	G	iв	ам	ами	ах			
ду́хи								
а	а	—	ам	ами	ах		і	
ї	G	iв	ям	ями	ях			
я	я	ь	ям	ями	ях			

115. *Singular Cases.* (*a*) *Nominative and accusative.* Even in Common Slavonic the nominative and accusative cases tended to coincide outside the *a*-declension. The *i- o- u*-stems had identical forms through loss of final -*s* -*m* from *-*is* *-*im*, *-*os* *-*om*, *-*us* *-*um*. All neuters (*o- n- s- nt*-stems) had identical forms for the two cases. In the *uv*- and masc. *n*-declensions the tendency to use the accusative for the nominative was already active in Old Bulgarian, and the old nominatives seem to have gone out in Russian definitely during the thirteenth century: NA*S*. любовь 'love' камень 'stone'/OB.N*S*. *luby kamy* A*S*. *lubŭvĭ kamenĭ*. The form N*S*. церкви 'church' is exceptional; it occurs in manuscripts down to the later fourteenth century, and must be accounted a descendant of the original *cĭrky >*cerki* (by palatalization of *k*) >*cerkvi* (on the analogy of other cases)/MR.NA*S*. церковь. It was by means of these nominative-accusative forms that the declensions became fused; and it was by reaction against the identity of form where sentient beings were concerned that the genitive-accusative arose [see section 66(*a*) iii].

The genitive is also used in the partitive sense (дать хлеба = *donner du pain*) and in negative constructions (нет хлеба = *il n'y a pas de pain*). Some of the uses are curious from the Western point of view; e.g. Маши здесь нет? 'isn't Masha here?' (as though 'isn't there any M. here?'). The position in standard Russian with negative verbs is that the object is put in the genitive except when the negative involves the verb alone and does not extend to the object; e.g. не читаю книги 'I am not reading *the book*'/не читаю книгу 'I am not *reading* the book (sc. merely glancing through it)'. Polish on the other hand uses the genitive after all negative verbs. In Old Russian the genitive was found in examples where the partitive sense could not be called self-evident: живота вѣчьнааго имате 'ye have eternal life' 1056–57, Іанъ посла наю (G*D*.) к тобѣ 'John sent us two to thee' 1354. In the older manuscripts the accusative is found with positive verbs, but the two cases stand side by side in убиша Овъстрата (G*S*.) и сынъ (A*S*.) его 'they killed O. and his son' (14th cent.). The accusative is found, though rarely, in Russian dialects, and in the fixed phrases выдать замуж 'give in marriage', выйти замуж 'to marry' (of a woman). The extension of the gen.-acc. to the plural of *o*-stems and to the plural of feminines is the result of later analogy, and in it the animate class covers only persons, not animals, in Ruthenian. On the other hand, trees, games and coins are often given the same treatment as animals: WR. мае рубля 'he has a rouble'.

(*b*) *Vocative.* The vocative was obsolete by the sixteenth century, and has now been fused with the nominative. It has remained in ecclesiastical use: отче Боже Христе Иисусе, сыне божий 'Son of God', царю 'O heavenly King' владыко 'O Lord'. In the sixteenth

century господине 'my lord(s)' брате 'my brother(s)' are merely
apostrophes, used without reference to number: скажите, брате, чья
то земля? 'say, brothers, whose is this land?' Examples of the nominative for the vocative are frequent from the twelfth century onward:
Хоразинъ Виосаида/-е -о 'O Chorazin and Bethsaida'. Vocatives are
frequently encountered in old documents where the nominative
should appear: заложи церковь Сьмьюне (VS.) Дывачевиць 'S.D.
founded the church' 1282, придоша (*alii et*) Петре (VS.) Водовиковиць
'there came (others and) P.V.' (14th cent.), Савке рече 'S. said' (14th
cent.), etc. In Ruthenian and White Russian there are many survivals
of the vocative of *o/u*- and *a*-stems: Ruth. лисе 'O fox' учителю 'O
teacher' мухо 'O fly' роже/рожо 'O rose'.

In view of the equation of nominative and accusative, the vocative
may take the place of the latter: аче гдѣ изнаидуть или тать или товаре
(VS.) 'if they find anywhere either thief or goods' 1392. This is a feature of folk-songs in North Great Russian, from the Onega region.
Similarly, in Serbocroat folk-songs the vocative is frequently found
for the nominative, for metrical convenience.

(c) *Genitive, dative, locative.* These three cases were fused in the
i-stems of Common Slavonic (-*i* G. ⟨**eis/ois*? D ⟨? L. *-*ēi*), but the
consonantal stems distinguished GL. -*e* ⟨G. *-*es*, L. ?/D. -*i* ⟨-**ēi*. In
monosyllables the locative -и is frequently stressed under the
Fortunatov-de Saussure law; e.g. в пыли 'in the dust'. (Cf. locative
in -ý below). In Old Russian the influence of the *i*-stems on the consonantal stems caused the dative flexion to extend to their genitive and
locative also. The *a*-stems in Old Russian showed G. -*y/ě* DL. -*ě/i*.
These were not normal hard/soft pairs and they were rationalized as
G. -*y/i* DL. -*ě*, since -*ě* was common to both varieties. DL. -*iě*, however, has become -*ii*. The same situation arose in the dual and plural:
OR.NAP. -*y/ě* NAD. -*ě/i* became -*y/i* -*ě* respectively. Between the
eleventh and the fourteenth centuries the genitive singular vacillated:
Отроковичи (ч=ц) 1095 Захарии 1157. In the earlier documents GS.
-*ě* is predominant, but by the fourteenth century it had become rare.
For -*ě* which was proper to Russian and West Slavonic there also
appeared -*ja*=OB. -*ę*: изъ лодья 'out of the boat' на конець земля 'to
the end of the earth'/съ шиѣ 'from the neck down' до шие 'up to the
neck'/изъ гробли 'out of the grave' 1377. DL. -*ě* also dates from the
eleventh century; госпожѣ 'to the lady' 1095, землѣ 'to the land' 1215,
нуже 'to the need' 1285. DL. -*i* was still frequent in the fourteenth
century, and is to be found in Modern White Russian, West Ruthenian
and some South Great Russian dialects (notably that of Putivĺ). Ruth.
GS. бур-i DL. -i imply the original GS. -*ě* coupled with the later DLS.
-*ě*. In North Great Russian D. -*ě* has spread to the *i*-declension: *peče
grjaze* (печь 'stove' грязь 'mud'). In the hard declension there was a

special confusion of genitive and dative in the Novgorod region, where it still persists. D*S*. -*ĕ* was found in place of G*S*. -*y*: отъ владыцѣ 'from the bishop' 1305, у Вьлнѣ у рѣцѣ 'by the river Vilna' (14th cent.). Conversely, the use of G. -*y* for DL. -*ĕ* is found in the fourteenth and fifteenth centuries: на онои страны 'on that side' (14th cent.), ко святыма Козмы (*y* for *ĕ*) и Дамьяну 'to Sts. C. and D.' 1400. This usage is quite frequent in Modern North Great Russian dialects and also in that of Putivĺ in the south, and it is found sporadically in the declension of definite adjectives: въ Юрьевское волости 'in the Juŕev district' (14th cent.).

L*S*. -*ĕ* (of *a*- and *o*-stems), like N*P*. -*i* L*P*. -*ĕch* (of *o*-stems), induced the second palatalization, i.e. *k g ch* >*c z s*, and *sk* >*st*: OR. вълцѣ(хъ)/ вълкъ 'wolf' руцѣ/рука 'hand' женьстѣ/женьска 'womanly'. After the palatalization of *k' ǵ ch'* these sounds were restored by analogy, beginning as early as the twelfth century: женьскѣ 1073, Дъмъкѣ 'to Domka' 1096. These restitutions were normal in fourteenth century manuscripts from North Russia, and they now cover the northern and central region, including the Moscow dialect. At Orel and Kursk are found *c st*. In White Russian and Ruthenian the older mutation persists: Ruth. DL*S*. NA*D*. мýсі/NA*P*. мýхи NA*S*. мýха 'fly' (Ruth. *i* <*ĕ*, и=*y*), L*S*. дýсі/дух 'breath'.

Between the hard masc. *o*-stems and the *u*-stems there was a complicated series of transactions, through which gradually the modern declension was determined. The singular cases involved (putting the *o*-forms first) were: G. *a/u* D. *u/ovi* L. *ĕ/u* V. *e/u*, and to these have to be added in the plural: N. *i/ove* G. -/*ov*. This matter has already been discussed in section 112 (*iii*) in general terms. During the Old Russian period these forms were fluid. The most stable feature was the genitive -*u* which was attached to some forty words that either belonged originally to the *u*-declension or had become attributed to it. They may, of course, have included original *o*-stems, and the use of G*S*. -*u* with an original *o*-stem was frequent in Old Russian: G*S*. отъ льну 'from flax' (Lat. *linum*) 1073, воску 'of wax'. By the sixteenth century a distinction had been effected on the basis of meaning; G*S*. -*u* was appropriated to nouns denoting divisible matter: MR. мáло нарóду 'few people'/мнéние нарóда 'the people's opinion', фунт чáю 'a pound of tea'. It also occurs in some adverbial phrases: с вúду 'by sight', без тóлку 'without sense', с нúзу/вéрху 'from below/above', óт роду 'from birth', úз дому 'out of the house'. In Ruthenian G*S*. -*u* is limited to things. Certain Ruthenian words have both terminations: огорóд 'garden' лист 'leaf' цьвіт 'flower' сир 'cheese' рід 'family' нарíд 'people' мост 'bridge' вíтер 'wind' стíл 'table'; a considerable number have only G*S*. -*u*: гóлод 'hunger' прúклад 'example' суд 'judgment' мур 'wall' цýкор 'sugar' óцет 'vinegar' (г)орóх 'pea' дím 'house' бík 'side' сад 'garden' час 'time' and others. The D*S.* *-ovi* was a form recommended by its clarity. It is found frequently in Old Russian: Данилови 1270, мастерови 'to the artisan' 1230. It is rare in Great Russian and White Russian dialects, but is normal in Ruthenian: лисови 'to the fox'. The employment of L*S.* *-u* was more capricious. It was appropriated by nouns that happened to end in *-sk:* Полоцку 1407. It is found in some fixed adverbial expressions: в саду 'in the garden' на мосту/берегу/лугу/краю/полу 'on the bridge/bank/meadow/corner/floor', в . . . году 'in the year . . .', в углу 'in the corner'. The constant stress on the locative case-ending (from *-ēu$) is due to de Saussure's law and to analogy. In Ruthenian a number of words, chiefly indicating persons or days of the week, have G*S.* *-a*/LV*S.* *-u:* парох 'parson' батенько 'daddy' ученик 'scholar' вівтóрок 'Thursday' ручник 'handkerchief' вовк 'wolf' and others.

Though the *u*-declension was hard only, its flexions are given soft alternatives by analogy: D*S.* *-evi* L*S.* *-ju.*

Домóй 'homewards' (OR. домовь) has been explained as a loc. in *-ĭ*, but OB. *domovi* is certainly dative.

(*d*) *Instrumental.* In the *i*-declension the masculines and feminines differed in the termination, and the distinction has been maintained: I*SF.* *-'ju*/M. *-em* (путём only). I*SF.* *-oju*/*eju* survives in Ruthenian and has not been completely displaced in Modern Russian. The alternative modern forms *-oj*/*ej* are due partly to the weakening of the final vowel and its absorption, partly to the analogy of the definite declension of adjectives, in which *-oj* has become the ending of oblique singular cases of the feminine. CSl. *-ŭmĭ* and *-omĭ* give R. *-om* (with hardening of the final consonant). In Old Russian -ъмь is the form most frequently used, and when -омь occurs it may be ascribed to the usage of Old Bulgarian. Ruth. *-om*/*em* come from *-ŭmĭ*/*ĭmĭ*, since otherwise *ō ē*, lengthened by compensation for loss of final *jer*, would give *i*.

115A. *Accent.* Change of stress within the paradigm, resulting from the historical processes described above and the workings of analogy, while presenting a complicated picture is nevertheless reducible to certain 'laws' allowing of singularly few exceptions. The position in the singular is as follows:

(i) *Masculines.* Some nouns stressed on the last syllable of the nominative shift the stress to the ending of all the other cases; e.g. старик 'old man' G. старикá etc. The only other shift is to the locative in *-u*, which (found as a rule only in nouns with monosyllabic nominatives) occurs as a rule only in such nouns as do not otherwise shift the stress in the singular; e.g. сад 'garden' G. сáда etc. L. саду.

(ii) *Feminines.* Apart from the occasional locative in stressed *-i*, no shift occurs save in the case of some nouns stressed on the ending of the nominative, which move the stress to the first syllable of the accusative; e.g. водá 'water' вóду, земля́ 'earth' зéмлю, сторонá 'side' стóрону, сковородá 'frying-pan' сковороду.

(iii) *Neuters.* No shift occurs.

116. *Plural Cases.* (*a*) *Nominative and accusative.* Masculine *i*-stems originally distinguished N*P*. -*ĭje*/A*P*. -*i*, but the feminines had only NA*P*. -*i*. The accusative displaced the nominative in the masculine from the thirteenth century, and was the only form known in the sixteenth. Earlier substitutions were: *MNP*. дьни 'days' (11th cent.) три 'three' (1073); from the thirteenth century: *MNP*. люди 'people' 1262 пути 'ways' 1271, but людье путье гостье 'guests' звѣрье 'beasts' татье 'thieves' червье 'worms' are all found in 1377. The *r*-stems had N*P*. -*e*, which passed to -*i* under the influence of the feminine *i*-stems. In Old Russian there are examples of the use of the nominative for the accusative in this and other declensions: съзъвавъ князи (-*i* for -*ě*) и люди 'having gathered the princes and the people' 1215, три (-*i* for -*ĭje*) на два и два на трие (-*ĭje* for -*i*) 'three on two and two on three' 1357.

The feminine *a*-stems had OR.NA*P*. -*y*/*ě*, which became -*y*/*i* in the manner indicated in section 115 (*c*): рабыни 'slave-girls' 1215, блудници 'courtesans' 1311, птици 'birds' 1354, убиици 'murderers' 1355. It has also been noted already that the rise of *k' ģ ch'* helped to cancel some of the effects of the second palatalization in Russian declensions.

The *o*/*u*-stems have OR.N*P*. -*i*/*ove* in the hard declension. Examples of -*ove* with *o*-stems go back to the twelfth century: N*P*. посоловѣ 'envoys' Татарове. This flexion is fairly frequent in North Great Russian dialects, rare in White Russian, but common in Ruthenian. A few nouns have retained the old nominative ending: сосéд 'neighbour' чорт (чёрт) 'devil' pl. сосéди чéрти. These plurals are treated as soft forms: сосéд-ей -ям, черт-ей -ям. The plural of друг 'friend' preserves in the form друзья́ the palatilization formerly characteristic of this declension. Some neuters in -ко have an analogical plural in -ки : я́блоко 'apple' я́блоки.

MNP. -*e* survives with collectives in -*jane*: горожáне 'townsfolk'.

The old acc. pl. (=nom. pl. in appearance) has been preserved in certain fixed expressions like произвести в офицéры 'promote to the rank of officer' in which, by analogy, real nom. pls. in -и -а -я are also used. Cf. готóвился в профессорá, а попáл в члéны зéмской упрáвы 'he trained to be a professor and ended up as a member of the local council'. The expression в гóсти means 'on a visit', and in где уж нам в молоды́е лезть 'it's not for us to ape the young 'uns' the nominative of the adjective is similarly employed.

(*b*) *Genitive.* The *i*-stems developed their genitive in -*ej* (<-*ĭjĭ*/ Ruth. -ий), and this has affected the feminine *r*-stems. By analogy, some soft masculine *jo*-stems have acquired a *GP.* *-ej*, which has spread to soft neuters: оленей (олень 'stag') морей (море 'sea'), сыновей (сын 'son'). Masculine *o*-stems have generally adopted the termination *-ov* of the *u*-declension: *MGP.* народов 'of the peoples'/ *N.* сёл 'of the villages', Ruth. лисів 'of foxes'; some *jo*-stems have an analogical *GP.* *-ev:* соловьёв (соловей <*-ĭjĭ* 'nightingale') стульев (стул nom. pl. стулья 'chairs'); *-ov* is occasionally found with neuters: очко 'point' очков. The word стремя 'stirrup' has the exceptional *GP.* стремян.

(*c*) *Dative, instrumental, locative.* For these cases there are three types, corresponding to the *i*- *a*- and *o*-stems: *-em* -*'mi* -*ech*/-*am* -*ami* -*ach*/-*om* -*y* -*ěch*. There is no tendency in Russian to confuse these endings with the dual, nor much to identify them with each other. In those North-west Great Russian dialects which confuse *č*/*c* the dative and instrumental plural are confused; in other northern dialects, in White Russian, and in the southern dialect of Kursk, this is limited to the use of the dative for the instrumental: *s nam*/с нами 'with us'. The history of the three cases is that of the gradual extension of the *a*-forms to all declensions.

It was during the fourteenth century that the *a*-forms spread over the *u*/*o*-declension: на распутьяхъ 'at the cross-roads' 1354, книжникамъ 'to the scribes' 1355. In the fourteenth, fifteenth and even sixteenth centuries the historical forms are still encountered: въ сундукехъ 'in coffers' (*Domostroj*, 16th cent.). The weakness of the *o*-forms was their uncertainty. *IP.* *-y* lacked support in other declensions, though it invaded that of the neuter consonant-stems. The *o*-stems had properly OB.D. *-omŭ* L. *-ěchŭ*, and the *u*-stems D. *-ŭmŭ* *-ŭchŭ* (giving *-omŭ* *-ochŭ* when the *jer* was vocalized in South-west Bulgarian). Hence there was vacillation in the locative between OR. *-ъхъ*/охъ/ѣхъ, and the last was indistinguishable in sound from *-ехъ* <*-ьхъ* (of the *i*-stems). There was no such hesitation about the *a*-forms. Their taking the place of *u*/*o*-forms was an advance in precision. *IP.* *-y* is found in fairly modern literary usage: съ тесовыми вороты 'with wooden gates' (Puškin), and by contamination with *-ami* it produces *-amy:* dial. *slezamy* 'tears' *gorodamy* 'cities'. These mixed forms are widespread in North, South and White Russian. A mediæval example is безаконьнымы 'by the lawless' 1356, if it is not a scribal error.

The neuter consonant-stems tended to identify themselves in the plural with neuter *o*-stems. The history of their cases is thus the same as that of the *o*-stems.

The extension of the *a*-forms over the *i*-stems was later than over the *o*-stems and caused vacillations which are still present in that declension. Masculines passed over to the *jo*-declension in the singular, but that circumstance had no immediate effect on their treatment in the plural. In the first part of the sixteenth century all but путь 'way' had joined the *jo*-declension in the singular. But there were still found: гостей татей тетеревей I*P*. гостьми татьми, etc., declined according to the *i*-stems. As we have seen, the G*P*. -*ej* (OR. -ии) was extended to many *jo*-stems from the thirteenth century onwards: пѣнязии 'of monies' 1270, князии 'of princes' (14th cent.), MR. рубл-ей/ёв 'of roubles'. The L*P*. -*ech* was a less distinctive form, since it was identical in sound with -*ěch* in Russian, and the dative -*em* was easily confused with the same case of the *jo*-stems; but the instrumental has proved highly resistent as -'*mi*: лошадьми 'with horses' костьми 'with bones' людьми 'with people' дверьми 'with doors' детьми 'with children'. It has not, however, shown much power of expansion: I*P*. матерьми дочерьми are found as well as матерями дочерями 'by mothers/ daughters'; but that is the extent of the advance. The *a*-forms have monopolized the dative and locative in Modern Russian and Ruthenian, and they have spread to the greater number of *i*-stems, notably to all in -*ost* -*est*, and to those ending in a palatal (*č šč ž š*): частями 'by parts' ночами 'by nights'. Masculine *n*-stems passed into the *i*-class before joining the *jo*-declension, and feminine *uv*-stems were immigrants into the *i*-class; neither stem shows the I*P*. -'*mi* which is characteristic of the declension.

Borrowed neuters in -о -е (-э) are for the most part not declined (save sometimes in the colloquial): кино 'cinema' галифе 'riding breeches', etc.

116A. *Accent.* (Cf. 115A). (i) *Masculines.* Nouns which shift the stress in the singular likewise stress the endings of the plural, with the exception of a very few nouns (e.g. конь 'horse') in which the ending of the nominative plural only is not stressed. Certain nouns initiate the shift with the nominative or genitive plural; in either case all the remaining cases stress the ending; e.g. сады садов 'gardens' доктора докторов 'doctors' воры воров 'thieves'. Exceptional is the form люди 'people' which (like дети 'children') stresses the genitive but not the other plural endings: людей детей/людям детям. Nouns which stress the ending of the nominative plural and have zero-ending in the genitive stress the last syllable of this case; an example is волос 'hair' N*P*. волоса G*P*. волос D*P*. волосам.

(ii) *Feminines.* Some nouns which stress the ending of the nominative singular move the accent back in the nominative plural, either to the first syllable (e.g. сковорода 'frying-pan' N*P*. сковороды) or (in the case of certain polysyllables) to the penultimate syllable (e.g. сирота 'orphan' N*P*. сироты). In the latter type the stress remains on this syllable throughout the rest of the paradigm. In the former the stress may remain on the same syllable as the nominative plural throughout (e.g. жена 'wife' N*P*. жёны G*P*. жён D*P*. жёнам etc.) or it may shift to the ending of the dative and subsequent cases (e.g. сковородáм etc.); in any case there is a tendency to stress the last syllable of the genitive: сестрá 'sister' NP. сёстры GP. сестёр (DP. сёстрам/сестрáм). Many feminines in -ь initiate a shift of stress to the ending in the genitive plural, e.g. лóшадь 'horse' мать 'mother' GP. лошадéй матерéй DP. лошадя́м матеря́м.

(iii) *Neuters.* Many nouns in -o and -e shift the stress in the plural, e.g. селó 'village' NP. сёла, веретенó 'spindle' веретёна, óзеро 'lake' озёра, мóре 'sea' моря́. Subsequent cases regularly stress the same syllable as the nominative plural (сёл сёлам, веретён веретёнам, озёр озёрам, морéй моря́м). Nouns in -мя regularly stress the last syllable of the plural: и́мя 'name' NP. именá GP. имён DP. именáм etc. (But знáмя 'banner' has NP. знамёна etc.)

117. *Numerals.* 1.*M.* оди́н *N.* однó *F.* однá 'one', also used for 'a', 'alone', 'only', 'nothing but' (*MNP.* одни́; *FP.* однé (однъ)—disused since 1917) is by origin a demonstrative and follows that declension; пéрвый 'first' Ruth. пéрший.

2–4 (and 'both').

		N	A	GL	D	I
OR. *M.*	дъв-	а	а	ою/у		ѣма
NF.		ѣ	ѣ			
Mid.R. *MN.*	дв-	а	а	у(хъ)	ѣмъ/ѣма	ѣма
F.		ѣ	ѣ			
	тр-	и	и	ех	емъ/ема	еми/ема
	четыр-	е	е	ех	ма	ма/ьми
MR. *MN.*	дв-	а	NG	ух	ум	умя́
F.		е				
MN.	óб-	а	NG			
F.		е				
MN.	обó-			их	им	ими
F.	обé					
	тр-	и	NG	ёх	ём	емя́
	четыр-	е				ьмя́
Ruth. *M.*	дв-	а	NG	ох	ом	омá
NF.		і				
	тр-	и		ох	ом	омá
	чоти́р-	и		óх	óм	(о)мá

During the Middle Russian period the dative emerges as a distinct case with the plural ending. The locative also took a plural ending, and imparted it to the genitive: двухъ. Then *dvu-* replaced *dv-* as the stem, and formed IP. двумя́, by conflation of IP. *-mi* with ID. *-ma.* This form then spread to три четы́ре. In Ruthenian this type of declension is extended to 5–9 as an alternative: пят-ь 'five' GL. -й/ьóх D. й/ьóм I. -ьмá. 2nd–4th: второй трéтий четвёртый/Ruth. дрýгий трéтий четвёртий. Трéтий is declined like рыбий (see section 118). The form третéй (< -*ĭjĭ*) occurs in the expression сам-третéй ('self the third', i.e.) 'self and two others' and in третьёводни 'the day before yesterday' (dial.).

5–10. пять шесть семь (OB. *sedmĭ*) вóсемь (OB. *osmĭ*) дéвять дéсять are *i*-declension nouns (sg.) governing the following noun in the genitive plural; 5th–10th: пя́тый шестóй седьмóй восьмóй девя́тый деся́тый. Ruth: 6 шість 7 сім 8 вісім. Short forms of the ordinals occur in сам-шост 'self and five others' etc. ('Self and one other' is сам-друг). Other ordinal forms are во-пéрвых во-вторы́х etc. ('in the first place' etc.) and, with discrepant accent, впервóй 'for the first time'.

11–19. These were originally formed by a number capable of inflexion+на деся́те : пяти́ на деся́те (*GS.*) '15'. Then by hypertrophe of flexion, both numbers were made to agree: двумя́ на деся́тьма (*ID.*) 1307. This usage lasted till the seventeenth century, when пятинадеся́ти is attested. Now the flexion is restricted to the second element, and the whole is treated as a fem. *i*-stem: оди́ннадцать '11' двена́дцать '12' четы́рнадцать '14', Ruth. одина́йцять двана́йцять шісна́йцять. The genders of 1 and 2 are chosen arbitrarily, and 4 is contracted (also 6 in Ruthenian), while дéсять suffers a contraction not normally encountered in the development of Russian.

20–90. CSl.OB. *dŭva desęti* (*NMD.*) has been assimilated to fem. *i*-stems (sg.): два́дцать; CSl.OB. *tri desętę* (pl.) has also been assimilated to an *i*-stem: три́дцать. CSl.OB. *pęti desętŭ* (*GP.*) has been preserved as пятьдеся́т [p'ɪdɪsát], and so on upwards, both parts declined as *i*-stems. Девянóсто '90' has been explained as *dévjat̓ do sta* '9 to 100'/Cz. *devadesát* < *devętĭ desętŭ*. Сóрок '40' (Cz. *čtyřicet* < *četyre desętę*) is an innovation; either from MGk. σαράκοντα or ON. *serkr* (a number of skins, which were the Slav tribute to the Rurikids).

100: сто 200: двéсти (*ND.*) 300: три́ста (*NP.*) 500: пятьсóт (*GNP.*) 1000: ты́сяча 2000: двe ты́сячи (*FD.*) 5000: пять ты́сяч (*GFP.*).

Forms of the collectives described in section 69 extant in Modern Russian are the neuter singulars двóе трóе чéтверо etc. used in certain contexts with the genitive plural of the noun, e.g. двóе детéй 'two children', or as pronouns in such constructions as их бы́ло трóе 'there were three of them'. The oblique cases have plural forms: G. двои́х детéй D. двои́м дéтям etc. There are also the adverbs вдвоём 'two together' etc.

From the ordinal вторóй 'second' is derived the fractional number полторá 'one and a half' (lit. 'half of the second').

The adverbs одна́жды 'once' два́жды 'twice' три́жды 'thrice' appear to contain as their second element the verbal root *šĭd-* 'go', with *š* changed to *ž* by assimilation.

While all nouns, as we have seen, take the genitive singular after 2, 3, 4 (22, 32, etc.), adjectives take either the nominative-accusative or genitive *plural* with these numbers. Certain demonstratives may take the nominative-accusative with all numbers; e.g. заплатил все тридцать 'he paid all the thirty (roubles)'. Cf. те несколько строк 'those few lines', через какие-нибудь четверть часа 'in about a quarter of an hour'.

Distribution is expressed by по with the accusative or dative: по два рубля 'two roubles each'.

118. *Adjectives*. The definite and possessive adjectives are declined thus:

			SNV	A	G	D	L	I
OR.	добр-	M.	ъи/ыи	NG }	ого	ому	омь/ѣмь	ы(и)мь
		N.	оіе	N				
		F.	ая	ую	оѣ/ыѣ	ои/ѣи		ою
	син-	M.	ьи/ии	NG }	его	ему	емь	и(и)мь
		N.	еіе	N				
		F.	яя	юю	еѣ/ѣѣ	еи		ею
MidR.	нов-	M.	ой	NG }	ого	ому	омъ	ымъ
		N.	ое	N				
		F.	ая	ую	ые	ой		ою
MR.	молод-	M.	óй	NG }	óго	óму	óм	ы́м
		N.	óе	N				
		F.	áя	ýю		óй		
	бѣл-	M.	ый	NG	ого, etc.			
	син-	M.	ий	NG }	его	ему	ем	им
		N.	ее	N				
		F.	яя	юю		ей		
	Ивáнов-	M.	—	NG }	а	у	ом	ым
		N.	о	N				
		F.	а	у		ой		
	рыб-	M.	ий	NG }	его	ему	ем	им
	рыбь-	N.	е	N				
		F.	я	ю		ей		
Ruth.	дóбр-	M.	ий	NG	ого	ому	ім	им
		N.	е/ее	N				
		F.	а/ая	у/ую	оï	ій		ою
	гýс-	MN.	ій/е				ім	ім
	гýсь-	MN.			ого	ому		
	гýс-	F.	я			ій		
	гýсь-	F.			оï			ою

PNV	A	GL	D	I	DNAV	GL	DI
ии	ыѣ				ая		
ая	N }	ы(и)хъ	ы(и)мъ	ы(и)ми	ѣи }	ою	ы(и)ма
ыѣ	N				ѣи		
ии	ѣѣ				яя		
яя	N }	и(и)хъ	и(и)мъ	и(и)ми	ии }	ею	и(и)ма
ѣѣ	N				ии		
ые	NG	ыхъ	ымъ	ыми			
ьіе	NG	ьіх	ьім	ьіми			
ие	NG	их	им	ими			
ы	NG	ых	ым	'ыми			
и	NG	их	им	ими			
}i/ii	NG	их	им	ими			
}i	NG	ix	im	imи			

The spelling of the Russian adjectival flexions is traditional and obscures some of the principal features. The nom. sg. masc. of the definite declension is revealed under the accent to be -*oj* ($<$ *ŭjĭ*), G*S*. -*ogo*. When unstressed these become [əj əvə], which are represented by M*R*. -*yj* -*ago* (the latter till 1917) out of deference to Old Bulgarian orthography. In older spellings stressed -*ago* is also found, and there are surnames in -áго (and -ых). Many speakers use the spelling-pronunciation for -кий, -гий, -хий. In the plural, the distinction *M*. -*ye*/N*F*. -*yja* (abolished in 1917) dates only from the eighteenth century and is purely orthographical, since both are pronounced [ɨjə]. In the sixteenth century there was only N*PMF*. -*ye*, corresponding to A*PM*. -*ye* and N*APF*. -*ye* $<$-*yě* (with the usual soft equivalents).

CSl.N*SM*. -*ŭjĭ*/*ĭjĭ* appears somewhat rarely in Old Russian as -*ŭi*/*ĭi:* умьрыи 'dead' 1215, тои 1220 = тъи 1270, Сынъ Божьи 'Son of God' 1144. These endings develop normally into -*oj*/*ej*. Old Bulgarian lengthened *ŭ* to *y* and *ĭ* to *i* before *j*, giving -*yi*/*ii;* this was the general usage in Old Russian spelling and has been retained, quite conventionally, in Modern Russian. In stressed positions -*oj*/*ej* gradually predominated after the fifteenth century.

Some uncontracted forms are found in Old Russian in -ыи/ии- (I*SMN*. GL*DIP*. D*ID*.). They have been shortened. The demonstrative declension has continued to exert a powerful influence upon that of the definite adjectives. G*SMN*. -*ogo* D. -*omu* L. -*om* are forms due to analogy of G. того D. тому L. том/-*ago* -* umu* -*ěm*, the natural results of contraction in these cases. This result was attained by the eleventh century, as may be seen from the spellings Златоустого 'of Chrysostom' тоужего/чоуждего 'of the stranger' славьньому 'to the famous' 1073. Dissyllabic forms are sometimes heard in the Moscow dialect and in folk-songs: во славноем городе во Киеве 'in the famous town of K.'.

The feminine singular has also been reshaped under the influence of the pronouns. The forms were CSl.G*SF*. -*yě* (in Russian and West Slavonic/OB. -*yję*) DL. -*ěji* I. -*ǫjǫ*, with the flexions of both the indefinite adjective and the suffixed pronoun visible. The hard demonstrative pronoun had G*S*. *toě* D. *toji* L. *tojǫ*. In Old Russian G*SF*. -*yě*/*oě* were concurrent; the latter became -*oj*, and so identical with DL. -*oji* $>$-*oj*. The intermediate forms are rare, but тоеи is found in 1663. It is also heard in the modern Moscow dialect occasionally, and in the North Great Russian folk-songs. In White Russian it is restricted to the pronoun, the adjective having the fully contracted ending. Apparently similar forms of the demonstrative in Ruthenian are merely coincidental; they are due to the analogy of the possessive personal pronouns. I*SF*. -*oju* has been assimilated to the three other cases in the modern period of Russian.

In the plural we have to note the use of the acc. masc. for the nom., though the cases were correctly distinguished in Old Russian.

In theory there is a complete nominal declension of the indefinite adjective, but it is little used in the literary language apart from the nom.: *SM.* нов 'new' *N.* -о *F.* -á *PMNF.* -ы/син-ь 'blue' -е -я -и, where it serves merely as predicate together with 'to be' and similar verbs. There are traces of other cases in stereotyped expressions, e.g: среди бела дня 'in broad daylight', and in popular language, e.g. он её за белу ручку 'he (took) her by her little white hand'. A strengthened *jer* or a fill-vowel may appear in the short form of the masculine: умён 'sensible' (< *umĭnŭ*), зол 'cross' (< *zŭlŭ*). The short form of the soft искренний 'sincere' is *M.* искренен *F.* искренна etc. Certain adjectives, including those in -ский and -енький have no short forms (though cf. place-names like Смоленск and the adverbs in -ски from the short instrumental plural), and the long forms of adjectives are often used in the predicate though short forms exist. With the long forms, 'how' and 'so' are expressed not by the adverbs как and так but by the adjectives какой and такой: она такая хорошенькая 'she is so pretty!' The indefinite declension of adjectival participles has also been lost, and the definite participles have become adjectives.

Possessive adjectives are formed from masculines by means of the suffix *-ov/ev* and from feminines by means of *-in*: попов 'priest's son', Parsons' Андреев 'Anderson' сестрин 'sister's' Царицын 'Empress's town' (now Stalingrad). The suffix *-in* is also used with masculines, and occasionally the suffix used is *-ič*: братнин 'brother's' Фомин/ Фомич 'Thompson'. Based on these are the Russian patronymics, which agree in gender with the baptismal name: Пётр Павлович 'Peter son of Paul', Анна Павловна 'Anna daughter of Paul'. They are definite by nature, and so do not require further definition by means of a demonstrative. In fact, however, they follow a mixed declension, in which some of the cases follow the definite declension (*SMN.* loc. instr., *SF.* gen. dat. loc., *PMNF.* gen. dat. loc. instr.).

Another group with mixed flexions is that formed from the names of animals: рыбий 'fish-' -ье -ья. They are not definite by nature, but they are analogous to adjectives formed from such common nouns as 'sister' 'brother'. The suffix used is *-ij-*, attached to the noun-stem, and followed by definite (soft) flexions: *SMN.* gen. рыб- ьего instr. -ьим *SF.* acc. -ью *P.* nom. -ьи gen. -ьих, etc.

In the long (attributive) form of comparative adjectives the *-š-* of the oblique cases has spread in Russian to the *MN*: новейший/OB. *novějǐ*. Such forms are declined like normal soft adjectives: *FN.* новейшая/OB. *novějišija;* similarly высший (with analogical *s* for *š* from the positive высокий/OB. *vysǐjǐ*) etc. In the modern language these forms tend to be used only in fixed phrases or in senses not strictly comparative, e.g.

вы́сший 'superior'; they are in fact superlatives rather than comparatives, and the comparative attributive is usually expressed by means of the word бо́лее 'more' with the positive. Russian also present comparatives of this type apparently based on the addition of -*ějš*- to gutturals: строг 'strict' строжа́йший 'strictest', высо́к 'high' высоча́йший 'highest', то́нок 'fine' тонча́йший 'finest', together with analogical formations like ближа́йший 'nearest' from бли́зок 'near', short comparative бли́же. Superlative: наилу́чший 'best' (literary), преосвяще́нный 'most reverend'; normally expressed by са́мый + positive or comparative: са́мый краси́вый 'most beautiful' са́мый лу́чший 'best'.

The short (predicative) form of the comparative has been reduced in Russian to the neuter -*e* -*ěje* (giving Russian -ee or -ей) for all genders and numbers: дом нове́е 'the house is newer' кни́га нове́е 'the book is newer'; this form is sometimes used attributively, e.g. краси́вей мужчи́ны нет 'there is no more handsome man'. The addition of -*e* produces changes in the stem of the type shown in section 70 (*a*) iii: ху́же 'worse' вы́ше 'higher', and also specifically Russian developments (many of them analogous): бога́че (/богате́йший) from бога́т 'rich', чи́ще(/чисте́йший) from чист 'clean', то́ньше from то́нок 'thin, fine', бо́льше 'greater, more' (and бо́лее 'more', adverb), сла́бже and глу́бже from слаб 'weak' глубо́к 'deep' (perhaps under the influence of доро́же 'dearer' стро́же 'stricter' etc.) and so on. The prefix по has a weakening effect: помоло́же 'a bit younger'.

The superlative of the short forms is usually expressed by adding the word всех 'of all': э́та кни́га лу́чше всех (lit. 'this book is better of all'). The adverbial superlatives наибо́лее 'most' наиме́нее 'least' are however in frequent use; e.g. наиме́нее краси́вая же́нщина 'the least beautiful woman'.

118A. *Accent.* There is no accent-shift in the positive declension of attributive adjectives, all cases of all genders and numbers being stressed as in the nom.sg.masc.; but shifts are common in the short (predicative) forms, both as compared with the stressed syllable of the corresponding attributive adjective and as regards the various genders and numbers of the short forms. The latter shifts resemble those occurring in the past tense, which is itself a short adjective in form (see section 108 A), and are mainly of two types. In one, the stress moves to the ending of the feminine, neuter and plural, e.g. широ́к 'wide' широка́ широко́ широки́; in the other only the feminine ending is stressed, e.g. (весёлый 'gay'/) ве́сел -о -ы весела́. There are also mixed types. In the comparative the ending is regularly stressed if preceded by one syllable only, e.g. честне́е 'more honourable' древне́йший 'most aged'/здоро́вее 'healthier' почте́ннейший 'most respected'.

119. *Definite Article.* Some Russian dialects, especially in the north, have sought to compensate for the loss of the demonstrative sense of the definite declension (which has become merely attributive, without the sense of definition) by developing an enclitic definite article. There was already a tendency to such things in Common Slavonic: OB. *tŭ sĭ* are often used as demonstrative enclitics with hardly any value beyond definition (OB. *rabo-tŭ* 'this/the slave' *dĭnĭ-sĭ* 'this day, today'). The development of MB. *-ăt -to -ta -te* is independent of NGtR. *-t*, but is no doubt the result of realizing the same latent possibilities of Slavonic; it should be noted that there is an affixed article in the adjacent Roumanian and Albanian. At first the article was fully declined and differed from the demonstrative only in the weakened meaning: смердъ тотъ орати лошадью тою 'the serf to plough with the horse'. At Šadrinsk (Perḿ) it is still fully declined, though with some aberrations from the demonstrative pattern: *MSN. mužik-ot* 'the peasant' (G. *-á-to* D. *-ú-tu* I. *-óm-to* PN. *-í-te* L. *-ách-tu*) *FSN. doróga-ta* 'the road' (A. *-u-tu* G. *-i-to* etc.). It is found before the noun in folk-songs: без бою, без драки, без того кровопролитья великого 'sans war, sans fight, sans great bloodshed.' In literary Russian and in most dialects the enclitic is reduced to *-ot/to*, though *-tu* (acc. fem.) survived to the eighteenth century; прокотъ (прок 'profit') occurs in Gribojedov's *Gore ot uma* (1823). Almost any part of speech may take *-to* as an emphatic particle in Modern Russian: я-то? 'me, you mean?' в том-то и дело 'that's just the point' выйти-то? 'go out, eh?'. It may be added that in a sentence like вот они пистолеты the pronoun amounts to a definite article: 'here are *the* pistols'.

120. *The Demonstrative Declension.* This includes relatives, interrogatives, demonstratives, and indefinite pronouns:

			SNV	A	G	D	L	I
OR.	т-	M.	ъ(тъ)	NG	ого	ому	омь	ѣмь
		N.	о	N				
		F.	а	у	оѣ	ои		ою
		M.	(и)	-ь/NG	іего	іему	іемь	имь
		N.	іе	N				
		F.	(я)	ю	іеѣ	іеи		іею
MidR.	т-	M.	отъ	NG	ого	ому	омъ	ѣмъ
		N.	о	N				
		F.	а	у	оѣ	ой		ою
	с-	M.	(сесь/ сій/сей)	NG	его	ему	емъ	ѣмъ
		F.	и/я	ію/ю	еѣ/ее/ѣе	ей		ею
MR.	к-		(кто)	огó	огó	омý	ом	ем
	ч-		(что)	(что)	егó	емý	ём	
	вс-	M.	весь	NG	егó	емý	ём	ем
		N.	ё	N				
		F.	я	ю		ей		
Ruth.	т-	M.	ой	NG	óго	óму	ім	ím
		N.	о/е	N				
		F.	а	у	óï	ій		óю
	к-		(хто)	огó	огó	омý	ім	им
	ч-		(що)	(що)				
	вс-	M.	весь	NG	éго	éму	ім	ім
		N.	е	N				
		F.	я	ю	éï	ій		éю

NV	A	GL	D	I	DNAV	GL	DI
и	ы	ѣхъ	ѣмъ	ѣми	а / ѣ / ѣ	ою	ѣма
а	а						
ы	ы						
(и)	ѣ	ихъ	имъ	ими	(я) / и / и	іею	има
я	я						
(ѣ)	ѣ						
ѣ	NG	ѣхъ	ѣмъ	ѣми			
ѣ/и/я	ѣ	ѣхъ/ихъ	ѣмъ	ѣми			
эт-и	NG	их	им	ими			
е	NG	ех	ем	éми			
i	NG	их	им	йми			
i	NG	ix	ім	ими			

The principal words of the hard declension of demonstratives, etc., are: тот 'that' э́тот 'this' он -ó -á 'he, it, she' (see section 121) кто 'who?' оди́н 'one' сам 'self'/soft: сей 'this' чей 'whose' что 'what?' весь 'all' мой твой свой наш ваш 'my, etc.' The accusative of самá is самоё (cf. её). For the use of сам with short ordinals, see section 117. Чей is declined like тре́тий: GSM. чье́го etc. The GF. всея́ in Всея́ Руси́ 'of all Russia' is the ChSl. equivalent of OB. *všeję. Other pronouns, like кото́рый 'who, which' не́который 'a certain' вся́кий 'each', follow the definite declension of adjectives. CSl. *kŭjĭ appears in the obsolescent кой 'which' and the derived не́кий 'a certain'. For ка́ждый 'each' see section 124.

The simpler demonstratives are also used as enclitic particles: *tŭ-tŭ* > тот (э́тот with epideictic prefix), *kŭ-to čĭ-to* > кто что, *sĭ-sĭ* > MidR. сесь; *tŭ-jĭ* > Ruth. той, *čĭ-jĭ* > чей (stem чь-), *sĭ-jĭ* > сей have the definite suffix. Ruth. той та/тáя то/тóе show suffixed and suffixless forms side by side. In Ruthenian the hard forms have strongly affected the soft ones: мій gen. мо́го нáшого чóго céго/сьóго. The hard instr. тем has caused the substitution of *e* for *i* in the soft чем/OR. чимь. Кто had instr. цѣмь (still attested as late as the 14th cent.), for which кѣмъ was also found, with restored *k* and hard *m* (1334), MR. кем. OB. *čĭ-to* has gen. *čĭ-so;* OR. нѣтъ ни чьсо же таино 'there is nothing hid'. As there was no parallel for the genitive ending *-so* the case was rebuilt upon the nominative: кто : когó : : что : чегó. But *čĭso* (substituted for the nom.) gave *čšo ššo ščo* Ruth. що (also in a number of NGtR. dialects), cf. P.Cz. *co*. The instrumental чем is used for 'than', and чем . . . тем . . . is used like English 'the (more) the (merrier)'. The genitive тогó is the 'er' of the hesitant speaker; in this sense it is sometimes spelt товó. The interrogative что is sometimes distinguished by an accent from the conjunction что 'that'. The genitive of ничтó 'nothing' is the celebrated ничегó, meaning 'all right, not bad, doesn't matter'. кто with a verb in the singular is frequently used as relative to a plural: всех тех, кто отка́зывается 'of all those who refuse'. The negative pronouns insert a preposition after the negative prefix: ни о кóм 'about no one'. Что (and чегó) often mean 'why'.

Indefinite pronouns and adjectives are formed by adding the neuter *-to:* чтó-то 'something', or by adding *li-bo:* чтó-либо 'anything (you like)', or a suffix -нибудь (*ni+bud́* imperative of быть) : чтó-нибудь 'anything', or lastly by prefixing кой (*kŭjĭ*): кóе-что 'something or other'. In some constructions the simple forms кто что чей (like the adverbs когдá 'when', etc.) are used in the indefinite sense.

FND. nom. acc. *tě* took the place of the old plural forms after the end of the thirteenth century: тѣ спасáються 'those are saved' 1282. In the fourteenth century *MNFP.* nom. acc. *-ě* was common to тъ оди́нъ онъ самъ; it is the source of Ruth. -*i* (воні/воні 'they' самі/самй alternate in that language). In modern literary Russian те все,[*] but otherwise the plural is in -*i* (чьи самй) or *MN.* -*i*/*F.* -*ě* (они/онѣ'), though the latter distinction has been abolished since 1917. The vowel *e* or *i* is carried through the cases of the plural so as to agree with the nom. pl. те : тех : : эти : этих. The forms in *i* were proper to soft stems, and represent an invasion of the hard declension by them. The interchangeability of *ě*/*i* is attested in old documents: всимъ 1328 (Moscow), своемъ 1397 (Kiev), своеми 1562. In some NGtR. dialects loc. моём instr. моим appear as *моём моём* (pl. *моёch моёmi*). On the other hand, many GtR. dialects, together with White Russian and Ruthenian, have loc. pl. -*ych* (Ruth. -их) on the analogy of adjectives: *tych odných samých.*

---

[*] Все is the one word in which the abolition of ѣ can lead to ambiguity. In many contexts it is not immediately apparent whether neut. sg. всё or pl. все is intended. Of late there has been a marked increase in the use of the diaeresis in this and other words; some modern texts indicate every case of *ё*. The old spelling also distinguished between міръ 'world' and миръ 'peace'.

121. *Personal Pronouns.* These are:

	SNV	A	G	DL	I	PNV
OR.	я(зъ)					
м-		я		и(D)		ы
мен-		е	е			
мън-				ѣ	ою	
н-						
в-						
т-	ы	я		и(D)		ы
себ/теб-	е	е		ѣ/е		
соб/тоб-				ѣ	ою	
в-						ы
MR.	я	меня́	мсня́	мне	мной	мы
(себ/соб-)	ты	тебя́	тебя́	тебе́	тобо́й/ою	вы
Ruth.	я	мене́	мене́	мені́/мині́	мно́ю	ми
	ти	тебе́	тебе́	тобі́	тобо́ю	ви

1. OB. *azŭ* 'I' is not often found in Old Russian. The loss of -*z* was presumably due to the effect of syntactical combinations on a monosyllable. The other cases have a different stem, which appears as *men/mn/mno-*. The nom. мы (L. *mēs*) perhaps takes its initial from the singular; its initial may have been originally **w*, as in the dual вѣ < **wē*. The enclitic forms (ADS. ADP.) are now encountered only in dialects, but AS. мя has no doubt influenced the GS. меня́/мене́.

2, and reflexive. The stem *tob-* is proper to the instrumental, but has spread to the dative-locative in Ruthenian. For -*e* we find -*ě* (gen. dat.) from the eleventh century onwards, thanks to the identity of these sounds and probably to the analogy of the noun declensions (L. -*ě*): менѣ 1056–57, тебѣ 1095. In some NGtR. dialects (as at Onega) -*i* takes the place of -*e*: сёби. The instrumental -*oju* has been shortened to -*oj* by weakening of the final vowel, as in nouns, demonstratives and adjectives. The dative of the reflexive pronoun is used idiomatically in such expressions as сидите себе́ 'just go on sitting', слу́шают да пьют себе́ 'they listen and just go on drinking'. Reciprocal relations, if not expressed by the reflexive, employ the word друг 'friend': друг дру́га 'one another', друг с дру́гом 'with one another', etc. It should be noted that мы с ва́ми, lit. 'we with you', means 'you and I'.

The oblique cases of 3 pers. он etc. are taken, as in other languages, from the demonstrative **jĭ* (gen. его́ dat. ему́ gen. pl. их etc.). After prepositions they prefix the *n* originally terminating the prepositions *sŭ(n) vŭ(n) kŭ(n)*: у него́ 'at his place' к ним 'to them'. The locative never appears without accompanying prepositions and so always presents this *n*: (о) нём, (в) ней, (на) них. The *n* does not appear when the pronoun stands for a possessive adjective: у него́/у его́ отца́ 'at his

A	GL	D	I	DNV	A	GL	DI
/асъ	асъ	ы/амъ	ами	ѣ	а	аю	ама

A	GL	D	I	DNV	A	GL	DI
ıs мы/насъ)				a	(as вѣ/ва)		
ас	нас	нам	нáми				
ıс	вас	вам	вáми				
ıac	нас	нам	нáми				
с.							

(pron.) place/at his (adj.) father's place'. The only form requiring comment is the gen. sg. fem.: OB. gen. *jeję* acc. *jǫ*. Corresponding to gen. *jeję* in East and West Slavonic was *jejě* (еѣ 1073), Ruth еï'. The modern form её [jıjó] appears to be due to the influence of masc. neut. eró [jıvó], and as eró was used for the accusative, even of neuters, её took over the functions of the acc. fem., and the Russian equivalent of *jǫ* disappeared. The spelling ея was used for the genitive till 1917 under Church Slavonic influence.

When the preposition по takes the dative of nouns it rather curiously takes the locative of the corresponding pronouns. Reflections of the short forms of the pronouns occur sporadically in colloquial speech.

(iii) INDECLINABLES

122. *Adverbs.** Many of the forms found in Old Bulgarian (see section 73) are absent in Russian, or only appear in that language as borrowings. From the neuter of a word corresponding to OB. *tolikŭ* 'so great' is derived, with shortening of the *i*, the adverb тóлько 'only'. A prefixed *s* (? preposition *sŭ*) gives стóлько 'so much'. From *kolikŭ* 'how great' is derived скóлько 'how much'. (This use of *s*- is only found in ESl.; cf. Ruth. скílько). Каκ 'how' and таκ 'so' appear to be the masculines *kakŭ takŭ* used analogically (OB. *kako tako*); таκ is also used for 'just, simply, in any case', and каκ ни means 'however (much,

*Modern Russian grammar distinguishes between adverbs and particles on the one hand and 'modal' or 'parenthetic' words and particles on the other; in some cases one and the same word may be used in either function, an example being the word 'definitely', which is used adverbially in *He definitely refused* and 'modally' in *He is definitely mad*. In the present work, modal words and particles are discussed under the more conventional heading of Adverbs and Particles.

etc.)'. Adverbs from adjectives have the o/e of the neuter (though not always the same stress as the neuter adjective; cf. Serbocroat): приятно 'pleasantly' крайне 'extremely', save for those in -ский, which end in -и (OB. -y, IP): политически 'politically'. Much use is made of the preposition по : по-новому 'in new style', по-английски 'in English, по-моему (/моему) 'in my opinion', почему 'why' (conjunction потому что 'because'), поэтому 'for this reason'; with comparatives: поскорее 'as fast as possible'. Instrumentals: весной 'in spring', утром 'in the morning', ночью 'at night', таким образом 'in such a fashion, so', etc. Здесь 'here' represents sĭ-dĕ-sĭ, and тут 'here' tu-to. The usual word for 'today' is сегодня, G. of сей день 'this day' and therefore pronounced [śivódńə]; the colloquial намедни 'the other day' represents the locative construction onomĭ dĭni; теперь 'now' derives from *to-pĭrv-; cf. Cz. teprv(e) and P. dopiero 'only' (used in the temporal sense of German erst). Other adverbs worthy of mention are иначе 'otherwise' (OB. inako); тотчас and сейчас 'at once' (час 'hour' originally meant 'time'; cf. Cz. čas); вчера 'yesterday' (OB. vĭčera; cf. večerŭ 'evening'); уже 'already' (OB. u-že ju-že; cf. L. jaŭ), which also appears colloquially in the forms уж and ужо, the latter meaning 'later on' or 'just wait till I get hold of you!'; еще 'still, yet', which is sometimes unaccented еще [jɪš':ə] and occurs in the curious expression ещё бы 'rather! not half! of course!'; пока 'for the time being', which is also used as the conjunction 'while' and (with a negative verb) 'till'; it seems to derive from a form поколя (cf. OB. koli 'how much, when'); куда 'whither' (OB. kǫdu kǫdě 'whence'), откуда 'whence', сюда 'hither'—but всюду 'everywhere', also везде (vĭsĭ-dě); домой 'home (-wards)' (see section 115), similarly долой 'down' (OR. доловь); прочь 'away' (OB. proči 'remainder'); очень 'very', the origin of which is wrapped in mystery; весьма 'quite' (OB. vĭsĭma); даже 'even' (OB. da-že ne 'before'); впрочем 'besides' (прочий 'other, remaining'; cf. прочь above); авось 'perhaps' (a-ovo-se) and небойсь 'I dare say' (не бойся 'fear not'), which occur together in the saying авось небойсь да как-нибудь 'I expect we shall manage somehow'; едва 'hardly' (OB. jedva); еле 'hardly' (<je-lě); чуть (чуть-чуть) 'almost, hardly' and ничуть 'not at all', from the infinitive čut (MR. чуять 'to sense, smell'); вряд(-ли) 'hardly' (ряд 'row, rank'); точь-в-точь 'exactly' (точка 'point, dot'); кругом 'round', an instrumental form of круг 'circle' with a different stress from the normal instrumental кругом; однажды 'once' etc. (see section 117); пожалуйста 'please' [see section 99 (a)]; вон 'out' (cf. вне 'outside'; it is not the same word as вон meaning 'lo'). Adverbial expressions include то и дело 'now and again', мало-по-малу 'little by little', только что 'just' (temporal), как раз 'just', а то 'otherwise, or else', как же! 'undoubtedly!', того (и) гляди 'before you know it', куда как 'ever so', cf. куда лучше 'ever so much better'.

123. *Prepositions and Prefixes.* Most of these occur both in their Russian and in their Old Bulgarian (Church Slavonic) form. They appear under different guises according to the treatment of the *jers;* e.g. в во (in some cases Church Slavonic) вн-ушйть 'suggest' (*vŭn uši* 'into the ears'); вз- вс- воз- вос- взо- from *vŭz(ŭ)*, reduced to в- in встать 'stand up' всáдник 'horseman'; чéрез/чрез. *Děla* is replaced by для 'for' from **dĭla* (lit. 'along of'; cf. дóлгий 'long', OB. *prodĭliti* 'prolong' etc.), with ,which are connected вóзле 'beside, by, near' (*vŭz-dĭl-*) and пóдле 'near' (*po-dĭl-*). In addition to the literary (Church Slavonic) мéжду are found colloquial меж and промéж (from **medj-;* cf. S. *měd*); the prefix appears as между (-нарóдный 'international'), меж (-зýбный 'interdental') and, in a few words, междо-, e.g., междоусóбие 'feud'. The latter form perhaps originates in this word, as a result of dissimilation (у-у $>$ о-у); a like dissimilation may have occurred in полоýмный 'half-witted', unless this word represents a Greek παλαβώμενος. Обо is used before certain monosyllables and in certain compounds: обо мне 'about me', обойтú 'to go around'; об is always used before vowels and occasionally before consonants: бúться об заклáд 'to bet'. Пере-/пре-, only the latter being used in the superlative sense (прекрáсный 'beautiful'). Пéред/пред. Роз-/раз- [see section 88(*b*)]. The non-nasal *on-* (see *vŭn,* section 74) occurs in онýча 'legging' (root *u-* 'put on footwear' in об-ýть etc.). Prefix вы- is used as well as из-. Compound prepositions are of two types: (i) вдоль 'along' (доль 'length'), вмéсто 'instead of' (мéсто 'place'), вокрýг 'round' (круг 'circle'), вопрекú 'in spite of' (ChSl.; OB. *prěkŭ* 'transverse, contrary'), впередú 'in front of' (cf. пéред), напрóтив 'opposite' (прóтив 'against'), óколо 'round' (Sl. *kolo* 'wheel'), позадú 'behind' (cf. за, зад 'back part'), сверх 'above' (верх 'top'); (ii) из-за 'from behind', из-под 'from under'. Пóсле 'after' represents *po-sĭ-lě* [see section 73(*d*)]. Мúмо 'past'; cf. минýть 'to pass'.

124. *Particles and Conjunctions. Interjections.* Several of the forms listed in section 75 do not appear in Russian; -*žde* occurs in (ChSl.) тóждество 'identity' (*tožde* 'idem'), and -*žĭdo* in кáждый 'each' (OB. *kŭ-žĭdo,* G. *kogo-žĭdo*). Ведь 'after all' has already been explained as deriving from the CSl. (OB.) *vědě* 'I know', and вишь (colloquial, also ишь) 'look!' as probably representing the athematic imperative of вúдеть 'see'. Вот 'see here/there, here/there is' represents, with prefixed *v* (cf. вóсемь), a form *o-to, o-* being an ablaut-form of the epideictic *e-* found in э́тот etc. (P. *ot, oto*); the more colloquial вон 'see there, there is' is a similarly prefixed *ono.* Да normally means 'yes'; it is also used in the sense of 'and, but' and to introduce imperatives; нет 'no, there is not' (in latter sense also нéту) represents **ně-tu* from **ne-(j)e-tu* 'is not here'. Éсли 'if' is from есть ли; more colloquial forms are колú (cf. OB. *koli* 'how much, when') and éжели.

For лишь 'but' cf. лишить 'to deprive' лишний 'superfluous'. Таки 'nevertheless' is frequently suffixed to some other word: я-таки 'I however' всётаки 'all the same'. Однако 'however'; cf. OB. *jedĭnače* 'yet'. Пусть 'let' (see section 104). Хоть хотя 'though, at least, at any rate, even'; present gerund of хотеть 'wish'. Чу 'hist!'; see section 99(b). Ну 'well', но 'but', connected etymologically with *now* and *new*. Пока 'while'; see section 122. The word разве, which in OB. (*razvě*) is a preposition meaning 'apart from', is used in Russian to introduce dubitative questions: разве он ушёл? 'do you really mean to say that he has gone away?' By itself it means 'really?'. Разве may be replaced by неужели (lit. 'not already eh?'), and colloquially by нешто (>не-уж-то). The -те of the second person plural, which we have already observed added to the first person plural imperative, also appears in полноте 'that will do' (полно 'full') нате 'there you are!' (на 'there!'). The emphatic же, which appears in the adverbs тоже and также 'also', is frequently reduced to -ж: чтож? 'what then?'. И 'and' often means 'even', and ни ('neither') 'not even'; не то . . . не то . . . is used for 'either . . . or . . .' and suggests uncertainty, не то что means 'let alone, much less', and не то чтоб 'not what you'd call . . .' (Как) будто means 'as if, as it were' (будь 'be'). Мало того is used for 'what is more', and мало того что for 'let alone that, not merely that'. Спасибо 'thank you' represents спаси Бог ('God save'). Значит, lit. '(it) means', is frequently used for 'therefore, and so, in other words, that is to say', and the pronoun это often means 'in this case, in such a case, you know'. Чего доброго means 'I shouldn't be surprised if'. The word бишь (= баешь, from баять 'to say') occurs in как бишь его (зовут)? 'now then, what's his name?' and то бишь 'it is, that is to say'. Стало-быть means 'consequently, and so', and благо 'seeing that'. The colloquial чай 'I expect' is a reduced form of the first person singular of the verb чаять 'to expect, hope for'. Reported speech is colloquially indicated by the particles мол (from молвить 'to say') and де (скать) from *dějati* (meaning in Old Bulgarian 'to put', but used elsewhere for 'to say', e.g. Slovene *dejáti*) and сказать 'to say'.

As regards the interjections, all that needs mentioning here is the way in which some of them have developed into other parts of speech (just as, conversely, other parts of speech have developed into interjections; cf. English *woe!*). From ax 'oh', for instance, are derived the verb ахать (pf. ахнуть) 'to say "oh"' and the adjective аховый 'surprising, no good whatever'; and the same interjection occurs in the adjectival phrase не ахти какой 'not so very wonderful' (lit. 'not oh to thee such a').

C. WORDS

125. *Russo-Slavonic.* During eight centuries the vehicle for cultured speech and expression was not Russian but Russo-Slavonic or, in its liturgical form, Church Slavonic. This was essentially the Old Bulgarian language, modified upon Russian soil by Russian speech-habits and settled as a convention, varied for different purposes. All religious works used it in its more absolute form. Works of travellers, such as the Daniel who visited Jerusalem, were not regarded as documents of culture, and were written in a language not far from the cultured vernacular. Chronicles occupied an intermediate position in their style. The chanceries also established norms for official use, incorporating a certain number of vernacular elements. Ordinary speech would no doubt be in the vernacular, but the speech of educated persons when speaking formally took on a Slavonic tinge; and there was a considerable range of subjects, including all those which transcended the daily routine of concrete experience, which could not be discussed without drawing upon this special vocabulary.

In round terms, about half the Russian lexicon of today is more or less Russo-Slavonic. The Romance elements in English and the Slavonic in Rumanian are, perhaps, somewhat more numerous; but they can be more easily distinguished. They belong to a different family of languages, whereas those which have been imported into Russian are cousins-german. They might have been replaced by Russian words, element for element, at the time of importation (a thing which could not have happened in English or Rumanian), but once settled they seem so natural that in some instances they can with difficulty be detected. They may, in fact, be formed on Russian soil, since the slightly alien elements of formation are associated in Russian minds with certain ranges of thought. They increase spontaneously as the style rises.

In the English parallel we find that the Latin of the Mediæval Church and culture was mediated to us through Norman-French in a form then more acceptable to our speech. Similarly, Greek theological terms were Slavicized by the Bulgarians before they passed into Russian. The Orthodox Church, unlike the Roman, did not insist on the use of a single liturgical language; nor, on the other hand, was there a Greek Renaissance comparable to the Latin Renaissance of the west, nor was Russia, at grips with the Tatars, able to share in such a renaissance. Russian, in consequence, does not show like English a second alien stratum succeeding the first. Our later borrowings were in much better Latinity; the Russians have only sought from Greek the technical terms of the most modern civilization, borrowing rather from cosmopolitan usage than from Hellas.

The relationship between the two dialects being as it were cousinly, it is not surprising to find a considerable group of words which are neither Russian nor Church Slavonic, but a compromise between the two. Roots of the one sort combine with trimmings of another: перебраниться 'quarrel'/оборона 'defence' is Russian in *pere-*/OB. *prě-*, but Church Slavonic in *bran-*; сотоварищ 'co-partner' has a Church Slavonic prefix, while вытрезвляться 'sober up' has a Church Slavonic root with a Russian prefix *vy-;* in здравый 'sound, sane' only the *z-* ($<sŭ$ by loss of vowel and assimilation) is Russian. The numerous prefixes and suffixes borrowed from Church Slavonic, and used with complete freedom today, have contributed to this result: *črez- pre- pred- raz- so- vo- voz-* in such words as собор 'cathedral'/сбор 'gathering' вопрос 'question' восход/всход 'ascent' чрезвычайный 'extraordinary'/через 'across'; verbal nouns in *-anie -enie*/R. *-ańe -eńe*, adjectives in *-nnyj -nnij*, participles in *-jaščij -uščij*/R. *-jačij -učij*, superlatives: делание 'deed' играющий 'playing', etc. While the effect of Church Slavonic is generally literary, these features appear in quite common words also: прежде 'before' сладкий 'sweet' время 'time' are the ordinary words for these very common concepts. In the declension of the adjective there are or have been Russo-Slavonic forms, such as N*S.* *-yj* G*S.* *-ago* (see section 119). In some case endings R.WSl. *-ě* corresponded to OB. *-ję*, for which the Russo-Slavonic equivalent was *-ja*. Hence G*SF.* моея душа was in use in the seventeenth century and even well into the eighteenth among cultured persons/R. моей души.

The absence of Russian full vocalism (R. *torot*/OB. *trat*) is a ready indication of alien influence. Church Slavonic roots include *blag- bran- breg- brem- chlad- chrabr- chran- drag- glav- grad- glas- kratk- mlad- mrav- plam- plen- prazd- slad- smrad- sram- sred- stran- straž- šlem- treb- trezv- vlad- vlas- vrag- vrat- vred- žreb- zlat- zrak-*, etc. They make doublets with Russian stems in such a manner that the simpler concept is expressed by the Russian form and some nuance by the Church Slavonic: голова 'head'/глава 'chapter, cupola, chief', ворота 'gate' (царские) врата 'gate of sanctuary', беременная 'pregnant'/бремя 'burden', ошеломить 'stun'/шлем 'helmet' (OR. шеломъ). The Russo-Slavonic word is more abstract, secondary, more generalized, more archaic, etc., than the purely Russian form. The nuance may be very fine: солод 'malt'/сладок 'sweet' shows generalization in the Russo-Slavonic, but only in so far as an adjective is more general than a noun.

Other signs of alien influence are the appearance of CSl. *ŭ/*ĭ* as *o*/*e* in weak position, the preservation of *é* before hard consonants (/R. *ë*) and the use of *šč* (for OB. *št*) *žd*/R. *č ž*. The former resulted from the practice of transcribing and reading liturgical books. It was the custom to transcribe the *jers* long after they had ceased to be pronounced in Old Bulgarian, and to read them in Russian (when not final) as *o/e*. Hence вопи́ть 'lament'/OR. впити, упова́ть 'trust' (P. *ufać* ⟨*upйvati*⟩), со́ты (pl.) 'honeycombs' (OB. sg. *sйtй*), мно́жество 'crowd' (P. *mnóstwo* ⟨*množistvo*⟩), and similar words, show signs of Russo-Slavonic. An interesting doublet is о́тчество 'patronymic/оте́чество 'fatherland' (⟨*otičistvo*). By conservation of *é* before hard consonants we identify the same influence upon не́бо 'sky'/нёбо 'palate', предме́т 'object', пеще́ра 'cave', перст 'finger'/оди́н как пёрст 'all alone', пе́кло 'burning pitch, hell', etc. We must not take into account, to the credit of Russo-Slavonic, those cases in which stressed *é* stood before an originally soft consonant which has now become hard: оте́ц 'father' ⟨*otici*, душе́вный 'sincere'(-*evinyji*),пе́рвый 'first'/OR. пьрьвыи. The third criterion is one which often expresses itself in doublets: ме́жду/OR. межу 'between', наде́жда/наде́жа 'hope' надёжный 'reliable', граждани́н/горожа́нин 'citizen', чу́ждый/чужо́й 'foreign', мощь/мочь 'strength', пеще́ра 'cave'/Пече́рский (monastery), неве́жда 'ignoramus'/неве́жа 'boor'.

Since Russian and Old Bulgarian agreed on most points the origin of many words is not to be demonstrated. It is possible that a good enough dictionary (which does not exist) might show when and under what circumstances each word came into circulation, and consequently how much it is indebted to the literary Russo-Slavonic tradition. For the present it is merely to be set down as probable that cultural words of long standing are likely to be Russo-Slavonic, even in the absence of external signs. On the other hand, there are examples in which the demonstration applies to the average and not to the individual. Among prefixes meaning 'out of' Russian has a preference for *vy-* and Old Bulgarian for *iz-*, though both belong to the common store; but it is impossible to say that вы́бить 'knock out'/изби́ть 'massacre' reflects a difference of dialect. *$\hat{O}rz$- is found in рост 'stature'/расти́ 'grow', and it is not more than plausible to attribute the difference to the intervention of Russo-Slavonic in the second.

126. *Turko-Tatar and other Loanwords.* The languages of the Turko-Tatar group are remarkably conservative. 'In the Turkish group', says J. Deny in *Les Langues du Monde*, 'only Yakut and Čuvašian appear aberrant. It follows that the forms of words of Common Turkish which we can reconstitute are remarkably like the forms of words of various dialects now spoken.' It is possible to make a distinction between the northern languages and the southern, of which latter Osmanli Turkish is the most important. The latter has profoundly affected Bulgarian and Serbocroat, but not Russian. The Russian translations have been with a number of northern dialects, such as those of the Pečenegs, Polovcy, Džagatais and above all the Golden Horde. One is largely prevented by the strong family

resemblance of this group of languages from seeking to define the
source of any particular word.

Within this class of borrowings it is convenient to include those
words for which Turko-Tatar languages were merely intermediaries.
Some were Greek, borrowed directly or through Persian. Persian
words express many of the most important cultural concepts available
to the Tatars; and as the Persians anticipated them in adopting the
Moslem religion it was through Persian that a large vocabulary of
Arabic terms found its way into Turkish. For the Mediæval Russians,
however, all this was Turko-Tatar; the Golden Horde filled the whole
Orient as they viewed it.

At an earlier time the Slavs had been in contact with Iranians upon
the steppe or in the White Russian plains. This had led to very ancient
borrowings (see section 2). At that time the eastern horizon was
composed of Aryans in the steppe and woodlands of South Russia and
Finns in the forests of the centre and north. The Tatars lay wholly
outside the world of the primitive Slavs. Between the fourth and sixth
centuries, however, a succession of Turanian tribes—Alans, Huns,
Avars (Обры)—crossed Southern Russia and were entangled in the
Great Migrations. As a result of this the oldest stratum of Turko-
Tatar loanwords is common to all Slavonic peoples: R. клобук 'cowl'
OB. *klobukŭ* P. *kłobuk* Cz. *klobouk* 'hat' S. *klòbûk* < TT. **kalbuk* T.
kalpak. In this form the word has suffered metathesis, though not of
the normal variety; when reborrowed later it did not suffer this change:
R. колпáк 'night-cap' MB. *kalpák*, cf. MGr. καλπάκι Magyar *kalpag*.
After the Slavonic peoples had divided, the Turanian migrations
continued—Bulgarians coming from the Volga into Moesia, Magyars
(but they were a Finno-Ugric people) advancing towards Hungary,
Pečenegs, Khazars and Polovcy into South Russia. Words then
borrowed had varying areas of diffusion: T. *san* 'appearance, honour'
> OB. *sanŭ* R. сан 'rank' приосáниваться 'assume a dignified air'. One
of the words borrowed in this period was лóшадь 'horse' Ruth. лошá
'colt' < TT. *alaşa*, which seems to have been brought by Vladimir
Monomach from his travels among the Vjatiči at the beginning of the
twelfth century. There was an important horse-market for the nomads
at Kiev. The bulk of the words which entered Russian probably did so
as a result of the dominion established over the steppe and open woodland by the Golden Horde. It is a record of the military superiority
of the nomads and of the unfamiliar way of life which they revealed to
the Slavs. Osmanli Turkish words have also entered Russian, but at a
much later date and in smaller numbers.

The oriental words borrowed by the Russians from the Turkish
tribes, whether original parts of their vocabulary or not, are generally
names of things: of animals and metals native to the east, terms

appropriate to nomad life, military and religious expressions, and some oddments referring to ships, measures and institutions.

Birds and animals: OR. крагуй 'sparrow-hawk' (TT. *karagu*) корга 'crow, hag' (T. *karga*) бёркут 'golden eagle' (TT. *burgut*) лошадь 'horse' (TT. *alaşa*) ишак 'mule' (T. *eşek* 'ass').

Trees and materials: карагач 'elm' (T. *kara ağaç* 'black tree') сабур 'aloes' (TT. *sabr* from Arab.) изюм 'raisins' (T. *üzüm*) OR. харалуг 'steel' (T. *karalık* 'blackness') булат 'Damascene steel, sword' (from Pers. *pūlād*) алтын 'three copecks' (T. *altın* 'gold') дёньга 'coin' pl. дёньги 'money' (T. *damga;* a doublet is тамга 'stamp' from which is derived таможня 'customs-house') жёмчуг 'pearl' (T. *inci*, perhaps of Chinese origin) изумруд 'emerald' (T. *zümrüt*) нефть 'naphtha' (T. *neft*, from Greek) алмаз 'diamond' (T. *elmas*, from Greek ἀδάμας).

Nomad life and customs: казак 'Cossack' (T. *kazak*) кочевать 'lead a nomad life' (T. *göçmek*) хан/хаган 'khan' орда 'horde' (T. *ordu*) юрта 'yurt' (T. *yurt*) сарай 'shed' (T. *saray*) ям 'post-house' (TT. *yam;* adj. ямской) башмак 'shoe' (T. *başmak*) кафтан 'long coat' (T. *kaftan*) тюльпан 'tulip' (Pers. *dulbend* 'turban') утюг 'flat-iron' (T. *ütü*) чекан 'stamp, die' (TT. *çakan*) арбуз 'watermelon' (T. *karpuz*) кукуруза 'maize' (T. *kokoroz*, a word of mysterious origin) буза 'buckwheat beer' (T. *boza*).

Military: кинжал 'dagger' (T. *hançer*, from Arab.) ятаган 'yataghan' (T. *yatağan*) богатырь 'warrior, hero' (Pers. *bahadur*) караул 'sentry' (T. *karakol*) гайдамак 'bandit' (T. *haydamak*).

Religious: бусурман/мусульманин 'Moslem' арап 'negro, Moor' калёка 'beggar, cripple' (?TT. *kalak*).

Colours: карий 'brown' (T. *kara* 'black') бурый 'chestnut' (TT. *bur*) алый 'bright red' (T. *al*).

Musical: (Ruth.) кобза 'eight-stringed guitar' (T. *kopuz*) дудка 'reed pipe' (?T. *düdük;* the word may be anomatopœic).

Measure: аршин 'ell' (T. *arşın*).

The Ukrainian peoples of the steppe were not released from nomad and Turkish dominion until the eighteenth century was well advanced. They have, consequently, a number of loanwords not found in Great Russian. Among them the most celebrated is *caviar* (Ruth. кав'яр), which has become universal.

There are later, specifically Osmanli, loanwords also: янычар бей паша башибазук фирман диван каюк/кайк сераль etc. (T. *yeniçeri bey paşa başıbozuk ferman divan kayık saray*, the last word giving the doublet сарай listed above), which are common European currency.[*]

---

[*] F. Miklosich, *Die türkische Elemente in den südost- und osteuropäischen Sprachen* (Vienna, 1884); K. Lokotsch, *Etymologisches Wörterbuch der europäischen Wörter orientalischen Ursprungs* (Heidelberg, 1927).

The word балбе́с 'dolt' and the бельме́с occurring in ни бельме́са не смы́слит 'he doesn't understand a thing' represent TT. variants of the same word (T. *bilmez* 'ignorant').

Among borrowings from East European languages are: (from *Finnish*) морж 'walrus' (*mursu*, whence perhaps English *morse*); (from *Hungarian*) ку́чма 'cap with flaps' (*kucsma*); (from *Lithuanian*) валáндаться 'to slack' (*valandà* 'hour'), пáкля 'tow' (*pãkulos*); from *Polish*) ве́нзель 'woven monogram' (*węzeł* 'knot' = R. у́зел), венге́рский 'Hungarian' (*Węgry* = OR. Угре, whence the *Ugro-* in *Ugro-Finnish*) and possibly, though incredibly, вóдка (*wódka*). Curious borrowings from the Classical languages are: куроле́сить 'to play pranks' (from the *Kyrie eleison* in the church-service), ерундá 'nonsense (Latin *gerundium*) and колбасá 'sausage' (? Hebrew *kol-basar* 'every sort of meat'; there are similar words in other Slavonic languages). Other words from Greek are Росси́я 'Russia' (Ρωσσία), кровáть 'bed' (κραββάτιον), кáторга 'penal servitude' (κάτεργον), кит 'whale' (κῆτος), ле́нта 'ribbon' (λέντιον); from Latin оце́т 'vinegar' (*acetus*, while у́ксус 'vinegar' is from Greek ὄξος), индю́к 'turkey' (*indicus*), колядá 'Christmas and New Year festivals' (*calendæ*) and (*via* Germanic) котёл 'cauldron' (*catillus*), ре́дька 'radish' (*radicem*), тюрьмá 'prison' (P. *turma* 'dungeon' Germ. *Turm*, Latin *turris*). The only borrowings from Celtic appear to be слугá 'servant' and perhaps скок 'leap'.

Among the less obvious borrowings from other European languages are: (from *German*) шля́па 'hat' (*Schlapphut*), ве́ер 'fan' (*Fächer*, but influenced by ве́ять 'to waft'), рыдвáн' sort of carriage' (P. *rydwan* from *Reitwagen*), арáпник 'whip' (P. *harapnik* from *herab*), ефре́йтор 'corporal' (*Gefreiter*), эфе́с 'hilt' (*Gefäss*), верстáк 'joiner's bench' (*Werkstatt*), винт 'screw' (P. *gwint* 'worm of screw' from *Gewinde*, popularly associated no doubt with вить 'to screw'), крахмáл 'starch' (P. *krochmal*, from *Kraftmehl*), бунт 'insurrection' (P. *bunt*, from *Bund*), таре́лка 'plate' (P. *talerz*, from *Teller*); (from *Dutch*) трюм 'ship's hold' (*'t Ruim*, complete with definite article), руль 'rudder' (*roer*, with dissimilation of liquids), дюйм 'inch' (*duim* 'thumb'), зóнтик 'umbrella, parasol' (*zonnedek;* a back-formation is зонт); (from *English*) ми́чман (*midshipman*), пиджáк 'jacket' (*pea-jacket*) гóндек (*gundeck*), вокзáл 'railway-station' (ultimately from *Vauxhall*), аврáл 'all hands on deck' (*over all*), френч 'burberry' (Lord *French*), стэк 'riding crop' (*stick*), вере́йка (*wherry*), and there is an intriguing theory that дёшев 'cheap' (long form дешёвый) derives from an English *dog-cheap;* (from *French*) сюртýк 'frock-coat' (*surtout*), куря́житься 'to swagger, bluster' (*courage*), блáнжевый 'flesh-coloured' (*blanche*), шине́ль 'overcoat' (*chenille* 'sort of dressing-gown') лафе́т 'gun-carriage' (Germ. *Laffette*, from *l'affût*); (from *Italian*) лаж 'agio' (French *l'agio*, from *aggio*), картóфель 'potato' (Germ. *Kartoffel*, from *tartufola*); (from *Spanish*) ломберный стол 'card-table' (French *l'hombre* 'a card game' from *hombre* 'man'), енóт 'raccoon' (*gineta*, from Arabic); from *Portuguese* comes perhaps апóрт 'sort of apple' (*?Oporto*).

127. *Word-formation.* The suffixes set forth in section 78 are well represented in Russian, either in the native form or in borrowings from Old Bulgarian or both. Few points require noting. The suffix -*ěne* appears in Russian in its analogical form -*jane* (славя́не 'Slavs'). -*ěnǔ* appears as -ян(ный), e.g. деревя́нный 'wooden' (OB. *drěvěnyjǐ*), see section 86. -*ežǐ* figures in native words as -ёж (падёж 'murrain'), in borrowings as -еж (падéж 'grammatical case'); both words from *pad*- 'fall'. Except in the word дитя́ 'child' the diminutive ending -*ę* is lengthened in the singular to -*en-ǔkǔ* (as though from an *en*-stem): котёнок 'kitten' G*S*. котёнка/NVAP. котя́та (<-*ęta;* the old forms of the singular are found in White Russian and Ruthenian, but cf. Ruthenian names in -енко). -*ište*, used as in OB. in учи́лище 'school' (presumably borrowed), is also used as an augmentative (кулачи́ще, from кула́к 'fist'). -*ištǐ* in its Russian form -ич gives patronymics: Петро́вич 'son of Peter' Ива́нович 'son of John'. (Surnames in -ович -евич are usually from Polish and are accordingly stressed on the penultimate.) -*ǐje* (-*ije*) gives -ие in borrowed and -ье in native Russian words. -*ǐji* appears as -ья (судья́ 'judge'); -*yńi* as -ыня -иня (боги́ня 'goddess'). Some feminines are formed with the suffix -иха; e.g. купчи́ха 'merchant's wife' from купéц; others with the ending -(ь)ша; e.g., генера́льша 'general's wife', профéссорша 'professor's wife'. The short form of the adjective in -*ǐskǔ* gives the numerous place-names in -ск.

Russian is notable for its use of augmentatives and diminutives, as such or in an affectionate, depreciatory or ironical sense. Among the suffixes may be mentioned -ик : дóмик 'little house', -чик (from first palatalization of the *-*ǐk*- giving -*ǐčǐ*+-*ǐkǔ*): голу́бчик 'dear' from гóлубь 'pigeon', -ок (from -*ǔkǔ*): лесóк 'little wood', -ек (from -*ǐkǔ*): конёк 'little horse', лесóчек, double diminutive of лес 'wood' from лесóк by first palatalization, -ка (from -*ǐk-a*): крова́тка 'small bed' from крова́ть, -очка (from -*ǔk-ǐk-a*): Ни́ночка 'little Nina', -ко (from -*ǐk-o*): я́блочко by first palatalization from я́блоко 'apple', -шко: окóшко 'little window' (apparently based on óко 'eye'; 'window' is the derived окнó), double diminutive окóшечко; -це/-цо (from -*ǐce*): зéркальце 'small mirror' from зéркало, -ышко: пёрышко 'small feather' from перó, -ашка: старика́шка 'nasty old man' from стари́к 'old man', -ишка/-ишко: пальти́шко 'shabby old overcoat' from пальтó (French *paletot*), -ище: кулачи́ще 'big fist', -уха: стару́ха 'old woman', -ен(ь)ка: бабёнка 'peasant woman' from ба́ба, Ка́тенька 'Katie' from Ка́тя (itself a diminutive), -уша: Лизу́ша 'Lizzie' from Ли́за,

-юша: Олю́ша from Óля, dim. of Óльга, -ушка: ба́бушка 'grand-
mother', -юшка: дя́дюшка from дя́дя 'uncle'.

The diminutive forms of Christian names present a high degree of
mutilation and abbreviation; e.g. Cáша from Алекса́ндр, Кóля from
Никола́й.

Diminutives in -ище and -ишко of masculine nouns retain their
masculine gender; e.g. кулачи́ще above (from кула́к 'fist'), уе́здный
городи́шко 'a wretched little district capital'.

D. STYLE

128. *The Slavonic Sentence.* The order of words in a Slavonic
sentence was entirely free. In the principal clause that word went first
upon which the speaker's mind was dwelling particularly. A great deal
of our material is narrative, and therefore the verb (the active element)
is mostly to be found leading the sentence: OB. *glagolaaše bo emu:
izidi, duše nečistyj* 'for he said to him, Depart, unclean spirit'. The
subject often followed the verb. In subordinate sentences, however,
the conjunction or relative of subordination headed the sentence; the
verb either followed the opening word or was delayed until the end of
the sentence. A dative generally preceded an accusative; the attributive genitive preceded, and the partitive followed, its noun, and demonstratives might precede or follow. A considerable use was made of
enclitics: OB. *že bo li* and oblique cases of the personal pronouns.

The linking of sentences was loose, in the manner called paratactic
(exemplified by Homer). The following verses of St. Mark v. will help
to define this manner:

2. *i izlězŭšju že emu is korablja, abie sŭrěte i otŭ grobŭ člověkŭ duchomĭ nečistomĭ, 3. iže žilište iměaše vŭ groběchŭ, i ni žeľeznomĭ ožemĭ ego niktože ne mogaaše ego sŭvęzati . . . 9. i vŭprašaaše i: kako ti estŭ imę; i glagola emu: leǵeonŭ mĭně imę estŭ, jako mnozi esmŭ.*	2. καὶ ἐξελθόντος αὐτοῦ ἐκ τοῦ πλοιοῦ εὐθέως ἀπήντησεν αὐτῷ ἐκ τῶν μνημείων ἄνθρωπος ἐν πνεύματι ἀκαρθήτῳ, 3. ὃς τήν κατοίκησιν εἶχεν ἐν τοῖς μνήμασι, καὶ οὐδὲ ἀλύσει οὐκέτι οὐδεὶς ἠδύνατο αὐτὸν δῆσαι . . . 9. καὶ ἐπηρώτα αὐτόν, Τί σοι ὄνομα; καὶ λέγει αὐτῷ, Λεγεὼν ὄνομά μοι, ὅτι πολλοί ἐσμεν.

The Greek text shows that this is a translator's style: each word and
turn is rendered by a corresponding word and turn in the same place.
Yet the translator keeps to his own idiom. He renders the genitive
absolute by a Slavonic dative absolute in verse 2, and uses an instrumental for Gk. prep.+dative in the same. In the Greek the clauses are
mostly principal. The Slavonic translator follows this usage not
merely because it is in the original, but because it corresponds to the
genius of his own tongue. The relative clause in verse 3 is less

subordinated than in the Greek. OB. *iže* was still recognizably a demonstrative, and its oblique cases have survived as the third personal pronoun of the modern languages. As in Homer, it admits of translation 'who/he, indeed', whereas Hellenic ὅς was purely relative 'who'. When compelled to subordinate a phrase, the Slavonic translator relied on his declined participles, as:

4. *za nje emu mnogo kraty pǫty i* *oži železny sŭvezanu sǫštju prě-* *trĭzaachǫ sę otŭ njego oža želě-* *znaa i pǫta sŭkrušaachǫ sę.*

4. διὰ τὸ αὐτὸν πολλάκις πέδαις καὶ ἁλύσεσι δεδέσθαι, καὶ διεσπάσθαι ὑπ' αὐτοῦ τὰς ἁλύσεις καὶ τὰς πέδας συντετρίφθαι.

Lit.: 'For this (reason)—he many times with fetters and iron bonds being bound (*dat. abs.*)—there were broken from him the iron bonds and the fetters were shattered.'

The absolute construction allowed the subordination of one clause, but the other two (governed in Greek by the same conjunction) had to become principal.

The verses quoted illustrate the principles of word-order. In the ninth verse the verb comes first (apart from the conjunction) in the two narrative clauses. In the interrogation, *kako* 'what?' (lit. 'how?') comes first, and the noun is postponed to the end of the sentence; but in the reply the essential word *legeonŭ* 'Legion' is announced at once. Similarly, in the second half of verse 3: 'and no man could bind him, no, not with chains' is rendered 'and not even with iron bonds (him) anyone could him bind', so that the necessary emphasis is secured by placing 'iron bonds' early. In this the Slavonic translator was following the Greek word for word, but it was not the less appropriate to his own style, which required him to announce his concepts in the order of their interest to him. The one caveat which must be entered is, perhaps, that the task of coping with a highly organized tongue like Hellenistic Greek was beyond the native resources of Old Bulgarian, particularly in the matter of subordination, and that the translators may have used their participles with more ingenuity than would be found in the colloquial.

129. *Kievite Prose.* It was these resources that Russian writers inherited when they began to frame Russian literature. The Russian vernacular differed, however, in having already lost the feeling for declined participles: идущи 'going' is found in 1073 with a masc. sg. subject; идуще (*sic*) же ему въспять 'as he was going back' (14th cent.) (OB. *idǫštu*) is a defective dative absolute. Russian writers could not indulge in participial constructions without artificiality, and consequently tend to write more paratactically even than the Bulgarian translators. It is the easier to do because their material is suited to simple narrative, with a predominant position allotted to finite verbs,

and much direct speech. This is exemplified by the Chronicle formerly attributed to Nestor, which gives the historical traditions of Kiev to the year 1118. It exists in two fourteenth-century forms: *Povĕsť vremennych lĕt* and the *Načalnaja lĕtopiś* (Laurentian MS. 1377). The relatively late date of the manuscripts prevents us from drawing too precise inferences from this work; but it is legitimate to note that a simple narrative style in a disciplined language had been evolved in the service of the Rurikid princes. The authors suppress their own personality; they compose annals in which, generally, each year is complete in itself, so that the more important ones form historiettes, as in the *Anglo-Saxon Chronicle*, which are told with vigour, pith, and dramatic force. The *Poučenie Vladimira Monomacha* ('Instructions of V.M.') (c. 1110) is in the same style; but it is more hortatory, and reveals a strong personality. The *Choždenie igumena Daniila v svjatuju zemlju* (1106–8) ('Abbot Daniel's journey to the Holy Land') is written in a yet simpler manner, since books of travel were not regarded as literature. It may be taken as a specimen of the speech of the educated classes with its leanings toward Church Slavonic. The style includes expressions of confession and exhortation suited to the author's religious profession, together with evidence of a capacity for direct observation and simple statement (e.g.: 'Saved by the will of God, I went to the holy city of Jerusalem and saw the whole land of Galilee and the holy places'). A mild sectarian malice enlivens his remarks concerning the Latin clergy, who took first place in the ceremonies at Jerusalem.

These and other works in prose exemplify the literary achievement of Kiev, apart from verse. They show that a satisfactory medium of expression had been found for the matters then requiring record; the colloquial had been given form, and the alien elements had been assimilated and assigned their place. Had society remained undisturbed, Russian prose would have passed through the same phases as that of France or England, advancing at the same time according as more matter was drawn into writing and more use was made of classical resources (in this case Greek). The ruin of Kiev in 1240, first by internal dissensions and then by Tatar conquest, drove literature into the monasteries, where the liturgy tended to petrify Church Slavonic, while the chanceries used an official language for business purposes only. The two styles thus drew more and more apart; that of literature became a deadening convention. There is no such dichotomy apparent in the Kievite documents, in which the Church Slavonic manner must have corresponded with normal cultured expression.

130. *Prince Igor's Expedition* (*Slovo o polku Igorevĕ*). Until 1940 it might have been said that this celebrated work was accepted by almost all competent critics as a unique survival of the secular poetry of Kiev.

The manuscript was discovered in 1795, three years after the Tmutarakań stone (of alleged date 1068), and was carefully edited under the patronage of Count Musin-Puškin, who had already consecrated a memoire to the affairs of the principality of Tmutarakań (1794). The Russian power was then spreading into the Tamań promontory, beyond the Sea of Azov. Karamzin took a copy of the manuscript, and it was examined by Malinovskij before it was lost in the Great Fire of Moscow. Among the scholars who have accepted the work as genuine we may cite Sreznevskij, Peretc and Speranskij. There have been doubters from the time of the discovery, but they have been overwhelmed by the weight of authority and (it must be said) by the conviction generated by the brilliance of the poem itself. A. Mazon's Le Slovo d'Igor (Paris, 1940), however, has opened the whole question afresh and, in default of the original manuscript, proof of genuineness has become exceedingly difficult.* The authenticity of the Tmutarakań stone is no longer accepted, thanks to the unfavourable testimony of epigraphists. That of the Slovo is associated with it by the circumstances of the discovery, and by the prominence given to Tmutarakań in the poem.

Loss of the manuscript is a first obstacle to certainty upon this point. Another is the uniqueness of the Slovo in Kievite literature. It is the only source for many words and turns of phrase, mythological conceptions and stylistic devices, for which the predominantly clerical literature of Old Russia provides no parallel. This is as things should be if the Slovo were indeed the sole survivor of a brilliant lost literature of heroic poems; but it is also as things would be if the Slovo were a pastiche. Its only peer is the Muscovite Zadonščina, which celebrates the encounter of the Russians and Tatars on the field of Kulikovo in 1380. The verbal similarity of the two pieces is such that one or the other must be a plagiarism. Those who hold that the Slovo is authentic complain that the Zadonščina uses the language and situations of the older poem without skill or taste. But the manuscript history of the Zadonščina is well attested. The oldest form is preserved from the fifteenth century, and there are versions from the sixteenth and seventeenth centuries. The language of the Slovo is not exactly that of any surviving manuscript of the Zadonščina, but it resembles very closely that of the sixteenth-century MS. 2060 of the Moscow Historical Museum. There are other testimonies to the narrative of Kulikovo, but the Slovo remained completely unnoticed until its

* Mazon advances the theory that the Slovo was an eighteenth-century forgery. See Slavonic Review, xxiv, No. 63. S. P. Obnorskij's detailed account of its linguistic state (Očerki po istorii russkogo literaturnogo jazyka, Moscow, 1946) presumes the authenticity of the poem. Much depends on a sentence in an Apostle (Acts and Epistles) of 1307, which might be taken from the poem, or vice versa.

brusque discovery in the last years of the eighteenth century. Upon the charge of plagiarism, therefore, the onus of proof lies upon the partisans of the *Slovo*.

The discoverers assigned to their manuscript a tentative date in the sixteenth, or late fifteenth, century. Since *č/c* and *š/s* are confused (лучи русиць сморци сыновча чепъ шизый), editors were compelled to postulate an intervening redaction (14th or 13th century) made at or near Pskov. The simplification of the group -*vl*- to -*l*- is another northern feature of the language. The list of princes could hardly have been completed before the end of the first quarter of the thirteenth century, though the author speaks as if Igoŕ (d. 1202) were still alive. No specifically Kievite dialect features have been identified.

Russian and Slavonic forms are found side by side, with some preference for the Slavonic equivalents: славію/соловію 'nightingale' вратъ/ворота 'doors' забралѣ/заборолѣ 'visor' преградиша/прегородиша 'they impeded' болотомъ 'marsh'. The *jers* are confused in мъгла 'mist' (Gk. ὀμιχλή). They are generally retained in stressed positions, but *o/e* are also found. *Ri* has hardened to *ry*, but *k* remains a wholly velar consonant which cannot be set before *i*: рыскати 'run about'; кыкати 'clamour' Кыевѣ 'at Kiev'. The dual is used for наю 'of us two' соколома 'with two falcons' мужаимѣся 'let us two show bravery', and the aorist and imperfect used for aorist are frequently in evidence: успе 'slept' рече 'said' бѣ/бяшетъ 'was' рокотаху 'thundered'. The ethic and possessive datives and the instrumental of comparison are also used.

The *Slovo* is commonly printed as prose and described as if it were such. But it has a marked accentual rhythm, and the clauses run parallel. They can often be arranged so as to show lines of three (and sometimes two or four) accents. It is not the rhythm of the North Russian heroic folk-songs (*bylíny*) which are devoted to the exploits of Kievite heroes of earlier date than Igoŕ. Their lines are longer, and the prosodic accentuation is less marked. They are, on the other hand, as Speranskij has shown, regularized by their melodies. It is to be noted, in view of some other suggested parallels, that Macpherson's *Ossian* is in strongly accented prose, with a basis in the English ballad metre. Those who maintain the authenticity of the *Slovo* may find in its uniqueness a justification for its isolated prosodic technique.

The author's style is rapid, forceful and brilliant. No scepticism can diminish the credit of his creative achievement, beside which the phrases of the *Zadonščina* seem so jejune. The author uses the Homeric epithet with mastery when speaking of the 'eight-thoughted' Jaroslav, and he is almost Pindaric when he uses 'six-winged' as an equation for three falcons. Heroic periphrase is used in 'Dažbog's child' (for Igoŕ), and Vsevolod is regularly introduced by the epithet

буй туръ or яръ туръ 'the valiant (or fiery) aurochs'. The *editio princeps*
explains the first epithet as equivalent to богатырь 'hero'. Powerfully
constructed phrases are devised to echo the crash and fury of
action, and alliterations give firmness to the rhythm. The use of the
inner object, the doubling of words that signify action, and parallelism
enrich his style. The headlong construction of the poem itself, sug-
gesting the inspiration of a rhapsode, helps to win the reader's assent.
The first editors remarked with complaisance that this poem had come
to prove that the Russian heroes of olden time had, like those of
Macpherson, their *bards*. In this remark sceptical critics read an
acknowledgement of one of the sources of this poet's inspiration. His
apostrophes to various heroes and rivers, his use of lyres that play by
themselves, and his accumulation of misty omens and images resemble
the style of Ossian, while (it is claimed) some epithets can be justified
from *bylíny* which were in process of collection in the latter half of the
eighteenth century. A stylistic matter of particular importance is his
criticism of the old poet Bojan for his use of kennings and stereotyped
phrases. Bojan is named also in the *Zadonščina*, and it is hard to resist
the evidence that the citations in the *Slovo* are from that work. That
poet's name is South Slavonic. He might have immigrated into Russia
in Kievite times, but it is also possible he was one of the many South
Slavs who left the Balkans in the fourteenth and fifteenth centuries
under the pressure of the Turkish victories.

The doubt concerning the authenticity of the *Slovo* is not such as to
diminish its worth as creative literature or its influence in literary
history (since that was only felt after Musin-Puškin's time). But it
prevents us from citing the *Slovo* as a sample of a lost heroic literature,
and until it is removed there can be no credence given to the numerous
scholarly and ingenious emendations and interpretations which have
been added to those of the *editio princeps*.

MIDDLE RUSSIAN (1500–1700)

131. *The Chancery Styles*. In preceding paragraphs the history of
Russian sounds and forms has been carried down to modern times for
the sake of continuity of exposition. It is now fitting, however, to call a
halt and to survey Middle Russian, the language of the princes of
Muscovy. The sixteenth century was, in Russia as in other parts of
Europe, an age of energetic changes which were reflected in the
language also. By the end of the fifteenth century the Muscovite
princes had rounded off their domain by the reduction of Great
Novgorod (1478) and the acquisition of its vast, indefinite hinterland
in the dense conifer forests that stretched from Archangel to Perm and
the Urals. So Novgorod was added to Vladimir, Suzdal, Rostov, Tver,
which were Muscovite domain in the fourteenth century, and to

Jaroslavĺ, Rostov, Vjatka, Pskov, Rjazań and Smolensk; the series of annexations concluded with the capture of Novgorod Seversk in 1523. Russia had become a State. In the latter half of the century this new State hurled itself upon its old oppressors in the east and south-east. Ivan IV's capture of Kazań in 1552 was rapidly followed by the seizure of Astrakhan in 1556, and that by the Cossack Ermak's conquest of the original Siberia, the Tobol Valley, in 1581. What the discovery of the New World was to Spain, the opening of Siberia was to Russia—a broad outlet for adventure. Russia differed from Western Europe, however, in enjoying at this time no humanistic renaissance. The Greeks who fled from Byzantium brought nothing of their classical culture to the land civilized by the Greek Church. There is no such flowering of all the arts, including the art of polite living, as accompanied the similar explosion of economic and State-building energy in the west.

The concept of the State had its counterpart in language. For use in the Muscovite chancery there was built up an official style (прика́зный язы́к), which was thoroughly nationalistic in its applications. It was not literary, nor unified beyond the needs of official business. This absence of second intention allowed it to reflect more accurately the speech-habits of the time. Legal documents embodying arguments and judgments record with accuracy the statements actually made in court. A party declares: 'He said anything that came into his head' (что ему вѣтръ нанесъ на ротъ, то говорилъ 'what the wind brought to his mouth, that he said' 1525), and the vivid colloquialism is a guarantee of the faithfulness of the whole record. There is no trace of Church Slavonic in such pieces. There is no aorist or imperfect. The perfect is found as much without auxiliary as with it, especially in the third person; for the other persons either the auxiliary or a pronoun might appear: язъ взялъ 'I took'/есми зжогъ 'I burned' купили есмя 'we bought'. The active participles had become gerunds. The infinitive was in -ti, but with an evident tendency to contract: собрати и молвить 'to gather and discuss'. Hardening was more frankly admitted than in the modern orthography: (з)жог/MR. жёг 'burned', вышолъ/MR. вышел 'went out', дѣлаешъ/будешь (2S.).

In its nominal flexions this sixteenth-century Russian had reached a definite form, but not that of the present day. The i- a- o-declensions formed three distinct patterns, and there had not yet occurred the invasion of all oblique cases of the plural by a-flexions. The details may be studied in the paradigms already offered. The examples of Middle Russian all correspond to the period from 1500 to 1550, which was one of relative calm and consolidation. There were vacillations in Middle as in Modern Russian. The u-declension was still recognizable, at least in the gen. sg.; but in the loc. voc. sg. and nom. pl. there was a law for each word. Masculine *i*-stems retained their old forms in the plural, though their singulars had already passed to *jo*. The record was still incomplete: ка́мень 'stone' had G*S*. камени/камня. Distinction of gender had been erased from the plural, and in the singular gender had been made to conform very closely with declension. The old neuter collectives in -*ĭje* were still in use: братье/MR. бра́тья 'brethren', but the later usage was not unknown. The dual lingered in a weakened form. Два 'two' was still declined as a dual, but dual nouns like очи '(two) eyes', while retaining DI*D*. очима, took their gen. loc. form from the plural: gen. оче́й.

Russian was thus a national language in official use, but it was variable according to occasions or persons. A will was more stylized than a record of pleas. The Tsar wrote with some elegance, preferring -*ja* to R. -*ě* where there would be OB. -*ę*: всея/всеи Руси 'of all Russia'. That was a shibboleth of good Muscovite society until far into the eighteenth century. A Novgorod merchant puts on paper his native *cókańe* (*c* for *č*): проце/проче 'further', and assimilates the reflexive pronoun to the infinitive: дожидатца 'wait'. More curious than these are other practices showing the extreme scrupulousness of the Tsar's civil service in adaptations and translations. Polish documents are in the Polonized White Russian of that court (вшитки панове 'all the lords', маетъ мовити 'has to declare', абыхмо ѣхали 'that we should go' 1503). The stilted German or Latin of the Austrian Court was rendered by the neat device of turning the pompous phrases into Church Slavonic. Letters from Tatary were rendered word for word, with a free use of Tatar words and turns of expression, and a colourfulness otherwise foreign to Russian correspondence.

132. *The Literary Styles.* The literary styles were radically different from this robust national speech of the official classes, with its background of the vernacular. As we have seen, there was no humanistic renaissance to call attention, as in the west, to the superiority of living over dead styles. A book was a convention shared by few. Books so composed were not either numerous or important, and later writers of the Russian classical age looked back across them to the *Slovo* as the only authentic record of Russian style. Still, in an energetic age, the books that were written could not lack some interest of subject or temperament, if not of elegance.

For the latter half of the sixteenth century the best authority is the *Domostroj* (*Oeconomicus* or *Book of Household Management*), composed by the archpriest Silvestr at the wish of the Tsar. Its author aspired to no heights. His language is practically the same as that of the chancery. He uses or omits the auxiliary in the same fashion, retains the sibilants due to second palatalization/MR. *k ǵ ch*, has infinitives in -*ti* but gerunds for active participles, uses the acc. for nom. in дцерь 'daughter'/MR дочь, knows the *u*-plural in сынове/сыновья, and in соромота 'shame' is more true to the vernacular than MR. срамота. His counsels are of a Hesiodic naïvety, though doubtless needed at the time, and as his purpose is severely practical he uses the very words he expects his uncouth pupil, the Muscovite paterfamilias, to repeat, leaving a blank for the names. So he inculcates respect for the Tsar and for religion, the correction of children, the obedience and consultation of wives, rule over servants and the patient endurance of sicknesses which there was no medical science to cure.

Kotošichin's *Sočinenija* (*Description of Russia*, 1666) is a work of quite another cast. It is salted with malice, especially against the Romanov princesses who knew so little of the art of society during the reign of Aleksej Michajlovič. The author has adopted the style appropriate to a formal composition on a mundane subject. He draws on the bank of Russo-Slavonic for such obvious archaisms as the imperfect tense: зряху 'saw' пребываху 'resided'. The *a*-flexions had not overflowed into the *o*-declension in his time: домѣхъ/MR. домáх '(in) houses'. He had even a style of a sort; his sentences being long and shapeless, with delayed verbs, perhaps under German influence. His acuteness and *animus nocendi*, however, serve him fairly well in place of eloquence.

A third writer is hardly more than an ejaculator on paper. It is the archpriest Avakkum Petrovič (1610–81), a bigoted opponent of Peter the Great's decree concerning the cutting of beards. Avakkum's *Žitie* (*Autobiography*) and *Poslanie* (*Epistle*) record his indomitable dislike of the order and all the sufferings brought upon him by his intractable conscience. He was a champion of the old modes of life, and both his taste and his profession encourage him to retain more Church Slavonic elements than the courtly Kotošichin: the aorist (приидоша 'arrived' изгнаша 'drove out' быстъ 'was'), единъ/одúн 'one', по граду/гóроду 'through the city', вѣмъ 'I know', ти enclitic, сирѣчь 'that is', аще 'if, емлетъ 'takes', виждь 'see'. But the use that he puts these things to is more vernacular than his contemporary's manner. He has perfect tenses without auxiliary, я 'I' as well as язъ, дочь 'daughter' and городъ 'town' according to the vernacular, the article (голову-ту въ землю хоронитъ 'hides his head in the ground', дѣтенки-тѣ 'the little children'), and the expletive -*su*: чаю-су 'I hope'. The man was accustomed to addressing Russian citizens and peasants in a way they could understand. His sentences are close-clipped, and follow the simplest models. He shows himself to be a popular preacher in the vigorous turns of his phrases, in his exclamations and asides and arguments *ad hominem*, and in the vividness of his imagery.

MODERN RUSSIAN (from 1700)

133. *Peter the Great and the Material Conditions of the Language*. The first Russian newspaper, *Russkija Vědomosti*, began to appear under official sanction in 1703 (Jan. 2). Peter the Great himself marked passages in foreign newspapers that ought to appear in this journal. Its style is that of a bulletin, but necessarily colloquial. The topics of a newspaper were varied—a presentation of an elephant to the Shah, the unpopularity of Jesuits in China, discovery of copper ore and naphtha near Kazań, a Cossack raid, etc.—and meant the entry of fresh interests into Russian letters. This periodical appeared in Moscow; at the new capital of St. Petersburg the *Peterburgskija Vědomosti* was first issued in 1711 (May 11). Meanwhile, in 1705, the first books had been issued in the new civilian alphabet (гражда́нская а́збука). This was less a reform of the alphabet than an improvement of its shapes. The thick and thin strokes were made more even and spaced more openly, having in mind the best Italian alphabets; certain letters, e.g. p, were made more like Latin letters despite their different meaning, and scribal flourishes were eliminated. The orthography remained almost as it was. But, though highly conservative, this innovation was of great importance. All our alphabets have, in the last resort, a religious sanction: the Vulgate, the Koran, the Hebrew Bible, etc. The Tsar's innovation established a distinction between the religious alphabet, for use in the liturgy, and the more legible letters for civilian use. By so doing it tended to liberate lay literature from clerical prejudice, and to open up the possibility of its future development.

More important than either of these changes was the impression left by Peter the Great that an entirely new era had opened for Russia. 'Our culture', wrote Puškin, 'appeared of a sudden, like the Russian nobility, in the eighteenth century.' The new life could hardly have appeared in more dramatic circumstances. Peter the Great pitched his new capital outside the racial limits of Russia, in districts where the Finnish language still predominated. Germans, Dutchmen, Frenchmen and Scots entered his service and that of the Empress Catherine, as every effort was made to acquire and utilize the resources of occidental culture in statecraft, science, architecture and the military art. There was a tremendous rush of new ideas into Russian life, and they had to be accommodated in the language. The tempo quickened throughout the eighteenth century. 'After Lomonosov', said Makarov, 'we became acquainted with a thousand new things. Foreign ways begat in our minds a thousand new concepts. More than two-thirds of the Russian lexicon passed out of use. What could we do? We had to look for new modes of expression.'

The new modes of expression came first by simple importation from the west. The bureaucracy was essentially German, but it was drawn from the Gallicized Germans of the petty States, for whom the German language had none of the higher cultural implications. French influence was therefore predominant, though often at second hand; and behind French was the prestige of Latin. Latin was still a diplomatic and academic language in Germany and Poland. The eighteenth century has thus come to be called the Latin-French period of Russian literature, and Polevoj recognized in Karamzin not the first author to make adequate use of Russian resources, but 'the transition from the Latin-French epoch to the purely French epoch'. That is to say, with Karamzin, apart from the use of pure Russian there was direct access to the main source of new cultural ideas in France.

These phenomena are reflected in the lexicon. There is no need to make a detailed list of words which declare themselves to the reader on any page of a Russian book or newspaper. The German words are often bureaucratic, such as штémпель 'stamp' штаб 'staff' мáрка 'mark (coin), postage-stamp' ландвéр 'landwehr, militia'. The German verbal suffix -ieren provides a means of adapting to Russian an infinity of foreign terms. The Russian suffix is -ir-ovať: асфальтúровать 'to cover with asphalt'. In other cases the German mediation is seen in some phonetic feature, such as Germ. š before a consonant at the beginning of a word (e.g. штат 'State'). More important were the direct French borrowings. These are found in all stages of acclimatization in Karamzin, those least advanced being left in their original alphabet: имажинация сентимент *tourment énergie épithète* экспрессия экселировать. Russian words began to be used in French senses: for example, a style could be плóский (*plat*, not physically 'flat' as the Russian term properly implied); быть не в своéй тарéлке is a mistranslation of *ne pas être dans son assiette*, where *assiette* means 'mood, state of mind'; трóгательный is French *touchant*, and so on. These sorts of expressions abounded in the language of the fops and beáux (щёголи, щегольскóй 'elegant'), which was, strange to say, one of the contributive elements to the Russian national style. A distinctive manner arose in the *salons* among the 'best people' who surrounded *les dames illustrées* (свéтские дáмы). When Puškin was asked what he thought of the intelligence of one of these ladies, he said, 'I don't know. We talked French!'

In the nineteenth century this kind of importation continued chiefly on the technical side; commercial, scientific, industrial. Russian has thus a large vocabulary of those cosmopolitan words to which no specific home can be given: актинúческий 'actinic' аллигáтор 'alligator' антитéза 'antithesis' артéрия 'artery', etc. When precision is possible, the word is generally found to be French: акушёр

'obstetrician' (*accoucheur*) аплодировать 'clap' (*applaudir*) а́рмия
'army' (*armée*). Italian musical and architectural terms and English
and Dutch commercial and nautical words are also characteristic,
though minor, parts of the modern vocabulary.

It is not to be supposed that these innovations went unopposed. The
purists proposed alternatives for these 'barbarisms': а́втор/сочини́тель,
аудито́рия/слушали ще, актёр/лицеде́й, ассисте́нт/помо́щник, адресо-
ва́ться/обрати́ться, etc. Their criterion predominated in the Russian
Academy's dictionary, both with regard to barbarisms and to
vulgarisms, but it involved no fewer difficulties than it removed. An
actor is not precisely a 'character-maker', nor an auditorium a 'place of
hearing'. The Slavonic terms could only be used in a new and precise
acceptation, and that could hardly be done without some system of
mnemonics, whereas the foreign word contained *ipso facto* the precise
connotation desired. A further difficulty was that the content of the
Slavonic lexicon was not rich enough to provide the necessary new
terms without having recourse to archaic and obsolete words, which
were, under the circumstances, less familiar than the foreign words in
the Gallicized society of the Russian capitals.

134. *Lomonosov and the Three Styles.* A decisive date in the history
of Russian was that of the issue of Lomonosov's *Rossijskaja gram-
matika* (1755). To his contemporaries and successors in the eighteenth
century he seemed to have given laws to the Russian language. That
was a characteristic concept of the age. It would probably be more
correct to say that Lomonosov revealed the inherent regularity of the
Russian tongue to persons who had taken it too much for granted. The
language had been in full use, as we have seen, in the chancery of
Ivan III at the beginning of the sixteenth century, and it had played
its part even earlier. But a spoken language is more fluid and various
than a dead one, and Russians of the eighteenth century might well
contrast the immutability of Russo-Slavonic with the 'lawlessness' of
the vernacular. Even after Lomonosov there was room for debate
concerning the Russian standard; but that one existed there was no
doubt. There was no doubt, because he had himself exemplified it.
According to Karamzin, Lomonosov was the only Russian 'classic'.
There might be blemishes in the odes (and Puškin came to the conclusion that he was a great man, but not a great poet), his prose might
have unwieldy sentences, and he might have no breath for the
epic; none the less, Lomonosov had written authentic Russian
(чистымъ русскимъ языкомъ) and his works were satisfying and
definitive.

For this reason Lomonosov was approved by the 'westerners', and
he was the delight of the 'slavophils' because of his respect for Church
Slavonic. This was expressed in the dogma of the 'three styles'.

Mediæval rhetoricians distinguished between the high (Latin), middle (courtly vernacular), and low (popular) styles. Lomonosov obtained this doctrine from France in its eighteenth-century transformation and applied it to Russian literature ('три штиля, высокій, посредственный и низкій'). The high style was Russo-Slavonic. It was suitable for Greek poems, odes and prose dissertations upon important themes. The middle style was to be used for theatrical pieces which had to bear an evident relation to normal conversation ('человѣческое слово'), and made use of Church-Slavonic for elegance along with elements of the low style for verisimilitude. The low style was suited for common purposes, such as comedies, impromptu epigrams and songs. It was purely Russian. All three styles were literary, however, and did not admit of vulgarization.

The essential notion was that of the 'middle' style, since it recognized the mixed character of Russian. From it developed the literary and academic norms. After Lomonosov, the 'high' style could not be distinguished from the liturgical language. The 'low' style suggested that certain derivations from the norm would carry certain implications, but other varieties (e.g. regional) have been discovered and exploited.

These views led to the *fin de siècle* controversy between the traditionalists ('slavophils') and the innovators ('westerners'). Their differences extended far beyond the borders of literature and language, but within those limits they could be defined with some precision. The main point at issue was the position of Russo-Slavonic. According to some 'slavophils' this language of books was the kernel of the literary dialect. Its rights, in the higher departments of letters, were absolute. It had been adopted and perfected by the Slavs for intellectual expression, and the Russian colloquial was no more than a phase of the same language specially adapted for the common and vulgar affairs of life. The 'westerners', and especially Karamzin, took the liberty of doubting whether this language was Russian at all. In their view it was merely Old Serbian, and therefore had no rights over Russia. Karamzin's *Letters of a Russian Traveller* (*Piśma russkago putešestvennika*, 1791–2, 1797) lay within the territory always accredited to the vernacular, but they were proof of the charm of Russian and of its capacity for the most varied themes. His *History of Russia* (*Istorija gosudarstva rossijskago*), however, was a work in the 'high style', but in Russian. Russian was capable of all forms of literature, and its use involved the rejection of literary history in Russia with the single exception of the *Slovo o polku Igorevě*. The modern facts required modern words; and not so much words, according to Makarov, as content, thoughts, emotions, pictures and poetic elegance.

Го measure the distance between the two manners of composition
we may cite some lines quoted by Admiral Šiškov to prove the
impossibility of composing elegant verse in Russian:

Russo-Slavonic	Russian
ю́ная де́ва трепе́щет	молода́я де́вка дрожи́т
к хла́дну се́рдцу вы́ю кло́нит	к холо́дному се́рдцу ше́ю гнёт
. . .	. . .
еди́ный млад, други́й с брадо́й	оди́н мо́лод, друго́й с бородо́ю

'The young maiden shivers; she bends her neck to the cold heart;
. . . one was a youth, the other had a beard.'

In these phrases, save for the prepositions and for a single word, the
Russian writer thought in one set of forms and had to alter them
conscientiously to another series. Quite apart from the special
æsthetic qualities of these lines, the process was one in which sponta-
neity was impossible, and the original source of pleasure dried up.
But centuries of use had invested the Russo-Slavonic literary tongue
with qualities of its own, including a certain dignity not admitted in
the vernacular. The solution of this deadlock was impossible along the
lines of controversy. It had to be settled, like all ultimate questions of
literary style, by the authority of a great poet.

135. *Puškin* (1799–1837). These were the elements of the problem
of Standard Russian as they presented themselves to Puškin. He was
convinced, like the 'westerners', that Russia had suddenly become a
nation in the reign of Peter the Great, and that such a nation demanded
its national language and literature. On the other hand he was disposed
to accord more respect than they to Russo-Slavonic. In his opinion the
Slavonic literary style was indivisible, and had been adopted in the
eleventh century by the Slavonic people (not by any specific branch of
them) with a fresh lexicon, new harmonies, and rational structure
derived from the Greek. Such a model endowed the Slavs even more
richly than the occidental nations, who depended upon Latin for their
inspiration. He thought that this language had remained inviolate
until the reign of Peter the Great. It had not suffered from the Tatar
invasions nor from the Polish-Lithuanian dominion over White
Russia and the Ukraine. But it was not the national speech of the new
nation.

Until shortly after 1820 Puškin was single-minded in his allegiance
to the new literary language of Karamzin, and only employed Church
Slavonic features for comic effect or for parody. He was more critical
of Lomonosov than older men who had better reason to appreciate the
greatness of the advance made. 'In Lomonosov', he wrote, 'I esteem
a great man, but not, in the last analysis, a great poet. He had
understood the veritable source of the Russian tongue and of its

beauty: that is his principal service.' He rejected entirely the thesis of the 'three styles'. But the high, almost mystical value he set upon the Slavonic dialect drew him towards experiments in it. He began to assert the need for synthesis between the Russo-French literary mode and the Russo-Slavonic of books. He admitted also the semantic values of other Slavonic vocabularies as a possible source of enrichment of Russian, and looked for the emergence of suitable lyrical and narrative styles from the mingling of these different types of expression. But while numbering Russo-Slavonic among the sources from which the poet might draw, he resolutely rejected the notion that it was the essential dialect of Russian culture. It was fitted, he thought, to offer pictures and symbols, themes and expressions, for both prose and verse. They were, indeed, by virtue of the supposed Greek reformation of the eleventh century, parts of the process of Europeanizing Russian thought. They were, moreover, essential parts of Russian, viewed as a historical creation. Russo-Slavonic might be used in narrative to mark certain social features and types. Its rhetorical forms were admissible in critical writing, and in the lyric both Russo-Slavonic and Biblical Slavonic afforded nuances for the 'oriental style', helped to express pathos, marked the epic tone, helped to sharpen antitheses and to give shades of meaning and symbols. The general background of all Russian expression was given by the 'neutral' dialect of educated society, but this speech, he thought, should go further towards assimilating elements of the Russo-Slavonic heritage.

He had to deal also with the French invasion of the Russian language and with the jargon of the beaux and salons (щегольские фразы). To the authority of the salons or of the illustrious ladies who presided over them he would not bow, but he had to admit the fact of their existence and of their necessity in some part. The new life demanded new expressions; in so far as it was a European life it required European, i.e. French, expression. 'Frenchmen write as they speak', Karamzin had written, 'but in many fields Russians must learn to speak as men of talent write'. There were French words which imposed themselves, either because there could be no satisfactory equivalent (éли с большим аппетитом 'they ate with a good appetite') or because they were part of the social scene (шампанское). More often it was possible to give French words Russian equivalents which were neither archaic nor monstrous, but suitable for the conversation of ladies. It was more important to nationalize certain French connotations by employing Russian phrases in new senses: обман/*illusion*, залог/*gage*, в мыслях (мóлвила) *en pensée*, отдáть сéрдце/*donner son cœur*, слóво надéжды/*mot d'espérance*. The French language had had an immense sentimental and intellectual education which had given to its simplest words the power of uniting into significant groups; Puškin acquired the same flexibility for Russian. Finally, it is from the brief French sentence that Puškin derives his own prose style, which rejects the involutions of German prose as seen in Lomonosov and the unambitious shapelessness of so much Russo-Slavonic.

Like other languages, spoken Russian had vertical dialects. Puškin held firmly to the general principle of educated expression, the language of the 'best people', but with some freedom to welcome more racy elements. He gave a democratic complexion to the national language, unifying the literary styles by denying their traditional divisions, adding artistic touches from the colloquial reservoir, and purifying and ennobling the common tongue by new artistic creations. He adapted the grammar and the nuances of the common tongue to the ideals and style of the literary manner. In particular he made the freest use of expressions denoted as vulgar by the dictionary of the Academy. He was willing to use the language of 'wafer-makers and corn-chandlers', but with a difference, since he considered that Russian had become somewhat debased in their mouths.[*]

136. *After Puškin*. With Puškin the Russian language had been fully constituted not merely as the speech of the Russian nation, which it had been in the fullest sense since the sixteenth century, nor as that of the directing classes, but with the capacity to express the whole range of thoughts proper to a complex modern society. With him, therefore, our historical sketch ends. But there are one or two points to be added by way of appendix. Puškin's romanticism differs from that of contemporary poets in Germany and England in its lack of popular models. Karamzin has translated ballads transmitted to him through Herder and Bürger, but neither he nor Puškin was in a position to know the extraordinary wealth of Russian *byliny* which were secretly recited in the huts round Lake Onega. Karamzin and Puškin wrote short stories after French precedents, without knowledge of the greater part of the vivid Russian *skázki*. These stores of 'pure' Russian became available after the middle of the nineteenth century, and showed how it was possible greatly to reduce the debt to France by shifting the interest to genuinely native themes. Elegant society became less important as Dostoevsky scrutinized the human heart and Tolstoy preached his doctrine of love. The artistic values came to be sought much more in the purely Russian part of the lexicon.

In May 1917 the Provisional Government promulgated a simpler system of spelling. The letters ѣ o i were dropped, and so was ъ wherever it was otiose. The use of ё was considered desirable, but not

---

* See V. Vinogradov, *Jazyk Puškina* (Moscow-Leningrad, 1935). Since these words were printed G. Vinokur has given a masterly description of all phases of literary Russian in *La Langue russe* (Paris, 1947; Russian text, Moscow, 1944).

compulsory; failure to comply with this suggestion has been a cause of doubt (see section 120). Prefixes ending in *z* changed *z* to *s* in compound words before voiceless consonants (расска́з 'tale'/разска́зъ [before 1917]). In the declension of adjectives *GSMN. -ago/jago* and *NPNF. -yja/ija* were dropped, leaving only *GSMN. -ogo NPMNF. -ye* and their soft equivalents. Similarly, among pronouns, они́ одни́ became available for the neuter and feminine as well as the masculine, and the spelling of A*SF*. её was extended to the genitive/older G*SF*. ея. The question of word-accent was not touched in this decree. In practice an accent (acute or grave) is used to distinguish e.g. у́же 'narrower' from уже́ (уже́) 'already'.

Soon after this order was given the October Revolution was carried through, with notable effects upon the language which we cannot attempt to measure at this date. Obvious points are the sudden flourishing of initials in the form of words, as оги́з = объедине́ние госуда́рственных изда́тельств 'Unified State publishing house', озе́т 'Society for the promotion of agriculture among toiling Jews', and of portmanteau words like Совнарко́м = сове́т наро́дных комисса́ров 'Council of People's Commissars', комсомо́л 'Young Communist League', Всерабо́тземле́с 'Union of Land and Forest Workers', зарпла́та 'wages' (=за́работная пла́та). Equally obvious is the effect of innovations in the literary language; though it is still difficult to determine how many innovations will be definitively adopted into common cultural use. Languages develop rapidly under the stress of strong experiences, and there is every reason to believe that we are contemporaries of one of the most active periods in the history of the Russian language.*

DIALECTS
[See also section 9(*a*)]

137. *White Russian.* The White Russian speech corresponds in part to the territory of marsh and river between the Pripet and the Dvina which was occupied by the ancient Dregoviči. They provide, however, only a portion of the linguistic substratum. In the region of Polock and Smolensk the original inhabitants were Kriviči (North Russians), while between Dnieper and Sož lay the Radimiči who were at first associated with the Vjatiči (East Russians). Certain Lithuanian tribes have also been submerged in this mass. It appears, therefore, that White Russia was constituted not by a tribal unit but by the political compression of peoples under the Lithuanian sovereignty. This process belongs to the thirteenth and fourteenth centuries. It was in the same epoch that Little Russian or Ruthenian took shape in the

---

* See Astrid Bœcklund, *Die univerbierenden Verkurzungen der heutigen russischen Sprache* (Upsala, 1940).

Carpathian Galicia. In certain respects the two languages concur in features which may be described as typically West Russian.

The White Russian speech was already in use for official purposes under the Lithuanian Olgierd (c. 1345), father of the Jagiello who ascended the Polish throne by marriage with the heiress Jadwiga in 1386. It had already reached its full phonetic and morphological development, but it continued to develop its vocabulary and syntax. The predominant position in the partnership of peoples was taken by Poland in the fifteenth and sixteenth centuries, and the Polish elements began to increase in White Russian, the more markedly when Poland espoused the cause of the Counter-Reformation. A White Russian literary language arose which was marked by Church Slavonic and Polish increments and differed considerably from that of the common people. Even the sounds and forms of the language were affected by Polish. A decline set in with the end of the seventeenth century, when White Russian began to go out of administrative and judicial use, though it continued in other respects until the end of the eighteenth century. This variety of the language has now died out. The popular dialect was in 1939 still used by over ten million people distributed between the Polish and the Soviet States. It has two sub-species: the north-eastern and the south-western; and there is a regional literature which takes the south-western variety as its standard. It is an official and literary language within the USSR.

The western frontier of White Russian has been described in section 9, since it is also the frontier of Russian against Polish. As against Great Russian it runs from south of Pskov to include Ržev in the former Government of Tveŕ, and then just south of Smolensk. It then takes in the western part of the former Government of Brjansk and descends to the Desna. North of Černigov the frontier turns west and is continued to the Polish frontier along the line of the Pripet. In this section White Russian divides from Ruthenian, with a comparatively narrow band of mixed dialect. As is well known, the Pripet marshes form an effective barrier between northerners and southerners on the west bank of the Dnieper.

The Cyrillic alphabet is officially used for White Russian, but a number of dialectal studies have also been carried out by means of an alphabet based upon Polish. There is a strong accent, and consequently reduction in the strength of unstressed vowels, which tend to pass to a neutral timbre (ákańe). Unstressed e also changes timbre (by jákańe): WR. нясу́/R. несу́ 'bear'. Where Russian has developed oj/ej from ŭjĭ/ĭjĭ, White Russian has y(j)/i(j): WR. злы 'bad' шыя 'neck'/R. злой шея. Highly characteristic is the semivowel ŭ, which has resulted from unstressed u before a consonant, from the preposition and prefix v, and from final l: ŭlećéła 'flew away' (R. улетéла) ŭśё 'all' (R. всё) *ŭžáŭ* 'took' (R. взял) *zrabiŭše* 'became' (P. *zrobił się*). As regards the White Russian consonants, one notices that the second palatalization still takes effect in declension: L*SMN. e* <*ě:* WR. на паро́зе, ў ла́ўце, на саце́/R. поро́г 'threshold' ла́вка 'shop' соха́ 'plough'. The fricative *g* (voiced *h*) is normal, as in Ruthenian: *hóły* 'naked'/R. го́лый. This sound is found also with the demonstrative particle (*h*)*e-:* WR. *hétak* 'so'/R. эта́к. As for the dental consonants, they show *dzékańe* and *cékańe*, i.e. the development of affricates from occlusive *d t* before front vowels, as in Polish: WR. хадзі́ць 'go'/R. ходи́ть. Examples of this phenomenon go back only so far as the fourteenth century, and in the sixteenth the dentals still remain in manuscripts, or take the intermediate form *dj tj*. In the present tense of verbs in *-*djǫ* a WR. *dž* (resulting from analogy) corresponds to R. *ž:* WR. гляджу́ 'I look'. The treatment of *r* varies according to dialect, some softening hard *r* and others hardening soft *r;* standard WR. has hard *r*. The tendency to harden final consonants (осмъ 'eight' любовъ 'love') is very pronounced in sixteenth-century manuscripts. Before a palatal glide [j], consonants are liable to be doubled as in some forms of Ruthenian: WR. вясе́лля 'rejoicing'/R. весе́лье.

The plural of the imperative of verbs still shows *e* for CSl. *ě*/R. *i*. The vocative is in much use: сы́нку 'O son' чалаве́че 'O man', and numbers 2–4 take after them masculine plurals and feminine duals (cf. use of pl. in P.Cz.). Much use is made of the enclitics ци/R. (dial.) ти (ethic dat.), and of чы in questions (P. *czy*).

138. *Ruthenian* (*Ukrainic* or *Little Russian*). The claim of Ruthenian to be regarded as an independent language, not a mere dialect, is considerably stronger than that of White Russian. It is not one based on ancient dissociation from Russian; nothing is to be gained by putting it on the same footing as Serbocroat or Czech. Its history is comparatively short, but it is individual. Though never attaining official status like White Russian in the Middle Ages, nor in modern times until the Revolution, it has become the expression of a distinctive mode of life, with folk-poetry and tales, ethnography and customs peculiar to itself, and an increasing body of literature of which the outstanding personage is the poet Ševčenko (1814–61). In the great city of Kiev it has had a capital for centuries, a capital still golden with the prestige of the oldest Russian civilization.

The territory originally occupied by the Русини was bounded on the north by the Pripet, on the east by the Dnieper as far as the Falls, on the south by a line from the Falls to the Dniester estuary, and on the west by the Prut and the Carpathians. This region was divided by the tree-line which ran diagonally north-eastward, crossing the Dniester a little above Kiev. In the one section, among the tributaries of the Pripet and the foothills of the Carpathians, there was woodland; in the other, the open steppe. In the wooded country were the *Drevljane*, *Volynjane*, *Duléby*, *Chorvaty*, *Bužane* and other tribes. The plains on the west bank of the Dnieper around Kiev were held by the 'plainsmen', *Poljane*. The importance of Kiev as the focal point of all the Russian waterways raised the *Poljane* to hegemony over the other tribes, especially when they were organized by the Rurikids. They fashioned the first Russian civilization. Out on the open steppe towards the mouth of the Dniester lay the *Tiverci* and *Uliči*.

The open steppe was favourable ground for the Turko-Tatar nomads. The Pečenegs and Polovcy cleared them of Russian colonists, who were forced back into the woodlands to the north. The *Poljane* held firm, however, until the rout on the Kalka and the destruction of Kiev by the Golden Horde in 1240. They too were driven north, to unite with the Vjatiči as East Russians, or north-westward into the Carpathians. Two principal centres arose in South-west Russia: Galicia (Galič) and Volhynia (around Cholm). Here the woods and broken ground and marshes prevented the Tatars from using their cavalry, and Russian principalities arose with some leisure to develop their culture. When larger states formed to the west of them, Galicia fell within the sphere of Poland and Volhynïa of Lithuania. This diminished Russia (*Ruś*) was known as *Málaja Ruś*, 'Little Russia', from the thirteenth century. In Galicia the word 'Ruthenian' was preferred. The 'Ukraine' was rather a geographical concept; it was the 'frontier' of colonization, which advanced with the decline of the nomads upon the steppe. Poltava and Černigov were bases for this movement back into the open plains. In the eighteenth century Ukrainian colonists advanced to Charkov and parts of the provinces of Voronež and Kursk. They reached the mouth of the Don at Taganrog and Rostov, but there encountered South Great Russians who had pressed down the river. Beyond the Don they reached as far as the Kubań.

The ancient literature of Kiev throws no light upon the Ruthenian language. It is in Church Slavonic, which was also no doubt the language of the educated classes whenever they gave care to their utterance. Only a few errata show traces of the vernacular, and what they reveal is common Russian matter. It is only by a chance transcription that we know that *g* was a fricative (*h*) in Kiev. Some dialectal peculiarities appear in the second half of the twelfth century in manuscripts executed in Galicia-Volhynia, notably in the Gospel of 1164. It is in the thirteenth and fourteenth centuries, however, that typically Ruthenian features are first evident (*o e ě* $>i$). Under Polish rule many Polonisms entered the written and popular speech, and the popular poetry was remodelled on an occidental principle (rhyme). Many Ruthenians wrote wholly in Polish. On the other hand, the business of colonization gave to the language a power of expansion denied to White Russian, and it developed a high degree of independence. There are many collections of folk-songs and legends of Carpathian Galicia and the Ukraine. Over fourteen thousand proverbs have been collected. Original works have been published, and there are important treatises on grammar and ethnology. Out of the many dialects there has been evolved a standard language for literary use. Its basis in the speech of former Austro-Hungarian territory is explained by political considerations. In Podkarpatská Rus (formerly part of Czechoslovakia) there was a movement to bring the vocabulary of the language closer to that of Great Russian.

The northern frontier of Ruthenian leaves the Polish language frontier in the region of Bielsk, and is separated from White Russian by the Pripet and a line north of Černigov. It is then divided from South Great Russian to the south of Kursk and Voronež. Thence the frontier turns south to the mouth of the Donec, and follows the Don. Rostov has a mixed language, thanks to the South Russians who have followed the stream to its mouth, but the Ruthenian tongue crosses the Don and reaches the middle course of the Kubań, whence it turns south-west to the Black Sea. There are Ruthenian colonies in the Crimea. Between the Dniester and Prut Ruthenians and Rumanians are mixed, and south of the Carpathians they shade into Magyar and Slovak communities. From the Carpathians the line turns east-north-east through the provinces of Lublin and Siedlce (Polish Galicia). In 1940 the total number of Ruthenians stood at something short of 40 millions. The distribution of a smaller total (33 millions) in 1924 was: Ukraine, 28½ millions; Galicia, 3½ millions (42 per cent. of the population); Bukovina and Hungary, ½ million each. There were also a few hundred thousand in Podkarpatská Rus.

The Ruthenian vowels are distinguished from those of Great Russian in some important ways. Original *e* and *o* and *ě* developed, under certain conditions, into long vowels, $\bar{e}\ \bar{o} >$ Ruth. *i* (section 86 *O E*). : íхати 'travel' лíто 'year, summer' вiл 'ox'/*GS*. волá кiсть 'bone'/*GS*. кóсти лiд 'ice'/*GS*. лéду. The northern dialects differ in these particulars. OR. *ě* > NRuth. *ie ié* and sometimes *ije* under the stress (свiет 'light' вiéтер 'wind'), though *i* is found in the loc. sg., and in the infin. *-iti/il* < *-ěti*. In the same region lengthened *o* and *e* are represented by *uo ue uy ui*: кýонь куóнь 'horse' вýил 'ox' (люд 'ice' мюд 'honey') leading to the simple vowel *u*: кунь вул. Though the end of the series differs from Standard Ruthenian the diphthongs represent older stages of the common speech. The substitution of closer for more open vowels is more general than this treatment of long or lengthened $\bar{o}/\bar{e}$. Normal *o/e* are represented by *u/ju* in examples which begin with the thirteenth century: купувати 'buy' таньцювати 'dance' (cf. по Божьюмъ 'in God's name' 14th cent.).

Initially *o-* >*vo-* >*vi-:* він(вон-ó -á with analogous в-) 'he (it, she)', вiвця 'sheep' (cf. воовьца въно 13–14th cent.). Finally -'*e* becomes -*je* or -*ja*, doubling the previous consonant in the latter case if it is not a labial (cf. White Russian): весiлля 'joy' життя 'life', and весiлé; cf. also лляти <*lĭjati* 'pour'.

The language differs from Great Russian and White Russian by the absence of *ákańe* and by the hardening of the two front vowels, though it should be noted that г к are slightly softened by i и e. Ruth. *e* (OR.*e/ĭ*) was not originally as soft as in the Moscow pronunciation of today, and is now generally hard, except when initial, after a vowel, after doubled letters, and in some endings. The sounds are distinguished as hard e/ soft e: де 'where'/есть 'is' мáе 'he has' весiлля <*-ĭje* щáсте 'happiness'. At a time when *e* was still soft after a palatal it became *ë* before a hard consonant, not only under the accent as in Standard Russian but in all cases: жóвтий 'yellow' жонá 'woman' чоловiк 'man'. This change does not take place before letters now hardened, which were soft in Mediæval Russian. Similarly, *i* was hardened except when initial and after a vowel, and at the same time *y* was brought forward in the mouth. The result is Ruth. и = R.WR. ы и(i). It is more open than *i* and closer than *e*, and resembles the vowel in Eng. *milk*. The precise value differs with dialect, however; it is represented by *y/i ï* for the soft sounds: лúхо 'evil' бúти 'strike' мúти 'wash' (R. мыть)/iм 'to them', поïтú 'go' and *i(ï)* from *o/e*. Traces of this development are found as early as the twelfth century and become frequent in the fourteenth. *I* is sometimes found for *u:* вúйти замiж 'marry'/R. зáмуж, and и dialectally for *e:* вiчiр 'evening' (OB. *večerŭ*).

In two particulars Ruthenian goes with White Russian: *ŭjĭ/ĭjĭ* > Ruth. ий/R. ой ей, and *v* and *u* (unstressed) may give *w u* (written в or у according to position): дóбрий 'good', у менé 'beside me, I have', мов [mɔu] 'speak' прáвда [práuda] 'truth'. OR. *rŭ/ri lŭ/lĭ* >may appear as Ruth. р/л-и/R. *ro/re lo/le:* слизá 'tear'.

The principal features of the system of consonants are also common to Ruthenian and White Russian, viz., fricative *g* (=voiced *h*), persistence of the second palatalization, development of final (of word or syllable) *l* >*ŭ* (в): гóлод 'hunger', LS. руцí/рукá 'hand' нозí/ногá 'foot', вовк 'wolf'. Occlusive *g* occurs in Polish words and some other foreign matter, and is now denoted by г̇. It occurs when *k* comes before a voiced consonant, and in the fourteenth century the occlusive *g* of foreign names was represented by *k* or *kg:* Олыг̇ѣрта G*S*./*Olgierd* 1350. Occasionally fricative *g* (*h*) has been lost: dial. орóх 'pea'/горóх тодí 'then'/R. тогдá. Foreign ф is normally replaced by Ruth. х/хв/хф or п: Хомá 'Thomas' Пилúп 'Philip'. A conspicuous feature is the doubling of consonants, except labials, before soft *je/ja*, already mentioned. The labials develop a following *l̓* in such cases, and *m̓* may become *mn̓:* мня <*mja*/мя (cf. Cz. *mě* [mn̓ɛ]).

Ruthenian largely agrees with Serbocroat in not unvoicing final consonants (except *h*): слід 'trace' is pronounced [śl̓id, śl̓idt].

As to the sibilants, *c* remains soft in the same places as in Old Russian and Common Slavonic, except when later hardened by the hardening of the front vowels: Ruth. G*S*. сóнця 'of the sun' царúця 'empress' отéць 'father'/купцéм 'by the trader'. CSl. *dj >*dž*, *zdj >*ždž*. The letter щ stands for hard *šč*. *C̓ ś ź* have the palatal sounds heard in Polish, but *t̓ d̓* are palatalized as in Russian. An apostrophe is used to separate hard consonants from following soft vowels.

3*S*. -*t̓* is found with verbs of classes iii 2 and iv, but is otherwise dropped: Ruthenian платúть 'pays' /пúше 'writes'. In some South Ruthenian dialects it is found in all cases, and there are dialects in which 3*S*. -*t̓* is hardened. The consonant is often omitted in the 3*P*. in Galicia. South of the Carpathians 1*S*. -*m* (гáдам/гáдаю 'think') links the Carpathian dialect to the neighbouring Slovak. 2*S*. -*š* is normal, with a few relics of the athematic conjugation in -*si -ś*. On the analogy of 2*S*. -*ś* has been formed 2*P*. -*t̓*/R. -*te*. 1*P*. -*mo* is normal, -*m* being rarely found; but in the Carpathian region the ending is -*me* as in Czechoslovak. The principal feature of the imperative is the survival of *ě* in the form of *i* in the plural; to it have been assimilated the verbs of iii 2 and iv: орíть 'plough ye', and so хвалíть 'praise ye'. The infinitive is normally in -ти, except for verbs in -чи (i 1), but -ть is also found. Verbs in -*ěti* (iii) have -іти. In the formation of the imperfective future there is an analytical form composed of infin. + иму 'I have to', etc. (хвалúтим-у,-еш, etc. 'shall praise') as well as the construction with бýду. The reflexive is sometimes assimilated to a previous -*t*: ведéтця 'is led'.

A few minor features of the Ruthenian conjugation are the assimilation of *byti* to *búdu*: Ruthenian бýти 'be' був 'was'; the loss of initial *i*- in мáю 'have'; the intrusion of initial *i*- in ишóвши 'having gone'; ишóв 'went' (*šĭd*-) from the pres. iдý, infin. iтú (cf. S. *išao*). In мóжу(ть) 'can' печý(ть) 'bake' we find the palatal consonant proper to the other persons of the tense; and in 3*P*. сплять 'they sleep'/R. спят there is softening of the labial on the analogy of 1*S*. сплю.

Ruthenian noun-declensions contain a number of special features. The survival of the vocative is notable: чоловíче 'O man' жíнко 'O woman' сíну 'O son'. D*S*. of *o*- stems is in -ови/dial. овí, the latter by contamination of -*ovi* and -*ě*. N*P*. -ове/и <ы/е <e/і <ѣ: G*P*. -*ovŭ* >-ів; DIL*P*. -ам-ами-ах in all declensions (but -ем -ьми -ех and -ох -іх < -*ěchŭ* are found in dialects). The *u*- and *o*- declensions have been thoroughly mixed, and the consonant-stems fused with them, either by generalizing the oblique-stem (iмéно 'name') or by declining by means of the nominative-stem (NA*S.* iмя́/G*S.* iм-я́ D*S.* -ю, etc., like *jo*-stems). In the *a*-declension one notes soft G*S.* -i < OR. -*ě*, and I*S.* -ою/ею. In Polish Galicia and the Carpathians IS*F.* -*oju* has become -*ou* -*oй* -*ov*: рúбов 'by a fish'.

The dual has survived in feminine and neuter declensions (NAV*D.* -i < -*ě*), and the ending -*ma* occurs in fixed phrases: пiд дверúма 'under the door'.

Short forms of the adjectives are rare, though more frequent in folk-songs. The long forms are sometimes reduced by loss of final -*j*, and many cases are affected by the passage of *ě* and lengthened *ē/ō* to Ruthenian i. G*SMN* -ого becomes -его in the northern dialects which border on Polish. In addition to сей/ceсь 'this' there is цей/оцéй < от сей (for от, cf. R. вот P. *oto* 'behold'). The flexions of numbers 2–4 are applied also to 5–9.

Literary Ruthenian has been carefully purified from Old Bulgarian phonetic forms, so that CSl. **per-* always appears as Ruth. *pere-*, never in a form borrowed from OB. *prě-*, CSl. **tort* always appears as Ruth. *torot*, and so on. Apart from this and what may be called dialect features, Ruthenian differs from Great Russian chiefly in its abstract vocabulary, which has in many cases been built up on principles other than those of Great Russian, sometimes (one suspects) purely for the purpose of being different.

For purposes of comparison we give here parallel passages in the three official languages (Russian, White Russian and Ruthenian) taken from *Izvestija* (Jan. 20, 1938):

Russian	*White Russian*	*Ruthenian*
По пункту пятому порядка дня—о назначении Прокурора СССР выступает депутат Г.И. Петровский. От имени Советов Старейшин Совета Союза. и Совета Национальностей депутат Петровский предлагает назначить Прокурором СССР депутата А.Я. Вышинского.	Па пункту пятаму парадку дня—аб назначэнні Пракурора СССР выступае дэпутат Г.I. Пятроўскі. Ад імя Советаў Старэйшын Совета Саюза і Совета Нацыянальнасцей дэпутат Пятроўскі прапануе назначыть Пракурорам СССР дэпутата А.Я. Вышынскага.	По пункту п'ятому порядка дня—про призначення Прокурора СРСР виступае депутат Г.I. Петровський. Від імени Рад Старійшин Ради Союзу і Ради Національностей депутат Петровський пропонуе призначити Прокурором СРСР депутата А.Я. Вишинського.

'On point 5 of the agenda (*ordre du jour*)—on the appointment of a Public Prosecutor (*procureur*) of the USSR Deputy G. I. Petrovskij speaks (lit. steps out). In the name of the Councils of Syndics of the Council of the Union and the Council of Nationalities Deputy Petrovskij proposes the nomination as Prosecutor of the USSR of Deputy A. J. Vyšinskij.'

Note.— (i)   Proper names take different forms in the three languages.
      (ii) WR. совѣт 'council' appears without *ákańe*.
      (iii) WR. прапанѵ́е <Lat. *proponere* P. *proponować*, with *ákańe*.
      (iv) Ruth. рáда <Germ. *Rat* P. *rada* 'council'.

139. *Great Russian.* (*a*) *South.* Viewed as a local speech, Great Russian is on the same footing as White Russian and Ruthenian, though its area and population are vastly greater. They are three divergent forms of one common Russian language which was substantially the same from the ninth to the twelfth centuries. It has also given the pattern of the standard literary language, the vehicle of administration and culture, according to the way it is spoken in Moscow. Moscow is on the line of division between North and South Russian, with a moderate *ákańe*. In one or two points the dialect of the city differs from the literary tongue, as for example in the transformation of *k ǵ* into *ŧ d́:* dial. *bid́í*/бегѝ 'run'.

The South Russian dialect proper is marked by strong *ákańe*, a tendency to turn stressed *ó* into *uo*, the interchange of *u/v/ł*, fricative *g* [γ], hardness of *ž š* even when doubled, and a tendency to soften *k ch* before the back vowels *a/u:* dial. *tóĺka*/тóлько 'only'. Thanks to the interchange *u/v*, -*vu*- may be reduced to *u:* dial. *déuška* 'maiden'. G*SMN.* -го is pronounced -γ*o/*γ*a*, but rarely -*vo*. 3*S.* -*ŧ :* *jid́óŧ*/идёт 'goes'. Past gerund -*mši/R.* -*vši:* dial. *ujéchamši* 'having gone away'.

The South Russian area is divided into three principal division. The north-western division (Kaluga, Tula) changes the timbre of unstressed *e* (to '*a* by *jákańe*) only before hard consonants: *śaló*/селó 'village' *ńasú*/несѵ́ 'bear'. In the eastern section (Rjazań, Tambov, Penza, Voronež, Saratov) the change of timbre of *e* occurs in all circumstances: *ṽadú*/ведѵ́ 'lead' and also *baŕaǵí*/берегѝ 'guard'. The frontier to the north of South Great Russian is defined by the north-western and eastern dialects as far as the Volga, after which the eastern frontier is defined by the eastern dialect which follows the river down to Stalingrad. There has also been some expansion of this dialect towards the Urals. In the southern variety (Orel, Kursk) unstressed *e* suffers dissimilated *ákańe*, that is, it becomes *i* when followed by a stressed *á*, but *a* when followed by another sound: dial.

źimla/земля 'land' but *ńasú*/несу́ 'bear'. It is this variant of South Great Russian which defines the northern frontier of Ruthenian.

(*b*) *North*. As the North Great Russian dialects have not given the literary standard their divergencies from it are the more striking. They have historical importance as being either the Old Russian northern dialect of Nóvgorod, Pskov, Polock and Smolensk, or extensions of the same. It was from North Russia that the first colonists were drawn for Perḿ and Siberia, and its speech has spread with its people. Moreover, North Russia is the place of refuge of discarded traditions, the home of *skázki* or legends which were evolved further south, and more especially of the traditional heroic poetry of the *bylíny*. The *bylíny* take for their oldest subjects the affairs of Kiev in the days of the Rurikids, and they still preserve traces of this distant origin (e.g. in knowledge of some historical persons, of the grasses of the steppe, etc.). Richard James collected the first known *bylíny* in Moscow, at the beginning of the seventeenth century. Many of the best strictly historical ones belong to the reign of Ivan the Terrible, and it seems probable that they reached their apogee in the sixteenth century. If so, they were the finest examples of imaginative literature of the time, compensating for the poverty of the extant works in Russo-Slavonic. But they fell out of favour, and were only recovered in the middle years of the nineteenth century round the cold shores of Lake Onega. In this last form they are examples of North Great Russian; but they are discrepant in some particulars, and display more information and imagination than are to be expected in their humble surroundings.

North Great Russian dialects are characterized by *ókańe* (*o* retaining its timbre when unstressed, and even being used instead of *a*: dial. *dolóko*/далёко 'far', *Ondréj*, *lokéj* 'lackey'. Unstressed and stressed *e* become *ë* before hard consonants, and *ë* is even found for original *ě*: dial. *bʹesóda* 'conversation'. There is a general tendency towards narrower vowels: *e* for *ja*: dial. *páńeť*/па́мять 'memory' *cédo*/ча́до 'child'; *i* for *e* in some parts: dial. *líbeḋ*/ле́бедь 'swan'; *i* for *ě* where *c* and *č* are confused: dial. *líto*/ле́то 'summer' *ḿisto*/ме́сто 'place' (*město*); *ju* for *jo* (*ë*): *lud*/лёд 'ice'. It is only in North Great Russian that contraction of vowels occurs as a regular feature: *ae oe ěe* > *a o e*: dial. *znaš délaš*/зна́ешь де́лаешь.

The principal feature in its consonants is the occurrence of *cókańe* and *čókańe*. The first is the use of *c* for *č* (as *cédo* 'child', quoted above); the latter is the use of *č* for *c* (as *ovčá*/овца́ 'sheep'). Both features are absent from parts of Novgorod, Tveŕ, Vladimir, Jaroslavĺ, Kostroma, Simbirsk and Kazań. There are dialects which have *cókańe* only. The double change is characteristic of the old Novgorod dialect, and examples can be traced back to the eleventh century. Occlusive *g* persists, and is sometimes even imposed on those words (*Gospód* 'lord' G*S. Bóga*) in which the standard was fixed by Kiev. *Ł* ending a word or syllable becomes *ŭ/v:* dial. *dóvgo*/долго 'long', *kólokov*/ колокол 'bell', as in South Russian, and there is the same tendency to palatalize *k* before *a/u:* dial. *dévočka* 'girl'. OR. *-ĭstvo -ĭskŭ* appears with softened *s: gréčeśki* 'in Greek', *otéceśvo* 'fatherland' *cárśvo* 'kingdom'. In part of the region soft *t d́* becomes *ć dź*, as in White Russian: dial. *búdźot*/будет 'will be'.

The peculiarities of conjugation and declension are fewer, since in these respects the *littérateurs* of Moscow adhered to northern traditions. 3*S*. *-t* is always hard. The reflexive *-sja -ś* is assimilated to a preceding *t*, and appears as *-si -sy -cy*, according to circumstances, but rarely as *-sa -ca*. In the *a*-stems, the dative and genitive are interchanged. In the plural of all stems, the instrumental takes the form of the dative (*-m* for *-mi*) in the whole *cókańe* area; otherwise it sometimes takes the form *-my* by contamination of OR. *-mi -y*, and in the *bylíny* I*P*. *-y* is found, though not in the living dialects; more rarely the dual *-ma* is used for instr. loc. plural.

An important characteristic is the use of the article. It is generally reduced to *-(o)t* or *-to:* dial. *dúm-ot* 'the idea' *drugój-ot* 'the other' *páreń-to* 'the lad', but in the region of Perḿ a considerable amount of the demonstrative declension survives. In the *bylíny* the word он is used enclitically as an article: свищет Соловей он по соловьиному 'Nightingale whistles in nightingale fashion', волх он догадливыл 'the magician kept guessing'.

The adjectives have only N*SM*. *-oj/ej*, being free from Church Slavonic influence, and so also G*SMN*. *-ovo/evo*. A final *-e* is often found transformed to *-ë*. In folk-poetry the uncontracted declensional forms of Old Russian sometimes occur: dial. *dobroej -oem -yim -yech*, and the genitive plural is occasionally in *-ef*. The comparative is in *-jae: skoráe* 'quicker'. Что 'what?' is rendered also by *što ščo što šč'o ššo šo*.

North Great Russian has five principal sub-dialects. The maritime variety of Archangel transforms *ja* to *e*, and pronounces щ as hard long *šš*. In the Olonec region (where the best *bylíny* have been found) *ě* becomes *i* before soft consonants, final *-ł >ŭ*, 3*S*. *-t́* survives. The western variety (North-West Russian) is that of Novgorod and Pskov (*ě >i*, weak *cókańe*, confusion of dat. instr. pl.). The eastern sub-dialect is that of Vjatka and Vologda, where *ě >e/ie : chleb/chlieb* 'bread'. The fifth area is that of Vladimir and the Volga.

Chapter VI

WEST SLAVONIC

(POLISH, WENDISH, CZECHOSLOVAK)

A. SOUNDS

140. *Stress, Length.* (i) The original Slavonic stress was light but variable, and it continued to be so in the West Slavonic dialect or language of the Elbe (Polabian) until its extinction in the eighteenth century: Polab. *jolövéića*/P. *jalowica* 'heifer', *püli*/P. *pole* 'field'. This type of mobile accent is still found in certain North Cassubian dialects [Cass. *jédniwe* (gen.sg.) 'one' *noví* 'new' *zámuzikują* 'will begin to play music']. Apart from these survivals of the archaic system, fixed accentuation is a distinguishing characteristic of West Slavonic.

A musical intonation has been developed, seemingly in independence, by Cassubian, which has also lost consonant-softness.

As explained in section 22, a relatively long Slavonic word was likely to have three grades of stress: strong (the stress-accent), medium and weak. The lighter the stress-accent, the more in evidence would be the medium stresses, until the point was reached at which an exchange was effected. Among the medium stresses was included the initial syllable. Properly speaking this would be at the beginning of a breath-group, when, the exhalation of breath having just begun, there would be a relatively lavish expenditure upon the first syllable. But any substantial word might find itself at the beginning of a breath-group, and all but enclitics have relatively tense first syllables. The change of accent has taken place in Czechoslovak and Wendish. Wendish is entirely surrounded by German, and Czechoslovak largely so; but it hardly seems necessary to attribute to foreign influence a development so much in the nature of things. That there was originally a mobile accent in Czechoslovak and Polish is clear from the weak and strong grading of the *jers*. This corresponds exactly with that in other Slavonic tongues. Yet the fixed accent must have established itself in the Proto-Czech and Proto-Polish periods. The fact can hardly be proved, since the spelling does not indicate the place of stress.

Once the initial stress had been established, a secondary stress developed in Czechoslovak at a certain distance from the principal one. (As diacritics are used to denote length in this language, we shall denote stress by other means, i.e. by the roman letters of the examples cited in italics.) The secondary accent falls on the second syllable away from the main stress: Cz. *napadal napadala* 'attacked' *Pivoda Kalivoda pronásledovati* 'pursue'. In Lower Wendish the secondary stress falls regularly on the penultimate: *cerẃeny* 'red' *powołanje* 'summons'. In the villages along the eastern border, i.e. in those nearest to Poland (Horno/Rogow, Drjějce/Wüstdrewitz, Radojz/ Radewiese and as far as Mužakow/Muskau on the Nysa/Neisse), the secondary accent is more and more in evidence. The Polish and South Cassubian principle of fixed stress on the penultimate is thus seen to be a development from the secondary accent which resulted from an earlier shift of stress to the first syllable. To this penultimate stress the Polish language offers few exceptions (e.g. in the foreign words *matematyka liryka*, etc., and in such verbal forms as *robilibyśmy* 'we should do', originally two words). There is a secondary initial accent in the longer Polish words: P. *macierzystego* (*GSMN.*) 'maternal'. When stress is laid on a word or an antithesis is given point, the secondary accent becomes principal: P. *nie ojczystego lecz macierzystego* 'not paternal, but maternal'.

(ii) Original quantities still survive, to some extent, in Czechoslovak. The clearest case is that of the *tort*-formula. It contains a diphthong, which is necessarily a long syllable; and in a general way a long syllable corresponds to (and in Russian *torot* is actually converted into) two shorts. The falling and rising tones placed the peak of stress as well as pitch upon the first and second elements respectively: falling ⌣ : —/rising — : ⌢. These distinctions of tone were converted into distinctions of quantity in Czechoslovak. The low, weak element of the falling tone was shortened and lost, leaving only a short vowel; but the final rise kept those vowels long: Cz. *hlas* 'voice' *vlas* 'hair' *břeh* 'bank' *dřevo* 'wood'/*dráha* 'road' *mráz* 'frost' *hrách* 'pea' *bříza* 'birch' *břímě* 'load'. Unstressed syllables behaved as though with falling intonation: *hlava* 'head' *brada* 'beard' (cf. R. *golová borodá*), but there are some irregularities, like *mléko* 'milk' *žláza* 'gland'/R. *molokó železá*. In the *ort*-group, difference of tone seems to have led (as in P.Wend.ESl.) to difference not of quantity but of quality: CSl. **ŏrstŭ* >**rostŭ*/**ólkomŭ* >Cz. *růst* 'growth'/*lakomý* 'greedy'.

Other cases of original length preserved in Czechoslovak are more difficult to demonstrate. The stressed syllable is absolutely longer than any unstressed one, and therefore the accent-shift confused relative quantities. The length of CSl. *ě* is represented by its diphthongization and (in Czech) ultimate solution as a narrow long vowel (*ě* >*ié*/*ie* >*í*) in many words. Comparison with other Slavonic languages shows that differences of tone survive as differences of quantity in Cz. *muka* 'torture'/*mouka* 'flour' *sud* (pl. *sudy*) 'cask'/*soud* (pl. *soudy*) 'tribunal' [cf. S. *müką*/*múka sûd*/*sûdovi*/*sûd* (*súdovi*)]. In

Cz. *mohu můžeš* 'can' there is a quantitative difference associated with originally distinct stresses (R. *mogú móžeš'*).

In some neuter *n*-stems, the stem-vowel is long in the nom.acc.sg., but short in the dissyllabic flexions: Cz. *rámě* 'arm' *břímě* 'burden' *plémě* 'tribe' (G*S. ramene břemene plemene*). An exception is *písmě* 'letter'. It is not easy to determine where the stress originally lay in the *n*-masculines and neuters. From other languages we have: Gk. ἄκμων 'anvil'/ἡγεμών 'leader', L. *akmuō* 'stone' A*S. ākmeni̯* G. *akmeñs* N*P. ākmens* G. *akmenų̃*. In Slovene there has been an accent-shift in these declensions: Slov. *tèle* 'calf' G*S. teléta, pléme* G*S. pleména*. In Russian the accent shifts between the singular and the plural: R. *plémja* G*S. plémeni*/NAV*P. plemená*. What is recorded by the Czechoslovak quantities is thus an accent-shift occurring at a time when there was still a free accent in Proto-Czech. So also the *r*-stem: Cz. *máti* 'mother' G*S. mateře*.

Among nouns of the *a*-declension there are differences of length which may be explained by the *tort*-formula, as above. In these and other words the length may vary within the declension, the quantity being, for instance, long in the nominative and accusative, and short in some of the oblique cases: Cz. *brána* 'gate' I*S. branou* (and so also *kráva* 'cow' *dráha* 'road' *sláma* 'straw' *vrána* 'crow'/R. *boroná* 'harrow' *koróva doróga solóma voróna*), *práce* 'work' I*S. prací, kůže* 'hide' I*S. koží, pára* 'steam' I*S. parou*, etc. There are some words which have a short vowel only in the gen.pl., and others which carry the long vowel throughout the declension. Not all such words are covered by the *tort*-formula; and whereas the long vowel can often be accounted for (e.g. CSl. rising *ě* >*ie* >*í* in *víra* 'faith'), its vacillation is unexplained. Generally speaking, when Czechoslovak longs and shorts do not correspond to Common Slavonic rising and falling (or short) syllables, one must assume the working of analogy or the effects of stress-shift.

(iii) The principle of compensatory lengthening for loss of *jer* is found in both Polish and Czechoslovak, though not under identical conditions. For *o* and *e* (and the nasal vowel in Polish) this leads to a change of timbre. In Polish the distinction of quantity has been eliminated, leaving only that of quality; in Czechoslovak both remain.

The Mediæval Polish system of secondary quantities is still alive in the North Cassubian dialects. It was at first imperfectly represented. The alphabet was based on the Latin model, which ignores differences of quantity. None the less, spellings occur like *Milees* (1155) *staan* 'state' (13th cent.), which seem to be attempts to show longer quantity. Jakób Parkosz (c. 1440) expressly asserted that 'omnes vocales modo longantur modo patulo breviantur'. By the sixteenth century, however, the distinction of length had become obsolescent: 'Antiqui

Poloni longas vocales geminabant, breves simplicibus pingebant' (Zaborowski, 1520). At about this time the acute accent was borrowed from Czech, where it represented length. The copyist of the St John fragment of 1516 vacillates: *oswieeca/swiécy wolee/volé*. He seems to have been embarrassed by signs denoting length where he found only difference of quality. The qualitative difference certainly goes back to the fourteenth century, when diphthongs appeared in the place of geminated vowels: *guor/gór* (gen.pl.) 'of mountains' *synvow/synów* 'of sons' *Buog/Bóg* (cf. OCz. *Buoh*/MCz. *Bůh*) 'God'. There is nothing to show greater antiquity for this difference of quality. Modern Polish spelling distinguishes only *ó* = [u]. This letter was usually left unaccented in the eighteenth century, but *é* was regularly used to denote a close [e] approaching [i]; the seventeenth century marked *á é*, the former to denote a sound approximating to [ɔ], and *ó* less often.

In Mediæval Polish there was only one nasal (*ǫ*). In the fifteenth century *ą* began to appear; later, *ę*. At first this latter denoted shorter length than *ą;* later, more open quality.

Compensation for loss of final *e* occurs in P. *któż* 'who then' *cóż* 'what then'. The commonest cause for compensation was the loss of final *jer* (nom.sg., gen.pl.): nom.sg. *mróz* 'ice' *chleb* (dial. *chléb* [χłip]) 'bread' *dąb* 'oak' *mąż* 'husband'/gen.sg. *mrozu chleba dęba męża*. Final nasal consonants impede the change in Polish: *dom* 'house' *zakon* 'order' *koń* 'horse'. Analogy works a like effect: *pęd* 'speed' : : *pędzić* 'hurry'. Words ending in a voiceless consonant are also generally exempted: *płot* 'hedge' *sęp* 'vulture' *chłop* 'yokel'. Gen.pl.masc. *-ów* < *-ovŭ: dębów* 'of oaks', cf. Cz. *hadů(v)* 'of snakes' *hradů(v)* 'of cities'. Gen.pl.fem.neut. - < *-ŭ/ĭ* causes compensation except in nasal stems: *ksiąg* 'of books'/*księga wód* 'of waters'/*woda rąk* 'of hands'/ *ręka pól* 'of fields'/*pole*, but *imion* 'of names' (nasal stem). New words and some others are excepted from this change: gen.pl. *strof/strofa* 'verse' *sof/sofa* 'sofa' *jędz/jędza* 'vixen' *gawęd/gawęda* 'talk'.

Compensation for the loss of *jer* in the diminutive suffix is irregular in Polish: *wózka* 'little cart' *dójka* 'milkmaid'/*wędka* 'fishing-rod'. Forms like *dąbek* 'little oak' *wózek* 'little cart' are due to the influence of oblique cases.

In Czech compensatory lengthening of the nom.sg.masc. of *o/jo-* and *i-*stems appears arbitrary: *chléb* 'bread' *sníh* 'snow' *Bůh* 'God' *kůň* 'horse' (where a final nasal is no impediment) *déšt* 'rain' *sůl* 'salt'/ *had* 'snake' *lev* 'lion' *Řek* 'Greek' *muž* 'man, husband' *meč* 'sword' *kost* 'bone' *čest* 'honour'. When lengthening takes place in Serbocroat it is associated with a falling tone in the stem-vowel: S. *Bôg* (gen. *Bôga*) 'God'; but it is not certain whether intonation affects the issue in Czech. The words compensated are those which have become monosyllabic by loss of final *jer*, but GPM. *-ů* (formerly *-ův*) always shows compensatory length. Compensation is not found in Cz. gen.pl. fem.neut. (though it is in Slovak). Perhaps the analogy of other plural cases, in which the stem remained short, prevented this change. In the dat.loc.pl. *-ům -ách/ích* there is compensation in the flexion. On the other hand, loss of *jer* causes metatony resulting in shortening in Cz. *kláda* 'log' gen.pl. *klad* and other words. Slovak gen.pl. *hranic* (*hranica* 'boundary') shows lengthening, which does not appear in Cz. *hranic*.

When a suffix is added in Czech, the lengthened vowel of the simple word may or may not be retained. The diminutive *-ko* regularly preserves such vowels, but with *-ka* usage is variable and apparently arbitrary. In dialects lengthening occurs with the participle in *-ł*: dial. *volál/volala*.

The semivowel *j* causes long vowels to arise (as in Serbocroat and Old Bulgarian): Cz. *půjdu* 'I shall go' *stůj* 'stop' *můj* 'my' dial. *náj-* (superlative prefix); cf. P. *mój stój* etc.

(iv) Lengthening due to contraction is also a feature of Old Polish and Czechoslovak. These contractions establish a clear distinction between West and East Slavonic. Among the most important of them are:

aja oja aje >*ā*: OB. *dobraja* Cz. *dobrá* P. *dobra*, OB. *stojati* Cz. *státi* P. *stać* (cf. *Joan* >Cz. *Ján* P. *Jan*), OB. *dělajetů* Cz. *dělá* P. *dziala*. Gen.sg.masc.neut. of adjectives Cz. *-ého* P. *-ego* (OB. *-ajego*) takes *e* from the pronominal ending CSl. *-ego*.

oje >*ē*: OB. *moje* Cz. *mé* P. *me*.

ojo >*ǭ*: OB. *sobojǫ* P. *sobą* Cz. *sebou*.

ěja >'*ā*: OB. *sějati* Cz. *sáti* P. *siać*.

ěje >'*e*: OB. *umějetů* OCz. *umie*/MCz. *umí* P. *umie*.

All the Polish long vowels have been shortened. These contractions are due to the loss of *j* between vowels, and have had an important effect on the declension of definite adjectives and the declension of nouns with stems ending in a vowel followed by a *j*-suffix. Uncontracted forms were found in Polish as late as the fifteenth century: OP. *znajemy* 'we know' *okopaje* 'will dig up' *umieje* 'knows how to'.

In Old Czech certain prepositions lengthened the initial vowel of a following noun: OCz. *kaapostolom* 'to the apostles'. Hence MCz. *vůbec* (*v obec*) 'in general'. *vůči* (*v oči*) 'in view of'. Prefixes are frequently lengthened: Cz. *národ* 'people' *výkres* 'design' *původ* 'source'.

(v) In Wendish there are no original long vowels still surviving, but vowels are narrowed under some conditions and also lengthened from secondary causes. The narrowing affects only *o e* in Upper Wendish. Lengthening occurs in a stressed open syllable (unless the next begins with *š s*), and by reason of a following *j w*. In Miklawusch Jakubica's

Lower Wendish New Testament (1548) the still surviving long vowels were marked by doubling the letter, with or without intrusive *h*: *zczuhutcz*/*sćuć* 'behead' *maasch*/*maš* 'hast'.

(vi) In Slovak a sort of balance has been established in adjectives according to which those with a short stem-vowel have a long vowel in the ending, as in Czech (e.g. Slovak *vel'ký* 'great' gen.sg.masc. *vel'kého* nom.sg.fem. *vel'ká*/Cz. *velký velkého velká*), but those with a long stem-vowel have a short vowel in the ending (Slovak. *krásny* 'beautiful' *krásneho krásna*/Cz. *krásný krásného krásná*).

141. *Oral Vowels.* It should be noted that in Standard Czech initial vowels are preceded by the glottal stop. A result is that prepositions are devoiced: Cz. *v Americe* 'in America' [f 'ámɛritsɛ]. In Czech dialects and in Wendish, initial vowels tend to prefix *v* or *h*, e.g. LowWend. *wóraś* 'to plough' (OB. *orati*) *hupiś* 'to drink' (*u-piti*). This feature is found sporadically elsewhere.

A. P. *pani* 'lady' *jagnię* 'lamb' *jajko* 'egg' *ziemia* 'earth' *dusza* 'soul'; UpWend. *bratr* 'brother' *jejko* 'egg' *duša* 'soul'; Cz. *máti* 'mother' *jehně* 'lamb' *duše* 'soul', *dej* 'give'.

In the languages affiliated to Polish the vowel *a* tends toward *o*. When lengthened in Old Polish *á* had the value of *å*. So Polab. *brot* 'brother' Cass. *barôn* 'ram' *pôn*/*pön* 'gentleman' Wendish Slovene *påun* Polab. *råtoj* 'ploughman'. OP. *czaas* 'time' *laas* 'wood' testify to differences of quality and quantity not now observed in the literary tongue. The Mazovian dialects tend to make *a* into *e*: P. *rano* 'morning'/Maz. *reno*.

In Wendish *a* has been maintained except between soft consonants, when it becomes *e* in Upper Wendish.

In Czech (but not Slovak) this tendency has gone further, since *a* is modified to *ě*/*ie* >*i* after originally palatal or soft consonants, and to *e* before *j* (Cz. *dej* <*daj*). The pronunciation of *a* (and *u*) after a soft consonant in Old Czech has to be inferred from later history, since the soft pronunciation is not at first clearly marked. Thus OCz. *zema* 'earth'/*zima* 'winter' employ the same letters for *ṁ*/*m* and '*a*/*a*. This kind of spelling is found in the twelfth century: *ialovica* 'heifer' 1130, *strasa*/*stráž(e)* 'guard' 1143. With the first years of the thirteenth century the palatalization is fully recognized: OCz. *berne* 'tax' 1208 *bernie* 1249 (*berně*), *Skalice* (<*-ca*) 1211 *chtwrtne* 'quarter' (measure) 1249 (*čtvrtně*). The palatal on-glide was quite perceptible, but has been absorbed by a previous palatal consonant in Modern Czech: Cz. *nouze* 'poverty' *bouře* 'storm' *vůle* 'will'. The process of eliminating the on-glide (dispalatalization) began in the fourteenth century. The instance of *vůle* shows that this occurred while *ĺ* was still distinct from *l*. When lengthened, *ě* became OCz. *ie* MCz. *í*: OCz. *dušiech* MCz. *dušich* (LP.) (12th cent. *dušách*).

O. P. ogrodu (*GS.*) 'of a garden' *ogród* 'garden' *mróz* 'frost'; Up Wend. *hora* 'hill' *hórka* 'hillock'; Cz. *Bůh GS. Boha* 'God', Slovak *Bôh Boha*.

In each of the main West Slavonic languages a lengthened *ó* has developed into a diphthong (*uo*), which is still heard in Wendish and Slovak, and is still represented in Czech spelling (*ů*); in Polish and Czech the diphthong has become a narrow vowel [u], which remains long in Czech but has been shortened in Polish. In the fifteenth century the diphthong was established in Czech spelling: *buoh* 'God' *duóm* 'house' *púost* 'fasting'. The letter *ů* is merely another form of the diphthong. In the sixteenth century *u* and *ú* are frequently found: *zakonum* (*DP.*) 'to the laws' *bůh dům*.

In Polish dialects *o* tends to develop into a diphthong (*uo*) after labial consonants. In Cassubian this occurs after labials and velars: *kuost* 'bóne' *puole* 'field' (with the narrower element made prominent). Further west, in Wendish Slovene, this becomes a diphthong of the mixed back-front order (*üö*), and in Polabian it becomes *ü*, which may further develop to *ö* before hard dentals: Polab. *nebü* 'heaven' *nüga* 'foot'. *O* is also found as *vå*: Polab. *vågard* 'garden'.

In the Czech of Prague initial *o- >vo-*.

E. P. *śnieg* 'snow' *deszcz* 'rain' *miasto/LS. mieście* 'township' *imienia GS./GP. imion* (*imię* 'name') 1S. *plotę/2S. pleciesz* 'plait'; LowWend. *ńebjo* 'heaven' UpWend. *pjerje* 'feather' LowWend. *wjasele* 'joy'; Cz. *nesete* 'ye bear' OCz. *řéci* 'to say'/MCz. *říci* OCz. *hňésti* 'kneed'/MCz. *hnísti* Slovak *žien* (gen.pl. of *žena* 'woman'), with compensatory lengthening, OCz. *nebeskeey* 'heavenly' (NASN.), OCz. *miesto/MCz. místo* 'place' OCz. *zpazenie/MCz. spasení* 'salvation', OCz. *miesto/MCz. město* 'town' OCz. *sẇet/MCz. svět* 'world'. In Prague *é* is pronounced *í*.

The vowels CSl. *ě/e* differed in West Slavonic as the diphthong *ie*/soft *e*. In Polish, as in Russian, soft and palatalized consonants united in one order, and in this respect there was no difference between *ě/e*. None appears in the earliest Polish documents. On the other hand, some difference of quality led to different results in the process of dispalatalization before certain hard consonants (*d t z s n ł r*), since in such circumstances CSl. *ě >P.'a* and CSl. *e >P.'o*: P. *miasto/imion*. (P. *e <i* develops like CSl. *e;* cf. the frequent dispalatalization of CSl. *ę* to P. *'ą*: P. *dziewiąty* 'ninth'). The two processes occurred in Proto-Polish; it is not certain whether they were contemporary. In the Bull of 1136, which is the first record of Polish, *ě >'a* occurs in *Bałouanz/Białowąs Balouezici/Białowieżycy Quatek/ Kwiatek*, etc. As dispalatalization does not take place before soft consonants, except by analogy, or before hard consonants other than those of the dento-alveolar order, this development has led to alternating stems in Polish declensions and conjugations which are partly due to analogy. It is characteristic of the whole so-called Lechitic group: Cass. *žona* 'wife' *sostra* 'sister' *cało* 'body' *vjara* 'faith'; Polab. *bol* (*⟨bělŭ⟩* 'white'/*sestra* 'sister' *med* 'honey' (*e* is not dispalatalized in Polabian, but *ǐ ę* are in Polab. *dăn* 'day' *dvăr* 'door' *desąt* 'ten'). The fact that this outlying member of the group should not have *e >'o* is an argument for regarding this change as later than *ě >'a*.

These dispalatalizations occur in Wendish only in the dialects of Sorau and Guben, spoken in an area now largely incorporated in Poland. The passage of *e >'o* is general, and not conditioned as in the Lechitic languages: LowWend. *śopły* 'warm' UpWend. *lód* 'ice' LowWend. *móŕo* 'sea' *pleśo* 'plaits'. The vowel *ě* remains before hard and soft consonants: LowWend. *běg*/UpWend. *běh* 'race' LowWend. *gwězda*/UpWend. *hwězda* 'star'. In unaccented syllables it appears as *(j)e* or *(j)ë* (a more open *e* not indicated in ordinary print): LowWend. *kupjela* 'bath' *zelězo* 'iron'.

In Czech the two vowels frequently remain quite distinct: CSl. *ě >* OCz. *ie*. The diphthong has become an open vowel (MCz. *ě* = [ɛ] with preceding soft consonant or intercalated [j]) when short, and when lengthened it has become the long narrow vowel (MCz. *í*). Examples of the simple long vowel go back to about 1300, but the spelling *ie* continued into the sixteenth century. Cz. *e* is without palatal on-glide.

U Y I. P. dwu (*GD.*) 'of two' *duch* 'spirit' *wody* (*GS.*) 'of water' *nowy* 'new' *kości* (*NP.*) 'bones' *rzeczy* 'things'; UpWend. *buk* 'beech' *błysk* 'lightning' *počinać* 'begin'; Cz. *duch* 'spirit' OCz. *běhún*/MCz. *běhoun* 'runner' *vysoký* 'high' *jazyk* 'tongue' *síla* 'force' *niť* 'thread'.

CSl. *u* remains in Polish. In Cassubian it often becomes a short *ě*, and in Polabian *eu: deusa* 'spirit'. In Lower Wendish *u >y* after labials, but the written style sometimes retains *u: kłobyk*/*kłobuk* 'hat' *rozym*/UpWend. *rozom* 'understanding'. It may develop further into *i: Libin*/*Lubin* dial. *witro* 'morning'. OCz. *ú <o* and *ojǫ* has passed through *au* to *ou: OCz. súd saud*/MCz. *soud* 'court' OCz. *hlavú hlavau* (*IS.*)/MCz. *hlavou* 'by the head'. The long vowel arose either by perpetuating original quantity or by lengthening during the history of Czech. It is normal in texts of the early fourteenth century, but with the beginning of the fifteenth it gives way to *au*, though still found as late as the end of the sixteenth century. The diphthong *au* is due to dissimilation, the first half of the long vowel (= *uu*) opening. It enters with the last quarter of the fourteenth century and lasts into the seventeenth: *Tropauss* 1373, *vykaupye* (3*P.*) 'ransom', *Kraupa* 1400, *Kaldeyskaw* 1470. Some writers preferred this diphthong as late as 1849. In the fifteenth century the diphthong had become *ou* by the

reassimilation of its two elements: OCz. *korowhwie* 'banners' (15th cent.)/MCz. *korouhve*. It was the most usual from the beginning of the seventeenth century. Meanwhile, *'u* preceded by a palatal developed into a front vowel, as did *'a*. At first this was not marked: the *u* of OCz. I*S. zemu/zimu* appeared the same, but was in fact different. Then came the sign *iu* (*yu*): *pokazyu sie* 'show myself' (14th cent.). In the same century forms like *zemy* (A*S*.) show the full development had taken place.

CSl. *y* persists in Polish as a separate sound; it is there a retracted *i* not unlike Ruth. и. As a result of the rise of soft velars *k ǵ* and (less often) *ch*, *y* is replaced by *i*: P. *ginąć* 'perish' *sługi* 'servants' *matki* 'mothers'. Conversely, *y* is substituted for original *i* as a result of the hardening of the palatals *sz cz szcz ż rz*: P. *oczy* 'eyes'. Before an *r* original *y* >*e* from the beginning of the fifteenth century: *cztery* 'four' *pasterz* 'herdsman'. In Wendish also the original pronunciation persists, but with exchanges for *u* or *i*. The oldest Czechoslovak transcriptions were by means of *ui*, as in Old Slovene: Cz. *Buitsow/Bydžov* 1186, *Buitic* 1196, *Buistrice* 1226. Hus (1406) used the sign *y*, and said the sound was made 'ponendo principium linguæ sub inferioribus dentibus et in medio elevando linguam per modum circuli'. The distinction of letter was maintained by the Moravian Brethren for their great Bible (1579–93), and it remains to this day. The sounds of *y* and *i*, however, are now identical, and are not some middle value as in Ruthenian but the forward vowel *i*. *I* >*y* in Cz. *blýskati* 'shine' and in dialects after *c z s*. In Prague Cz. *ý* is pronounced *ej*; cf. *ú* >*ou* in Standard Czech.

In Cassubian *y* has become generally the same as *i*, but after labials and liquids it is a short back *ě*. In Polabian, German influence has made accented *y* to sound as *åj*.

Loss of *i* sometimes occurs in Polish initially: *grać/igrać* 'play' *iglica*/OP. *glica* 'bodkin' *mieć*/OP. *imieć* 'have'; medially: *wieliki/ wielki* 'big'; and finally (2*S*. imperative and infin.): *chwal* 'praise' *bacz* 'heed' *mieszkać* 'dwell'. It appears as a semivowel in Cz. *jméno* 'name' *jho* 'yoke', etc.

Jers. The *jers* are lost in weak position, and in strong position they both originally became *e*: P. *dzień* G*S*. *dnia* 'day' *koniec* G*S*. *końca* 'end' *łeb* G*S*. *łba* 'head'; UpWend. (*són* 'dream') *dźeń* 'day'; Cz. *pátek* 'Friday' *den* 'day' *sen* 'dream' *orel* 'eagle'. It is characteristic of West Slavonic that the *jers* should both give *e* (apart from later changes affecting that vowel); Slovak, however, frequently has *o* <*ŭ* as in Russian and some forms of Bulgarian. Dispalatalization occurs as for original *e* in Polish and Wendish.

142. *Nasal Vowels*. P. *wąż* G*S*. *węža* 'snake' *sędzia* 'judge' *niosę* 'I bear' *będąc* 'being'; LowWend. *gus* 'goose' UpWend. *husyca*,

LowWend. *pěty* UpWend. *pjaty* 'fifth'; Cz. *ruka* 'hand' *pět* 'five' *pátek* 'Friday'; Slovak *päť* 'five'.

(i) CSl. *ǫ*/*ę* persisted into twelfth-century Polish, but with their timbres very closely allied (approximately nasal *ą̇*/*ä̇*). In the Bull of 1136 they are represented by a large variety of devices: *an en un/am em um/ o e u: Bałouanz Deuentliz Lunciz Sodouo Chomesa Chrustov/Białowąz Dziewiętlic Łęczyca Żądowo Chomięża Chrząstow.* The scribe had in mind two sounds, the one akin to both *a* and *o*, the other akin to *e*. The soft variant (*ę*) had been dispalatalized before hard dento-alveolars (*Bałouanz/Chomesa*, due to hard *z*/soft *ż*). This was a feature of all Lechitic languages. In the thirteenth century the transcriptions overlap, since CSl. *ǫ* is found as P. *an am a/en em e/on om o/un u y* and CSl. *ę* as *an am a/en em e/ on o/u/in.* A new sign for nasality (*ø*), sometimes barred, sometimes with a tick on each side, came into use to denote the single sound which had resulted from both ancient nasals: OP. *swøtego/świętego* 'holy' *sø/są, wilil iesm w mø duszø moiø/mię duszę moją* 'I poured out my soul within me' (Florian Psalter, 14th century). The scribe of the Puławy Psalter (mid 15th century) distinguished two nasal vowels: *tobø/tobą* (I.S.) 'by thee' *będę* 'I shall be'. The distinction implied was mainly one of length, and depended on the conditions stated in section 140. By the sixteenth century, however, a qualitative difference had supervened. P. *ą* had come to be pronounced again as [ɔ̃]. In 1568 it is said to be equivalent to Fr. *an* (and to Italian *an*, which is different in all but the backward position of the vowel), and in 1612 it is said to be as in Germ. *Bank Gesang;* but Germans are chided in 1600 for pronouncing *prostą* as if it were *prostam*, and in 1612 Germ. *on* is said to be its equivalent (*mąka=moncka*). In the seventeenth and eighteenth centuries there are denasalized spellings in *o* corresponding to pronunciations now heard: *wzioł=wziął* 'took' *minoł=minął* 'passed'. Meanwhile the short nasal *ę* had become a front nasal [ɛ̃]. Finally, the distinction of length was lost, and only that of quality remained. Before some following consonants in Modern Polish a nasal vowel develops a nasal consonant of the same class as the following consonant: *dąb* [dɔmp] *mądra* [mɔndra] *ręką* [rɛŋkɔ]. When final or before *l* it may be denasalized: *ręką* [rɛŋkɔ rɛŋkɔ] *minął* [mínɔł mínəł].

In Cassubian CSl. *ę* remains nasal before hard dento-alveolars, where it is dispalatalized: *mjąso* 'meat' *čąsto* 'often'. Otherwise (i.e. before palatals, velars and labials) it was narrowed to *i*, and then denasalized to *i*: *pisc* 'fist' *cygnie* 'pulls'/P. *pięść ciągnie.* CSl. *ǫ* became Cass. *ą: rąka* 'hand'. In Polabian there were also two nasals: *ą* < *ę* (before back consonants and final and < *jǫ*), and *ǫ* < *ę* (before hard front consonants and < *ǫ*): *mą* (A.S.) 'me' *mąsü* 'meat'/*pǫty* 'fifth' *jǫzyk* 'tongue' *rǫkǫ* (A.S.) 'hand' *gǫs* 'goose'.

(ii) In Czechoslovak and Wendish CSl. *ǫ* >*u*, *ę* >*ja* (*'a*), with certain further modifications. The vowel *u* remains unaltered, save that long OCz. *ú* >MCz. *ou*: Cz. *bloud* 'fool'. After the labials short *'a* appears as *ä* in Slovak: Slovak *päť* five' *pamäť* 'memory' *sväzok* 'volume'. In Czech and in Upper Wendish *ja* (*á*) >*ě* before an originally soft consonant: Cz. *pět* 'five' UpWend. *pjeć*. In Lower Wendish the vowel *ě* is found in all instances: LowWend. *měso*/UpWend. *mjaso* 'meat' LowWend. *pěty*/UpWend. *pjaty* 'fifth'. The vowel *ě* lengthens to OCz. *ie* MCz. *í*, so that CSl. *ę* corresponds to (*j*)*a*/*ě*/*í* according to later developments: Cz. *pátek* 'Friday' Slk. *piatok*/*pěst* 'fist'/*říditi* 'direct'.

143. (*a*) *Tort*. P. *gród* 'town, castle' *groch* 'pea' *głos* 'voice' *głowa* 'head' *brzeg* 'bank' *mleko* 'milk'; UpWend. *broda* 'beard' *hłód* 'hunger' *srjeda* 'middle'; Cz. *hrad hlava břeh mléko*.

(i) In Polish and Wendish the same solutions have been obtained. In Old Polish prepositions were vocalized before words of this series: OP. *ode młodości* 'from youth up' *we śród* 'amidst'/*w strumeniu* 'in the stream'. This is an indication that the presence, or recent presence, of a fugitive vowel in the initial syllable was still recognized: *mᵒło-sᵉre-*. P. *śród* is a special development from **śrzód*.

In Polish place-names there are traces of another procedure: *Karwina*/P. *krowa* 'cow', and possibly also in *chabry*/*chrobry* 'brave' (**charbry?*). In Cassubian the forms deriving from *tort* are various: Cass. *groch* 'pea' *droga* 'road' *parg* and *próg* 'threshold', *-gard(a)* in place-names. Otherwise the development is as in Polish. Further west, Polabian has *stárna* 'side'/*bórzda* 'furrow'/*gord* 'castle' *korvó* 'cow'/*brüöda* 'beard' (an isolated solution); *gluod* 'hunger'; *brég* 'bank' *bréza* 'beech'; *mlåko* 'milk'. In the last word *telt* has been treated like *tolt*, and this also occurs in Cassubian (cf. R. *molokó*): Cass. *młoć* 'grind'/P. *mleć*. The western branches of the Lechitic group thus show important differences from Polish and Wendish. CSl. *tort* must have given *tårt* as a first stage of the future developments *tart* and *tort*, but *tolt tert telt* suffered metathesis in the usual way.

(ii) On the other hand, Czechoslovak agrees with the South Slavonic languages in replacing CSl. *tort tolt* by *trat tlat*. Again the middle point of the development must have been the vowel *å*, viz. *tort* >*tårt* >*tåråt* >*trat*. CSl. *tert telt* > Cz. **trět *tlět*, the former giving palatal *ř* (OCz. *třět*), with later dispalatalization of the vowel (MCz. *třet*). Both *a* and *ě* have become liable to lengthening in Czechoslovak, resulting in *á* and OCz. *ie é*/MCz. *í é*: Cz. *hrad* 'castle' *brána* 'gate' *vlas* 'hair' *vláda* 'government' *břeh* 'bank' *břímě* 'load' *mříti* 'die' *mlíti* 'grind' *mléko* 'milk'.

(*b*) *Ort-*. P. *radło* 'hoe' *łakomy* 'greedy' *łabędź* 'swan'/*rość* 'grow'; *łoński* 'last year's'; UpWend. *łakomc* 'climber'/*rość* 'grow'; Cz. *radlo lakomý labuť růsti roz-*. The different results seem to agree with a difference of tone in Common Slavonic: CSl. *órt-* >*rat-*/*órt-* >*rot-*. There is no similar difference in *ert- elt-*, but the latter shows some discrepancies. R. *lébeď* OB. *lebędǐ* imply **elbendǐ/olbondǐ* >P. *łabędź* Cz. *labut;* and Cz. *lebeda*/P. *łoboda* 'green orach' differ in the initial syllable.

In Polabian the difference of tone gives different results: Polab. *råtoj* 'ploughman' *Låbi* 'Elbe'/*rüla* 'ploughland' *rüst* 'grow' *rüz* 'separate'.

(c) *Tŭrt.* P. *gardło* 'throat' *bardzo* 'very'/*śmierć* 'death' *mierzić* (pronounced -*rž*-) 'disgust' (OP. *śmirć mirzić*), hardened in *martwy* 'dead', *tłusty* 'stout' *dług* 'debt' OP. *słuńce* (MP. *słońce*) 'sun' *mowa* 'talk' (OP. *mołwa*) *pełny* 'full' *wełna* 'wool'/*wilk* 'wolf'; Wend.Low. *gjardło*/Up. *hordło* Low. *ẃerch*/Up. *wjeŕch* 'top' Low. *twardy*/Up. *twjerdy* 'hard' Low. *carny*/Up. *čorny* 'black'; Cz. *prst* 'finger' *vlk* 'wolf' *vlna* 'wool' *plný* 'full'/ *chlum* 'hill' *slunce* (Slovak *slnko*) 'sun'/ *černý* 'black' *čert* 'devil' *žernov* 'millstone' (OCz. *črný črt žrnov*).

There were no sonants in Common Slavonic, but for the West Slavonic forms it is necessary to start from sonant *r/l* in both hard and soft types, viz. WSl. *trt/tr̥t tl̥t/tl̥t*. The simplest consequences of this situation are found in Old Czech, where the qualitative difference has been lost, and there remain only OCz. *tr̥t tl̥t*. At a later period vowels have developed: *l̥* (*ŭl/lŭ*) >MCz. *lu*, *r̥* (after *č ž* and in some isolated cases like *trest* 'reed') >MCz. *er*.

In Polish and Wendish *r̥* has been hardened, before hard dentals in Polish and more generally in Wendish. Hence alternations like P. *śmierć/martwy*. The difference between MP. *śmierć*/OP. *śmirć* is only orthographic for some speakers, since the former is often given a close pronunciation (*ié*) approximating to *i*. The result is that WSl. *trt* >P. *tart* and WSl. *tr̥t* >P. *tirt* (unless later hardened). Similarly WSl. *tl̥t* >P. *tłut* and WSl. *tl̥t* >P. *tilt*. But these later correspondences are traversed by some other considerations. WSl. *tl̥t* has been confused with *tl̥t* in many instances, and after a labial it then results in *tełt* (*pełny*). After labials, also, original *tl̥t* may become OP. *tołt* (OP. *mołwa* MP. *mowa*).

In Cassubian and Wendish Slovene *trt/tr̥t* were distinguished: Cass. *gardło/smirc* (but hardened in *cwiardy* 'hard'); but *tl̥t* alone was found: Cass. *polny wołk*, Wendish Slovene *pouny vouk*. The same is true of Polabian: *garnak* 'milk-pot'/*dérzat* 'hold' (hardened in *tjårde* 'hard') *tåusty* 'stout' *våuk* 'wolf'.

144. *Czechoslovak Sonants.* CSl.OB. *sedmǐ osmǐ* >OCz. *sedm osm* (monosyllables)/MCz. *sedm osm* (dissyllables—also pronounced *sedum* (*v*)*osum* : : GS. *sedmi osmi* (dissyllabic declensional forms), This leads to full vocalization in some dialects: dial. *sedem osem*. Similarly, MCz.

blázen 'madman' *bázeň* 'fear' *kázeň* 'discipline'/OCz. *blázn bázň kázň*
and Cz. *bratr* 'brother' *mysl* 'mind' *mohl* 'could' were monosyllabic in
Old Czech, but are now dissyllabic, with sonant r̥/l̥. A medial sonant l̥
has developed in *slza* 'tear', which was monosyllabic in Old Czech.
Vocalization of medial sonants occurs in dial. *smert* 'death' *pelný* 'full',
and in Cz. *pluk* 'regiment' *žert* 'jest' *žertva* 'victim' *červ* 'worm', etc.
The earliest example of this vocalization is *czerven* 'June' 1251, but
the examples increased throughout the fourteenth and fifteenth
centuries. Czech dialects show that sonant r̥ was sometimes long, and
that sonant l̥ had two qualities and two lengths in parts of the area;
Slovak still distinguishes length in sonant *r* and *l*.

145. *Velars and Postpalatals.* MP. *ptak* NP. *ptaki* 'bird', *brzeg* 'bank'
brzegi, *ręka* GS. *ręki* 'hand', *noga* GS. *nogi* 'foot', *kielich* 'chalice'
geografia 'geography', *chytry* 'cunning'; UpWend. *wulki* 'big'/Up
Wend. *dołhi* LowWend. *dłujki/długi* 'long' LowWend. *duchy*
(NAP.) 'spirits'/UpWend. *duchi*; Cz. *žák* 'pupil' *soudruh* 'comrade'
hoch 'lad'/NP. *žáci soudruzi hoši*; Slovak DLSF. *ruke* 'hand' *nohe*
'foot'/Cz. *matce mouše dráze* (*matka* 'mother' *moucha* 'fly' *dráha* 'way').
UpWend. *khlěb* 'bread'; in this language initial *ch-* has become
aspirated *k*, and *ě* represents the diphthong [iə].

(*a*) *Palatalization of k g ch.* Ky gy have palatalized in Polish to
ki gi; in Cassubian they have developed further into *ći dži*, and in
Polabian to *ti di*: P. *kij* 'stick' Cass. *ćij*/Cz. *kyj. Chy* normally remains;
in *wymachiwać* 'brandish' *rozdmuchiwać* 'blow away' etc. the suffix
-iwać is due to the analogy of *k/g+iwać* (*oczekiwać* 'await'). The Polish
change can be dated as of the fifteenth century: *drugich* (mid. 15th
cent.)/*wszystky* (14th cent.). In Lower Wendish this palatalization
is as in Polish, but Upper Wendish has normally *chi*. The restoration of soft forms of the velars helped to eliminate some of the effects
of second Slavonic palatalization from the declensions of nouns and
adjectives, as in Russian. In Czech there has been no such development. However, the hardening of *e* has led to the reinstatement before
it in Slovak of hard *k g*.

West Slavonic differs from East and South Slavonic in the fact that
ch >*š* in both Slavonic palatalizations: P. *dusza* Cz. *duše* 'soul' P.
musze Cz. *mouše* (DLSF.) 'fly'.

Foreign words had provided *k̓ ǵ* even in Old Bulgarian (OB. *k̓esaři*
'Cæsar' *gazofilakija* 'treasury'). They produce palatals before *e* in
Polish, except in the most modern borrowings.

(*b*) *Velar fricative h.* In the sixteenth century an occlusive *g* was
often written with a diacritic in Czech (*synaǧoǧa* 'synagogue'). It was
limited to foreign words, and even among these the more intimate
have a fricative velar (*hrabě* 'count' <Germ. *Graf*). Native Czech
words took the fricative pronunciation in the period between the

middle third of the thirteenth century and the first third of the fourteenth, fully three centuries after this feature had appeared in South Russia: Cz. *gora* 'hill' 1228 *gore* 1213/*hora* 1241/*ogarzie* 'hounds' 1322. Later loanwords used *k* to denote the occlusion: *Aukšpurk* 'Augsburg' *kvalt* 'power' (Germ. *Gewalt*). In contact with the dentals *k* might become fricative: *vetký*/*vetchý* 'frail'. In Czecho-slovak dialects *h* is frequently lost before *r l n*, especially in initial position: *onedy*/*onehdy* 'lately' *rozen*/*hrozen* 'grape' *Řek* (literary Czech) *ʃ*'Greek'. In Old Czech *h* was used in combination with other letters to help denote peculiarly Slavonic sounds, and it often appeared intrusively: OCz. *Habraham Hemma Kabrhel* 'Gabriel'; cf. also the intrusive initial *h-* before vowels in Czech and Wendish (section 141).

In the fifteenth and sixteenth centuries the influence of Czech upon Polish was strong and led to the introduction of *h* into Polish, the more readily since it was already a feature of the Ruthenian of Polish Galicia: P. *hańba* 'disgrace' *hardy* 'haughty' *rohatyna* 'javelin' *hrabia* 'count'. There were instances of confusion of *k*/*g* with *ch* at the same time, but they were never more than sporadic. A spelling-mistake common in Modern Polish is the confusion of *h* and *ch*.

146. *Dentals and Alveolars.* (i) As observed in sections 39–41, the Common Slavonic dentals and alveolars had three variant pronuncia-tions: hard, soft, and palatalized. In principle what occurs in Western Slavonic is the coincidence of the soft and palatalized varieties in palatal sibilants. The latter tend to become 'hard', that is, normal or self-sufficient, without a glide of the nature of [j] between the sibilant and the following vowel. The original soft dentals and alveolars—those before a front vowel—developed into palatals later than the originally palatalized forms—those before the semivowel *j;* and this has led to minor discrepancies in the sibilants which result from them: P. *t*/ *ć* (originally soft), *c* (originally palatalized), *d*/ *dź dz*, *ł*/ *l*, *r*/ *rz*, *n*/ *ń*, *s*/ *ś sz*, *z*/ *ź ž*. Wendish agrees with Polish in general, but in Czech (though not Slovak) we have to reckon among 'hard' vowels *e* (CSl. *e ĭ ŭ*) and the *jers*, which disappeared without permanently softening the preceding consonant. The two dentals have remained less developed in their soft forms: Cz. *t*/ *t c*, *d*/ *ď dz* >*z*, and the distinction of types of *l* has been lost. (ii) Before the hard dentals and alveolars the vowel *e* has been 'hardened' in Polish and Wendish (section 141 *E*). In Czech the hard consonants prevent the further palatalization of (*j*)*a* <CSl. **ę* (section 142, ii). (iii) The groups *tl dl* persist in West Slavonic: P. *padł* Cz. *padl* 'fell', P. *płótł* Cz. *pletl* 'wove', P. *modlić się* Cz. *modliti se* 'pray', P. *radło* 'ploughshare', Cz. *radlo*, P. *szydło* Cz. *šidlo* 'awl'.

T D. P. *to* 'that'/*ciało* 'body' *chcieć* 'want', *lód* 'ice'/*łabędź* 'swan' *działo* 'deed', *noc* 'night' (**noktĭ*) *moc* 'might' (**mogtĭ*); UpWend.

ćělo/LowWend. *śělo ćichi/śichy* 'quiet', UpWend. *swěca* 'candle', UpWend. *dźowka*/LowWend. *źowka* 'daughter', UpWend. *mjeza* 'border'; Cz. *tak* 'so' *tma* 'darkness' (dial. *t'ma*)/ *mlat'* (imperative) 'thresh' *svíce* 'candle' *noc* 'night', *náhoda* 'chance'/*cid'* (imperative) 'polish' *mezi*/Slk. *medzi* 'between'. Infinitives in -*kti *-*gti* (Class I i) become P. -*c*/otherwise -*ć*.

In Polish the palatalization of the soft vowels only occurred by the beginning of the thirteenth century. In the Bull of 1136 the dentals remain: *Chotan*/MP. *Chocian*, *Deuentliz*/MP. *Dziewiętlic*. In the middle of the twelfth century there occurs *Bartozege/Bartodzieje* and in the first years of the next century *Chocan Braces/Braciesz*. In foreign loanwords and in the modification of consonants by syntactical union with vowels the palatalization is attested from the same period. The Bull of 1136 probably represents by *t d* in this position not the hard dentals, but dentals modified by a sibilant off-glide (t^s d^z) which were already on the way towards full palatalization. CSl. *stj *zdj >P. *szcz żdż*: P. *puszcza* 'wilderness, forest' *gąszcz* 'thicket' *jeżdżenie* 'riding'.

In Lower Wendish the process of palatalization has been carried one step further. Instead of an affricate sibilant, a fricative (*ś ź*) has developed

In Czechoslovak *t d* (and also *n*) are soft before *i*, and are not marked by a diacritic; *t d n* are also soft before Cz. *ě*, the glide being marked as part of the vowel (*tě dě ně*). The dentals are hard before Cz. *e* <CSl. *e *i and before CSl. *i >Cz. -: Cz. *den* 'day'/P. *dzień* R. *deň*, Cz. *tma* 'darkness' *kost* 'bone' *deset* 'ten'. Where *t d* occur they are due to a lost *i*, not to loss of *jer*; it is a feature of the imperative: Cz. 2S. *mlat'* 'thresh' *řid'* 'direct'. The plural is formed upon the singular: *řid'te*. In Old Czech and in modern dialects the full palatalization of the soft dentals takes place: OCz. *czizucz* 'thousand'/*tisíc hnuczi/hnouti* 'move' *nawracz/navrat'* 'return', dial. *kosć* 'bone' *mać* 'mother'.

R. P. *rzecz* 'thing' *krzyż* 'cross' *zwierzę* 'animal' (*rz*=MP. [ž], a sound which includes a touch of the West English 'inverted' *r*, or when unvoiced [š]); UpWend. *křidło* (*ř*=[š]), LowWend. *kśidło* 'wing'; Cz. *říci* 'say' *řádek* 'row' *zvěř* 'animal' (*ř*=[ř]; vibrant voiced sibilant palatal, which is unvoiced when final or in contact with a voiceless consonant). Slovak has hard *r*.

The Polish and Wendish forms represent developments beyond the result attained in Czech. The value [ř] was common to all three tongues, and is still represented in Polish spelling by the digraph *rz*, formerly used also in Czech, and in Upper Wendish by the Hussite sign *ř*. Though the sound was once common to all the West Slavonic languages except Slovak, it was not a feature of West Slavonic itself.

At that time (6–9th cent.) the sound must have been a much softened *ř*, which had not yet acquired a sibilant pronunciation. So it was in the time of the Polish Bull of 1136 (*Dobrenta* = *Dobrzęta*), and when Wendish names obtained their German equivalents: Germ. *Krimnitz*/ LowWend. *Kśimice*, Germ. *Krausnick*/LowWend. *Kšuświca*, Germ. *Krischa*/UpWend. *Křišow*. So also in OCz. *Kriwoplath* 1154, but with assibilation: *Lukohorsany Orsechow* (*s* = [ž]) 1237. Examples of *r rr* for *ř* persist through the thirteenth century in Czech, though they dwindle rapidly after 1300. The distinction between P. *rz*/*ż* persisted until the eighteenth century, as may be attested by the absence of orthographic confusion before that time. The vibrant was heard in Lower Wendish in the sixteenth century: *prczyschel*/*pśišel* 'came' (1548), but it had already been reduced to a simple sibilant in Upper Wendish by the fifteenth century (*pschisaham* 'swear' 15th cent., *pźeto* 'therefore' 1627). Slovak with its hard *r* presents the same development as Serbocroat and Slovene.

L. P. *koło* 'wheel' *starzał* 'grew old'/*dolina* 'valley', *kolanko* 'knee' *kolonista* 'colonist'; Wend. *Přiluk* (Germ. *Preilack*)/*Lěskej* (Germ. *Lieske*); Cz. *mile* 'pleasantly' *milo* 'pleasant'.

There was no normal alveolar *l* in West Slavonic. The hard form was a hollow or 'dark' *ł* (rather like that in Eng. *milk*) alternating with a soft or palatalized *l*. So it is in Polish and Wendish; this 'palatal' *l* (P. *lato* 'summer' <*lěto*) is still the nearest to normal West European *l*, and is so used in acclimatizing loanwords. In Old Czech the two sounds were distinguished by Hus (1406), who wrote: 'unde sciendum quod *l* generatur apponendo linguam ad superius palatam sive dentes æqualiter tenendo, seu inferiores extra protendendo, vel e contra; sed *ł* generatur linguam in fine sub dentibus ponendo et superiores dentes ultra inferiores protendendo'. The definition marks the palatal quality of *l*, while, for *ł*, the advancing of the upper part of the mouth would bring the arch of the tongue into the velar region. The reduction of *l ł* to a single (normal) *l* took place towards the middle of the sixteenth century: *nalezlo se* 'it was found' *léto* 'summer, year' *powolaw* 'having summoned' (all from V. Hájek, 1541). The distinction is sometimes marked in the Moravian Brethren's Bible (1579–93), and grammarians persisted in making the distinction, though often incorrectly. The method of showing consonantal variations adopted by Hus was to put a point above the non-Latin form. The barred *ł* is the relic of an older looped *l*. In present-day Czechoslovak dialects those of West Moravia agree with Czech, but *ł* is found more frequently as the Polish border is approached. According to Hus the Slovaks had no palatal *l*. At present there are three sounds of this nature in Slovak dialects; *l ľ ł*, of which the last may become *u*: Slovak dial. *dau* 'gave'.

N. P. imion (GP.) 'of names'/*niebo* 'sky' *koń* 'horse'; Wend. *wino* 'wine'/*nizki* [ńíśki] 'low'; Cz. *národ* 'nation'/*nic* 'nothing' *báň* 'dome' *kůň* 'horse'.

In Czech the soft consonant is sometimes due to analogy: *kůň* takes *ň* not from CSl. *-*ňi (which would have given *-n*), but on the analogy of GS.NAP. *koně* GP. *koní/koňů* IP. *koni*. The palatal quality of *ň* is not indicated by a diacritic before *i*.

S Z. P. *rosa* 'dew'/*rość* 'grow' *piszesz* 'writest', *rozłóg* 'plain'/ *wzierać* 'look into' *źle* 'ill' *wyżycie* 'sustenance'; UpWend. *pisać* 'write'/1S. *pišu;* Cz. *stáří* 'age' *kost* 'bone'/*píšeš* 'writest', *zvěř* 'animal'/*vožen* 'carted'.

The passage of **sj *zj* to *š ž* had already taken place in Common Slavonic. In addition to the palatals *š ž* that language had hard *s z*/soft *ś ź*, and the distinction is accurately reflected in Polish. In Czechoslovak, however, originally soft *ś ź* have hardened.

147. *Labials. P B V F M.* The letter *f* has been added partly to represent a non-Slavonic sound, partly to denote a sound due to the unvoicing of Sl. *v*, e.g. in P. *ufać* 'trust'< *upúvati.*

The labials are hard (*p* etc.) or soft [P. *p(i)* etc.]. Before the semiconsonant [j] they have not usually generated a palatal *l* in West Slavonic as in Russian, Slovene, Serbocroat and some forms of Old Bulgarian. In the oldest Czech documents the softened sound was not represented graphically, so that OCz. *zema* 'land'/*zima* 'winter' only reveal their different qualities in the sequel; MCz. *země/zima*. After the introduction of diacritic points, these are sometimes employed even when under modern conditions (e.g. before *i*) the softening is taken for granted:OCz. *piekna* 'pretty'/MCz. *pěkná*. So the Czech grammarian Nudožerský stated in 1603 that *p m v* in *pjše mjsto wjra* (*j=i*) were 'liquidæ molles'. The intrusive *l* is not entirely unknown in Polish: P. *kropla*/OP. *kropia* 'drop' *grobla*/OP. *grobia* 'dyke' *przerębla* 'hole in ice'. The precise timbre of soft *p* etc. varies according to dialect. In the south they are palatalized labials, as in Wendish, but in the north they are labials followed by a palatal semiconsonant, which is liable to pass into another consonant (*pi/pś bi/bż wi/ź*: dial. *żara/wiara* 'faith'). Softened *m* becomes, under those circumstances, *mi/mń*, and this helps to account for occasional confusion of *m/ń*: P. *niedźwiedź* 'bear'/Cz. *medvěd*. Cz. *mě* is pronounced *mně*.

Final labials have become hard. In the sixteenth century they were still soft in Polish where they had been soft in Common Slavonic: OP. *krew* 'blood' *cerkiew* 'church' *kilku ziem* (GP.) 'of several lands'; it was especially so in the case of imperatives, in which the consonant had become final through loss of *-i: mów* 'speak' *odstęp* 'desist'. As late as the nineteenth century Mickiewicz printed *jedwab'* 'silk' *jastrząb'* 'hawk'. So too in Wendish final *p b m r* may be marked soft (*ṗ* etc.) though they are pronounced hard; final *ẃ* is pronounced *j* and is sometimes so written.

148. *Sibilants.* The palatalization of velars and dento-alveolars resulted in the possession of a considerable number of sibilants by the West Slavonic languages. These sibilants have followed certain common lines of development. In Polish dialects there is a tendency to confuse the alveolar or prepalatal type with the mediopalatal, as in White Russian and North-western Great Russian: *c/cz z/ż.*

P. *sz ż rz cz dż* have been hardened, that is, they have become normal prepalatals or mediopalatals, not followed by a *j*-glide before the following vowel. The change is noted when they take the hard *y* for the soft *i:* P. *czysto* 'cleanly' *życie* 'life' *przysada* 'admixture' *dżdżysty* 'rainy' *szydło* 'awl'.

In Old Czech the sibilants were soft, and as such they had power to palatalize the following vowel. They have been hardened at a later date, and that only in West Czech and in the standard literary (Czech and Slovak) languages. In this the course of development was: *duš'a* 'soul' >*dušě* >*duše*/Slovak dial. *duša.* In this way OCz. *ě* after sibilants has been replaced by MCz. *e,* and *ě* is found only after *t d v n m* (*mě,* as we have seen, being pronounced *mňe*): OCz. *rucě*/MCz. *ruce* (DL*S.*) 'hand' OCz. *nozě*/MCz. *noze* (DL*S.*) 'foot'. The affricates OCz. *dz dž* were like P. *dz dż:* OCz. *przyrodzenye*/MCz. *přirozeni* 'nature' *zrodzeni* 'birth' 1466. They have become fricatives.

New affricates (*ć dż* or *č dž*) have developed in eastern dialects out of Cz. *t' d': ćicho čicho*/Cz. *ticho* 'quietly', *dziedzina džedžina*/Cz. *dědina* 'hamlet' Slovak dial. *dziävka* 'girl'. In some dialects *ś ź* are found before front vowels, and in others *si zi* have hardened to *sy zy,* as in Wendish.

149. *Final Consonants.* These are unvoiced, save to some extent in Wendish. As this is not made evident by the spelling it constitutes an exception to the phonetic character of Czech orthography. Alternations occur like P. *łeb* [łɛp] 'pate'/G*S. łba,* which give rise to secondary alternations like the diminutives P. *łepek/łebek.* Final Cz. *h=ch.*

150. *Consonant-Groups.* (*a*) Double consonants became single or were dissimilated, but new doublings have arisen, e.g. in *-nn-:* P.Cz. *panna* 'maiden' P. *sanny* '(road) usable by a sleigh' Cz. *vonný* 'fragrant'. Other doubled consonants are *kk* in P. *lekki* 'light' and *łł pp* in proper names: *Radziwiłł Jagiełło Łappo.* In Czech dialects *dn* yields *nn,* which may be dissimilated to *rn:* Cz. *bednář* 'cooper'/dial. *bennář bernář.* Double consonants, including those of adjacent words, are normally pronounced single in Czech but double in Polish.

Labials tended to disappear by assimilation before *n t s* as early as in Common Slavonic times: P. *sen* 'dream' (**sŭpn-*) *osa* 'wasp' Cz. *hynouti* 'perish' (**gybnǫti*). Dentals assimilate to affricate palatals: Cz.

svěcký 'worldly' (*ts* > *c*) *děcko* 'child' *dvanáct* 'twelve', and sibilants to other sibilants: P. *boski* 'divine' (Cz. *božský*), P. *mnóstwo* 'multitude' (Cz. *množství*). P. *mówić* 'speak' has lost *l* through assimilation/Cz. *mluviti*.

As in all other Slavonic languages, three-consonant groups tend to become two-consonant groups by loss of the middle consonant, but occasionally by loss of the first element.

With regard to voicing or unvoicing, the general tendency is for the first consonant to assume the nature of the second, but *v* (P. *w*) may assume that of a preceding consonant, *ř* (P. *rz*) does so, and *n m j r l* are relatively unaffected. These assimilations are not usually recognized by the spelling when they occur within the modern speech, but they do sometimes appear in sporadic variations. P. *dech* 'breath' answers to *tchórz* 'coward' through its gen.sg. (*tchu* < *dchu*); cf. P. *krtań* 'larynx'/R. *gortáń*, P. *swadźba* 'marriage'/OB. *svatĭba*, P. *pchła* (< **płcha*) 'flea'/OB. *blŭcha*, the exceptional P. *gwoli* (< *kwoli*) 'for the sake of' *grzeczny* 'polite' (< *k rzecz-*).

With regard to hardness or softness the results are more variable. In Polish all labials hardened in groups: *pnia* (GS.) 'of a stem' (**pĭnja*), *prawda* 'truth' *krzywda* 'wrong'. When the group results from loss of *i* there is discrepancy between Old and Modern Polish: OP. *robmy*/MP. *róbmy* 'let us do'. Palatals retain their softness in Polish: *nieśmy* 'let us bear' *plećmy* 'let us plait'. Similarly the sibilant in *kość* 'bone' *śpiew* 'song' *ślub* 'wedding' (**sŭlubŭ*), softening before soft consonants when necessary. P. *k ģ* were, however, still hard when this process was operative, and so do not soften sibilants: P. *bliski* 'near' *grząski* 'quaggy'. Soft *ś ź* remained before *ń ĺ*, but before CSl. *ň ľ* they may become *š ž*: P. *drażnię* 'I tease' (trom *drażnić*). P. *ć dž ść* > *j* before *c cz s*: P. *zamoście* 'tract beyond a bridge'/*Zamojski wiejski* 'rural' (**vĭsĭskyjĭ*), *ojczyzna* 'fatherland' (**oćczyzna*), *zdrajca* 'traitor' (**zradźca*). In this way GS. *ojca*/NS. *ociec* 'father' gave the analogical NS. *ojciec* 'father'; CSl. **tĭstĭ* OP. *cieść* 'father-in-law' has GDS. *tści-a -owi* (with *t* hardened in the consonant-group), whence the analogical NS. *teść*. Original P. *ť ď* retained their soft quality after the loss of the *jer*, finally or before other than dental or palatal consonants: P. *pamięć* 'memory' *spowiedź* 'confession' *ćma* 'darkness'/*widno* 'it is light' *radca* 'adviser'. [The hardness of *d* in *jeden* 'one' (OB. *jedĭnŭ*) is due to the analogy of forms in *jedn-*.] They remain soft before *w* (which tends to assimilate to a previous consonant, as remarked), but there are variations from the norm as the result of analogy: P. *dźwięczyć* 'tinkle' *lędźwie* 'loins'/*ledwie* 'scarcely' : : *ledwo*. P. *l* becomes *ł* before dentals or palatals: *łza* 'tear' OP. *słza* (**slĭza*), whence GP. *łez* (not **ślez*). There are, however, examples of the retention of soft *l* in a group: *wspólny* 'common' *okolny* 'circulatory'. So *r* varies: P. *orła* (GS.) 'eagle' (**orĭla*), *wierna* 'true' (**věrĭnaja*) *morski* 'maritime' (Cz.

mořský)/*burzliwy* 'stormy' *jutrznia* 'matins' *wewnętrzny* 'inner'
opatrzność 'providence' (OP. *opatrność* Cz. *opatrnost*).

In Czech, qualitative assimilation is affected by the general tendency
to harden consonants, which is not universal as in Serbocroat but
usually occurs wherever there was originally *e* or *jer*. Cz. *ř* corresponded to all soft and palatalized instances of *r*. Therefore Cz. *orel*
'eagle'/P. *orzeł* must be explained as due to the analogy of GS. *orla*,
where *ři* hardened before hard *l*.

(b) *Dissimilation and epenthesis.* Original **sr *zr *nr* >*str zdr ndr:*
Cz. *stříbro* 'silver' *Jindřich* 'Henry', P. *strumień* 'stream'. More rarely
there is epenthesis of *g* (*zgł* for *zł*) or *š* (*ršč* for *rč*: P. *świerszcz* 'cricket'
Cz. *čvrček*). Mediæval Latin frequently inserted *p* in the groups *mn*
mt ml ms, and this scribal practice was followed in spelling Mediæval
Polish and Czech. At a distance *l---l r---r* were dissimilated; and so is
k---k in P. *biszkopt* 'biscuit' (*biszkokt* <*bis coctum*). Dissimilation of
sounds in contact occurs in Polish: *szcz* for *zš* (OP. *wszczedł*), *cht tch*
for *kt tk* (OP. *wiotchy*/MP. *wiotki* 'frail'), velars for dentals before
liquids (OP. *ostydnąć*/MP. *ostygnąć* 'cool off'), *t* for *č* in *potciwy* (16th
cent.)/MP. *poczciwy* 'honest'.

B. FORMS

(i) VERBS

151. *Classes of Verbs.* The infinitive remains full in Czech -*ti*.
Verbs of class I i resolve **-kti *-gti* into Cz. -*ci*. In Polish, Slovak and
Wendish the vowel of the infinitive-ending has been shortened and then
lost, modifying the previous consonant. The Polish infinitive is in -*ć*,
except for -*c* in class i 1; Slovak -*ť* (and analogical -*cť* where Czech has
-*ci*; UpWend. -*ć* (-*c* in i 1), LowWend. normally -*ś* (with the former
affricate converted into a fricative; see section 146 *T D*).

A. Athematic. See section 152.

B. Thematic. (i) 1. *k g*: P. *piec* 'bake' *móc* (sometimes spelt *módz*) 'be
able'/*pie-kę -czesz mo-gę -żesz;* UpWend. *pjec* LowWend.
pjac/UpWend. *pje-ku -češ* LowWend. *pjeku* (obsolete) *pjac-om*
-*óš;* Cz. *péci moci*/*pe-ku -češ mohu můžeš.*

2. *t d*: P. *wieść* 'lead'/*wiodę wiedziesz;* UpWend. *plesć* 'weave';
Cz. *vésti*/*vedu vedeš.*

3. *p b v*: P. *grzebać* 'scrape' *skubać*/*skuść* 'pluck' *pleć*/*plewić* 'weed'
show change of conjugation (OP. *grzebię skubę plewę*/MP.
pielę); UpWend. *plěč* LowWend. *plaś;* OCz. *hřebsti*, Slovak
hriebsť, Cz. *zábsti* 'freeze'.

4. *s z*: P. *nieść* 'carry' *leźć* 'crawl'/*niosę niesiesz lezę* (OP. *lazę*);
LowWend. *njasć*/*njasom* (*njasu*); Cz. *nésti*/*nesu.*

5. *m n*: P. *dąć* 'blow'/*dmę, wziąć wziąść* (analogical) 'take'/*wezmę*

weźmiesz; UpWend. *żeć* LowWend. *żeś* 'reap'/*žnju;* Cz.
pnouti se 'shoot up'/*pnu, počiti* 'begin'/*počnu.* The infinitives
in Czech have generally been rebuilt upon the present stem.

6. *l r:* P. *drzeć* 'tear'/*drę drzesz, kłuć (kłóć)* 'prick'/*kolę;* Low
Wend. *pŕeś* 'deny'/*pru prjoš;* Cz. *tříti* 'rub'/*tru třeš.*

7. *vowel:* P. *bić* 'strike'/*bij-ę -esz, czuć* 'feel' *myć* 'wash'; Low
Wend. *piś* 'drink'/*pij-om -oš;* Cz. *bíti*/OCz. *bij-u -eš* MCz.
bij-i (colloquial *biju,* by analogy).

(ii) *n:* 1. *vowel:* P. *ginąć* 'perish'/*ginę,* Cz. *minouti* 'pass, miss'.

2. *consonant:* P. *ciągnąć* 'pull'/*ciągnę;* UpWend. *wuknyć* Low
Wend. *huknuś* 'learn'/*wuknu huknjom;* Cz. *tisknouti* 'squeeze'
/*tisknu.*

(iii) *ě:* 1. *ěj:* P. *istnieć* 'exist'/*istnieję;* these verbs pass to (iii) 2 in
UpWend., and tend to the same in LowWend.; Cz. *uměti*
'know how'/OCz. *uměju* MCz. *umim,* similarly MCz. *rozu-
mim* 'understand' *smim* 'am allowed to' (used like German
dürfen); but *spěti* 'hurry' is conjugated *spěji* etc.

2. *i:* P. *cierpieć* 'suffer'/*cierp-ię -isz, słyszeć* (analogical *-eć* for *-ać*)
'hear'/*słysz-ę -ysz* (by hardening); UpWend. *lećeć lećić* 'fly'/
leć-u -iš; Cz. *viděti* 'see'/OCz. *vizu* MCz. *vidím,* OCz.
slyšěti MCz. *slyšeti* (by palatalization).

(iv) *i:* P. *mówić* 'speak'/*mów-ię -isz uczyć* 'teach'/*ucz-ę -ysz* (by
dispalatalization) UpWend. *palić* 'burn'/*pal-u -iš;* Cz.
prositi 'entreat'/OCz. *proš-u -iš* MCz. *prosím.*

(v) *a:* 1. *-aj-:* P. *czytać* 'read'/*czytam* 3P. *czytają;* UpWend.
dźěłać 'do'/*dźěł-am* 3P. *-aju;* Cz. *dělati*/OCz. *dělaju* MCz.
dělám, sázeti 'plant'/OCz. *sázěju* MCz. *sázim.*

2. *-j-:* P. *pisać* 'write'/*pisz-ę -esz;* UpWend. *pisać*/*pišu;* Cz.
tesati 'hew'/OCz. *teš-u >-i* 2S. *-eš.*

3. *zero:* P. *brać* 'take'/*biorę bierzesz;* UpWend. *brać*/*bjer-u -ješ;*
Cz. *bráti*/*beru bereš* (with *r* for *ř* by analogy).

4. *-j-:* P. (*dawać* 'give')/*daj-ę -esz;* UpWend. *kać so* 'repent' Low
Wend. *kajaś se* (obsolete)/*kaju kajom.*

(vi) *ova:* P. *budować* 'build'/*buduję;* UpWend. *kupować* 'buy'/
kupuju; Cz. *kupovati*/OCz. *kupuju* MCz. *kupuj-i -eš.*

152. *Athematic Verbs.* *Es/s.* The scheme of the present tense is:

Indicative

	S1	2	3	P1	2	3	D1	23
P.				jest		są		
	jest-e-	m	ś		śmy	ście		
LowWend.				jo				
	s-	om	y		my	ćo	u	mej	tej
Cz.				je(st)				
	js-	em	i		me	te	ou	

The present indicative has been rebuilt in Polish on the basis of the form *jest*. In Old Polish there were found also *jeść* (rarely) ana *je;* OP. *nie* ($<$*ne je*) 'is not'. The Cz. *nenі* 'is not' results from prefixing *ne* to *nі* $<$*ně* $<$*ne je*, OP. *nie*. The rest of the tense was based in Old Polish on the root *jes-* (*je-śm -ś -smy -ście* D1. *-swa* 23. *-sta*). The softening of the *s* in *jesteśmy* is due to the analogy of *jesteście*. The remodelled forms began to appear in the fifteenth century (*przeniesieni jestmy* 'we have been transferred' 1438), and the older forms die out in the sixteenth century. Occasionally forms are found based on the 3*P. są: sąsmy sąście*. The endings *-m -ś -smy -ście* serve as enclitics attached to the participle in *ł* to make the past tense (*byłem* etc.) and the conditional (*byłbym*), normally without shifting the stress (*byłabym*). They may be added to particles: *żebyście byli*/*że bylibyście* 'that you would be'.

The plural originally was in **s-*, which appears in *P*3. OCz.Slk. *sú* and also in OCz. *P*1. *sme* 2. *ste*. This led to forming a singular in *s-*, as in Wendish: OCz. *S*1. *sem* 2. *si*, Slovak. dial. *šem ši šme*. On the contrary, MCz. *jsou* has been assimilated to the other persons. Dialectically *S*1. *-ch P*1. *-chmy* are enclitics modelled on the aorist: dial. *že-ch*=*že jsem*. Gerund: *jsa, jsouc-*.

Aorist and Imperfect

		*S*1		23	*P*1	2	3	*D*1		23
OP.	by-	ch		-	chom	ście	chą	chowa		sta
LowWend.Aor.	bu-	ch		-	chmy	śćo	chu	chmej		štej
Impf.	bě-	ch		šo						

Conditional

				2 s	3-			
MCz.	by-	ch		2 s	3-	chom	ste	-

Future

			2	3			
P.	będ-	ę					ą
	będz-		iesz	ie	iemy	iecie	
Cz.	bud-	u	eš	e	em(e)	ete	ou

Imperative

P.	bądź		-		my	cie	
		niech będzie			niech będą		
LowWend.	buź	(i)	(i)	my	ćo		mej	tej
Cz.	budʼ-		-		te		

The retention of the aorist and imperfect tenses and of the dual number is a characteristic feature of Wendish, whose isolation and lack of development in literature have led to archaism. There was no trace of the imperfect in Polish at any time, apart from the *P3. bychą*, transferred to the aorist. OB. *S23. bystŭ* also was unrepresented. Beside *P1. bychom* there was found, as in Wendish, *bychmy* : : OP. *jesmy*. It passed out of use in the course of the fifteenth century. There remained the enclitic of the conditional mood *-by*, attached to the participle in *l* or to a particle and followed by the enclitic endings of the present tense: P. *byłbym* (fem. *byłabym*) 'should be'. This usage began in the sixteenth century (*wolałbym* 'I would rather' 1527/*radbych umiał* 'I would fain be able'). The latter usage lasted till the seventeenth century. There is no trace in Polish of a form like OB. *bimĭ* (conditional). The aorist gave way to the perfect: P. *byłem*, etc. Infin. *być*; UpWend. *być buć*, LowWend. *byś*. The future and imperative are from CSl.OB. *bǫdǫ*, with compensatory lengthening for loss of *jer* in the imperative (see sect. 140 iii). Gerund: *będąc* (OP. also *sąc*); adjective: *będący*; noun: *-bycie* (UpWend. *byće*, 'being'). The past part. pass. occurs only in compounds: *przybyty* 'having arrived, increased'.

The aorist has ceased to function as such in Czechoslovak, and has become a conditional, there being no trace of anything like OB. *bimĭ*. It has not lost its inflexions, save in the *P3*. In the modern language, and particularly in colloquial speech, are found such conditional forms as *byl bych býval* 'I should have been' and even *byl bych býval byl*. The imperfect was also current in the older language: OCz. *S1. bie-ch* 23. *-še*, etc., occasionally contracted: *bíše*, and there was an alternative aorist: OCz. *běch S23. bě*. Examples occur as late as the fifteenth century. The future and imperative tenses have their root in *bud- ⟨bǫd-*; gerund: *budouc-* as well as *jsa*. There are no enclitic forms of the present, but the full forms have suffered loss of vowel by reason of their unaccented nature. They are employed with the participle in *l* to form the past tense, except 3*SP*. (*on dal* 'he gave').

The passive is expressed by the reflexive of verbs, or by the past part. pass.+the present tense of the auxiliary: P. *to nam przez kapelana oznajmiło się i objawiono jest* 'this was declared to us and revealed by the chaplain'. It is equivalent to the Latin perf. pass.: *constitutus sum rex*=OP. *postawion jeśm krol*. The neuter served to form impersonal expressions, from which the auxiliary is now omitted: P. *pogrzebano go* 'he has been buried' ('it has been buried him').

153. **Ēd- etc.* P. *jeść* LowWend. *jěść* Cz. *jísti* 'eat', P. *dać* LowWend. *daś* Cz. *dáti* 'give', P. *wiedzieć* LowWend. *wěžeś* Cz. *věděti* 'know', are conjugated thematically except in *Sl.* P. *dam jem wiem*, LowWend. *dam jěm wěm*, Cz. *dám jím vím;* in *P3. dadzą jedzą wiedzą*, LowWend.

daže jěže wěže, Cz. *jedí vědí*, the original dental closing the stem re-appears. Polish -*dz*- for -*dž*- is due to analogy. P. *mam* 'have' OCz. *jmám*/MCz. *mám* forms a parallel to *dam*. This has in Czech, and had in Old Polish, a long vowel by compensation for loss of *jer*. It was thus analogous to the long vowel resulting from the contraction of -*ajǫ* >OP. long nasal *å*, which was thus induced to adopt the -*m* of the athematic verbs: OP. *wołaję* >OP. *wołą* : : *dåm* >MP. *wołam* 'call'. A further analogy gave *umieję* >MP. *umiem*, cf. *wiem*. So also Cz. *dělám* 'do' *umím* 'know how to' *trpím* 'suffer'. In Slovak this -*m* has spread also to uncontracted verbs: Slovak. *nesiem* 'I bear'. Conversely, Cz. 3*P*. *dělají* has given rise to 3*P*. *dají*/OCz. *dadí dadie*, Slovak *dadia*. Gerund: Cz. *dada dadouc*-.

*Ei/*i* 'go' has become entirely thematic: P. *idę* (infin. *iść*—an analogical form) Cz. *jdu* (*jíti*), with past tenses from *šĭd-*: P. *szedłem* Cz. *šel* (*šel* <*šedl : : *šla* <*šdla) *jsem*. Cz. *míti* 'have' had a diphthong formerly: OCz. *mieti*, whence MCz. *měj* 'have thou' *měl* 'had', in which the vowel was short and so did not close to *i*. Other tenses were: OCz. impf. (*j*)*mějiech*, aor. *jměch*. From the infinitive new frequentative formations have been made: Cz. *S1*. *mívám*, past part. act. *míval*.

154. *Thematic Present Indicative.*

		$S1$	2	3	$P1$	2	3	$D1$	23
P.	gin-	ę	iesz	ie	iemy	iecie	ą		
	pisz-	ę	esz	e	emy	ecie	ą		
(iii 2)	cierp-	ię	isz	i	imy	icie	ią		
	leż-	ę	ysz	y	ymy	ycie	ą		
	um-	iem	iesz	ie	iemy	iecie	ieją		
(v 1)	koch-	am	asz	a	amy	acie	ają		
Low Wend.	njas-	om/u	oš	o	omy	ośo	u	omej	otej
	piš-	u	oš	o	omy	ośo	u	omej	otej
(v 1)	žěł-	am	aš	a	amy	aśo	aju	amej	atej
Cz.	nes-	u ⎫	eš	e	em(e)		ete	ou ⎫	
(vi)	běduj-	i ⎭						í ⎭	
(iv) pros-		ím ⎫	íš	í	íme	íte	í ⎫		
um-		⎭					ějí ⎭		
(v 1)	děl-	ám	áš	á	áme	áte	ají		

The nasal vowel of *S1.P3.* became the indifferent Polish nasal *ø*, from which developed short *ę* and long *ą* (section 142 i). These two persons were originally hard and the others soft, which led to modification of the final consonant of the stem (*drę drą*/*drzesz* 'tear' *mogę mogą*/*możesz* 'can' *piekę pieką*/*pieczesz* 'bake'). In verbs of classes iii 2 and iv the vowel of the ending is *i*. After palatals which have hardened, *e* replaces *ie*, and *y* replaces *i*. The group *aje* contracts to *a* and *eje* to *ie*; *S1*. long nasal *å* then became -*am* : : *dam*, and *umiem* corresponds to *wiem; P*3. remains uncontracted. The contracted forms began to appear in the fourteenth century, but uncontracted forms did not disappear until the seventeenth (OP. *wolaję umieję*). *P*3. *noszą*/R. *nósjat* owes its consonant to *S*1. *noszę*/2. *nosisz*, where it is due to CSl. **sj >š;* cf. *dadzą* (section 153).

The dual endings were OP. 1. *-wa* 23. *-ta*/OB. *-vě -ta -te.* The first person was affected by *dwa* 'two' and the masculine dual in *-a.* Of the distinction between the other two persons there is no trace in Polish. This number went out of use during the course of the fifteenth century. It persists in Wendish, where *D*1. *-mej* has *m* from *P*1. *-my*, and *D*23. *-tej* alternates with *-taj*. In Czech the dual was OCz. *D*1. *-vě/va* 23. *-ta*; but *D*1. *-ma* also occurred: *wstanma* 'let us arise' (15th cent.).

The tense has been affected in Czechoslovak by contraction and palatalization. By the former *aje >á, eje >*OCz. *ie* MCz. *í;* but *uje* remains uncontracted. Palatalization occurs in *S*1. *-u P*3.OCz. *-ú*, preceded by a palatal consonant. The development is *'u >iu >i* (*'ú >iú >i*). The fully developed forms appear in the course of the last third of the fourteenth century, and establish themselves in the fifteenth. In some dialects *o* appears for *u* (*neso* 'I bear'), and palatalization does not take place (*malujo* 'I paint'). In Silesia, under immediate Polish influence, the soft form is *-em >-ym* : : P. *-ę*/MCz. *-i.*

*S*1. *dám* has generalized final *-m* to other conjugations. No examples occur before 1300. They begin to show in the second half of the fourteenth century, and are established by its end. In Slovak all verbs take final *-m*, as (with few exceptions) in Serbocroat; but in Modern Czech its use is restricted to (i) contracted verbs: OCz. *dělaju* 'make' *sázeju* 'set' *uměju* 'know how'/*dělám sázím umím*, (ii) verbs of class iii (infin. *-ěti*): OCz. *trpu* 'suffer'/*trpím* and those of class iv (*-iti*): OCz. *prošu/prosím*. Very early forms are *neuczinym* 'I shall not do' *spym* 'I sleep' (between 1325–50).

*SP*3. *-tŭ* loses its consonant in West Slavonic. Occasionally *t* is found in Old Czech, more often with the plural than with the singular, and it is then sometimes shown with a diacritic (*t̓*). It may then represent an enclitic demonstrative particle: OCz. (*člověk*) *newezmet=non sumet=* 'will not take'.

CSl.*P*1. *-me/mo/mŭ/my* was a variable termination. From the first came Cz. *-me*, obligatory in those verbs which have *S*1. *-m* (*S. dělám/P. děláme*) and also in Slovak where *S*1. *-m* has been generalized to all conjugations (Slovak. *S. nesiem/P. nesieme*). CSl. *-mŭ >*Cz. *-m*, which alternates with *-me* after *e*: Cz. *nesem*(*e*) 'we bear' *pějem*(*e*) 'we sing'. It might be lengthened to *-my*: OCz. *mamy* 'we have' *damy* 'we shall give', Moravian dial. *mamy volamy* 'we call'. It might also be vocalized as *-mo*: Slovak dial. *budemo mámo vidímo* (cf. Ruthenian).

P2. -*te* remains firm in Czech, but in dialects palatalization takes place in proportion as the Polish border is approached: -*t'e* -*će* -*će*, -*t'o* -*ćo:* dial. *plećeće plot'ot'o*/Cz. *pletete* 'you plait'. In one Moravian dialect -*ta* has been introduced from the dual.

P3. -*ǫtŭ* >OCz. -*ú* >-*au* >-*ou*, -'*ǫtŭ* >OCz. -'*ú* >MCz. -*í*, -'*ętŭ* > OCz. -'*á* >-*ie* >MCz. -*í*. This palatalization had not taken place in eastern and Slovak dialects, where either the old forms persist (Slovak *chvália* 'they praise') or a partial palatalization gives -*ä*. Transition dialects towards the Polish border show *P3.* -*o* -*jo*/-*om* -*jom* : : P. -*ą* -*ią:* dial. *robio* 'they toil' *chodźum* 'they go'. Another dialectal innovation heard in Prague is the extension of -*ějí* to other verbs than those of the type *uměti:* dial. *trpějí trpěj*/Cz. *trpí* 'they suffer'. Yet other dialects have *P3.* -*ijó*/*ijau*/*ijou*. Prague Czech uses the analogical endings -*u* -*ou* for -*i* -*í* (dial. *píšu* 'I write').

155. *Imperative.*

		S23	P1	2	D1	2
P.	pisz-	-	my	cie		
	kocha-	j	jmy	jcie		
	ciągn-	ij	ijmy	ijcie		
LowWend.	syṕ-	-	my	śo	mej	tej
	źěła-	j	jmy	jśo	jmej	jtej
	hukn-	i	imy	iśo	imej	itej
Cz.	nes- ⎫ chval- ⎭	- (*nesiž*)	me	te		
	děle- (<děla-)	j	jme	jte		
	bd-	i	ěme	ěte		

The athematic endings had been CSl. *S2.* *-*jĭ* *P2.* -*ite*, and the thematic were *S2.* -*i* *P2.* -*ěte*/*ite*. They were reduced to a single series -*i* -*ite* in Polish at a very early date. This usage remained normal until the fifteenth century: P. *wrócicie się* 'return ye' (15th cent.). In the previous century, however, the next stage had been reached, namely, the shortening first of final -*i*, and then of the corresponding vowel in the plural: OP. *nies-i* -*icie* 'bear'/MP. *nieś* -*cie*. Both treatments of the imperative were concurrent in the fourteenth century: *pojdzi* 'go' *dowiedzi* 'prove'/ *wstań* 'arise' *bądźmy* 'let us be'. Because of the hardening of final labials in Polish we find *cierp* 'suffer'/Low Wend. *syṕ* 'strew' (this *ṕ* is soft only in spelling). There is no consistency in the loss or preservation of the vowel in Old Polish, and therefore nothing to show whether (as in Russian and as seems probable) the vowel was better preserved when the stress-accent originally fell on it. After another vowel it was reduced to a semivowel, and after two consonants it was preserved: Low Wend. *hukni* 'learn'. In Polish this -*i* became entangled orthographically with the closed *é* in the form *éj*, which has ultimately come to be spelled *-ij: wspomni/wspomnéj/ wspomnij* 'remember'. In the last form it presents an apparent correspondence with *dziełaj* 'do', etc. Between the fourteenth and sixteenth centuries the vowel might be lost in these conditions also: OP. *wytargńcie* 'pull' *padńmy* 'let us fall', cf. UpWend. *wukń wuk(ń)će* 'learn'.

The development of the mood in Czech was, in the main, similar. The vowel *ě* was more resistent, and is now found in the standard speech after consonant groups. It invaded the territory of *i* before the historical record began; the contrary substitution of *i* for *ě* is a characteristic of modern Moravian dialects. Full forms in *-ite* occur as late as the fifteenth century. *Dělej* for *dělaj* is due to the effect of *j* on preceding *a* (see section 141).

*S*2. **-ois* 3. **-oit* both gave CSl.OB.*S*23. *-i*. The confusion of persons spread also to the plural and dual in Old Polish, but there was great inconvenience in not knowing to whom a given command referred. For instance: *pojcie Bogu wszelika ziemia, chwalcie ji niebo i ziemiu* 'sing to God all the earth, let heaven and earth adore him' (14th cent.) only becomes grammatically clear on comparison with the Latin *jubilate/laudent*. So too: OP. *błogosław dusza moja Gospodzina/ błogosław wszelkie ciało imię jego* 'Praise God, o my soul'/'let all flesh praise his name' offer identical renderings of Lat. *benedic/benedicat*. This ambiguity lasted in Polish until the seventeenth century, though it is rare in the poet Kochanowski (1530–84). From the sixteenth century it tended to be solved by letting *niech(aj)*+3 pres.indic. take its place, and from the seventeenth century *niech(aj)* might be used with the first person also: *niechaj mieszkam* 'let me dwell' *niechaj służywa* 'let us two serve'. *Niechaj* 'let' originally meant 'don't care', (Sl. **chajǫ* 'care'). This latter development has not persisted. In some dialects *bodaj* (= *Bog daj*) 'God grant' serves the same turn, and at various mediæval dates there existed for Lat. *sine* 'let' OP. *daj, daj at, przepuści aci, przepuść, pozwól*. On the other hand, Lat. *noli* 'do not' was also rendered by *niechać;* at first with infin.: *niechajcie źle czynić* = *nolite malefacere*, and then with the indicative: *niechać skazują* 'let them not condemn' 1400. The suffix *-ać* represented *a ci* OP. *at(i)* = *et tibi*, cf. OB. *as(i)* = *et sibi*, an ethic dative.

In Czech 3*SP*. imperative is expressed by *at* < *ati* or *necht* < *nechati*+present indicative.

156. *Present Gerunds.* CSl.OB.N*SM*. *-y/ę;* of these the former was ambiguous and went out of use, and was replaced by the unambiguous *-ę* (masc.neut.). It is found in some Polish fragments of the sixteenth century, without reference to declensional type: OP. *mogę* 'being able' *sę* 'being'/OB. *mogy sy*. There was also the form *-a* in fourteenth-

century Polish, which may have been borrowed from Czech: OP. *ida* 'going' (cf. Cz. *nesa* 'bearing'). These forms have all ceased to be employed. In Upper Wendish -'*o* <-*ę:* UpWend. *wjedźo* 'leading' *bjerjo* 'taking'. These are used predicatively. In Lower Wendish the same effect is obtained by adding the suffix -*no* to the participle in -*cy*. CSl.(OB.) *těšę* 'comforting' *trpę* 'suffering' >OCz. *těš'a trṕa* >MCz. *těše trpě*. Before the process of palatalization took place, that is, in or before the twelfth century, this soft -'*a* produced an analogical hard -*a*: Cz. *nesa* 'bearing', which may have affected Polish as above noted. These are masculine singular gerunds.

CSl.A*SM*.   *-*oťi/ęťi* >OP. -*øc* >MP.-*ąc:* *cierpiąc* 'suffering'/OB. *trpęšťi*. This is the normal Polish gerund. Its definite form is an adjective: *kochający* 'loving' (*N. -e F. -a*). In Czechoslovak the vowels were denasalized, but remained distinct in quality: Cz. *nesouc těšíc* *trpíc*/OB. *nesǫšťi těšǫšťi trpęšťi* (*ǫ* >*ú* >*ou*, '*ǫ* >'*ú* >*i*, '*ę* >'*a* > *i*). These are feminine and neuter singular gerunds.

The sign of the plural is -*e* for all genders in Czech: *nesouce trpíce* *umějíce* 'knowing how to'.

CSl.*SF*.   *-*oťi/ęťi* would give OP. -*øcy* >-*ęcy:* OP. *płaczęcy* 'weeping'. This was the more common ending of the gerund until the sixteenth century, and it still alternates with -*ący* in some Polish dialects. It was in the seventeenth century that -*ący* prevailed. Under such conditions they are used without varying the flexion, i.e. as gerunds, as distinct from the verbal adjective in -*ąc-y e a*. So Lower Wendish *pletucy/plećecy* 'weaving'; OCz. *nesúci těšíci trpíci*. In Old Czech this feminine was opposed to the masc.neut. in -*a/ě;* but in the modern language the final vowel is lost and the neuter coincides with the feminine. The loss of the vowel is explicable on the theory of the survival of *nesouc* etc. <A*SM*. *nesoťi. Verbal adjective: Cz. *nesouci*.

157. *Infinitive and Supine*. P. -*ć* (-*c* <*-*kti* *-*gti*); UpWend. -*ć/* LowWend. -*ś* supine -*t;* Cz. -*ti* (-*ci*) supine -*t*.

Since final consonants are unvoiced, infin. -*ć* (-*c*) is sometimes spelt -*dź* (-*dz*) in Polish, in order to mark the correspondence with other forms in which voiced consonants occur: OP. *idź=ić* (*idę*)/MP. *iść* 'go', *módz/móc* (*mogę*) 'be able'. Verbs of the first class suffer modification of some final consonants before the infinitive flexion: the velars unite with it to give -*c*, the dentals *t d* become *ś* (*pleść* 'weave' *wieść* 'lead' *płótł wiódł*), and the sibilants become soft (*nieść* 'bring' *gryźć* 'gnaw'/*niósł gryzł*), while the original nasal diphthongs are represented by nasal vowels: *dąć* (*domti) 'blow'/*dmę miąć* 'crumple'/*mnię*. Verbs in -'*ati* (after an originally soft consonant) are liable to appear in Polish as verbs in -*eć* as a result of analogy: *widział* (from *vidělŭ*, with dispalatalization): *widzieć* (*viděti*) 'see' : : *leżał* (*ležalŭ*): P. *leżeć*/OB. *ležati*. In the verbs of Class ii (*n*-suffix) the nasal appeared in the infinitive, but not in the aorist or in the forms directly depending on the aorist, such as the participle in -*l*. This led to an anomaly in Polish after the disappearance of the aorist, and to the extension of the nasal consonant to the participle: *ciągnąć* : : *ciagnął* 'pull'. Often both forms are found: *kwitnął/kwitł* 'bloomed' *prysnął/prysł* 'burst'. This reacted in turn upon the infinitive, giving doublets: *biegnąć/biec* 'run'. From this also came intrusive -*n*- in *paść* (*padti) 'fall'/ *padnę*.

The infinitive in Czech is in -*ti* (velar-stems in -*ci*), which is some-times found in mediæval manuscripts represented by -*tyu* -*tie* (*datyu* 'give' *wzyetie* 'take'/*dáti vzíti*) since palatalization had reduced these endings to -*ti*. In dialects shortened forms of the infinitive occur: dial. *kupovat' kupovat* 'buy' *sázet'* 'set' *śedać* 'sit'. After a soft consonant infin. *-'*ati* palatalized to Cz. -*eti: sážati* >*sázeti*. The length of the vowel before the flexion varies according to principles not wholly determined. When the infinitive is a dissyllable the vowel is normally long (*dáti* 'give' *bráti* 'take'), but the compounds of these dissyllables may have long or short vowels (*napásti* 'graze' *vylézti* 'creep out' *vyrůsti* 'develop'/*nastati* 'approach' *ustlati* 'make a bed'). The only short dissyllables are: *moci* 'be able' *jeti* 'ride' *pěti* 'sing' *spěti* 'hurry'. Where there has been contraction the vowel is long: *báti se* 'fear', and there is a similar length in the past participle in -*l* (*bál*). In Class iv (-*iti*) both lengths are current: -*iti/íti;* but in Class iii 2 (-*ěti* past part. -*ěl*) OCz. -*ieti* becomes MCz. -*íti*. OCz. -*yti* is always short, but -*ýti* increases with the centuries; -*outi* is always long. In those eastern dialects which drop the final vowel the stem-vowel is sometimes lengthened for compensation: Moravian *hónit'*/Cz. *honiti* 'hunt'. A purely personal innovation was the attempt by J. Kollár (1793–1852) to create a perfect infinitive in -*vš-eti: vidě-vš-eti*=*vidisse* 'to have seen'.

A supine exists in Lower Wendish (but not in Upper Wendish) and in Czech as a complement to verbs of motion: Cz. *jíti spat* 'to go to bed'. The stem-vowel is short in Czech.

158. *Past Tenses*. The participle in *l* distinguishes genders in the plural in Polish, Czechoslovak, and Upper Wendish: P. *cierpiał -o -a* PM. *cierpieli* NF. *cierpiały;* UpWend. *brał -o -a* PM. (persons and animals) *brali* M. (things) NF. *brałe* DMNF. *braloj*, LowWend. PMNF. *brali* DMNF. *brałej;* Cz. *bral -o -a* OCz.PM. -*li* NF. -*ly* DM. -*la* NF. -*le*/MCz. PM. (persons and animals) *brali* M. (things) F. *braly* N. *brala* (OB.PM. -*li* N. -*la* F. -*ly* DM. -*la* NF. -*lě*).

The suffix was originally adjectival, but very few such adjectives survive: P. *były* 'former' *stały* 'constant'. They were more numerous in Old Polish: OP. *zabiłego człowieka* 'of a slain man'/MP. *zabity*, OP. *zginęłych*=*mortuorum*/MP. *martwych*. Otherwise this form was specialized for use with the auxiliary to form past tenses and the conditional. In Old Polish, auxiliaries of the third person were in use, though now disused, and those of other persons might be omitted if the subject was named by a pronoun or if the auxiliary had appeared in a previous clause. They are attached in reduced, enclitic forms which are still partly independent of the participle: *gdyśmy byli w Paryżu/gdy byliśmy* 'when we were in Paris', *ja byłem/jam był* 'I was'. To express the conditional the enclitic particle *by* is used, with the auxiliary of the first and second persons: P. *czytałbym* 'I should read', with past conditional: *byłbym czytał*. Here also the enclitic is mobile: *jabym czytał* 'I should read', *człowiek, któryby był gotów* 'a man who would be ready', *choćby dał* 'though he gave'. The enclitic suffix does not normally cause the stress to shift: *czytałbym któryby*. The impersonal form of the conditional is formed of *by* and the passive past participle *-no*: P. *mówionoby* 'one would say'.

Certain final consonants assimilated in the infinitive reappear in the participle: *kwiść* 'bloom'/*kwitł pogrześć* 'bury'/*pogrzebł oblec* 'put on clothes'/*oblekł*. The principle of compensation for loss of final *jer* may affect the masc.sg.: P. *trząsł/F. trzęsła* 'shook' *niósł/*fem. *niosła* 'bore'. The hard alveolar *ł* dispalatalizes a previous *e: niosłem/ nieśliśmy, plotłem/pletliśmy* 'wove', *darł/drzeć* 'tear'. After a consonant final *ł* is not clearly heard; hence OP. *umar* 'died' *rzek* 'said', cf. Cz. dial. *nes* 'bore'. In standard Czech all varieties of *l* have fused, but they remain distinct in dialects, and *-l* has developed to dial. *-u: umreu* 'died' *byuo* 'was' *čekau* 'awaited'; whence the velar quality has spread to the preceding vowel: dial. *buł/*Cz. *bil* 'struck'. In Old Czech final *l* after a consonant did not form a syllable; from later sonant *l* in such cases has come dial. *-el -ol -yl -al.* Cz. *jsem* is enclitic, but unattached, and so is *bych* (condit.; past: *byl bych*). The third-person auxiliaries are always omitted, the others sometimes. Peculiar to Czech is the use of the *singular* past tense when one person is addressed by the (formally) plural pronoun *vy: Vy jste byl/byla* 'you have been'.

159. *Past Participles.* (*a*) *Active.* CSl.*MNS.* -(*v*)*ŭ* >OP. *w:* OP. *obróciw się* 'having turned round', OP. *rzekw* (an analogical form) 'having said'. Sometimes the *ł* of the parallel past participle intruded: OP. *wyszedłw* 'having gone out'. Forms like *rzekw wyszedłw* were common in the fourteenth and fifteenth centuries, but are now disused. CSl.*FS.* -(*v*)*ŭši* >P. -(*w*)*szy*, now indeclinable: MP. *począwszy* 'having begun'; *upadłszy* 'having fallen' *przyniósłszy* 'having brought' are based on the *-ł* participles. As all these forms were felt to be closely akin to the participle in *-ł*, the intrusive *ł* became frequent in the first half of the sixteenth century, and again in the nineteenth century; but it is the exception in the second half of the seventeenth century and in the eighteenth. In the fourteenth and fifteenth centuries the *w* proper to vocalic-stems appeared also after consonants: OP.

szedwszy 'having gone', and with intrusive *l:* OP. *wszedłwszy* 'having entered'.

Vocalic-stems in Czech: *M. zača-v NF. -vši P. -vše* 'having begun', *vzav* etc. 'having taken' *mlev* 'having ground' *kryv* 'having covered'. Apart from cases of contraction the vowel is short. Consonant-stems: *M. vez NF. -ši P. -še* 'having conveyed'. Verbs of the second class sometimes have doublet forms: *pad/padnuv* 'having fallen'. Old Czech texts show no signs of the definite declension of this participle, but in Modern Czech this is formed by means of the suffix *-i:* MCz. *přispěchavší lékař* 'a doctor who had hurried to the spot'.

(b) *Passive.* The distribution of the participle between the suffixes *t* and (*e*)*n* is as in Old Bulgarian (see section 57 *c d*). In Polish *-t* has been extended to verbs of class ii: *zgǐnięty* 'dead' (*ię* for *ę* by analogy). There are some doublets: *kłuty* 'stung'/*kolony*, *miełty* 'ground'/ *mielony*, *pełty* 'weeded'/*pielony*, the former being used as late as the seventeenth century. Both suffixes effected dispalatalization: *tarty* 'rubbed'/*trzeć*, *widziany* 'seen'/*widzieć*, *wiedziony* 'led' OP. *pogrzebion* 'buried' *raniony* 'wounded'. Cz. *mnut* 'rubbed' *trt* 'rubbed' *kryt* 'covered' *dělán* 'done' *prošen* 'begged' *trpěn* 'suffered'. From the participle definite adjectives may be formed: Cz. *krytý* 'covered' *řečený* 'said'. In Czech, especially in the eastern dialects, the use of *t* has spread to verbs now in *-ati: sát* 'sown' *hřát* 'warmed'. In Slovak softening of the consonant before *-jen* has been eliminated, as in Slovene and Modern Bulgarian, by analogy: *razený* 'struck' (*raziť*)/ Cz. *ražený*.

160. *Verbal Noun.* P. *cięcie* 'blow' *czytanie* 'reading' *plecienie* 'plaiting' (without dispalatalization as in the participle *pleciony*); LowWend. *piśe*/UpWend. *piće* 'drinking' UpWend. *rězanje* 'cutting' *khwalenje* 'praising'; Cz. *začeti* 'beginning' *řčení* 'saying'. In Polish verbs of class ii (*n*-suffix), doublet verbal nouns occur: P. *ciągnienie*/ *ciągnięcie* 'pulling'.

161. *Imperfect and Aorist.*

Aorist

	S_1	23	P_1	2	3	D_1	23
LowWend. spleś-e- nahukn-u- hup-i- nasyp-a-	ch	-	chmy	śćo	chu	chmej	štej

Imperfect

	S_1	23	P_1	2	3	D_1	23
LowWend. pleś-e- hukń-e- pij-a-/syp-a-	ch	šo	chmy	śćo	chu	chmej	štej

These two tenses are alive only in Wendish. P_3. -*chu* belongs to the imperfect: OB. -*cho*/aor. -*šę*, and P_2. -*ščo* D_{23}. -*štej* show contamination of the imperfect and aorist terminations (OB.P_2.impf. -*šete*/ D_2. -*sta* 3. -*ste*); D_1. -*chmej* has been influenced by the plural -*chmy*. The imperfect is the past tense of imperfective verbs and the aorist that of perfective verbs (the latter shown above with prefixes s- na- hu- $\langle u$-$\rangle$. In the aorist the stem-vowel e results from carrying e through the declension, in face of OB. *o/e;* LowWend. *u* corresponds to OB. *ǫ* (Cl. ii); *i a* persist. In the imperfect only contracted vowels appear: Wend. '*e* $\langle$*ěa/ě*, *a* $\langle$*aa*.

When the historical period opened in Polish the two tenses were so far decayed that a complete paradigm can be formed for neither. S_1. aor. *mołwich*/impf. *mołwiach* 'said' *widziech* 'saw', attested only for two verbs. S_3. impf. -*sze* only; D_3. aor. -*sta* only: OP. *włożysta* 'they two put in'. P_3. -*chą* (impf., and used for aor.) is used quite freely: OP. *idziechą* 'they went'. A precise notion of aspect is wanting; Lat. *loquebatur* = OP. *mołwich/mołwiach* indifferently. As the latter are formally in the first person, a confusion of person also is implied. As between OP. *zapłakachą* 'wept'/*szukachą* 'were seeking', the difference of tense depends not on tense-ending but on the verbs themselves (perfective/imperfective).

Both tenses were retained for a longer time in Czechoslovak. Cz. *bych* (auxiliary of the conditional) is a sigmatic aorist still in use. The asigmatic aorist was most imperfectly preserved in Old Czech, but the sigmatic was normal. As to persons, S_2. was rare, and $P_2.D_{12}$. unattested; $S_{13}.P_1$. were in frequent use, but P_3. was rarer: OCz.S_1. *id/jíd* 'ate' *pad* 'fell' *léz* 'climbed' *táh* 'tugged' *zdvíh* 'lifted', 3. *vede*/ *véde* 'led' *wyleze* 'climbed out', P_1. *jidom/jídom* 'ate' *sědom* 'sat', 3. *nesú* 'brought', D_3. *bodeta* 'stabbed'. P_3. -*chu* (OCz. *brachu* 'took') is an imperfect form used also for the aorist, and -*šte šta/ste* sta are used indifferently. As in Wendish, OCz. *e* corresponds to OB. *o/e:* OCz. *vedech* 'I led'/OB. *vedochŭ*. In Old Czech the vowel of the imperfect was *ie*, resulting from *ě* (*ěa*) and by palatalization from '*a:* OCz. *nesiech* 'I was bearing' *lajiechŭ*/OB. *laachŭ* 'I was scolding' *dělajiech*/OB. *delaachŭ* 'I was doing'. In the last example, Czech contraction gave -*ajie*- $\rangle$-*á*-, which vowel spread to other classes of verbs: OCz. *dělách* : : *beriech/brách*. The stem used was the present. The tense was current in the fourteenth and fifteenth centuries: *myšleše* 'he was thinking' *kupováàch* 'I was buying'.

The two tenses were gradually eliminated. In the fourteenth-century *Alexandreid* the simple tenses/periphrastic forms were 71 to 29; but this division was not uniform for all persons. Even then the periphrastic forms were normal for $S_2.P_{12}.D_{12}$.; S_1. shows an equilibrium, but SP_3. show a ratio of 4 to 1. In the fifteenth century

Hus uses the aorist only for biblical quotations, and the translator of Comestor let his instinct for periphrastic forms lead him into doubled imperfects [imperfect+auxiliary in the same tense: *biesse krztiesse*(!), as if *erat baptizabat*(!) 'was baptizing', *když dva měsiece biechu minušta* 'when two months had passed'; in this latter there has also been confusion of numbers: pl.+dual]. The complete disappearance of the tenses was probably a feature of the late sixteenth century, and examples from Doležal (d.1764) are no doubt to be discounted as deliberate archaisms. Popular poetry, as collected in 1814, retained these tenses by traditional recitation: *slibovachu* 'promised' *měch* 'had'. In eastern dialects the aorist and imperfect flexions are sometimes added to the participle in *l*: dial. *litałach* 'I (fem.) flew' *věděłch* 'I knew'.

(ii) NOUNS, ADJECTIVES, PRONOUNS

162. *Gender and Declension.* The redistribution of nouns among the declensions so as to identify form with gender has been more fully carried out in Polish than in Wendish or Czechoslovak. Apart from the 'natural' masculines in *-a*, the state of affairs in Modern Polish has come to be that nouns are masculine if the nominative ends in a hard or soft consonant [G*S*. -(*i*)*a*], neuter if ending in the vowels *o e ę*, and feminine if in *a i* or a soft consonant (G*S*. -*i*/*y*).

(i) Of original *i*-stems only the feminines remain in Polish, save that P. *ludzie* <*ludije* 'people' IP. *gośćmi* 'with the guests' and other forms show the retention of endings originally proper to masculine *i*-stems. They have even been extended by analogy: IP. *końmi* 'with horses'. CSl.(OB.) *pǫti* 'way' survives only in the derivative *pątnik* 'pilgrim'. These masculines have left many more traces in Czech and Wendish plurals. The whole declension is affected by contraction and assimilation so as to present few changes of flexion in Polish or Czech. In the latter, final *i* was lost without permanently softening the previous consonant. In Polish, where this softening takes place with -*i* <**-i* or **jo*, a strong analogy was established between masculines of the two groups, an analogy absent from Czech. The hardening of sibilants in later Polish has given rise to a soft/hard alternative within this originally wholly soft declension: P. *kość* (G*S*. *kości*) 'bone'/*rzecz* (G*S*. *rzeczy*) 'thing'. In colloquial Czech there is a tendency, not revealed in the literary language, to eliminate this declension by transferring all its masculines to the *jo*-type, and all its feminines to *ja*. The *uv*-stems were assimilated to feminine *i*-stems, and show further colloquial assimilation to (*j*)*a*-stems: Cz. *konev*/*konva* 'jug' *mrkev*/*mrkva* 'carrot' *bukva* 'letter'.

Feminine *r*-stems have taken *i*-flexions. P. *macierz* 'mother' derives from CSl.(OB.)A*S*. *materi;* but CSl. **dŭťi* OB. *dŭšti* 'daughter' has been transferred to the *a*-declension through the diminutive *córka*, cf. also *matka*. LowWend. *maś/maśeŕ* and also *maśeŕa*. Cz. *máti/matka* 'mother', *dci/dcera* 'daughter', *net* 'niece'.

Masculine *n*-stems, using the accusative for the nominative, have been transferred to the *jo*-declension in Polish. In Lower Wendish *kameń* 'stone' has a colloquial G*P. kameń*, preserved in a few phrases, as well as the analogical forms *kameni* and *kameňow*. The survival of this type is more complete in Czech, since Cz. *kámen* 'stone' *kmen* 'stem' *kořen* 'root' *plamen* 'flame' *hřeben* 'comb' *ječmen* 'barley' *pramen* 'source' *tř(e)men* 'stirrup' have, to some extent, a double declension in the singular; but in the plural they are wholly *jo*-stems. Wend. *(d)żeń* 'day' Cz. *den* have mixed *i/jo*-declensions.

The *s*-stems have passed over to the *o*-declension, some with and others without a longer form of stem for the plural: P. *słowo* (G*S. słowa* N*P. słowa*) 'word', *niebo* (G*S. nieba/*N*P. niebiosa*) 'sky'; Wend. *słowo* N*P. słowa*, LowWend. *ńebjo* UpWend. *nebjo* LowWend. N*P. ńebja/*UpWend. *njebjesa* (and LowWend. *ńebjaski* 'heavenly'); Cz. *nebe* (cf. *moře*) D*S. nebi/*N*P. nebesa* (cf. *města*) with soft singular and hard plural declensions.

The *n*- and *nt*-stems are declined alike. They are influenced by soft (*jo*) neuters in the singular, and by hard (*o*) neuters in the plural. In Czech a number of *n*-stems have been transferred to *o*-neuters by a declension based on the oblique stem: Cz. *jméno* 'name'/OCz. *jmě*, colloquial *břemeno* 'load' *rameno* 'upper arm' *plemeno* 'tribe', etc./*břímě rámě plémě*. On the other hand a number of foreign masculines have been added to the *nt*-stems: Cz. *kníže* 'prince' *hrabě* 'count', P. *książę/ hrabia* (from Czech). Cz. *dítě* P. *dziecko* 'child' have Cz. N*P. děti* P. *dzieci*, which follow the *i*-stems.

(ii) Among the *a*-stems those in *-ьja >OB. *-ьji* have sometimes been rationalized: P. *sędzia* 'judge' (*sǫdьja*) is a 'natural' *a*-masculine, but it borrows declensional forms from the definite adjective (gen. *sędziego* etc.). On the other hand * *-'ja* (OB. *-'i*) gives P. *-i* : *gospodyni* 'land-lady' *bogini* 'goddess' *pani* 'lady' *ksieni* 'abbess' *prorokini* 'prophetess', Cz. *paní* (OCz. *knieni*)/*hospodyně prorokyně bohyně*.

(iii) the hard and soft *o*-declensions give masculines and neuters. With the masculines have been fused the *u*-stems, case by case, and there is no definite principle behind the differences revealed in the declension of single words. The *u*-flexions do tend to be associated with living beings, and in Czech the neuters are free from them in the literary language, though not in the colloquial (especially dat. sg., gen. pl.).

163. *Number.* (*a*) *Dual.* Wendish preserves the dual intact. There are more traces of this number in Czechoslovak than in Polish: Cz.G*D. prsou* 'of the breasts' *kolenou* 'of the knees' *ramenou* 'of the shoulders'

(the usage is limited to paired parts of the body). The locative and dative tend to take plural endings, and the nom. dual is felt to be a plural, and to be fit for use with low numbers: Cz. *oko* 'eye' *ruka* 'hand' *noha* 'foot' have dual-plurals N. *oč- uš-i ruc-e/nohy*, G. *oč- uš-i* (OCz. *-iú*), *ruk- noh-ou* (OCz. *-ú*)/*ruk noh*, D. *oč- uš-ím ruk- noh-ám*, I. *oč-uš-ima ruk- noh-ama*, L. *oč- uš-ích ruk- noh-ách/ou*. Cz. *dvě stě* '200' is dual. In popular speech the ID. *-ma* tends to invade the plural, as in Serbocroat, but it is limited even so to the single case of the instrumental. Mixed forms arise in dialects: Cz. dial. D. *rukoum* L. *nohouch*, based on GLD. *-ou*+DP. *-m* LP. *-ch*. Similarly in Polish: *dwieście* '200', *ocz- usz-* N. *-y* G. *-u* I. *-yma*, *ręc-* N. *-e* I. *-oma* (*ręku* as LS. in *w moim ręku* 'in my hands')/plural forms G. *ócz oczów usz(ów) rąk* I. *ocz- usz- ręk-ami*. The dual has not affected the usage after '3' and '4' as in East and South Slavonic; after these numbers Czech and Polish employ the nom.-acc. pl.: P. *trzy konie*/R. *tri konjá* S. *trî kònja*.

The dual persisted in Polish until dates varying from the fifteenth to the eighteenth centuries. It was protected by close association with '2': OP. *dwa krola* 'two kings' *dwie lecie* 'two summers' *dwie żenie* 'two women' *dwie oczy* 'two eyes', etc. The dative case took plural forms (*-m*) as early as the fifteenth century, to mark it off from the instrumental; the latter persisted into the sixteenth century. The gen.-loc. dual also persisted through the sixteenth century. Nominative duals were found in the sixteenth century, but the accusative lasted as late as the eighteenth, and is still to be heard in Polish dialects. In Czech the dual was still current in the sixteenth century, in immediate contact with '2'.

(*b*) *Collectives*. The collective neuter singular *-ije* was equated to the masculine plural of *i*-stems *-ije*: P. *kamienie* 'stones' : : *ludzie* 'people'. The abstract fem. sg. *-a* was also used to describe a collectivity, and P. *szlachta* 'noblemen, noblesse' is still declined as a fem. sg. (G*S*. *-ty* D*S*. *-cie* etc.). For the most part such words have come to be deemed plurals, and parallel to *i*-plurals: *brac-ia* 'brothers' : : *dzieci* 'children' AG. *-i* D. *-iom* I. *-(ć)mi* L. *iach*. So also *ksiądz* 'priest' pl. (coll.) *księża*. P. *czlowiek* 'man' has pl. *ludzie* 'people'. Abstract neuters serve as collective plurals: *królestwo* 'king and queen' as (well as 'realm') *państwo* 'sir and madam' (and 'gentry') *rodzeństwo* 'relatives, kin': e.g. *państwo Wolscy* 'Mr. and Mrs. Wolski'.

164. *Paradigms of Nouns.*

I-stems

	SNA	GDLV	I	PNV	A
P. (F) kość					
⸱ kość-	-	i	ią	i	i
rzecz	-	y	ą	y	y
LowWend.					
(F) kósć	-	i	u	i	i
rěč	-	y		y	y
(M) luź-				e	i/e
Cz. (F) kost	-	i	í	i	i

Consonant-stems

	SNV	A	G	DL	I
P. (N) imię	-	-			
imien-			ia	iu	iem
imion-					
LowWend.					
(M) źeń	-	-			
dń-			a	oju	om
dn-					
(F) maś	-(i)	-	i	i	
maśer-	-′	-′	′e	i	′u
(N) zwěře/znaḿe		-			
zwěřeś-/znaḿeń-	-		a	u	om/im
zwěřet-/znaḿeń-					
Cz. (F) neť					
neteř-	-	-	e	i	í
(M) den	-	-			
dn-			e	i	em
kámen	-	-			
kamen-			e	i	em
(N) rámě	-	-			
ramen-			e	i	em

G	D	I	L	DNAV	GL	DI
		mi				
i	iom		iach			
y	om	ami	ach			

G	D	I	L	DNAV	GL	DI
i/ow	am	ami	ach	i	owu	oma
ow				y		
i	om/am	imi	och/ach			
í	em	mi	ech			

PNV	A	G	D	I	L	DNAV	GL	DI
a	a	-	om	ami	ach			

PNV	A	G	D	I	L	DNAV	GL	DI
y	y	ow	am	ami	ach	a	owu	oma
'e	'e	'ow	'am	'ami	'ach	i	'owu	'oma
a	a	ow	am	ami	ach	i	owu	oma

PNV	A	G	D	I	L	DNAV	GL	DI
e	e	í	ím	emi	ích			
ové/i	y	í/ů(v)	ům	y	ech / ích			
y	y							
a	a	-	ům	y	ech			

					UV-stems
	SNV	A	G	DL	I
LowWend.					
(F) cerk-	ej=eẃ				
cerkw-	ja	ju	'e	i	ju

					A-stems
	SN	A	G	DL	I
P. (F) wod-	a	ę	y		ą
wodzi-				e	
dusz-				y	
ziem-	ia ⎫	ię	i	i	ią
gospodyn-	i ⎭				
(M) cieśl-	a	ę	i	i	ą
monarch-					
sędz-	ia	ię	i	i	ią
		iego	iego	iemu(D)	im
				im(L)	
LowWend.					
(F) ryb-	a	u	y	'e	u
rol-	a	u	e	i	u
kólń-					
Cz. (F) žen-	a	u	y	ě	ou
⎧daň	-	-			
⎩dan-			ě	i	í
duš-	e	i	e		
pan-	í	í	í	í	í
(M) sluh-	a	u	y	ovi	ou
soudc-	e	e	e	ovi/i	em

PNAV	G	D	I	L	DNAV	GL	DI
'e	jow	jam	jami	jach	i	jowu	joma

V	PNAV	G	D	I	L	DNAV	GL	DI
o	y	(wód)	om	ami	ach			
io	ie	-	iom	iami	iach			
o	e(NV) ów(A)	ów ⎱	om	ami	ach			
io	owie iowie	ów iów ⎰	etc.					
a	y	ow ⎱	am	ami	ach	'e	owu	oma
a	e	ow ⎰				i	'owu	'oma
o	y	-	ám	ami	ách			
i	ě	í	ím	ěmi	ích			
e	e			emi				
í	í	í	ím	ími	ích			
o	ové/y (A.-y)	ů(v)	om	y	(z)ích			
e	ové/i (A.-e)	ů(v)	om	i	ích			

O/U-stems

	SN	A	G	D	L	I
P. (M) pan-	-	G	a	u	u	em
kogut-	-	G	a	owi		em
koguc-					ie	
ogród	-	N				
ogrod-			u	owi		em
ogrodz-					ie	
król	-	G	a	owi	u	em
kamien-	-	N	ia	iowi	iu	iem
(N) drzew-	o	o	a	u	ie	em
zdan-	ie	ie	ia	iu	ie	iem
morz-	e	e	a	u	e	em
LowWend.						
(M) dub-	-	N	a	u	'e	om
syn-	-	G	a	oju		om
kóń-					u	
(N) słow-	o	o		u	'e	om
mór-	'o	'o		'u/'oju	'u	
Cz. (M) had-	-	G	a	u/ovi	u/ovi	em
hrad-	-	N	u/a	u	u/ě	em
muž	-	G	e	i/ovi	i/ovi	em
(N) měst-	o	o	a	u	ě/u	em
mor-	e	e	e	i	i	em
(M) Jiř-	í	G	í / ího	í / ímu	í / ím	ím

PNV	A	G	D	I	L	DNAV	GL	DI
owie	G							
y	N							
		ów	om	ami	ach			
y	N							
owie	G							
ie	N	i	iom	iami	iach			
a	a	-	om	ami	ach			
ia	ia	-´	iom	iami	iach			
a	a	(mórz)	om	ami	ach			
y	N							
i	G	ow	am	ami	ach	a	owu	oma
e		-						
a	a	-/ow				e		etc.
'a	'a	'ow				i		
i/ové	y							
y	y	ů(v)	ům	y	ech/ích			
i/ové	e	ů(v)	ům	i	ích			
a	a	-	ům	y	ech			
e	e	í	ím	i	ích			
í	G	{ í / ích }	ím	ími	ích			

165. *Singular Cases.* (*a*) *Nominative.* NVA*SN.* Cz. *rámĕ* 'upper arm' shows palatalization of OCz. -'*a* <-*ę* and a long stem-vowel. Similarly, *ja*-stems become Cz.N*SF.* -*ĕ*/*ę* (the latter by dispalatalization after palatals): Cz. *duše* OCz. *dušĕ.*

It is probable that among *ja*-stems the oldest Polish distinguished two qualities of the vowel (*a*/*ǻ*), according as the stress fell on the flexion or the stem: OP. *dusza* 'soul' *świeca* 'candle': OP. *dolǻ* 'luck' *trześniǻ* 'cherry' : : R. *dušá svečá* : *dólja čeréšnja.* The pronunciation -*ijǻ* is found in modern dialects and Old Polish for loanwords in Lat. -*ia:* P. *oracyjǻ opinijǻ.* It also corresponded to original -*ĭja* in the names of officers: OP. *sędziǻ* 'judge'/MP. *sędzia.* In these words the vowel *a* has been restored/OB. *sǫdĭji,* and Polish has added to their number German loanwords obtained through Czech: P. *hrabia* 'count' <Cz. *hrabĕ* (*nt*-stem) <Germ. *Graf.* They have alternative flexions borrowed from the pronominal declension. CSl.(OB.) -*ńi* is represented by P. -*ni*/Cz. -*nĕ* <-*ńa:* P. *bogini* 'goddess'/Cz. *bohynĕ.* There are many masculines in -*a:* P. *Sapieha monarcha* which follow the feminine declension in the singular and the masculine in the plural.

The ending *-*ijos* >-*ĭjĭ* is found in P. *Jerzy* Cz. *Jiři* 'George', the latter having alternative pronominal flexions. Neut. -*ĭje* >OP. -*ié* MP. -*ie,* OCz. -*ie* MCz. -*í:* P. *miłosierdzie* 'pity' Cz. *dĕlání* 'doing'.

In the *o*-stems compensation for loss of final *jer* occurred in both Old Polish and Czech. In both it induced a qualitative change, by which the stem vowel took on a narrower pronunciation, and it is this qualitative distinction which alone survives in Modern Polish: P. *dąb*/GS. *dęba* 'oak' *Bóg*/GS. *Boga* 'God', Cz. *chléb* 'bread'/GS. *chleba,* *Bůh*/GS. *Boha, sníh* 'snow'/GS. *snĕhu.*

(*b*) *Accusative.* With the exception of a few words like P. *pani* 'lady' A*S. panią,* the acc. sg. fem. is -*ę* in Polish. In Old Polish, however, so long as nom. -*a*/*ǻ* were distinguished, there was a corresponding distinction between acc. fem. -*ę*/*ǫ.* In the sixteenth century usage vacillated: *pracę*/*pracą* 'work' *wieżę*/*wieżą* 'tower' (A*S.*). In the seventeenth century the distinction failed, but A*SF.* -*ą* was described as 'elegantius' in 1690. In Czech soft A*SF.* -*i* results from palatalization of -*ǫ:* OCz. *duš'u* (**duš'ǫ*) *dušiu* MCz. *duši.* After some consonants the vowel is lost in the off-glide of the consonant: Cz. A*SF. báň* 'dome'.

In the *o*- and *u*-stems the accusative had the same form as the nominative in Common Slavonic, and this led in time to the adoption of the genitive for living things. The accusative was retained in Polish until the sixteenth century, though usage was already vacillating in the fifteenth. The acc. sg. masc. was rarely used in Old Czech of persons, but it continued in use with male appellatives (class-names like *andĕl* 'angel' *biskup* 'bishop' *syn* 'son'). Animals still took the acc. sg. in seventeenth-century Czech, and the group included *bĕs* 'devil' *duch* 'spirit'. In Modern Polish the gen.-acc. is used of persons in both numbers, and of animals in the singular; in Modern Czech it has still not invaded the plural. There are some relics of the accusative in fixed phrases: P. *iść za mąż* 'to marry' *wsiąść na koń/konia* 'to mount a horse', Cz. *na kůň*. On the other hand P. *koń stanął dęba* 'the horse reared' is a gen.-acc. used for a thing, and a relic of the old vacillations.

It was chiefly through the accusative that transfers of declension took place. CSl.A.S. -*ĭ* derived from *-*m̥* *-im* *-jom*, and so helped the passage from the consonantal type, through *i*-declension, to *jo*-declension. The oblique cases in Czechoslovak still show many variant flexions as evidence of incomplete transfer in the last stage of the series.

(c) *Vocative.* VSF. -*o*: P. *wodo* 'O water' *zemio* 'O land' *sędzio* 'O judge', Cz. *ženo* 'O woman'/soft -*e*: *duše* 'O soul'. For some masc. names in -*a* the vocative has taken the place of the nominative: P. *Jagiełło Kościuszko*. These are to be distinguished from P. *Jaśko Jasio Grzymko tat(k)o* 'daddy' etc, in which the -*o* represents the original use of the neuter with diminutives (cf. *dziecko* 'child'); cf. Cz. *dítko Stýblo Hromádko*. Pet-names take VSF. -*u*: *Zosiu* 'O Sophy'. VSF. -NSF.: P. *pani* 'O lady'/*boginio* 'goddess'. In the sixteenth and seventeenth centuries there tended to appear a soft fem. voc. -*i* (OP. *ziemi* 'O land' *lutni* 'O lute'), but it has died out again.

The *o/u*-stems had VSM. -*e/u*. In Old Polish -*u* occurred with *u*-stems, but not throughout all the class: OP.MP. *synu* 'O son' *domu* 'O house'. To avoid altering a velar by first palatalization VSM. -*u* is often preferred to -*e* by both Polish and Czech; another criterion in Polish is to associate VSM. -*e* with persons and -*u* with things. There are exceptions both ways, and the history of the vocative is a history of individual words. In the fifteenth century there was a reaction towards -*e* which lasted until the seventeenth: OP. *królewicze* 'O prince' *panicze* 'O squire'. From Common Slavonic times -*ju* was the vocative of *jo*-stems, and it spread in Polish to *i*- and *n*-stems before the historical record opened: P. *ogniu* 'O fire' *kamieniu* 'O stone'.

The vocative has been wholly lost in Slovak and almost completely in Wendish.

(d) *Genitive.* Neuter *s*-stems have their suffix only in the plural: P. *niebo* 'sky' GS. *nieba*/NP. *niebiosa*, Cz. *nebe* GS. *nebe*/NP. *nebesa*. In Czech the word has been transferred to the soft declension in the singular. Polish *n*- *nt*-stems take soft flexions in the singular (GSN. *imienia* 'of a name') and hard flexions in the plural (NP. *imiona* 'names'). The masculines of this declension are variable in Czech: *hřeben* 'comb' GS. *hřebene* (consonantal)/*hřebenu* (*u*-declension), etc.

Ja-stems had their gen. sg. originally WSl.ESl. -*ě*/SSl. -*ę*, like the nom.-acc. pl. of fem. *ja*-stems and the acc. pl. of masc. *jo*-stems:

Wend. *role* 'of a field' Cz. *duše*. In Polish this genitive was universal until the sixteenth century, and was still found in the seventeenth and eighteenth: *nieba i ziemie* 'of heaven and earth' (18th cent.). Forms in *-i* are concurrent as early as the fifteenth century. From nominatives in *-å -ni* there was G*S*. *-ej* in use from the fourteenth to the sixteenth centuries: *dobrej wolej* 'of good will'.

The *o/u*-stems distinguished their genitives as *-a/u*. G*SM*. *-u* is historically correct in such words as P. *wierzchu* 'of the top' *wołu* 'of a bull'. (It should be noted that the acc.-gen. of this word is *woła*). G*SM*. *syna* 'of the son' may be due to its place between two genitives in *-a* in P. *w imię Ojca i Syna i Swiętego Ducha* 'in the name of the Father, the Son and the Holy Ghost'; but all nouns of persons take G. *-a* in Polish, and there is a contrary tendency to specialize *-u* to names of things. This coincides with another tendency to increase the use of *-u* at the expense of *-a:* OP. *luda*/MP. *ludu* 'of the people' *boku* 'of a side' *biegu* 'of flight'. The beginning of hesitation is found in the thirteenth century: *przebytk-a/u* 'of a sojourn' (13th cent.). Usage was crystallized by Polish writers of the sixteenth century. Polish *i-* and *n*-stems were assimilated: P. *gościa* 'of a host' *kamienia* 'of a stone', though old writers sometimes used G*S*. *-u:* OP. *żołędziu* 'of an acorn'. Neuters in *-ije* OP. *-ié* gave G*S*.OP. *-iaa -iå* MP. *-ia:* OP. *przyściaa/przyściå* (16th cent.). In Czech *-a* is used of persons, *-a -u* of animals and things, with a marked increase of the latter as time progressed. The former is more common in Moravia and Silesia. It is used in Standard Czech for names of places, months, days of the week, and a list of miscellaneous nouns.

Slovak has most exceptionally borrowed the gen. sg. *-u* (of masc. *u*-stems) for the 'natural' masculines in *-a:* Slovak *sluha* 'servant' gen. *sluhu*.

In Polish the genitive is used after all negative verbs. In Czech, on the other hand, the accusative (which may, of course, in form be a genitive) is used, except in the partitive sense: *nemám penize* 'I haven't *the* money'/*nemám peněz* 'I haven't *any* money'.

(*e*) *Dative*. The dative and locative of *a*-stems are identical, and as that is also true of *i*- and consonant-stems, these cases are distinguished only in the *o/u* declension. The masculines of that type have the usual doublet-forms in the dative: P. *-u/owi* Cz. *u* (palatalizing to *-i*)/*ovi*. The distinction by origin was maintained, with vacillations, in Polish as late as the sixteenth century; but the new tendencies were producing doublets as early as the fourteenth: OP. *syn-owi/u Bog-u/owi*. The tendency was to increase the use of *-owi*, as the more distinctive flexion, at the expense of *-u*, but Kochanowski (1530–84) still has many examples of *-u* where more recent Polish employs *-owi*. The same century witnessed an extension of *-owi* to neuters, but this has died out again: MP. *ku południowi* 'to the south' (neut.) : : D*SM. dniowi*. The flexion *-u* now appears with a number of monosyllables (D*SM. Bogu bratu chłopu* 'to the peasant' *księdziu* 'to the priest' etc.) and nouns with fugitive *e* (*lew* 'lion' D*S. lwu, ojciec* 'father' D*S. ojcu, sen* 'sleep' D*S. snu*, etc.). Old *i*-stem masculines have been fully assimilated to *jo*-stems in Polish. In Czech *-ovi* is specialized to living things: Cz. *bratrovi* 'to a brother' *Janovi* 'to John' *Tomášovi* 'to Thomas' *Benešovi* 'to Beneš'. Notable datives in *-u* are: *Bohu člověku* 'to the man' *Kristu* (nom. *Kristus*), *pán-u/ovi* 'to the gentleman'.

In Old Wendish the dative derived from *u*-stems was *-owi/ewi*, but the soft alternative was assimilated to the hard from early times. A special feature of Wendish is the loss of *w* before *i*, which gave D*SM. -oj/u* (from *o*-stems). The latter has influenced the former to give the alternation *-oju/u*, and *-oj* is obsolete. It was sometimes spelt *-oj'* under the false impression that it was a shortening of *-oju*.

(*f*) *Locative.* The *o/u*-stems have L*SN.* P. *-(i)e/u*, Cz. *-ě/u* (and *-ovi* : : dat.). The use of L*S. -u* increased in Polish after the fifteenth century, and its present repartition is arbitrary. It serves to avoid palatalization in stems that end with a velar or dental: *o księdzu* 'about a priest' *w Bogu* 'in God'. A distinction of meaning is effected in L*S. w domie* 'in the house' (as an edifice)/*w domu* 'at home'. The soft form (CSl.OB. *-i* <*-joi*) continued to leave traces as late as the fifteenth century: OP. *na stolcy* 'on the stool' *w gaji* 'in the grove', but has been eliminated in favour of *-(i)u*, which is also found with *i*- and *n*-stems. In Czech the two endings are arbitrarily distributed. D*S. -u* is proper to living things, names of months, many nouns ending in velars or *r* (to keep the stem unmodified), etc. L*S. -ě* used of a personal name implies a calendar date : *o svatém Janě* 'on St. John's day'; it is proper to things, places, and stems ending in a labial or dental. After *l s z c š ř* it is dispalatalized (*-e*). Some of the masculine *n*-stems have L*S. -ě/u* as well as *-i*. The last is that of their original declension.

(*g*) *Instrumental.* The feminine instr. sg. is in P. *-ą* OP. *-ø*, OCz. *-ú* > *-au* >MCz. *-ou* OCz. *-'ú* >MCz. *-í*. As both *jers* gave WSl. *e* the distinction between CSl.OB. *-emĭ/imĭ/ŭmĭ* disappeared, and *-omĭ* > *-om* was left isolated and also disappeared. An *o* reappears in Wendish as a result of dispalatalization before the hard final consonant. Neuters in *-ĭje* had I*S. -ĭjemĭ* >OP, *-im* (OP. *udręczenim* 'by torture'), which has become MP. *-iem* by analogy. Examples of this substitution occur in the fourteenth century, and only *-em* is found in the seventeenth.

It is to be noted that masculine and neuter declensions tend to fall together, and feminine declensions to stand apart in all the cases of the singular. As that is true also of the adjective it forms a principal structural division in these languages.

Polish nouns in -*um* of Latin and Greek origin (e.g. *gimnazjum*) are not declined in the singular.

166. *Plural Cases.* (*a*) *Nominative and accusative.* The nominative, vocative and accusative are identical for feminine *i*-stems, consonantal stems and the *a*-declension. Masculine *i*-stems distinguish the nom.-voc./acc., but show alternative forms which identify them: Cz.NV. *host-é*/A. *hosti*/*y*, LowWend.NV. *luže*/A. *luž-i*/*e*. Similarly masc. *n*-stems: Cz.NV. *dn-i*/*y* A. *dn-y*/*i*, LowWend.NVA. *dny*. For the *a*-stems the identification of nominative and accusative is of Common Slavonic date. The separation of plural from singular (as a system of differentiated flexions against one of largely unified flexions) allows mental-dissociation of the forms of the same word in the two numbers. Thus *n*-neuters have a soft system of flexions in the singular and a hard one in the plural, and *s*-neuters preserve the suffix only in the plural.

The relations of singular and plural reach their extreme of complexity in the nominative of masculine *o*/*u*-stems. It is not merely that there are alternative flexions, as throughout the singular, but that the plural ending is selected according to quite different criteria. The nominative endings in Polish are -*i*/*y* -*owie* -'*e* -*e* -*a*, and in Czech -*i* -*é* -*ové* -*ě*/*e*. The ending P. -*owie* was originally proper to *u*-stems. In the fourteenth and fifteenth centuries it was freely used for the names of things: OP. *krajowie* 'countries' *biczowie* 'whips', and the usage lasted into the sixteenth century: OP. *tronowie* 'thrones' *orłowie* 'eagles'. It is now used for names of persons, and, in the face of persons in -*i*/*y*, for those who command a degree of respect: MP. *królowie* 'kings' *synowie* 'sons'/*chłopcy* 'peasants'. In Czech the flexion was OCz. -*ove*, used of persons or living things, which became -*ové* by contamination with -*é* of the masc. *n*-stems: Cz. *synové* 'sons' *chlapové* 'fellows' *hadové* 'snakes'. Dialectally this appears as -*ovi* and (Slovak) -*ovie*, whence by assimilation to collectives in -*a* comes Slovak. -*ovia*, e.g. *synovia* (cf. R. *synovjá*). The flexion -*ové* is associated with monosyllables in Czech.

In Polish *i*/*y* correspond to the *o*-declension: P. *sąsiedzi* 'neighbours' *orły* 'eagles' *wilki* 'wolves' *koguty* 'cocks'. NP. -*i* occurs for original -*y* after velars, which are then preserved. In Old Polish these velars suffered palatalization until as late as the eighteenth century: OP. *ptacy* 'birds' *wilcy*/MP. *ptaki wilki*. Palatalization takes place in Modern Czech: Cz. *soudruzi* 'companions' *žáci* 'pupils' *bratři* 'brothers'. The ending was often lengthened to -*ij*: OCz. *mistřij a bratřij*, sometimes analogically written -*iu* -*ie*. In Old Czech the flexion was applied to living and lifeless objects. AP. -*y* gave a nominative which was rarely used in Old Czech, but increased as a flexion for things, and appears steadily in national names and place-names in

-any: Čęchy 'Bohemia' *Uhry* 'Hungary' *Rakousy* 'Austria' *Hradčany.* In Polish N*P. -y* is used with hard nouns denoting animals or things, but *-(i)e* with soft nouns: *lwy* 'lions'/*palce* 'fingers' *gołębie* 'doves'. The *i*-declension gives P. *ludzie* 'people' *goście* 'guests', cf. Cz. *lidé hosté andělé* 'angels' *židé* 'Jews' *-tel*/pl. *-telé.* P. *kraje* 'countries' *dziedzice* 'heirs' *węże* 'snakes' are old soft accusatives (WSl. *-ě*).

A number of names in *-ani* are old loanwords in Czech: *děkani* 'deans'. Latin or Græco-Roman neuters have alternative plurals in *-y/a* in Polish (*poemat-y/a*), and those in *-ans* have pl. *-anse:* P. *kwadranse* 'quarter-hours'. Lat. *-arius*/pl. *-arii* gave OP. *-arz*/pl. *-ary*, but MP. *-arze* is reformed upon the singular: OP. *piekary* 'bakers' /MP. *piekarze*, OP. *koniary* 'horse-coopers' *świniary* 'swine-herds'.

Other plurals are the result of the collective/singulative principle. This occurs with the suffix *-'an-in-:* P.S. *Słowianin* P. *Słowianie*, cf. *poganin* 'heathen' P. *poganie*. The corresponding Czech singulative was *-ěnin*/pl. *-'ane;* but this has been modified. The singulative in Modern Czech is *-an: měšťan* 'townsman', with pl. *-ané* (by contamination with *-é* above): *měšťané Slované Pražané.* A neut.sg. collective in *-ie*, now treated as a plural, is P. *kamienie* 'stones'. Collectives in *-a* were originally declined as fem.sg. *a*-stems, and that is still true of P. *szlachta* 'nobles' (with a little-used alternative pl. *szlachcice*). P. *bracia* 'brothers' is declined like the *i*-stems (AG. *-i* D. *-iom* I. *-'mi* L. *-iach*); *księża* 'priests' (sg. *ksiądz*) has hard endings (AG. *-y* D. *-om* I. *-mi* L. *-ach*) as a result of the hardening of *ż;* and *książę* 'prince' (R. *knjaż*) is assimilated to the *nt*-stems: AGS. (by contraction of the stem) *księc-ia* DL. *-iu* I. *-iem* NP. *książęta* etc. In Czechoslovak the neuter pl. *-a* may be used of masculine lifeless things: Cz. *záda* 'back' *oblaka* 'clouds'. In Old Polish this ending applied to certain official titles: *podkomorza* 'chamberlains' *podczasza* 'cup-bearers' (15–16th cent.), the singulars of which were neuters in *-é< -ije* (or in *-i*); they now have masc.pl. *-e:* MP. pl. *podkomorze*/sg. *podkomorzy.*

The acc.pl. of hard masculines in *o* was P. *-y*/soft *-e:* P. *syny chrześciany* 'Christians' *kanclerze* 'chancellors'. The former was extended to several soft masculines: P. *przyjacioły* 'friends'/*przyjaciele pieniędzy* 'money', and *-y* and *-e* afford accusatives for words in *-ans*. Occasionally, but rarely, *-ej* is found in Old Polish texts for the nom.-acc. of *ja*-stems, and between the fourteenth and seventeenth centuries forms in *-ie* (NVAPF. *koście/kości*) appear sporadically. MP. *wsie/wsi* 'villages' are still concurrent. In the fifteenth century P. *macierze* 'mothers' was sometimes replaced by *maciory : :* GP. *maciór.* The *uv*-stems had NAVP. *-i* in the fifteenth century, but *-ie* in the sixteenth: OP. *cyrekwi* 'churches' *brwi* 'brows'/*cerkwie chorągwie* banners'. P. *brwi* is still in use.

(b) *Genitive.* The genitive plural never serves for an accusative in Czech. In Polish that usage was unknown before the sixteenth century (OP. *posłał katy* 'he sent executioners').

The genitive sign was a final *jer.* This was liable to confusion with the nominative singular of many words, though it was quite distinctive in the *a*-declension: P. *woda* 'water'/GP. *wód*, Cz. *žena* 'woman'/GP. *žen.* It was not inconvenient when the plural stem differed from the nom-sg.: P. *imię* 'name'/GP. *imion* Cz. *nebe* 'cloud'/ GP. *nebes.* The *o*-neuters also were quite distinctive: P. *drzewo* 'tree'/ GP. *drzew*, but the *o*-masculines were liable to confusion of cases. Among instances of stems differing in the two numbers were the *i*-stems and the *u*-stems. These gave GP. *-ij-ĭ* and *-ov-ŭ*, but, by regarding the whole ending as a flexion, this resulted in P. *-i* Cz. *-i* and P. *-ów* Cz. *-ů(v).* The latter was found in older Czech documents as *ov/ow ó uov uo ův ů*, which shows the origin of the modern sound in a diphthong resulting from narrowing the pronunciation of *o*. The form *-ův* was formerly retained at the end of sentences and before vowels.

The flexion P. *-i* corresponds to NAVP. *-ie:* P. *kamieni* 'of stones' *niedźwiedzi* 'of bears'. Polish neuters in *-ie* have GP. *-i* (*-y*) or without suffix: *stuleci* 'of centuries' *pokoleń* 'of generations'; natural masculines in *-ia* have GP. *-i* (*sędzi* 'of judges'), but might lose the flexion on the analogy of other *a*-stems (*sędź*), and that sometimes occurred with *i*-stems: P. *dań* 'of gifts' *goleń* 'of shins' (16th cent.); the *r*-stem *macierz* 'mother' had GP. *maciorz* (15th cent.)/MP. *matek* from *matka*, and among the *uv*-stems were GP. *krwi* (14th cent.) *krwiej* (16th cent.) *chorągiew* (15th cent.). In Czech the ending *-i* has become normal with *ja*-stems; Cz. *duši* 'of souls' : : *kosti.*

Old genitives without flexion in the fifteenth and sixteenth century were OP. *sąsiad* 'of neighbours' *god* 'of festivals' *akt* 'of acts' *kamion* 'of stones'. P. *przyjaciół* 'of friends' is still in use, and so is *-czas* in *dotychczas* 'till now' (adv.). Neuters are P. *lat* 'of years' *mórz* 'of seas' *serc* 'of hearts', etc. The extension of GP. *-ów* from *u*-stems to *o*-stems had taken place before the opening of Polish records, and it has been introduced into the neuter declension also. It was attached to Latin loanwords: P. *aktów* 'of acts' *gimnazjów* 'of secondary schools', and even intrudes into the feminine declensions: OP. *myszów* 'of mice' *pieśniów* 'of songs' (18th cent.). Masculine *a*-stems take their gen.pl. in *-ów*, though formerly suffixless, and by this means have come to be declined in the plural like *o*-stems: *monarchów* 'of monarchs', whence *monarchowie* 'monarchs'. The suffix has spread to all declensions in Wendish. In Czech GP. *-ů* is occasionally found with neuters, and it affects colloquially other oblique cases (as in L. *-ůch*). It was most often written *-ó* in the fifteenth century, while *-uov* ranged from the fourteenth to the sixteenth, and -ŭ(v) has prevailed since the sixteenth.

(c) *Dative, instrumental, locative*. The Polish language has imposed a considerable degree of uniformity upon its oblique flexions by making them almost all D*P.* -*om* I*P.* -*ami* L*P.* -*ach*. The dative is then quite obviously distinct from the instrumental, and it is unlike the instr.sg. in -*em*. I*P.* -*mi* occurs with some *i*-stems (P. *kośćmi* 'with bones'/*rzeczami* 'with things'), and has even been extended to some *jo*-stems (P. *końmi* 'with horses').

In the fourteenth and fifteenth centuries D*P.* -*em* <-*ŭmŭ*/*ĭmŭ*/*emŭ* and -*am* <-*amŭ* were concurrent with -*om* <-*omŭ* and -*emŭ*: *gościem koniem ludziem podkomorzem dzieciem*/*koniam ustam ciemionam zwierzętam nogam duszam czeluściam*/*panom królom morzom wodom ziemiom kościom*. Usage vacillated in the sixteenth century. The instr.pl. of masc.neut. *o*-stems was OP. -*y*, which is still encountered in some fixed phrases: P. *dawnymi czasy* 'in olden times', *wielkimi bogi* 'by the great gods', *pan nad licznymi pany* 'lord above many lords', *pod twemi skrzydły* 'under Thy wings'. It was found in feminine declensions in the fifteenth century, and later survived as a poetic licence. I*P.* -*mi* is proper to *i*-stems, but is restricted even there to *kość* 'bone' *dłoń* 'palm' *nić* 'thread' *gałąź* 'twig' *ludzie* 'people'; otherwise -*ami* is used. Outside of the *i*-declension it is found in I*P.* *końmi* 'with horses' *braćmi* 'with brothers' *przyjaciółmi* 'with friends'. In the fourteenth century it was in use with masc. *o*-stems, and even with neuters: OP. *językmi* 'with tongues' *chlebmi* 'with loaves' *gwoźdźmi* 'with nails' *polmi* 'with fields' *imionmi*/*imienmi* 'with names'; this is still the position in Slovak. The mediæval attitude was one of experimentalism, without attachment to one form. The same is true of the locative plural, for which -*ech* -*och* rivalled -*ach*. The first still survives in territorial expressions: P. *w Niemczech* 'in Germany' *w Prusiech*/*Prusach* 'in Prussia' *we Włoszech* 'in Italy'. Old Polish vacillations (14th–16th cent.) were : *w grzeszech* 'in sins' *w uściech* 'in the mouths' *w polech* 'in the fields' *w robociech* 'in works' *w gęślech*/*gęślich* 'on dulcimers' *w pokolenich* 'in generations' (contracted from -*ijech*) and *w ogródkoch* 'in gardens' *w poloch* 'in fields' *w siercoch* 'in hearts' *po imionoch*/*imienoch* 'by names' *na rękoch* 'on hands' *w gęsloch* 'on dulcimers'. OP. -*ech* represents the -*ěchŭ* of *o*-stems, and -*och* the -*ochŭ* which existed as a variant for -*ŭchŭ* in the parent speech and enjoyed the support of dat. -*om*. Kochanowski showed aversion for -*och*, and it has disappeared from the modern speech.

The development of Wendish is like that of Polish, save that dat. -*am* is preferred for feminine nouns.

In Czech the ancient pattern of oblique plural endings is more fully retained. Special features are the effect of palatalization (Cz.

duš -im -emi -ích) and compensatory lengthening (*žen-ám -ách*). The mutual interference of dual and plural flexions in colloquial Czech and Slovak is a link with Serbocroat, where the dual ·-*ma* has ousted the dat.instr.loc. plural. This ending tends to be construed as an instrumental, in which role it is more sonorous than -*mi*. On the other hand D*P*. -*m* L*P*. -*ch* afford distinctions not present in the dual. These cases of the plural therefore ousted DL*D*. -*ma*, and so helped to destroy that number, but I*D*. -*ma* tends to replace I*P*. -*mi* in common speech. There is a strong colloquial tendency to spread the endings -*ám* -*ami* -*ách* to all declensions, and instead of I*P*. -*y* (of *o*-stems) there is frequently found I*P*. -*mi*/*ami* or I*D*. -*ma*/*ama*/*oma*. Old Czech loc.pls. were in -*iech* <-*ěchŭ*, -*ech* <-*echŭ*, -*och* <-*ochŭ*, resulting in -*éch*/*ích* -*ech* -*och*. MCz. -*ech* (of *o*-stems) must rather be explained as a borrowing from *i*-stems, where -*ech* <-*ĭchŭ*, since -*ech* <-*ŭchŭ* is not attested in old writings. Slovak makes much use of L*P*. -*och*.

167. *Numerals.* 1: P.Cz. *jeden* LowWend. *jaden* UpWend. *jedyn* is declined as a demonstrative. In Low Wendish it is often used as an indefinite article. In the plural P.Cz. *jedni* is used for living masculines, P. *jedne* for masc. things and fem. and neut., Cz. *jedny* for masc. things and fem., *jedna* neut. LowWend. *jadne* in all usages. 1st: P. *pierwszy*, LowWend. *předny* and *ṕerwy*, UpWend. *prěni*, Cz. *prvý* and *první*.

2–4

		N	A	G	L	D	I	
P. dw-	(*M*)	aj/a	NG⎫				⎧u/oma	(oba)
	(*N*)	a	a ⎬	u(ch)	G	u/om	⎨u/oma	
	(*F*)	ie	ie ⎭				⎩u/iema	
trz-		ej/y	y	ech	G	em	ema	(czter-)
LowWend.								
dw-	(*M*)	aj/ej	NG⎫					
	(*NF*)	ě	ě ⎬	eju	I	I	ěma	(hobej/wobej)
tś-	(*M*)	o	NG	och	G	om	omi	(styŕ)
(*NF,M.* things)		i	N	ich		im	imi	(styr-)
Cz. dv-	(*M*)	a	N⎫					
	(*NF*)	ě	N⎭	ou	G	I	ěma	(oba)
tř-		i	N	í	ech	em	emi	
čtyř-		i	N	-	ech	em	mi	

The use of *dwa* with dual cases of the noun lasted to dates varying according to case from the fifteenth to the eighteenth century in

Polish: OP. *dwa króla* 'two kings' *dwu synu* 'of two sons' *o dwu apostołu* 'about two apostles' *dwiema bratancioma* 'to two nephews'. It is now construed with the plural: *dwaj/obaj/obydwaj synowie* 'two/ both sons'. In the impersonal construction the genitive is used: P. *tych dwuch panów przyjechało* 'these two gentlemen have come'. GL. *dwuch* is from dual *dwu*+pl. *dwóch*. The instrumental flexion has ousted the proper plural forms of '3, 4': OP. *trzema dnioma* 'in three days'. There is a tendency for *dwu/obu* to spread to all oblique cases. In Wendish the locative has been identified with the instrumental, and in Lower Wendish there is a difference of vowel between living masculines/masc. things, fem. neut. In Upper Wendish this affects only the nom.-acc. cases. From the sixteenth century in Czech the locative of *dva* has been *dvou* or dial. *dvouch* (OCz. *dvú*); Slk. *dvoch*. Mixed forms are also found in the dialectal instr. and dat. *dvoum dvouma oboum*. The distinction of declension between Cz. *tři* (*i*-stem) and *čtyři* (consonant-stem) appears in the genitive and instrumental. 2nd–4th: P. *drugi trzeci czwarty* UpWend. *druhi třeći štwórty*, Cz. *druhý třeti čtvrtý*.

5–10: P. *pięć sześć sied(e)m osiem/ośm dziewięć dziesięć*. Their declension has been influenced by the dual *dwa*: GDIL. *pięciu*, instr. also *pięcioma*. The noun follows in the gen.pl. UpWend. *pěć šesć sedym wósym dźewjeć dźesać*. Cz. *pět šest sedm osm devět deset*. 5th–10th.: P. *piąty szósty siódmy ósmy dziewiąty dziesiąty*, UpWend. *pěty* etc., Cz. *páty devátý desátý* (*šestý* etc.).

11–19: P. *jedenaście* etc., Wend. *jednasće* etc., Cz. *jedenáct*. 11th–19th: P. *jedenasty* etc., Wend. *jednasty* etc., Cz. *jedenáctý* etc.

20–90: P. *dwa-dzieścia* (nom.du.masc.) *trzy-/czter-dzieści* (nom.pl.) *pięć-* (etc.) *dziesiąt* (gen.pl.), UpWend. *dwaceći* etc., Cz. *dva-/tři-/ čtyři-cet pa-/še-/sedm-/osm-/deva-desát*. 20th–90th: P. *dwu-/trzy-/ czter- dziesty pięćdziesiąty* etc., Cz. *dvacátý* etc.

100–1,000,000: P. *sto, dwieście* (dual), *trzy-/cztery-sta* (NPN.) *pięćset* (GP.) etc. *tysiąc, dwa tysiące, pięć tysięcy, miljon*, LowWend. *sto* (*hundert*), *dwě sćě* (*dva hunderta*), *styri sta, wósym stow* (GP.) UpWend. *tysac* (*towzynt*), Cz. *sto, dvě stě, tři/čtyři sta, pět set* etc., *tisíc* (with *ti-* for *ty-*), *dva tisíce, pět tisíc, milion.* 100th etc.: P. *setny dwu-/dwóch-setny trzech-/czterech-setny, pięćsetny* etc., *tysiączny, dwutysięczny, trzytysięczny, miljonowy*, Cz. *stý dvoustý tří-/čtyř-/pěti- stý osmistý devítistý, tisící dvoutisící* etc., *miliontý*.

In addition to the cardinal and ordinal numbers there are the collectives: P. *dwoje czworo* etc., Cz. *dvojí čtverý* etc., and the fractions: P. *pół* Cz. *půl* 'half' P. *półtora* 'one and a half', P. *połowiczny* Cz. *polovični* 'half' (adj.), P. *kwadrans* 'quarter-hour', etc. Cz. *půl* may be the origin of the name of the dance *polka*.

168. *Adjectives.* The definite and possessive adjectives are declined thus:

		SNV	A	G	D	L
P. now-	(M)	y	NG ⎫	ego	emu	ym
	(N)	e	e ⎬			
	(F)	a	ą ⎭	ej	ej	ej
tan-	(M)	i	NG ⎫	iego	iemu	im
	(N)	ie	ie ⎬			
	(F)	ia	ią ⎭	iej	iej	iej
LowWend.						
now-	(MN)	M.y/N.e	NG	ego	emu	em
	(F)	a	u	eje	ej	ej
tśeś-	(MN)	M.i/N.e	NG	ego	emu	em
	(F)	a	u	eje	ej	ej
Cz. piln-	(MN)	M.ý/N.é	NG	ého	ému	ém
	(F)	á	ou	é	é	é
pěš-	(MN)	í	NG	šho	ímu	ímu
	(F)	í	í	í	í	í
Petrův	(MSN)					
Petrov-	(MN)	N.o	NG	a	u	ě
	(F)	a	u	y	ě	ě

In Italics: definite flexion

Palatalization of the consonant occurs in the personal nom.pl.masc.: Cz. *drazí* (*drahý* 'dear') P. *dobrzy* (*dobry* 'good'), cf. OB. *dra(d)ziji dobriji.*

The indefinite declension of adjectives has become quite extinct in Slovak and almost so in Polish. A few isolated words have special predicative forms: P. *zdrów* 'healthy' *gotów* 'ready' *godzien* 'worthy' *pełen* 'full' *wesół* 'gay' *świadom* 'aware' *syt* 'sated' *łaskaw* 'kind' *rad* 'glad' *kontent* 'pleased'. The indefinite neuter is more often found: P. *łatwo* 'easy' *trudno* 'difficult, what cannot be helped' *ciepło* 'warm'. In Old Polish there were many more indefinite adjectives: OP. *bogat* 'rich' *wolen* 'free' *młod* 'young'. In the fourteenth and fifteenth centuries other cases than the nominative were in use. The indefinite form is exemplified also in P. *samotrzeć* 'three together' *półtora* (= *pół wtora*) 'one and a half' *półczwarta* 'three and a half'.

The definite declension has become proper not merely to attributive adjectives, whether defined or undefined by an article, but to predicates also. The contraction of endings has removed the evidence of composition: OP. *dobr-y é ǎ* MP. *-y -e -a*/CSl. *-ŭ-ji* etc. The corresponding pronominal cases caused the flexions *-ego -emu -ym* to enter the declension of adjectives. In former times pronoun and adjective differed here in quantity, since the adjectival flexions were due to contraction: OP. *dobrégo/tego.* Former adjectives now surviving as place-names are declined as nouns, but in the fourteenth and fifteenth centuries some nouns took adjectival flexions (*sędziego* 'of a judge' is

PNV	A	GL	D	L	DNAV	GL	DI
i/e e e.	NG e e	ych	ym	ymi			
i/ie ie ie	NG ie ie	ich	im	imi			
e e	NG e	ych	ym	ymi	ej	eju	yma
e e	NG e	ich	im	imi	ej	eju	ima
M.í/N.á é	*M.é/N.á* é	ých	ým	ými			
í	í	ích	ím	ími			
M.i/y/N.a y	*M.y/N.a* y	ých	ým	ými			

still normal); Latin names continue to be so handled: *Aleksego Więciencemu* (15th cent.).

The survival of indefinite forms is more considerable in Czech, but not for all adjectives, nor even theoretically constituting a complete declension: Cz. hard *chud -o -a* 'poor'/soft *pěš -e -e* 'foot-'. The soft type survives only in relics: Cz. *anděl Páně* 'the angel of the Lord' (indeclinable), and in place-names: *Kněž-most Kněž-ves* etc. Examples of hard adjectives in the indefinite form, used only as predicates, are: Cz. *živ* 'alive' *dobrotiv* 'kindly' *znám* 'known' *mlád* 'young' *zdráv* 'healthy' *hrd* 'proud' *nemocen* 'ill' *silen* 'strong' *mrtev* 'dead'. The indefinite declension is complete for possessive adjectives in *-ův* or *-in* (*matčin* 'mother's' *Olžin* 'Olga's'), except in the instr.sg. masc.neut. and the gen.-loc. dat.instr.pl., which have been borrowed from the definite declension. The indefinite accusative is found in phrases like Cz. *Štěpán viděl nebesa otevřena* 'S. saw the heavens opened', and adverbially in *daleko* 'afar' *na levo* 'on the left'. The indefinite genitive exists only adverbially: Cz. *docela* 'quite' (*celý* 'whole') *zdaleka* 'from afar' (*daleký* 'distant') *znovu* 'anew' (*nový* 'new'; *znovu* is an example of the *u*-gen. in adjectives). The indefinite instrumental occurs adverbially in Cz. *málem* 'almost' *skorem* 'nearly' The locative appears in *pilně* 'diligently' *vesele* 'cheerfully', etc.

Evidence for the contraction of definite flexions in Czechoslovak is still given by the long quantity of the vowels. The pronominal declension has influenced the same cases as in Polish, and palatalization has modified those cases which showed '*a* or '*u* in Old Czech.

The comparative adjective may be used, as in German, to express 'fairly', 'rather': Cz. *starší* 'older'/'elderly'. The superlative is formed by prefixing *naj-* (Cz. *nej-*).

169. *The Demonstrative Declension*:

		SNV	A	G	D	L	I
P.							
t-	(*MN*)	M.en/N.o	NG	ego	emu	ym	
	(*F*)	a	ę		ej		ą
k-		to	G	ogo	omu	im	
cz-				ego	emu	em	
c-		o	o				
	(*M*.on/*N*.ono)	NG		jego/go	jemu/mu		
				niego	niemu	nim	
	(*F*.ona)				niej		nią
				jej			
wsz	(*M*)		}	ego	emu		{ ym
	(*N*)	e	e }				{ em
LowWend.	(*M*)	(wón)	NG }	jogo	jomu		
	(*N*)	(wóno)	N }				
	(*MN*)					ńom	nim
	(*F*)	(wóna)	ju	jeje	jej		
						ńej	ńeju
Cz. t-	(*M*)	en	NG }	oho	omu	om	ím
	(*N*)	o	o }				
	(*F*)	a	u		é		ou
k-		do	G	oho	omu	om	ým
č				eho	emu	em	ím
c		o	o				
(jenž) j-	(*M*)	(en)	ej/G	eho/ho	emu/mu		ím
	(*N*)	(e)	e				
						něm	
	(*F*)	(e)	i	í	í		í
						ní	

The principal pronouns in the demonstrative and interrogative-relative group in Polish are: P. *ten* 'this' *ów* 'that' *on* 'that, he' *kto* 'who', which are all hard, and soft: OP. *jen* 'that' *wsze* (*N*) 'all' *co* 'what'. *Ten*, *jen* have suffixed -*nŭ*, and *kto* has the demonstrative suffix -*to;* other pronouns are formed with suffixes or prefixes: P. *któż* 'who then' *cóż* 'what then' *tamten* 'that' *nikt* 'no one' *nic* 'nothing'. *Co* < G.S. *čiso*, used as nominative; *co za*+nom. 'what sort of?' is a Germanism (*was für ein Mensch* 'what a man' cf. Russian; Czech has *co za*+

PNV	A	GL	D	I	DNAV	GL	DI
M. ci							
MN. e	NG⎱						
		ych	ym	ymi			
e	e ⎰						
(*M.*oni/one)	NG-⎫						
		ich	im				
(*NF.* one)		nich	nim	nimi			
	(*M*) ech						
e	e	ecn	em	emi			
⎰(wóni)	je/G⎱						
⎱(wóni)	je ⎰	jich	jim		(wónej)	jeju	jima
		nich	nim	nimi			nima
(wóni)	je						
i/y	y	ěch	ěm	ěmi			
a	a						
y	y						
(i/e)	e⎤						
(e)		ich	im	imi			
(e)	e⎦	nich					

acc.). *Wsze* is completely declined only for things and is defective for persons. The missing personal forms are obtained from the compound *wszystek*. Pronouns with definite declensional endings are: P. *który* 'which' *jaki* 'what sort of' *taki* 'such' and the possessives *mój twój swój nasz wasz czyj* 'whose'. *Czy* is an old case of the pronoun *čĭ-* specialized as a conjunction ('whether, or') and to introduce direct questions, and with *-li* it gives *czyli* 'or'.

P. *tego temu : :* vowel in nom. *ten*, aided by the analogy of the soft declension. These flexions have passed into the definite declension of adjectives. P. *tym tych : :* soft *nim nich*, by means of the alternation soft *i*/hard *y*. The loc.instr.sg.masc.neut. were distinguished in Old Polish (I*SMN. jim*/L*SMN. niem*) until the end of the fourteenth century. P. *ci* (by palatalization of the dental) is used for human male subjects. The declension of the soft demonstrative was defective in Old Polish. The nom.sg. appeared with suffixes: OP. *jiż jen jenże*. It is now derived from another pronoun: MP. *on*. The mediæval plural was P.*M. jiż(e) N. jaż(e) F. jeż(e)*. The locative singular and plural have *n-*, derived from prepositions originally ending in *-n* [as *sŭ(n)* 'with'], and there are alternative forms with this *n-* for the genitive and dative. Until the spelling-reform of 1936 the instrumental distinguished masc./fem.neut.pl. (*tymi/temi nimi/niemi*) and instr.-loc.masc./neut. (*tym/tem*). The dat.-loc.fem.sg. has fused with the genitive, which remains quite distinct in Wendish. OP. loc. *czem*/instr. *czym* corresponded to OB. *čemĭ/čimĭ*, and on that analogy was formed OP. *kiem/kim* (OB. *komĭ/cěmĭ*), with the new palatal *k*. After the fourteenth century the cases were fused, giving MP. *kim* and *czem*. The same fusion has taken place in the adjectival declension. Conversely, the genitive and dative of *co* have been remodelled upon *kto*, giving *czego* (OB. *čiso*) *czemu : : kogo komu*. In P. *co zacz* 'what kind of man is he' the *-cz* is an enclitic accusative (=*čĭ-*). The possessive pronouns *mój twój swój* have full and contracted variants: G*SMN. mojego/mego* F. *mojej/mej* I*SMN. moim/mym* F. *moją/mą*.

In Czech the demonstrative NA*SM. t* occurs only in OCz. *vetčas* 'at that time' (*ve t čas*). Otherwise it was strengthened by suffixes: OCz. *tet* MCz. *ten tenž tenže tenhle tento*, or with prefixes: *toten tuten tamten*. So also *jenž*, which retains its value as a relative pronoun, *onen* 'that', *an* 'and he' (*a+on*), *kdo, týž* 'same' (=*tŭjĭ že*), etc. *Kdo* 'who' has *d* for *t* on the analogy of *kde* 'where' (R. *gde*) *kdy* 'when'. Cz. *týž* 'same' *taký* 'such' *takový* 'such' *ký* 'what a' *který* 'which, who' etc. are definitely declined. Cz. *sám* 'self' follows a mixed definite-indefinite paradigm. The soft relative *jenž* could also be demonstrative in Old Czech. The initial *n-* of the locative spreads in the colloquial to any case but the nominative, and gives an enclitic masc.acc. *-ň*

($<$-n+$j\breve{\imath}$). Enclitic -$\check{c}$ is found in Cz. *proč* 'why?' *pročež* 'therefore' *načež* 'whereupon' *zač* 'what for?' *začež* 'this being so' OCz. *pocz* 'therefore'. *Co* 'what?' is from the genitive, as in Polish; and there is a possessive *či* ($<$*či-jĭ*) 'whose?' The old demonstrative *s* 'this' is found in Cz. *dnes* 'this day, today' and OCz. *sen;* it gives Cz. *letos* (A*SN.*) 'this summer', *zimus* 'this winter' and OCz. *sí noci/s'noci* (D*SF.*) 'this night'. As in Polish the ancient *vĭšĭ* 'all' has lost ground to a derivative in the nominative and accusative: MCz. *všechen.* The oblique cases of the simple stem survive: G*SMN.* *všeho* F. *vše* etc., though the suffix may be carried through the paradigm. Other suffixes in use with this word are :-*cek* (Slovak -*cok*) -*tek* (Slovak -*tok*) -*cen* -*ken* -*cken* -*tken* -*keren* -*ckeren* -*cheren.*

The hard G*SMN.* -*oho* D. -*omu* L. -*om* exist with variant soft forms (-*eho* -*emu* -*em*) in the declension of *ten kdo.* G*SF.* *té* $<$*tojě has parallels (*tý/ty téj/tej*) in the colloquial; and similarly D*SF.* *té* (for *toji*)/*ty.* I*SMN.* *tím* $<$OCz. *tiem* $<$*těmĭ;* I*SF.* *tou* $<$OCz. *tú* $<$*to,* dial. *tô* and *tum/túm* near the Polish border under the influence of Polish nasals. N*PM.* *ti* $<$*toi is restricted to human males; for animals and inanimates *ty* has been taken into the nom. from the accusative. A*SMF.* *ty* $<$*tons F. **tans.* N*SF.* *ty* (acc. for nom.) is found as *te tý. tie tye tyé* in the dialects. G*LP.* *těch* $<$*toisu is often written OCz. *tyech tijech* in manuscripts, but the vowel was certainly short, as it would otherwise have become *i.* D*P.* *těm* is sometimes hardened to *tem tym.* I*P.* *těmi* is confused with the dual in dialects and also liable to harden: *těma tema tymi tyma.* In Old Czech the dual read: NA*M.* *ta* N*F.* *tě* GL. *tú* DI. *těma.*

In colloquial Czech there is a tendency to use *ten,* etc., as a definite article, particularly before superlative adjectives.

Reduplicated forms of the soft declension (*jejich* etc.) are attested from the fourteenth century. OCz.G*D.* *jeju* is probably a secondary formation, though it is paralleled in Old Bulgarian. G*SMN.* *jeho* had a variable accent which has given rise to differences in the contracted forms: *j'ho ho jeh'; jej* $<$*jejĭ; čeho* is a new formation/OB. *čĭso.* In Slovak the vowel of *co* persists through the paradigm (G. *čoho* D. *čomu* L. *čom*). The locative and instrumental are kept distinct in Czech, unlike Polish: *čem/čím.* Czech *co* appears in Slovak as *čo.* Other dialectalisms are *jomu ňom : : tomu tom.*

Before the epoch of the palatalization of -'*a* -'*u* the possessive adjectives *můj tvůj svůj* suffered contraction, as in Polish, and have acquired doublet forms: N*N.* *moje/mé* F. *moje/má,* G*SMN.* *mého* F. *mé,* D*SMN.* *mému* F. *mé,* L*SMN.* *mém* F. *mé,* I*SMN.* *mým* F. *mou. Náš* 'our' *váš* 'your' follow the soft pronominal declension.

170. *Personal Pronouns:*

	SNV	A	G	DL	I	PNV	A	GL	D	I	DNAV	GL	L
P.	ja												
m-		ię		i(D)		y							
mn-		ie	ie	ie	ą								
n-							as	as	am	ami			
t-	y												
c-/s-		ię		i(D)									
cieb-/sieb-		ie	ie										
tob-/sob-				ie	ą								
w-						y	as	as	am	ami			
Low Wend.	ja												
m-		'e	'e	'e(D)		y						ej	
mn-		'o	'o	'e/'o	u								
n-							as	etc.				aju	ama
t-	y												
ś-			i	i(D)									
s-		e	e	e									
teb-/seb-		'e	'e	'e	u								
tob-/sob-					u								
w-						y	as	etc.				ej	etc.
Cz.	já												
m-			ě	i(D)		y							
mn-		e	e	ě	ou								
n-							ás	ás	ám	ámi			
t-	y		ě	i(D)									
s-			e	i(D)									
teb-/seb-		e	e		ou								
tob-/sob-				ě									
v-						y	ás	etc.					

OP. *jaz* 'I' occurs occasionally in the fourteenth century, but the mediæval and dialect form was more often *jå;* OCz. *jaz.* The forms P. *mię mi tię ci się si,* and their congeners in Wendish and Czechoslovak, are used enclitically; of P. *ci* there is a variant *-ć:* P. *toć było dobre* 'that was good (for thee)'. In the third person there are similar enclitics (*go mu*). The stem *men-* has been eliminated. In Czech the stems *teb- seb-/tob-sob-* have been exchanged in the dative and instrumental. The locative fell in with the dative in Common Slavonic.

CSl.(OB.) acc.pl. *ny vy* is not found, except in OP. *poświęci ny=*'ut sanctificemur'; their place is taken by the original gen.-loc. CSl.(OB.) *vě* 'we two'/*va* 'ye two' is imperfectly represented in West Slavonic. In OCz. *va : : dva* is found alongside *-va/vě* in verbs; OP. *wa* 'we two' dates from before the records begin. In Wendish *m* is borrowed from the plural. A fifteenth-century etymology *swadźba = swać wa* 'marry us two' is evidence of the survival of *wa* as an accusative. There is no trace in Polish or Czech of CSl.(OB.) acc.dual *na*. G*D*.OP. *naju waju* O*Cz. najú >naji vajú >vaji*, DI*D*.P. *nama wama* Cz. *náma váma.* They were in use in Poland as late as the seventeenth century.

(iii) INDECLINABLES

171. *Adverbs* (see section 73). These are formed from adjectives in Czech by means of the suffix *-ě: rychlý* 'quick' *rychle, hloupý* 'stupid' *hloupě, drahý* 'dear' *draze*, those in *-ský* taking *-sky: česky* 'in Czech (fashion)'. In Polish the ending *-o* is preferred after gutturals: *głęboki* 'deep' *głęboko/dobry* 'good' *dobrze*, and adjectives in *-ski* take the (DL) form *-sku: po polsku* 'in Polish (fashion)'. The adverb-system described in section 73 is well represented in these languages: Cz. *kde* (pr. [gdɛ]) 'where' from *kŭde* (P. *gdzie*), *zde* 'here' from *sĭde* (cf. R. *zdeś*), *všude* 'everywhere' from **vĭś-ǫde* (cf. OB. *kǫdě* 'whence'), *jinde* 'elsewhere' (*jiný* 'other' <*inŭ*), *někde* 'somewhere', *nikde* 'nowhere', *kam* 'whither', *sem* 'hither', *tam* 'thither, there' (P. *tam* 'there'), *kdy* (pr. [gdi]) 'when', relative *když*, from **kŭdy* (P. *gdy* relative), *nikdy* 'never' (P. *nigdy*), *tehdy* 'then' from **tŭgdy*, also *tedy* [whence P. *(w)tedy* 'then'], *teda* 'then, so' and *ted*' (colloquial) 'now', *(i)hned* 'at once' (whence P. *wnet*) from *inŭgd-* with metathesis, *vždy* 'always' from **vĭśĭdy, kudy* 'which way', cf. OB. *kǫdě* (P. *dokąd* 'whither'), *tudy* 'this way' (P. *tędy*), *odkud* 'whence' (P. *skąd*), *odsud* 'hence' (P. *stąd*), *posud* 'this far', *odevšud* 'from everywhere' (P. *zewsząd*), *jak(o)* 'how, as' [P. *jak(o)*], *tak* 'so' (P. *tak*, also means 'yes')' *nějak* 'somehow', *nijak* 'in no way' [P. *nijak(o)*], *nikterak* 'in no way' (from *který* 'which' from **kŭ-ter-*), *jaksi* 'somehow' with *-si* D. of reflexive pronoun (P. *jakoś*), *jakkoliv* 'however' (P. *jakkolwiek; cf.* OB. *koli* 'how far'), *nikoli* 'not at all', *kolik* 'how much' (cf. R. *skól' ko*), *tolik* 'so much' (P. *ile* 'how much' from relative **jĭlě*, whence *tyle* 'so much', *tylko* 'only', *kilka* 'some'), *velmi* 'very' (from *vel-* 'great'), *sice* 'it's true' (used like Germ. *zwar*), cf. OB. *sice*, neut. of *sicĭ* 'such'. Other forms are *nyní* 'now' (P. adj. *niniejszy* 'present' with assimilated *ni-*), *ještě* 'still, yet' (P. *jeszcze*), *teprve* 'only', used like Germ. *erst* (P. *dopiero;* Cz. form from **tŭ-pĭrv-*, cf. R. *teper* 'now'), *až* 'when' from *a-že* (P. *aż* 'till'), *zas(e)* 'again' from *za se* (P. *zaś* 'but, however'), *dnes* 'today' (P. *dziś* ? <**di-sĭ*, also explained as from *dĭnĭ-sĭ*), *včera* 'yesterday' (P. *wczoraj*, with suffixed *-i* found elsewhere in Polish and other languages), *zítra* 'tomorrow' from *z-jutra* (P. *jutro*, cf. R. *útro* 'morning'), *letos* 'this year' (P. *latoś*), *již, už* 'already' (P. *już*, R. *užé*), *právě* 'just' (P. *prawie* 'almost'), *téměř* 'almost' (connected with *míra* 'measure'), *jen(om)* 'only' (from *jedn-* 'one'), *najednou* 'all of a sudden', *snad* 'perhaps' (P. *snać* 'apparently, maybe', cf. OB. *snadĭ* 'from the

top'), *také* 'also' (from *takŭ*), *též* 'also' (from *tý-ž* 'the same' <*tŭ-jĭ že;*
P. *też*), *sotva* 'hardly', *zvlášt́* *zvláště* 'specially' from *vlast(nĭ)* 'own',
i.e. 'that in one's power' (P. *zwłaszcza*), *přece* 'still, yet, but' from
před se 'before oneself' (P. *przecie-ž*), *ovšem* 'of course' from *o vĭšemĭ*
(P. *owszem* 'on the contrary', also 'no doubt'), *vŭbec* 'generally', used
like Germ. *überhaupt*, from *v obec* ['into the generality'; *obec* 'community' from **obĭtj-*, cf. R. (ChSl.) *obščij* 'general'; P. *wobec* is a
preposition meaning 'in view of'], *trochu* 'a little', acc. of *trocha* (P.
trochę), *stranou* 'aside' (I.S. of *strana* 'side'), *nahoře* 'upstairs' (*hora*
'mountain'), *vpředu* 'in front' (cf. *před* 'before'), *vpravo* 'to the right'
(*pravý* 'right'), *zdaleka* 'from afar' (*daleký* 'distant'), *potom* 'then' (*po
tomĭ* 'after that', P. *potem*), *proč* 'why' (*pro či* 'for what'), etc. Other
Polish forms are *tu tutaj* 'here' (cf. OB. *tu* 'there'), *teraz* 'now' (<*tŭ
razŭ* 'this time'), *kiedy* 'when' (<**kŭgdy* with loss of g), *zawsze*
'always' (*za wsze* 'for all'), *inaczej* 'otherwise' (cf. OB. *inače*), *jednak(že)*
'however' (*jednaki* 'identical' from *jedn-* 'one'), *ledwie* 'hardly'
(probably from contamination of words like OB. *jed(ŭ)va* and *lě*
'hardly'), *wiele* 'much' (from *vel-* 'great'; cf. Cz. *velmi* 'very'), *bardzo*
'very' (**bŭrzo* 'quickly', Cz. *brzo*), *niemal* 'almost' (*mały* 'small'),
nawet 'even' (*wet*, also found in *wet za wet* 'tit for tat' *odwet* 'revenge',
from Germ. *Wette*), *dopóty* 'so far' (from a plural of the pronoun *tŭ*),
dopóki 'as long as' (from *kŭjĭ*). A few (Lower) Wendish forms are
how 'here' (*ovŭ* with prefixed *h;* cf. S. *óvde*), *gromaže* 'where together'
(cf. Cz. *dohromady* 'together'), *znowa* 'next year' (in other languages
similar forms mean 'anew'), *něto* 'now' (?*nyně-to*); some of them are
characterized by a great accumulation of suffixes, e.g. *wělgickano* 'very
much indeed' (*vel-* 'great'), *lěbdycka* 'hardly'.

172. *Prepositions and Prefixes* (see section 74). The strong *jer* and
fill-vowel is represented in Czech and Polish by *e*, therefore Cz.
P. *bez/beze* 'without', Cz. *ode-jíti* 'go away', etc. P. *bez* (for **biez*)
appears to be due to the unstressed nature of the word. For OB.
(ChSl.) *črěsu/črězu* these languages have Cz. *přes* P. *przez* LowWend.
pśez 'through, over' by contamination with *pře- prze-*, unless one
assumes a Sl. **perzŭ;* Cz. also has *skrz* 'through', cf. Ruth. *skrož*/R.
skvož, and Slk. *cez* is presumably based on *črězŭ*. For OB. *děl´a* Czech
and Polish like Russian have **dĭl´a:* P. *dla* 'for' Cz. *dle* 'according
to'. **jĭz* gives the expected Cz. *z* (cf. *jho* 'yoke' from **jĭgo*); in Polish
this preposition has been confused with *sŭ*, both giving *z(e)*, though
the prefix is sometimes *s-*. Cz. *k(e)* and also *ku*, P. *ku*, with *-u* probably due to the ending of masc. and neut. dat. singulars.
P. *między* 'between', with intrusive nasal, Cz. *mezi* Slk. *medzi*
appear to represent the LS. of **medja*. Cz. P. *od(e)* 'from' for
otŭ by generalization of the assimilation to a following voiced consonant. *Pro* has disappeared from Polish and is replaced as a prefix by

prze- save in a very few words like *prorok* 'prophet' no doubt borrowed from abroad. (Cf. Slk. *pre* 'for'). Similarly *przeciw(ko)* 'against'/Cz. *proti.* Cz.P. *roz-* from **ŏrz-.* Cz. *v* appears as *u* before *v*, e.g. *u viře* 'in the faith'. Cz. *vy-* P. *wy-.* Prepositions in Czech take the accent (*dò toho* 'up to that' etc.) except (usually) *dle* 'according to' *kol* 'round' (also found in forms *kolem okolo;* cf. R. *ókolo* ⟨*kolo* 'wheel') *krom* 'except' (also *kromě,* OB. *kromě*), *skrz* 'through' *stran* 'concerning' (connected with *strana* 'side'); in Polish this only happens (and then not always) when the preposition forms the penultimate syllable in the group preposition+pronoun, etc.: *dò tej* 'to that (*F*)', *podè mną* 'beneath me'. Compound prepositions are e.g. P. *zamiast* 'instead of' (*miasto* 'place') *podług* 'according to' (cf. OB. *po-dļgŭ*), *sprośród* 'from amongst' (*sŭ-po-*serd-*), *gwoli* 'for the sake of' (⟨*k woli* 'to the will'), Cz. *uvnitř* 'inside' (*vŭ-vŭn-jŏtř*) *vŭči* 'in view of' (*v oči* 'into the eyes').

173. *Conjunctions and Participles* (see section 75). In Czech *a* is used for 'and', and *i* (Polish 'and') means rather 'and even'; Slovak *aj* 'and' combines the two. Cz. *ač(koliv)* P. *acz(kolwiek)* 'though' (*a-či*). P. *albo* 'or' (*a-li-bo*). Cz.P. *ale* 'but' (*a-lě*). Cz. *anebo nebo* 'or' (*a-ne-bo*), *nebot'* 'for, since' (*-t'*⟨*ti,* ethic dative). Cz.P. *ani* 'neither, nor' (*a-ni*). Cz. *ano* 'yes' (*a-no*); the colloquial word is *jo* from Austrian German, and Polish uses *tak* ('so'). Cz. *arci* 'indeed' (*a*+*rći* 'say'), *at'* 'let' (*a-ti;* see above). Cz. *avšak, však* 'but, however', P. *wszak(że)* 'yet, nevertheless' (*a-*viśakŭ,* cf. OB. *vĭsěkŭ* 'every'). P. *bo bowiem* 'for' (*wiem* 'I know'). The particle *že* is widely used, often in the form *ž:* Cz. *aniž* 'without' (e.g. *aniž bych věděl* 'without my knowing'), P. *cóż* 'what then?'; it serves as the conjunction 'that' (Cz. *že* P. *że iż* from *i-že*). The particle *-žĭdo* in OB. *kŭžĭdo* 'each' has been treated as in Russian: Cz. *každý* P. *każdy* 'each'. *-li* is used in Czech to express 'if' and introduce indirect questions: *jste-li nemocen* 'if you are ill', *nevím, je-li to pravda* 'I don't know whether that is the truth'; it also occurs in Cz. *jestli(že)* P. *jeśli jeżeli* 'if' (cf. R. *ésli éželi*), Cz. *zdali* 'whether'. In Czech the negative *ne* is prefixed to verbs: *nevidím* 'I don't see' *neviděl jsem* 'I didn't see', and also occurs in *nýbrž* 'but', used like German *sondern* [*ný-* for lengthened *ne* (*né*) pronounced Prague-fashion, *-brž* from *brzý* 'quick']. Cz. *pak* 'then', cf. OB. *paky* 'again'. Other forms: P. *czy* 'whether', also used to introduce direct questions (a form of the pronoun *čĭ-*); *czyli* 'or' (Cz. *či čili* 'or'); P. *lecz* 'but' (*lě-čĭ*); Cz. *poněvadž* P. *ponieważ* 'because' (cf. OB. *po ńeže;* suffixes *-va-že*); P. *więc* 'so', connected with *więcej,* adverbial form of *większy* 'greater', OB. *vęštĭji* ⟨**vętį-;* P. *choć chociaż* 'though'. As the last two forms are based on the present gerund *chotę* of the verb *chotěti* 'wish' (which in any case appears in Czech and Polish in forms corresponding to *chŭtěti:* Cz. *chtíti* P. *chcieć*), they would appear to be borrowed from Russian.

C. WORDS

174. *Western Elements in Vocabulary.* The West Slavonic languages lie within the orbit of occidental civilization: Latin as to fundamentals, Catholic as to faith, and Germanic as to secondary qualities.* Bohemia was the nucleus of the Luxemburg dynasty's power during the mediæval Roman Empire. It won a conspicuous primacy in arts and letters over other Slavs during the fourteenth, fifteenth and sixteenth centuries; its influence was strongly felt in Poland. The disasters of the seventeenth century coincided with the rise of Poland under strong kings. Polish literary life was reinspired by the Latin Renaissance and the Jesuit system of education. In its relations with Lithuania, White and Little Russia, however, Poland retained more contact than Bohemia with the Slavonic east, and the elements which compound its vocabulary are the more complex.

Some oriental words in Polish are parts of universal European speech, as *basza* 'pasha' *janczar* 'janissary', but others are more particularly due to the Ukrainian connexion: P. *baszłyk* 'hood' *bohater* 'hero' *bukłak* 'leather bottle' *wojłok* 'saddle-cloth' *ułafa* 'soldier's pay' *sajdak* 'quiver'. They are associated historically with the Ruthenianisms of Polish, including many words in which *h* stands in the place of P. *g*. Both sets of words are small in comparison with the vast number of Latin, French, German, and even English borrowings which stand out at a glance upon any page of the dictionary. They are, moreover, limited to naming things of a low stage of culture, and these things have less and less reason to be mentioned.

Any page of the dictionary will reveal the polyglot state of Modern Polish. The borrowings are present also in Czechoslovak, but they are less evident. Czech has imitated from German a strong antipathy to the foreign word in its foreign form, and many borrowings are disguised as pseudo-Czech compounds. Even in Czech, however, the foreign words are quite numerous.

A few examples may be cited at random: P. *buazeria* 'wainscot' Fr. *boiserie*/Cz. *táflování* (Germ. *Tafel*) *deskování* (Cz. *deska*), P. *buchta* 'bay' Germ. *Bucht*/Cz. *záliv*, P. *buduar* Cz. *budoar* Fr. *boudoir*, PCz. *bufet* Fr. *buffet*, P. *bukiet* Fr. *bouquet*/Cz. *kytice*, P. *bukszpryt* 'bowsprit' Dutch *boegspriet*/Cz. *čelen*, P. *bulion* Fr. *bouillon*/Cz. *hovězí polévka*, P. *bula* Cz. *bulla* MedLat. *bulla*. In Polish there are immediate Latinisms like P. *alumn* 'pupil' *biszkopt* 'biscuit' *korygować*

---

* As Dr. Johnson was aware. "He observed that the Bohemian language was true Sclavonick. The Swede said it had some similarity with the German. JOHNSON: 'Why, Sir, to be sure, such parts of Sclavonia as confine with Germany will borrow German words; and such parts as confine with Tartary will borrow Tartar words.' "

'to correct'; Latinisms modified by French, as the numerous àbstracts in -ja, Fr. -ie: P. aluzja kuracja; immediate Gallicisms, like P. afera 'swindle' afisz 'poster' galimatias 'nonsense'. German words are numerous: P. pudel Cz. pudlik 'poodle', P. szwajcar 'porter' Germ. Schweizer/Cz. vrátný, P. szpulka Cz. špulka 'spool' Germ. Spule, P. sztaba Cz. štáb 'bar, rod' Germ. Stab. French and Latin words often show traces of German mediation: P. cetnar Cz. centnýř Germ. Zentner Lat. centenarius 'hundredweight'. Among other elements of vocabulary are English words connected with shipping, commerce or articles of English origin, Italian words for the arts, and the pseudo-Greek compounds which express nineteenth-century thought and invention.

The principle of translation of parts has been present in Polish at all epochs, though less often applied than in German or Czech. Thus to P. chemia telefon teleskop correspond Germ. Chemie Fernsprecher Fernseher, Cz. lučba (chemie) telefon dalekohled (teleskop). Translation was one. of the procedures applied in Old Bulgarian, and so is found in old religious words: P. Bogurodzica (Θεοτόκος) błogosławić (εὐλογεῖν) wszemogący (omnipotens), OP. sąmnienie (conscientia) Cz. svědomí, spowiedź (confessio) Cz. zpověď'. A special group of crypto-Latinisms is formed of the grammatical terms which began to be widely used in the fifteenth century, and which have passed into Russian also: P. spadek (casus) namiastek (pronomen) sprzężenie (conjugatio), all used in 1542 (Glaber). The names of months and days are fabricated from Polish and Czech materials, though the calendar is undoubtedly of Latin origin: P. kwiecień (kwiat 'flower') Cz. duben (dub 'oak') 'April', P.Cz. listopad ('leaf-fall') 'November', P. wtorek 'Tuesday' ('the second day') Cz. pondělí 'Monday' (po+neděle 'after Sunday') etc. The purpose of the translation in the latter case may have been to avoid mention of heathen deities.

On the other hand, the readiness of the Poles to adopt foreign expressions was proverbial as early as the sixteenth century. A writer then complains that they are forward to utter signor with every word in Italy, par ma foi in France, and nosotros caballeros in Spain. The new words were often given purely Polish senses, as P. rezon 'boldness'. They easily acclimatized themselves so as to propagate families by Polish prefixes and suffixes: P. bezceremonialność 'frankness' rezonować 'argue' bisować 'cry encore (bis)' romantyczność 'romance' romansopisarz 'novelist'.

We must notice a few points in historical perspective. Christianity came to the Western Slavs as a result of the mission of Methodius in Great Moravia before the schism of the Churches. Its inspiration was from the south, with a preponderance of Old Bulgarian expressions; its organization was from the west, Latin and German: P. Bogurodzica

OP. *licemiernik* 'hypocrite' *cerkiew* 'church' *mięsopust* 'carnival'/ *proboszcz* Germ. *Probst* 'provost', *mnich* (cf. *Munich*) 'monk', *klasztor* Germ. *Kloster* Lat. *claustrum* (Cz. *licoměrník církev masopust profous mnich klášter*). Alongside them were some simple terms of lay culture, already current in the thirteenth century: P. *łaty* 'laths' *czynsz* 'rent' *grosz* 'groschen' *bednarz* 'cooper' *garbarz* 'tanner'.

Czech cultural hegemony in Poland during the fourteenth and fifteenth centuries is reflected in P. *obywatel* Cz. *obyvatel* 'citizen', P. *hardy* Cz. *hrdý* 'haughty', P. *wesele* 'joy, wedding' Cz. *veselí* 'joy', P. *serce* Cz. *srdce* 'heart'/native OP. *obywaciel* dial.*gardy* OP. *wiesiele sierce*. The foreign pronunciation of these words was considered to give a nuance of elegance to conversation.

The Latin Renaissance of the sixteenth and seventeenth centuries, Poland's Golden Age, is reflected in the numerous Latinisms of the epoch: P. *adwersarz archa defensor dekret dyscypuł impressor insuła kondycja kreatura mandat posesja respondować sentencja symulacja*. It was, for instance, a mark of elegance to replace *ojczyzna moja* 'my fatherland' by *patria moja*. These humanistic words came from Italy, but purely Italian words, outside the arts, were few; of the sixteenth century were: P. *kuradent* 'toothpick' *wirydarz* 'garden' (modelled on Lat. *viridarium*). German military terms flooded the vocabulary of war as a result of the fame of reiters and lansquenets: P. *anszlak* 'attack' *glanc* 'sheen' *kryksman* 'warrior', Cz. *glejt* 'safeguard'. Along with them came terms for organization: P. *burmistrz* 'mayor' *ochmistrz* (Germ. *Hofmeister*) 'steward'. The Czech influence was still effective in such loanwords as P. *hnet* 'at once' *kterak* 'how' *złatohław* 'gold brocade'.

In the eighteenth century France became the focus of cultural interest for the Western and Eastern Slavs and also for the German States. The source of new loanwords was France, but they sometimes showed marks of their travel through Germany. Polish words of the period derived from French are: P. *konkurent kondolencja krytyka denegować obserwować tentować fawor honor animusz notować*. In seven pages of one Polish author (S. Konarski, 1764) no less than sixty-four such neologisms have been counted. A great many of them have gone out of use, but the stream has been constant, and some have been replaced by others of the same formation: P. *denerwować* 'enervate' is precisely parallel to *denegować*. Even where Polish resources might have sufficed to express the idea, the foreign word has often been adopted as the readiest method of introducing new or modified cultural conceptions.

175. *Word-formation.* The suffixes listed in section 78 have been preserved and developed in West Slavonic. Little needs to be noted, but here are a few points, chiefly from Czech: The feminine -*iji* is

retained in the form -*i* in Cz. *paní* P. *pani* 'lady'. The feminine -*yńi* has remained in Polish (*bogini* 'goddess', etc.) but has been altered analogically in Czech as elsewhere (*bohyně; -ně<-ňa*). The dental is preserved in the suffix -*dlo:* Cz. *mýdlo* 'soap' (*mýti* 'wash'), P. *mydło*. OB. -*ište*, suffix of place, appears in its Czech form -*iště* from -*išče* (*hřiště* 'playground', *hráti si* 'to play', dative-reflexive verb), while -*isko* is used as an augmentative (*chlapisko* 'a big chap'; cf. this use of -*išče* in Russian), and in Polish -*isko* is used for 'place where' (*bojo-wisko* 'battlefield'). -*ství* (OB. -*istvьje*) is the usual abstract suffix (*bohatství* 'wealth'/P. *bogactwo* R. *bogátstvo*), while -*stvo* has a collective meaning (*ptactvo* 'birds' from *pták*). *-*itjo*- (OB. -*ištĭ*) appears in its West Slav form -*ic* (Cz. *dědic* P. *dziedzic*. 'heir' from *děd dziad* 'grandfather'). Besides -*ář* from -*aři* (e.g. *rybář* 'fisherman') Czech has -*íř* (e.g. *malíř* 'painter'), originally in borrowed words (Germ. *Mahler*). The ending -*ák* is very common and extremely active in Czech: *voják* 'soldier', *gestapák* (colloquial) 'gestapo-man', *koncentrák* (colloquial) 'concentration-camp'; so too is -*och*, as in *slaboch* 'weakling' (*slabý* 'weak') and many other words. The addition of the latter suffix sometimes causes considerable mutilation of the word to which it is added; e.g. *hoch* 'lad' from *holý* 'bare' (*sc.* '-faced'), F. *holka* 'lass'. A back-formation from words like *Pražané* 'people of Prague' gives the singular *Pražan;* similarly *Angličan* 'Englishman' (R. *angličánin*) etc. A compound -*ár-na* (P. -*iarnia*) expressing 'place where' gives words like *kavárna* (P. *kawiarnia*) 'café', in which connexion it is important to note that *pisárna* means 'office', a place where writing (*psáti*) is done.

Chapter VII

SOUTH SLAVONIC

(SLOVENE, SERBOCROAT, BULGARIAN)

A. SOUNDS

176. *Stress, Tone, Length.* (*a*) *Bulgarian free stress.* As in Russian, a free stress accent operates in Modern Bulgarian, without either tone or quantity. The Slavs who occupied Mœsia approached from the north-east in company with Proto-Russian tribes, and were, no doubt, the most easterly of South Slavs. It is tempting to suppose that tone and length had already been weakened in the eastern and south-eastern Slavonic area at an early time. Whether Old Bulgarian had tone and length is hard to say. There were probably vowels intrinsically different in duration, but variations of pitch may no longer have given intervals on a definite scale. It is, at least, certain that the Old Bulgarian scribes had to hand Greek diacritics which represented length and tone according to grammatical theory, though not in current Greek practice, and that they used them for other purposes.

Though the stress-accent is free, its mobility is somewhat less in Bulgarian than in Russian. The elimination of declension has removed one principal cause of stress-shifts. The stress still varies by number and gender (though decreasingly in gender), and in consequence of suffixing the article; it varies, too, among the derivatives of a given root: B. *krástavica* 'cucumber', *krastavičár* 'cucumber-seller'; *ézero* 'lake' pl. *ezerá*. The neut. pl. -*a* had a latent rising tone, and took to itself the stress of a previous short or falling accent. Hence the stress-shift between the singular and plural. But the tendency to uniformity has caused some neuters to take the final accent in the singular (B. *mesó* 'meat'), or to admit both accents (B. *nébó* 'sky'), or to shift back an originally final singular stress (B. *sélo*/R. *seló* 'village'). Note, parenthetically, that an accent written in Bulgarian signifies stress only; more than one accent on a word indicates not two stresses but alternative stresses. The law of the latent rising final tone applies also to the suffixed article: B. *duch* 'breath'/*duchắt*, *brat* 'brother'/*brátắt* (since the latter stem had a rising tone), and to the stress of words with the plural ending in -*ove*.

The *tort*-formula had added another cause of stress-mutation to Russian, by increasing the number of syllables involved. This circumstance is absent from Bulgarian. Stress shifts to the article, however, from original falling tones (*tȏrt), but not from original rising ones (*tórt): B. *gradắt* 'the city'/*gráchăt* 'the pea'.

The stress of *a*-stems tends to be made uniform: B. *žení* 'women' : : *žená*, though the dialects often retain the original variability (*žéni*), and some restrict it to the vocative. The rationalization of stress in the definite declension of adjectives is younger than the processes of contraction and assimilation: B. *mlád* 'young' *mladó mladá mladí*/with article: *mládijat mládoto mládata mládite* (whence, more usually, *mládo mláda mládi*).

Verbal stress was always more steady than that of nouns, and in some instances Bulgarian has made uniform paradigms that vary in Russian: B. *móga móžeš* 'can'/R. *mogú móžeš'*. The present and aorist stems of some verbs differ in place of stress as a result of their original independence: B. *móga*/aor. *možách*. As the imperfect has come to be associated in the minds of speakers with the present, it has also modified its stem and its stress: B. aor. *možách*/impf. *móžech*.

The Macedonian dialects show a tendency towards fixed stress. Some limit the places available to the last three syllables (as in Greek): Maced. *krastávica* 'cucumber' (also *krastavíca*)/B. *krástavica*. Bulgarian anteparoxytones are sometimes heard with a double stress as double paroxytones, which leads to a paroxytonic stress in the end of the development. In the immediate neighbourhood of Salonica and at Dojran (the region which gave the Old Bulgarian dialect) stress is restricted to the last two syllables. This regularization seems to be modern. Transitional Serb-Bulgar dialects in the crescent from Prizren to the Timok tend to agree with Bulgarian as to accentuation.

(*b*) *Intonation in Serbocroat and Slovene.* The Serbs and Croats descended to the Balkans from the middle Carpathians, where they were in contact with West Slavonic tribes. The Slovenes of Slovenia were split apart from the Slovaks by the irruption of the Magyars into Greater Moravia. Their north-eastern dialects are still allied to Slovak in some interesting ways. Now, the characteristic accentual mark of West Slavonic, as we have seen, is quantity, old and new; the quantities have disappeared from Polish but remain in Czechoslovak. So many dialects have variable stress that the tendency to define stress is to be considered only a secondary sign. The characteristic mark of Serbocroat and Slovene, which distinguishes them sharply from Bulgarian (and is supported by the different treatment of CSl. **ĺ *ď*), is musical pitch. Pitch, however, to be variable, requires quantity and stress. In all this these two languages show a high measure of conservatism. Standard Serbocroat and Slovene have suffered certain shifts, and so cannot, without correction, represent Common Slavonic practice, but the dialects of Istria and the Dalmatian coast

(Ča-Serbocroat, *čákavština*) still faithfully represent, on the whole, not merely Common Slavonic but, so far as it can be known, Indo-European accentuation (with the exceptions due e.g. to the effects of de Saussure's law).

(i) Ča (*čákavština*). In this dialect the place of the accent is entirely free; in particular, nothing prevents the stress from falling on the final syllable. There are short stressed syllables, which function as falling tones and are marked by the double grave accent ˵ appropriated by Vuk Stefanović Karadžić to short falling tones, though there are no short rising tones (ˋ) as in standard Serbocroat (*štòkavstina*). (The double grave accent is here represented by a diaeresis.) Long syllables may have rising tones (´) or falling tones (^): Ča. *böb* 'bean' G*S*. *bobä* (R. *bobá*), *kût* 'corner' G*S*. *kūtä*/Što. *böb* *bòba*, *kût kúta*. Serbocroat generally preserves falling tones; from which it follows that Ča (˵ ^) are ancient. Further confirmation may be obtained as to place of accent from Russian and Bulgarian, and sometimes from Sanskrit; as to quality from Greek, when the final syllable is accented, and from Lithuanian, after allowance is made for the exchange of rising and falling tones in that language. On the other hand, all Serbocroat dialects convert original rising long tones into falling shorts, so that it follows that rising long tones in Ča are of more recent origin.

There are three principal causes for the emergence of new rising long tones in this dialect. Firstly, the contraction of two syllables of which the second bore the stress; the unstressed syllable had a low tone, and therefore rose to the height of the second: *bojäli* >Ča. *báli* 'feared', *dvaèset* >Ča. *dvájset* 'twenty'. (Naturally, a stressed and unstressed series contract to falling long: Ča. *jedanâjst* <*jedanäest*.) Secondly, old rising shorts were lengthened under some conditions. Original rising long vowels became falling shorts in Proto-Serbocroat, but if, for any reason, this falling short should be lengthened, it gave a new rising long vowel. Such lengthening took place before a liquid (*l ĺ r m n ń*) or *j* in the same syllable: Ča. *kónj* 'horse' G*S*. *stárca* 'of an old man' *kráj* 'end' *divójka* 'girl' *bárka* 'boat'/Što. *kònj stârca krâj djèvôjka bârka*. When *j* stands for -*ij*- and follows another consonant, lengthening always takes place. Thirdly, recession of stress. On the loss of final *jers* the tone shifted to the preceding syllable, especially in nom.sg.masc. and gen.pl.fem.: Ča. *súd* 'judgment' G*P*. *gríh* 'of sins'/ G*S*. *súdä* N*S*. *grîhä* (where long vowels remain long), and G*P*. *žén* 'of women' (where a short vowel is lengthened/N*S*. *ženä*). When the loss of final *jer* in the gen.pl. left a consonant-group resolved by strengthening a preceding *jer* or by inserting the fill-vowel *a*, Ča accentuation vacillates: G*P*. *otác*/*ötäc* 'of fathers'/N*S*. *otäc*. There is variable stress in the definite adjective: Ča. *čist -î -â* 'clean' or *čìst-ī -ä* (indefinite: *čìst -a*). In the verbal conjugation stress was withdrawn when the original pretonic was long, but not when short: Ča. *pítāmo* 'we ask' (recessed)/*kopâmo* 'we dig'. Verbs of class iii 2 assimilate the first personal stress to the others: Ča. *píše-n -š -* 'write'/R. *pišú píšeš' píšet*. In all these examples the recession of the accent is due to causes quite different from those operating in Što.

(ii) Što (*štòkavština*). The original accentuation is found also in the Una Valley and along the left bank of the Sava as far as Županja. In South Serbia and South and East Montenegro also the primitive conditions prevail. There is found there a rule of recession, not from all final syllables but from final open vowels, in which cases long syllables receive a long rising tone and short syllables a falling tone: *svíla* ‹*svīlä* 'silk'/*sèstra* ‹*sesträ* 'sister'. Next come dialects which retract the accent from both a final open syllable and a final closed short syllable: dial. *pötok pòtok* ‹*potök* 'brook'. In these areas the long syllable takes a long rising tone, but the short syllable may be rising or falling. All these are stages in the evolution of the final Što solution, exemplified in the standard speech, in which accent-shift occurs also from a final long syllable. There is thus a general retraction characteristic of Standard Serbocroat, as fixed by Karadžić, and valid for Hercegovina, the South-West, Central Serbia (Šumadija) and the Banat.

As fully developed in Standard Serbocroat the tonic system includes shorts falling (̈) and rising (ˋ) and longs falling (^) and rising (′). The signs were applied by Karadžić. All syllables after the stress have a falling tone, which he left unmarked when short, but marked, somewhat ambiguously, with a circumflex when long (^). When more than one accent is written on a word, only the first marks a stress: S. *kòjî* 'which', *zàpîtâ* 'asked' *dôdê* 'came'. The unstressed long syllable is sometimes marked by the usual long diacritic (‾), which has the advantage that it can be placed above a pretonic long vowel, unlike Karadžić's circumflex: e.g. dial. *zīmä* 'winter' *žīvîm* 'I live'.

The tonic accent is recessive. It passes back one syllable towards the beginning of the word, and it should be noted that this applies equally to words borrowed from Turkish. Consequently, one can only be sure that the accent is primitive when it is one of those that fall on a first syllable, and there is external evidence (from Ča) to show that it is not due to recession. There can be no stress on a final syllable where there is more than one in the word. Original long rising tones became falling shorts. The rising long (′) and rising short (ˋ) tones of the present language are thus innovations. Original long falling tones remain: S. *glâs* 'voice' *snüjeg* (*snêg* in the *e-* dialect) 'snow' *dûb* 'oak'. In the transcription of *snüjeg*, we must allow for the effect of the full group, which is composed of two short elements, of which the first is a fifth higher than the second. The method of transcription (-*ije*-) shows that the general effect is a fall of pitch, and that half the whole vocalic effect amounts to the duration of a short vowel. The actual effect might have been more clearly rendered by a large circumflex or an acute followed by a grave (-*ijè*-).

Original long rising tones were shortened and made to fall: S. *kräva* 'cow' *räna* 'wound' *čüdo* 'miracle'. Long vowels which precede the original stress, and which have become stressed by recession of accent, are rising longs (´): S. gen.sg. *nága* 'naked' *žúta* 'yellow' (fem.) *cŕna* 'black' (fem.) *rúka* 'hand'/*nâg žût cȓn*.

Original short syllables in monosyllables due to the loss of final *jer* are lengthened and falling: S. *Bôg* 'God' *lêd* 'ice' *môć* 'power'/*GS. Böga* etc.

Certain consonants lengthen preceding vowels in the same syllable: at the end of words, *v j* (but not *v* when the tone was originally rising: *läv* 'lion' *növ* 'new'): *bôj* 'battle' *krâj* 'end', adjectives in -*āv* -*īv; any consonant followed by *j* <-*ij*-: *pêrje* 'plumage' *zȓnje* 'grains' *zdrâvlje* 'health', though in the next syllable; *l r n m* closing the syllable, or *v j* closing a syllable other than the last. A number of suffixes, however, do not share in this lengthening.

(iii) Slovene. In this language the tone is largely recessive, but upon principles unlike those of Ča- and Što-Serbocroat. The tones are three: short and virtually falling (ˋ), long rising (´) and long falling (ˆ). Under stress all short syllables are lengthened. A final rising tone shifts to a preceding syllable, i.e. the rise is anticipated and is at last attracted to the mediumly tense pretonic: Slov. *góra* 'hill' *bôs* fem.sg. *bósa* 'barefoot'/R. *gorá bosá*. There are a number of circumstances which prevent the tone-shift: it does not occur with neo-acute tones resulting from metatony; in the case of the ending -*é* <-*ije;* if the syllable has become final through loss of *jer*, or if *jer* has been lost in the pretonic syllable: Slov. *glavár* 'chief' *kupcà* 'of the merchant'. Conversely, a falling tone tends to be delayed and so transferred to a following syllable, which is lengthened thereby: Slov. *Bogâ* 'of God', *zlatô* 'gold' (S. *zlâto*; cf. B. *zlató*).

The full circumstances of tone-change in Slovene are obscure. It seems probable that original rising longs were shortened, and then lengthened in open syllables along with original rising shorts. In final open syllables no lengthening occurred. In closed syllables, other than the last, rising longs became falling longs: Slov. *dîmka/dìm* 'smoke'; this happened also when the following syllable was originally long (as I*SF. a*-stems, I*S.* pres.indic., definite declension of adjectives). A falling tone lengthened original short vowels: Slov. *Bôg* 'God' *nôč* 'night', and case-endings. When new long vowels have resulted from contraction the tone falls when the stress was on the first element, and rises when the stress was on the second: Slov. *igrâm* 'I play' R. *igráju*, instr.sg. *tó* 'by that' <CSl.*tojǫ̃*.

Musical tone has been lost in some forms of Slovene, e.g. in Styria.

177. *Hardening in Slovene, Serbocroat and Bulgarian.* The system of alternation between hard/soft forms of vowels and consonants has been entirely abandoned in Slovene and Serbocroat, and to some extent in Bulgarian. In Old Bulgarian it was well defined, and the scribes frequently marked its presence by placing a little semi-circle to the right of a consonant, linking it with the following vowel. This symbolizes the essential nature of softening. It affects both consonant and vowel, so that the one ends with an off-glide of the nature of [j] and the other begins with a [j] on-glide. The relation was one of necessity. The off-glide and on-glide being identical, it followed that a soft consonant was bound to lead to a soft vowel, and a soft vowel could only be preceded by a soft consonant. All consonants may be modified by the soft off-glide without necessarily changing their timbre or area of articulation, but some were modified in a palatal direction, and so palatalized, though still forming part of their original series. The last stage was the conversion of palatalized consonants, related to hard consonants by palatal modification, into palatal consonants which subsist as autonomous speech-units. As to vowels, softening was originally a feature of the front vowels *ę ě e i ĭ*, which are sometimes known as the palatal vowels.

Among these vowels, *e ĭ* became hard in Proto-Czech, as we have seen (section 141). When soft *jer* was lost, it did not normally leave behind a softened consonant, as in Polish or Russian. The vowels mentioned became normal front vowels, without previous on-glide, and therefore did not require palatal off-glide in the previous consonant. The tendency towards hardness is continued and fulfilled by Slovene and Serbocroat, in which the remaining front vowels became hard, that is, normal, and, *pari passu*, all consonants became hard. In the case of soft *jer* this is clearly indicated in early Serbo-Slavonic documents. Only one sign (ь) is used for both *jers*, because they imported no distinction. Both signs have been used in Modern Bulgarian script, but without effecting any distinction at the end of a word: MB. день 'day' is pronounced *den* (and now spelt ден) despite the soft *jer*. But there are dialects in which it is pronounced *deń*, and the history of Bulgarian shows that the process of hardening is most recent in that tongue. In it there are two variants of *ě*, viz. *'a* and *e*, due to the influence of the vowel of the following syllable. The opener type softens the preceding consonant in Modern (East) Bulgarian: MB. *běla běli* 'white' (*bála/béli*, now spelt бяла бели), *mlěko* 'milk' (*mláko*, now spelt мляко). This vowel retained its on-glide long enough in Serbocroat to develop into a diphthong or a dissyllable in

Je-Serbocroat (*jékavština*), which Karadžić adopted as the standard; the diphthong further developed into a vowel, either *i* or *e* (*ikavština/ékavština*). But in all three forms the vowel became normal and self-contained, implying no softening of the previous consonant. In Modern Bulgarian *ja ju* soften a previous consonant: MB. *Gánju* (*Gáňu*) *tja* (*ťa*). It is not so with S. *kúća* 'house', in which the final -*a* is a normal *a*, and is written as such. As a result of the normalizing of vowels in Serbocroat and Slovene it was possible for Karadžić to recognize and abstract the sound *j*, as a consonant or semivowel, and add it to the Cyrillic alphabet. With a break in logic, it has been used also in the groups *lj nj* to denote palatal *ľ ň*, which would have been better represented under their own signs (*ľ ņ* have sometimes been so used).

The phenomena of palatalization are not wholly conditioned by softness. Palatalized consonants have continued their natural line of development into palatals, unimpeded by the loss of softening; and the palatals, in their turn, have become normal in their types, and so 'hard'. They are marked by strong off-glides still, but these are of the sibilant nature (*ś* or *š*) appropriate to the pre- and medio-palatal positions. They are no longer accompanied by further off-glides of the nature of *j*.

Note. The premiss of the present work is that softness before front vowels was a Common Slavonic feature which has been preserved e.g. in Polish and Russian, partly preserved e.g. in Czech and largely lost in South Slav. It is, however, worth noting that a theory has been advanced according to which this softness *developed* in certain languages as a result of the change of certain vowels from front to back, the process being e.g. *te* >*t'o* followed by generalization of *t'* before front vowels. It is true that while such changes of vowel-quality are unknown in Standard Serbocroat and Ukrainian there are several in Polish (*e* >*o*, *ę* >*ą*, *ě* >*a*) and Russian (*e* >*o*, *ę* >*a*) and one in Czech (*ę* >*a*). A compromise-theory would suggest that the change of vowel-quality may have helped to *preserve* a Common Slavonic feature. A. V. Isačenko of Bratislava has drawn attention to the fact that softening of consonants is commonest in those languages which have relatively fewest vowels (e.g. Polish with 5 only, counting *ę* and *ą* as forms of *e* and *o*, and *y* as a form of *i*) and disappears in proportion with the increase in vowels (e.g. in Serbocroat, which—counting for instance *á â à ä* as four vowels, and including the sonant *r*—has 24). R. Jakobson of the Prague phonological school has discussed softness in non-Slav languages adjacent to the Slavonic area (e.g. East Lithuanian).

178. *Oral Vowels. A.O.* Slov. *kakô* 'how' *jágnje* 'lamb' *drevésa* 'trees' *devíca* 'girl'; S. *jàbuka* 'apple' *kàduna* 'Turkish lady' *jêtrva*

'sister-in-law' *dúša* 'soul'; B. *vratá* 'door' *búrja* 'storm' *igrája* 'I play', Slov. *ósel* 'ass', S. *žìvot* 'life' *òpêt* 'again' *ŏkolo* 'around'; B. *óblak* 'cloud' *podmógvam* 'I help' *pívo* 'beer'.

Unstressed *a* in Bulgarian tends to be pronounced [ə], as to some extent it does in Russian, and unstressed *o* to be pronounced [u]: [vrətá búŕə igrájə pudmógvəm pívu], though the latter is officially discouraged. The pronunciation [ə] may even be used for stressed *a*.

E. (i) CSl.OB. *ě*: Slov. *koléno* 'knee' *človéka* 'of a man' *povêst* 'tale' *potréba* 'need', the vowel usually being pronounced as closed [e]; S. *bijelo* 'white' *svijet* 'world' *djĕd* 'grandfather'; S.Serbian and Macedonian: Τριάδιτζα = OB. *Srĕdĭcĭ*, Πρίζδριανα = *Prizren*, Πριλέαπος = *Prilep* Δεάβολις = *Debol;* B. *bĕla bĕli* 'white', *vĕra vĕri* 'faith', *gnĕzdó* 'nest' (WB. *e/e*, EB. *'a /e;* the modern spelling had я or e). Unstressed B. *e* (*ĕ*) tends to [i], though this is also discouraged.

The Greek transcriptions show that *ĕ* had, in South Serbia and Macedonia, a very open pronunciation in stressed syllables, of the nature of *ia* or *ea*, possibly ['ä]. Rumanian words borrowed from Bulgarian, and native Latin words which show metaphony like that of Eastern Bulgarian, represent the sound by *ea*: Rum. *veac* 'age' *deal* 'hill' *searǎ*/pl. *seri* 'evening'. The pronunciation of stressed *ĕ* divides Modern Bulgarian into two main zones. In the west it is always *e;* in the east, from which it derives the standard pronunciation, it is *e* before originally soft consonants; before hard consonants it may, when stressed, become *'a:* WB. *béla béli*/EB. *bála béli*, but *čovék* 'man' and other words have the quality *e* even in East Bulgarian. By analogy one also finds *já* followed by front vowels. The West Bulgarian tendency may have originated in a small north-western focus, and have spread southwards and eastwards during the last two hundred years. South-west Bulgarian had a different pronunciation, as we have seen. In South-eastern Bulgarian (south of Tatar Pazardžik-Burgas and east of Tatar Pazardžik-Šer-Salonica) the pronunciation of *ĕ* is *ja jä* in all circumstances.

Serbocroat is divided into three parts (cutting across the division by the criteria *što ča kaj*) according to the treatment of *ĕ*. The most important is the central and southern region of the Je-dialect (*jékavština*), in which *ĕ* gave *je* with originally rising intonation and *ije* with falling intonation: S. *vjĕra* 'faith' *djĕlo* 'deed' [original rising longs becoming falling shorts, see section 176 (b) ii] *vijek* 'age' *tijelo* 'body'. But after *r, je* appears as *e: trĕbâ* 'it is necessary', and before *j* and *o* as *i: smìjati se* 'laugh' *bio* 'white'. To the east of these dialects, in the Šumadija and the border region from Prizren to Timok, *ĕ* > *e;* these are E-dialects (*ékavština*). To the west, along the shores of Istria and Dalmatia, *ĕ* > *i* (I-dialects, *íkavština*), but in North-west Bosnia and inland parts of Dalmatia *i/je* alternate, doubtless as the result of migration from South Serbia northwards. In the oldest Latin transcriptions of Dalmatian names *e* was employed: *Negovan Vera Belgrado*. Old Croat documents written in Glagolitic script have *i*: *naslidnika* 'heir' (GS.) 1392/S. *násljednîka*. In the island of Lastovo the distinction of *je/ije* is given as *je/jē*, and that was how it appeared in the poets of the Ragusan school (16th cent.). That there was an early division of Serbia into two regions, in the eastern one of which *ě e* both gave *e*, and in the western remained distinct (as *i je/e*) seems clear. It is not clear that any advantage arises from Leskien's method of explaining *i* and *je* by positing an originally close [e:], since the same result would be achieved through the diphthong [iɛ] resulting from fractioning the long vowel [ɛ:]. The closed *e* of Slovene does not support the hypothesis of a close vowel in Serbocroat, since it appears to be of recent origin.

Slov. *e* is as old as the oldest monuments (Freising, 10–11th cent.): *grechou* (gen.pl.) 'of sins' *vueruiú* 'I believe' *imeti* 'have'. There is nothing to indicate its exact quality. In parts of the modern area the long close *e* develops into a falling diphthong *ei*, which may dissimilate its parts and become *ai*. In Carinthia *ě >i ie*, a result which, under the special conditions of the dialect, implies original [ɛ:].

(ii) CSl.OB. *e*: Slov. *jélen* 'stag'; S. *tèći* 'flow' *jèdan* 'one' *ěto* 'behold'; B. *ézero* 'lake'.

Apart from the demonstrative element *e-* every initial Slavonic *e* becomes *je-*, though in Modern Bulgarian this has largely been lost (as in *ézero*). Foreign words have initial *e-*: S. *ekonòmičan* 'economic' *eksploàtisati* 'exploit' *evàndêlje* 'gospel'. In Bulgarian unstressed *e* tends to become [i]: [éziru]; cf. *ě* above.

U. Slov. S. *rúda* B. *rudá* 'ore'.

Y I. Slov. *sîn* 'son' *storíti* 'make'; S. *bìti* 'be' *bìti* 'strike'; B. *bivš* 'late, ex-', *ženíte* 'the women'.

Among the Freising documents one finds *y* represented as *ui*: OSlov. *buiti* 'be'/*bíti*, *bui/bi*, *mui/mî* 'we' (10–11th cent.). The spelling was based on the equation *ui*=Germ. *ü*. There are alternative spellings in *u* and *iu*. The sign transliterated *y* was used in Old Serbian documents: OS. *prěbyti* 'dwell' 1234–40, but its pronunciation was *i* as may be seen from the ultracorrection *s yněmi vsěmi* 'with all others'/ *iněmi* in the same text. Occasional confusion of *y/i* occurred dialectally even in Old Bulgarian (*rybě/ribě* 'fish' *pokrivaemŭ* 'we veil', 12th cent.). The distinction was, however, regularly maintained in the thirteenth century, and only after that did it fail in Bulgarian. Yet one Bulgarian fragment of the thirteenth century has no letter for *y*, though the conservative practices of Bulgarian men of letters helped to retain the sign as late as the beginning of the twentieth century.

Naturally it appeared often enough in the wrong place. In South-east Macedonia the vowel has persisted as *ăi* or has become *ă*.

Jers. Slov. *děž* 'rain' *dân* 'day' *mâh* 'moss'; S. *dân mähovina*; B. *den măch* (OB. *dĭnĭ mŭchŭ*). In S. it often appears as a fill-vowel: *fäkat* 'fact'.

In weak position the *jers* disappear. In strong position they vocalize to Slov. *a/e*, S. *a*, MB. *e/ă*. The difference in Slovene is one of quantity. The short vowel is written *e* and pronounced [ə], akin to MB. *ă*, in which case it may disappear from pronunciation and even from spelling: *kónčno* ⟨*konĭčino* 'finally'; but when lengthened the vowel becomes *a*. This is in conformity with the usage of the south and west, including Lower Carinthia and the literary dialect. In the east and north, however, *e* is found for both *jers*, as in Czech. This is another example of the function of Slovene to serve as a bridge between the Balkans and West Slavonic. The loss and confusion of the *jers* is attested for the tenth century by the Freising documents: OSlov. *zimirt*/OB. *sŭmŭtĭ* 'death' *dini den*/OB. *dĭnĭ* 'day' *selom*/OB. *sŭlomŭ* 'to the messengers'.

When the Serbs pressed into the Balkans in the sixth and seventh centuries they still had the two *jers*, as may be seen in the equivalence of Romance and Slavonic forms of place-names: *Buccari*/*Bàkar Civitatem*/*Càptat Càvtat Corcyra nigra*/*Kȑkar*. They are omitted in weak position from Latin documents of the eleventh and twelfth centuries, and in strong position they are confused: *sitnicus*/*sŭtĭnikŭ* 'captain'. By 1300 *a* appears for them in Glagolitic documents: *va ime otca* 'in the name of the Father' /*v* 1392. This spelling was current in Bosnia in the fourteenth century alongside the traditional orthography. This included but one symbol for both *jers* (ь) which was sometimes doubled in strong position: сьь 'this'. No doubt it represented an obscure vowel in many instances, e.g. when the vowel was short; but it has become a full vowel *a* in Serbocroat and the Serbo-Bulgar dialects from Prizren to the Timok: S. *dân* 'day' *sän* 'dream'. In Montenegro and South Serbia it is a dull vowel, akin in timbre to Fr. *eu* Germ. *ö*. In the north-west, among the Quarnero Islands and in Cres (Cherso), the resulting vowels vary between *a e* and *o*: *pës* 'dog' *otëc* 'father' (Vrbnik), *pös otöc* (Dobrinj), *dân* 'day' *denës* 'today' (Cres).

The tendency to confuse the *jers* was already felt in Old Bulgarian: OB. *šĭdŭ*/*šŭdŭ* 'having gone'. They were sometimes distinguished not on their own merits, but by reference to the nature of the vowel in the following syllable: OB. *vŭnŭ*/*vĭně* 'outside' *dŭva*/*dĭvě* 'two' *zŭlo*/*zĭli* 'bad'. The resulting obscure vowel in Modern Bulgarian is *ă* [ə]. The soft *jer*, when pronounced as a vowel, has been replaced by the sign for the hard *jer*. It was without significance at the end of a word, and marks softness of the consonant only when appearing between a consonant and vowel: Цóньо = *Cóño;* in some spellings it has been used before the masculine definite article; кóньтъ 'the horse' (now written конят). In some central dialects and occasionally in the Rhodope Mountains and in the north-east, this vowel becomes fully vocalized as *a:* dial. *daš* 'rain' *slánce* 'sun' *maglá* 'mist'.

There have also been hesitations in the literary language between *ă/e: dăn/den* 'day'. This is a dialectal feature of the north-east, the north-west, the south-west and Macedonia. A narrower range (Southwest Bulgaria and Macedonia) is that of the vocalization of *ŭ* as *o:* dial. (Prilep and Salonika) *dóš* 'rain' *von* 'outside' *nókot* 'nail'/*dăžd văn nókăt.* The two tendencies together mark Macedo-Bulgarian, and their presence in Old Bulgarian texts is a clear proof of dialect: OB. *sonŭ/sŭnŭ* 'sleep' *rabotŭ* 'that slave' *dĭnesĭ* 'today' *denetŭ* 'that day', -*omĭ/-emĭ* -*omŭ/-emŭ* -*ochŭ/-echŭ.*

179. *Nasal Vowels.* Slov. *govédo* 'ox' *bôdem* 'I shall be'; S. *gòveda* (pl.) 'cattle' *büdem;* B. *govédo băda.*

Denasalization has taken place in all three languages. The soft nasal *ę* has given *e* in all (in Slovene usually closed [e]), but the hard nasal *ǫ* has given varied solutions: Slov. *o* (usually closed [o]) S. *u* B. *ă/a.* The situation has been further obscured in Bulgarian by conservative (but largely unetymological) orthographies, which used the sign of the hard nasal vowel, though with the same value as the hard *jer* had achieved, that is, ѫ = ъ = *ă.* The first sign alone might be used initially.

There are dialectal differences in the Slovene derivatives of *ę,* viz., north-east *ä* (as sometimes in Slovak), Carinthia *je,* Upper Carinthia *ja,* Gorizia *a.* There are some traces of nasality in dialects: *mesenc/mésec* 'moon, month'. For *ǫ* the Freising documents, which were written partly under the influence of Old Bulgarian models (10–11th cent.), have *on/un o/u:* OSlov. *poronso (porončo)* OB. *poroǫčo*/MSlov. *poročíti* 'command' *dusú/dušo* (A*S.*) 'soul' *vueruiú* 'believe'. The modern solution *o* is exceptional among the standard forms of Slavonic languages, but it is continued dialectally through the Kaj and Ča dialects of Serbocroat.

There were nasal vowels in Serbocroat between the seventh and tenth centuries. They were lost in the eleventh, before Serbian records commence, but there are still traces of them in Ča. Foreigners heard *ę* as *e(n)* and *ǫ* as a very close *un: Mǫtimirŭ = Muncimirus* (9th cent.) Μουντιμῆρος (10th cent.)/*Mutimir* (11th cent.). Examples of nasalization persist to some extent in Istria and Dalmatia: Ča *dunbök/ dübok* (OB. *glǫbokŭ*) 'deep' *kolëmbat* (with intrusive nasal)/*kolèbati se* 'stagger'. CSl. *ę > e* extends through Yugoslavia into Western Bulgaria, and is normal for the Bulgarian literary tongue. At the

north-west end of this area, however, it becomes *a* after a palatal
(*š ž č j*), medially, but not finally: *jazik* 'tongue' *jačmen* 'barley'
(Fiume), *zajik* 'tongue' (Krk)/*jèzik jĕčmên*, but final -*e* <-*ę* remains in
Ča. *duše* (G.S.) 'of a soul' *pridoše* 'they approached'. CSl. *ǫ* >*u* is
general in the Ča and Kaj dialects (*čákavština, kájkavština*), but in
some northern Ča-dialects the treatment differs as to length, viz. *u*
(short)/*uo* (long): NČa. *küća* 'house'/*ruôka* 'hand' *puôt* 'road'.
Occasionally *o* is found: Ča. *gölob* 'dove' *ženò* (AS.) 'woman'/*gölûb*
ženu.

In East Bulgarian dialects *ę* >*e* >*a* not only after palatals (*š ž č j*),
but after all sorts of palatalized consonants: EB. *žáden* 'thirsty' *žátva*
'harvest, crop' *iḿa* 'name' *klátva* 'curse', as well as the normal *žéden*
žétva íme klétva. The Serbo-Bulgar dialects from Prizren to the Timok
have *ǫ* >*u* as in Serbocroat. Elsewhere the effect of nasality is seen in
a duller pronunciation of the vowel, which otherwise remains as open
as possible, giving, in the first instance, a relaxed nasal *ã* (like the
Portuguese nasal *ã am* in *lã cama*). This sound is heard in the region
of Salonica, in South-west Macedonia, and in Albania; it is sometimes
followed by a perceptible consonant before another consonant (as
with the Polish nasals): *ãm*. Other varieties of pronunciation are
sonant *m̨* and fully consonantal *am œm om:* dial. *zœmp zomp*
zmp̨/B. *zãb* 'tooth', dial. *rãnka*/B. *rãká* 'hand'. In the Central
Rhodope area the pronunciation is a very open *o*, which has been
transcribed *o o āō*, and in South-west Bulgarian there is a forward
pronunciation of the back nasal as *ä:* dial. *zäbi* 'teeth'. The two nasals
were both very open in Old Bulgarian (approximately nasal *å/ä*), and
were sometimes exchanged. In the literary language *ã* sometimes
appears as *a*. The outlying Siebenbürgen Bulgarian dialect dating
from the thirteenth century shows that it was the nasal of a final
syllable which was first weakened: *bande*/OB. *bodǫ* 'I shall be'.

180. (*a*) *Tort.* Slov. *grâd* 'city' *gràh* 'pea' *vrána* 'crow' *sládek* 'sweet'
sláma 'straw' *gláva* 'head' *glâs* 'voice' *mlâd* 'young' *bréza* 'birch' *brêg*
'bank' *mléko* 'milk'; S. *grâd kräva* 'cow' *vrân* 'raven' *vräna slädak*
släma gláva glâs mlâd plïjen 'booty' *brïjeg mlijèko;* B. *grad grach glavá*
glas brĕzá brĕg mlĕko (бреза́, бряг, мля́ко).

The common solutions are *trat tlat trĕt tlĕt*, and the latter give the
variant solutions of *ĕ* which differentiate Serbocroat dialects. In this
language there is found a constant set of differences due to tone. The
falling tone remains as a long falling tone, whether in one syllable or
in two: *vrân plïjen*. The original rising tone is converted into a short
falling tone: *vräna*. Thus, with regard to length, Serbocroat has longs
where Czechoslovak has shorts, and shorts for longs. The reason is
that the Serbocroat development has had tone and the Czechoslovak
length as the primary consideration.

(b) *Ort*. Slov. *ráma* 'shoulder' *ràz* 'away from' *rásti* 'grow' *ládja* 'ship' *lakèt* 'elbow'; S. *rälo* 'plough' *röb* 'slave' *lâḍa lâkat läkom* 'greedy'; B. *rámo rob ládija*.

The original difference of tone in the formula *ôrt/órt-* does not normally appear as a difference of vowel.

(c) *Türt*. Slov. *čȓv* 'worm' *dôlg* 'long' *sólnce* 'sun'; S. *gȑlo* 'throat' *bȓz* 'swift' *dȓvo* 'wood' *sûnce* 'sun' *bùha* 'flea' *smȓt* 'death' *cȓn* 'black' *pün* 'full' *žût* 'yellow' *sùza* 'tear'; B. *čȑäv dälg/dläg bärna* 'lip' *slänce* 'sun' *smärt* 'death' *pảlen* 'full'.

In such circumstances *rŭ lŭ* in Old Bulgarian stood for sonant *ŗ ḷ*. That is the point from which the modern South Slavonic tongues have developed, either retaining the sonant, or resolving it into a consonant preceded or followed by a vowel.

In Slovene the solutions of *ŗ ḷ* are *ŗ ol* (pronounced *ou*). In western Slovene dialects *ar* is found for *ŗ;* and in the extreme west and east *u* stands in place of *ol*. The latter is often pronounced *ou* in long syllables and *u* in short syllables, even in the standard language.

In Serbocroat the sonant *ŗ* is almost universal. At the beginning of words it sometimes vocalizes: S. *ŕḍa* 'rust' *r̂ž/ràž* 'rye'. During the middle ages the sonant was spelt in various ways: *r* in Glagolitic documents, *ri* in Cyrillic, occasionally *er* in Ragusa (13th cent.), and *ar* in Dalmatian Latin of the sixteenth century. All these spellings signify one sound, which was described in 1649: 'mortem aliqui scribunt *smart*, aliqui *smert*, aliqui alii sine vocali *smrt;* sed in communi usu loquendi non dicitur *smart* nec *smert*, sed modo quodam aspero ita ut vocalis non advertatur'. To imitate the sound this grammarian (Nicaglia) used the formula *rri*. There is an *i*-element in the pronunciation used in the island of Lastovo (*GP. prĩst* 'of fingers'/S. *pȓstâ*). It appears in eleventh-century transcriptions like *Tirpimir Girdan* Νοβόπριδον= *Növô Bȓdo*. In the Quarnero Islands the pronunciations vary: *ŗ ar er œr år ri*.

Initially *ḷ* >S. *la*, but occasionally *o: làgati* 'lie' *lâž* 'lie' *làžica/òžica* 'spoon' *priònuti* 'stick'. Between consonants it was 'dark' or hollow. In the Quarnero Islands it persists as a sonant: dial. *dḷg* 'long' *pḷn* 'full'. It is found in long syllables at Kneževac in South Serbia: dial. *vlk* 'wolf'. Among the Dalmatian Islands the sonant has been diversely vocalized as *el ol al*, whence also *e o:* dial. *dëg dög* 'long' *päln* 'full'. This diversity is found in Dalmatian documents of the eleventh century: *Vilkan Velkan*/S. *Vùkan*. Croatian Glagolitic documents of the fourteenth and fifteenth centuries have only *l: mlčanie* 'silence' *dlžan* 'due' *Vlkšić*. However, the development *ḷ* >*u* is already attested by Ragusan writers of the fifteenth century: *puni* 'full' *napuni* 'fill' (Menčetić and Držić's poems, early 16th cent.). From this *u* there developed a diphthong *uo* in Ragusan and Bosnian works of the seventeenth century (*suonce* 'sun'), but that represents a side-line. At first the timbre of the vowel resulting from *l* may not have been precise, as vacillations occur: *Vokac Vukac Vuokac, Volc Voch Vuoch.* The vocalization of final consonant -*l* >S. *o* was not contemporary with the vocalization of the sonant *l*, but later. In consequence, it has not yet completed its development over the Serbocroat area, since it is kept at Lastovo in the order of words *ja san rekal* 'I have said', but dropped in the order *reka san.* Elsewhere among the Dalmatian Islands final consonantal -*l* is dropped: dial. *bî* 'been' *pobëgnu* 'fled', whereas in the northern group of them, from Krk to Vis (Lissa), it is still regularly maintained: dial. *videl* 'saw' *rekal* 'said'. The earliest specimens of this change are found in Bosnia in the fourteenth century and at Ragusa about 1400: *veseo* 'joyful'.

181. *Final Vowels.* A peculiar feature of some forms of Serbocroat is the unvoicing of final vowels under certain conditions.

182. *Velars.* Slov. *deklè* 'girl' *drâg* 'dear' *dûh* 'spirit'; S. *nîškî* 'of Niš' *nëgo* 'but' *drügî* 'second' *htjëti* 'wish'; B. *kăm* 'to' *bogát* 'rich' *drúgi* 'others' *chljab* 'bread'. S.Slov. *h* <CSl. *ch* tends to become a pure aspiration (as Eng. *h*), especially in Serbocroat, where it is frequently dropped: *'òću* 'I will'.

There has been no development of soft velars (*ḱ ǵ ch*) as in Russian and Polish, save to some extent in Bulgarian, since the general hardening of vowels and consonants has made this unnecessary. S. *kïdati* 'rend' *gïnuti* 'perish' derive *i* <*y* without affecting the normality of the consonant. Owing to the absence of soft velars as such, Gk. Romance *ḱ ǵ* and Turkish *ḱ ǵ* (Magyar *gy*) are represented by S. *ć đ*: S. *ćèlija* 'cell' *ćïpûr* 'garden' *ćùmur* 'charcoal' *Đurađ* 'George' *däkon* 'deacon' *đâk* 'student' *đèrdân* 'necklace' *Màdâr/ Màdžâr* 'Magyar' (from *cella* κηπούρα *kömür* διάκ(ονος) *gerdan*).

183. *Dentals and Alveolars.* T D. Slov. *žito* 'corn' *kôst* 'bone'/*kóča* 'hut' *nôč* 'night' *môč* 'might', *dôm* 'house' *diják* 'student'/*méja* 'boundary'; S. *tïjelo* 'body'/*svijèća* 'candle' *nôć môć*, *djèlo* 'deed'/*Ča. mèja* Što. *mèđa;* B. *tëlo* [t́á...]/*svešt nošt mošt;* *dëlo* [d́á...]/*meždá.* Before *ja ju* the consonants are palatalized in Bulgarian: [t́álu] *tjutjún* [t́ut́ún] 'tobacco', and some Bulgarians palatalize these and other consonants before *e i*, though not so markedly as in Russian: B. *den* is thus pronounced as [dɛn] or [d́ɛn].

In the development of CSl. **t́ *d́* South Slavonic is opposed to West and East Slavonic, but is not united within itself. The Slovene forms are further developments of those in Serbocroat, but Bulgarian forms are independent. The pronunciation *t́* is said to occur in the Dalmatian Islands, in some regions, but in the same districts *d* has developed into *j*, as in Slovene. In most parts of Yugoslavia a sibilant off-glide has been developed, and *ć đ* are readily confused with *č dž*.

Conversely, in Ragusa and parts of Bosnia and Hercegovina the tendency is to discard *č dž* in favour of *ć đ*. In Bulgarian the development has been: **ť >tš >štš >št* and similarly **ď >žd*. The sibilant off-glide was anticipated before the dental and then lost in a soft off-glide (OB. *št žd*), which has since been hardened (MB. *št žd*). Akin to these developments has been that of **skj *sk*: Slov. *šč* S. *šć št* B. *št*. In Old Serbian documents the sounds are written *k g: pobeki/pobeći* 'flee' *se svagju/svađu* 'dispute' 1387. This is due to the close resemblance of *ť đ* and *k ǵ*, when the latter are strongly palatalized. It is the pronunciation current in Macedo-Bulgarian dialects: *brájka* 'brothers' *ǵavólite* 'the devils', and upon it is based the Standard Bulgarian gerund in *-ajki/-ejki*.

Medial *-dl-* sometimes occurs in Slovene (as in West Slavonic), not all instances being explicable by analogy.

L R N S Z. Slov. *lêp* 'beautiful' *ljudjê* 'people', *hríb* 'hill' *morjê* 'sea', *nebô* 'sky' *njíva* 'field', *nósiti* 'bear' *nósim.* 'I bear', *kázati* 'show' *kážem* 'I show'; S. *bȉo* 'been' *lȉjep ljûdi trî* 'three' *môre, nȅbo njȅgov* 'his', *nȍsiti nȍsîm, kázati kâžêm;* B. *lep ljúde, tri moré*/pl. *morjá, nebé bánja* 'bath', *míslene* 'reflexion'.

In Serbocroat *l*, final of a word or syllable, becomes *o*, except when analogy intervenes: *Bȉògrad <Bělügradŭ*. In Slovene final *l* tends to be pronounced as *w: rèkel* [rέkεw] 'he said'.

Slov.S. *lj nj* are palatal consonants, not combined sounds. S. *lj* results from CSl. **lj*, from secondary *lj* (<*-lij-*), from *l+je* (Je-dialect), and from intrusive *ĺ*: S. *pȍlje* 'field' *dávljênje* 'choking' *zdrâvlje (-ĭje)* 'health' *ljěto/lěto lȉto* 'summer'; Slov. *králj* 'king' *ljûb* 'dear' *vólja* 'will', but *zdrávje (-ĭje)*. Similarly, *nj* develops from CSl. **nj*, secondary *nj* (<*-nĭj-*) and *nje* in the Je-dialect. S. *bȁnja* 'bath' *pîtânje* 'question' *njemòta* 'dumbness'; Slov. *bânja znánje* 'knowing' *njíva*. Slov. *rj* is not a palatal *ŕ*, but a normal *r* followed by a *j*. In Bulgarian *r* is softened before *ja ju*: B. *morjá* (pl.) [muŕá] 'seas' *razorjá* [rəzuŕá] 'I ruin'/ *moré razorén*. Bulgarian also palatalizes *l n s z* before *ja ju*, and as *l* is hollow when final of a word or syllable or before a back vowel (including *ă*) the consonant has three varieties: *ĺ l ł* in *ĺak/lek/łak* ('medicine, easy, lacquer'). The development **sj *zj >š ž* is of Common Slavonic date. *S z* are softened in Je-Serbocroat before secondary *j*, and before *lj nj* they tend to palatalize: S. *mȉšljênje* 'thought' *kâžnjênje* 'punishment' *s njîm/š njîm:* 'with him'.

184. *Labials. P B V M*. Slov. *píjem* 'I drink' *pljuváti* 'spit', *bíti* 'hit', *žîv* 'alive' *življénje* 'living', *mâh* 'moss' *zémlja* 'land'; S. *píće* 'drink', *ljúbiti* 'kiss', *žîv življênje, mȁti* 'mother' *zèmlja;* B. *kórab* 'boat' *zemjá* 'land'.

The intrusive *ĺ* is a constant feature of Slovene and Serbocroat when a labial was originally followed by *j*. It was also the most usual result in Old Bulgarian, where (in the Zographensis manuscript, for instance) there are about 4 *zemli* to 1 *zemi*. The hesitation is evidence of dialectal variation, and it is upon that difference of dialect that the absence of intrusive *l* in Modern Bulgarian depends. The exceptions in the literary language are words borrowed or imitated from Russian or Church-Slavonic. These include the use of the ending *-enie*, fitted to form abstract nouns from verbs.

In Serbocroat initial *v* + consonant gives *u-*: *ùtorak* 'Tuesday' < *vŭtorŭkŭ*, and the preposition *vŭ* gives *u*.

F. F occurs in Slavonic only as a result of unvoicing *v* (B. *zdrav* [zdraf] 'healthy'), or in imitative words (S. *fŕkati* 'puff'), or as a reduction of B. *chv* (B. *chvalá* 'praise' [fəlá]) and S. *hv* in some dialects, or (in one WSlav. word) from *-pŭv-*. Otherwise *f* is foreign: Slov. *fant* 'boy' S. *fìldiš* 'ivory' *fìldžân* 'dish' *fìnans* 'revenue-officer' *feudalìzam filosòfija* B. *famílija fišeklík* 'cartridge-box' *Fráncija* (Italian *fante* T. *fil-dişi fincan fişeklik* etc.).

185. *Palatals.* Apart from the new palatals arising from dentals, there are those due to the first and second Slavonic palatalizations (*č ž š/c z s*). They become relatively hard in South Slavonic, but have no special history, save that *ž* has sometimes become *r* in Serbocroat and Slovene, e.g. Slov. *mórem* 'I can'.

B. FORMS

(i) VERBS

186. *Classes of Verbs.* These have been classified on the basis of Old Bulgarian in section 48. The old forms were continued in South Slavonic thus:

A. Athematic. See sections 187, 188.

B. Thematic.

(i) 1. *k g:* Slov. *péči* 'bake' *péčem;* S. *pèći pèčêm, mòći* 'be able'/ *mògu mòžeš;* B. *peká pečéš.*

    2. *t d:* Slov. *brésti* 'wade' *brédem;* S. *plèsti* 'plait' *plètêm;* B. *metá* 'sweep'.

    3. *p b v:* Slov. *grébsti* 'scratch' *grébem;* S. *grèsti grèbêm;* B. *grebá.*

    4. *s z:* Slov. *nésti* 'bear' *nésem;* S. *nèsti nèsêm;* B. *nesá.*

    5. *m n:* Slov. *péti pnèm* 'stretch'; S. *kléti* 'curse' *kùnêm;* B. *kălná.*

    6. *l r:* Slov. *mréti* 'die' *mrèm:* Sl. *mrijèti mrïjem, kläti* 'stab' *kòljêm;* B. *umrá mélja* 'grind'.

    7. *vowels:* Slov. *bíti* 'strike' *bîjem;* S. *bïti bïjem, čüti* 'hear' *cüjêm, pïti* 'drink' *pïjêm, plïti* 'swim' *plïjêm, krïti* 'hide' *krïjêm, düti* 'blow' *düjêm, znäti* 'know' *znâm.*

(ii) 1. *vowel:* Slov. *tóniti* 'sink' *tónem;* S. *tònuti tönêm;* B. *minúvam /mínávam* 'pass'.

 2. *consonant:* Slov. *vzdígniti* 'raise' *vzdîgnem;* S. *tïsnuti* 'press' *tïsnêm;* B. *dvígam.*

(iii) *ě:* 1. *ěj:* Slov. *umêti* 'know how to' *umêm;* S. *ùmjeti ùmĭjem;* B. *žívéja* 'dwell'.

 2. *i:* Slov. *letéti* 'fly' *letím;* S. *vĭđeti* 'see' *vĭdîm;* B. *tărpjá* 'suffer'.

(iv) *i:* Slov. *govoríti* 'speak' *govorím;* S. *nòsiti* 'carry' *nösîm;* B. *govórja.*

(v) 1. *a: -aj-:* Slov. *igráti* 'play' *igrâm;* S. *bívati* 'be' *bîvâm;* B. *bjágam* 'run'.

 2. *-j-:* Slov. *písati* 'write' *píšem;* S. *vézati* 'bind' *vêžêm;* B. *píša.*

 3. *zero:* Slov. *bráti* 'gather' *bérem;* S. *bräti bërêm;* B. *berá* 'take'.

 4. *-j-:* Slov. *dajáti* 'give' *dájem;* S. *käjati* 'avenge' *käjêm;* B. *lája* 'bark'.

(vi) *ova:* Slov. *kupováti* 'buy' *kupûjem;* S. *kupòvati kùpujêm*; B. *kupúvam.*

187. *Athematic Verbs.* **Es/s*. The present indicative runs:

	S1	2	3	P1	2	3	D1	23
Slov.	s-	èm	ì / jè		mò	tè	ò	và	tà
S.	(jè)s-	am	i / jë(st)		mo	te	u		
B.	s-	ăm	i / e		me	te	a		

In Serbocroat there are two forms, the one full, the other enclitic. The full form contains an innovation in 3*P. jèsu*/OB. *sǫ* MB. *sa* (pr. *să*) Slov. *sò.* 1*S. jesmĭ* hardened and gave a sonant (*jesm sm*), which has been vocalized separately by each language. The *t* of **sonti* is found in some Macedonian dialects: Maced. *set.* B. *săšti* 'same' is from the present participle; S. *süštî* 'in person, absolute' is from Church Slavonic.

Other roots give the infin: Slov. *bíti* S. *bïti,* act.past part.: Slov. *bîl bívši* S. *bïo bïvši* B. *bil,* aorist, imperfect and conditional; as well as the future: Slov. *bôdem bôm* S. *büdêm* B. *šte băda,* imperative: Slov. *bódi(te)* S. *büdi(te)* N. *bădi bădéte,* and future gerund (Slov. *bodòč* S. *büdûći*) and participle (B. *bắdešt*). From this stem comes also an impf. part.active in Modern Bulgarian: B. *băđel.* The Bulgarian gerund *bidéjki* results from confusion between the stems *bǫd-* and *by-* (cf. aorist B. *bidóch* below).

The aorist and imperfect have been lost in Slovene, which retains only an invariable *bi* for use with the past participle in *-l* to express the conditional. There is no trace of a form like OB. *bimĭ* (conditional) in any of these languages. The aorist and imperfect in Serbocroat and Bulgarian run:

		S1	2	3	P1	2	3
S. aor.	bï-	h	-	-	smo	ste	še
impf.	bjë- bïjâ }	h	še	še	smo	ste	hu
B. aor. condit.	be- } bi- }	ch	-	- }	chme	chte	cha
impf.	be-	ch	še	še }			

The old aorist B. *bich* is restricted to conditional uses: *az bich bil* 'I should be'. There is also an aorist with intrusive *d*, with stem *bid-*: B. *bidóch nakázan* 'I was punished'. In Serbocroat *bï* is frequently used in *P* 1 2 of the conditional (for *bïsmo bïste*), leaving *S* 1 *bïh*/*S* 2 3 *P* 1 2 3 *bï*. As the final *h* of *bïh* is frequently dropped, the effect is much the same as in Slovene and Russian, namely, that of one invariable form. The original distinction between the 3*P*. aor./impf. flexions is retained in Serbocroat (-*še*/*hu*), but lost in Bulgarian (-*cha*). Consequent upon that has been the spread of *ch* to the other persons of the plural. Impf. 2*P*. -*šete* has been lost.

188. **Ēd.*, etc. 1*S* **dōdmĭ* > CSl.(OB.) *damĭ* > Slov. *dám* S. *dâm* B. *dam* 'I (shall) give'; Slov. *jém* 'I eat' *vém* 'I know', OS. *vijem*/*jem*/S. *imâm* 'I have', B. *jam imam*. These are athematic forms, but, apart from 3*P*., all other persons are now thematic: *S*2 -*š* 3. - *P*.1 -*mo*/*me* 2. -*te* (*D*1. -*va* 23. -*ta*). The old athematic forms were eliminated in Slovene from the eleventh century (*vĕs* appears in the Freising documents); in Serbocroat they disappeared with the fourteenth century, when 3*S*. *dâ* was found alongside 2. *dasi vĕsi vĕsĭ* 3. *dastĭ;* the thematic endings are frequently found in Middle Bulgarian, but with final -*t* as a scribal anachronism as late as the seventeenth century. 3*P*. **dōdn̥tĭ* > OB. *dadętŭ* > Slov. *dadé* (and then *dadó* on the analogy of other conjugations), S. *dádê* (and then *dádû* from the fourteenth century, on the same analogy), B. *dadát*. From this person the stem in *d* was spread to other persons: S. *dádêm* B. *dadéš* etc. The dental was retained also in 3*P*. Slov. *jedó* S. *jēdû* OS. *vede*/*vedu* B. *jadát* MidB. *vĕdǫ* (13th cent.). A further complication was the presence of *da-j-*, from the root *da* with a thematic *j*-suffix; and this *j* was spread to other verbs: 3*P*. Slov. *dájo jéjo vejó*. Thus there was an apparent alternation *d*/*j* which caused *d* to spread to words in *j*: S. *znádêm* 'I know' *imádêm* 'I have'/*znaj- imaj-*. It was convenient in forming the stem of new aorists: S. *dädoh jēdoh imadoh*, B. *dádoch jádoch*/S. *däh jēh* B. *imach*. The imperfects followed suit: S. *imaðâh jēðâh*/B. *imach*. B. *jaž*(*te*), imperative, is the old athematic form. Otherwise the imperatives show intrusive *d* or *j*: Slov. *dàj*(*te*) *jédi*(*te*) *védi*(*te*) [OSlov. *vej* MSlov. *povêj*(*te*)], S. *dâj*(*te*) *imâj*(*te*), B. *dáj*(*te*).

The fact that most other persons were thematic in flexion allowed
1*S. dam* to exercise a vast effect upon all conjugations in Serbocroat
and Slovene, and upon some in Bulgarian. These took the flexion
1*S. -m*. Since by contraction *aje* >*a* it was possible to set up an
analogy between these contracted verbs and *dam*, which worked as
follows: *dĕlaješ* >Slov. *dĕlaš: dáš : : dám: dĕlam*/OB. *dĕlają̇*. In
Slovene this 1*S. -m* has spread to all conjugations, and has been
accompanied by the elimination, in many verbs, of the consonant-
mutation due to the change from hard/soft in *-ǫ/-eš*. The present
tenses have thus been notably rationalized. In Serbocroat contracted
verbs in *a* (v 1) were made to conform to this pattern by the thirteenth
century: OS. *rabotam* 'I work' *obladam* 'I conquer'; those in *i* (iii 2 and
iv) fell into line in the fifteenth century: OS. *učinim* 'I do' *vidim* 'I see';
but in other verbs 1*S. -u* appeared as late as the seventeenth century,
and is still found in *mògu* 'I can', *hòću/ću* ' I wish, will' and in two or
three less common verbs. In Modern Bulgarian the 1*S. -m* is found
only with verbs of classes vi and v 1 (*va* and *aj* >*a*): B. *kupúvam* 'I
buy' *polučávam* 'I receive' *polágam* 'I place'/R. *polagáju*. Otherwise
OB. *-ǫ* >MB. *-a*. But the forms in *-m* are widely distributed in
Bulgarian dialects, and are universal in Macedo-Bulgarian.

Though not athematic, the modern representatives of **chotją̇* 'I
wish' are conveniently mentioned here. They are used to form the
future tense in Serbocroat and Bulgarian. Serving as auxiliaries they
lose their accents (becoming enclitic or proclitic) and also the first
syllable. In Modern Bulgarian 3*S. šte* is used for all persons (B.
studéno šte mi bằde 'I shall be cold', condit. *štéše da mi e studéno* 'I
should have been cold' *šte perá* 'I shall wash'). A full conjugation
exists for the verb in the desiderative sense (*št- a eš e em ete at*): B. *šta
da píša* 'I want to write', impf. *štjach*, past.part. *štjal*. In Serbocroat the
full conjugation is used, and when the auxiliary follows its principal
verb, and is written with it, there is a veritable future tense flexion:
S.*Sl. -ću* 2. *-ćeš* 3. *-će* P1. *-ćemo* 2. *-ćete* 3. *-ćê* (OS. *-te*); infin. S. *hòtjeti*/
htjĕti.

189. *Thematic Present Indicative:*

	S1	2	3	P1	2	3	D1	23
Slov. páse- (iv) govorí- (v 1) dĕla-	m	š	–	mo	te	jo	va	ta
S. pjĕvâ- örê- (iv) gòvorî-	m	š	–	mo	te	(pjĕvajû) (örû) (gòvorê)		
B. per- (iv) nós- (v) bằrz- (vi) polučáv-	á ja am	éš iš aš	é i a	ém im ame	éte ite ate	át jat at		

*S*1.CSl.OB. -*ǫ* survived in OSlov. *mogǫ* 'can' *verujǫ* 'believe' *prošǫ* 'beg' *odpuščǫ* 'forgive' *obljubljǫ* 'vow', which were in use as late as the first half of the fifteenth century. It survives in Modern Serbocroat: *mògu* 'I can' *hòću* 'I wish' and a few other forms. In Modern Bulgarian -*ǫ*/*jǫ* appears as -*a*/*ja*, with an open vowel which is dull in East Bulgarian -*ă*/*jă*. There has been rationalization in MB. *nósja*/OB. *nošǫ*, on the analogy of *nósiš* etc.

From *S*l. *dam* a final flexion -*m* has been generalized in Slovene and Serbocroat and extended in Bulgarian as described in section 188. Before this -*m* there appears the characteristic vowel of the conjugation, as before -*š* -*mo* and the other persons. Hence the opposition between the first person and the rest as to quality of flexional vowel disappears, and the conjugation can be rationalized: S. *vĭdîm vĭdîš* 'see' *nösîm nösîš* 'carry', *pèčêm pèčêš* 'bake'/R. *vìžu nošú pekú*. The third person plural continues to have a hard vowel in many verbs, and then consonant-mutation is prevented in Serbocroat and Slovene: S. 3*P*. *pèkû* 'they bake'. The vowel *a* appears in class v 1, *i* in classes iii 2 and iv, and *e* in all others, with 3*P*. -*ju* -*e* -*u* respectively. Class iv 1 (S. *ùmijêm* 'I know how to') remains uncontracted in Serbocroat, and vacillates in Slovene (*umêm*/*umêjem*). In Class vi (*ova*) the suffix of the infinitive has been passed into the present tense in Bulgarian: B. *kupúvam*/S. *kùpujêm* 'I buy'.

*S*2. -*šĭ* > -*š*. When -*šĭ* is found in Middle Bulgarian or Old Serbian manuscripts it must be attributed to Church Slavonic influence, though archaizing writers continued to write it in Bulgarian as late as the nineteenth century.

*S*3. -*tŭ* >-. CSl. *-*tĭ* > R. -*t́*, but the ending was hardened at a remote date, before the separation of West and South Slavonic. Hard final *t* then tended to be lost. Its presence in Old Bulgarian may, even in the ninth century, have been an archaic feature, since forms without *t* are also encountered: OB. *bǫde* 'will be' *je* 'is' *ně* 'is not'. A few south-western Macedonian dialects, which are highly conservative, still retain -*t*. It dwindled in Middle Bulgarian texts. Dalmatian writers of the sixteenth and seventeenth centuries used a -*t* in this person which may be explained as an enclitic, not a flexion: OS. *budet Jerosolim tvoj* 'J. will be thine' (*bude*+*t* ⟨*ti*⟩). Otherwise final -*t* is lacking in Serbocroat and Slovene from the thirteenth century.

*P*1. Slov.S. -*mo*/B. -*me*. For the alternatives see section 53 *P*1. Forms in -*me* would find support in plurals in -*e*, and also resemble -*te*. In the Freising manuscripts -*m* (as in Czech) is found alongside -*mo*: *modlim* 'we pray'/Slov. *mo*(*d*)*limo*. The ending -*mo* is found in Slovak and Ruthenian, and so, if we discount the Magyar irruption, over a wide belt of Slavonic territory.

P2. -te.

P3. *-*ǫtĭ* >Slov. -o S. -u B. -at.* The final -t drops in Modern Bulgarian *sa* 'are', though retained in the south western dial. *set.* It is frequently dropped in Sofia (*sedjá/sedját* 'sit'), and in the south-west. It disappeared in Proto-Serbian (*budu hode* 12th cent.). In classes iii 2 and iv -ętŭ >S. -e: *vĭdê* 'see' *nösê* 'bear'. Contracted verbs do not contract in this person: S. *kùpujû* 'buy' *pítajû* 'ask' as well as *ùmijû* 'know how to'. The corresponding forms in Slovene are -o/e, but there has been a general extension of -jo to all classes of verbs: Slov. *bôdo/bôdejo* 'will be' *dêlajo pásejo govoríjo.*

D1. -va. The dual survives only in Slovene. On the analogy of *M. dvâ NF. dvê* there is a tendency to distinguish gender within this person as *M. -va F. -ve -vi.*

D23. -ta. In Old Bulgarian a distinction of gender also appeared in this person: *M. -ta NF. -tĕ,* and it also is found in Slovene.

The date of the disappearance of the dual in Bulgarian is hard to determine, since the language known as Middle Bulgarian does not represent an attempt to render current speech. In Serbocroat the dual disappeared at an early date, and only *sva sta* 'are' persisted into the fifteenth century.

190. *Imperative.*

		S2	3	P1	2	D1	23
Slov.	pás-	i	i	îmo	îte	îva	îta
	govôr-			imo	ite	iva	ita
	déla-	j	j	jmo	jte	jva	jta
S.	plèt-	i		imo	ite		
	pîtâ-	j		jmo	jte		
B.	per- ⎫	i			éte		
	nos- ⎬						
	bărza-	j			jte		

Save after a vowel, Slovene and Serbocroat have generalized the ending *P2.* -ite to all conjugations, and Bulgarian has generalized -ĕte. In Serbocroat this practice was normal from the fourteenth century. Some athematic imperatives survived into the fifteenth century (*veđ -te* 'know' *viđ -te* 'see'), and the loss of *i* is a characteristic of popular poetry and Dalmatian writers between the fifteenth and eighteenth centuries. Other persons of the imperative are obtained from the indicative by the use of *neka* or *da: S. neka pjëvajû* 'let them sing' B. *neka peré* 'let him wash' *da perém* 'let us wash' *da nósjat* 'let them carry'. Negative imperative: S. *nèmôj(te)* = Lat. *noli(te)*; a negative form of the verb *mòći* 'be able'. The velar stems are palatalized, second pal. in Serbocroat, first in Bulgarian. Personal endings may be attached to particles to make a sort of imperative: S. *nâte* 'there you have it' *hàjdemo hàjdete* 'come on' (T. *haydi*).

191. *Present Gerund and Participle.* Slov. *nesóč* 'bearing', S. *plètûći* 'plaiting', B. *perášt* (part.) *pérejki* (ger.) 'washing'.

Slovene has also gerunds in -*e* <-*ę*: Slov. *sedê* 'sitting' *molčê* 'being silent'. This gerund is frequently found in Serbocroat documents up to the seventeenth century; in the sixteenth century S. -*či*/*će* were alternatives: OS. *hodeće* 'going'. Dalmatian writers, perhaps as a result of Latin influence, sometimes declined the participle. OB. -*ǫšt*- >MB. -*ašt* and OB. -*ęšt*- >MB. -*ešt*. The latter is found colloquially as a doublet of -*ašt*, without reference to historical origins. In Macedo-Bulgarian the consonants of the gerund are *šč* and *k* according to locality; the literary language has *k*.

192. *Infinitive and Supine.* Infin. -*ti*, Supine (Slovene only) -*t*. Class i 1 (roots ending in *k g*) have infinitives in Slov. -*či* S. -*ći*. Slov. *téči* 'flow' S. *pèći* 'bake'. The final vowel may drop in both dialects, and this is the rule in Ča, where also -*sti* may become -*s*. In Što -*ti* is dropped before the enclitic of the future tense: S. *dä́ću* 'I shall give'; but -*ći* is retained: WS. *rèći ću* 'I shall say'. When the enclitic is attached to a pronoun or adjective the infinitive keeps its full form: S. *jâ ću pítati* 'I shall ask', *gdjë će se ròditi Hrìstos* 'where will Christ be born?'

The supine is used with verbs of movement in Slovene: *déklice prihâjajo plésat* 'the girls are coming to dance'.

In Bulgarian the final vowel had been lost in the twelfth century, leaving a hard -*t* indistinguishable from the supine. By the seventeenth century this -*t* had also gone; a few traces of this reduced infinitive remain. The infinitive was then rendered analytically by means of the present indicative and the particle *da*, which is also common in Serbocroat: B. *ískam da otívam* 'I want to go', S. *pòčeše da dòlazê*/*pòčeše dòlaziti* 'they began to arrive'. The analytical substitution of a phrase for an infinitive is also a feature of Modern Greek (*νὰ*), Rumanian (*să*) and Albanian (*të*). There can be no question of borrowing in the usual sense, and yet these congruent developments seem more than coincidental. They represent a common process of thought, due partly to living together in a given area, which has been worked out from different material and under the stress of different immediate causes. The loss of the infinitive flexion required adaptation also in the future and conditional: B. *šte ostána* 'I shall stay', *štéše da víkaš* 'thou wouldst have called'.

193. *Past Tenses.* The participle in -*l* is used to form the perfect tense: Slov. *jàz sem bîl*, S. *jèsam bïo*/*bïo sam*, B. *az săm bil* 'I have been'; the conditional with invariable *bi* in Slovene and at least partially

conjugated S. *bĭh*, B. (conjugated) *bich;* and the future in Slovene: *jàz bôdem govorîl* 'I shall speak'. [This construction is used in Serbocroat as a future perfect in dependent clauses: *käd büdêm dòšao* 'when I (shall) have come']. The perfect, preceded by *da*, is exceptionally used in Serbocroat to express unreal conditions in the past: *dä sam bïo tàmo* 'had I been there'. It is not used without auxiliaries (except sometimes in Bulgarian 3 *SP*), so that the participle in *-l* does not normally itself become a past tense, as in Russian. In Modern Bulgarian it has been affected by the semantic development of the imperfect and aorist. As these tenses have drawn apart in meaning (see sect. 196), they have also come to differ in form. The imperfect has been attached to the present stem of the verb, while the aorist remains in the aorist stem. From the imperfect stem thus obtained there has arisen an imperfect participle: B. *perél* 'washed' *nósel* 'bore'/ *pral nósil*.

The *l-* participle plays a great part in the peculiar Bulgarian idioms of indirect speech, which have presumably developed under Turkish influence. In these forms the auxiliary is omitted in the third person of the past tense. Examples are: ('he writes well' *toj píše dobré*/) 'they told me he *wrote* well' *kazácha mi, če toj* píšel *dobré;* ('he was ill' *toj béše bólen*/) *kazácha mi, če toj* bil *bólen*. In the first case Bulgarian agrees with English in using a sort of past tense in the reported clause; it should be remembered that in all other Slavonic languages the reported clause uses the same tense as the corresponding direct speech (lit. 'that he *writes* well, that he *is* ill').

194. *Past Gerund and Participle*. (*a*) *Active*. *-(v)ši:* Slov. *rékši* 'having spoken' *skrívši* 'having covered', S. *rèkâvši brâvši* 'having gathered.

These have become indeclinable, and therefore gerunds. They probably represent the nom. sg. fem. of the original participle. The participle in *-ŭ* persisted until the seventeenth century with root- and *n*-verbs (classes i and ii): OS. *rek* 'having said' *dvig* 'having moved'. This participle (save in the adj. *bivš* 'former, ex-') has disappeared from Modern Bulgarian, in which the adjectival function had been taken over by the *l*-participle in a way of which in other Slavonic languages there are only traces (*e.g.* P. *były* 'former').

(*b*) *Passive*. *-t/-(e)n-*. The distribution of these forms has been discussed in section 57. In Modern Bulgarian (as in Slovak) palatalization before *-jen* has been eliminated by analogy.

195. *Verbal Noun*. Slov. *délanje* 'working' *znânje* 'knowledge' *počétje* 'undertaking' *vpitjè* 'cry'; S. *bíće* 'being' *pokoljénje* 'generation'; B. *míslene* 'meditation' *vpísvane* 'inscription' *prigotovlénie* 'preparation' *bitié* 'existence'. Bulgarian forms in *-ie* are borrowed or imitated from Russian, and often include the epenthetic *l* of that language.

196. *Aorist and Imperfect.*

			S1	2	3	P1	2	3
S.	aor.	bï-	h	-	-	smo	ste	še
		ìmad-	oh	e	e	osmo	oste	oše
	impf.	bjë/bïjâ-⎫						
		ìmaɗâ- ⎭	h	še	še	smo	ste	hu
B.	aor.	pra-	ch	-	-	chme	chte	cha
	impf.	peré/nosé_⎫						
		bӑrza- ⎭	ch	še	še	chme	chte	cha

In the Freising documents and in other forms of Old Slovene these tenses are frequently encountered, not only in the sigmatic but also in the asigmatic forms: OSlov. *boido* (for *poido*) 'went' *be* 'was', *delase* (*delaše*) 'did', *pečachu* 'baked', *beše* 'was' *nošaše* 'bore'. There are now traces only in outlying dialects. In this respect Slovene is markedly contrasted with Serbocroat and Bulgarian, in which both tenses flourish, and have acquired new forms in both and new meanings in Bulgarian.

There has been interplay between the two sets of personal endings in both Serbocroat and Modern Bulgarian. *P3.* -*še/hu* remain distinct in Serbocroat, but are confused in B. -*cha*, whence -*chme* -*chte* also. *P2.* -*ste* is the aorist form used for both tenses in Serbocroat, whence -*smo*/OB. -*chomŭ*. The difference between the tenses is thus reduced to the second and third persons singular, but new differences have arisen through use of the present stem. In Old Serbian *P1.* -*homo* and -*hmo* occurred, though rarely: *zapisahmo* 'wrote down' 1347, *krstihmo* 'baptized' 1399, and from this came -*mo*, still used in the transitional Serbo-Bulgar dialects: dial. *rékomo* 'we said'. As late as the seventeenth century there were still found -*homo*/*hmo* -*hote* (*P2.* remodelled on the analogy of *P1*), but -*smo* -*ste* go back to the thirteenth century. In Middle Bulgarian -*chmy* is an alternative form as in Old Bulgarian: MidB. *rabotachmy* 'we worked', and in Modern Bulgarian -*chmi* is often the pronunciation given to the written -*chme*, though this may be due to the fact that the -*e* is unstressed, and so tends to become [i] (sect. 178).

Only the sigmatic aorists survive, and they do so in two forms: without vowel (S. *klêh* 'vowed' *mrïjeh* 'died', B. *dignach* 'moved') and with vowel (S. *plètoh* 'plaited', B. *plétoch*). Stems ending in a labial in Modern Bulgarian have *a* as vowel of support: B. *grébach* 'scraped'/S. *grèboh*.

The imperfect tense has developed divergently in the two languages. There was a tendency to associate the imperfect with the present stem in Serbocroat, which has been fully carried out in Bulgarian. In Serbocroat this results in distinctions of stem like S. *kùnijâh* 'was cursing' *mrâh* 'was dying'/*klêh* 'cursed' *mrĭjeh* 'died', or in mere doublet imperfects: S. *zòvijâh*/*zvâh* 'called' *köljâh klâh* 'stabbed'. At other times the presence of the aorist stem in the imperfect is evident: impf. *brâh* aor. *brâh*/pres. *bërêm* 'gather'. In this matter the perfective or imperfective nature of the verb is influential. S. *-âh* represents CSl.OB. *-aachŭ*: S. *pîtâh* 'asked' *hvâljâh* 'praised' *pèčâh* (i 1) 'baked'; this ending was then generalized to other types of conjugation: S. *grèbâh* 'scratched' *mrâh* 'died'. In S. *vïdâh* 'saw'/OB. *vidĕachŭ* the theoretical source would be **vidjaachŭ*. S. *-ijâh* is concurrent with them: S. *plètijâh* 'plaited'. In the sixteenth century they were written *-ĕch*/*iech*, depending on OB. *-ĕchŭ*, not on *-ĕachŭ*, and they owe the semivowel *j* to words which ended in it: OS. *umejah* MS. *ùmijâh* (*umĕj-achŭ*). The ending *-jâh* has the same origin, and is restricted to verbs of class ii 2: *tönjâh* 'sank'. S. *bjëh* (originally an aorist) was the only imperfect to retain *ĕ;* other forms of it are *bëh bëjâh* (*e*-dial.) *bïjâh* (*je- i*-dial.).

In Bulgarian the imperfect has been wholly transferred to the present stem: B. impf. *peréch* 'washed'/aor. *prach*. The vowels are *a* (OB. *aa*) and *ĕ* (OB. *ĕ*, of the shortened form). The aorist is always precise, and suited for categorical assertions. The imperfect is less definied, and so acquires a certain distinction of mood in Modern Bulgarian. It is suited to conditional and concessive clauses, in which no affirmation is made: B. *akó ostánech óšte málko u négo, štjach da zakăsnéja za vláka* 'If I stayed a little longer at his place, I should miss my train'.

(ii) NOUNS, ADJECTIVES, PRONOUNS

197. *Loss of Declension in Bulgarian* (cf. sect. 206). Declension has been almost entirely eliminated from Bulgarian. The language has not, of course, ceased to have cases, since case is the term for all methods of determining the relation between parties to an action and the action itself. The complex cases of Old Bulgarian have been replaced by new analytical devices; a suitable preposition is combined with the nom.-acc. as *casus generalis*. Pronouns have three cases. Nouns of family relationships and some personal names have four cases for the masculine, though not always for the feminine. In the colloquial there are many traces of the ancient oblique cases of the singular, so that certain old paradigms can be reconstructed from living dialect material. Paradigms are sometimes so composed that the presence or absence of the suffixed article constitutes a discrimination of case. The subject is normally singled out in speech, and therefore normally definite, with an article; the vocative defines itself, and needs no article;

the accusative and oblique cases are less likely to be defined. The article, in fact, like the ancient Greek article, is somewhat more of a demonstrative than in English; but a paradigm cannot be based upon its presence or absence as a criterion.

Names of male persons (though to a decreasing extent) and other masculine nouns when used in the sense of definition have an oblique case (the old gen.-acc. sg.) in -a/ja: B. Stoján GD. na Stoján(a) A. Stoján(a); zakón 'law' (na) zakóna '(of, to) the law'. Similarly: učítel -ja 'the teacher' gerój -a 'the hero'. The old dative is to a limited extent available for persons: DS. Stojánu or na Stoján(a), na učitelja/ učitelju 'to the teacher' (zakónu is obsolete). The vocative is in -e/ju: zakóne/učitelju geróju. In the plural there is but one case: zakóni učiteli gerói; with other flexions we have vólové 'oxen' méčové 'swords' koné 'horses' kralé 'kings' caré 'tsars'. Feminine nouns vary less: NGAS. žená V. žéno P. žení; but the dat. sg. appears in májce/májci 'to mother'. B. kắšta 'house' has loc. sg. kắšti. Neuters distinguish singular from plural: S. peró 'pen' P. perá, S. cveté P. cvetjá. They tend to normalize the accent.

The two Slavonic palatalizations affect Bulgarian nouns: VSM. Bóže 'O God' čovéče 'O man', NPM. săprúzi (săprúg 'husband') čovéci stomáci (stomách 'stomach').

Some nouns have two plurals with different meanings; e.g. list 'leaf, sheet of paper' pl. listá 'leaves' lístove 'sheets of paper' (and also neut. collective líste 'leaves, foliage'). For an apparent pl. -a which is really an old dual see the next paragraph.

The first move towards simplifying the declension in Bulgarian, as in other languages, was to eliminate the dual. It remains, however, in the form of the usual anomalies: paired parts of the body (răcé 'hands'/răkí in some dialects, nozé 'feet', kolené 'elbows' krilé 'wings' ramené 'shoulders' oči 'eyes' uši 'ears'), the dual numerals and the flexion -a after numerals in the case of masculine nouns. It should be noted that this -a does not shift the stress: dva gráda 'two towns'/ gradá (oblique case). Next came the elimination of oblique cases of the plural, leaving only the nom.-acc. The locative had lost its reason for existence, since it was always accompanied by a preposition, which performed all necessary semantic services. The instrumental in -i remains in adverbial uses: B. govóri rúski 'he speaks Russian', staréški 'in a senile fashion', naópaki 'contrariwise'. In the Rhodope mountains and some south-eastern dialects the dative lingers: dial. družínam 'to companies' žénamtěm 'to the women'. The genitive plural lost all distinctiveness with the loss of final jers. The partitive genitive is found dialectically after numbers: dial. dévet godín 'nine years', za mnógo godín 'after many years', and occurs in the literary pétstotin '500'. The accusative fell into the nom. pl. from which it differed only in *o*-stems, and as the vocative already coincided with the nominative, only the nom. pl. remained to this number.

The oblique cases of the singular have proved more resistant, though the locative soon disappeared. A tendency to construe the instrumental always with *s* made this flexion also otiose. It survives in the set phrase: (*idí*) *s Bógom/zbógom* 'adieu', and in adverbial expressions: B. *dénem* 'by day' *nóštem* 'by night' *sílom* 'by force', of which the last two are examples of analogical formations, since the nouns concerned are feminine. In folk-poetry the instr. sg. is in much use as an internal object: *tékom tečé*, *víkom víka* 'flows a flowing, cries a cry'. The dative is in occasional use with names of male persons, less often of females, as above noted, but the usual construction is *na*+nom. or gen. The genitive is well preserved in the masculine, though it has lost its possessive function to the possessive adjectives. As gen.-acc. it has widened its use in the case of male persons. The accusative and nominative tended to fall together in Old Bulgarian (*uv-* and masc. *n*-stems). B. *kámik kámăk* 'stone' retains a trace of OB. *kamy*, followed by a diminutive ending. Old *r-uv*-stems have become feminine *a*-types (B. *dăšterjá* 'daughter', dim. *štérka, cărkva* 'church'), and masc. *n*-stems have become *o*-types. The dialects still sometimes distinguish nom./acc. in the *a*-declension: dial. N. *sestrá* A. *sestră* 'sister', N. *reká* A. *rekú* 'hand'), but this is not general.

198. *Gender and Declension in Slovene and Serbocroat.* The main line of demarcation lies, not between the languages as such, but between Slovene with Kaj- and Ča- dialects of Serbocroat, and the Što-dialect. It is due to the complete reconstruction of the plural in Što. The old plural is intact in Ča and Kaj, and in Slovene the dual also is found.

As in other modern Slavonic tongues, gender has been largely identified with declensional forms. Masculine *i*-stems have passed into the *o*-declension, as from the fourteenth century, but I*S. pútem* 'by the road' *göstem* 'by the guest' remain, and D*P. ljudem* 'to people' was in use in the sixteenth century. OS.I*P. gostmi* was a form of the *i*-declension, but D*P. gost-em* L. *-eh* were due to the influence of *jo*-nouns, since CSl. *ĭ* in strong position >S. *a*. Slov. N*PM. puti gosti* were used in the thirteenth century, by confusion of nom. acc. pl., and Slov. *ljudjê*, M*P. trijê štirje*/F*P. trî štíri* '3 4' still show the ancient form of the masc. pl. Slov. *dân* 'day' has gone over to the *o*-declension, but shows a considerable diversity of stems: *dn- dnev- dnov-*, giving alternative forms for most cases.

Masculine *n*-stems have also passed into the *o*-declension. OS.N*S. kami* 'stone' *plami* 'flame' *prami* 'tuft' persisted as late as the sixteenth century, and by loss of the final vowel have given Modern South Serbian dial. *käm pläm krëm* 'flint'/S. *kämên plämên krëmên.*

Feminine *r*-stems are represented only by Slov. *máti/mater-* 'mother' *hčí/hčer-* 'daughter', S. *mäti kčí*. They have suffered assimilation to *i*-stems and later to *a*-stems, though still forming a class apart. OS. *ljubi* 'wife' was indeclinable (16–17th centuries). Fem. *uv*-stems have gone to the *a*-declension in Serbocroat, but show doublets in Slovene: *cérkev/cérkva* 'church'.

Neuter *s*-stems have become *o*-stems. S. *nëbo* 'sky' has pl. *nebèsa*, and in Slovene *-es-* is also found in singulars of the series: Slov. *perêsa* 'of a feather' *očêsa* 'of an eye' pl. *perêsa očêsa*. The ancient dual Slov. *očî* S. *öči* 'eyes' has been assimilated to feminine *i*-stems, while S. sg. *öko* pl. *öka* are now *o*-stems. Neuter *n*- and *nt*-stems are declined as *o*-neuters except for the difference of stem between nom. acc. sg. and the oblique cases of the singular and all the plural. In Slovene the *nt*-declension has affected also some masculines that happened to end in *-e:* Slov. *óče* 'father' G*S. očéta*.

Masculine *u/o*-stems have fused. In Slovene G*P. -ov* is from the *u*-stems. In Serbocroat *-ov/ev-* forms plural stems for masculine monosyllables: S. *gràdovi* 'cities' *mäčevi* 'swords'. The oldest Serbian had *vukove* 'wolves' *muževe* 'men' : : *sinove* 'sons', and *-ovi* replaced *-ove* gradually during the fourteenth to sixteenth centuries.

199. *Number.* The dual persists almost unimpaired in Slovene. The gen.-loc. remains in *náju* 'of us two' *váju* 'of you two', but is replaced by the plural forms in the declension of nouns. The latter therefore show only the nom.-acc. and dat.-instr.: N*DM. -a* N*F. -i,* DI*DMNF. -ma*, preceded by *i e o a* or a consonant: *míslima* 'with two thoughts' *nìtma* 'by two threads' *kostéma* 'with two bones' *klopéma* 'by two benches' *híšama* 'by two houses' *hríboma* 'by two hills'.

In Što-Serbocroat there are only relics of the dual apart from its use (an apparent gen. sg.) after numbers 2–4 and the fact that *-ma* has been substituted for the proper endings of the dat. instr. loc. pl. of all nouns and (to some extent) adjectives. The dual is used for paired objects: *öči üši* (G*L. -î/ijû*, DI. *-ima*), but *öka üha* in transferred senses ('eye of a bridge/needle', etc.). Gen. dual = gen. pl. *nögû* 'of feet' *rükû* 'of hands' *prsijû* 'of breasts'; *plèče* 'shoulder-blade' has a double declension: NA. *plëči/plëča* G. *plëčî/pléčâ*. Since the fourteenth century *öči üši* have been considered feminine plurals; G*LD. -u* was in use as a locative as late as the seventeenth century.

200. *Hardening of Declensions in Slovene and Serbocroat.* Only traces of the former distinction between hard and soft forms of the same declension survive in either language. They lie chiefly in the opposition *o/e* in the instr. sg. of masc. neut. *o*-stems and the nom. acc. sg. of neuters. I*S. -em* appears in Slovene after *c č š ž j lj nj rj*, in Serbocroat after *št žd -telj ž č*. Slovene *r* shows its original softness when a vowel follows (Slov. *pastírja* 'of a shepherd' *pastírju* 'to

a shepherd'/*pastír*), but in Serbocroat there are alternative forms: V*SM. -e/u* I*SMN. -om/em* (but always e.g. *cärem* 'by the tsar'). The fusion of hard and soft *a*-stems was gradual. The gen. sg. S. -*ê* dates from the beginning of the Serbian records, and *y/i* are found only in documents affected by Church Slavonic. Dat. sg. S. *i* was predominant in the south and west as early as the fourteenth century, concurrently with -*ě* -*e* (*ženě* 'to the woman' *službe* 'to service'); in the sixteenth century *i* was universal in those parts, and has since spread over all the area. Voc. sg. S. -*o* (used for soft equivalents) dates from the fifteenth century, though words in -*ica* remain exceptional (V. -*ice*). Acc. pl. S. -*e* dates from the earliest time; -*y/i* occur only under the influence of Church Slavonic. Ragusan writers sometimes preferred the original hard form. Feminine instr. sg. OS. -*ovĭ* (13th cent.) represented the sound -*ōu*, with the vowel lengthened by the *u* (<-*jǫ*). There was a soft variant OS. -*evĭ* (*voljevĭ*) which died out. Instr. -*ōu* then fused with instr. sg. masc. -*om* to give -*ôm* [Ča -*û(n)*].

201. *Paradigms of Nouns.*

I-stems

	SNA	GDL	I	V	PN	A	G	D	I	L	DNA	DI
Slov. nit- (*F*)	-	i	jo		i	i	i	im	mi	ih	i	ma
ljud- (*M*)			(pôtem)		je	i	i	em	mi	eh		
S. stvar-	-	i	i/ju	i	i	i	î	ima				

(S. stvar-: D, I, L = *ima* (braced))

Consonant-stems

	SN	A	G	L	D	I	V	PN	A	G	D	I	L	DNA	DI
Slov. máti	-														
mater-		-	e	i	i	jo		e	e	-	am	ami	ah	i	ama
okô	-	-													
očes-			a	u	u	om		a	a	-	om	i	ih	i	oma
oč-								i	i	i	em	mi	eh		
imê/déte	-	-													
imen-/detet-			a	u	u	om		a	a	-	om	i	ih		
S. kćî/mäti	-														
kćer-		-	i	i	i	i/ju	i	i	i	î	ima				
mater-		-	-	ê	i	i	om	e	e	â	ama				
plëme/táne	-	-													
plemen-/tanet-			a	u	u	om		a	a	â	ima				

(S. kćer-, mater-, tanet-: D, I, L = *ima* / *ama* / *ima* (braced))

UV-stems

	SN	A	G	L	D	I	V	PN	A	G	D	I	L	DNA	DI
Slov. cérkev	-	-													
cérkv-		a	o	e	i	i	ijo/o	e	e	-	am	ami	ah	i	ama

A-stems

	SN	A	G	DL	I	V	PNA	G	D	I	L	DNA	DI
lov. hîš-	a	o	e	i	o	e	-		am	ami	ah	i	ama
Ča. kräv-	a	u	ē	i	ūn	o	e	-	ān	ami	ah		
žen-	ä	ü	ï	ë	û	o	ï	-	ân	âmi	âh		
Što. žen-	a	u	ê	i	ôm	o	e	â	ama				

U/O-stems

	SN	A	G	D	L	I	V	PNA	G	D	I	L	DNA	DI
Slov. hríb- (M)	-	-	} a	u	u	om	{ i / a }	{ e / a }	{ ov / - }	om	i	ih	{ a / i }	oma
jezer- (N)	o	o												
Ča. čäs- (M)	-	-	} a	u	i	ōn	e	{ i / a }	{ i / a }	-	ōn	i	ïh	
lët- (N)	o	o												
Što. jelen- (M)	-	G	} a	u	u	{ om	c	i	e	â	ima			
sel- (N)	o	o						a	a					
orač- (M)	-	G				em	u	i	e					
polj- (N)	e	e				em	e	a	a }					

In view of the difficulty caused by the shifting and changing accentuation, intonation marks have been given in only a few instances. In Što-endings the circumflex denotes length.

202. *Singular Cases.* (a) *Dative-locative.* These cases were identical for feminine *i- a-* stems in Common Slavonic. As we have noted (section 200), their hard and soft forms were fused in Slovene and Serbocroat. They remain different in *u/o*-stems in Ča: dat. -*u*/loc. -*i*, but are fused in Slovene and Što (apart from intonation): Slov. DL*SM. hríbu*, Što. D*SM. grâdu* L*SM. grádu* (*hríb* 'hillock' *grâd* 'town'), DL*SM. gradíću*. The two cases were kept apart in the fifteenth century in Serbia, and by Ragusan poets in the sixteenth century. The latter use locative endings only for a few words, such as *svïjet* 'world' *sän* 'dream'. When found in seventeenth-century poets, the old endings must have been purely imitative.

(b) *Instrumental.* For the fusion of the masc. and fem. forms see section 200.

In Serbocroat, as in Czech, the genitive does not normally occur after negative verbs. In Slovene on the other hand, as in Polish, it is always used in negative clauses.

203. *Plural Cases.* (a) *Genitive.* A characteristic of Što is the addition of *â* to all genitive plurals except those of feminine *i*-stems. Feminine *r*-stems vacillate: *kćérî/mätêrâ*. Because of the loss of *jers* the genitive plural had zero-ending until the sixteenth century: OS. *žen duš lët polj imen nebes, sinov/kóstî*. This is still their state in the Ča-dialects.

From the fourteenth century there appear endings spelt with doubled
jers (ьь), which were doubtless pronounced as *jer* in strong position,
viz. *a*. The *a* begins to be written in the fifteenth century: *zeméljâ*
'of lands' *zŕnâ* 'of grains'. The problem is to account for what would
be a normal development of stressed *jer* in conditions for which
stress was certainly not normal. A long vowel appeared in the
i-declension (GP. *-î*), which may have offered a starting point for
-â in the *a*-declension, and then in others also; but the evidence
is insufficient to clear up the point. The creation of this form on
a suffixless gen. pl. is shown by the presence of the fill-vowel:
sestárâ 'of sisters', cf. R. *sestër*/OB. *sestrŭ*. In some Montenegrin
dialects the adjectival *-h* is added to *-â -î*, sporadic examples
appearing in the fifteenth and sixteenth centuries: *rabotah* (15th
cent.), *stvarih* (16th cent.).

(*b*) *Dative, instrumental, locative*. These cases remain distinct in
Slovene.

In Ča-Serbocroat only the endings of the *a*- and *o*- stems remain,
since the *i*-stems take the flexions of the *a*-stems in these cases: Ča. *-ân*
-âmi -âh/ón -i -ih. Ča. *-ih* <*-ichŭ*, the soft equivalent of *-ĕchŭ*. In some
Bosnian Što-dialects the hard ending *-ĕchŭ* >*-ijeh* >*-ije*: dial. *kolije* 'in
rings', and this has been extended to soft stems: dial. *na kòńije* 'on
horses'. In all the Yugoslav area the locative remained intact until
about 1600, when it began to conform to the already fused dative and
instrumental.

The stages of development in Što were the following: In the fifteenth century the dative and instrumental plural were already used
interchangeably, and the plural might be found after *dvâ òba*, where
the dual was required: OS. *dvjema gospodarom* 'to two masters',
objema rukami 'with both hands'. So, in the sixteenth century, dual and
plural were fused. Instr. pl. masc. neut. *-i* took the *-m* of the dative,
resulting in IPMN. *-im*, which formed a parallel to *-am* (dat. used as
instr.), and so aided the confusion of cases. The last step was the
adoption of the final vowel of the dual, giving *-ima*. The dual ending
-oma did not pass directly into the plural, but by a process of coales-
cence with IP. *-i*+DP. *-m*, as above described. The whole development was not complete until well into the seventeenth century, when
IP. *-i* was still found with *o*-stems. There was some confusion with
i-stems, giving forms like *gradovmi* 'with towns', while *-imi* appeared
within a narrow range in the seventeenth century. Examples of instr.
for dat. in the sixteenth century are: *k vrati* 'to the doors', *k ženami* 'to
women'. Some writers of the sixteenth century, and even later, prefer
-ma to *-ima*: *jajma* 'with eggs' *końma* 'with horses' *bregovma* 'with
banks'. The present result is DILP. *-ama* for *a*-stems/*-ima* for *o*- and
i- stems; it should be noted that this *-ima* causes second palatalization

like nom. pl. *-i:* S. *mòmak* 'lad' nom. pl. *mòmci* dat. loc. instr. pl. *mòmcima.*

204. *Numerals.* 1. Slov. *éden (èn) én-o -a;* S. *jèdan jèdn-o -a;* B. *edín edn-ó -á.* 1st. Slov. *pȓvi,* S. *pȓvî,* B. *părv*/def. *pắrvijat.*

2–4. B. *dva*/*NF. dve, tri, čétiri. Dvà* takes the masc. dual article: *dváta.* Otherwise the article is *-te(ch): trité gospoží* 'the three ladies' *četiridesetjách selá* 'the forty villages'. The old masc. dual *-a* of the noun (which, unlike gen. *-a,* nevèr attracts the stress) is used with all numbers, except those in *-ma* (originating in the DILD) which refer to men: B. *tríma lekári* 'three doctors', *šestíma učiteli* 'six teachers'.

	N	A	G	L	D	I	
Slov. dv-	*M.*â/*NF.*ê	â/ê	éh	éh	éma	éma	(obâ)
tr-	*M.*ijê/*NF.*î	î	éh	éh	ém	émi	
štír-	*M.*je/*NF.*i	i	ih	ih	im	imi	
S. dv-	*MN.*â/*F.*ïje	â/ïje	áju/éju	áma/éma			(öba, öbadvâ)
tr-	î	î	íju	íma			
čètir-	i	i	iju	ima			

The tendency in Modern Serbocroat is not to decline these numerals. From 5 upwards they are never declined. The masc. dual *-a* is employed in Serbocroat after 2–4, and is construed as a gen. sg.; in the sixteenth century this usage was extended to the neuters also: S. *dvâ plëmena* 'two tribes'/pl. *plemèna.* 2nd–4th. Slov. *drûgi trétji četŕti,* S. *drügî trècî cètvrtî,* B. def. *vtórijat trétijat četvắrtijat.* Distributive: Slov. *dvôj obôj trôj četvêr* (all other numbers taking the suffix *-er*), declined as adjectives; S. *dvöje öboje tröje čètvoro* are declined as adjectives but restricted to the neuter; forms *dvòjica,* etc., occur with the gen. pl. of nouns referring to male persons.

5–10: Slov. *pêt šêst sédem ósem devêt desêt;* S. *pêt šêst sëdam ösam dëvêt dësêt;* B. *pet šest sédem ósem dévet déset* (all ending originally in soft *jer*). 5th–10th: Slov. *péti ósmi,* etc., S. *pêtî,* B. def. *pétijat.*

11–19: Slov. *enájst dvanájst,* etc.; S. *jedànaest šèsnaest;* B. *edinádeset/ edinájset četirinájset.*

20–90: Slov. *dvâjset/dvâjsti, éden in dvâjset, trîdeset, štírideset, pêtdeset, šêstdeset,* etc.; S. *dvádeset, dvádeset i jèdan, četrdèset pedèset šéset/šezdèset, sedamdèset,* etc.: B. *dvádeset/dvájse(t) trídeset/tríjse(t), četirideset/četírise, petdesét, šestdesét/šejsé(t), sedemdesét,* etc.

100–1,000,000: Slov. *stô, stô in éden, dvê stô, tisóč, milijón;* S. *stô/ stötina, stô jèdan, dvjësta/dvïje stötine, pêt stötînâ, (tïsúča)/hìljada/ hìljadu, dvïje hìljade, pêt hìljâdâ, milîón, dvâ milióna;* B. *sto, sto i ednó, dvéste trísta čétiristótin, chiljáda, dve chiljadi, milión, dva milióna.* OS. *dvïjesti* '200' had the dual ending until the seventeenth century and is still in use in Ragusa (Dubrovnik). S. *hìljada* is from the Gk. χιλιάδα.

205. *Adjectives.*

	SN	A	G	D	L		I	PN	A	GL	D	I	DNA	D
Slov. lép-	M.i/N.o i/o	ega	emu	em		im	M.i/N.a e/a ⎱		ih	im	imi	⎰ M.a/N.i ⎱ im
	F.a	o	e	i		o	e ⎰					⎰ i ⎰
S. žût-	M.î/N.ô NG/ô	og(â)	om(e)	om(e)	îm	M.î/N.â ê/â ⎱		îh(G) îm(a)(DIL)			
	F.â	û	ê	ôj	ôm ê	ê ⎰					
òčev-	M.-/N.o -/o	a	u	u	îm	M.i/N.a e/a ⎱		îh(G) îm	(DIL)			
	F.a	u	ê	oj	ôm e	e ⎰					

Gen. sg. *-ga* (for *-go*) in both languages is due to the analogy of gen. sg. *-a* of the *o*-stems.

There is a full paradigm of the indefinite declension in Serbocroat: S. *növ -o -a*, 'new', *tûđ -e -a* 'strange', alongside the definite declensions: *növ-î -ô -â*, *vrûć-î -ê -â* 'warm'. The indefinite declension follows that of the noun except in the instr. sg. and gen. dat. instr. loc. pl. The gen. dat. loc. sg. of the definite declension may be used for the indefinite also. The loc. pl. has been separated from the genitive and associated with the dative and instrumental, under the influence of the dual forms in *-ima*. In the masc. neut. the forms I*S*. *-îm*, G*P*. *-îh* DL*IP*. *-îm* are derived by contraction from the Common Slavonic forms, but there also exist the flexions *-ijem -ijeh -ijem*, remodelled upon the demonstrative *tijem* ⟨*těmŭ*. The final vowels of the genitive and dative are sometimes dropped, which causes the dative to coincide with the locative. The dative is in *-omu* as well as *-ome*. DL*IP*. *-îma* is found most often when the adjective stands alone without noun.

In Bulgarian the indefinite and definite adjectives are distinct in the masc. *nov/nóvi*, but not in the neut. fem. *nóv-o -a*. In dialects and folksongs G*SMN*. *-ago/ogo/ego* and D*SMN*. *-omu* are in frequent use; and there are also forms based on the nom. sg., G. *-igo* D. *-imu*.

The possessive adjectives have the mixed declension of indefinites. They are of the usual types: S. *ivanov bratòvljev* 'brother's' *òčev* 'father's' *sèstrin* 'sister's'; and they have been extended to the pronouns also: S. *njègov* 'his', B. *négov*.

Adjectives drawn from the names of animals (and some other nouns also) have a special suffix: S. *lìsičî rêp* 'fox tail', *tičî glâs* 'bird's voice', *jučerašnjî hljëb* 'yesterday's bread'.

Comparatives: Slov. *dràžji* 'dearer' *lêpši* 'fairer' *čistéjši* 'cleaner'; S. *cŕnjî* 'blacker' *slàvnijî* 'more famous' *ljèpšî* 'morc beautiful'; B. *pó-sílen* 'stronger'. Superlative prefix: Slov. *náj-* S. *nâj-*, B. *naj-*. Correlative 'than': Slov. *kò kòt kàkor nêgo* (after negatives), S. *nëgo od*, B. *ot*.

206. *The Demonstrative Declension.*

	SN	A	G	D	L	I	PN	A	GL	D	I	DNA	G	DI
ov. t-	M.â/N.ô	NG/ô	èga	èmu	ém	ém	î/â	ê/â	} éh	ém	émi	{â/ê / ê}		éma
	F.â	ô	é	i/éj	ó.	ê	ê							
k-	dó	ogá	ogá	omú	òm	òm								
k-	áj	áj												
č-			èsa	èmu	ém	ìm								
nj-	MN.	èga	èga	èmu	èm	ìm		ih/je	ih	im	imi		u	ima
		(gà/nj	ga	mu)										
	F.	ó	é	i/èj	ó									
. òv-	M.âj/N.ô	NG/ô	og(â)	ome	om(e)	îm	î/â	ê/â	} îh(G)	îm(a)(DLI)				
	F.â	û	ê	ôj	ôm	ê	ê							
k-	ö	òga	òga	òme	òm(e)	îm(e)								
št	ö/ä	ö/ä												
č			èga	èmu	ëm	îm(e)								
nj-	MN.	NG.	èga	èmu	èmu	îm(e)		îh	îh(G)	īma(DLI)				
			(ga	mu)				(ih)	(im)(D)					
	F.	û	ê	ôj	óm(e)									
			(ju/je	je	joj)									

NSM. S. *tâj ònâj* 'that' *òvâj* 'this' OS. *saj* 'this' are due to the analogy of the definite adjectives, *tŭ-jĭ* giving *tâj*, since *jer* in strong position becomes *a*, and a vowel lengthens before *j*. *Saj tâj* have been noted from the fourteenth century (1332, 1398), but *ònâj òvâj* only from the fifteenth. Neuter *kŭ-* (cf. Lat. *quod/quid*) similarly formed Slov. *kâj* 'what', and *kaj* is found in the transition Serbo-Slovene dialects of the north (Varaždin), which are called *kájkavština* on that account. Ča-dialects stressed the soft form of the pronoun (*čĭ-*), giving *čä* and the regional name *čákavština*. *Štòkavština* comprises the region where 'what' is pronounced *štö* or *štä*, derived from *čĭto* by dissimilation: *št* < *tšt*. Since the thirteenth century *štä* has stood after a negative prefix (*nìšta* 'nothing'), as if it were a genitive in *-a*. The same process of stressing *jer* gives Slov. *tâ*, Ča. *sa* (сьь храмь 'this temple' 14th cent.). The Ča-dialects have also an interrogative adjective (*k-î -ô -â* 'which?') and an enclitic relative: Ča. *krozač zač* 'why?'/Što. *zäšto*, and an enclitic demonstrative: Ča. *zat vinograd* 'beyond that vineyard'. OS. *tko* 'who?' is the result of metathesis, and is recorded in the thirteenth century, followed by *kö* from the fifteenth; Croat still uses *tkö*.

Gen. sg. *čìso* is represented by Slov. *čèsa*, with *-a* on the analogy of GSMN. *-a* in the *o*-declension; the same analogy has produced S.

tŏgâ kòga svèga. Hard and soft forms have interchanged in S. *joj njôj*
(OB. *jeji*) and Slov. *tèga tèmu* Ragusan *tega ovega.* Where *ĕ* was
involved this gave the usual alternatlvès *ije/i,* but *i* spread to the
e-dialects at an early date, so that the expected third alternative is-
missing. The cases involved are instr. sg. masc. neut. and gen. dat. loc.
instr. pl.: e.g. I*SMN. tijem/tîm kijem/kîm.*

Particles added to relatives and demonstratives in Old Serbian were
-r(e) ⟨*-že, -zi,* and *-a -i* to the instr. sg.: OS. *nitkore* 'no one', *tima* (14–
15th cent.), *sa svima/sàsvîm* 'quite', *ovzi* (13th cent.), *tizi/tizijeh* (16th
cent.): Slov. *kdòr* 'who' (rel.); for *kdó* 'who' cf. Cz. *kdo.*

The corresponding demonstratives and relatives in Bulgarian are
tózi/tója 'this' *ónzi/ónja* 'that', *kój* F. *kojá* 'who?' *koé* 'what?' pl. *koí,*
kójto 'who, which' (rel.), *tój* (⟨*tŭjĭ*) F. *tja* (apparently *ta* affected by *ja*)
N. *to* pl. *te* 'he, she, it'. They are formed by means of suffixes, like the
parallel forms in Slovene and Old Serbian. They have commonly four
cases: nom. acc. gen. dat., though the acc. has often the form of the
gen.: N*M. toj* A. *négo/go* G. *na négo* D. *nému/mu,* N*N. to,* N*F. tja* A.
néja/ja G. *na néja* D. *nei/i* (usually spelt *ì* to distinguish it from
the conjunction), N*P. te* A. *tech* (*tjach*)/*gi* G. *na tech* D.
tem/im. The possessive form of this pronoun is formed from the
genitive: M*NS. négov* F. *néjn* P. *téchen* 'his, her, their'. Of the
demonstrative there exist G*SMN. togóva togózi, na tózi,* D*SMN.*
tomúva, na tózi, etc. The attribution of grammatical gender to the
relative pronoun is a notable innovation (A*SM. kogó* N. *koé* F. *kojá,*
D*SM. komú* N. *na koé* F. *na kojá*), the genitive case being provided by
the possessive S*M. čij* N. *čié* F. *čijá* P. *čii.* There is also *što* 'what?'

207. *The Article in Bulgarian.* Though the postpositive article is
highly characteristic of Bulgarian, it is not unique in the Slavonic
world. It is due to two tendencies of the Common Slavonic language:
to subjoin demonstrative enclitics to words by way of emphasis, and to
denude them gradually of demonstrative meaning. More than one
particle was available for the purpose (OB. *sĭ tŭ onŭ vŭ*), and these
variants are still alive in the archaic dialects of the Bulgarian south-east
and west: dial. *godína-ta/va/na* 'the year'. In these dialects there
remain also several cases of the article G*SMN. toga/togo* D*SMN.*
tomu I*SMN. tum* D*SF. tuhi* (for *toi*) G*P. tĕch* D*P. tĕm.* To use *-to*
with the plural in a collective sense is a characteristic of the colloquial
idiom. The literary language has S*M.* (*ă/ja*)*t* N. *-to* F. *-ta* PMF. *-te*
(*N. -te* with adjectives, *-ta* with nouns), the article standing with noun
or adjective according to which comes first. The masc. sg. *-t,* following
a *jer,* puts that *jer* into strong position; it therefore vocalizes as *ă/a:*
B. *zakónăt* 'the law', and retains its original hardness or softness: B.
gerójat 'the hero'. In B. *četiridesetjách selá* 'the forty villages', *-tjach* is
in the gen. pl. because of *četírideset.*

The feminine article -*ta* always draws the stress from the noun: *kost/kosttá* 'the bone' *nezavísimost* 'independence'/*nezavisimosttá*.

The position in the modern literary language (though this rule is not always observed in speech) is that the genitive in -*a* (-*ja*) serves for the oblique cases of the singular of masculine nouns with the definite article: *zakónăt* 'the law' GD. *na zakóna* A. *zakóna*. Similarly when a preceding adjective takes the article: *bálgarskijat zakón, na bálgarskija zakón.*

208. *Personal Pronouns.*

	SN	A	G	DL	I	PN	A	GL	D	I	DN	AGL	DI
ov.	jàz												
mèn-		e	e	i	ój								
m-		e	e	i(D)		î	⌣				ì(dva/e)		
n-							âs	âm	ámi			áju	áma
s-/t-	i	e	e	i(D)									
sèb-/tèb-		e	e	i	ój		⌣						
v-						î	âs	âm	ámi		i(dva/e)	áju	áma
	jâ												
mèn-		e	e	i									
mn-					ôm(e)								
m-		e	e	i(D)		î	⌣						
n-							âs	äm(a)	äma(IL)				
s-/t-	i	e	e	i(D)									
sèb-/tèb-		e	e	i									
sòb-/tòb-					ôm		⌣						
v-						î	âs	äm(a)	äma(IL)				
	az												
mén-		e/-	e	e									
m-		e	e	i									
n-							íe	i/as	as	am/i			
s-/t-	i	e		i									
séb-/téb-		e	e	e									
v-							íe	i/as	as	am/i			

Slov. *jàz* occurs also in Ča-dialects at some points on the Istrian mainland; B. *az* is also found in the Island of Silba; otherwise S. *jâ*. DL*S*. B. -*ě* is historically correct; Slov. S. -*i* is by analogy of *a*-declension nouns (S. DL*S*. *žēni*). The original flexion survived to the sixteenth century as *mne*, alternating with *mni/mani* (OB. *mǐně*). The stem of the genitive has spread to this case, and where -*e* survives in Montenegro it is assimilated to the genitive: GDL*S*. *mène tèbe sèbe*. The instrumental has been lost in Bulgarian. In Slovene it takes the genitive stem (*men- teb- seb-*) but with final accentuation and loss of the final vowel: Slov. *menój*/OB. *mŭnojǫ, tebój sebój*. The original stem survives in Serbocroat, where the ending has developed: *-ojǫ* > *-oju* > *-ōu* > *-ôm*, with *m* from instr. sg. masc. as in the case of the instr. of the *a*-declension (section 200). The enclitic forms are used as possessives in Bulgarian: *májka mi* 'my mother' (3*S. sestrá ì* 'her sister' *brat mu* 'his brother' 3*P. kắštata im* 'their house'). CSl.OB. *my vy* survive in Slov. S. *mî vî*, and have driven from the dual CSl.OB. *vě va* in favour of *mi-*/*vi- dva/dve*. In Bulgarian the nominative of the first person plural has been reformed upon the accusative: *nie*. For form cf. *vie* 'you'. In the other languages the gen.-loc. *nas vas* has ousted the original accusative. D*P. B. nam vam* enclitic *ni vi* correspond to OB. *namŭ vamŭ ny vy;* Slovene retains *nâm vâm*, and Serbocroat had *nam vam ni vi* in general use until the seventeenth century. They are still found in dialects of Montenegro and Hercegovina, and in the literary speech S. *nam vam* serve as enclitics, while the full forms are taken from the old dual. In the sixteenth century the dative and instrumental were confused, and the dual forms introduced into the plural. The original genitive dual remains in Slovene.

(iii) INDECLINABLES

209. *Adverbs* (see section 73). As exemplified by the Serbocroat forms, these words reproduce with minor variations the Slavonic pattern. Adverbs derived from adjectives usually have the form of the indefinite neuter, save that the two sometimes differ in accent, e.g. *lijepo* 'beautifully'/*lijèpo;* those from adjectives in *-skî* take *-skî. Kȁko* 'how' *tȁkô* 'so' *nȉkȁko* 'in no way' *nëkȁko* 'somehow', etc. *ĵako* is used for 'how' and (with different accent) *ĵȃko* for 'strongly, very'; cf. Roumanian *tare* 'strong' from Lat. *talis*. For *bäš* 'just' cf. OB. forms in *bŭch-. Kȁda* 'when' is based on *kŭda, cf. *tȁdâ* 'then' *säda* 'now'; for 'always' there is *svägda* (and *üvjek* < *vïjek* 'age'). Other adverbs of time are *zìmûs* 'this winter' *zîmi* (an old locative) 'in winter' *ljëtôs* 'this summer' *dànas* 'today' *večèras* 'this evening' *sütra* 'tomorrow' (*ütro*/*jütro* 'morning') *jütrôs* 'this morning' *jüčĕ* 'yesterday' [from *viče(ra)*] *sïnôć* 'tonight' *nòćas* 'last night' *onòmad* 'the other day' (< *onomï dïne*, cf. R. *namédni*); of place *gdë* 'where' (from *kŭdĕ; B. kȁdé* is from *kǫdĕ*) *küd*/*kùdâ* 'whither' (< *kǫd-*) *svùdâ* 'everywhere' *tämo* 'there' *òdâklê* 'whence' (cf. OB. *otŭ kol-*); of degree *kȍliko* 'how much' *tȍlikô* 'so much'. The Sl. *ješče* 'yet' (R. *eščë*) appears as *jöš(te)*, by contamination with a variant **ošče;* cf. B. *óšte*. The Slovene word for 'when' is also based on **kŭda: kàdar* (*r* < *ž*), cf. *zdàj* 'now' (*sï-da-i*), but Bulgarian has *kogá* from *kogda* with loss of *d*. Slovene *àmpak* 'however' comes from *a-nŭ-pak-;* for Slovene *sicèr* 'indeed' (*r* < *ž*) cf. Cz. *sice*. A number of Serbocroat and Bulgarian adverbs are borrowed from Turkish, e.g. S. *badàva* 'in vain' *džäbe* 'gratis'.

210. *Prepositions and prefixes* (see section 74). Most of these forms compare with those of Old Bulgarian, and the prefix *vy-* is missing as from that language. The Serbocroat strong *jer* and fill-vowel being *a*, *bez* appears as *bez/beza*, *kŭ* as *k/ka*, etc. Before a *k* Slovene *k* is pronounced and written *h* (cf. a similar pronunciation in Russian); for this preposition Bulgarian has a form *kăm*. There is a Serbocroat preposition *črez* 'through', but it is normally replaced by *kroz* (cf. Cz. *skrz* and, with loss of *r*, Slov. *skoz*). In Bulgarian *iz* frequently (and confusingly for those familiar with other Slavonic languages) means 'through': *iz Bălgárija* 'through Bulgaria'. The Serbocroat prepositions compounded with *iz* are used in the sense of, and more frequently than, the simple prepositions from which they are formed: *između* for *među* 'between' (B. *meždu* Slov. *med*), *ispod* for *pod* 'under', etc. The Bulgarian *s* 'with' and *v* 'in' are usually pronounced *săs* and *văf;* the Slovene *z* (cf. Polish) and *v* (which in Serbocroat has given *u*) are not linked as in other languages to a following word but are pronounced *zᵊ vᵊ*. *Vŭzŭ* 'up' is used, as in Old Bulgarian, in the Serbocroat form *uz* as a preposition; elsewhere it is only a prefix. In Slovene the prefix **orz- (raz)* 'apart' is also used as a preposition.

211. *Conjunctions and particles* (see section 75). *A* and *li* combine in Serbocroat in the word *äli* 'but' (/Cz.P. *ale* ⟨*a-lĕ*). Serbocroat *àko* means 'if', and *dä* is used for 'yes' and for the conjunction 'that'; the same word is used in Bulgarian for 'yes' and to introduce clauses replacing the infinitive, but otherwise 'that' is *če*, while Slovene has borrowed for 'yes' the German *ja*. *-žde* in its Serbocroat form *-đe* appears in *takóđe(r)* 'also', in which the final *r* is from *ž(e)*, a form it frequently takes in this language and in Slovene; cf. *jër(bo)* 'for, since' from *jež(e) bo*. The Slovene *in* 'and' is from *i-nŭ*. The Serbocroat expression for 'because' is *zàtô što*, the Bulgarian (with change of order) *zaštóto* (Slov. *zakàj* = 'for what'). A number of Serbocroat and Bulgarian particles are borrowed from Turkish, e.g. S. *jök* 'no' (coll.), *afèrim* 'bravo'.

C. WORDS

212. *Turkish Loanwords.* Within the South Slavonic group Slovene stands apart from Bulgarian and Serbocroat by reason of the source of the foreign element in its vocabulary. The language developed under the Austrian suzerainty, and the colloquial employs German loan-words, even when the native lexicon suffices. So duplicates arise: Slov. *krojáč/žnídur* 'tailor' *liják/tráhtar* 'funnel' *mílo/žéfa* 'soap' (Germ. *Schneider Trichter Seife*). The oriental element is unimportant.

In Serbocroat and Bulgarian the latter element considerably modifies the appearance of the two languages. Their literary applications

in modern times have been expressions of occidental thought, so
that the eastern contribution is the less apparent. But in colloquial
usage and in folk-songs there are signs everywhere of the long
Turkish domination. It is naturally more apparent in songs from
Moslem districts, such as those in Hercegovina, since there some of the
most stimulating national motives were not at work. The loanwords
are specifically Osmanli, whereas those of Russian are Turko-Tatar.
The difference of dialect is not very pronounced, because of the
remarkable conservatism of the Turanian language-group. Osmanli
forms are convenient even for the study of Russian borrowings, since
they are more accessible, and satisfy the rough purposes of comparison.
Still, the difference of origin is there. In the South Slavonic languages
it is demonstrable for the words which are due to Osmanli organization
in peace and war. Such words are B. *vilajét* S. *vilájet* 'province' T.
vilâyet, B. *sandžák* S. *sàndžak* 'district' T. *sancak* 'flag', B. *vezír*
'visier' T. *vezir*, B. *pašalǎk* S. *pašàluk* 'pashalik' T. *paşalık*, B. *agá*
'lord' *agalǎk* 'lordship. T. *ağa ağalık*. Military terms form an important group: B. *bajrák* 'flag' *bajraktár* 'standard-bearer' T. *bayrak
bayraktar*, B. *iničerin* 'janissary' T. *yeniçeri*, B. *deli* 'mad' *delibašijá*
'hot-head' 'member of light troops', S. *dèli dèlija* 'hero', T. *deli* 'mad'
baş 'head'. Administrative terms include: B. *charáč* S. *hàrâč* 'poll-tax'
B. *charačár* 'tax-gatherer' T. *haraç*, B. *ilám* 'written verdict' T. *ilâm*,
and such words as B. *altǎn* 'gold' T. *altın*, B. *bakǎr* 'copper' T. *bakır*,
B. *bešlík* 'five-piastre piece' T. *beşlik* (*beş* 'five'). There are also the
names for persons in certain social grades: B. *ekímdžija* 'doctor' T.
hekim+*-ci*, B. *kadǎna* 'Turkish woman' T. *kadın*. In addition to these
there are the names of a wide range of miscellaneous objects: B.
kalpák 'fur cap' T. *kalpak*, B. *kat* 'storey' T. *kat*, B. *kebáb* 'roast meat'
T. *kebap*, B. *gerdán* 'collar' T. *gerdan*, B. *gajtán* 'braid' T. *gaytan*, B.
bakšíš 'gratuity' T. *bahşiş*. The Serbian words are very similar to the
Bulgarian, but show the typical recession of stress.

Only a small group of words may be attributed to the original
Turko-Tatar influence exerted through the Bulgar conquest of the
Danubian basin. The names of the first Bulgarian princes were of this
sort; but their conversion to Christianity was also a gain to Slavonic
prestige. The oldest Bulgarian vocabulary included B. *bíser* 'pearl'
belég 'sign' *čertóg* 'bridal chamber' *bǎbrek* 'kidney' *san* 'honour'.

213. *Word-formation* (see section 78). The OB. suffix *-ištĭ* appears in
its Serbocroat form as *-ić*, which gives the numerous surnames
(mostly patronymics in origin) in *-ić -ović -ević*. (Bulgarian surnames
have the form of the possessive adjective in *-ov -ev*, and there is a
legend that Serbian graveyards have at times been converted into
Bulgarian ones by the process of deleting the *-ić*.) *-ilivǔ:* S. *štèdljiv*
'economical', etc. *-ěninǔ* appears as *-janin*, as elsewhere: S. *grȁđanin*

'citizen'. -*yñi*, in the form -*inja*, is frequent in Serbocroat: *Ènglêz* 'Englishman' - *Ènglêskinja* 'Englishwoman'.

The most striking feature of Serbocroat and Bulgarian word-formation is the extent to which Turkish suffixes have been incorporated, firstly being taken over in complete Turkish words and then, by a process of abstraction, added to native roots. Examples of the latter process are (-*luk*): *bezobràzluk* 'impudence' (*bezòbrazan* 'impudent') *pr̃sluk* 'waistcoat' (*pr̃si* 'breast', unless, as has been suggested, the first element is the German *Brüstchen*).

Much use is also made of the Greek verbal ending -*izō* in the form S. -*isati* B. -*isvam*, particularly in the case of verbs borrowed from Turkish: S. *kurtàl-isati* 'to save' (T. infinitive *kurtar-mak;* S. has dissimilated the second *r*). The borrowed verb frequently incorporates the -*d*- of the Turkish perfect: B. *utledìsvam* 'I iron' (T. infinitive *ütüle-mek*).

214. *Bulgarian and Rumanian.* The extension of Bulgarian influence over Rumanian represents the one great advance made by Slavonic languages at the expense of other civilized tongues. Russian, though it has international vogue and has assimilated Finns, Turks, Mongols and Caucasians, has made only a limited contribution to the vocabularies of occidental nations. But Old Bulgarian effected a partial conquest of one Romance area. The Rumanians, descendants of Trajan's colonists in Dacia, were pastoral nomads at the beginning of mediæval history. They were known to the Slavs by the name **Volchŭ* (S. *Vläh*) which was also the name given by Poles to the Italians (*Włoch*); the word appears to be the same as *Volcae*, cf. *Welsh*. Their ancient mode of life is still that of the fragments dispersed in Macedonia. Over such communities the Bulgarian Slavs, organized into a rude State in imitation of that of Constantinople, and endowed with loftier conceptions by conversion to Christianity, had a decided cultural advantage. They spread the new religion among the Wallachs, who had lost contact with Roman Christianity. Three-fifths of the Modern Rumanian vocabulary, including many important cultural terms, is Slavonic. The forms taken by these words reveal their immediate origin in East Bulgaria, and to a considerable extent also their date from the Middle Bulgarian period. The Cyrillic alphabet was in use in Rumania until the middle of the nineteenth century, and the subsequent adoption of the Roman character has been effective through the formation of new letters to correspond with Bulgarian antecedents.[*] Thus until the spelling-reform otiose *jers* were represented by *ŭ* and *ĭ*. The dull neutral vowel resulting from stressed

---

[*] It is interesting to note that in Soviet Moldavia the Cyrillic aphabet is once more used for Rumanian. The same change from Latin to Cyrillic has also occurred in the case of the Turco-Tatar and some other languages of Soviet Asia.

jer is rendered by *ă*, while *â* and *î*, representing a sound very like that of Russian ы, when followed by *m* or *n* frequently correspond to the Old Bulgarian nasals. Other letters found in Rumanian include ş = Sl. *š*, *j* (as in French) = Sl. *ž*, *ţ* = Sl. *c*, *c* (before front vowels) = Sl. *č*, *h* = Sl. *ch*, and the group *ea* has the sound of East Bulgarian *ě* before hard consonants, though it results also from a normal Romance development. CSl. **ĭ *ď* B. *št žd* are represented in Rumanian by *şt jd*.

Examples of the above-mentioned correspondences are as follows: For B. *št žd:* Rum. *moştean* 'heir' *ştirb* 'jagged' *grajd* 'stall' *odăjdii* 'vestments'/OB. *moštĭnŭ štṛbŭ graždĭ oděžda*. For the *jers:* Rum. *văzduh* 'air' *vădoviţă* 'widow'/OB. *vŭzduchŭ vĭdovica* MB. *văzduch vdovíca*, with the alternative *e* in Rum. *oţet* 'vinegar' MB. *océt*. For *ǫ ę:* Rum. *muncă* 'toil' *sîmbătă* 'Saturday' *Dîmboviţă*/OB. *mǫka sǫbota dǫbŭ* 'tree'/MB. *măka săbota* dial. *sămbota dăb* 'oak'; *sfînt* pl. *sfinţi* 'saint'/OB. *svętŭ*/MB. *svet*. It is clear that at the time of borrowing the nasals were still distinct in timbre, and still different from the obscure vowel *ă*. For *ě:* Rum. *veac* 'age' *deal* (with a curious semantic shift) 'hill' *leac* 'remedy', *vecinic* [véčnik] 'eternal'/OB. *věkŭ dělŭ* 'part' *věčĭn-ĭkŭ*). Furthermore Rumanian *f* represents the spoken Bulgarian *f* which corresponds to the written *chv-:* Rum. *fală* 'glory' B. *chvalá*. A notable coincidence in syntax is the strong tendency to get rid of the infinitive by means of *să* with the finite verb. There is a postpositive article in both languages, and some scholars have endeavoured to assign to this development a common cause.

The loanwords from Bulgarian to Rumanian embrace almost all departments of physical and material life, as well as those for religion and higher culture. The terms for the house and household management, for trade, clothes, ornaments, food and drink, state and church, as well as a large number of the commonest everyday expressions, show how profoundly Bulgarian had modified the outlook of the Dacian Latins.

215. *Bulgarian and Hungarian.* Slavonic, chiefly in its Bulgarian form, has also contributed in large measure to the vocabulary of Hungarian; e.g. *goromba* 'rough' (OB. *grǫbŭ*) *barázda* 'furrow' (OB. *brazda*) *beszéd* 'speech' (OB. *besěda*) *drága* 'dear' (OB. *dragŭ*) *ebéd* 'dinner' (OB. *obědŭ*) *medve* 'bear' (OB. *medvědĭ*) *gazda* 'farmer' (OB. *gospodi* 'lord') Pest (OB. *peštĭ* 'oven'; cf. Germ. *Ofen* for *Buda*); and also appears to have influenced Hungarian syntax, e.g. in the use of *meg* and *volna*.

216. *Albanian.* Many Albanian words are of Slavonic origin, though here Serbocroat has frequently tended to be the vehicle of transmission. Examples are *ças* 'moment' (OB. *časŭ*) *strehë* 'roof' (OB. *strěcha*) *porosis* 'order' (OB. *poročiti*) *godis* 'hit' (OB. *goditi*) *breg* 'hill' (OB. *brěgŭ* 'bank'; S. (*ekav.*) *brêg* 'hill').

217. *Literary Macedonian*. This language, which is now in official use in Yugoslav Macedonia (capital Skoplje), is written in the Serbo-croat form of the Cyrillic alphabet (e.g. ja jy for я ю), and the representatives of CSl. *ť *ď are transcribed *kj gj*. CSl. *ŭ* frequently appears as *o; ch* is replaced by *j*. The grammatical system is more or less that of Standard Bulgarian, with suffixed article, loss of cases and the rest, the one characteristic peculiarity being the use of a pronoun-object *before* together with a noun-object *after* the verb. (Cf. Albanian and—further afield—Spanish).

FOR FURTHER STUDY

Apart from references in general works on linguistics and comparative philology (Brugmann, de Saussure, Meillet, etc.), and in philological journals, the main sources available in non-Slavonic languages of information on general and special aspects of Slavonic philology and linguistics are the following:

VONDRÁK, V. *Vergleichende slavische Grammatik*. Göttingen, I, 1906; II, 1908.

MEILLET, A. *Le slave commun*. Paris, 1924; second edition, revised by A. Vaillant, 1934.

MIKKOLA, J. J. *Urslavische Grammatik*. Part I only; Heidelberg, 1913.

HRUBY, V. *Vergleichende Grammatik der slavischen Sprachen*. Hartleben, Vienna, Leipzig. A comparative sketch with extracts in the various languages, it is useful in some ways.

BERNEKER, E. *Slavisches etymologisches Wörterbuch*. Heidelberg, 1908–1914. First volume and part I of second volume only. Completed to *morŭ*, it may to some extent be supplemented by the (Russian) *Etymological Dictionary of the Russian Language* of A. PREOBRAŽENSKIJ, Moscow, 1910–1916, completed as far as the word *suleja* and thus covering words in *v, z*, and *ž:* and by R. TRAUTMANN's *Baltisch-slavisches Wörterbuch*, Göttingen, 1923. F. Miklosich's *Etymologisches Wörterbuch der slavischen Sprachen*, Vienna, 1886, like his *Vergleichende Grammatik der slavischen Sprachen*, Vienna, 1868–1876, is now largely out of date.

BERNEKER, E. *Slavische Chrestomathie*. Strassburg, 1902; passages in the older forms of the various languages and in dialect, with glossaries.

BROCH, O. *Slavische Phonetik*. Heidelberg, 1911. See also TROFIMOV and JONES, BOYANUS and SWEET on Russian phonetics. There are Czech, Polish, and Serbocroat phonetic readers in the "London Phonetic Readers" series (University of London Press).

EKBLOM, *Der Wechsel* (j)e-o *im Slavischen*. Uppsala-Leipzig, 1925.

LESKIEN, A. *Untersuchungen über Quantität und Betonung in den slavischen Sprachen*, I, II, Leipzig, 1885, 1893.

LIDÉN. *Ein baltisch-slavisches Anlautgesetz*. Göteborg, 1899.

MAYER, K. *Slavische und indogermanische Intonation*. Heidelberg.

MIKKOLA, J. J. *Berührungen zwischen den westfinnischen und slavischen Sprachen*. I, Helsingfors, 1894.

TORBIÖRNSSON. *Die gemeinslavische Liquidametathese*. Uppsala, I, 1901; II, 1903.

Articles in the *Encyclopædia Britannica* and other encyclopædias, in *The Slavonic Review*, and in philological journals and publications such as the *Archiv für slavische Philologie* (edited for many years by V. JAGIĆ, later by E. BERNEKER), the *Zeitschrift für slavische Philologie* (ed. M. VASMER), the *Revue des études slaves*, the *Travaux du cercle linguistique de Prague*.

There is a French version of the standard work (in Czech) on Slavonic prehistory, L. NIEDERLE's *Slovanské Starožitnosti* (*Slav Antiquities*). See also V. THOMSEN, *The Relations between Russia and Scandinavia*, Oxford, 1877, and among more recent works on Russian history, e.g., G. VERNADSKY's

Ancient Russia (Yale University Press) and B. H. SUMNER's *Survey of Russian History*, London, 1944. Sir B. PARES' *History of Russia* includes a useful bibliography.

On the individual Slavonic languages:

JAGIĆ, V. *Entstehungsgeschichte der kirchenslavischen Sprache*, Berlin, 1913.

JAGIĆ, V. (ed.) *Quattuor evangeliorum codex glagoliticus olim Zographensis*. Berlin, 1879.

JAGIĆ, V. (ed.) *Quattuor evangeliorum versionis palæoslovenicæ codex Marianus*, Berlin-St. Petersburg, 1883.

LESKIEN, A. *Grammatik der altbulgarischen (altkirchenslavischen) Sprache*, 3rd ed. Heidelberg, 1919. LESKIEN's *Handbuch der altbulgarischen (altkirchenslavischen) Sprache*, 6th ed. Heidelberg, 1932, includes texts and a vocabulary.

MARGULIÉS, A. *Der altkirchenslavische Codex Suprasliensis*. Heidelberg, 1927.

MEILLET, A. *Etudes sur l'étymologie et le vocabulaire du vieux slave*. Paris, 1902-5.

MEILLET, A. *Recherches sur l'emploi du génitif-accusatif en vieux slave*. Paris, 1897.

MIKLOSICH, F. *Lexicon palæoslovenico-græco-latinum*. Vienna, 1862-5.

VONDRÁK, A. *Altkirchenslavische Grammatik*. 2nd ed. Berlin, 1912.

VONDRÁK, A. *Kirchenslavische Chrestomathie*. Göttingen, 1910.

VAN WIJK, N. *Geschichte der altkirchenslavischen Sprache*. I, Berlin, 1931.

MLADENOV, S. *Geschichte der bulgarischen Sprache*. Berlin-Leipzig, 1929.

MEYER, K. H. *Der Untergang der Deklination im Neubulgarischen*. Heidelberg, 1920.

JAKOBSON, R. *Remarques sur l'évolution phonologique du russe comparée à celle des autres langues slaves*, Paris, 1927.

MAGNUS, L. *The Tale of the Armament of Igor* (text and translation with introduction and notes, Oxford University Press, 1915).

MARTEL, *Michel Lomonosov et la langue littéraire russe*. 1933.

MAZON, A., *Emplois des aspects du verbe russe*. Paris, 1914.

MEYER, K. H. *Historische Grammatik der russischen Sprache*. I, Bonn, 1933.

UNBEGAUN, B. *La langue russe au XVIᵉ siècle*. Paris, 1935.

VINOKUR, G. *La langue russe*. Paris, 1947.

KARSKIJ, E. F. *Geschichte der weissrussischen Volksdichtung und Literatur. Grundriss der slav. Phil. u. Kulturgeschichte*. Berlin-Leipzig, 1926.

LESKIEN, A. *Serbokroatische Grammatik*. I, Heidelberg, 1914.

MUCKE, E. *Historische und vergleichende Laut- und Formenlehre der niedersorbischen (niederlausitzisch-wendischen) Sprache*. Leipzig, 1892.

LORENTZ, F. *Geschichte der pomoranischen (kaschubischen) Sprache. Slavischer Grundriss*, Berlin-Leipzig, 1925. See also *The Cassubian Civilization* (F. Lorentz, A. Fischer and T. Lehr-Spławiński), London, Faber and Faber, 1935.

ROST. *Die Sprachreste der Draväno-Polaben im Hannöverschen*. Leipzig, 1907.

SCHLEICHER, A. *Grammatik der polabischen Sprache*. 1871.

The descriptive grammars in French by A. MAZON, HENRI GRAPPIN's *Grammaire de la langue polonaise*, Paris, 1942, and the *Grammaire de la langue bulgare* by BEAULIEUX and MLADENOV are recommended. G. SCHWELA's *Lehrbuch der niederwendischen Sprache*, Heidelberg, 1906, gives the modern spelling.

Those who can read Slavonic languages will wish to consult the writings (either in separate works or in the encyclopædias—e.g., the Russian *Enciklopedija slavjanskoj Filologii*, the Polish *Encyklopedia Polska*—and journals—e.g., the Czech *Slavia*, the Polish *Rocznik Slawistyczny*—published in these languages) of ALFEROV and GRUZINSKIJ, BRANDT, BUDDE, BUSLAEV, DURNOVO, FORTUNATOV, GALACHOV, GOLOVACKIJ, GROT, GRUNSKIJ, GUDZIJ, IL'INSKIJ, ISTRIN, JAGIČ (=JAGIĆ), KARINSKIJ, KARSKIJ, KOLOSOV, KOZLOVSKIJ, KRYMSKIJ, KUL'BAKIN, LJAPUNOV, OBNORSKIJ, POGODIN, PORŽEZINSKIJ (=PORZEZIŃSKI), POTEBNJA, PREOBRAŽENSKIJ, PYPIN, SELI-ŠČEV, SOBOLEVSKIJ, SOKOLOV, SPERANSKIJ, SREZNEVSKIJ, ŠACHMATOV, UŠAKOV, VASIL'EV, VINOGRADOV, VINOKUR, VOSKRESENSKIJ, VOSTOKOV and ZELININ in Russian; of

BUZUK, HANCOV, SMAL-STOCKYJ (author of the descriptive *Ruthenische Grammatik*) and ŽILYNŚKYJ in Ruthenian; of

BUZUK in White Russian; of

BAUDOUIN DE COURTENAY, BENNI, BRÜCKNER, FISCHER, KURYŁOWICZ, LEHR-SPŁAWIŃSKI, ŁOŚ, NITSCH, ROZWADOWSKI, SŁOŃSKI, SZOBER and UŁASZYN in Polish; of

FLAJŠHANS, FRINTA, GEBAUER, HUJER, MATHESIUS, NIEDERLE, PÁTA (on Wendish), POLÍVKA, SMETÁNKA, TRÁVNÍČEK, WEINGART and ZUBATÝ in Czech; of

BELIĆ, DANIČIĆ, IVŠIĆ, MARETIĆ, REŠETAR and SKOK in Serbocroat; of

NAHTIGAL and RAMOVŠ in Slovene: and of

CONEV, MILETIČ and MLADENOV in Bulgarian.

To the above the authors of the present work are in large measure indebted.

LIST OF SLAVONIC WORDS

The following list gives page-references to Old Bulgarian, Russian and some other etymologies occurring outside the sections in which forms concerned are dealt with (*i.e.*, under Pronouns, Numerals, Adverbs, etc.). The order is that of the English alphabet, accents of all kinds being disregarded. Students will find it helpful if they amplify this list by including references to other words and forms.

zělo OB, 95
želǫdĭ OB, 161
žëlud' R, 161
žemčug R, 261
žena OB, R, 95, 127, 135, 136, 177
žeravi OB, 53, 161
Zerbst, 29
zerno R, 19, 54
zęti OB, 126, 159
zga R, 200
židovinŭ OB, 164
zima OB, R, 80, 94
Žitomir, 192
živ(ŭ) OB, R, 80, 95

zjat' R, 126
zlato OB, 161
zmiji OB, 160
znat' R, 94
zob Slov, 83
zǫbŭ OB, 83, 160, 162
zoloto R, 54, 161
zolovka R, 159
zont(ik) R, 262
zorit' R, 202
zub R, Cz, S, 75, 83, 160, 162
žuravl' R, 183
zvěri OB, 125